Chinese Thought and
Institutions

Contributors

T‘UNG-TSU CH‘Ü

W. T. DE BARY

WOLFRAM EBERHARD

JOHN K. FAIRBANK

CHARLES O. HUCKER

E. A. KRACKE, JR.

JOSEPH R. LEVENSON

JAMES T. C. LIU

BENJAMIN SCHWARTZ

HELLMUT WILHELM

ARTHUR F. WRIGHT

C. K. YANG

LIEN-SHENG YANG

CHINESE THOUGHT AND INSTITUTIONS

Edited by

JOHN K. FAIRBANK

Phoenix Books

THE UNIVERSITY OF CHICAGO PRESS

CHICAGO AND LONDON

THE UNIVERSITY OF CHICAGO PRESS, CHICAGO & LONDON
The University of Toronto Press, Toronto 5, Canada

FOREWORD

SINCE 1951 the two editors of this series of publications have made use of grants of money from the Ford Foundation to extend and improve studies of cultures, and especially of the great civilizations, that they might become more truly comparable with one another. The undertaking has taken several directions: the encouragement of research with methods likely to be applicable cross-culturally; the criticism and testing of such methods already proposed or in use; and the provision of assistance to groups of specialists who might be advancing studies of one civilization in ways leading to a less compartmentalized and more nearly integrated description of that civilization and to dependable comparisons with others.

Such a group of specialists happily appeared to us in the Committee on Chinese Thought (as it is now known) of the Far Eastern Association. Here was a body of specialists, self-organized and vigorous, whose work led along just the paths conducive to the ends of our more general and inclusive project. These specialists in Chinese civilization were a continuing group with similar interests and assumptions, disposed to exchange ideas and results and to do so at length and more than once. They would continue in effective intellectual co-operation. Next, they had a conception of their subject matter that was favorable to the general ends in view: they were concerned, not with Chinese philosophy as a segregate body of propositions expressed by Chinese thinkers, but with "Chinese thought"—the "relations between political and biographical events and the development of ideas." They thought of "thought" as ideas, and also as institutions and action, to be studied together; and they were disposed to make the attempt together, criticizing and helping one another over a period of years. Moreover, they were ready to turn to social scientists, not for conclusions or doctrine, but for suggestions and stimulation in guiding their own work as specialists toward a comparability with studies of other cultures and civilizations—a comparability to be realized in the future, not self-evident or already achieved. Thus they constituted an important link between the specialized scholar, historian, or humanist and the comparative anthropologist or sociologist. These men knew what Granet and Weber had written about China and Chinese bureaucracy; they would neither accept nor

v

disdain these writings; they would adhere to their own scholarly carefulness while listening to and correcting those early generalizers.

One of the first decisions as to the expenditure of the money that had been provided for comparative work in the study of civilizations was that which made possible a conference of the Committee on Chinese Thought held in Aspen, Colorado, in 1952. There resulted the first publication in the present series: *Studies in Chinese Thought*, edited by Arthur F. Wright (1953). The book clarified some of the kinds of historical problems which Sinologists might attack with a justified hope that the results would move toward the more holistic understanding of Chinese civilization and toward the comparison of that civilization with others. That book was explorative; it suggested many lines of research. The present volume (the eighth in the series under our general editorship) has more concentration of topic and consistency of purpose. In the second undertaking the Committee chose to direct its attention to the interrelations of ideas, especially Confucian ideas, and to the political institutions and actions of China; the focus is on the Confucian state. In Professor Fairbank's excellent Introduction one may read of the several ways in which this topic receives treatment in the thirteen contributions: some deal with the relation of ideas to the exercise of state power; others relate Confucian teachings or other ideas important in China to the scholar-official—that enduring class of men who in their persons and careers connected ideas and institutions for two millenniums. The Committee, on its own initiative, obtained the participation in its work of Dr. Herbert Goldhamer, who was for the task just the right sociologist, being well read, skeptical, and discriminating.

The general editors are grateful to the Committee for this second and advanced production and to Dr. Goldhamer for his help. We thank also Mr. Herman Sinaiko, who put his critical skill and knowledge of Chinese to the task of preparing the manuscript for the press.

ROBERT REDFIELD
MILTON B. SINGER

TABLE OF CONTENTS

NOTES

INDEX

CONTRIBUTORS

T'UNG-TSU CH'Ü taught at the National Yunnan University and the National Southwest Associated University, both in Kunming. In 1945 he came to the United States to do research in the Chinese History Project at Columbia University and later joined the University of Pittsburgh. His work has combined the approaches of law, sociology, and anthropology in a historical framework. His books in Chinese include *Chinese Feudal Society* and *Chinese Law and Chinese Society*. A forthcoming book in English is entitled *Law and Society in Traditional China*.

WILLIAM THEODORE DE BARY took his B.A. at Columbia in 1941. After naval service in the Pacific and postwar study at Yenching and Lingnan universities in China, he completed his Ph.D. at Columbia in 1953. He is now Assistant Professor of Chinese and Japanese and Chairman of the General Education Program in Oriental Studies, Columbia College. His major interest is in Chinese and Japanese intellectual history. His publications include a study and translation of the seventeenth-century Chinese thinker Huang Tsung-hsi, a volume of *Readings on Japanese Thought*, and other studies and translations.

WOLFRAM EBERHARD took his doctorate in sociology and Chinese at the University of Berlin, and in 1934 went to China and taught in government universities in Peiping. In 1937 he went to Turkey to teach and remained there for a decade before coming to the University of California at Berkeley in 1948, where he teaches sociology with an emphasis on Asiatic societies. He has published a number of monographs and books, pursuing a broad range of interests in both Chinese and Turkish folklore, Chinese astronomy, the nomadic invasions of China, and other aspects of its literary, cultural, and social history. Most recently in English he has published a general *History of China* and *Conquerors and Rulers* (on problems of the barbarian invasions).

JOHN K. FAIRBANK studied at Oxford and Peiping (1929–36) and since 1936 has been teaching at Harvard University, where he is Professor of History, specializing on modern China. He recently spent a year in Kyoto and Tokyo as a Guggenheim Fellow. His publications include *The United States and China, Trade and Diplomacy on the China Coast, China's Response to the West* (with S. Y. Teng), and a number of bibliographical and documentary volumes in collaboration with others.

CHARLES O. HUCKER has done postdoctoral research at the Academia Sinica in Taiwan and at the Kyoto University Research Institute of Humanistic Sciences in Japan. He has been Assistant Professor of Modern Chinese Literature and Institutions at the University of Chicago, specializing in early modern Chinese history and traditional political institutions. His writings include a long monograph on the censorate of the Ming dynasty. He is now Associate Professor of Asiatic Studies at the University of Arizona.

E. A. KRACKE, JR., received his training in Far Eastern history and languages in Peiping, at the Sorbonne, and at Harvard, where he took his Ph.D. He is now Associate Professor of Middle Chinese Literature and Institutions at the University of Chicago. His research has been primarily on Chinese institutional history, with a special interest in the Sung period. In addition to numerous articles and reviews, he has recently published *Civil Service in Early Sung China*.

JOSEPH R. LEVENSON received his Ph.D. from Harvard, where he was a member of the Society of Fellows. He is now Assistant Professor of History at the University of California. His major interest is the intellectual history of modern China. In addition to a number of articles and reviews, he is the author of *Liang Ch'i-ch'ao and the Mind of Modern China*.

JAMES T. C. LIU was on the staff of Yenching University, Peiping, and since coming to the United States has taught at the University of Washington and at Yale. He is at present Associate Professor of History and Sponsor of Far Eastern Studies at the University of Pittsburgh. His services as a Historical Consultant, International Military Tribunal, Tokyo, led him into studies of modern Sino-Japanese diplomatic relations, but his main interest is in Chinese political thought and institutions of the traditional period.

BENJAMIN SCHWARTZ, following wartime service in the Pacific, took his Ph.D. at Harvard, where he is now Associate Professor of History. He is best known for his work on the development of the Communist movement in China, on which he has published *Chinese Communism and the Rise of Mao*, *A Documentary History of Chinese Communism* (with C. Brandt and J. K. Fairbank), and various articles. His primary interest, however, is in the whole range of intellectual history in China and also in Japan, and his further research is proceeding along this broad line.

HELLMUT WILHELM received his doctorate from the University of Berlin, with a thesis on the seventeenth-century scholar Ku Yen-wu. He lived many years in Peiping and taught at several of the major universities in China, particularly the National University of Peking. He has published widely in the field of Chinese studies and is at present teaching Chinese history and literature at the University of Washington, Seattle, where he is also a member of the Modern Chinese History Project, specializing on the nineteenth-century statesman Tseng Kuo-fan.

ARTHUR F. WRIGHT received his early graduate training at Oxford, Harvard, Kyoto, and Peiping before returning to Stanford University, where he is now Associate Professor of History. As a historian of China he has pursued special interests in the history of Chinese Buddhism and in intellectual history, particularly of the medieval period. In addition to publishing a number of articles and monographic studies, he has been editor of the *Far Eastern Quarterly*, 1951–55, and Chairman of the Committee on Chinese Thought of the Far Eastern Association since 1951, editing its first symposium, *Studies in Chinese Thought* (Chicago, 1953).

C. K. YANG (Yang Ch'ing-k'un) took his M.A. in sociology at Yenching University, Peiping, in 1934 and his Ph.D. in the same subject at the University of Michigan in 1939. He taught at the University of Washington, 1944–48, became Chairman of the Sociology Department at Lingnan University at Canton in 1948, and since returning to the United States has become Associate Professor of Sociology at the University of Pittsburgh. Aside from publications in Chinese, he is the author of *A North China Local Market Economy, Meet the U.S.A.,* and several manuscripts awaiting publication.

LIEN-SHENG YANG studied at National Tsing Hua University and received his Ph.D. from Harvard University, where he has taught since 1942 and is now Associate Professor of Far Eastern Languages. His principal interests are Chinese history and philology, with special emphasis on the economic history of China. He is the author of *A Concise Dictionary of Spoken Chinese* (with Y. R. Chao), *Topics in Chinese History,* and *Money and Credit in China: A Short History,* as well as numerous articles and reviews in the *Harvard Journal of Asiatic Studies* and elsewhere.

A NOTE ON ROMANIZATION

ACCURATE TRANSCRIPTION of Chinese sounds in English letters being practically impossible, the standard Wade-Giles system of romanization is a purely conventional device. It is replete with bothersome diacritical marks like the aspirate and circumflex, which form an esoteric symbolism known neither to the Chinese people nor to Westerners but only to the international fraternity of sinologists, who differ widely in the degree of their devotion to it. The choice between Hsuntse and Hsün-tzu, or Chu Yuan and Ch'ü Yüan, could be settled in favor of the simpler forms, to the joy of linotypists, were it not for the problem of using the dictionaries. We have therefore simplified the Wade-Giles system by omitting all diacritical marks *except* the aspirate and the diaeresis on final *ü* (to distinguish *yu* and *yü*, *lu* and *lü*, etc.) or where necessary to avoid ambiguity in consulting dictionaries (e.g., by retaining the distinction between *chun* and *chün* or between *chuan* and *chüan* while omitting the diaeresis in *chueh, hsueh, yuan, yueh, yun,* etc.). The chief exception to our exceptions is *hsün;* we feel that the philosopher Hsün-tzu should remain Hsün-tzu.

J. K. F.

CHRONOLOGICAL CHART

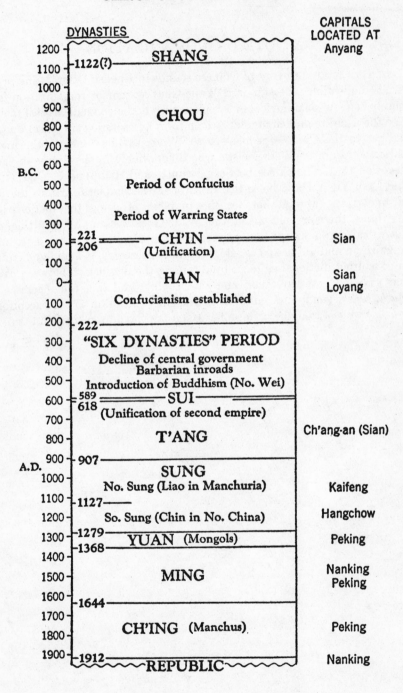

DYNASTIES

CAPITALS LOCATED AT

B.C.	Dynasty	Capital
1200	SHANG	Anyang
1100	1122(?)	
1000		
900	CHOU	
800		
700		
600		
500	Period of Confucius	
400	Period of Warring States	
300		
200	221 CH'IN 206 (Unification)	Sian
100		
0	HAN	Sian Loyang
100	Confucianism established	
200	222	
300	"SIX DYNASTIES" PERIOD	
400	Decline of central government Barbarian inroads	
500	Introduction of Buddhism (No. Wei)	
600	589 SUI 618 (Unification of second empire)	
700		
800	T'ANG	Ch'ang-an (Sian)
900	907	
A.D. 1000	SUNG No. Sung (Liao in Manchuria)	Kaifeng
1100	1127	
1200	So. Sung (Chin in No. China)	Hangchow
1300	1279 YUAN (Mongols)	Peking
1400	1368	
1500	MING	Nanking Peking
1600		
1644		
1700	CH'ING (Manchus)	Peking
1800		
1900	1912	
	REPUBLIC	Nanking

INTRODUCTION: PROBLEMS OF METHOD
AND OF CONTENT

JOHN K. FAIRBANK

IN PENETRATING the neglected field of Chinese political thought, these papers deal less with the formulations of classical texts than with the use of Confucian ideas in political struggles and sociopolitical institutions. Rather surprisingly, these studies have been produced by historians, with some sociological assistance, rather than by political scientists. The latter, though in a discipline which seems not to be moribund, have generally succeeded thus far in avoiding the challenge of the Chinese political record—in spite of the fact that it is not only easily accessible in our libraries but represents, after all, the most long-continued experience of government, in the most populous of states, in human history.

This remarkable parochialism on the part of Western political science, I suggest, has resulted from a mistaken doctrine of scientific universalism which forbids "regional" specialization. Political scientists trained in the data, concepts, and languages of Western political life, having divided their science into logical nonregional categories, have thereby estopped themselves from studying politics among the majority of mankind, who happen always to have lived in the Asian region. In economics, the overriding necessity of the development of underdeveloped areas has recently permitted American economists to create the new economics of development, which just happens to apply mainly to Asia, without stooping to regionalism. No doubt some future need for understanding government in Asia will permit a similar happy growth in political science.

Meanwhile, in this volume, working primarily as regional-specialist historians, we have found ourselves on an exciting and often confusing intercultural frontier, where the analytic skills of social science are as necessary as the intimate and particular knowledge of the humanist. We have had to keep facing two ways. To penetrate the well-kept but forbidding reaches of Chinese historical literature, we have needed the careful methods and endless patience of the sinologist. At the same time, to make sense of Chinese political phenomena in terms meaningful to modern social science, we have had to study aspects of the latter, particularly in the area of the sociology of knowledge.

1

Trying to develop a new field of learning, while endeavoring to keep up with other rapidly growing fields, is no doubt the common state of modern scholars. Our experience thus far in the study of Chinese thought may be of interest to a wider audience than the growing company of China specialists. The following introductory pages indicate something of the origin, method, and content of our effort.

1. Origins and Methods

The Committee on Chinese Thought, now a committee of the Far Eastern Association, Inc., was organized in 1951 in the belief that Western scholarship had dangerously neglected the role of ideas in Chinese society and history. While a number of classical texts and historical works had been translated or studied, rather little attention had been paid to the interplay in China between ideas and institutions, or to the analysis of the influence of ideas on events, careers, and policies in their historical unfolding. With the postwar growth of Chinese and Japanese studies in the United States, it seemed possible to mobilize a diversity of minds and skills and seek new approaches which would relate the work of the sinological specialist more closely to that of philologists, philosophers, sociologists, psychologists, and others who had for the most part neglected Chinese studies. The original suggestion for this endeavor came from Mortimer Graves of the American Council of Learned Societies. Arthur F. Wright of Stanford became chairman of the new Committee, and, with the support of the project for Comparative Studies of Cultures and Civilizations, directed by Robert Redfield, the first Conference on Chinese Thought was held at Aspen, Colorado, in 1952.

As indicated in Arthur Wright's Introduction to the resulting volume of papers (*Studies in Chinese Thought*, American Anthropological Association Memoir No. 75 and University of Chicago Press, 1953), that conference seemed to open up many avenues for systematic analysis—the history of groups of thinkers, the history of certain key terms and ideas, the history of values, of situations of intellectual choice, of foreign ideas in China, the history of nonlinguistic symbolism. Guided by this experience and stimulated by the cordial reception given its product, the Committee was able to hold a second conference, on the general theme "The Relationship between Ideas and Institutions in China," at Steele Hill near Laconia, New Hampshire, during the week of September 3–10, 1954.

Several procedures proved their value at this second conference as at the first: all papers were distributed and read beforehand, discussion of each paper was initiated by a formal analysis presented by another conference member, and a selective and condensed (not verbatim) record of the discussions was prepared each day by an able *rapporteur* (Mr. Stephen Hay of the Harvard Graduate School). The subsequent revision of papers could thus take advantage of several hours of critical comment around and about each subject. Such methods made possible a balance of ordered thought and free inspiration among thirteen discussants during the week's sessions. (We were impressed with the fact that several man-years of research and the wisdom of many lifetimes were thus brought together at a total cost equivalent to roughly one year's support of one scholar.)

In methodology our chief effort was to make available, to our conference members, the informed criticism of a social scientist from outside the field of Chinese studies. We assumed that, no matter how much one may try to induce the miscegenation of disciplines, the actual formation of ideas must still occur in an individual mind. Moreover, to be effective in research on China, new ideas of interdisciplinary reach must come to the minds of individual sinologists. Seeking critical concentration rather than a discordant confrontation of several disciplines, we therefore invited a single sociologist, Dr. Herbert Goldhamer of the Rand Corporation, to act as consultant to the conference members. The latter in most cases sent him briefs and queries drawn from their researches as these progressed during the early part of 1954, and benefited from his comments before, as well as during, the conference.

In our approaches to the research problems dealt with in these conference papers, I suppose we exhibit the variety characteristic of Western historical studies in this second half of the twentieth century. Each author chose and developed his own topic. The resulting papers do not fit into an over-all scheme; at best the volume is semiplanned and semicohesive. Yet the authors undoubtedly share a considerable body of assumptions, both as to the general role of ideas in the historical process and as to the special problems to be met in studying the relationship of ideas and institutions in Chinese history.

To begin with, we assume that the ideas with which we have dealt, as perceivable in recorded Chinese writings, all had their existence and significance in Chinese minds as part of the general and inclusive manifold of contemporary Chinese events—thought was one component of the historical process, one part of a whole. Each of us might choose different words in order to define by abstraction the role which ideas played both in the stream of a thinker's action and in the social scene. But we believe that comprehension of history, in both its unique particularity and its underlying generality, is more than a matter of abstract terms, factors, and definitions: we generally subscribe to the suggestion of Mr. Schwartz, with which this volume opens, that in the last analysis we must seek to understand men's ideas in their original context of connotation, attitude, and feeling, in their close interconnection with unique times, persons, and places. It is not enough merely to seek genetic explanations as to causal factors or to confine ourselves to criticism of the validity of a man's ideas; the historian must try to understand the inner world of the individual thinker, and the explicit content of his thought, assuming meanwhile that his response to his circumstances included a limited degree of free and unique creativity. This means that our comprehension, in this field of Chinese studies where so relatively few facts are known, must flow from a further amassing of humanistic fact and painstaking interpretation, as well as from the application of social science theory of a general nature. Our first danger is that, in imitation of more advanced Western studies, we may try too soon to reach a comparable level of generality and abstraction.

Second, our effort to comprehend the explicit content and historical relevance of Chinese thought makes it especially necessary that we also comprehend ourselves as observers. This is made difficult by the cultural gap, beginning initially with the linguistic gap, which intervenes between us in the present world and individuals in the Chinese past. Our own everyday assumptions and commitments as observers today are more than usually foreign to the historical scene we are studying in China. This is because China, of all the great cultures, has been the furthest removed from the Western tradition. Thus, for example, Western thinkers on the social order have often tacitly assumed the supremacy of law within the state. Max Weber could posit his discussion of bureaucracy on the exercise within the state of a dominant and effective "legal authority." But when he came to his discussion of Chinese bureaucracy, he naturally had to begin with the absence in China of any "systematic, substantive and thorough rationalization of law."

Our own process of thought, as we attach significance to the Chinese record, must be characterized, I think, by a sort of oscillation, in which our attention continually shifts back and forth, contrapuntally, between the particular ideas of a Chinese individual and the broader circumstances surrounding and preceding them, and between this integral slice of Chinese history as a unit and our own conceptual understanding of the historical process in general. Each step in such an oscillation leads us into problems. Beginning with the particular statements in Chinese of the thought of a historic Chinese personage, we confront the linguistic and metalinguistic problems of translation, some of which were discussed in the volume for the first conference; problems of textual authenticity and accuracy, of punctuation, of grammar and syntax, of classical quotation and allusion, of rhetoric and sentiment, and the like. To these textual problems must be added layer upon layer of problems of context—the writer's situation of the moment, his previous career, the tradition behind him, the Chinese society of his time, and so on. Inevitably we are faced with the broad question of the cultural circumstances, the social institutions and events, in the midst of which his ideas were recorded in writing. Partly these circumstances are to be grasped as matters of fact, through specific historical detail; partly they must be understood in the long sweep of China's whole history, through interpretations, constructions, and patterns which we think we discern in the political, economic, social, intellectual, and cultural experience of the Chinese people. In this stage of our process there is no logical stopping place short of the total historical comprehension of the human story on earth; we must use our understanding of the whole historical process, such as it may be.

Thus the oscillation of our attention leads us from the Chinese text through successive layers of context, at varying levels of abstraction, to our concepts of Chinese historical periods, of Chinese culture in general, and of all human history, until finally, as in any process of translation, we narrow our focus, select our terms, and arrive at the concrete written text of our own statement in English. In this procedure conceptual exactitude is not only as important as exactitude of translation but indeed cannot be divorced from it. There is thus no easy or simple circuit for Truth to follow in moving from one time and culture to another. The process of our comprehension is continual, always approximate and never finished.

2. Concepts and Propositions

As every historical researcher knows, it is less difficult to amass factual data, on the one hand, and to understand generalized concepts, on the other, than to fit them all together in an integrated, articulate account. The "application" of concepts to a historical situation may yield results very similar to those of the successive generations of Western travelers to China who have taken with them, mentally prefabricated, the observations and conclusions which they have subsequently found there. Against this evil, Herbert Goldhamer at the end of our second conference suggested a useful antidote. He concluded:

There is a danger that sinology will be corrupted by social science in the same way that social science is corrupting itself: by studying concepts and books, ignoring the concrete data of life. This danger takes two forms: (1) the strong tendency of seeking to be guided by the concepts themselves, whereas concepts should first be tested against empirical data; (2) the tendency to attach meaning to a word instead of first taking a social reality and then finding a word for it.

To meet this danger of apriorism and reification of concepts, Mr. Goldhamer offered the practical suggestion that researchers should seek to relate their data less to concepts than to propositions:

Key concepts are not so stimulating to research as are propositions which challenge your data and force you to either prove or disprove them. A broader collaboration, both within sinology and between sinology and other disciplines, might lead to the proving of propositions, providing the specifications were agreed upon beforehand. Propositions must not be held too rigidly; they should be understood as hypotheses still to be proved. Problems must be broken down into very specific propositions in order to make sense to men working in other dynasties, histories, or disciplines. This procedure dictates, in sufficiently rigid form, the type of data needed to solve the problem.

In short, the test of action or operability (called for by the positive verbal nature of propositions) should be applied to our problems; and the latter should be formulated in such a way as to make this possible. This excellent advice, though no doubt inspired in part by the inadequacy of our discussions, will of course be found only partially exemplified in our papers.

Certain further problems faced by researchers in intellectual history are discussed in the first paper by Mr. Schwartz. Arguing that philosophic assumptions must underlie all delimitations of disciplines, he defines intellectual history as focused upon men's "conscious responses" to their situations. Historic "situations" he sees as full of ambiguities, and men's responses to them include attitudes and feelings as well as ideas, which are not entirely "caused" by a situation and which themselves help create it. Thus, for instance, he sees Marxism-Leninism serving both as a body of animating ideas and as a mere rationalization or ideology in the Chinese Communist movement; papers that follow will show Confucianism serving in a comparable dual role in traditional China.

3. Main Divisions and Trends of Content

In content our papers will be seen to range over a wide area, reflecting the varying capacities and interests of the authors. They fall into two main groups, the first of which is an unusual series of historical monographs illustrating the relation of ideas to the exercise of state power. These papers deal with six different periods during the two millenniums of the Imperial era from Han to Ch'ing. In each case they analyze the use made of certain ideas in the process of government, particularly in the struggle for power among the bureaucracy.

Mr. Eberhard explores the political function of astronomy at the Han court. Building upon his own earlier monographs, he shows the essentially political, rather than scientific, interest which lay behind the recording of eclipses, droughts, fires, and other portents of nature. Not only were portents connected with human events on the assumption that they indicated a disturbance of the normal harmony between celestial and terrestrial actions, they were also taken to be warnings of "Heaven" (and hence possibly of a personal deity?) either against the conduct of emperors or against imbalance and impropriety in the administration of government. Thus they formed a kind of institutional check upon imperial absolutism ("despotism") and were included in the dynastic annals as part of the process by which Chinese historians used their account of past events to provide a "mirror" or guide for future political conduct. Some portents were fabricated, and in any case the explanations of them varied greatly among the official recorders and according to the theories invoked. Yet, since they applied to the conduct of the government and not solely to the emperor, portents could be used as political tools by one faction against another. Finally, the Han use of a luni-solar calendar of minimal value for agriculture, constructed according to symbolic criteria to show the magical powers of the dynasty, underlines the conclusion that early Chinese astronomical "science" was oriented to political ends and therefore stunted as true science.

Where Mr. Eberhard studies the institutionalized use of the ideology of portents by Han astronomers, Mr. Wright next appraises the ideological justifications utilized by the vigorous founder of a new dynasty. In reunifying China after A.D. 581, the first Sui emperor's various uses of Taoism, Confucianism, and Buddhism seem to have reflected the hierarchy of problems which he saw before him and also the assumptions in his mind as he dealt with them, both as to the efficacy of the written symbols of the Chinese language and as to the inherited system of values represented by them. In analyzing the emperor's ideological assertions and acts of policy, Mr. Wright thus appraises his intellectual inheritance as well as the major motifs of his career and character. He then provides an exemplary summary of the economic, political, and cultural problems of the early Sui period which the ruler had to meet. Within this historical framework, finally, he traces the ways in which Taoism, Confucianism, and Buddhism were used for ideological purposes, as a "suasive accompaniment to the exercise of power."

The next three papers of this group form a trilogy on the relationship between Confucian thought and the imperial power, operating as two primary influences upon the conduct of the official class. Mr. Liu's study of an early Sung reform movement led by Fan Chung-yen highlights the factional power struggle between the idealistic bureaucrat's claim of superior ideological authority and the career-minded bureaucrat's opportunistic manipulation of the emperor. By enlisting the emperor's personal power, on which all officials were ultimately dependent, the opportunists could thwart the reformers. Yet Confucianism constantly generated an impulse toward the reform of the conduct of the imperial administration. Mr. Liu recounts the efforts of Fan Chung-yen and his friends to foster Confucian studies, to improve the recruitment of officials through examination and the sponsorship system, and to better the administration of local government—all of which aimed at the application of their political ideology. His analysis puts forward a typology of bureaucrats and a paradigm of the power structure, and suggests how different types of bureaucrats relied upon certain sectors of power. What the idealistic bureaucrats sought was an "ethocracy" in which their moral ideological authority would attain overriding power. When translated into political action, this aim inevitably became a threat not only to antireformers but also to the emperor's personal rule and, accordingly, was checked though never extirpated. This suggests an important type of dynamism inherent within the Confucian state.

As another example of Confucian idealism in action, Mr. Hucker analyzes the political activity of the philosopher-officials associated with the famous Tung-lin (sometimes translated "Eastern Forest") Academy of the late Ming period. He describes first the institutional weakness and administrative decay at the Ming court and the power struggle which arose within officialdom there. Within this conflict of cliques he then traces the emergence of moral issues and their espousal by the politically oriented scholar-officials of the Tung-lin group; this led to a moral crusade against the less principled opposition groups and was climaxed by the violent destruction of the Tung-lin crusaders at the hands of the vile eunuch, Wei Chung-hsien. Mr. Hucker's study of the personnel and the issues uncovers a larger pattern of common moral purpose which moved these philosopher-officials to invoke the traditional Confucian morality against misuse of the emperor's power and misconduct among officialdom. The eventual liquidation of the reformers by a eunuch who temporarily wielded the imperial power was shortly, and in Confucian terms quite logically, followed by the collapse of the last great purely Chinese dynasty.

The third paper of this trilogy, by Mr. de Bary, studies *A Plan for the Prince*, written in 1662 by the political theorist Huang Tsung-hsi. This reformer's prescription for China's ills (as so recently evidenced in the Ming collapse) was posited on the exercise of a benevolent though still despotic imperial power. It provides an eloquent, critical summary of the Confucian political ideal. Reforms to make the law something more basic than a mere dynastic tool; to raise the status of ministers, restore the prime ministership, and curb the eunuchs; to sponsor public schools open to all and improve the examination system; to reform the lower levels of bureaucracy; to revise land tenure and land taxation, and the like—were all to be carried out from above by a monarch ruling "for the people," as urged originally in the Confucian classics two thousand years before. The ancient ideals of the ruler's virtue and of a harmonious social order, rather than institutional checks and balances, were to make such reforms possible. While Huang's ideas were sometimes bold and later of influence, they were comparable to those of Fan Chung-yen and of the Tung-lin movement in staying well within the age-old framework of the Confucian state.

My own paper concerns the recent collapse, under the treaty system of a century ago, of the traditional theory and also the practice by which the Chinese empire when under non-Chinese emperors had been administered by a mixed Chinese and foreign officialdom. Joint administration under barbarian dynasties of conquest had become a Confucian institution with regular and identifiable features, many of which reappeared briefly in the period of the British invasion of China during and after the Opium War. Early European contact, before the unequal treaties, had been assimilated to this tradition, and the treaties did not disrupt it immediately: synarchic tendencies manifested themselves in the conduct of Sino-Western relations after the opening of the treaty ports. But the ideas and assumptions which underlay the tradition of joint administration by Chinese and invader were soon disrupted by the influx of Western ideas, primarily by the modern concept of nationalism implicit in the treaty system itself.

The second group of papers concerns the role of ideas in China's traditional social order, particularly those which affected the official class. Going back to ancient China and the origins of the Confucian official class, Mr. Ch'ü first describes the ideology which accompanied the class structure of the feudal period. The rationalization that the superior man labored mentally, especially in governing others, while the small man labored physically, and was governed, fitted the facts of the feudal system. After that system passed away, this distinction of classes persisted under the empire after 221 B.C. The status of superior man or of small man was determined no longer by ascription but henceforth by achievement—in virtue and ability, eventually as evidenced in examinations. These two status groups, differentiated by occupation, prestige, and power, did not form a simple "two-class society"; those who were ruled actually included several classes. But the official ruling class, in China's traditional social structure, continued to hold the top position both in actual power and in prestige, as well as in the social theory of Confucianism.

After the Sui-T'ang revival of central power, the Confucian state increasingly recruited its officials through examinations. Mr. Kracke examines the shifting relationship between the ideal and the reality of the examination system. Although civil service appointments were often made through the methods of protection (*yin*), recommendation, sale of office, and otherwise, the use of the examination method expressed the ideal, and may have indicated the degree, of social mobility into officialdom. In the early period of free, interregional competition, up to the end of the Sung in 1279, the rising number of examination candidates from commercial Southeast China and the growing proportion of new talent there (from nonofficial families) suggest that the urbanization process promoted social mobility in the civil service. Under the Mongols (1279–1368), ostensibly impartial quotas were used to penalize the most anti-Mongol region, South China. Under the Ming and Ch'ing, to 1911, quotas by regions according to their population density provided still another way of acknowledging the validity of the goal of equal opportunity.

Thus sanctioned and selected, the Chinese officialdom with its

Confucian way of thought remained the dominant class in an institutionally monolithic state in which no divisive dualism of church and temporal power ever became established. Mr. C. K. Yang, in analyzing the relationship between Confucianism and Chinese religions, finds that Confucianism was not entirely rational or agnostic but actually accepted and incorporated a number of supernatural elements; that it dominated the field of ethics and kept itself separate from religion; and that Chinese religions either were kept weak through lack of centralized organization (in the case of "specialized" religions like Taoism and Buddhism) or were kept under the nonreligious control of the Confucian state (in the case of "diffused" religions like ancestor worship and the cult of Heaven). No priestly class ever succeeded in challenging Chinese officialdom.

The persistence and proliferation of basic concepts concerning the social order, from even before the time of Confucius, are illustrated in a case study by Mr. L. S. Yang. He traces the forms and uses of the concept of "response," "return," "reciprocate" (represented by the character *pao* [for Chinese characters see the Index to this volume]), noting its use in social relationships of various sorts—by the knights-errant of early times, in the famous Five Relationships of Confucianism, between nature and man (including the idea of divine retribution, the sharing of fate, and the Buddhist *karma*). This ramified concept had its application in family life, where rewards and punishments were shared by the whole group reciprocally and filiality was inculcated as the return due to parents; in man's rationalized relation to Heaven; and in personal relations, especially among officials, where it supported what Westerners call "nepotism" or "favoritism."

The remaining papers concern the aesthetic expression of the scholar-official in literature and painting, respectively. Mr. Wilhelm connects the sudden predominance of the *fu* (or "rhyme-prose") genre of writing in the Han period with the contemporaneous rise of the scholars to assume the institutionalized status of imperial officials or, at least, of membership in the ruling class. He doubts the exclusive connection of the Han *fu* with the Ch'u school of literature and suggests it was a legacy of the philosophical School of Politicians. Most *fu* are political in their ulterior content, and many concern specifically the relationship of ruler and official. Institutionally the *fu* functioned as a vehicle for the scholar's expression of criticism by indirection. One type of *fu* in particular voices the frustration of the scholar who is prepared for official service but, failing to "meet the proper time," remains unemployed by his imperial master. This comparatively neglected genre of Chinese literature can thus be related to the development of Han political institutions, and those which express the scholar's frustration indicate one of his occupational hazards.

Another view of the scholar-official class, from an unusual angle, is afforded by Mr. Levenson's paper on its theories of painting. He sees the scholar-officials of the Ming and early Ch'ing periods as conservative and unspecialized amateurs, in whom were conjoined the highest social status and cultural values. As painters they scorned professionalism but studiously followed traditions of "spontaneity." By a "routinization of intuition" these Confucian intellectuals followed the Ch'an (Zen) tradition of Buddhist anti-intellectualism. They did not paint nature directly but the inherited representations of nature, which resulted in stylistic eclecticism and syncretism. This amateur tradition was destroyed only when the impact of the West and the rise of modern Chinese nationalism wiped out the unspecialized, omnicompetent type of scholar-official himself—as marked eventually by the abolition of the examination system and so of this whole class.

4. The Political Orientation of Chinese Thought

Needless to say, the reader will be ill-advised (and my colleagues thoroughly dismayed) if he accepts the foregoing panorama as representing either the scope or the depth of the following papers. Yet from this hasty look one may derive certain impressions which the papers themselves may reinforce: from first to last the mountainous written record of Chinese history has been the product of scholars who have by and large identified themselves with the official class. This class depended in theory and in practice upon the exercise of supreme power by the Son of Heaven (or, as Westerners say, the emperor). The dynamism of the Confucian state came partly from the conflict between the sordid reality of personal elitist government and the Confucian ideal of the emperor's virtuous rule (the Chinese version of benevolent despotism). This Confucian ideal, seeking the harmonious order of society, gave the thought of Chinese scholars a primarily sociopolitical orientation. The fact that the social order was to be maintained not merely by law or by force but primarily by the personal conduct of the ruler and of his officials, exemplifying traditional Confucian ideals, had the effect, I suggest, of exacerbating their political-mindedness. Participation of the scholar class in the institutionalized processes of an essentially personal government required that it be constantly attentive to its personal conduct, which was always at the same moment political conduct.

Perhaps this explains how the present contributors, invited to prepare papers on "The Relationship of Ideas and Institutions in China," have produced these studies which center around the role of ideas in Chinese *political* life. They all make plain the central role of the state, at least in China's literate and recorded experience. In one study after another, both in this volume and elsewhere, the Confucian state—certainly no more loose a term than "Christendom" or "the West"—emerges as the main focus of China's long history. The emperor heads it, but under certain checks and sanctions; the ruling class serves it, though at the whim of the emperor; religion, ethics, and social relationships are dominated by its system of thought; reformers and rebels seek no more than to realize its original ideals; the non-Chinese peoples of Eastern Asia participate in it as rulers or ruled. This great political tradition is what Mao has inherited today and what Western scholars have barely begun to study. The economic institutions of traditional China, on the concrete level, are perhaps best known to us, along with the classical statements of Confucian ethical thought, at the other extreme of abstraction. In between lies the comparatively unexplored region where scholarly thought and state institutions interpenetrate in historical situations of the sort discussed in these papers.

5. The Varieties of Research Problems

Each of our papers demonstrates a certain approach to understanding the political-social role of ideas, whether it be the operational assumption underlying a court institution (Eberhard), a ramified concept of social conduct (L. S. Yang), the ideological measures used to justify a new dynasty (Wright), the applications to political life of the Confucian ideals invoked by a group of active reformers (Liu, Hucker), or a scholar's attempt by theory to ameliorate the imperial despotism (De Bary). By such studies the ground is being prepared for one of the great feats of scholarship—a connected study of the evolution of political thought and institutions as it has occurred over three continuous millenniums of recorded history in the single society of China. Examples of this evolution in these papers show its variety and movement within the framework of a homogeneous cultural inheritance—the class structure of Chou feudalism persisting but modified under the empire (Ch'ü), portents of nature viewed more rationally but retaining ritual if not magical value (Eberhard), religious developments inveterately absorbed or neutralized by Confucianism (C. K. Yang), examination quotas responding to the urbanization of the Sung period (Kracke), scholar-painters turning Sung creativity into Ming stereotypes (Levenson); and, running through several papers, the persistent efforts of the scholar-official class to devise institutional checks upon the despotic power of the ruler.

A firmer grasp of such multiform intellectual developments in traditional China is prerequisite for any evaluation of the ideological prospects for Communist China. They can be grasped, we believe, only by pluralistic methods and multiple projects adapted to the problems and the materials confronting each researcher. But out of such efforts, both individual and co-operative, should come scholarship capable of depicting and appraising the Confucian state and its present-day heritage.

THE INTELLECTUAL HISTORY OF CHINA
PRELIMINARY REFLECTIONS

BENJAMIN SCHWARTZ

THE FOLLOWING reflections, somewhat abstract and sententious in nature, have arisen out of an attempt to prepare a study of the intellectual history of China in the twentieth century (what is contemplated is actually a study of topics in twentieth-century intellectual history). The reflections fall roughly into two categories—reflections on the concept of intellectual history in general and on modern China as a field of intellectual history. The two categories, while very much involved in one another, may nevertheless be treated separately.

1. A Concept of Intellectual History

"Intellectual History" has always been a particularly hazy area of human inquiry. The term has been appropriate to a variety of uses, all of them legitimate in themselves but often quite different from one another in content. So muddy is the concept that some statement concerning one's own use of the term would seem to be incumbent on anyone venturing into this area.

There are at least two problems involved: (1) How is one to define the scope and limits of the field? (2) How does one conceive the relationship between the field in question and other disciplines?

To consider the second question first, one may, of course, conceive of intellectual history as a sort of autonomous process which concerns itself with thought exclusively, without ever raising the question of its relationship to other fields of human experience. The present writer must confess to a prejudice against such an approach *within the field of history*. Within the field of history, intellectual development—like all other historical studies—must be considered as part of a total existential complex. One may focus on one area, but one must be acutely conscious of the whole penumbra. On the other hand, one can hardly touch the problem of the relationship of "thought" to other areas of experience without becoming involved in philosophic discourse and without revealing one's philosophic presuppositions. Our American academic community is, to be sure, full of people who are convinced that they are untainted with the sin of having philosophic assumptions. They achieve this amazing belief by invoking the magic word "science" on every possible occasion. What generally happens, of course, is that in dealing with the relationships among the disciplines they simply take their own unexamined assumptions for granted. Whitehead has defined the criticism of assumptions as the central task of philosophy. So long as one is convinced that one has no assumptions or that one's own assumptions are simply "science" pure and simple, this task will, of course, never be performed. In the following paragraphs I should like to make as explicit as possible a few assumptions concerning one view of intellectual history.

In defining the focus of intellectual history, this writer has found it rewarding to think in terms of men's conscious responses to the situations in which they find themselves. Both these terms—"conscious response" and "situation"—call for further elucidation.

The word "situation" can be applied to perennial features of men's situations in all times and places—to the great universal human themes of birth, death, love, etc., or to the specific social and cultural situations of given times and places. Men are born into specific societies with specific institutions, specific cultural conditions, specific intellectual currents, etc. One might raise the question whether there are not certain choice spirits (a Spinoza or Shakespeare comes to mind) who may orient themselves primarily to the universally human rather than to their specific historic situation. Thus in that generation of notable figures which spanned the late nineteenth and early twentieth centuries in China (Yen Fu, T'an Ssu-t'ung, K'ang Yu-wei, Chang T'ai-yen, and others) there was one—Wang Kuo-wei—who, in his youth at least, disdained the overwhelming concern of his contemporaries with the current political plight of China and concerned himself with the perennial problem of the meaning of human existence, desperately seeking answers in Kant, Schopenhauer, and Nietzsche. It is not difficult to prove, however, that Wang Kuo-wei did not, after all, escape from his historic situation. The facts that he was a scion of a scholarly family, that he was no longer satisfied with traditional Chinese solutions, and that he came in contact with Japanese who happened to be interested in German philosophy are all circumstances which bind him to his time and place.

While it may be accepted as axiomatic that one can never escape an orientation to one's historic situation, it does not follow that the relation between the situation and the various conscious responses to it is a simple causal nexus, that a given situation simply "causes" a given response.

Historic situations as they are actually faced existentially are full of ambiguities. They are highly problematic and indeterminate in nature and are quite enigmatic on the question of which response is the most adequate. Of course, once a given conscious response has come to prevail, the historian can glibly allege a neat causal nexus, eloquently proving that all other responses were doomed to failure. What is here being challenged is the very notion that this retrospective view is necessarily closer to "reality" than the perspective which attempts to capture the situation as it may have appeared *in processu,* in its unresolved state. From the point of view of intellectual history as here conceived, it is, in fact, the latter perspective which is the more "real," since it reflects the state in which men actually make their conscious responses.

The general term "conscious response" may not be the happiest, but it has been used rather than "thought," "ideas," or "ideology" to indicate that intellectual history as here conceived involves more than the exercise of intellect. It also involves those areas of conscious life which have variously been called "emotional attitudes," "pathos," "propensities of feeling," etc. It will be readily admitted that all these are involved in men's conscious responses to their situations. Arthur Lovejoy includes this whole range of responses under the heading of the "history of ideas," but one cannot help feeling that he has stretched the meaning of "idea" well beyond its meaning in ordinary usage. To cite a concrete instance of what we have in mind, Lu Hsün—that key figure in modern China's intellectual development—during his youthful days in Japan conceived a tremendous affection for Nietzsche. In attempting to reconstruct from Lu's contemporary writings, later reminiscences, and the testimony of others the exact nature of his attachment to Nietzsche, one is led to the tentative conclusion that he was not really committed to the whole system of Nietzscheanism as a Weltanschauung, nor did he share all the preoccupations and exasperations of Nietzsche. What seems to have attracted him, above all, was a certain emotion-charged image of the sensitive, spiritual hero confronting a stupid and vicious world—confronting "the mob." This pathos which can be found in Nietzsche, but which can also be found in others with quite different views, seems to have struck a sympathetic chord in the sensitive and somewhat bitter young man. It has been reported that at the same time he was also very much enamored of Byron's poetry. Thus what Lu Hsün found in Nietzsche was not a whole body of doctrine but a certain welcome pathos. While such a pathos is not an idea in the strictly intellectual sense, it is certainly of immediate interest to the intellectual historian as here conceived.

This focus differs somewhat from the focus of the history-of-ideas approach, for the latter, as practiced by Lovejoy, concerns itself mainly with the relations of ideas to ideas (although, as pointed out, the concept of "idea" is very broadly conceived, either in historical or in logical terms, to encompass the historic vicissitudes and logical implications of ideas). Thus in his *Great Chain of Being* he follows the vicissitudes of certain Platonic ideas down through the ages. He uncovers the various guises in which these ideas have appeared and clarifies the tensions which have developed between these ideas and other ideas within the European stream of thought. In all this, he remains strictly within the stream of thought, and, while there are strong implications that these ideas have exercised a profound influence on other spheres of human behavior, this influence is not spelled out.

While granting the fruitfulness of this approach, our focus here is more on ideas within the context of men's responses to their life situations. The relationship of ideas to ideas cannot be overlooked, since the intellectual tendencies of previous generations and of one's contemporaries form an integral and important part of the situation itself. On the other hand, there are included within this situation givens which lie outside the stream of thought—institutions, technological facts, political conditions, and the like.

However, while the focus of intellectual history as here conceived differs somewhat from that of the history-of-ideas approach, the high respect for the *content* of ideas which that approach demands might well be emulated by anyone who turns his attention to this field. One of the besetting sins of intellectual history, as it has been practiced, has been an irresponsible dilettantism in dealing with ideas. One hurriedly identifies some body of ideas by some conventional name such as "liberalism" or "romanticism" and then leaps to an "explanation" of these ideas in terms of their presumed genetic antecedents. To assign causes is a much simpler operation than to determine as accurately as possible *what* men *think*. The history-of-ideas approach advances the simple proposition that so long as one deals with ideas one must make an honest effort to understand what these ideas are, painful and laborious as the effort may be. If one is dealing with vague thoughts and ill-defined ideas, it is important to be able to detect this vagueness and lack of definition. To understand the conscious responses of men to their situations, one must make a serious attempt to understand their ideas, for, no matter how mistaken men may be, they tend to believe that they act on the basis of their ideas.

The stress laid in the history-of-ideas approach on the meaning of words—on not resting content with semantic monsters like "nature" or "romanticism," which are so richly laden with levels of meaning that they are almost meaningless—is particularly relevant, it seems to me, to the intellectual history of modern China. On the side of the Chinese tradition, it is quite misleading, for instance, to cover the thought and attitudes of men like Chang T'ai-yen and K'ang Yu-wei with the simple label "Confucianism." This applies with even more force to Western ideas in China. We must not rest content with such murky categories as "liberalism," "socialism," "evolution," or "democracy." To say, for instance, that Yen Fu was a liberal during his earlier period does not relieve us of the necessity of attempting to analyze the various strands of thought which he espoused—their implicit logic and mutual consistencies and inconsistencies as well as his own perspectives on the whole range of thought with which he dealt. Are Social Darwinism and the Liberalism of John Stuart Mill mutually compatible? How indeed does Yen Fu conceive of Mill's ideas?

Regarding the "controversy over science and humanism"[1] which raged in certain intellectual circles in China during 1923, one might sum up the position of one side by saying that its protagonists believed that all human problems were amenable to the application of the scientific method. A closer look at their writings reveals, however, that Ting Wen-chiang is an exponent of Pearson's philosophy of science, that Hu Shih is an exponent of Dewey's pragmatism, that Ch'en Tu-hsiu considers himself a dialectic materialist, and that Wu Chih-hui is a sort of humorous exponent of an eighteenth-century type of materialism. In terms of their subsequent development, these differences were to loom much larger than their common devotion to the catchword "science." Modern Chinese intellectual history is particularly rich in this type of semantic pitfall, and Lovejoy's cautions are peculiarly relevant to it.

The ideal goal, then, of the intellectual historian as here conceived is to achieve as thorough an understanding as possible of the conscious responses of the individuals or groups with which he is in dealing. In the first instance, this means to attempt to see their situations as they see them, to attempt to understand their ideas as they understand them. This is, of course, an ideal—and a remote ideal at that. There are all sorts of reasons for doubting the possibility of realizing it. Can we really participate vicariously in the mental and emotional processes of others? Do their written records really furnish us with adequate clues? Probably the most one can achieve are a few insights here and there seen as through a glass darkly, and yet the striving toward this ideal is the main *raison d'être* of the intellectual historian.

Those who are inclined to leap to genetic explanations of thought may feel that one can avoid the necessity for this sort of hazardous and uncertain undertaking by getting down to the solid bedrock of cause. Unfortunately, however, in order to establish a causal nexus, one must know the "what" of the effect as well as the "what" of the cause. To say, for instance, that a given attitude reflects a given class background, one must know what the attitude in question is. Those who leap immediately to the cause simply grossly underestimate the difficulties of achieving an understanding of the effect.

Beyond this, our hesitancy to resort immediately to genetic explanations springs from an assumption that the conscious responses of men to their situations are something more than the effect of the historic situation as a whole or of any genetic explanation that can be brought forth. What is here being posited is a limited freedom—a limited creativity of men in their conscious responses. This does not mean that this freedom is not hedged in by a multitude of factors— biological, psychological, social, and so on. It does mean that the task of the intellectual historian is somewhat less modest than that of providing corroborative data to confirm the validity of a given sociological, economic, historical, or anthropological theory.

It is perhaps a trite objection to consistent determinisms to point out that the determinist no less than others is determined by the conditions which he describes—trite, but not easily refuted. Karl Mannheim, after heaping considerable scorn on the notion that man's conscious life plays any role other than that of reflecting the sociohistoric process as he conceives it, after disposing of the thought of everyone who disagrees with him as "ideology," suddenly, in the final section of his *Man and Society*,[2] posits the existence of a group of planners—all presumably duplicates of himself—who are free of all taint of particular interest and all limiting conditions. They are, as it were, disembodied pure intelligences able to remold society in the light of unadulterated reason. The emergence of these pure and untainted minds is, of course, itself presumably the end product of the sociohistoric process, which indicates, incidentally, how close Mannheim still is to Hegelian-Marxist utopianism in spite of his seeming scorn of utopianism. History will be redeemed through the sociologists rather than through the proletariat. Thus we are offered, on the one side, the image of a man in the pre-Mannheim era whose thought is nothing but a reflection of its sociohistoric antecedents and, on the other, the image of the post-Mannheim planner unconditioned by factors of time and place. A view which begins by denying to thought any precarious creativity ends by assuming a type of freedom which is humanly inconceivable. Mannheim's is not the only determinism which thus passes over into its opposite.

However, if it is not the first task of the intellectual historian, as here conceived, to provide corroborative evidence for some genetic theory, this does not mean that he is not interested in the light which a consideration of background factors may throw on the conscious responses of the individuals or groups he is studying. He should, as best he can, attempt to gauge whether the various genetic theories which he encounters do or do not, in fact, help to an understanding of the concerns and preoccupations of his subjects. He should not, however, be satisfied with a vague plausibility or arbitrary correlation. A good example of such arbitrary correlations is provided by some of the vulgar Marxist class analyses in which the Chinese Communists indulge. K'ang Yu-wei, to cite one instance, has been assigned to the bourgeoisie. Now this obviously has nothing to do with K'ang's class origins, which were clearly mandarin, or with the role he played throughout his life, which was that of the mandarin for the most part out of office. It is true that after 1898 he had financial contacts with overseas Chinese who can be called bourgeois, but this was in his postbourgeois "feudal" period. To call him "bourgeois" because of the content of his thought is to assume that some clear definition of bourgeois thought is available—which is, of course, not true. The illusive nature of this class imputation is simply covered by the arbitrary obiter dictum that "objectively" K'ang belongs to the bourgeoisie. The bases of such "class analyses" are so vague that it has been possible to assign Chiang Kai-shek now to one class and now to another. Such arbitrary correlations are by no means confined to the Marxist-Leninists.

On the other hand, where significant facts can be adduced in support of a given correlation, it may be signal aid to the intellectual historian. It has often been pointed out, for instance, that the bulk of the intelligentsia in twentieth-century China is of official-scholar background. This fact may well help to explain some of the common predispositions and persistent habits of this intelligentsia—its aversion to business as a vocation, its high regard for the political vocation, certain elitist tendencies, etc. To the extent that such predispositions are common, this explanation is most helpful. The explanation does not necessarily determine in advance, however, which of those predispositions are likely to survive and which to be reversed. Chinese communism seems to represent the continuation of some of these predispositions and the destruction of others. Nor is a consideration of these common predispositions at all helpful when we are coping with profound differences within the intelligentsia—between, let us say, Lu Hsün and the liberals of the "Crescent" (*Hsin-yueh*) group, or between K'ang Yu-wei and Chang T'ai-yen.

Thus, to the extent that genetic hypotheses drawn from various disciplines concretely and specifically help the intellectual historian in his attempt to understand, they are most welcome to him. It is not, however, his primary task as an intellectual historian to furnish confirmation of one hypothesis or another. The other disciplines may, of course, use the data he is able to furnish for their own purposes.

Furthermore, having assumed that men's conscious responses are not completely determined from behind, we shall venture an even bolder assumption, namely, that men's conscious responses to situations constitute one of the dynamic factors in changing situations. It is, of course, possible to write intellectual history without making this assumption. Santayana, who explicitly and vehemently denies the capacity of thought to affect other areas of human activity, seems to find the value of intellectual history in the sardonic aesthetic pleasure which it provides. Since he has absolutely no desire to "transform man," he can, unlike Mannheim, maintain this point of view quite consistently.

This assumption has not been made in ignorance of the vast problem of the relation of ideas to power interests or in ignorance of the distortion and transformation which ideas often undergo when they become enmeshed with power interests, in brief, the problem of the conversion of ideas into ideologies. On the contrary, the problem is a genuine problem not to be disposed of by such simplistic formulas as (*a*) that in considering the actualization of ideas one can ignore the transformation which they undergo when they become enmeshed with power interests or (*b*) that all ideas are from beginning to end nothing but rationalizations of power interests. What is needed above all, in the absence of any general theory which will do justice to both poles of the dichotomy, are concrete studies of the ways in which specific ideas relate themselves in time to specific constellations of power. A study of the rise of Chinese communism, for instance, has led the present writer to the view that neither (*a*) nor (*b*) is a useful

assumption in attempting to assess the role of ideas in that movement. It has rather appeared that, while some elements of the Marx-
ist-Leninist complex have actually molded the thought, emotions,
and behavior of the leaders of the movement, other elements have
become a ritualistic dead letter or mere rationalization. Marxism-
Leninism has created, shaped, a new ruling group and at the same
time has been twisted and manipulated to serve the interests of that
group. It has played the roles both of animating idea and of animating ideology. Other ideas may relate themselves in other ways to the
social conflicts of their time and place. Concrete studies, unburdened
by simplistic assumptions, are likely to prove of most help in dealing
with this most thorny subject at this time.

Having made these undefended assumptions concerning the relations of thought to other areas of human experience, we might venture some opinion concerning the relations of intellectual history, as
here conceived, to the question of the validity of thought. The most
obvious observation which comes to mind is that it is not the business
of the intellectual historian to validate thought but rather to understand it. Unimpeachable as this proposition may be, to state it is not
to escape the formidable difficulties involved in acting on it. Our own
judgments are bound to influence our understanding. We may be
inclined, for instance, to lay particularly heavy weight on genetic
factors in accounting for thought which does not appeal to us. John
Dewey in his vehement hostility to the contemplative ideals of Plato
and Aristotle simply disposes of their thought, at one point, as the
product of a slave society. "It seems to me," he states, "that this
genetic method of approach is a more effective way of undermining
this type of philosophic theorizing than any attempt at logical refuta-
tion could be."[3] (Since then the same method has been used by Communists to dismiss Dewey as the voice of monopoly capitalism.)
Now, this haste to dismiss the thought of Plato and Aristotle in terms
of its "causes" actually springs from a passionate feeling that they
are wrong and not simply from a passionless desire to "explain" their
thought. It is, nevertheless, the faith of the intellectual historian, as
here conceived, that however involved we may ourselves be in the
issue which we are considering we may nevertheless—up to a point—
suspend our own views long enough to attempt to achieve an understanding of the preoccupations and lines of reasoning involved in the
thoughts of others. A certain possibility of self-transcendence is here
assumed.

Actually, a conscious awareness of our own commitments may help us, to some extent, to draw a line between our own views and our attempt to comprehend the views of others. At best, of course, a certain residue of personal interpretation is bound to remain. Yet it is doubtful whether this conscious involvement is quite as prejudicial to the cause of objectivity as the illusion that one has reached a state of Olympian detachment from those ideas that agitate the individuals, groups, and periods which one studies. There are those who are firmly convinced that they have available methodologies which free them from any possible concern with questions of validity. Dilthey seems to have felt that his general lack of commitments resulting from his historicism made it possible for him to present a passionless yet sympathetic picture of the most diverse times and places.[4] Is it likely, however, that Dilthey would have furnished a truly trustworthy and cool account of modes of thought which called his historicism into question? Has Karl Mannheim ever been able to present a painstaking or accurate account of philosophies which assume the metahistoric validity of human thought? To do so would have been to face the realization that the premises of his *Wissenssoziologie* constituted merely one set of metaphysical propositions among others.

In brief, then, while it is true that the ideal of the intellectual historian is to understand and not to judge, yet, if he is honest with himself, he will be aware of the fact that he is not free of commitments on various issues which he encounters in the course of his studies. While these commitments are bound to color his understanding to some extent, he can make an effort to distinguish in his own mind between his commitments and his attempt to understand the conscious responses of others. On the other hand, the illusion of complete noninvolvement, with all the self-deceptions it nourishes, is more detrimental to objectivity than a lively sense of involvement controlled by the desire to understand.

I have attempted here to defend a conception of intellectual history which grants it a degree of independence from both the realm of genetic explanations and the realm of validification. No attempt has been made, however, to deny its close relationship to both these realms. The basic assumptions of this conception may be summarized as follows:

1. The focus of intellectual history does not lie merely in the area of thought conceived of as a self-contained process. It is concerned with men's total conscious responses to their life situations.

2. The ideal of the intellectual historian is to achieve as complete

an understanding of the inner world of his subjects as possible. He is not, in the first instance, interested in "explaining" their thought in terms of its supposed genetic causes, and he even assumes a limited freedom of men in this area. He is, however, interested in genetic hypotheses to the extent that they truly shed light on background factors in the thought of his subjects.

3. Regarding men's conscious responses as one of the dynamic factors in human behavior as a whole, he is interested also in the relationship of ideas to other areas of human activity.

4. While rejecting the illusion that he stands somehow outside and above any views on the validity of the thought he encounters in his investigations, he nevertheless attempts to draw a line between his own judgments and his attempt to understand the thought of others.

2. Twentieth-Century China as a Field of Intellectual History

Having ventured certain unsupported reflections on the scope and limits of intellectual history as a field of study, I should now like to consider briefly some more specific problems—not entirely unrelated to the issues considered above—which come to mind in contemplating twentieth-century China as a field of study.

The first question which comes to mind is: To what extent does twentieth-century China constitute a legitimate time unit? It is notorious that historians can generally provide eloquent reasons for the most diverse ways of cutting the melon of history. Without pressing the matter too hard, it seems to me that the period of the turn of the century constitutes one legitimate dividing point, among others, in modern China's intellectual history. It was a period in which certain notable figures—Yen Fu, Liang Ch'i-ch'ao, and others—began to manifest an interest in Western thought as thought. (In the case of Lin Shu it was an interest in the whole new range of sensibilities available in Western literature.) This was in contrast to the "Self-strengtheners" and "Western Affairs" experts who had been interested in Western thought only to the extent that it was relevant to a mastery of material technology or social technology (e.g., industrialism). This is, of course, a most imperfect division at best. Traces of intrinsic interest in Western thought can be found before this. There is also the whole problem of the ideology of the Taiping Rebellion. However, it is only at the end of the century that the change in question comes to occupy the center of the stage. Furthermore, however varied, fragmentary, and confusing the intellectual life of the period may be, there are certain constant elements in the historic situation confronted by the articulate intelligentsia. Underlying all the intellectual confusion there is an enduring spiritual and intellectual crisis involving the relations of traditional Chinese modes of thought and values to various strands of thought out of the West.

To those who are attracted by periods when cultures are in high bloom, twentieth-century China may well seem a wasteland. A period in which traditional modes of thought are in trouble and obliged to defend themselves as best they can, and in which the major energies of the intelligentsia are involved in the process of assimilating strands of thought from the West, may not seem to offer material of absorbing interest to the historian of thought.

Nevertheless, twentieth-century China does offer fascinating avenues of inquiry to the intellectual historian as here conceived, since his interest lies not simply in the content of ideas qua ideas but in the total conscious responses of men to their situations. Even to the "historian of ideas" as such, twentieth-century China offers abundant material for reflection. This is particularly true of the writings of that generation which overlapped the two centuries—K'ang Yu-wei, Chang T'ai-yen, T'an Ssu-t'ung, Yen Fu, Wang Kuo-wei, and others. These were men who had genuine roots in Chinese traditional culture, who used a linguistic instrument still saturated with traditional modes of thought, and who were, nevertheless, already open to the influence of Western modes of thought. It is challenging to ponder what happens when Yen Fu translates a word as ambiguous in the Western tradition as is "nature" with a word equally ambiguous in the Chinese tradition—*t'ien*. It is equally fascinating to read the commentaries he interlards in his translations, in which he compares Western concepts with Chinese concepts or illustrates Western concepts with examples drawn from Chinese experience. It is fascinating to reflect on the pioneer efforts in comparative philosophy which one finds in Wang Kuo-wei's youthful essays on Kant, Schopenhauer, and Nietzsche, or to find in Chang T'ai-yen's essay on evolution a treatment of that subject in terms of the Mere Ideational (Vijñanavadin) school of Buddhist philosophy. To those interested in novel juxtapositions of ideas, in their mutual consistencies and inconsistencies and immanent logic, these writings offer rich opportunity for fresh inquiry. While the writings of subsequent generations are by no means so rich in problems of this type, the very transfer of Western ideas and systems to a new environment allows us to view these ideas in new perspectives. European Marxists during the latter part of the nineteenth and early part of the twentieth centuries were not overwhelmingly concerned with the problem of the "Orient" in Marx or even with the whole discussion of "precapitalist societies." Among Chinese Marxists, these problems have perforce come to occupy the center of the stage. What have been the implications of the shift in emphasis for the Marxist system as a whole? What happens to Dewey's pragmatism in the hands of Hu Shih, confronting conditions radically different from those in twentieth-century America?

In addition to providing new opportunities for inquiry in the area of the "history of ideas," twentieth-century China raises highly significant questions in the area which we have chosen to regard as central, namely, the area of the responses of men to their situations, the concerns and preoccupations which lead to the acceptance of one strand of thought and the rejection of another. Why have certain Western ideas been warmly received in China while others have been met with cold indifference? Before any fruitful inquiry can take place in this area, we must be ready to reject glib and plausible answers provided in advance of any close inquiry into the evidence. We must also reject, it seems to me, the simply dichotomy "Chinese traditionalism versus Western modernism." Neither pole in this dichotomy constitutes a monolithic whole. On the Chinese side, a close scrutiny indicates that Chinese traditionalism was no monolith. The literati who confronted the West in the nineteenth century were divided among themselves. Some were still ardently wedded to the Han Learning scholasticism; some still clung to Neo-Confucianism. Others supported the *Kung-yang* school, while still others had a lingering interest in Buddhist metaphysics, and so on. There were, of course, also eclectic combinations of all these elements. On the Western side, to speak of some one entity which can be labeled the "modern West" is even more misleading. The Western intellectual world which confronted Yen Fu, Liang Ch'i-Ch'ao, and others was bewildering in its fragmentation. To remind ourselves of just a few cross-currents— eighteenth-century types of liberalism were still strong in western Europe, yet nineteenth-century reactions against this liberalism had long set in. It was thus not anomalous for Yen Fu to translate both Montesquieu and Huxley. Socialism according to its various schools was already highly crystallized, as were various schools of conservative antiliberalism. The belief in historic progress was widely cherished, but the attacks of Schopenhauer, Nietzsche, and others had already taken place. Social Darwinism was being interpreted simultaneously in an individualistic and a nationalistic sense. Cutting across all this was the aesthetic reaction against modern industrial utilitarianism.

Thus the question which confronts us is seldom that of why "Western modernism" is accepted or rejected but why such and such a current finds favor while another is rejected. So overwhelming has been the prestige of Western ideas as a whole, however, that even neotraditionalists are as likely to seek support in Bergson, Bertrand Russell, or Spann as in the Chinese classics.

The following is a random selection of some of the problems which come to mind within this area: Why did Lu Hsün, at a relatively early age, cut himself off almost contemptuously from western European literary influences? Why was Ch'en Tu-hsiu unable to come to terms with the Maoist version of Chinese communism? Why does the May Fourth period (1919 and after) seem to mark not merely a high point but in some senses a terminating point in receptivity to Western ideas? One is often struck by the fact that major modes of thought which were, with modifications, to dominate the Chinese intelligentsia for the next thirty years were already on the scene in the immediate post–May Fourth period. Except for scattered individuals and small groups, one does not have the impression that new developments in Western thought subsequent to World War I and the Russian Revolution have exercised any great influence in modern China. How can one account for the amazing success of academic Marxism in China after the early twenties?

The answers which one may attempt to provide to such questions do not, of course, enjoy the support of scientific proof. The type of problem considered is so portentous and significant, however, that some effort to cope with them seems justified.

One of the most obvious values of the intellectual history of twentieth-century China presumably lies in the light it may shed on the course of recent history. One cannot, of course, assume that it does shed any light unless one assumes that men's conscious lives do indeed affect other areas of their behavior. If one does assume that the acceptance of Marxism-Leninism by large segments of the Chinese intelligentsia has been a vital factor in shaping the course of events (in other words, that what has happened is not simply the product of "Oriental Society," Fitzgerald's wheel of history,[5] or other nonconscious forces), then a study of the total intellectual milieu within which Marxism-Leninism caught hold and spread is indeed most pertinent to an understanding of the course of events.

Whatever may be the values of twentieth-century China as a field of intellectual history, there can also be no doubt that this field is beset with pitfalls and difficulties, particularly for the Western novice. Leaving aside for lack of space the obvious pitfalls provided by the Chinese language—both *ku-wen* and *pai-hua*—let us consider one or two other difficulties which are not readily surmounted.

One is a difficulty which is, to some extent, inherent in intellectual history as an enterprise but which is peculiarly relevant to China, namely, the fact that intellectual history tends to be the history of intellectuals, a relatively small segment of the whole society. The question whether those who write or express themselves publicly do indeed, in some manner, reflect the thought of the society as a whole is in itself a most formidable one. In countries like twentieth-century China, in particular, one is confronted with the specific problem of an alienated intelligentsia—an intelligentsia which thinks thoughts and uses a language quite alien to the masses as a whole. It is true, of course, that since the May Fourth period many elements of this intelligentsia have been frantically eager to establish a rapport with the masses. This is true not only of leftists but also of supporters of traditional values, like Liang Sou-ming, who are convinced that these values have survived only among the rural masses. There is a large body of literature which attempts to communicate to us the lives of the masses, and yet one always suspects that this literature reflects the preconceptions of the urban authors more accurately than it reflects the lives of the masses. The fictional writings of a man like Lu Hsün undoubtedly give us genuine glimpses into the lives of nonintellectuals, but he is much more interested in portraying the horrible effects of the "old society" upon them than in giving us insights into their inner world. Recently there have appeared some Japanese studies of popular secret societies in the twentieth century which may cast some light on the inner world of certain segments of China's nonintellectuals. There are also village studies which attempt this task. In the end, however, we must admit that a study of China's intellectual history in the twentieth century will concern itself mainly with those who have left written testimony. Limited as such an undertaking may be, it has its own justification. The group in question is a highly strategic group in the society as a whole. While it may be alienated from its society, it is not isolated from it, and the context of its thought is provided by the whole Chinese world in which it lives.

Another difficulty, which has already been mentioned in our general discussion of intellectual history, lies in the whole question of involvement. Are we not too intimately involved in the history of twentieth-century China to achieve any perspective? This question has often been raised with regard to all studies in contemporary history, but it probably applies with particular force to modern China.

It is true, of course, that in dealing with more remote periods factual documentation is likely to be fuller. "More of the facts are in" (although this is not always the case in intellectual history). However, unless the historian of the more remote period confines himself to the most minute type of monographic study, the question of interpretation always arises. It has often been observed that history is constantly being rewritten from the perspectives of the present. In the case of China, however, our involvement arises out of a common world crisis which engages the passions of us all. The only recourse we have is to cling to the faith that one can overreach one's self long enough to achieve some degree of understanding.

There are numerous other pitfalls which make any attempt to deal with this field tentative and uncertain. The crucial nature of the subject, however, which involves nothing less than the confrontation of civilizations, should embolden us to make the attempt.

PART I

The Role of Ideas in the Exercise of State Power

THE POLITICAL FUNCTION OF ASTRONOMY
AND ASTRONOMERS IN HAN CHINA

1. The Question of Despotism and Its Limitations
in Ancient China

A. THE PROBLEM

IN MOST of the early high civilizations of the world, observation of
celestial and other natural phenomena has played an important role.
This fact has given rise to a number of theories to explain it. Theories
which try to find a general explanation, valid for all civilizations of
this kind, can be divided roughly into two main types:

1. *Psychological theories:* The main reason for the interest in astronomy and astrology was the existence of "classificatory thinking"
or "associative thinking," also called an "archaic" or "prelogic" type
of thinking (Lévy-Bruhl), combined with the belief in a "celestial-
terrestrial parallelism" (A. Jeremias). Theories of this type began to
appear around 1910 and were developed mainly in the twenties. Perhaps the typical expression can be found in the books of Th. W.
Danzel.[1]

2. *Economic theories:* The main reason for the interest in astronomy and astrology was the need for a functioning calendar system
which would enable the ruler and his bureaucracy to give orders to
the population as to when it should begin to plant, to harvest, and so
on. Usually, theories of this type are connected with the theory of
"Oriental society" which stresses the importance of irrigation and
state direction of waterworks. Perhaps the typical expression of this
type of theory can be found in the earlier writings of K. A. Wittfogel.[2]

While China plays an important role in all these comprehensive
theories, no one theoretician has done real research on the basis of full
sets of original documents. Special studies in Chinese astronomy,
astrology, and calendar systems began in the early years of the century and developed again mainly in the twenties. Main foci of interest were:

1. The age of Chinese astronomy and the question whether it developed in China or was influenced by the West. I mention here the
names of men like L. de Saussure, H. Maspéro, E. Chavannes, Sh.

Shinzō, I. Tadao, and Tung Tso-pin, among others. In connection with this was raised the question of the age of Chinese civilization and especially of certain historical texts.

2. The role of astronomy and astrology or the "sciences" in general in Chinese thinking, especially political thinking. Here again interest soon turned to the examination of Chinese texts and their reliability. Work along this line has in the main been done by J. J. M. de Groot, A. Forke, Ku Chieh-kang, W. Eberhard, and H. Bielenstein, among others.

The following discussion intends to remain within the narrow framework of this second approach. It will, furthermore, limit itself to the Former Han period (206 B.C. to A.D. 8) and make only a few references to earlier or later periods. The problems to be discussed are: (1) what were the positions assigned to the ruler and to government in the cosmos during the time under consideration, and (2) what was the function of astronomy or astrology, and astronomers or astrologists, in relation to ruler and government?

In spite of the extensive literature on Chinese emperors, little attention has been paid to clarifying, for a given period of time, the concept of emperor[3] so that a comparison with similar concepts in other civilizations can be made. Was the Chinese emperor a despot?[4] A god-king? A combination of temporal and spiritual ruler? A representative of his nation? Or was he dissimilar to all of these and other possible forms known elsewhere? Exploration seems to be called for by recent discussions of the despotic character of the Chinese government.[5]

This question is intimately connected with the question of the character of the Chinese gentry: was the gentry a group of bureaucrats and "scholars" which depended solely upon the emperor and derived its economic and political power from him,[6] or had the gentry economic and political power resulting from its own structure? We do not attempt to discuss or to solve the whole problem here, but wish to pose it as a question and to explore only one of several possible approaches toward an answer for one specific period, the Han period. For later periods the situation and the answer are certainly different.

It is an interesting question whether monarchies in the preconstitutional period included within themselves institutional checks on the power of the ruler and, if so, what these checks were; and thinkers in such societies seem to have been aware of the importance of this point. As Wittfogel has pointed out, such checks could be constitutional or societal, and societal checks could be provided by independent centers of authority, or intragovernmental influences, or a "right of rebellion" or election of the despot. They could be provided also by laws of nature and patterns of culture. I would prefer to include "patterns of culture" in the category of societal checks but, in any case, regard this classification of checks as useful. However, in order to avoid the word "constitutional," with all its connotations, I would prefer classification under the categories "institutional" and "functional." The term "institutional" would include Wittfogel's "constitutional" checks but would include also other checks which have been given formalized expression in the shape of moral rules, philosophy, standard practices of behavior in certain standard situations. Such institutional checks may in certain situations be set aside and disregarded, but their existence or nonexistence is an important fact. Functional checks are those which have not found formalized expression; the behavior or the actions of certain social groups may, for instance, constitute such functional checks; by definition, functional checks operate in all applicable situations. They may coincide with institutional checks and strengthen them.

Medieval Europe had a system of institutional checks on the ruler in Christianity and the Christian church: the Bible offered moral standards which were regarded as binding for everybody, including the kings, if these wanted to uphold the claim to rule "by the grace of God." The Church was the organization which took over the duty, and had the power and prestige, to exercise criticism of a ruler who violated basic moral standards. And with the backing of Christianity and the Church individual administrators could also attempt to check the ruler in his actions. Thus, absolute as well as constitutional monarchies could exist.[7]

In the Islamic world, on the other hand, the situation was very different. Owing to the character of the Koran as a collection of regulations for the correct life of the individual, the individual, as Von Grunebaum recently pointed out,[8] was not responsible for state and society as long as the government sustained a framework in which the correct life could be lived. The ruler might be sinful and his acts unlawful, yet it was regarded as perfectly all right for a state official with literary and stylistic training to operate in the service of any state and for its aims. In such a society, although moral checks existed in the religion, no institutional framework provided for an efficient check on the ruler by the citizens. It was in such a society that a despotism (defined as unchecked personal rule) could develop.[9]

(Absolutism may be defined institutionally as personal rule in the interest of the state.)

In India a theory of government had evolved in which spiritual authority and temporal power, although both united in the king with the act of coronation, were separated conceptually.[10] As temporal ruler the king might be good or bad; as spiritual authority he was ruler by divine right and was controlled by a higher power—dharma.[11] This system provided for the possibility of criticizing the ruler when he violated dharma, while offering few possibilities for a criticism of the political actions of the ruler.

The king in ancient Egypt was regarded as a god[12] or an embodiment of the deity.[13] He had, therefore, absolute power over the land and its inhabitants.[14] He was the sole source of authority, but he could not act arbitrarily. He lived under the obligation to maintain *maat*, which is interpreted by H. Frankfort as "the right order,"[15] the inherent structure of the world. And justice is a part of this right order. The king, as a god, controlled social as well as natural forces.[16] Violations of the "right order" could be established, and servants of the king or citizens of the realm could be criticized for violating it, but, institutionally speaking, the king could hardly be criticized, since he was an embodiment of god.

In contrast to this concept, which also made despotism possible, the king in Mesopotamia derived authority from divine election[17] and acted as a servant of the gods who directed human affairs.[18] He had to represent the people before the gods and to administer the realm. The gods sent him signs to indicate whether or not they approved of his actions. In the case of bad signs, the king, as a poor servant of the gods, was in danger. The priests had to interpret the signs of the gods; they had to interpret also the answers the gods gave to the king's questions asked by the oracles.[19] Here the priests had great power in checking the actions of the king, and, as long as such a system prevailed, despotism was impossible. In addition, the power of the ruler was checked by law: law was regarded as divine, and even kings had to obey it.[20] A ruler had to supervise and amend laws, in order to bring the code up to date, but was not the source of law.[21] We remember that Egypt did not develop a law code.

Do similar checks exist in China, where we do not find a group of priests or a revealed book-religion with an organized church?[22] In other words, was ancient China a despotic state or could the power of the emperor be checked institutionally? At first glance, China after the feudal Chou period seems to have been a "despotic state";

at least, the Ch'in dynasty has often been regarded as such. It was exactly from this period that China had a fully developed law code. Although the Ch'in dynasty used the law as a means of control, it is indicated that everybody was subjected to the law, including the members of the elite. But, as K. Bünger has shown, the ruler did not "use his power to make whatever laws he and his aides deemed fit,"[23] as a true despot would have done,[24] but accepted a code which had been developed by his predecessors. All dynasties accepted the codes of the preceding dynasties, modifying or enlarging them only as far as might be necessary.[25] Bünger further shows that the promulgation of a code was not, institutionally, a one-sided action of the ruler but an "act of agreement" between ruler and ruled.[26] Laws were developed by Confucianist scholars in agreement with the moral system, and promulgated by the ruler. In promulgating a law and in deciding law cases, the ruler was bound by the moral system.[27] In this, we tend to see a check upon the ruler.

There is another argument that China after the Chou period was a despotic state because the ruler had the title *huang-ti*, which may tentatively be translated as "August Lord" and which contains the term *ti* used for *shang-ti*, the "Lord above," or *t'ien-ti*, the "Lord of Heaven,"[28] thus indicating a relation between the ruler and the highest deity. Moreover, the ruler was commonly called *t'ien-tzu*, "Son of Heaven."[29] Legends in connection with the founders of some of the early Chinese dynasties also indicate that the dynastic founder was not the child of human parents but was born of a human mother in a miraculous way.[30] Such a person[31] would, logically, be different from ordinary human beings, as was the Egyptian king, and not subject to any human law or criticism. Such a ruler would, therefore, be a "despot." The justification of revolution against him and of the creation of a new, legitimate dynasty would be very difficult.

In fact, at least at the time of Mencius, if not earlier,[32] the term "Son of Heaven" was regarded as symbolic: the ruler had mysteriously received a "mandate" from heaven (*t'ien-ming*) by which he was made the legitimate ruler. The mandate could be taken away from him and given to another man who would then be the legitimate ruler. The former, who was still ruling, would suddenly—and perhaps without being aware of it himself—have become an imposter to whom obedience was no longer owed. Mencius attempted to find a criterion by which to decide at what point the "mandate" had changed, and for him "popular opinion," i.e., the reaction of the educated elite, became the criterion. Thus, in Mencius' time the term

"Son of Heaven" was not taken literally and may already have been close to the clearly figurative definition of the *Po-hu-t'ung* (chap. 1), centuries later: "The King has Heaven as his father and Earth as his mother; he is the Son of Heaven."[33] The original thought—that a ruler is not an ordinary human being, since "Heaven" is his father—was revised[34] to refer only to ancestors of the few noble clans of antiquity which were supposed to have ruled China before the historical dynasties. Dynasties of historical time then tried only to prove their descent from one of these noble clans; pretenders tried the same, of course. Thus, the Han dynasty claimed to stem from Emperor Yao's family;[35] the Hsin dynasty of Wang Mang claimed to stem from Emperor Shun;[36] etc. In this formulation, the ruler was a human being but descendant from an original ancestor who had a supernatural father. As there were a number of families in the same situation, new dynasties could originate from a number of noble families, and a revolution was conceptually possible.

Another aid toward rationalization along the same line was a text in *Han-shu* (chap. 100a, p. 5a) that gave five signs which qualified Kao-tsu to be the creator of the Han dynasty: (1) he was a descendant of Emperor Yao (see above); (2) he had special bodily marks which indicated his mission; (3) heavenly signs appeared; (4) he had a good character; and (5) he was capable of selecting good helpers. This list is a mixture of old traditions and rational thinking.

At the time this text was written a completely different set of concepts had already emerged. Seals had been in use in offices during the Chou dynasty,[37] and in Han times even private persons had seals.[38] As in Near Eastern civilizations, sealing a document had the same meaning as a signature does today, and a document had to have a seal in order to be a legal document. The emperor had an imperial seal which he used to legalize documents; an emperor without a seal was not an emperor.[39] We know that the imperial seal of the Han dynasty came into the possession of Wang Mang,[40] and this was a decisive step on his way to the throne. According to Chinese tradition, the original imperial seal remained in China until the end of the Sui dynasty. It was then taken by the T'u-chueh, who returned it in 630, and in the tenth century it was definitely lost.[41] Wang Mang was the first to introduce the ritual of legitimate change of dynasty: the last ruler of the dynasty turns over the seal and other symbols of imperial power to the first ruler of the new dynasty in an impressive public ceremony.[42] In this conception the emperor is a human being who becomes ruler by being invested with symbols. During the investment ceremony the resigning ruler justifies his resignation by stating that he does not feel worthy to continue to rule and that the new ruler is the worthiest man in the world. Here arise possibilities for an institutionalized system of criticism.

B. PORTENTS OF NATURE AS A CHECK ON THE RULER

K. Bünger has shown in his above-quoted article that Chinese law already at its inception was not an arbitrary creation of a despot but a codification of earlier customary or other rules. The ruler could change only details; for example, only the type and measure of punishments. From the Han period on, according to Bünger, law was permeated by Confucianist moral standards. Such law presented a limitation on the power of the ruler. But it did not yet allow for criticism of the ruler. The concept of the ruler as the worthiest man in the world evidently opened up possibilities for criticism in a period when rationalization had progressed so far that the concept of the ruler as "Son of Heaven" was no longer taken literally. In a society in which the idea of a popular vote was not known,[43] the decision as to who was the worthiest man could be made by the deity only. As in Babylonia, where the ruler was "god's agent,"[44] the deity indicated its approval or disapproval by omens, or, in other words, astronomers could express criticism by explaining celestial or other signs.[45]

The Chinese, like the Pythagoreans and many other civilizations, including our own, believed in a "harmony" of nature: the course of natural phenomena is determined by individual laws which can be combined under one general law.[46] As the Chinese as well as the Pythagoreans had already attempted to express some of their laws in mathematical terms, the one general law was also conceived of as a mathematical law, generally as a number which included all numbers, the "Great number."[47] But instead of attributing apparent discrepancies, i.e., unusual celestial or natural phenomena, to inadequacies of the theories, such phenomena were thought to be the result of human activity, human interference in the balance of nature. Therefore, instead of correcting or adjusting the theory, men sought the sources of human interference.[48] China never developed the concept of the ruler as a god, as Egypt did. In such a case the ruler would have been able consciously to direct natural phenomena. The old concept of the ruler as "Son of Heaven" could imply that (a) his father, Heaven, used unusual phenomena to warn him in advance of a coming danger, in which case the phenomenon would have to come not after human action had taken place but as soon as action was planned, or (*b*) the celestial father could blame him for wrong actions by causing unusual phenomena, in which case the actions or at least some active preparation had to take place before the phenomenon occurred. The phenomenon might also be a castigation or punishment because of the direct harm it would do to the population (e.g., a drought or a flood). This concept could be retained even if the concept of "Son of Heaven" were replaced by a symbolic meaning given to the term or if the ruler were conceived of only as a very worthy human being. The underlying idea in all cases would be that the ruler was responsible for the normal functioning of nature. Another possibility is that (*c*) the phenomena do not concern the ruler personally but warn others of coming dangers, or (*d*) they make known publicly the wrong actions of others. These persons may be statesmen of the imperial court or administrators or feudal lords in the provinces. In this case, the emperor would not necessarily be regarded as personally responsible for the normal functioning of nature but would rather be regarded as the "state," represented by the administrators.

Our basic thesis is, therefore, as follows: we hypothesize that, in a society in which human beings are given the blame for disturbances of natural harmony, attribution of responsibility might reflect prevailing concepts of power vested in the ruler or in the elite collectively. The astronomers were regarded as interpreters of celestial signs. They were, of course, members of the elite. We hypothesize that, if they were regarded as mere tools of a despotic ruler, they might tend to fabricate good omens for him and/or unlucky omens for the bureaucracy; if, however, they were members of a responsible government under a ruler, their interpretations of celestial signs might blame the ruler as well as the rest of the responsible government.

We now propose to study lists of abnormal phenomena of the Han period and to try to find out to what degree they can clarify the issues discussed in the preceding pages.

2. *The Data concerning Natural Phenomena*

A. STATISTICAL ANALYSIS

The phenomena which were regarded as "signs" are called *tsai* or *i*, "catastrophe" or "unusual event"; in the texts we have used, *tsai* and *i* designate unusual natural phenomena of more or less severe impact upon mankind.

We start the investigation with the question, What is contained in the information on abnormal natural phenomena and what conclusions may be drawn from these data in relation to our problems? As we have translated and discussed abnormal phenomena in a previous study,[49] we give here only two examples of such texts, representing two typical basic forms of statement.

In the summer of the first year of [the reign-period] T'ien-han [100 B.C.], there was a great drought. In the summer of the third year [of the period T'ien-han, i.e., 98 B.C.] there was [again] a great drought.

Before this, the Erh-shih general [i.e., Li Kuang-li] had attacked Ta-wan [i.e., a state probably close to Ferghana], and had returned. In the first year of T'ien-han one started to exile people [to this distant place]. In the second year [of T'ien-han, i.e., 99 B.C.] in the summer, three generals attacked the Hsiung-nu. Li Ling [i.e., one of the generals] surrendered and did not return [*Han-shu*, chap. 27*ba*; 409*d* of the K'ai-ming ed.].

In the 6th month of the fourth year of Emperor Wen [i.e., 176 B.C.] there was a great snowfall.

Three years later, Ch'ang, King of Huai-nan, planned rebellion. It was discovered; he was removed and died on the way [to the assigned place].

The *Commentary to the I Ching* (*I-chuan*) of Ching Fang says: "Snowfall in summer is a warning that subjects start rebellion" [*Han-shu*, chap. 27*bb*, p. 412*b*].

The first part is a description of the event. It is followed by one or several "explanations" which often, as above, allow us to calculate exactly how many years there were between the event and the human action with which it was felt to be connected. In other cases, such as the second explanation of the second example, dating is possible only by inference.

Unusual phenomena of the Han period are systematically recorded in the "Han Annals" (*Ch'ien-Han-shu*, cited as *Han-shu*) in three places: (*a*) In the annals proper (*pen-chi*, chaps. 1–12). They are chronologically arranged and reported together with facts of political importance. They include celestial phenomena (eclipses, falling stars, etc.), terrestrial phenomena (droughts, floods, locusts, etc.), and other abnormalities. (*b*) In the chapter on the Five Elements (chap. 27). Here they are arranged according to topics and, within the topics, chronologically. Things recorded are, again, celestial as well as terrestrial and other phenomena. (*c*) In the chapter on astronomy (chap. 26). The arrangement is according to topics and, within the topics, chronologically. Things recorded are only such celestial phenomena as falling stars, irregular movement of planets, obscurity of the sun or the moon, unusual cloud formations, etc. Series *a* and *b* record portents from 206 B.C. to A.D. 5, while series *c* ends in 5 B.C.

We have arranged the data in Table 1, taking five years as the time unit, to enable us to represent them graphically (see Chart I). This

TABLE 1

Portents of the Han Period

Explanation.—The stub column gives the years, in five-year intervals. Column (*a*) gives the number of portents recorded in *Han-shu*, chaps. 1–12, for each five-year period. Added is the percentage of portents, calculated in percentages of the total sum of portents for the whole period of 211 years. Column (*b*) gives in the same form the portents and percentages taken from *Han-shu*, chap. 27; (*c*), from *Han-shu*, chap. 26; and (*d*) gives the number of portents (but no percentages) recorded in *Shih-chi*, chaps. 8–12. As the data in column (*c*) end in 5 B.C., the percentages are adjusted to cover the same period as those in columns (*a*) and (*b*).

Years	a		b		c		d
206–201	3	1.42%	3	1.34%	2	2.99%	..
200–196	1	0.47	1	0.45	1	1.49	..
195	8	3.78	5	2.24	2	2.99	..
190	9	4.26	7	3.13	0	0.00	..
185	4	1.89	3	1.34	0	0.00	..
180	5	2.37	9	4.02	0	0.00	3
175	5	2.37	6	2.68	0	0.00	..
170	1	0.47	1	0.45	0	0.00	..
165	2	0.95	1	0.45	1	1.49	1
160	2	0.95	3	1.34	6	8.96	..
155	5	2.37	5	2.24	4	5.97	7
150	9	4.26	6	2.68	8	11.94	8
145	6	2.84	5	2.24	1	1.49	10
140	9	4.26	4	1.79	2	2.99	..
135	7	3.31	5	2.24	3	4.48	..
130	4	1.89	4	1.79	0	0.00	..
125	3	1.42	4	1.79	0	0.00	..
120	5	2.37	3	1.34	0	0.00	..
115	9	4.26	5	2.24	1	1.49	..
110	1	0.47	2	0.89	2	2.99	4
105	2	0.95	4	1.79	1	1.49	1
100	0	0.00	5	2.24	0	0.00	—
95	5	2.37	5	2.24	0	0.00	
90	8	3.78	4	1.79	0	0.00	
85	5	2.37	5	2.24	1	1.49	
80	5	2.37	10	4.47	2	2.99	
75	4	1.89	6	2.68	6	8.96	
70	3	1.42	5	2.24	4	5.97	
65	1	0.47	1	0.45	0	0.00	
60	4	1.89	1	0.45	0	0.00	
55	4	1.89	2	0.89	0	0.00	
50	6	2.84	3	1.34	3	4.48	
45	2	0.95	9	4.02	1	1.49	
40	6	2.84	5	2.24	0	0.00	
35	11	5.20	9	4.02	1	1.49	
30	10	4.73	14	6.26	3	4.48	
25	7	3.31	4	1.79	2	2.99	
20	6	2.84	9	4.02	0	0.00	
15	9	4.26	12	5.36	2	2.99	
10	2	0.95	9	4.02	4	5.97	
5–1 B.C.	7	3.91	12	5.36			
A.D. 1–5	6	2.84	8	3.58	(2.99)		
211 years	211	100%	224	100%	64 (adjusted to 67)	100%	

42

CHART I

THE PORTENTS OF THE HAN PERIOD, AS REPORTED IN SERIES *a*, *b*, AND *c*. EACH COLUMN REPRESENTS A FIVE-YEAR PERIOD. THE PRESENTATION IS IN PERCENTAGES OF THE TOTAL. KEY: SERIES *a*: ———; SERIES *b*: ———; SERIES *c*: - - - .

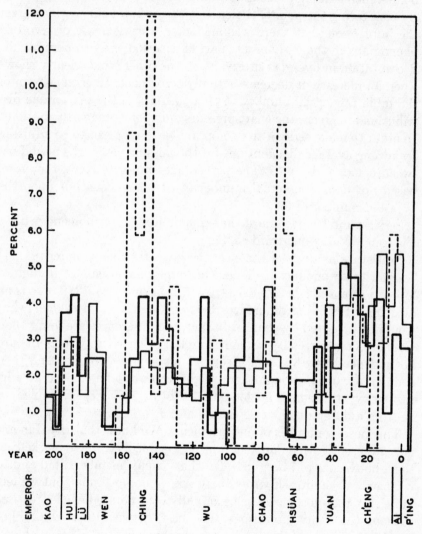

arrangement disregards the length of rule of individual emperors, which is indicated in Chart I on the abcissa. This arrangement seems preferable to the arrangement used by H. Bielenstein,[50] who represented by a point the arithmetic mean per year of the total phenomena recorded for an individual ruler and then connected these points, disregarding in his graph the differences in the length of rule. By connecting the points, Bielenstein arrived at a curve which gives the impression that there was an increase or decrease of recorded phenomena in the early or late part of a period of an emperor's rule. Presentation in five-year intervals, on the other hand, clearly shows when an increase or decrease actually took place. In each column of the table the actual number of phenomena and the percentage distribution are given; the chart presents only percentage distributions. In order to make series a to c comparable, series c had to be adjusted by adding average distributions for the missing years (the period between 5 B.C. and A.D. 5. The percentages in series c are, therefore, based not upon the actual number of 64 phenomena but upon the adjusted number of 67.

Series a and b have almost the same number of phenomena, while c has roughly only one-third as many.

Statistical analysis of these series[51] gives the following results: (1) There is no pronounced evidence of temporal consistency of high or low ratios of a to b in sequence ($p = 0.1$ on run test). (2) There is no evidence of striking differences between series a and b, over what would be expected by chance. In fact, the differences are fewer than would have occurred by random sampling. Conceivably the series are not independent. (3) Even if series a and b are combined and then compared with c, though there might appear to be considerable irregularity, still there is no good reason for regarding c, as sampled, to be from a different universe than a and b.

This poses a number of new problems. We know that the Han annals were edited by Pan Ku, who is assumed[52] to have worked on them between A.D. 74 and 84. To what extent he only edited and to what extent he himself wrote the work we do not know, but we feel quite sure that in some cases he actually incorporated whole treatises without too many alterations. The best-known case is the bibliographical chapter of the annals, which, it is believed, is based almost completely upon an earlier, independent work by Liu Hsin.[53] Chapter 27 of the annals is a systematic treatise[54] on the Five Elements, divided into a number of paragraphs, each of which starts with a discussion of theory and ends with a number of "illustrations." This chapter is clearly a unit and seems to stem essentially from the hands of Liu Hsiang (76–8 B.C.) and his son Liu Hsin (killed A.D. 23), i.e., it is some seventy years earlier than Pan Ku's final edition, assuming that Liu Hsin finished the treatise around A.D. 10. It seems unlikely that he finished it much later. Chapter 27 contains not only portents of the Han period but also phenomena of the Ch'un-ch'iu period. We know that Liu Hsiang and his son worked into their treatise all the phenomena which were recorded in the *Ch'un-ch'iu* and the *Tso-chuan*. We know, on the other hand, that they reported some phenomena (eclipses) which did not in reality happen,[55] and inserted these into the classics which they edited. We believe that these and possibly other insertions were made for political reasons.[56] Likewise, we might assume that they had similar lists covering the Han period down to their own lifetimes and used these lists as their second universe, which is the one concerning us here. We cannot prove this assumption, however.

The phenomena in series *b* (chap. 27) are to a large extent—but not completely—the same as in series *a*. Thus, series *a* cannot have been the universe from which *b* was drawn, nor vice versa. The events in series *c* differ strongly from those mentioned in series *a* and *b*. Out of the first twenty-five cases mentioned in series *c*, only *one*, the first one, is also mentioned in series *a*.

To complicate the situation still more, another list may be introduced. The *Shih-chi* contains data on phenomena covering the period from 206 to roughly 100 B.C. (in chaps. 8–12). These data are in the annalistic account of the Han dynasty in *Shih-chi*, therefore in the text which is parallel to series *a* from the *Han-shu*. But, while series *a* contains 100 phenomena for the period between 206 and 100 B.C., the *Shih-chi* series (*d*) contains only 34. Series *c* contains the same number of phenomena as *d*, but the portents as well as the distribution differ. Series *d* differs in its character from *a*, *b*, and *c*, in that it has no phenomena recorded for the period from 206 to 179 B.C. and, again, none between 140 and 111 B.C., i.e., for periods in which the other series had several clear-cut peaks. Therefore, although the *Shih-chi* (*d*) was finished more than one hundred and fifty years before the *Han-shu*, series *a–c* from the *Han-shu* are not copied from series *d*. Theoretically, series *a–d* could have taken their data from a common universe, as was suggested by the statistician, and for the time after 100 B.C. series *a–c* could have continued to use the same universe. This, however, seems very unlikely for two reasons: (1) *Han-shu* 26 (series *c*) is a well-structured chapter on astronomy, containing much technical information. Just as the chapter on bibliography is based upon Liu Hsin's catalogue of the imperial library, this chapter seems to have been written by a person who had access to the collection of data at the imperial astronomical office. (2) The explanations of some of the phenomena state explicitly that some of them were recorded not in the capital city but by "meteorologists" in the service of feudal lords in the provinces.[57] To some of the phenomena, explanations are given in chapters other than those used for series *a–d*. In those places it is often clearly stated that the event was made known to the emperor in a memorandum of a dignitary.[58] We assume, therefore, not that *one* central list of phenomena was kept, which was the common universe for series *a–d*, but that several independent lists existed, compiled by different central and provincial offices or excerpted from memoranda submitted by officials. The historians, i.e., the authors of chapters 8–12 of *Shih-chi*, 1–12 of *Han-shu*, 27 of *Han-shu*, and 26 of *Han-shu*, made use of these diverse lists.[59] The fact that the phenomena were selected, and selected in slightly different ways, indicates that subjective factors influenced the selection. In addition, at least in series *b*, strong reasons have been adduced to show that the authors added some phenomena.[60]

In view of the assumption that *Han-shu* 26 (series *c*) is in the main the work of a pre–Pan Ku author who made use of collections of data preserved in the astronomical office, a few words may be added on the position of this office in the bureaucracy, although we feel unable, at this point, to draw important conclusions. In Han bureaucracy the astronomical office was a special subdepartment in the "Ministry of Imperial and State Sacrifices" (*T'ai-ch'ang*). The officials who directed the observations, the *Ling-t'ai ch'eng* and the *Ming-t'ang ch'eng*, were in rank 13, i.e., fairly low. In the same ministry the office of historiography was located, and its chief was in a much higher rank (No. 7). The same arrangement seems to have existed before Han times, if we are allowed to take the statements of the *Chou-li* as a reflection of the basic form of Chou institutions as planned, but not necessarily as they functioned in actuality. According to these statements of the *Chou-li*, the astronomical office was located in the "Ministry of Spring," which corresponded to a ministry of imperial temples and state sacrifices, similar to the *T'ai-ch'ang* ministry. Again the office of historiography was in the same ministry. In T'ang times the *Men-hsia sheng*[61] contained one branch of historiography, reporting on the emperor's actions and utterances, while the *Chung-shu sheng*[62] contained the main office of historiography. Astronomy was brought, together with the calendar and the control of clocks, into the *Mi-shu sheng*, i.e., the Secret Secretariat, which, in the main, controlled the archives, libraries, and collections of documents, and in which one branch of writers wrote the texts for prayers and inscriptions. Here astronomy was more, but not completely, separated from historiography, and the office may be regarded as an office for keeping the ruler informed—a kind of reference bureau, like the libraries and archives.

B. INTERPRETATIONS OF THE DATA ON NATURAL PHENOMENA

Although a fair number of all phenomena are reported without commentary, there are many which are interpreted. For *all* cases in series *b* (*Han-shu* 27), explanations of a general character are given, because all cases of natural phenomena are classified under paragraphs of a theoretical character. The underlying theory is a development of the "theory of the Five Elements" as designed by Tsou Yen and others, combined with ideas taken from interpretations of the *Shu-ching*. These theoretical paragraphs are fairly general.[63] In addition, a goodly number of individual phenomena are connected with more detailed explanations, which often differ quite widely from what we should expect from theory. Even cursory reading shows that the margin for explanation within the framework of theory is very wide. There are few cases where the theory of the Five Elements is strictly applied. We will not enter here into a detailed analysis of this situation, since, for our purposes, only those cases can be used for which we have a detailed explanation with historical implications.

The portents in series *c* (*Han-shu* 26) are explained only in part; the enumeration in the text is not classificatory but classificatory-chronological. The phenomena in series *a* (*Han-shu* 1–12) and *d* (*Shih-chi* 8–12) are interpreted in only a few cases. This interpretation is sometimes direct, in so far as the ruler refers in a proclamation to the portent and proposes some action. Sometimes indirect interpretations are given: immediately after recording a portent another event, e.g., the death of an emperor, is recorded. In cases where the second event (according to the theory as expounded in *Han-shu* 27) is the event which is correlated with the portent, we are on safe ground in assuming that the second event in *Han-shu* 1–12 or *Shih-chi* 8–12 was regarded as connected with the portent. In other cases, we have refrained from connecting portents with events recorded in the same texts a few lines later, although, if we assume that the reason that phenomena were recorded in the text was the wish to express a criticism of the ruler or the government, we might logically assume that the historical facts mentioned after or before the phenomenon contain the object of such criticism.[64]

It might be added here that on such an assumption, in our opinion, hinges the evaluation and interpretation of Chinese historiography. The annalistic parts of the dynastic histories (*pen-chi*) are *not* biographies of the rulers. They are not even full records of court activities.[65] A superficial comparison of the "biography" of Emperor Wu of the Han dynasty as given by the *Shih-chi* and by the *Han-shu* makes this clear. The picture we get from the *Shih-chi* is that of a man whose main interests were magicoreligious activities, a man whose qualities seem to be quite doubtful. The picture which emerges from the *Han-shu* is that of a great military leader and great statesman.[66] Into the records of political and other court activities are inserted records of abnormal phenomena, most of which seem to us to be of no importance at all. We might, of course, take this at face value and conclude (*a*) that Chinese official historians had no real historical understanding because they were unable to separate politically important events from completely unimportant events, some of which could never in actuality have happened, such as the appearance of a dragon in a well in the provinces; and (*b*) that the Chinese, their historians included, were ridden by superstitions of a kind which is found among primitive peoples. As Confucius is credited with editing the *Ch'un-ch'iu*, and I see no proof to the contrary, he, too, would have been a man of the same caliber. It is the merit of O. Franke[67] to have adduced proof for the old Chinese opinion that the *Ch'un-ch'iu*, as well as later official dynastic histories, by the use of a special terminology and by the insertion of certain, seemingly unimportant, reports, became "mirrors," guides for political behavior, based upon a system of ethics. It is O. Franke's theory which has been the starting point for this entire discussion.

We now propose to analyze first some samples, taken from series *c* and *b*, before we proceed to a more general, comparative analysis.

1. We selected, as one example, the first twenty-five phenomena reported in series *c*, covering the period from 206 B.C. to 141 B.C. Of these cases, only the first one is mentioned also in series *a*. Of the twenty-five phenomena, twenty-three had negative and two had positive implications. The two "lucky omens" are the first two cases. These are interpreted as heavenly signs favoring the creator of the dynasty who was still struggling against the adherents of the old dynasty. We might note at once that "lucky omens" are very uncom-

mon and happen in all our series only at the beginning of the Han dynasty, when the dynasty had still to fight for final recognition, and at the end of the dynasty, when the signs are lucky omens for the coming dynasty of Wang Mang but are at the same time unlucky omens for the Han dynasty; that is, both situations are in principle quite identical, and "lucky omens" are, in a sense, also "unlucky omens."[68] In addition to these two instances among the first twenty-five portents, there are a very few other good omens scattered about, e.g., in 165 and 164 B.C. (series *a*) and under Emperor Wu around 116 and 113 B.C. These lucky omens are not different in kind from the unlucky portents; these cases have to be explained individually.[69] We propose to disregard in our further discussion the few "exceptions" of this type.

As far as the cases are fully explained, they are supposed to be connected with events of unlucky character for the emperor (six cases), princes and feudal lords in the provinces (eleven cases), the palace (two cases), and the empress (one case). The type of event which the celestial phenomena supposedly indicate varies: the emperor will be besieged for seven days by enemies; the emperor will die; there will be a revolt in a province; a feudal state will be destroyed, etc. The phenomena vary between the possible and the impossible: the planet Mars entered a special sector of the sky; there was a conjunction of Jupiter, Mars, and Mercury; the sky opened itself, etc.

2. We selected as a second example all fires reported in series *b* (*Han-shu* 27), covering the period between 191 B.C. and A.D. 5. A total of nineteen fires is mentioned. Sometimes there were several fires, at the same time but in different places, which the author of series *b* regarded as interrelated. The fires are all of the kind that destroyed parts of the palaces, imperial ancestor-halls, temples, or other symbolic buildings or grounds. No ordinary fires are mentioned.

Of these nineteen fires, fifteen are mentioned in series *a*, four are not mentioned. The last three cases of fire are interpreted as indicating the coming of Wang Mang as first ruler of a new dynasty; they are, therefore, unlucky omens for the existing dynasty but lucky omens for the coming dynasty and its supporters. The text explains them in the second meaning. Generally, the fires are seen as the result of wrong actions taken by the emperor (three cases) or the empress (two cases), or they indicate unlucky events which will affect the ruler (six), the empress (two), the crown prince (two), princes or feudal lords (five), or chancellors or other court dignitaries (five). (Often the unlucky event points at several of these persons at the same time; therefore, the sum of the numbers in parentheses is more than nineteen.) In a few cases the emperor makes use of the catastrophe by noting it in a declaration and asking the officials to come up with a criticism of policy; in one case he proposes a reduction of expenditures for the court.

This raises an important question: Could or did an emperor "order" portents as justification for some action? In many cases the possibility that the ruler "ordered" portents can be rejected, i.e., in all cases in which the portent was regarded as the consequence of wrong actions or incorrect behavior of the ruler or members of his own family. The eclipses which were "fabricated" (see below) were certainly not ordered by the ruler, because they predicted evil for him as a result of wrong action. In other cases the possibility of ordered portents exists; a clear-cut proof, however, seems quite difficult to obtain. The case of Wang Mang, in which we know that he ordered portents favorable for himself, is in another category, because this action of Wang Mang took place before he made himself emperor. We would expect a greater number of "lucky omens" if the ruler had omens fabricated, and such cases are very rare. If, however, the ruler had omens produced to justify some action, this would prove that he was not a despot but depended upon the consent of a social stratum which had its own power.

3. We have studied as a further example the first twelve eclipses mentioned in series *b*, covering the years between 204 and 173 B.C. All of them are also mentioned in series *a*. Eight of them are reported in series *b* without explanation. The eclipses announce unlucky events for the emperor (one case and, possibly, after interpolation with the context of series *a*, two more cases), the empress (one case with possibly one more after interpolation), or feudal lords (two cases and possibly three more after interpolation). In three cases the emperor exploited the event to issue proclamations in which he mentioned the event and used it as justification to dismiss the chancellor, to ordain an amnesty and a limited liberation of some categories of slaves, or to invite new politicians to come to the court and to reform the army. The most interesting fact about this series of eclipses is that five out of the twelve eclipses never took place, as can be ascertained by calculation.[70] In two cases out of these five the emperor died shortly afterward, in two others the emperor exploited them in the above-mentioned way, and in the last case the eclipse was regarded as indicating unlawful behavior of feudal lords and led to their subsequent punishment. As we have no reason to doubt the authenticity

of the proclamations, we might assume that in the two cases earlier mentioned the eclipses were "invented" at the time, in order to justify the proclamations or in order to influence the ruler to perform certain actions. But in the two other cases it is not easy to assume that people at the time invented an eclipse months before the death of the ruler in order to make him believe that he was supposed to die. Here the assumption that a later historian invented the eclipse after the death of the ruler seems much more logical.[71]

In most of the cases where an explanation of a phenomenon is given in series *a* or *d*, it is given in a subsequent proclamation of the ruler. This proclamation normally starts with the ruler's self-accusation: "Recently Yin and Yang were disturbed, wind and rain did not come in time. This is [the result of] my lack of *te* [spiritual power]."[72] The form of these "self-accusations" suggests that they are a conventional formula and do not have to be taken at face value. They serve as an introduction for political actions, such as cancellation of debts of citizens (85 and 79 B.C.), reduction of luxury (71 B.C.), reduction of expenses in the central administration (83 B.C.), or any other actions which naturally infringed the vested rights of some persons. It should be remarked here that in the years after 67 B.C. the ruler issued such proclamations almost year by year, while the text does not explicitly report single phenomena. The proclamations in these cases contain only general references to such portents. The historian may have judged it unnecessary to mention the phenomena separately.

If we compare the explanations of some of the portents as reported in different parts of the *Han-shu*, or even the explanations given by different persons and quoted in *Han-shu* 27 (series *b*), we find strong inconsistencies. The appearance of two moons in 32 B.C. was explained by Ching Fang as proving that the women around the emperor were too influential, the ruler too weak; by Liu Hsiang as proving that the ruler was too weak, the ministers too strong; by Liu Hsiang's son Liu Hsin as proving only the strength of the ministers. All these explanations are reported in the same paragraph of *Han-shu* 27. When in 26 B.C. a bird was reported to have burned its nest, this was connected by the author of *Han-shu* 27 with the murder of the crown prince by the empress Chao and her sister; by Ching Fang with the cruelty of the emperor; and by another person with the coming into power of Wang Mang (which happened some thirty-five years later).[73] In this, as in a number of similar cases, it is clear that the explanations were not given in 26 B.C. and were not memorialized to the emperor;[74] no one could foresee in 26 B.C. that Wang Mang would overthrow the dynasty in A.D. 9; Chao Fei-yen was not yet in full power and had not yet killed the crown prince. It seems to me very unlikely that a memorandum to the throne directly accused an emperor of cruelty. These explanations, therefore, were made by the historian, i.e., one of the many persons involved in the composition of the text which finally was edited by Pan Ku in the late first century A.D.

There are other cases too: two fires in imperial buildings in 53 and 46 B.C. are connected by Liu Hsiang[75] with the favors given by the ruler to Shih Hsien and the unfair treatment of Hsiao Wang-chih. Shih Hsien, incidentally, was an enemy of Liu Hsiang, who belonged to Hsiao Wang-chih's clique.[76] In connection with the second fire, however, series a[77] reports two imperial proclamations in which the ruler deplored the fact that nobody had criticized his actions, and asked for more thrift in the central administration. This seems to show that the reference to Shih Hsien was made by a historian after the event.

Series b mentions an eclipse in 178 B.C. without any other remark than that it happened in a part of the sky which corresponds to the area of Yueh (South and Southeast China). Series a,[78] also mentioning this eclipse, brings in an imperial proclamation with the usual self-accusation. The emperor appointed a number of persons of high repute to guide him, referred to wars, and ordered changes in defense. These wars took place mainly in the north. In 178 B.C., therefore, the eclipse was not considered to be connected with the area and the state of Yueh. In all cases in which series b gives an explanation for an eclipse or any other phenomenon unlucky events follow. The author(s) of series b, therefore, seems not to have believed that by issuing a proclamation the situation could be remedied, but rather that the omens had predicted the predestined future development. The ruler, however, at the time of the portent wished to give the impression that by issuing a proclamation the impending evil could be averted.

Summarizing the results of an investigation of all phenomena which are explained in series a–d, we can state:

a) Abnormal natural phenomena were believed, at the time they happened and later, to be connected with unlucky events.

b) The explanation of the meaning of a phenomenon at the time it happened was in some cases different from the explanation given by a later historian.

c) Even later historians and theoreticians did not always agree on the meaning of a portent: they used slightly different theories, and even the standard theory of the Five Elements was not exact enough to oblige astrologists to produce only one explanation.

d) Portents are sometimes considered to be connected with supposedly wrong actions of other persons, such as the empress, imperial concubines, princes, feudal lords, and court officials. They express a criticism, therefore, not of the emperor as an individual but rather of the government. Not only the ruler but frequently members of the government suffer bodily harm for their incorrect actions which are reflected by portents.

We can now go one step further and say:

e) Portents could, at the time they happened, be used as a political tool by one faction at court against another faction.

The biography of Liu Hsiang is very revealing in this respect. In his and his faction's fight for power an earthquake and an unusual star saved them from prison and brought them back into office. But when, half a year later, another earthquake happened, Shih Hsien and the other members of the opposing faction seemed inclined to exploit it against Liu Hsiang's faction; Liu got frightened and asked his relatives to give the emperor a report on portents and their meaning in which Shih Hsien was blamed for the earthquake.[79] The opponents branded this report, which, they felt, was written by Liu Hsiang, as calumny, and Liu was deprived of his rank. Here, and in the following reports on Liu Hsiang's political life, it is clear that the portents were used as political tools. What is not clear, however, is whether men like Liu Hsiang or the emperor really believed in portents. Sometimes one is strongly inclined to doubt this.[80]

C. THE TIME RELATION BETWEEN PORTENTS AND EVENTS

In a fair number of cases it is possible to find out exactly how many months or years lay between a portent and an event which was believed to be related to it. In the case of the above-mentioned twenty-five cases of series *c*, the events always happened after the portent. The time lag was between one month (in two cases) and nine years (one case). In the whole series *c* the time lag varied between one month and eleven years, with an average around two years.

In the case of the twelve eclipses mentioned above, the event was also always after the portent, the time lag being between one month (one case) and nine years (one case). In the case of the nineteen fires the situation was different; in some cases (six out of nineteen) the event was up to four years prior to the portent, while in all other cases the event ranged from several months or as many as twenty years *after* the portent to which it was supposed to refer, to four years *before* the phenomenon. This gives rise to serious questions. If the portent followed after the event (which is on the whole comparatively rare), we might conclude that the event, i.e., a human action which was not in harmony with the "course of nature" (*tao*), was regarded as the cause of the phenomenon: the action disturbed the balance of nature, thus producing the phenomenon. This would serve to demonstrate the existence of the concept of parallelism, in the sense that an upset balance of human affairs is reflected by an upset balance of nature. However, the causal relation which was seen between the two manifestations of disturbance does not permit one to speak of a concept of absolute parallelism[81] but may be imagined to be represented by the two parallel sides of a lozenge; a third side then stands for the causal relation. If, as in the majority of cases, the phenomenon occurred before the human event had occurred, three explanations seem possible:

a) Applying the concept of this "lozenge-shaped parallelism" with a disturbance of human affairs at the starting point, one is forced to think that a human disturbance existed before the phenomenon occurred. In this case a cause for the later human event already existed at the time of the portent, for example, a rebellion might already be planned but this fact might not yet be publicly known at the time of the portent. This would make psychological attitudes and thought constitute potential causes of disturbances in the balance of nature. As the person in question was not the emperor alone, and a large number might as well be regarded as the cause for unbalance, we might assume that in theory the actions of any human being might be regarded as potentially disturbing to the harmony of nature. If the disturbances were assumed to be the result of the working of some "law of nature," the size of the portents should, in a hierarchical society such as the Chinese, be found to be in relation to the status of the person(s) who caused it. It has not been possible to show such a relationship. It seems to us that one is almost compelled, by implication, to postulate the existence of a concept of a personal deity which has insight into the feelings and thoughts of men, and causes the portents. This seems to fit better than the extended application of the concept of parallelism.

b) The imperial proclamation of 178 B.C.[82] states: "I have heard that Heaven produced people, and set up rulers for them, in order that they may care for them and rule them. If the ruler of men has no *te* [spiritual power], if the exercise of government is not balanced, Heaven shows him [i.e., the ruler? or them?] portents, in order to warn him [them?] against bad government." If we try to explain this and similar statements, we must conclude that the ruler is held responsible for good government, because he is invested by Heaven to care for the population. Portents happen when the ruler has no *te* or when the government is not balanced. The latter anomaly may be considered to indicate that the officials are as responsible for good government as is the ruler.

Here another interesting problem emerges: in which sense were rulers or officials "responsible"? In the case just discussed they seem to be regarded as responsible in the sense that an official accepts responsibility for failures beyond his control. In the majority of cases, however, actions of the ruler or others (such as too much interest in the life of the harem instead of interest in affairs of the state; a planned rebellion; favoritism shown to an unworthy individual, etc.) for which they clearly had personal responsibility are explicitly mentioned. On this question, too, no clear attitude seems to have existed in Han times.

On the basis of the case just discussed it seems clear that the events which occurred after the portents were not interpreted as having been caused by the portents, nor would secretly planned actions be taken to be the cause of the portents. A bad government would lead to those events. In other words, one cannot speak of parallelism at all, but rather of the concept of a causal relationship between unbalance of government and later catastrophic human events. The portent enters in as a warning from Heaven, as a purposive attempt to indicate to the ruler that balance on earth must be restored lest serious catastrophies follow. If we take the quoted and similar texts at face value and not as merely conventional, insincere self-accusations on the part of the ruler, we are forced again to assume a belief in the existence of a personal deity, "Heaven," who "warns," as is expressly stated in a fair number of texts. On the other hand, attempts such as those made in series *b* by Liu Hsiang, Liu Hsin, and perhaps others, to find "scientific laws" by which to calculate the meaning of a portent, seem to speak against the concept of a personal god or would seem to admit only of the concept of a deity bound by self-imposed "laws." In spite of these reflections we would not postulate on the basis of these data alone the existence in Han times of a concept of a personal deity and of predestination.

c) In a number of cases it seems impossible to assume that the action to which the portent was supposedly referring was even planned at the time the portent happened. In such a situation one might, for the third explanation, conclude that the Chinese in Han times believed in the existence of a supernatural power or a personal deity who could foresee actions, even when they were not yet planned by men, and that the future course of actions was believed to be predestined by the deity and/or abstract power. This would mean that man could not do anything against the impending unlucky event, could not prevent it. Indeed, the reading of series *b* (*Han-shu* 27) strengthens this belief: there was no case recorded in which the calamity had been avoided by quick action after the portent, although in series *a* (*Han-shu* 1–12) the rulers seem to wish to express their belief that immediate action promises such success.

It seems most logical to assume that the Chinese during this period did not have uniform and clear concepts in this respect. Some seem to have believed that quick action after a portent, or "reaction upon the warning of Heaven," would lead to success; others, and, we may add, apparently in the main the later historians who wrote after the event, believed that the calamities came anyhow, because the right type of action was never taken. Some seem to have believed that actions as well as plans for action produced portents, following certain laws which could be detected. Others seem to have believed that a kind of predestination existed.

However, the fact that we know both that portents were fabricated and that portents were used in the power struggle between factions opens another perspective: at least some of the persons who reported portents in memoranda, or who wrote them into the historical records, may not have believed in portents at all but may have used them merely as political weapons. This conclusion, however, does not justify the inversion of the statement, namely, that portents were not memorialized or not recorded in history if the official or the historian had no use for them in his political fight or his criticism. On the one hand, some "portents," such as an eclipse or a palace fire, could hardly remain hidden to even the most disinterested ruler, and, on the other hand, the possibility that the historian could utilize a portent to explain an event that happened as much as thirty-five years later gave him almost unlimited choice to utilize any portent.[83]

If we should try today to make a similar analysis of our popular "superstitions," of "dream books" or astrological treatises, we would probably come up with a similarly confused picture; an analysis of our scientific literature would give a consistent one. It is possible that in the case of Han China this whole field of omens was not included in "scientific" thinking but was regarded as "politics" only; it is also conceivable that the Han period was a period of transition from thinking in limited categories, each with its own inherent logic, to thinking on the basis of a generally accepted, unified system of logic.

D. THE OBJECTS OF CRITICISM BY PORTENTS

If we return to our chart, a number of "peaks" are clearly recognizable. The peaks of series *a–c* correspond to some extent. We may now study the kinds of topics used to explain these accumulations of portents. We begin with series *b:*

1. A peak is visible for the period between 195 and 185 B.C. The portents in this period do not criticize Emperor Hui (194–88) but criticize unlawful actions of Empress Lü and her family, mainly their actions against feudal princes of the emperor's clan.

2. A peak between 180 and 170 B.C. does not indicate criticism of Emperor Wen (179–57) but refers only to the revolts of feudal princes, starting in 174 and culminating in 154. The "warnings" begin twenty-five years before the main revolt and continue to 143, i.e., the year in which Chou Ya-fu, one of the two main proponents for centralization and fighters against feudalism, was forced to commit suicide. Ch'ao Ts'o, the other proponent, was executed in 154 B.C.

3. A peak around 115 to 110 B.C. is visible. The "warnings" given in the explanation to the portents had already started in 136 and warn continuously against the excessive wars of Emperor Wu (140–87). These wars started in 133 and culminated around 105.

4. A peak around 100 and 90 B.C. is connected with (*a*) the murder of the crown prince and the scandal connected with it, and (*b*) wars in distant Central Asia. The murder of the prince occurred in 91; the wars, 104–90.

5. A peak between 80 and 70 B.C. is visible. The "warnings" are directed this time (*a*) against a revolt of a feudal prince in 80 (these warnings begin in 84 and end in 78); (*b*) against the claim of the successor, the Prince of Ch'ang-i, who became ruler for a few days in 74 and was soon deposed. Most warnings are directed against the Prince of Ch'ang-i, fewer against the regents. "Warnings" start in 85.

6. A small peak exists between 70 and 65 B.C. It is related to the revolt by the clan of the regent, Huo Kuang. Warnings begin in 69; the action starts in 66.

7. A peak in 45–40 B.C. indicates (*a*) the origin of the power of the

Wang clan (warnings begin in 48; Wang Mang was born in 45); (*b*) a criticism of Shih Hsien and his group, who were enemies of Liu Hsiang and killed Ching Fang (warnings begin in 46 and last until 36; the eunuch Shih Hsien loses power and dies around 32).

8. Peaks in 35–25 and 20–10 B.C. These peak periods belong together and indicate (*a*) the ascendance of the Wang clan to power (warnings start strongly in 32; in 32 five uncles of the Emperor Ch'eng [32–7] received key posts; the warnings accompany the ascendance of each single member of the Wang family until 8 B.C.); (*b*) the warnings criticize the love affair and marriage of Emperor Ch'eng with the later Empress Chao (this anti-Wang clique is blamed for the murder of the sons of Emperor Ch'eng by a former marriage; Empress Chao is killed in 6 B.C.; the murder of the prince takes place in 12).

9. A peak between 5 and 1 B.C. This is a continuation of the warnings against the Wang family, now against Wang Mang personally; it is also a criticism of Tung Hsien, the homosexual love-object of Emperor Ai (6–1 B.C.).

Series *c* (*Han-shu* 26) shows a different pattern from series *b* (*Han-shu* 27). The criticism here is directed:

a) Against the revolt of the feudal princes in 154 (as in series *b*).

b) Against the King of Liang who wanted to become successor to the throne in 146. (Emperor Wu, who became ruler in 140, was still a baby at that time. *Han-shu* 27 [series *b*] does not criticize this.)

c) Only weakly against the Prince of Ch'ang-i and the regents in 74 B.C.

d) Not strongly against the Wang clan.

Series *d* (*Shih-chi* 8–12) offers again a different pattern:

a) No criticism is expressed against the first three rulers (Kao, Empress Lü, Hui).

b) There are more portents under the rule of Emperor Ching (156–41) than in the similar series *a*. They cover almost his whole regency, with cumulations at the beginning and at the end of his rule. The historian(s) seems to have wanted to blame the emperor personally, because (differing from series *a–c*) the portents set in quite suddenly with his ascent to the throne and end as suddenly while, in the other series, the portents start earlier, under his father, and refer to the rebellion of the feudal lords, not to the emperor. It is interesting to note that Chang Fu, a scholar of the Chin period, already observed that the *Shih-chi* (series *d*) differs from the *Han-shu* (series *a*) in the evaluation of the personality of the key figure, Ch'ao Ts'o.[84]

c) For the following period (Emperor Wu), series *d* concentrates on the year 110 B.C. In this year a special sacrifice was offered. As the author(s) of this chapter describes Emperor Wu as a person interested only in magic, it seems likely that a criticism of this specific sacrifice was intended. The parallel text in series *a* credits Emperor Wu mainly with military exploits and hardly mentions his preoccupation with magic. Portents in series *a–c*, as far as explained, have no connection with his magical interests.

In the general judgment of later Chinese historians, the darkest periods of China in the period under study are (*a*) the usurpation of Empress Lü, because, according to the Chinese belief, no woman can be a legitimate ruler of the country, and (*b*) the usurpation of Wang Mang, because he took away the throne from the legitimate dynasty by fraud. Our analysis of the portents, however, shows that the earliest text (series *d*) does not raise objection at all against Empress Lü by using portents against her; series *a* and *c* also do not object to her. Only series *b* seems to be mildly concerned, but far less strongly about the empress than about the reappearance of feudalism. Series *c* does not object strongly to Wang Mang, and even series *b* is divided in its evaluation and only in parts is against Wang Mang. We may interpret this as another proof that, perhaps with the exception of series *d*, the portents really do not criticize the ruler but rather men in his government. Therefore Emperor Wen, who is later regarded as the ideal ruler of the whole period, saw relatively many portents, but they seem not to have been directed against him.

Although statistical analysis seems to speak for a common source of the data in series *a–c*, analysis of the "meanings" of the portents as reported in different series shows that the different authors of the different parts of the text interpreted history differently. A comparison of the "meanings" of portents in series *a–c* as against *d* confirms this strongly. Incidentally, study of the alleged meanings of portents may be helpful in clarifying the basic values held by the authors of historical works.

Another result of an examination of the chart is that series *a–c* do not show any clear relation between the person of an emperor and peaks of portents: the ups and downs of portents seem to be relatively independent of the rule of specific rulers.

E. THE CRITICS

The data we have presented lead us to assume that the explanations given for a large number of portents were fabricated by historians who wrote after the events happened and who even, in some cases, fabricated portents in order to criticize specific events. However, in a number of cases we have the memoranda submitted to the ruler immediately after the portent had happened. It is conceivable that one or more officials at court had the right or duty to analyze portents and to report on them: such persons might be chiefs of special bureaus, e.g., the astronomical office. Series *b* (*Han-shu* 27) clearly mentions fifteen persons who submitted memorials in connection with portents or who explained portents. We give below the essential data on each of these men.

1. LIU HSIANG. He gave oral warnings in 32, 28, 17, 12, and 9 B.C. He lived from 76 to 8 B.C. and occupied different posts during the years 32–9. His biography states clearly that he favored, whenever possible, members of the imperial clan to which he himself belonged, and criticized the relatives of the empresses (*Han-shu*, chap. 36, p. 452). He was a specialist in omens and did research on omens in the classical literature, especially the *Ch'un-ch'iu*, on which he wrote a book. He criticized the emperor, a member of his own clan, not because he held an office connected with astronomy or meteorology but because of his function as an official. In addition, comments of his are recorded concerning portents which happened in 204, 193, 188, 179, 178, 168, 157, 154, 145, 139, 135, 134, 80, 78, 77, 74, 69, 45 (twice), 43, and 40 B.C.

2. LIU HSIN. Son of Liu Hsiang. He is quoted for the year 32 B.C., but, as he came to have influence only around 6 B.C., he did not submit his report in 32 B.C. He was executed in A.D. 23. He specialized on research in the *Ch'un-ch'iu* and the *Tso-chuan*, and stood in opposition to his father, who was not in favor of the *Tso-chuan*. Because he had studied together with Wang Mang, he favored him and rose together with and through him. His explanations of portents, therefore, were not directed against Wang Mang. From at least 6 B.C. on, however, he planned to betray his school friend. With reference to the "apocryphal" texts, he changed his name in 6 B.C. and took a name which, according to these texts, was the name of the first ruler of a new dynasty to come after Wang Mang (*Han-shu*, chap. 36, p. 453 ff.). His attempted revolt in A.D. 23 is certainly connected with this change of name. It is interesting to note that one of his pupils was a certain Li Shou (H. Bielenstein, *Restoration*, p. 102), who belonged to the clan which actually nominated the later Emperor Kuang-wu as the candidate of the coming dynasty. It cannot be proved, but it is certainly possible that Li Shou was responsible for giving the future emperor the same name that his teacher Liu Hsin took in 6 B.C.; Kuang-wu was born one year later, in 5 B.C.

3. CHING FANG. He was a pupil of a "meteorologist" at the provincial court of Liang, i.e., a specialist in omens. He was appointed in 45 B.C. because of his general education. He memorialized on portents between 43 and 37 B.C. His criticism was against certain officials at court, not against the ruler. He quickly ran into opposition when he recommended control of officials. The emperor tried to save him by giving him a provincial post, but another memorandum, sent to the ruler, caused his execution as well as the execution of a relative by a marriage which had linked Ching Fang to a feudal lord in Huai-yang. He clearly was the victim of a struggle for power. (Biography in *Han-shu*, chap. 75, p. 547*ab*.) He is quoted, from his own

book, on portents for the years 193, 172, 155, 154, 131, 98, 80, 78, 74, 43 (twice), 32, 28, 15, 12, 7, 5, and 4 B.C. and A.D. 1 and 3.

4. SUI MENG. He was executed in 74 B.C., when he announced to the emperor that a new dynasty would come. The execution was caused not by the emperor but by the regent, who was afraid of his own position (*Han-shu*, chap. 75, p. 546*b*). T. T. Som, *Po Hu T'ung* (Leiden, 1949), Volume I, Table 7, states that he was trained in the same school as Tung Chung-shu.

5. TUNG CHUNG-SHU. He warned the ruler in 135 B.C. against feudal princes, in connection with a portent. He lived *ca.* 179–104 B.C. (see also T. T. Som, *Po Hu T'ung*, Vol. I, Table 7). He is famous for his commentaries on the *Ch'un-ch'iu*, in which he paid special attention to portents.

6. HSIA-HOU SHIH-CH'ANG. He warned the ruler in 104 B.C. and explained omens to him (cf. in general Som, *op. cit.*, Vol. I, Table 2).

7. HSIA-HOU SHENG. He warned the ruler in 74 B.C. He was the son of Shih-ch'ang and learned his knowledge of portents from his father. His father was teacher of the prince that he warned, the prince who later became the ruler. The ruler became furious and wanted to kill Hsia-hou Sheng, but, because the faction which opposed this ruler assumed erroneously that Hsia-hou Sheng was on their side, they saved him and honored him greatly when they succeeded in dethroning the ruler (*Han-shu*, chap. 75, p. 546*da*).

8. KUNG SUI. He, too, warned the ruler in 74 B.C. He was appointed to attend the prince because of his knowledge of classical literature. When the prince became emperor, he asked Kung about certain portents. Owing to the fact that Kung criticized the ruler on this occasion, he was saved from death when two hundred members of the ruler's entourage were executed after the ruler had been dethroned (*Han-shu*, chap. 89, p. 586*cb*).

9. KU YUNG. He commented on one portent which happened in 188 B.C.; in 35 B.C. he warned the empress in connection with portents, spoke up against Empress Chao in 32 and 30 B.C., and criticized the emperor, mainly because of his preference for Empress Chao, in 17, 15, 13, and 12 B.C. He was an adherent of the Wang clique. He spoke for a member of the imperial family (*Han-shu*, chap. 85, p. 570*cb* ff).

10. TU CH'IN. He warned in 30 B.C. against Empress Chao. He was the son of an official. He had only low appointments, but a strong interest in the theory of the elements (*Han-shu*, chap. 60, p. 3*a* ff.). He was an adviser of the Wang clan.

11. TU YEH. A friend and relative of Tu Ch'in. He warned in 3 B.C. against an empress who was anti-Wang. He specialized in astrology (*Han-shu*, chap. 85, pp. 9*b*–11*a*). He was related by marriage to Chang Ch'ang, a high official who specialized in the *Ch'un-ch'iu* and *Tso-chuan*, as did Liu Hsin and other friends of the Wang clan (*Han-shu*, chap. 76, pp. 6*a*–9*b*, and chap. 88, p. 12*a*). The wife of this Chang Ch'ang was a daughter of Ssu-ma Ch'ien, the editor of our series *d* (Wang Kuo-wei, *Kuan-t'ang chi-lin* [Shanghai: Commercial Press], chap. 11, p. 12*a*).

12. YANG HSUAN. He warned in 32 B.C. against the Wang clan.

13. YANG HSIUNG and LI HSÜN both warned in 5 B.C. against a chancellor who was anti-Wang. Yang Hsiung was a famous poet and writer, who collaborated closely with Wang Mang, until his suicide in A.D. 18 (*Han-shu*, chap. 87*a*, *b*). He fabricated a book parallel to the *I Ching*, applying theoretical principles based upon a calendar made for Wang Mang's dynasty. Li Hsün specialized in astrology and belonged to the same school as Ching Fang (Som, *op. cit.*, Vol. I, Table 2, and *Han-shu*, chap. 75, pp. 9*a* ff.).

14. CHEN FENG. He warned the ruler in 26 B.C. and blamed Empress Chao. He was one of the closest collaborators of the Wang clan, together with Liu Hsin, but had much more courage than Liu Hsin. He rose to highest honors but was later forced to commit suicide because of an act of his son (*Han-shu*, chap. 99*b*, p. 8*a*–*b*).

15. WANG YIN. He warned the ruler in 19 and 17 B.C. and blamed Empress Chao. He was a member of the Wang clan who rose to highest honors (*Han-shu*, chap. 85, p. 4*b*, and chap. 98, pp. 4*b*–5*b*).

This list shows clearly that (*a*) the critics did not criticize merely because this was a part of their official function; (*b*) they had the most diverse positions in the bureaucracy (any high dignitary seems to have been in a position to "warn" the ruler); (*c*) most of the critics were specialists in astrology or meteorology and were well trained in private schools (they belonged to different schools); and (*d*) most of them had outspoken political loyalties and utilized their "science" for the realization of their political aims.

3. The Political Character of the Calendar

Before summing up the results of the foregoing discussion, another function of astronomy (now taken in a narrower sense of the word) has to be looked at: the question of the development of a good calendar. It has been stated that this, indeed, was, because of the demands of an irrigation economy, one of the most important functions of Chinese astronomy: in order to have well-functioning irrigation and agriculture, a good calendar had to be developed.

Without discussing the origins of Chinese calendar systems, or the relation between calendar and irrigation in other societies, the following observations can be made concerning the calendar systems of the Han.

Basically, the Han calendar was a moon calendar with solar adjustment, i.e., each month began with the new moon, and the year had twelve full lunar months. This leads necessarily to a year of roughly 354 days. Adjustments, i.e., intercalations of full months, gear the moon year to the solar year. For an agricultural society such a calendar is extremely impractical: the beginning of the year or of any single month can oscillate within the limits of a full moon month, i.e., if the New Year is fixed to the first new moon after winter solstice, New Year's Day can fall on any day between December 22 and January 19, and, in the same way, all other months can oscillate. The intercalation of a full month somewhere in the year made this type of calendar unusable for the farmer. He could not, for example, plant his rice on the first day of the fifth month because in one year this might be too late, while in another year it might be too early.

He, therefore, relied upon basic signs of nature, such as the return of migratory birds or the appearance of a large fixed star, rather than upon the calendar. The *hsia-hsiao-cheng* ("little calendar of the Hsia dynasty") is a good example of such "natural calendars." The different *yueh-ling* which are preserved contain data on the reappearance of birds or animals as well as on the appearanse of constellations which are concise enough to make these books useful to a farmer, even though the general calendrical structure of the *yueh-ling* is useless to him.

All Chinese calendars which were in existence during or before the Han period are basically identical. Their main difference is in the beginning of the year. This is the point on which the Hsia, Shang, and Chou calendars differ. The Chou calendar seems to have been more influenced by purely astronomical thinking than the Hsia calendar. The Chou calendar ties the beginning of the year closely to the date of the winter solar solstice, a logical position for a calendar which pays great attention to the course of the sun. The so-called Hsia calendar starts the year in the spring, a logical position for a calendar which wants to serve agriculture; but in its internal structure the Hsia calendar is a luni-solar calendar like the others and, therefore, too imprecise to be of help to the farmer.

On the other hand, it can easily be shown that the Chinese were capable of developing a pure solar calendar. If an astronomer intends to make any astronomical calculation, for example, to calculate the date of the next new moon or the next eclipse of the moon or sun, he has to start from the movement of the sun. An examination of the formula which the Han astronomers used for their calculations[85] shows that they developed a pure solar calendar system for their calculations and then converted it into the "civil" calendar of a luni-solar character. If the function of Chinese astronomy had been to provide a tool for the farmer, this "astronomical" calendar would have been the ideal tool, because the seasons were fixed in this calendar. The fact that the Chinese retained the luni-solar calendar until the twentieth century indicates that their interests were different. We must assume that they followed an old tradition which had fixed the popular festivals and observances of a religious cult by the phases of the moon.[86]

There are other features of the Chinese "civil" calendar which speak against its functional value for a farming society. A simple calendar can achieve either one of two goals: it can disregard the position of the moon and pay attention to the position of the sun ("agricultural calendar"), or it can disregard the position of the sun and pay attention to the moon only. In this latter case, by simply looking at the moon, the citizen knows which day of the month it is. Such a calendar is valuable for festivals but not for farmers. Combined calendars usually achieve both goals in part. Units smaller than the month, e.g., the week, can also be used in similar ways. Our own week is a poor attempt to adjust a short period to the course of the moon (four weeks equal approximately one revolution of the moon). The Chinese cycle of ten (the ten celestial stems) in pre-Chou times was possibly an attempt to adjust to the course of the sun (thirty-six cycles of ten, roughly one solar year). But already in Shang texts the cycle had lost this function; in its combination with the twelve earthly branches, it formed the sexagenary cycle. Although theoretically this cycle could have been used to express the position of the sun and therefore could have been useful for the farmer, it actually served only "bureaucratic" functions. It was a handy, short system to keep the daily records straight. From the date according to the sexagenary cycle, no farmer could ever know whether he should start planting or not.

What, then, is the main importance of the popular calendar books which were so widely used until recent times?[87] The short fragments of Han calendars are a synoptic list of the months and of the cyclic dates (sexagenary characters) for the days of the month. They were tools to help the local bureaucrat keep straight the correspondence between the days of the month and the days of the sexagenary cycle; without such lists he would not know the cyclic date of a given day, and he needed this knowledge for his reports. The fully developed calendars of the T'ang period and down to the present time are purely astrological, like our former "almanacs": they indicate which action should or should not be taken on a given day.[88] They do not primarily help the farmer.

The calendar of the Han period was changed several times. If the function of the calendar was to help farming and irrigation, we should assume that it was changed in order to introduce still better, more exact, data, in order to achieve this aim more perfectly.

In fact, the changes are of differing character. One of the main changes was that of the date of the New Year. If we try to analyze the reasons for this change, we find that in Han times six different systems were known.[89] The three main systems were connected with (a) the position of the Great Dipper, (b) a specific color, (c) a specific symbolic number, (d) a specific musical flute, and (e) a specific historical dynasty.[90] The change from one dating system to the other depended not upon the feasibility of the calendar for irrigation or agriculture but upon the theory that, as nature changes, symbolic colors, numbers, flute-lengths, and dynasties change, in accordance with the theory of the Five Elements.[91] Until 104 B.C., in spite of earlier protests, the Han dynasty simply continued the calendar system of the earlier Ch'in dynasty, on the assumption either that the Han stepped in for the Ch'in, whose "time" was not yet up, or that the Ch'in never really existed as a legitimate dynasty, so that the Han were the continuators of the Chou. From 104 B.C. on, however, a new approach was accepted, by which the Han dynasty started a new period either as the next after the Ch'in or, regarding the Ch'in as a kind of "intercalation," as the next after the Chou. Without entering into the intricacies of these speculations here, it may be clear that here, too, political and not economic or other reasons were the motive for change.

Another type of change of calendar was one caused by a change in the basic astronomical data. Here, we would assume that, as time went by, better and better data were supplied by observation and the calendar thus improved as a more useful tool step by step.

On the contrary, however, no such tendency can be seen. The calendar of Liu Hsin, developed around the birth of Christ, is slightly better than the calendar of 104 B.C., but the Later Han dynasty (A.D. 25–220) then introduced a calendar similar to that of 104 B.C., i.e., an inferior calendar. And the calendars of Liu Hung and Wang Fan (second and third centuries A.D.) are still less accurate than the Later Han calendar.[92] The reason for this fact is that the Chinese astronomer was not primarily interested in improving the exactness of the calendar but tried very hard to find a solution which satisfied the basic demand for a functioning calendar and also incorporated all the symbolic numbers. For purely speculative, symbolic reasons, the calendar of the Later Han dynasty is based upon the number 4 and fractions of 4, while the calendar of Liu Hsin operated for the same reason with fractions of 1539. A calendar had to meet all the above-mentioned speculative requirements, so that it became a symbol of the magical powers influencing the dynasty. A new dynasty, representing different magical powers, therefore, had to have a different calendar, incorporating other speculative numbers, and so on. That the result in some cases was a better, in other cases a poorer, calendar was of little importance. This point makes understandable the belief which continued into modern times—that to develop a new calendar is a revolutionary act, committed by persons who have already planned to depose the dynasty. Liu Hsin's development of the *San-t'ung* calendar is a clear case: there can be no doubt that he developed it for the coming dynasty, which (perhaps ultimately against his own intentions) was that of Wang Mang, just as Yang Hsiung developed on parallel basic data a new *I Ching*, the *T'ai-hsuan-ching*, for the new dynasty because the classical *I Ching* was believed to be based upon the calendar of 104 B.C.

This study again proves that the function of astronomy, as expressed in the calendar, was political. Astronomy was used as a tool, in this case to develop a calendar which expressed the magical powers which the dynasty represented. The fact that our own society retains a completely outmoded, impractical calendar should help us in understanding the attitude of the Han Chinese.

4. Factors Militating against a Development of Science

We observed that the attitude of Chinese astronomers toward their calendar ultimately prevented scientific progress. Improvement of calendars was regarded as a revolutionary act and was punished.

This is a point of great interest. Those astronomers who prepared calendars certainly had a body of solid scientific knowledge.[93] The formulas which they used for their calculations compare not unfavorably with the knowledge of Greek astronomers. They certainly had a genuine interest in the field and acquired special training through private tutors. The reason why they did not develop their knowledge into a unified scientific system seems to be that they were not interested in pure science for science's sake. They did not spend time in developing abstract laws or in studying the process of thinking (logic). But they also were not interested in applied technical sciences, e.g., in developing theoretical tools which could be used to control the flight of a cannon shell or to direct ships safely across the sea. Their central interest was in politics, and all known "scientists" mentioned above were also personally deeply involved in politics— usually they had a job in the government. It is easily understandable that they tried to apply their scientific knowledge to politics and that this was a dangerous field. Here, again, developments before our eyes should help us to a better understanding of the situation in Han China. Already in the beginning of the third century B.C. the father of Chinese science, Tsou Yen, had entered this field by connecting dynasties with specific elements and by stating that the Five Elements alternate according to special rules which he and his successors tried to find. This knowledge was, because of its dangerous character, handed down from teacher to pupil in secret, and was laid down in secret books. Only from time to time, when the experts in this secret science thought that time for action had come, do we hear of this group, usually with the concluding remark that the man was executed. This secret school, which specialized in calculating the duration of dynasties in order to be able to predict the end of the ruling dynasty and the character, or even the person, of the creator of the new dynasty, reached its high point in the late first century B.C. A great literature was created: some books have been so thoroughly destroyed that we know the names only; other books came into the open in the disturbances during the reign of Wang Mang and were used politically for the legitimization of the Later Han dynasty. These books are called the "Apocryphal Books" because they seem to be commentaries on the classics, but their comments differ widely from the accepted commentaries. We cannot here discuss in detail all the personalities involved in this school of secret, revolutionary science;[94] we only want to say that they played an important role during the Later Han.[95] It can be proved that the rebellion of the "Yellow Turbans" at the end of the Later Han dynasty was directly influenced by this secret school. Only after the middle of the third century A.D. did the influence of this school upon politics decrease.[96]

This secret school, which had a life of some five hundred years, characterized very well the situation of Chinese scientists; their interest in politics, the reasons for which we cannot investigate here, led them away from theory and pure science and brought them quickly into a position which the ruling dynasty regarded with extreme suspicion. They therefore became the nucleus of antidynastic and revolutionary movements and were persecuted and finally crushed by the government forces. These movements were in part led by members of the elite, who represented a minority faction; in part they were popular mass movements, such as the "Yellow Turbans." Down to late medieval times, it is in the ideologies of such popular movements that we find over and over again thinkers who used scientific premises. Just as the astronomers, astrologists, or meteorologists were motivated by an interest not so much in science as in politics, so the government sponsored these scientific fields only in so far as they were politically loyal, i.e., as long as they did not develop new ideas. New ideas were conceived as new tools for the political struggle and therefore suspect. Science, therefore, was hampered in its development. What was achieved, over and above applied "political science," was the result of the hobbies of certain individuals; it remained hidden in their occasional writings, as a curiosity, and it was not systematized, discussed, clarified, enlarged, or applied in nonpolitical fields.

5. The Domination of Political Interest

We may now try to summarize the results of the above discussion. We repeat that our conclusions rely upon only a narrow, selected set of data, and therefore cannot be accepted as valid for all periods of Chinese history.

We know that certain offices in the central administration made astronomical and meteorological observations. Our data say nothing about these offices and their functions. It may be that they provided lists of abnormal phenomena, but this cannot be proved from our data. Some provincial lords had their own specialists, persons with special training and, as far as we can judge, not incorporated into the regular ranks of provincial bureaucracy.

Some portents were memorialized by court officials to the emperor. These persons were politicians, usually with a special training in astrology, astronomy, or meteorology, divided into several different schools. Still other portents were known to the emperor, perhaps because he personally observed them or because some of his servants reported them, and the emperor asked a specialist about the meaning of the portent. And, again, other portents may not have been known to the emperor but appear only in the history books. At least some of these were fabricated by historians.

It was assumed that the emperor was personally responsible for calamities of nature, although there is an indication that sometimes he was regarded as responsible only "ex officio." All members of the bureaucracy could blame him for a calamity or a portent and thus induce him to change his attitude. By doing this, they exercised an institutional right. It is another question whether this right to criticize the ruler was an effective check. In some cases it was apparently effective. Thus the ruler in Han times, institutionally speaking and according to our definition, was not a despot. We could prove, furthermore, that not only the ruler but also any other member of his government could be regarded as personally responsible for a portent or calamity of nature. Thus we might conclude that the government, with the ruler as its head, was held responsible. Whether the exact distribution of responsibility between ruler and government was ever clearly formulated by Han thinkers cannot be established by our method.

The fact that portents were used by some faction within the bureaucracy as a weapon against other factions in their struggle for power seems to indicate that these groups did not regard the ruler as the sole source of power, as earlier theory has assumed.[97]

The question whether the educated elite of the Han believed in portents or not is hard to decide. The fact that some portents were fabricated, that others were used in factional struggles to prove the arguments of one or the other side, makes us inclined to assume that at least some persons did not believe in portents at all.

The theory of the connection of portents with human life is not clearly developed. Expressions like "Heaven warned," together with a tendency to connect a portent with an event in human life which was not even planned, seem to indicate that at least some persons believed in a personal deity which sent portents as warnings. Other cases can best be interpreted by assuming that a human activity disturbed the harmony of nature and thus produced an abnormal natural phenomenon. Such cases, however, are by no means in the majority. Still other cases can be interpreted by assuming that some Chinese believed in a kind of predestined fate: portents indicate future catastrophies which always will occur, i.e., which cannot be prevented. We might say that this attitude is the most "scientific" one, because the attempt to calculate the time and character of the catastrophe could be made, if there was a belief in "laws of nature." No text used by us has a consistent approach or even a clear definition of the basic assumptions. It is quite obvious that the specialists were interested only in the political application of their observations and not in philosophical reasoning or scientific abstractions.

The cases in series *b* are systematically arranged in a framework which starts with an explanation of the "theory of the Five Elements." It has been shown in another place[98] that this theory did not have a uniform form in Han times but that different schools had quite different opinions. The explanations of the portents in series *b*, however, do not strictly apply the theory; no attempt is made to develop a procedure by which clear-cut "laws of nature" or systematized science could be applied to any case in order to get a clear-cut result. Some explanations often simply apply the basic Yin-Yang theory of the two opposing complementary forces, together with primitive analogies. Each portent, therefore, could easily be explained in quite different ways, as the texts prove. We may conclude

that the specialists had no real interest in the development and refinement of scientific laws; they were interested only in "applied political science," i.e., applied not in technology but in politics only.
For political application, too great clarity would have proved a
hindrance rather than an asset.

Our final conclusion is, therefore, that the function of astronomy,
astrology, and meteorology, as defined in these chapters, was purely
political: on the basis of a vague belief that there was a connection
between abnormal natural phenomena and social life, there grew up a
practice of utilizing this belief as a tool in the political struggle. Some
schools of scholars tried to develop certain general rules, but the very
interest they had in politics prevented them from developing a real
science of correcting incorrect observations, redefining and sharpen-
ing their theories. The study of the calendar has led us to the same
conclusions. And perhaps still more typical was the role played by
the antidynastic scientists, the secret school which developed at the
same time that the first real interest in science developed in China.

THE FORMATION OF SUI IDEOLOGY, 581–604

ARTHUR F. WRIGHT

1. Introductory Assumptions

THE SUI DYNASTY, which came to power in 581, lasted less than forty years. Yet its achievements were prodigious, and its effects on the later history of China were far-reaching. It represented one of those critical periods in Chinese history—paralleled perhaps only by the Ch'in dynasty (221–207 B.C.)—when decisions made and measures taken wrought a sharp break in institutional development in the fabric of social and political life.[1] The Sui reunified China politically after nearly three hundred years of disunion; it reorganized and unified economic life; it made great strides in the re-establishment of cultural homogeneity throughout an area where subcultures had proliferated for over three centuries. Its legacy of political and economic institutions, of codified law and governmental procedures, of a new concept of empire, laid the foundations for the great age of T'ang which followed.

There are many ways in which a historian may attempt to interpret such an age of profound and rapid change, and many types of inquiry are needed if we are to understand fully the dimensions of the problems which the Sui faced, the meaning of the solutions they found, and the long-term effects which their measures had. The ideology which a regime adopts generally suggests the hierarchy of problems which the holders of power believe they face, the social groups whose consent or support is regarded as necessary for the success of the regime. And shifts in the emphasis of ideological pronouncements tend to suggest the rulers' changing estimates of their problems and of their sources of support. It is with this in mind that I propose to analyze the sequence of ideological measures by which the Sui dynasty sought to justify and consolidate its rule. The period covered is the reign of the first emperor, Wen-ti (ruled 581–604), and the ideological measures fall into two phases: those aimed at the consolidation of Sui rule in North China and, after the conquest of South China in 589, those directed at unifying north and south into a new universal empire.[2]

This type of inquiry is beset by many difficulties. Our information is fragmentary on group and individual beliefs and attitudes, on the

prevailing climate of opinion, and on the class and geographical distribution of the various groups to which ideological appeals were
made. For the Sui, as for other periods of Chinese history, a more
coherent picture of the process of communication among groups and
individuals is urgently needed. Historians of China are increasingly
skeptical about the real effect on individual or social behavior of the
orders and pronunciamentos emanating from the capital and enshrined in the dynastic histories, yet, despite the abundance of material, case studies of the local effects of central government measures
have not been made.[3]

One of the most serious difficulties in the study of ideology is in
understanding the assumptions on which a power-seeker or power-
holder makes his ideological assertions—particularly his assumptions
as to the efficacy of such assertions. In our own time the manipulation of words for the purposes of power has become a "science," and
this tends to make us read into past situations too sophisticated an
intent and too developed a technique. Yet in China, from very early
times, the importance of verbal statement in attaining or holding
power has been emphasized by all statesmen and political thinkers.
The weight and authority of written symbols—efficacious in the natural world and in the world of men—has made the manipulation of
these symbols one of the major preoccupations of Chinese statesmen
and rulers. Thus, while we must guard against the distorting intrusion of current ideas, we must allow for the fact that the millennial
symbols of Chinese political and social values were thought by those
who used them to have a potency which we, at least until recently,
would not have attributed to "mere words."[4]

If a sequence of ideological measures is conditioned by the power-
holders' estimate of the climate of opinion and by the urgency with
which different problems present themselves to a regime, it is also
shaped by the power-holders' assessment of the relative appeal of the
various symbols which influence behavior. The authority of value
symbols in Chinese history—as in the histories of other societies—is
not constant, and consequently they have an ever shifting relative
power to shape the behavior of men. For example, take an appeal to
the Confucian ideal of the *chün-tzu*, "the princely man." The ideological use of this verbal symbol probably was persuasive with the
upper stratum of Han society. Yet in the subsequent period of disunion the ideal was devalued; the symbol not only lost its positive
power but among some social groups produced nothing but ribald
laughter.[5] The Sui developed its ideology in a period when many of

the old values of the age of Han had passed away, when many of the older symbols no longer elicited approval or affected behavior. It was a period in which the rise of the religions of Buddhism and Taoism meant that large segments of the population could be moved by appeals to the values of those faiths. We shall see that Sui ideology is compounded of verbal and ritual-symbolic appeals to the ranking values of Buddhism and Taoism and to the residual values of what I can only call "endemic Confucianism."[6]

Another intangible and important factor in ideology formation is the character of the person who judges the problems facing him, appraises possible responses from those groups whose approval and support are sought, and chooses to stress the assertion of some ideas and give only perfunctory lip service to others. The judgment of problems and the estimate of responses may be governed by limited information and by extreme personal bias; in such cases—for example, the later Kuomintang's assertion of Confucian values—the ideological measures meet with little response, and the ideology fails in its principal purpose. In all cases of ideology formation the personal factor—the effects of background, training, and temperament on the individuals responsible for ideological measures—are as crucial as they are difficult to measure. But if we make an effort to characterize the individual most concerned with ideological choices, we shall be somewhat less likely to go astray in our analysis of the sum of those choices which is his ideology. We shall see, for example, that Sui Wen-ti was a cautious and calculating man, by no means certain of his right to supreme power. And these traits, together with the other characteristics to be discussed below, comprise one of the factors which make his ideological measures strikingly different from those of a bold and self-confident monarch, such as Han Wu-ti.

In these pages I shall first attempt to characterize Wen-ti and—through a brief study of his life and the lives of his closest advisers—to discern those biographical-environmental factors which governed his view of his problems and the ideological measures he took. I shall then analyze some of the ideological measures which were aimed at gaining the support and approval of important social groups and which, in some cases, clearly aimed at the solution of certain specific problems facing the regime. The reader should bear in mind the exploratory and tentative nature of this essay. It has been written on the basis of limited research in a short period, and many of its findings may be drastically revised on the basis of further study. The categories in which I have sought to analyze a sequence of events are likewise experimental, and I claim for them no more than their usefulness—as I now see it—in ordering a complex group of related phenomena.

2. Problems of the Early Sui Period

In discussing some of the problems which faced Wen-ti and his advisers, I shall give the somewhat greater attention to those at whose solution ideological measures were directed. And, while recognizing that each of these problems has a long history, I shall attempt to keep historical excursions at a minimum and concentrate attention on the closing years of the period of disunion and the first twenty-three years of the Sui. Problems of the frontier peoples, particularly the T'u-chueh, and plans for the extension of Sui dominion over Central Asia undoubtedly affected some of the ideological measures of the Sui. It is likely, for example, that an emphasis on the Buddhist sanctions of Sui rule would have been an ideological move of considerable value vis-à-vis the Buddhists of Central Asia whom the Sui might attempt to incorporate into their universal empire. Yet it now seems to me that the primary problems of the early Sui, and particularly those which were the object of ideological measures, lay within China proper. Thus, while a later study might deal with Sui ideology in relation to Central Asian expansion, the present paper will be concerned largely with domestic problems and the ideological measures taken to aid in their solution.

The great tradition of Chinese political theory makes no provision for a pluralistic society. Its principles, its formulas for action, are based on the assumption that unified government based on a homogeneous society is the norm for civilized life. And an integrated system of social institutions is meant to affirm and embody the values held throughout the whole society. The barbarians are barbarians so long as they remain outside this community of mores and values and maintain institutions which embody another and inferior system of values. While political disintegration was thought of—in terms of various life-cycle analogies—as periodically inevitable, reunification, by the same analogies, was regarded as inevitable.

When the North China plain—the heartland of Chinese civilization—fell to barbarians in 312, the Chinese suffered a damaging psychological blow.[7] The very ground on which their way of life, their system of values, and their institutions had developed was no longer theirs, and they were obliged to move into the Yangtze Valley and below.[8] The emigrants (and for generations they behaved like *émigrés*) settled in the few "civilized" areas; around them were open lands, aborigines' settlements, and a new sea frontier. In this new environment, and in the company of the literati whose families had come at an earlier date, the Chinese emigrants argued and reargued the debacle of the Han empire; they experimented with philosophies which explained the failures of the past and offered hope for the future. Out of the problems of a new environment and out of the philosophic ferment of an age of uncertainty, the Chinese in the south developed new attitudes and new values. The individual attained new importance; neo-Legalist political ideas commended themselves to a succession of southern despots; hereditary right replaced the Han standard of personal merit as the principal qualification for power and place. A new and alien religion, Buddhism, came to dominate the thinking and the lives of Chinese of all classes, while the religion of Taoism—based on a combination of folk beliefs, proto- (or pseudo-) science, and mystic philosophy—competed with Buddhism for adherents and deeply affected the lives of rural communities.

Thus south China in the sixth century was far from the unified homogeneous society that had been the Han ideal. Southern statesmen might protest the "legitimate" descent of their regime from the Han and might perpetuate the orthodox traditions of music and ritual, but they knew that theirs was a far different culture from that of the Han. And if they reiterated their "legitimate" claims to a China-wide dominion based on common values universally held, they had only to look at their own society to see that the classic basis for universal rule was not there. And when they looked north across the Yangtze at the homeland of Chinese civilization, they saw an area that had been under barbarian dominion for nearly three hundred years; the effects of barbarian rule, the development of new institutions in the north, made the reconstitution of a Chinese ecumenical empire, the re-creation of a homogeneous society, seem like the most improbable of dreams. And, as time went on, fewer and fewer Chinese, in the increasingly prosperous and comfortable south, dreamed or planned a new united empire or a new unified society.

In the north, wave after wave of non-Chinese invasions had left their mark on every aspect of life. Racial diversity and racial tensions divided society. Non-Chinese regimes oscillated between becoming more Chinese and attempting to return to the steppe customs of their forefathers. But the trend, during three hundred years, was for the barbarians to become more Chinese in culture and institutions. The propelling forces in that direction were three. (1) Han institutions developed in and for the agrarian society of North China had proved their utility for organizing a prosperous state and a productive economy; they were clearly better than any of the nomadic and semi-nomadic institutions that were the heritage of the invaders. (2) The northern conquerors dreamed of the conquest of the whole of China; if a ruler had energy or ambition, he worked toward that goal for himself or for his house. To organize and carry out such a plan meant the use of Chinese statecraft, of Chinese military strategy, the study of the lessons of Chinese history. The illiterate Shih-lo (sovereign of the Later Chao, A.D. 319–33)—with his hold on the north still far from assured—sitting in his camp and having the *Ch'un-ch'iu* and the *History of the Former Han* read to him,[9] is the forerunner of countless barbarian warlords of the next two hundred and seventy years who were to plot, plan, and organize—with ever more sophistication —the unification of China under their rule. (3) The gentry houses of Chinese descent—those who had chosen to remain in the north— steadily developed power and influence as the non-Chinese rulers turned to them for knowledge and political skill. These families used their power to secure offices for their family members and to promote policies that would protect their landed interests and re-establish in every segment of state and society the Chinese customs and values which would ensure their continuance as a Chinese-type elite.

Yet if certain institutions from the Han persisted or reasserted themselves in modified form in the north, the changes had been sweeping. Chinese and non-Chinese customs and habits were intermingled at all levels of society. Despite their reading of the Chinese classics and histories, the rulers of north China valued military abilities over civil virtues. Their regimes were dominated not by an educated elite but by hereditary nobles often bound to the ruler by racial or clan ties. Though Chinese from northern gentry families often gained posts of importance, the jealousy or racial antipathy of a non-Chinese noble might at any time bring dismissal or death. A gentry official's patient work toward the creatiou of a Sinicized state might be suddenly nullified by a ruler's tactical or emotional return to the policies of his steppe ancestors. In the north, too, Buddhism had invaded every aspect of life; it had made millions of converts, while its clergy accumulated influence in court and countryside. Religious Taoism had formed its communities, and its influence at court had set off a major proscription of Buddhism in 446.

To sum up, neither the north nor the south was a unified or homogeneous society. In both areas social values and habits, political behavior, and institutions were varied and diverse. Neither could claim that it was a working example of the Han state and society with unchallengeable rights to extend itself to universal dominion. Neither could appeal to the population of the other in terms of Han values and institutions, because such an appeal would meet, not automatic and uniform acceptance, but reactions as diverse as the cultures had now become. Out of this disunity, this pluralism, the Sui was to create a unified empire, to achieve an order that a sober Chinese historian could describe, in terms of the Han ideal, as a "Great Harmony" (*Ta-t'ung*).[10] What we have just said may indicate something of the magnitude and complexity of the task and the impressiveness of Sui Wen-ti's achievement. His biography, to which we now turn, will help us to understand the way he saw these problems and the way his ideological measures to deal with them were developed.

3. Yang Chien (Sui Wen-ti): Biography and Formative Influences

Yang Chien was born on July 21, 541, at P'ing-i in Shensi, northeast of Sian. His father, Yang Chung (507–68), was the descendant of Chinese officials who had served the Mu-jung rulers of Yen (384–436) and later the To-pa emperors of Northern Wei.[11] Yang Chung was ennobled during the reign of the emperor Hsiao-wu (532–34) and was re-enfeoffed by Yü-wen T'ai (506–56) for military contributions to the latter's bid for power.[12] Yang Chien was born in a Buddhist temple, the Pan-jo Ssu (Temple of Prajñā).[13] He was put in the care of a nun called Chih-hsien, who looked after him until he was thirteen.[14] During the persecution of Buddhism (574–78) the nun took refuge in the Yang household, where she carried on her religious life in secret.[15] It is said that, after his rise to power, Yang Chien fondly recalled the nun, his preceptor (*A-she-li:* Sanskrit "Ācārya"), and ordered a biography written of her.[16] The *Sui-shu* says that he entered the imperial college, T'ai-hsueh—a school usually reserved for the sons of nobles and high officials—and that he was standoffish in manner, even with his own relatives.[17] If our other sources are correct, his education in formal official Confucian studies was very brief, for at the age of fourteen *sui* he entered the service of an official.[18] From the few facts we know of his early life, together with the repeated statements by historians on his lack of learning and lack of enthusiasm for the Confucian arts, it seems likely that his upbringing and education were under Buddhist influence. Such a background accounts in part for Yang Chien's predisposition toward Buddhism and for his tendency to stress appeals to Buddhist values in the development of his ideology.

Yang Chien, in his twenties, rose rapidly in official life, seeing some service in local posts as well as in the capital.[19] But perhaps the most significant event of this period was his marriage, in 566, at the age of twenty-five, to the daughter of Tu-ku Hsin—a powerful non-Chinese noble who had been forced to commit suicide by the Northern Chou dictator, Yü-wen Hou.[20] Yang Chien's wife was in many respects a typical northern woman of the period. She was strong-minded, an economical and autocratic household manager, never slow to intervene in political and dynastic affairs.[21] She was jealous and a fanatic on the subject of monogamy: Yang Chien was never allowed the extramarital diversions customary among Chinese autocrats. When he was once tempted, his wife had the girl killed, and Yang Chien rode angrily off to the hills. He said to his friends with a heavy sigh, "My wife is the Son of Heaven and allows me no freedom."[22] There was considerable truth in the observation of members of the palace staff that there were "two emperors."[23] She is said always to have accompanied him to the vestibule of the audience hall; from there she sent in a eunuch to observe and report all that went on, and, when something displeased her, she rebuked her imperial husband.[24] Although she was sometimes capable, on principle, of sacrificing her personal feelings to state and dynastic interest,[25] she was, like her husband, deeply suspicious of everyone, and her implacable hatred brought ruin to many, including the greatest statesman of the early Sui, Kao Chiung.[26]

It is important for our present study that this strong and influential woman was a devout Buddhist. She took the vows of a lay adherent from one of the palace clerics in 595, and her patronage of monks and temples was a major preoccupation.[27] At the time of her death the sycophantic historian Wang Shao proclaimed that she had become an avatar of Avalokiteśvara.[28] Under the empress' influence, but fully in accord with the emperor's views, the private life of the imperial family was strongly colored by Buddhism. In 585 an imperial order provided that four sermonists (ch'ang-tao) and three monks of great virtue (ta-te) were to be invited each month to read the scriptures in the Ta-hsing-shan Palace. Services were held each night, and the emperor and empress, together with the courtiers, attended the scripture readings in person; if they had questions on the meaning of a sacred text, they put them to the monks.[29] The imperial princes were assigned eminent monks as their personal mentors or chaplains and were encouraged (or ordered) to become patrons of temples and communities.[30]

The preponderance of Buddhist influence in his background and in his daily life undoubtedly accounts in part for Wen-ti's anti-Taoism, for competition and conflict between the two religions was endemic.[31]

The suddenness and speed of the rise of Yang Chien to imperial power had a profound effect on his outlook and his ideological measures. In 577, when he was thirty-six years old, Yang Chien was a high official under the vigorous Emperor Wu of the Northern Chou and was the father-in-law of the crown prince. Yang Chien's honors and offices were no more impressive than those of a dozen other men of his class.[32] North China was reunified by Emperor Wu's conquest of the Ch'i in 577, and it must have appeared that the Chou was destined for further success and expansion. But the emperor died in June, 578, and was succeeded by his capricious and lascivious son, Pin, "who managed in the brief space of two years to destroy all his father had built."[33] This son, who ruled under the name of Hsuan-ti, went through the ritual of abdicating in favor of his six-year-old son on April 1, 579, but continued to hold the reins of government. Whatever Yang Chien's ambitions may have been, his hand was forced by events at court in June, 580. Yü-wen Pin had violated the wife of an imperial prince, had driven the latter to rebellion and death, and had made the unhappy widow his fifth empress. It then appeared that Pin was determined to eliminate Yang Chien's daughter in order to raise the position of the new empress. The daughter's life was saved only by the impassioned personal pleas of her mother. Shortly thereafter Pin, obviously still meaning to have his way, threatened to exterminate the whole Yang family.[34]

On June 8 it became known that Yü-wen Pin was seriously ill. Yang Chien's friends—one of whom had been chief official of the "abdicated" emperor—forged an order for Yang Chien to appear at the imperial bedside. The emperor shortly died, and Yang Chien's friends urged him to assume the regency. He agreed, after much hesitation, perhaps influenced by his wife's remark that he was "riding a tiger."[35]

During the rest of the summer Yang Chien's bid for power was challenged by supporters of the Yü-wen; strong forces took the field against him, and even two of his palace confederates began to waver. But his rivals were divided and showed a lack of vision and drive. Perhaps, as Boodberg suggests, the adherence of Kao Chiung, able and energetic leader who co-ordinated the military forces of the northeast, was of critical importance.[36] Rival forces were defeated one by one, important groups rallied to Yang Chien, and on January 3, 581, Yang Chien assumed the title of *wang*. The last of the elder princes of the blood were killed in January, and on March 4 Yang Chien ascended the throne and established the Sui dynasty.[37]

In less than a year Yang Chien had, through shrewdness, utter ruthlessness, and astonishingly good luck reached the pinnacle of power. But he had not had the time to make careful plans for usurpation or to follow the time-honored conventions which, if followed, would have given him assurance in his new and awesome role. As a result he had a lifelong fear of the consequences of his hybris, and he was ever apprehensive lest a similar combination of favorable circumstances and good luck bring a rival to power and end the Sui as suddenly as he had ended the Chou.[38] He was obsessed by fear of the jealous gods and deeply suspicious of officials and relatives who accumulated any power or popularity. He was suspicious of his sons, and, impressed by the damage done by the wayward princes of the Chou, he kept the imperial princes and their families under tight surveillance and control.[39] As we shall see, his ideological measures are marked by his craving for reassurance and by his obsessive urge to use any sanction to establish his right to rule in the eyes of the millions whose destinies he now controlled.

Suspicious as he was, Wen-ti was yet capable of warm attachments to old friends; when he finally decided to take an adviser into his confidence, he did not capriciously withdraw his trust. Among those whom he trusted, two are important both for their sustained direct influence on Wen-ti and for their role in the formulation and execution of his policies.[40] A brief consideration of these two statesmen may shed some light on the ways in which they influenced the formation of Sui ideology.

Kao Chiung (555–607), who rallied to Yang Chien in the critical summer of 580, was of northeastern origin, and his father had entered the service of Tu-ku Hsin, father of the future empress.[41] Kao Chiung's father had adopted the Tu-ku surname.[42] Kao Chiung, who was an able youth, gained his first military honors in the conquest of Ch'i in 577. From the time of his adherence to Yang Chien in 580 until his degradation in 599 through the intrigues of the empress, Kao Chiung was the emperor's most trusted minister and confidant. His was the plan—both psychological and military—for the conquest of the south. Despite the gaps in existing records, he is probably to be credited with many of the sweeping measures of economic,

social, and legal reform which solidified the Sui seizure of power. The
authors of the *Sui-shu* judged him to be a model prime minister, the
official most responsible for the achievement of peace and prosperity.[43]

It is always difficult, through the formalized anecdotes and phrases
of Chinese biography, to discern a man's character and outlook. But
a tentative appraisal of Kao Chiung is possible. Although his biography attributes to him the use of the well-worn phrases of Confucian
political argument, he was not regarded as a "learned Confucian."
We do not find his name associated with the commissions for the
reform of education, ritual, and the like—tasks that required Confucian training. He was rather a man of practical statecraft. His
measures, such as the reform of the system of collecting and recording taxes, were brilliantly conceived and rigidly enforced.[44] There is a
strong strain of authoritarianism in these measures, a rigor that re-
calls the great Legalist statesmen. When Tu Yu (735–812), writing
from a Legalist viewpoint, classes Kao Chiung among the six great
statesmen of Chinese history, it is on the ground that he accomplished brilliantly the objectives of a Legalist government: enrich-
ment of the state, strengthening of the armed forces, fostering a program for a strong autocratic government (*hsing-pa-t'u*) and the
like.[45] And Tu Yu groups Kao Chiung not only with such earlier
Legalist statesmen as Kuan Chung and Shang Yang but with the
great architect of Northern Chou rule, Su Ch'o (498–546).[46] It is
said that Kao Chiung regarded himself as the heir of Su Ch'o's statecraft and that many of Kao's measures can be regarded as the fulfilment of Su Ch'o's principles, as laid out in his Six Articles.[47] It may
be that the long collaboration between Kao Chiung and Su Wei was
based on a common esteem for the latter's father.[48] Yet, despite Tu
Yu's evaluation, Kao Chiung was not a "classical" Legalist any more
than Su Ch'o had been. Balázs has brilliantly demonstrated that in
this period Legalists and Confucians were in accord on the necessity
of treating the lower classes harshly with all the rigor of the law; only
when the Legalists insisted on the universality of law and equality
before the law did they part company with the Confucians.[49] Kao
Chiung was not in this sense a Legalist, but, while favoring certain
measures for the restoration of social morale which may loosely be
termed "Confucian," he consistently advocated harsh legal sanctions
and rigorous centralized control. It is perhaps his influence in this direction that accounts for the sad comment of the *Sui-shu* that after a
brief period in positions of power the Confucian scholars gradually

lost their influence at the Sui court and were replaced by men of a Legalist outlook.[50]

And, as in the case of his royal master, Kao Chiung's authoritarian outlook was accompanied by belief in Buddhism. Kao Chiung once said that on his retirement he would lead the life of a Buddhist ascetic and devote himself to reading the scriptures.[51] He was the patron of the great cleric Hsin-hsing and is said to have taken religious instruction in his leisure hours.[52] It seems likely that he favored those Buddhist ideological measures which he felt would contribute to his goal of a unified, stable, and prosperous society. And I venture the hypothesis that he favored all measures which strengthened the central power and gave it additional sanctions in the eyes of the population. The build-up of Wen-ti into a Ćakravartin king—the ideal Buddhist monarch, who, using the true teaching, builds a universal and happy empire—was, in the times in which he lived, one of the most effective ways to gain one of the primary goals of authoritarian statesmen: recognition of the supreme and unchallengeable authority of the monarch.

Su Wei (540–621) was the son of the famous Su Ch'o. He was commended to the emperor, early in the Sui, by Kao Chiung. The emperor liked and trusted him and gave him one difficult assignment after another. Although vigorous and hard-working, he was harsh and autocratic and was at various times accused of nepotism, forming cliques, and enriching himself.[53] He was by no means the calm, humane, self-disciplined official that had been his father's ideal.

At the same time, he, like his colleague Kao Chiung, urged upon the emperor policies strongly influenced by Su Ch'o's ideas. Appealing to the authority of his dead father, Su Wei advocated equitable *corvée* and tax regulations and the moderation of the severity of existing laws,[54] and these recommendations were adopted. It was Su Wei, too, who urged economical court and bureaucratic institutions, and this became one of Wen-ti's consistent policies. Early in the Sui, Su Wei quoted his father's dictum that the *Classic of Filial Piety* sufficed both for the formation of individual character and for governing a state.[55] Only a few months later Wen-ti ordered an old friend who had got into trouble "earnestly to read" that work.[56]

Whatever may have been Su Wei's influence in the early period when certain Confucian formulas were becoming part of Sui policy, it is likely that both Confucianism and Su Wei's influence on questions of ideology waned after 590. In that year he sought to force the conquered population of the south to memorize "five teachings" which he had apparently phrased insultingly. This was one of the provocations for widespread revolts against the Sui conquerors.[57]

But if, as seems likely, the Confucianism which Su Wei combined with his authoritarian political principles found little favor after 590, Su Wei probably had few objections to the increased ideological use of Buddhism. He, like his father before him, was something of a Buddhist.[58] If anything like the connection between authoritarianism and Buddhism which I have suggested above should prove correct, then Su Wei, like Kao Chiung, would have welcomed the additional Buddhist sanctions for an autocratic omnipotent ruler.

These are some of the biographical facts, some of the formative influences, that made Wen-ti what he was and affected his ideological measures as well as the other policies of the Sui. Before turning to his ideological measures, let us sum up, as best we can, the character and outlook of the man. He was, as we have suggested, fearful of the jealousy of the gods and suspicious of the motives of men. He sought reassurance for himself and justification for his regime from every possible source. His violent rages, followed by sudden remorse, suggest a basic sense of insecurity.[59] His heavy reliance on his wife might be similarly interpreted. His suspicion of his sons is, up to a point, explicable in terms of the recent history of China, with its vicious court intrigues and frequent parricides.[60] But Wen-ti's feeling about his sons is clearly abnormal and obsessive. He was somewhat anti-intellectual, impatient of "academic" argument, and had the northerner's distrust of fine manners and literary elegance.[61] He had the *arriviste*'s drive to succeed and the insecure man's reluctance to delegate authority.[62] He slaved over the business of government all day and into the night. He lived an austere life, indulging in few amusements and no extravagances. And this austerity, which he sought to impose on his family, was likewise based in part on the fear that, if they enjoyed too freely the benefits and privileges of their position, fate would strike them down.[63] His anti-intellectualism, his autocratic temper, his Buddhist piety are linked, for the Buddhists offered ways to salvation that did not depend on intellectual distinctions, and Buddhism offered a whole range of sanctions for the autocratic exercise of supreme power. Confucians might mutter moral strictures on his bloody and abrupt rise to power, but the Buddhists assured him that he came with the blessings of potent unseen beings and that acts of penance would exorcise the evil effects of his violent deeds.

Yet, for all his uneasiness and obsessive fears, he was a superb ad-

ministrator, remarkably sober and clear-headed among the tensions
and intrigues of the court. He was a shrewd judge of the talents and
the weaknesses of those who served him. And his decisiveness and
common sense stand out on the pages of history, helping to account
for the impressive record of achievement he left behind. We shall
have further insights into the character of the man as we turn to a
consideration of some of the measures he took to deal with the manifold problems he faced.

4. The Formation of Sui Ideology

The problem of winning support for a new dynasty in China has
always been a serious one. Wen-ti, like other dynastic founders, was
faced with all the complexities of this perennial problem. Three aspects that are particularly related to his ideological measures might
be noted. (1) The careful step-by-step approached to the imperial
position, in which attention to all the expected symbolic and ritual
prescriptions was required if his following was to be reassured and
consolidated. Actually the rapidity of his rise was such that much of
this had to be hurried through in a very short period; this meant that
even after he assumed the throne he had to take extraordinary measures to reassure himself, his officialdom, and the populace. (2) The
demonstration within a very short time that his regime enjoyed the
favor of Heaven, the gods, and the spirits. This involved not only
ritual-symbolic acts but also the production of convincing evidence
that the balance and harmony of the Chinese world were being restored. Measures to ensure the beneficent working of natural forces
were many: Heaven sustained its mandate only to the virtuous, and
evidence had to be forthcoming that the regime would employ virtuous men at all levels. Heaven and the spirits of nature favored only
those who nurtured the people, and measures for the relief and re-
habilitation of the countryside had to be rapidly taken lest Heaven,
working through the oppressed and the disaffected, should withdraw
its mandate and confer it on another. (3) The new regime had step
by step to prepare the way for the conquest of the south, not only
militarily, but by establishing a claim to a universal mandate that
would outweigh the pretensions of legitimacy of the southern dynasty; this had to be so contrived that it would invigorate the northern forces in attack, undermine southern morale, and prepare the
way for the assimilation of the southern population, not as permanently subjected and occupied people, but as potential partners in
the enterprise of a reunified empire.

The *Huang Sui Ling-kan Chih* is an instructive introduction to the ideological use of the three traditions of Taoism, Confucianism, and Buddhism. It is a kind of omnibus collection of symbols, portents, and canonical texts which sanctioned and justified the newly created dynasty. Its contents and the uses made of it suggest both the extraordinary range of Sui ideology and the compulsion the dynasty felt to justify its position to the whole population.

It was compiled by a Taoist, Wang Shao, whose facile and timely production of favorable portents reassured Wen-ti throughout his reign. It was made up of selections of popular songs, quotations from the prognostic texts, the *Lo-shu* and *Ho-t'u*, quotations from the divinatory texts and apochrypha, mysterious signs of Heaven's disposition to confer the mandate, plus passages from the Buddhist scriptures.[64] The emperor ordered that the book be distributed far and wide throughout the empire. Wang Shao, after a ceremonious handwashing, burned incense and read it aloud—in the manner used for chanting the Buddhist sutras—to the assembled representatives of the provinces (*Ch'ao-chi-shih*), who were, we may presume, expected to report to the polyglot population of the empire these proofs of the dynasty's claims.[65] There was a precedent for the compilation and wide distribution of such a work in the career of Wang Mang (A.D. 6–22), whose usurpation was planned with all the care lavished on the moves in an international chess tournament.[66] But Wen-ti's ideological measures were as different from Wang Mang's as were the problems they faced. Let us turn to Wen-ti's use of each of the traditions whose adherents' approval and support were needed by the new dynasty of Sui.

A. TAOISM

It is extraordinarily difficult, in the present state of knowledge and of terminological usage, to distinguish clearly what is "Taoist" from that Taoist-Legalist-Confucian amalgam that is known as "Han Confucianism." But certain measures of Wen-ti were clearly directed at winning the support of the communities of religious Taoists which had existed since the Later Han, while others sought to reassure those educated subjects who were philosophic Taoists or who were persuaded of the validity of one or another branch of Taoist "science."

The immediate background of Wen-ti's use of Taoism—as of Buddhism—is the Northern Chou persecution of 574–78, which proscribed both religions, destroyed their temples, images, and books, and secularized their clergy. At the end of his sweeping order of proscription, the Chou emperor had said, "That which is not re-corded in the Ritual Canon is to be completely extirpated."[67] This order, asserting the ultimate authority of the Confucian ritual canon, struck at the personal beliefs and community organizations of millions of people throughout north China.

Early in his reign, despite his recorded contempt for Taoist adepts, Wen-ti took measures for the revival of Taoism. During his reign some two thousand adepts were ordained,[68] and early in the Sui the capital had ten Taoist monasteries and six nunneries.[69] But there is no evidence that strong encouragement was given to the re-establishment of Taoist communities and temples at the local level. In 582 the Hsuan-tu kuan was set up in the heart of the new capital.[70] This institution had two purposes. It served as a central organ for government control of Taoist activities and the Taoist clergy. Also—like the T'ung-tao kuan of the Northern Chou of which it was the direct successor[71]—it functioned to preserve for the dynasty Taoist "scientific" skills in astrology, geomancy, calendric calculation, and the like.[72] It is significant that the first calendar of the Sui, whose adoption and promulgation was one of the important symbols of the dynasty's establishment, was prepared by a Taoist adept, Chang Pin.[73] This man had earlier influenced the Chou Emperor Wu in favor of Taoism and of Taoist prognostics,[74] and he had been one of those who produced astrological "evidence" favoring Wen-ti's seizure of power.[75]

The first Sui era-name—on whose selection I suspect Chang Pin had an influence—was a term used for one of the Taoist "kalpa."[76] The use of a Taoist term in the dating of official documents, on monuments, in the written calendar officially circulated throughout the country and beyond, might have seemed to some, early in the dynasty, to indicate partiality toward Taoism and to portend its use in political and social policy.

But ideological measures based on Taoism proved to be very limited. One of these was the promotion of the cult of Lao-tzu. In one of his first ideological pronouncements, which will be discussed in detail below, Wen-ti said, "We make humble obeisance to the transforming power of Tao and concentrate our mind on pure tranquillity. We revere the one and indivisible truth of Sakyamuni; We honor Lao-tzu's ideal of attaining one-ness."[77] Note the reiteration of words suggesting oneness, indivisibility, etc. We shall see that these are the most persistent themes of all Wen-ti's ideological statements and they reflect the dominant preoccupation of his whole reign: the attainment of political and cultural unity. The salute to Lao-tzu in this edict is recognition not only of the force of an appeal for unity backed by the authority of his name but also of the unique position which Lao-tzu had gained in Chinese thought and religion. On the one hand, the book attributed to him was revered and intensively studied by virtually all educated Chinese in the period of disunion; its ideas had been a major focus of intellectual life. On the other hand, Lao-tzu had been apotheosized into the deified founder of religious Taoism; in the course of his apotheosis he had become associated with a host of folk deities and culture heroes, and in hundreds of Taoist communities he was the object of worship.[78]

Wen-ti, like the T'ang founders a generation later, recognized the power of Lao-tzu's appeal to large segments of the population. In 586 he ordered his favorite writer of public documents to compose and set up a stele inscription at Lao-tzu's "birthplace" in Hao-chou (northwest Anhwei), and it was about this time that he ordered a high official to investigate the historic remains at the site and build a new hall of worship there.[79] Imperial veneration of Lao-tzu and care for his shrine dated back at least to A.D. 165,[80] so that Wen-ti not only was appealing to those who admired or worshiped Lao-tzu but was demonstrating his right to resume one of the ritual functions of the Han emperors. We shall see that in this sort of act Wen-ti tended to appeal to the least common denominator of the various traditions he used and to avoid the use of exclusive ideas or particular cults.

While Wen-ti, with his many fears and anxieties, took comfort from Taoist prognostics and sought to gain support for his rule by their publication, he was well aware that the oracle texts and apocrypha—of which the Taoist adepts were the authoritative interpreters—could be used by others to "foretell" or to justify the overthrow of the Sui. In 583 he felt obliged to execute an old friend whose subversive designs had been fostered by favorable evidence in an oracle text.[81] In 593 he forbade the private possession of all such texts; they presumably still remained in the hands of official diviners who were under state scrutiny and control.[82]

In summary, Wen-ti did not make extensive ideological use of Taoism. Both his personal prejudice against Taoist adepts (and fear of their power) and, I believe, a realistic estimate of the greater potency of other ideological possibilities led him to concentrate most of his attention on Confucianism and Buddhism.[83]

B. CONFUCIANISM

Wen-ti's ideological uses of Confucianism were numerous. They can be divided into two main types. The first is a group of ritual acts and pronouncements that were meant to justify his usurpation, establish important symbolic links with the last great unified empire of Han, and bring every kind of ritual-symbolic support to his regime. These were directed at the educated classes, at the present and potential officials of the Sui empire, at the aristocrats and great families whose loyalties had been to the Northern Chou or the Ch'en (557–89) and whose support Wen-ti required. The second group of acts was intended to re-establish a body of political principles and standards of behavior which, if accepted by the rulers and the ruled, would ensure the reconstitution of a stable state on the basis of Confucian ideals and behavioral norms. Since, as we have noted, a state based on a pluralistic society was incompatible with Chinese social and political theory, this second group of acts had the double purpose of political unification and social integration.

As we have noted in the biographical sketch of Wen-ti, he had no taste for Confucian studies and was often impatient at long-winded arguments laden with classical quotations. And, I suspect, while he admired and probably adopted some of the political principles of the great Su Ch'o, he was not greatly impressed by the Northern Chou creation of an archaistic façade of government nomenclature based on the *Rites of Chou*, especially when this came to involve the alienation of large segments of the northern population through the proscription of Buddhism and Taoism. But he knew the latent power of Confucianism, the endemic Confucianism of orderly family and community relationships which could bring harmony to society, and Confucian political theory, which provided the most complete body of sanctions available for one who would govern a unified Chinese empire.[84]

Thus early in his reign he brought together Confucians of many schools and put them to work bulwarking his regime. As the *Sui-shu* says, at that time people did not consider a thousand li too far to go to find a Confucian master, and the sound of lectures on the classics could be heard incessantly on the roads; such an upsurge of Confucianism had not occurred since the Han and (San-kuo) Wei. Yet, as it sadly says, in Wen-ti's later years this brilliant flowering faded and Legalist principles were exalted.[85] This is a rather clear indication of Wen-ti's attitude toward Confucianism: he used its sanctions to legitimize and consolidate his empire, but his character and background, his advisers, and the urgency of his many problems inclined him toward the authoritarian rigor associated with Legalism and inclined him at the same time to Buddhism, which salved his personal conscience and provided its special sanctions for a supreme autocrat.

It is difficult to select the most important among the ritual-symbolic acts—our first group of Confucian ideological measures—because each year of Wen-ti's reign was punctuated by many such observances. The year preceding his seizure of the throne was marked by a number of the essential ritual-symbolic steps toward supreme power. Then, on January 3, 581—an auspicious *chia-tzu* day at the start of a sexagenary cycle—he was given, in the name of the helpless Chou dynasty, the rank of Prince, and received the nine gifts symbolic of special imperial favor from the child emperor who was his puppet.[86] On March 4—another *chia-tzu* day—he received the eight imperial seals, donned the appropriate robes and hat, and informed Heaven in the south suburb of his acceptance of the mandate.[87] Shortly thereafter he took the prescribed steps of conferring posthumous imperial titles on his father and mother and established an imperial ancestral temple (*t'ai-miao*), on canonical lines, at which he made the appropriate regular sacrifices.[88] In 587 he returned to his native village and worshiped at the village shrine, not only demonstrating his respect for one of China's oldest fertility cults but renewing a custom sanctioned by the Han ceremonies carried on in Kao-tsu's old village.[89] In keeping with the elaborate symbolism that had been absorbed into Han Confucianism, the Sui adopted the color red, the element fire, and worshiped the Fire Emperor in the south suburb each spring. Here, too, was another symbolic link with the greatness of Han, for they too had ruled by the virtue of fire.[90]

These and a hundred other observances had to be guided by codified ritual—prescriptions which would order the imperial ritual year according to the most authoritative texts and which would mark the Sui as a great and orthodox dynasty and, at the same time, order the emperor's relations with his ancestors, with Heaven, Earth, and the nature spirits, in the interests of universal harmony. The emperor set up a commission of learned Confucians at the beginning of his reign, and its chairman was the president of the Board of Rites. The chairman pointed to the deficiencies in both southern and northern traditions of ritual scholarship and proposed returning to the canonical texts and building on them.[91] The emperor approved, and the commission and the Board of Rites consistently labored to provide the court with rules and prescriptions so that the Great Sui could lay authoritative claims to be operating within the sanctified structure of canonical ritual.

In concluding this very preliminary exploration of ritual-symbolic acts, it may be interesting to consider two which Wen-ti was reluctant to sanction or perform. The first of these was the building of a *ming-t'ang*, or cosmic house. In 593 he ordered the president of the Board of Rites to start discussions on the design and building of a cosmic house.[92] The construction of such a building on the basis of the symbolism of the "Ordinances of the Months" (*Yueh-ling*) of the *Book of Rites* (*Li-chi*) may have been attempted under the Ch'in, but it is typically a Han institution. It was, in a sense, a model of the universe, and imperial worship in it was to dramatize the charismatic power of the emperor, to symbolize his relationship to the five forces, the five direction-color-element "emperors," his role in ordering the sequence of seasons, and the beneficent and timely working of natural forces throughout the land. Wen-ti was obviously interested in such a symbolic assertion of ultimate power, but he found that his ritual specialists could not agree, and with characteristic caution he finally refused to order its construction.[93] He was not one to risk unbalancing the cosmic forces by adopting a design whose efficacy and canonical authority were in doubt.

The second of his ritual-symbolic evasions was more significant. The *feng* sacrifice at the most sacred mountain of China, T'ai-shan, was an ancient ritual, and by the Later Han it had come to signify a report to August Heaven on the achievements of the dynasty, a solemn acknowledgment of the mandate and all the vast responsibilities it involved.[94] A secondary, but still important sacrifice to Earth (*Shan*), was usually made on the same occasion and included the mountains, rivers, and other deities as well as Sovereign Earth. The emperor Kuang-wu of the Later Han had at first refused to make the T'ai-shan sacrifices, on the ground that there was still discontent among the people of the empire for which he was answerable to Heaven. But in A.D. 56, after elaborate preparations, he finally performed the sacrifices.[95]

When he was urged, in 589, to perform these sacrifices, Wen-ti spoke of the smallness of his accomplishment, the meagerness of his virtue, and said that his performance of the *feng* sacrifice would be empty verbiage and offensive to the supreme ruler on high, Shang-ti; he thereupon ordered that there should be no further talk of the *feng* and *shan* sacrifices.[96] But in 594, after the consolidation of his conquest of the south, he finally ordered the president of the Board of Rites to establish proper procedures; when this was completed, Wen-ti commented on the magnitude of the undertaking and the inadequacy of his virtue.[97] The imperial progress to the east, through the most populous and important part of the Sui domain, shortly began.

En route, the emperor inquired into the ills of the population then suffering from severe drought. In the first moon of 595 he finally worshiped at T'ai-shan, asking Heaven's pardon for his faults (which had brought on the drought).[98] But he was apparently still fearful of the full solemn sacrifice on the top of the mountain, which might seem, in the light of the problems still before him, presumptuous and likely to bring down Heaven's wrath. So he limited himself to a ceremony resembling that made annually to Heaven in the south suburb of the capital—this at the foot of the mountain—and a special sacrifice at the shrine of the Green Emperor, associated with east-spring-growth-wood, etc.[99] Thus the progress to the east toward T'ai-shan demonstrated to all the people along the route that the emperor was confident of his mandate, while his avoidance of the supreme ritual communion with Heaven may have pleased some of the sticklers for ritual among his officialdom and certainly assuaged his own deep-seated fears of the consequences of presumption.

Measures for the reinculcation of Confucian social values were numerous and frequent. Very early in the dynasty incentives were given to conduct which exemplified Confucian virtues; filial sons, obedient grandsons, widows and widowers who did not remarry were ordered exempted from taxes and *corvée*.[100] Schools of Confucian studies were established at the local level, and a national college (Kuo-tzu-hsueh) for the sons of nobles was set up in the capital and at one time had an enrolment of over a thousand.[101] In 587 a quota of three scholars yearly was levied on each province (*chou*), and these young men were sent up to the capital for examination and official appointment.[102] The system of schools, the provincial quotas, and the capital examinations had a dual purpose. One was to give the central government a reservoir of trained men so that the ruler need not be dependent on the few entrenched families which had long monopolized public office. The second was to promote social and intellectual conformity by rewards of place and prestige to those who excelled in Confucian scholarship and displayed Confucian principles in their personal behavior.[103]

The way the system was supposed to work is well illustrated in the story of Governor Liang Yen-kuang. This official had had a notable success in a stable province in southwestern Shensi and had been singled out for special recognition. He was later transferred to be governor of an area in northern Honan which included the old Ch'i capital of Yeh. With the fall of the Ch'i in 577, the officials and literati of the area had moved west, presumably to be nearer the new political capital at Ch'ang-an. The new governor found that the "tone" of the Yeh area was now set by artisans, merchants, and the descendants of criminals, who were under hereditary disabilities. The governor's mild methods, which had been effective in his previous post, were ridiculed, and he was regarded as a "hatted sugar lump" (colloquial, "softy"). He was removed from office, but soon asked to be allowed to return and try again. This time he started a vigorous campaign of exposing evil doings, so that the tough elements fled and order was restored. Then he brought in Confucian scholars and set up schools in every village. He personally participated in examinations, praised the diligent and rebuked the idle. When he recommended a candidate to go up to the capital, he gave a farewell feast in the suburban temple and helped the man on his way with money and goods. "Whereupon the atmosphere completely changed; officialdom and people were happy and contented and there were no more litigants."[104]

Achievement of this sort was used to further the spread of Confucian standards of official morality and social life. To all successful officials Wen-Ti gave well-publicized promotions. To one he gave an imperially sealed letter of commendation which was broadcast throughout the empire. To another—a district magistrate in the central province—he gave rewards of grain and cloth and personal commendation in the presence of all the district magistrates of the same province. On another's success the emperor addressed the assembled delegates of all the provinces: "His will is fixed on consolidating the dynasty; he loves and cherishes our people. To do thus is to be blessed by High Heaven and the spirits of the ancestral temple. If we should disregard and fail to reward him, High Heaven and the spirits of the ancestral temple would certainly punish us. It is proper that all of you take him as your master and your model."[105]

These and related measures had in view the complex of social and political objectives we have noted above. Until 589 these efforts were limited to North China, where the development of a peaceful society on the basis of Confucian values not only served to stabilize the area but furnished an ideological argument in Confucian terms for Wen-ti's right to conquer the south. Preparations for the conquest went on for eight years. While Wen-ti maintained the most ostentatiously "proper," ritually sanctioned, formal relations with the dynasty in the south, economic, military, and psychological preparations for the attack went forward. In 588 Wen-ti issued the edict justifying the conquest he was about to attempt. He had 300,000 copies made and distributed widely throughout the area south of the Yangtze; in addition, he dispatched an imperially sealed letter to the Ch'en ruler, listing the twenty crimes of an oppressive emperor which made it no crime but a duty imposed by Heaven to relieve him of his throne.[106]

The text of the broadcast edict contains no reference to Buddhism and none to Taoism. It is a direct appeal for support in classic Confucian moral-political argument. The Ch'en regime is guilty of bad faith, wastefulness, licentiousness (many concubines), oppression of the people, interference with agriculture, execution of upright remonstrators, extermination of blameless families, disregard of Heaven, contumely toward the five elements, heterodox religious practices; the appearance of ghosts and the occurrence of natural disasters are the signs of the withdrawal of Heaven's mandate.[107]

It is not possible to assess Wen-ti's inner confidence in the argument. His trusted adviser, Kao Chiung, seems to have believed in and acted on one of the time-honored practices of dynastic transition, for, despite the fact that it alienated the powerful Prince of Chin, Kao Chiung insisted on the execution of the favorite of the last Ch'en ruler, arguing that King Wu of Chou had killed the favorite of the last Shang emperor.[108] But whatever the degree of conviction in the rightness of their cause among Wen-ti and his advisers, the ideological choice was this: they adopted the most complete and sanctified doctrines for dynastic change that were available, those that were enshrined in the Confucian classics and histories. It is about this time that Wen-ti's use of Confucianism reaches its high point and begins to decline. For other purposes, for other problems such as the pacification of the conquered south and the overcoming of cultural diversity, he made increasing ideological use of other traditions, notably Buddhism.

C. BUDDHISM

As in the case of the other two traditions, the use of Buddhism was governed in part by the recent history of North China, notably the Northern Chou persecution of Buddhism and Taoism. While this persecution had created sufficient discontent[109] to make a reversal of policy appealing to one who sought power, Wen-ti must have been well aware of the abuses of clerical privilege that were in part responsible for the persecution. Even the most partisan Buddhist chronicles admit this. Wen-ti was a devout Buddhist, but he was also a shrewd and calculating man in pursuit of great power and universal dominion. What we shall find in the account that follows and what appears in all the Buddhist chronicles is a calculated and selective revival of Buddhism. The available figures indicate that, in numbers of clergy and in religious establishments, the Buddhist church was not in Wen-ti's reign allowed to grow to the vast proportions it had had during much of the period of disunion.[110] From beginning to end Buddhism was under firm state control, and support of Buddhism, as well as the ideological use of Buddhism, were calculated in terms of the problems facing the dynasty.

The Northern Chou government had, in the final years of its power, taken steps to modify the proscription; certainly it was aware of the tensions and disaffection which that sweeping measure had created among the population. Tsukamoto believes that the influence of Cheng I, chief official of the abdicated but omnipotent Emperor Hsuan, influenced this reversal of policy. And Cheng I was an old friend of Yang Chien, a close confederate in his seizure of power.[111] The steps taken were for a limited and controlled revival. Restrictions on Buddhist worship among the people were removed. State-supported temples, Chih-hu ssu, were built in Ch'ang-an and Loyang, and a hundred and twenty monks were selected to live in them and "practice their religion for the good of the state."[112] But other Buddhist building was not permitted. The monks were not to shave their heads—a practice which violated the sanctity of the body enjoined by filial piety—and they were obliged to wear secular clothing. The name of the temple, drawn from a poem in the *Book of Songs* which celebrates love of parents, symbolized the fact that Buddhism was to operate within the framework of Confucian values.[113] Because of these restrictions, many former monks refused appointments to the state temples, and this very limited and restricted revival of Buddhism probably was insufficient to allay the discontent of Buddhist believers generally.[114]

Within a few days of assuming the prime ministership, Yang Chien called the monk Fa-tsang down from his retreat and, a month later, ordered this eminent cleric—who had boycotted the Chou official temples—to collaborate with a nobleman in examining candidates for the priesthood. The one hundred and twenty selected clerics were to be ordained along fully canonical lines and returned to their places of residence.[115] And, in the same critical days following his seizure of power, he issued an order that qualified former monks and Taoist adepts would be selected to resume the practice of their religions.[116] Several of the monks who advised him in the formulation of new religious policies were members of powerful northern families, men who enjoyed great popularity and prestige among the Chou ruling class.[117] Thus, even before his accession, Wen-ti was bidding for the favor and support of north Chinese of all classes who had suffered from the Chou persecution. But even at a time when he desperately needed widespread support, he was carefully providing for state screening and control.

The symbol of religious centralization and state control was the metropolitan temple, Ta-hsing-shan ssu.[118] It occupied an entire ward in the heart of Ch'ang-an. And across the principal north-south street was the Taoist Hsuan-tu kuan, which occupied half a ward. These were impressive visible evidences of the Sui reversal of Chou religious policy. As soon as he occupied his new capital in 583, Wen-ti made available a hundred official temple name plates—and gave orders that anyone with the means to build a temple might take one.[119] Religious building went forward rapidly, and this building reveals a good deal about the relative appeal of Buddhism and Taoism to the residents of the capital and about the relative imperial favor the two religions enjoyed. There were soon 64 Buddhist monasteries and 27 nunneries, but only 10 Taoist monasteries and 6 nunneries. By the end of Wen-ti's reign, significantly, the proportion had further shifted in favor of Buddhism; there were then 120 Buddhist establishments and only 10 Taoist.[120]

Before turning to some of the Buddhist ideological measures of Wen-ti's reign, we might briefly consider the kind of Buddhism he favored. It would appear that Wen-ti appealed to the most general principles of Buddhism, to those doctrines that were accepted by all Buddhists regardless of their special interests or affiliations. And these appeals are nearly always accompanied by warnings against sectarianism. Buddhism could hardly serve Wen-ti's purpose as a reunifying ideology if it were itself allowed to become divided into hostile sects.

Hsin-hsing, who came to the capital early in the Sui and was patronized by the great minister Kao Chiung, was an immensely popular and impressive preacher. It was widely believed toward the end of the period of disunion that the last of the three stages of Buddhism had been reached, that the period of the "extinction of the dharma" was at hand. Buddhist clerics and intellectuals had different views as to what the proper religious attitude and activity should be in such a period. Hsin-hsing developed his own theory, and it found a wide audience. But two features of that theory brought government proscription. One was the claim to have the *sole* formula for salvation (which is, I suspect, a universal characteristic of apocalyptic sectaries). The second was the doctrine that no government worthy of the respect and co-operation of orthodox Buddhists could possibly exist in this age of extinction of the dharma. The first of these features was divisive and productive of fanaticism. The second was subversive of a regime that sought Buddhist sanctions. Thus in 600, some years after the founder's death, the teachings of Hsin-hsing and the circulation of his writings were officially proscribed.[121] On the other hand, the syncretic teachings of the founder of T'ien-t'ai Buddhism won particular favor from both Sui rulers; this relationship is complex and has been the object of much scholarly research. What is important for the present essay is the salient fact that Wen-ti favored the type of Buddhism that would best contribute to the solution of his problems. T'ien-t'ai had been developed in the south, and its founder had been favored by the Ch'en court; Wen-ti's public homage to the founder sprang as much from a desire to mollify southern Buddhists as from the intrinsic appeal of a kind of Buddhist *Summa theologica* for the needs of the time.

One of the earliest edicts which makes ideological use of Buddhism is that of the intercalary third moon of 581. It opens with a typical reiteration of the unity of purpose among religions, and it expresses the imperial esteem for the "indivisible truth of Śakyamuni" and "Lao-tzu's ideal of attaining one-ness." It goes on to state the emperor's commitment to the salvation of all the world and to the attainment of nonaction (the ideals, respectively, of Mahāyāna Buddhism and Taoism). It then pays tribute to the ideals and teachings of the ascetic recluses of both religions. And then it salutes the mountain fastnesses which harbor divine spirits and are beloved of recluses, the dwelling places of the immortal sages. Finally, it orders that a Buddhist monastery be built at the foot of the five sacred mountains and of the famous mountains which were the tutelary divinities of various provinces and that manors (*T'ien-chuang*) be set up to support the new establishments.[122]

The mountains of China are not only the homes of spirits and, in the Taoist tradition, the dwelling place of the immortals who there receive supernatural inspiration; they are also themselves deities which protect and stabilize the regions over which they preside.[123] The emperors of China regularly saw to it that these mountain divinities were propitiated, particularly those of the five major mountains. But this is the first instance of the use of Buddhist monks for the carrying-out of this important function. It automatically set up Buddhist establishments in key centers throughout the empire, associated Buddhism with the most important and enduring nature divinities, and signalized the competence of Buddhist monks to maintain some of the most important relationships with the forces of the natural world, the responsibility for which rested ultimately with the emperor.[124] This measure may also be seen as complementary to the network of official temples which were ordered established in the years before 585 and which brought centers of state-supported Buddhism to many areas of North China.[125]

An edict of 583 suggests the ways in which the spiritual life of the empire was to be unified in state-supported institutions—temples that were named uniformly Ta-hsing-kuo ssu, for the old fief of the Yang family—and in regularly observed services and religious abstinence.

To value life and hate death is the basis of kingly government. [Similarly] in the teachings handed down in the Buddhist tradition good acts (karma) are what one should put his faith in. To those endowed with life and intelligence only life is valued. (?) It is proper that We encourage the empire with one mind to seek salvation. In the capital and in the various *chou* let temples be officially erected. Every year, in the first, fifth and ninth moons, regularly from the 8th to the 15th days let there be religious services at the temples. On the days of these services, among the people far and near, let there be no killing whatever of any living thing.[126]

In the seventh and eighth moons of the year of his accession, 581, Wen-ti ordered Buddhist temples and inscribed steles set up at three scenes of his late father's military victories (and at one other place) and on the battlefield where he had crushed the last major resistance to his seizure of power. At the same time he ordered regular services for the repose of the souls of the war dead. In the first of these edicts he pays tribute to his father, reviews the natural and moral indications of the Sui's right to the mandate, praises martial virtues, and introduces an idea which he consistently propagates in public acts and pronouncements throughout his reign:

With the armed might of a Ćakravartin king We spread the ideals of the ultimately benevolent one [i.e., Buddha]. With a hundred victories in a hundred battles. We promote the practice of the ten Buddhist virtues. Therefore We regard the weapons of war as having become like incense and flowers [presented as offerings to Buddha] and the fields of this visible world as becoming forever identical with the Buddhaland.[127]

This statement and others which appear in the second edict establishing battlefield temples have two ideological purposes. One is to lay claim to a sanction for supreme power that existed in Buddhist tradition—that Wen-ti was a divinely ordained Ćakravartin king, a turner of the wheel of the law, that his actions were sanctioned by the

high goal of a universal Buddhist dominion.[128] The second purpose
was to create a new attitude among the people toward death in
battle—particularly important in view of the demands of frontier
defense and the massive attack on the south which Wen-ti had begun
to plan. It is ironic that Buddhism, the great religion of peace and
compassion, should have been put to such a use. But the idea that
the welfare of the war dead would be safeguarded in regular services
at official shrines was a useful antidote to the Chinese abhorrence of
a violent and bodily disfiguring death and an unmourned, unmarked
grave far from the ancestral altars of the family. Moreover, the battlefield monument to the victims of a righteous victory had the sanction of the greatest of Buddhist universal monarchs, Aśoka of the
Mauryas. As we shall see, the figure of Aśoka, as enshrined in Buddhist legend, had a persistent appeal for Wen-ti in his efforts to build
a peaceful and united empire under an all-powerful divinely sanctioned emperor.[129]

The image of Wen-ti as a Cakravartin is carefully built up in reiterated pronouncements and in symbolic acts. Nowhere are Wen-ti's
pretensions to a Buddhist divine mission more clearly stated than in
his order of 585: "The Buddha entrusts the true dharma to the rulers
of states. We, being honored among men, accept the Buddha's
trust."[130]

While Wen-ti was being presented as a Cakravartin king waging
righteous wars for the welfare of all mankind, he was also being publicly endowed with the character of the Mahā-danāpati, the pious
and munificent patron of the Buddhist religion. The restoration of
the temples destroyed by the Chou,[131] the order for the repair and
re-installation of images,[132] the royal patronage of temples and clerics
which fill the pages of the biographies of Sui monks—all these, plus
the publicly announced taking of the layman's vows (*p'u-sa chieh*,
involving the Bodhisattva's vow to work for the salvation of all creation),[133] endowed him with the character of Mahā-danāpati and
gained him the epithet of "Bodhisattva Son of Heaven."[134]

The creation of this related group of images—drawing upon the
sanctions of all Buddhist traditions—had two ideological purposes.
One was to proclaim to the Buddhists of all China Wen-ti's claim to
be regarded as the great and good king whose reign was a fulfilment
of Buddha's own prophecy that in the time of the decay of the
dharma (*mo-fa*) a great sovereign would appear in the land of China
who "would be able to bring all sentient creatures within the land
of China to abide in the dharma of Buddha and to plant in them the

roots of goodness."[135] Nor was the parallel to Aśoka—sage-king, Ćakravartin, Mahā-danāpati, master of one of the four continents—intended to be lost on the Buddhist communities of China.[136] The second purpose of this early Sui build-up of Buddhist sanctions was to prepare the south for conquest. The reversal of the Chou proscription certainly must have won for the Sui emperor a measure of approval among southern Buddhists. And one of the notable omissions in these assertions of Buddhist sanctions is the statement that the emperor *is* the Tathagata, a formula used by the Northern Wei to sanction their rule and overcome the conflict between royal and religious law. While the south had become accustomed, especially under Liang Wu-ti, to the notion of a Ćakravartin-Mahā-danāpati emperor, southerners had long viewed the Northern Wei formula as heterodox and outlandish.[137]

The effectiveness of this appeal to the south cannot be estimated. The actual conquest of 589 was followed by strict and harsh measures of the Sui conquerors against the Buddhist clergy of the south which had been particularly favored by and loyal to the Ch'en ruling class. In the subsequent uprisings—for which, as we have noted, Su Wei's attempt to force Confucian teachings upon the populace was one of the provocations—many of the southern clergy joined the rebels.[138] After the suppression of rebellion, measures were taken to mollify southern Buddhists. An edict of 590 called for the reordination by the Sui of southern clergy.[139] The numerous subsequent measures of the Sui have been thoroughly studied by Tsukamoto; their total effect was to sponsor the revival of Buddhism in the south, by the patronage of southern clerics to reduce the animosities that had existed,[140] and through strict but smoothly contrived measures of control to make sure that the southern clergy did not again become part of any movement of rebellion against the Sui.

An edict of 591 illustrates the ideological use of Buddhism in the wake of the conquest of the south. Its aim, as I see it, is to stress common religious activities toward a common religious goal—a goal toward which the emperor himself is striving—and thus reduce the tensions and conflicts between the two disparate cultures of reunited China:

The ideal of the Tathagata's teaching is uniformity (*p'ing-teng*), and the thoughtful care of the Bodhisattvas is fundamentally without distinctions. Therefore they are capable of saving all species, of bringing salvation to living creatures. Our position being that of a sovereign among men, We have continuously glorified the Three Treasures. We have ever spoken of the ultimate principle and have disseminated and clarified the Mahāyāna. All the teachings [dharma] are open and clear;

in their substance there is no distinction between "we" and "they." How much less in religious works should there be a distinction between public and private. Now and hereafter, let all those who would engage in building works of religious merit, within the wide world be as one in carrying out their charitable building. [In doing this] according to their vows, let no divisions arise. All the many ways to truth will return as one to the indivisible, and the worlds of the ten directions will all attain bodhi. . . .[141]

The dramatic pronouncement of January 5, 594, in which the emperor terms himself simply "such a one, disciple of Buddha," reviews the disasters of the Chou persecution and reiterates the emperor's moral and pious aims. After the announcement of a huge offering of silk by the emperor and empress for the repair of images and sutras and of offerings by nobles and commoners of a million cash, it concludes: "I pray that all the Buddhas and all the dharmas and all the great worthies and all the saintly monks will bear witness and receive this disciple's penance."[142] Here speaks the munificent *danāpati*, a pious and penitent Buddhist whom all his devout subjects throughout the land should revere and emulate. This was an appeal that was meant to transcend divisions of race and class, region and culture.

On July 21, 601, Wen-ti's birth date in terms of the sexagenary cycle recurred. The previous year had been one of a deepening crisis in his relations with his sons—a relationship poisoned with suspicion and intrigue—and it had been haunted by the fear that he would not survive beyond the allotted span of sixty years which, in Chinese count, was completed in July of 600.[143] But at the end of that year he had survived, and he had at last made what he thought at the time was a wise decision and had elevated his son Kuang to be crown prince; at the New Year he adopted a new era-name with overtones of longevity.

On his birthday in 601 he launched the first of a series of Buddhist undertakings through which he sought further personal reassurance. At the same time he sought to solidify the Buddhist sanctions for his rule and, through a country-wide co-ordinated celebration, to dramatize and strengthen the unity of culture and values he sought to build. On this day he issued two edicts. One was a critical and disillusioned review of his efforts at Confucian education, which commented on the failure of the schools to produce men suited for government service and ended with an order for the abolition of the T'ai-hsueh and all local schools in the provinces and districts.[144] This meant, in effect, the abandonment of the primary institutional device for the propagation of Confucian values in the local communities of the empire.

The other edict of the same day and its sequels suggest that he now intended to concentrate his efforts on building a homogeneous society based on Buddhism. In this edict he says:

We contemplate with awe the perfect wisdom, the great mercy, the great compassion [of Buddha] that would save and protect all creatures, that would carry across to deliverance all classes of beings. We give our adherence to the Three Treasures and bring to new prosperity the holy teachings. It is our thought and concern that all the people within the four seas may, without exception, develop bodhi and together cultivate fortunate karma, bringing it to pass that present existences will lead to [happy] future lives, that the sustained creation of good causation will carry us one and all up to wondrous enlightenment. . . . .[145]

The edict then gave instructions for the dispatch of commissions headed by eminent monks, who were to be both specialists in the interpretation of supernatural signs (dharma-lakśana) and able preachers, to proceed to thirty provincial capitals throughout the country. En route they were to be accompanied by a secular official, by two servants and five horses, and they were each to carry 120 chin of frankincense. They were to carry with them holy relics and upon arrival select a suitable and important site and build a reliquary pagoda. Noon of the fifteenth day of the tenth moon was set for the simultaneous enshrining of the relics in the thirty pagodas; all the monks and nuns of the empire were to adhere to strict abstinence, and all offices of the government save the military were to suspend business for seven days and engage in religious services in honor of the relics.[146]

Before the dispatch of these commissions the relics were placed by the emperor himself, with great ceremony, in costly double jars and stamped with the imperial seal. In the course of this ceremony the emperor took the disciple's vow to hold to the true dharma, to protect and maintain the Three Treasures, and to seek the salvation of all living creatures.[147] At the time set for the simultaneous enshrinement throughout the country there was another scene of great pomp and magnificence at the palace; 367 monks from the great Ta-hsing-shan temple moved in procession to the imperial palace; after the emperor had worshiped, he led the civil and military officials to partake of a sumptuous maigre banquet.[148]

In the following year of 602 there was a similar distribution of relics to fifty-one more localities where special pagodas had been built. This time the relics were to be enshrined on Buddha's birthday, and similar prescriptions for the participation of clergy and laity were handed down.[149] And a third distribution, again on Buddha's birthday, was decreed in 604.[150] For all the reliquary commissions influential and able monks were chosen, and it was specified that they should spread their faith among the people. The reliquaries were to be the visible and permanent symbols of the dynasty's devotion to Buddhism, and the surviving texts of inscriptions celebrating these enshrinements stress the pious vow that the imperial ancestors, the emperor and empress, the imperial heirs, officialdom, commoners, and all creatures may one and all attain the blessed fruit of enlightenment.[151] And while the pronouncements emphasized the unity of all classes in a common religious endeavor, the distribution missions carried the same message to all parts of the empire (see Fig. 1).[152] There appears to be ideological significance in the selection of monks for the reliquary commissions. Of the 69 identified by Sasaki, all without exception had suffered in some way from the Northern Chou persecution, and they were able to give eloquent testimony to the benefits and favors which the Great Sui had shown their faith.[153]

The emperor expected that the enshrinements would be the occasion of auspicious wonders, that there would be signs of the favorable disposition of the gods toward the dynasty, signs that would feed the aging emperor's lifelong hunger for reassurance and that, made known to his people, would emphasize the divine sanction of Sui rule. Local officials throughout the empire duly reported the fortunate miracles which occurred at the time of enshrinement, and an imperial prince headed a commission to compile these for publication.[154]

Throughout all the pronouncements and reports, references to Aśoka are frequent. One locality reported that those excavating a site for the new shrine discovered strange writing, which read, "Buddha reliquary of the Ćakravartin sage-king."[155] The sequence of elaborate ceremonies was strongly influenced by the example of Aśoka. The effort at synchronized enshrinement throughout the empire was patterned on Aśoka's achievement (with supernatural help) in building 84,000 reliquaries in a single day.[156] The provision of rich and costly containers for the relics was modeled on Aśoka's procedure.[157] One source asserts that the plans and regulations for the relic distributions "were entirely in accord with the standards established by King Aśoka."[158]

The whole galaxy of Aśokan symbols clearly was meant to impress the population with the glory, the piety, and the divine mission of the Sui monarch, and the widespread ceremonies, including nobles, clergy, officialdom, and commoners, were meant to dramatize the unity of the empire in a common faith and a common allegiance to a divinely appointed ruler. This was the last and greatest effort of

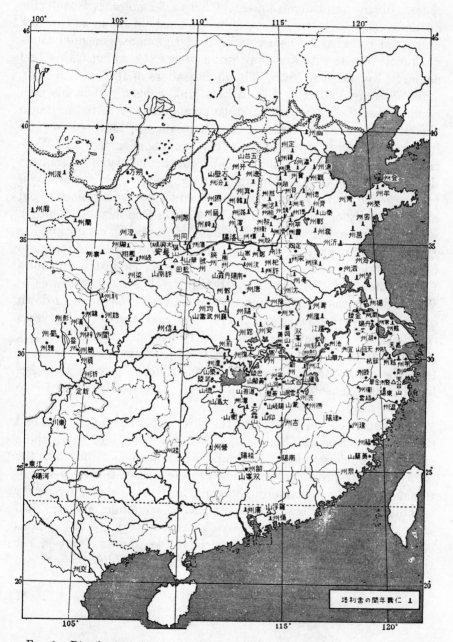

Fig. 1.—Distribution of reliquary pagodas built by government order in the years A.D. 601–4. (Reproduced by courtesy of Professor Yamazaki Hiroshi.)

Wen-ti to use Buddhism as an ideological means of unifying the races, cultures, and diverse areas of his vast empire. It is difficult, again, to estimate its real effect. Shōtoku Taishi in Japan was greatly impressed by what he heard and linked the state-sponsored Buddhism of Wen-ti with the impressive prosperity which China had achieved by the year 600.[159] The ambassadors of the three Korean states each requested a relic to be suitably enshrined in his own country, and for a moment Buddhist symbolism was introduced into the tributary relationship.[160] A thorough study of local records and inscriptions may help toward an understanding of the effect of Wen-ti's ideological use of Buddhism. Yet from the history of subsequent decades we know that Buddhism had only limited effectiveness as an ideology, and we are inclined to raise the question which Bloch asked after his study of the Aśoka inscriptions, "Is Buddhism compatible with temporal power?"[161] or to ask a still more complex question, "Is Buddhism, transplanted in China and adapted in a thousand ways to Chinese thought and values, an effective ideological instrument for a Chinese monarch?" Perhaps the Buddhist ideological measures of Wen-ti did, in the manner intended, contribute to the breaking-down of cultural and racial and regional barriers, and perhaps, in the years of Wen-ti's reign, they were the most effective instrument for doing this. But, in the end, it was a revived Confucianism, borrowing much from the other two traditions, that was at last to provide the basis for the homogeneous society and unified state which endured into modern times.

The ideological use of each of the three traditions by Wen-ti had its peculiar purpose. Though contradictory and ill-assorted, these publicly enunciated ideas and symbolic acts each contributed to the solution of the problems which the Sui faced. But this congeries of measures would not have brought a high level of unity and prosperity without the strong and intelligent social, economic, and political measures which the early Sui carried out. Ideology is—in China as elsewhere—one suasive accompaniment to the exercise of power. For the Sui, as for other periods of human history, its relative weight can be assessed only when the total history of the age is known.

AN EARLY SUNG REFORMER: FAN CHUNG-YEN

JAMES T. C. LIU

1. Introduction: Confucian Idealism and Power Structure

AMONG THE many significant developments during the early Sung period, following trends which originated in the T'ang, was the greatly increased number of degree-holders who rapidly advanced to high government positions. A considerable number of them did not have a bureaucratic family background.[1] The question naturally arises: Did these scholar-officials of nonbureaucratic extraction develop a political idealism which reflected their social origin and also added new significance to the Confucian tradition that they revived?

The answer to this question requires a general analysis of the political nature of this bureaucracy. The power which the bureaucrats shared was a derivative one, essentially dependent upon the ultimate power of the emperor. Many bureaucrats "degraded themselves by becoming utterly subservient to the emperor. . . . They did not themselves attempt to take over political power but found security by subordinating themselves to the mercy of the imperial court."[2] This is why the proud emperor T'ang T'ai-tsung (627–49) was able to declare that "all the talents and heroes in the empire are in my bag." Such a sociological analysis does not take into account the small but highly significant number of officials who persevered in their idealistic beliefs. It should be remembered that the traditional Chinese historiography maintains a dichotomy of good and bad officials. Evidence confirms, on the one hand, the unhappy fact that the idealistic scholar-officials were invariably outnumbered and, on the other, the important point that they were usually in a political position to carry on their struggle for a better empire. Many of them came up from modest circumstances, remained true to their social origin, and served the empire only in accordance with their Confucian principles, often at great personal risk. Without such a fine crop of idealists in any given period, the Chinese bureaucracy, instead of maintaining an appreciably high standard of government administration, could hardly have functioned at all.

A core problem in Chinese political history is: Why and how did these worthy scholar-officials fail to realize their ideals? One major explanation, I suggest, is to be found in the power structure.[3] The theoretical postulates of the present essay may be briefly stated here. Within the power structure of the Chinese empires, conflicts normally arose at two levels: (1) conflicts between the ultimate power of the emperor and the derivative power entrusted to the bureaucracy and (2) conflicts among the bureaucrats themselves, ranging from personal antagonisms to policy differences.[4] The idealistic elements who demanded reforms inevitably intensified the conflicts at both levels, which were closely connected. Reforms would fail when there was neither enough trust from the emperor nor effective support in the bureaucracy.

The emperor depended on the bureaucrats by necessity. He would be wise to draw into his government talented and learned individuals who might otherwise be a potential threat. However, he invited them to share only the burden of responsibility and not his ultimate power. This paradox created tension. The tension was at a minimum with the majority of career-minded bureaucrats, who gladly accepted the responsibility in exchange for personal and family privileges. This was not the case with the idealistic scholar-officials. Their very idealism, an element alien to the power structure, tended to disturb it. They believed in the Confucian principles as the supreme authority, to which even the ultimate power of the emperor should be subservient. As the guardians of the doctrine, they asserted their right to pronounce judgment and to offer guidance on state affairs.

Seeking to translate their political theory into reality, the idealistic scholar-officials relied mainly upon persuasion exerted on the emperor. Persuasion, though lacking in binding force, is of course the most commonly used means in politics under various forms of government. In China, it had a peculiarly long and deeply rooted tradition. Nevertheless, in order to be effective, persuasion had to be supported by articulate public opinion (*shih-lun* or *kung-lun*) among a cohesive group of officials. Then persuasion would amount to effective political pressure and exert a power of opinion such that the idealists might succeed in placing the emperor "in the bag" of Confucianism.

The bureaucracy was beset by personal frictions, mutual antagonisms, political differences, and even disputes on the correct interpretation of Confucianism. Yet it was the only political arena. No other "constituency" existed elsewhere in which the idealistic scholar-officials could build up their political strength. Their only hope was to transform the bureaucracy into a politically inspired body. This was why the leaders of reform movements tried to draw into the bureaucracy persons with ideological devotion and political zeal. Such a step was usually taken in the name of administrative reform. The reform leaders naturally had a practical concern for efficient and high standards of administration in order to strengthen the state.[5] However, beneath the drive for a better administration was a much deeper impulse to change the bureaucracy's very nature.

When an attempt was made to reorganize the bureaucracy, factional controversy would flare up. In this, one may discern a typology of the bureaucrats involved. On the one side would be a reform faction, comprising both genuine idealists and self-seeking opportunists who rode on their coattails. Those who were opposed to the reform did not necessarily form one faction. Some were true conservatives who disagreed in principle, some were a conscientious type of administrator who were politically timid and disliked political discord, but many others would obstruct the reform because it threatened their vested career interests.[6]

Quite apart from the complex typology of bureaucrats, the most vital issue which underlay the factional controversy concerned the very nature of the bureaucracy. The idealistic scholar-officials, who hoped to build up political cohesion within it, invariably lost because they suffered from a fatal disadvantage. Their political aspirations could be easily misconstrued as a dangerous threat to the ultimate power of the emperor, if not to his personal security. The career-minded bureaucrats, in order to protect their personal interests, were never slow in using this malicious but effective weapon to express their loyalty to the emperor and at the same time to frighten him into dismissing the reforming idealists. The bureaucracy would thereupon return to its normal course and remain a subservient administrative machine. Thus, Confucian idealism was essentially defeated by the complex intricacies of the power structure.

These theoretical postulates may be tested in the case of Fan Chung-yen (989–1052). The early Sung period produced a remarkable crop of scholar-officials of nonbureaucratic extraction. These developed a new political idealism within the Confucian tradition which led to the first reform movement of the Sung empire in 1043–44. In spite of its failure, the prestige of Confucian idealism was paradoxically enhanced. Through educational and social channels, one generation after another was later prepared to carry on the perpetual struggle, in the belief that it was the only true way to serve the empire and its people.

The Confucian idealism, clothed in the traditional terms of its ancient heritage, acquired new meaning and significance through these

early Sung pioneers. They developed a practical utilitarian spirit and
an active political interest.[7] Unfortunately for China, their political
defeats were followed by similar setbacks in the Southern Sung period (1127–1279). Many scholars then retreated into metaphysical
speculation (*tao-hsueh*) or into Neo-Confucianism, with the elements
of utilitarian spirit and political interest missing. Many disastrous
political tragedies during the Ming empire followed, such as the persecution of the *Tung-lin tang* ("Eastern Forest party").[8] Nevertheless, the political consciousness of the scholar class, its awareness of
"the responsibility to take care of the world," which had been established in early Sung, was smothered by neither frustration nor persecution. A regained emphasis upon the study of the classics and of
history during the Manchu period brought forth a new crop of political thinkers, like Huang Tsung-hsi,[9] who acknowledged with great
respect their primary indebtedness to the early Sung reformers.

2. The Significance of Fan Chung-yen

Fan Chung-yen, the privy councilor in 1043–44 who initiated the
first important large-scale reform of the Sung period, played a leading role in more ways than one. It was he who precipitated the first
factional controversy in the history of that empire. While provisional
prefect of K'ai-feng, the national capital, in 1036, Fan frequently
raised his voice beyond his proper jurisdiction. Among other matters, he submitted to the emperor a "chart on all officials' promotion
and demotion" (*pai kuan t'u*), which openly criticized Prime Minister Lü I-chien for indulging in favoritism. Lü charged Fan with
"sowing discord between His Majesty and the court ministers and
promoting factionalism."[10] The latter was a convenient political op-
probrium. Fan and those who actively supported him were repri-
manded in court and demoted to serve in various local offices. However, their political misfortune actually brought them enhanced
prestige, as learned scholars and officials with considerable following
in the country.

After a successful military assignment on the Shensi border, Fan
was finally appointed a ranking court minister in 1043. Many scholars and other officials greeted his rise to power with great enthusiasm.
Shih Chieh wrote a famous poem commemorating "the advance of
the worthy . . . and the removal of the crafty," which circulated
throughout the empire for decades thereafter.[11] By the explicit command of the emperor, Fan submitted his ten-point memorial out-
lining the reform program. This reform memorial of 1043 was read,

studied in schools, and admired throughout the land as a classical piece.[12]

To reform the bureaucracy, Fan replaced a large number of officials, especially in local government. It was now his turn to be criticized for favoritism. When he was removed from power the next year, the factional line was so bitterly drawn that it kept the next generation of statesmen in political division. Factional controversy during the T'ang dynasty had been a struggle between the old aristocratic gentry and the newly risen degree-holders.[13] This first factional controversy in early Sung was not the same. It arose largely between the entrenched bureaucrats of the career-minded type and the idealistic elements who advocated reform. The situation became more complicated when Wang An-shih's gigantic reform (1069–73) stirred up a different factional alignment. The original followers of Fan, in disputing Wang's interpretation of Confucianism and the radical features of his reform, now found themselves to be the conservatives and in effect on the same side with the career-minded bureaucrats. By this time, the fame of Fan had already passed into history and was respected by all. The conservative leaders, such as Su Shih, looked upon Fan as their "hero."[14] On the other hand, Wang An-shih in the early days of his career was considered to be a follower of Fan's faction. In Wang's own words, Fan was "the teacher for an entire generation."[15] As Lü Tsu-ch'ien in the Southern Sung period pointed out, "it was the defeat of Fan's program that precipitated such a radical reform as Wang's."[16] The true measure of Fan's historical position lies precisely in his being the unanimously acclaimed source of political reformist inspiration.

The complicated division of factions during the reform of Wang An-shih should not becloud the basic issue between the Confucian idealists, of whichever variety, and the career-minded bureaucrats. It reappeared many times either in open conflicts or at the root of political storms after the Sung period. Viewed as a thread through the maze of Chinese political history, Fan's role in introducing reform and its attendant factional controversy assumes even greater importance.

Fan's second significance was his promotion of Confucian learning. By sponsoring prominent scholars, he helped to make their thought known to the court and the country. Among them, three scholars, Hu Yuan (993–1059), Sun Fu (992–1057), and Li Kou (1009–59), were especially important. Hu Yuan had his students major in the classics and elect a minor in practical subjects such as economics, military science, irrigation, mathematics, or astronomy. They would "discuss learning together," somewhat as in a seminar, and "deliberate on current events" to see how Confucian theories could be applied. Through Fan's recommendation, Hu taught at the Imperial Academy for many years.[17] When the local government units were ordered to establish public schools, the third point in Fan's reform memorial, Hu's system was designated as the model in the hope that this type of school would produce more idealistic scholars with practical knowledge rather than career bureaucrats.

Sun Fu likewise advocated the active application of Confucianism in practical matters.[18] To him, the kind of formal literary composition used as the standard in the state examinations was no true test of knowledge and as useless as Buddhism and Taoism. When the state examination system came into political controversy, Sun was dismissed from the government for his radical ideas. He taught wherever Fan invited him to and continued to inspire many of Fan's followers. Shih Chieh was one of those whose zeal aroused so much antagonism that it became a liability to Fan's faction.[19] This showed, however, the amount of enthusiasm which Confucian idealism was capable of generating.

Li Kou, whom Fan respected more than the other two scholars, was especially systematic, realistic, and broad-minded.[20] Li criticized other scholars, including Sun, for their nonutilitarian metaphysical speculation based on the *Book of Changes*. He brushed aside Mencius' objection to the discussion of "advantages" (*li*) as an exaggeration. No Confucian virtue could be divorced from its practical value. "How can benevolence (*jen*) and righteousness (*i*) work to the exclusion of advantage?" Nor did Li neglect the importance of law. He believed that "the people obey, not so much the emperor, as his laws." In fact, he agreed with the Legalist school to the extent of upholding hegemony (*pa shu*) as a good method of governing. In times of exigency, such as the Sung empire experienced, he did not see how one could insist upon the princely way (*wang tao*) as the only ideal and neglect military power just because the latter happened to resemble the hegemony which ancient Confucianism had detested. Since circumstances differed, the sole criterion was which method would more readily achieve a stable order. Finally, Li was emphatic on the role of the emperor, who "should realize that the Mandate of Heaven was not for his selfish interest but for the interest of millions of people." It was no accident that Fan recommended that Li set up the regulations of the Imperial Ancestral Hall (*ming t'ang*), where the ceremonies were believed to exercise a moral and psychological restraint upon the emperor.[21]

Fan's contribution to the spread of Confucian idealism was fully appreciated by Chu Hsi. Among Chu's fifteen laudatory references to him, Fan was credited with being the first pioneer "to enforce vigorously the discipline of integrity and honor, thus raising the morale [*ch'i*, or political consciousness] among the scholars."[22] In comparison with the T'ang scholars who degraded themselves in courting favor by "sending their essays to high-ranking officials," the Sung scholars indeed had more self-respect and political faith.[23] Chu's most important comment on Fan and his scholar friends appeared in a passage on the sociointellectual history of China:

The honor and integrity (*ming-chieh*) upheld in the Han dynasty, the studied casualness (*k'uang-tang*) indulged in during the Wei and Chin periods, the literary composition (*tz'u-chang*) valued in the time of T'ang, all had their respective faults and should not be condoned. . . . True Confucian learning began to flourish under the present dynasty. . . . Good interpretations first appeared with Fan Chung-yen, and then Sun Fu, Shih Chieh and Hu Yuan.[24]

The high esteem which Chu Hsi had for Fan was shared by succeeding generations. It eventually brought Fan into the Confucian Hall by an imperial edict in 1716.[25] Far more important than this ritual honor was Fan's famous maxim, which, significantly, he formulated after his fall from power: "A scholar should be the first to become concerned with the world's troubles and the last to rejoice in its happiness."[26] This maxim became an article of political faith deeply imprinted in the mind of the scholar class. As recently as a decade ago, it was often assigned as an essay topic in modern schools.

The third significance of Fan's work lay in his promotion of schools. Fan well remembered the hardships he had gone through in getting an education. While in local government offices, he invariably established schools for the underprivileged. The imperial order given at his suggestion in 1043 for all local government units to do this was unfortunately not carried out everywhere because of the lack of funds.[27] Education remained largely limited to the private schools established by individual scholars. Only those who had enough means went there. And, being rather removed from the active political scene, the teaching veered toward metaphysical speculation. The inadequacy of school facilities for those of humble circumstances was a major reason why Confucian idealism failed to win a stronger foothold in politics.[28]

Finally, Fan made a significant contribution to Chinese familism. Friends suggested to Fan that he should buy an estate at Lo-yang for his retirement, as many other high officials had done. Instead, Fan bought land in Soochow, the native place of his clan, and set up a charitable estate (*i-chuang*) to give relief not only to the clan members but also to their relatives and neighbors in the community. Separate funds were also provided for a charitable school (*i-hsueh*) for youngsters who could not get an education otherwise. Both became renowned institutions which still functioned among a number of clans in the first quarter of the present century.[29]

The charitable estate had "profound purposes."[30] Frustrated in government and politics, Fan intended to pursue his social ideals by himself. With the large aristocratic families disappearing in Sung society, little influence existed on the community level to check the local officials, who became more unrestrained in abusing the common people.[31] Fan strengthened the clan organization probably as a protection against such abuses. The Chinese familism from the Sung period on, under revived Confucian influence, represented the small gentry.[32] Moreover, Confucian idealism regarded the family, the clan, and the community as the training ground for potential political leadership. Fan taught his own sons "to earn respect in the community, to demonstrate at home an ability to rule the people and to maintain integrity, thus to earn a justifiable recommendation for official appointment."[33] Political defeat taught Fan the need of a base for scholar-officials to exercise their leadership in social welfare while in voluntary or forced retirement.[34] The clan organization was the answer.

These manifold efforts of Fan were not his alone but sketch a broad panorama showing the width and depth of the revival of Confucianism. It took on new meaning in Chinese social life with the endeavor to strengthen the small gentry familism. Above all, it inspired a continuous political struggle for reforms.

3. The Reforms of Civil Service Recruitment

Under the Sung empire, the large gentry ceased to dominate politics. The two main gateways to officialdom were the "protection" system (*yin*) and the state examinations. To Fan, who came up the hard way through studies and examinations, the "protection" appointments, totaling thousands every year, appeared to be abusive privileges accorded the family members of high-ranking officials. The bureaucracy was overcrowded by their sons, nephews, secretaries, even by young children and family doctors. The few remaining vacancies would go to unscrupulous careerists who resorted to devious means of favoritism. The poor scholars who had struggled for decades through the examination system would have to wait for an appointment many long years in vain.[35]

Though "protection" appointments had been moderately curtailed several times before, Fan, in the second item of his ten-point memorial of 1043, demanded further "reduction of the favorities." The high titular officials should be allowed the nomination of only one son at the administrative level, and only on the occasion of an imperial celebration, instead of several sons on numerous occasions as before. Their other sons and relatives related by blood should be given only probationary titles without actual appointment to office. Ranking local officials and military officers, after serving for some years, would qualify for the same privileges, according to a prorated scale. Henceforth, no one who entered the civil service through the *yin* privilege should ever be made an academician or censor. These sensitive offices close to the emperor should be reserved for the learned scholar-officials. In a separate memorial, Fan suggested that "protection" appointees with probationary titles, upon reaching twenty-five years of age, should go to the classes held at the Directorate of Education and take an examination within half a year. A similar provision had long existed on paper, though each year only a dozen persons ever took the trouble to attend these classes. Fan wanted the rule enforced rigidly. If the "protection" appointees should fail in three successive examinations, their last chance to get an appointment would be on the recommendation of three sponsors who could testify to their integrity and good conduct. Otherwise, the door of officialdom should be closed forever to these unworthy young men.[36]

Fan's proposals were not very strict. The high-ranking officials frequently made the claim, with some validity, that their family members, having been long exposed to public affairs in the home environment, were in reality better prepared for civil service than those from nonbureaucratic backgrounds who came up through the examination system.[37] Fan only demanded that the *yin*-privilege appointees should have additional training in the Confucian classics and should produce some concrete proof of their competence either by examination or through sponsorship. The *yin* system was much curtailed and never regained the prestige it had enjoyed before among official circles. Though it must have hurt the feelings of many high-ranking officials, they could not oppose Fan effectively on this matter. With the revival of Confucianism, schooling, examination, and sponsorship were accepted as the standard features of the civil service.

Fan was not happy either with the state examinations, the other gateway to officialdom. When he was a minor official in 1030, Fan had already voiced the criticism in a memorandum to the prime minister that "at the present time, literary form has little to do with the principles of Confucianism. Social custom inclines toward skilful superficiality. This is why examination and selection are having difficulty to find enough talent. . . . Reading the beautiful literature of the Six Dynasties, one can readily understand why these regimes declined."[38] From a strict Confucian viewpoint Fan believed that there was an inverse correlation between ornamental literature and good government. He suggested that the state examinations should emphasize the broad interpretations of the classics, the dynastic histories, current events, and political principles such as the problems of the princely way and hegemony in government. The last point was Li Kou's idea. Incidentally, neither Li Kou nor Sun Fu were successful at the examinations. To Fan, who respected the profound learning of both, the system and its standard appeared bad enough to require thorough reform.[39]

After Fan attained power, the examination system soon became a burning political issue. The third point in Fan's reform memorial affirmed that the examinations should be based upon knowledge of those classics which "embody the principles for governing the state and the people." Fan also offered the compromise that, for the time being, poetry and prose should still receive due consideration, so that no one would be penalized by a sudden change in the standard. The most interesting part of Fan's proposal was the stress upon the actual conduct of the candidates. Neither written nor oral tests could tell whether the candidates really lived by Confucian principles. Fan wanted part of their grade to be based upon reference reports from the local government on the character and conduct of the candidates. Likewise, the public esteem which candidates had won among officials and scholars should also count in their favor. For this reason, Fan objected to the pasting of a piece of paper over the name of each candidate. This was originally designed to insure impartial grading. But Fan believed this constituted an injustice by excluding the judgment of the character and attainment of the candidate according to public information. As to favoritism in grading, it would be defeated by having open discussion among the examiners, with the name of the candidate fully known.[40]

Strenuous objections greeted the proposed reform of the examination system. Some career-minded bureaucrats who had obtained their degrees under the existing standard of literary form resented the proposal as a personal insult. Others opposed it because it would obviously favor the type of Confucian scholarship which the followers of Fan represented. The opponents raised the objection that it would be exceedingly difficult to determine the grades of essays which put forth various interpretations on the meaning of the classics, whereas it was much easier to grade poetry and prose objectively by the rhyme and phonetic rules. They used further a clever political argument that, since the examination system had worked well enough under previous reigns to recruit talent, there was no reason why it should be changed now.[41] The malicious insinuation was that those who advocated reform were being disrespectful toward earlier emperors as well as contemptuous of numerous degree-holders past and present. Once the dispute degenerated from the level of policy issues to that of politics involving personalities, the case of the reformers was lost.

The dispute had another connected phase. Fu Pi, a close colleague of Fan, believed that the candidates could hardly prove themselves with justice on a single day in the final court examination. Much depended on those officials near the emperor who might exercise undue influence. He made the proposal, therefore, that the Ministry of Rites should report the final grades to the emperor, who would give his approval in an audience without an examination. The suggestion was countered by a smearing retort that Fu was being contemptuous of the emperor.[42]

These tactics of slander revealed a recurring pattern: the career-minded bureaucrats used the emperors, past and present, as a weapon against the reformers as well as a shield for themselves. In other words, those who had entrenched themselves in the power structure under the existing system effectively opposed change by invoking the ultimate power of the emperor. Though the number of "protection" appointments was reduced through Fan's efforts, the examination system remained much the same, with little emphasis upon the classics, history, and political principles and hardly enough preference for idealistic elements.

4. The Reforms of Local Government

The centralizing trend of the Sung empire made officials prefer positions in the capital, where chances for further promotion were far better than in the offices of local government. Fan believed this to be a grave mistake. "To rule the empire, administrators and prefects are the most important officials." Only good officials in these offices "can spare the people from suffering."[43]

Fan was himself an able administrator. His irrigation project was such a success that it drew admiration even from Lü I-chien, his political enemy.[44] On economic matters, Fan admired Sang Hungyang of the Han period, Kao Ying of the Sui, and Liu Yen of the T'ang.[45] On the one hand, he shared the physiocratic belief that merchants tended to encourage wasteful luxuries and took excessive profit from the agricultural population. On the other hand, he preferred private trade to state monopoly, as in the case of salt during his military governorship in Shensi.[46] Fan's attention to economy also influenced his attitude toward religion. As far as the religious teachings of both Buddhism and Taoism were concerned, Fan was quite favorable toward them, as evidenced by his poems and the prefaces he wrote for religious literature.[47] But he objected to the growth of Buddhist and Taoist establishments, because they took away productive manpower:[48]

The commodity prices have gone up high. Many believe it to be a natural result of the increased population. I disagree. More population also means more people to be engaged in productive work. Why should the increase in population become a burden? . . . There are too many soldiers who are not really useful and there are Buddhists and Taoists loafing around. . . . All depend on the peasants for food and clothing. This is why prices have gone up higher and the peasants have become poorer.

Fan also devised a realistic way to use for the common welfare of the people the wealth held by religious groups.[49] When he was the administrator at Hangchow during a serious famine, he persuaded the Buddhist temples to engage in building projects which had a cheap labor cost and at the same time could provide much needed employment—an approach which has a familiar modern ring.

Fan devoted more than half of his famous reform memorial to local government affairs. Its sixth to its tenth points urged the increase of productivity by land reclamation, irrigation, mulberry cultivation for silk, and other improvements; the recruitment of local militia who would be given military training when the farming season was over; special orders for relief by tax exemption to be carried out in earnest; a re-examination of the codes and statutes to eliminate injustice caused by mistakes, confusion, and conflicts; and the reduction of the people's labor service by the consolidation of several neighboring subprefectures into single units. But more important than anything else was the personnel problem in local government, on which Fan lay particular emphasis in the fourth and fifth points in his memorial.

Corruption in local government, Fan believed, stemmed partly from the inequity of the salary scale. While officials in the capital were very well paid, better than during previous dynasties,[50] the local officials did not receive much. The office landholdings, which constituted a part of the income of the latter, often varied in size and did not match the rank. This caused a great deal of competition for the better-provided offices and bitter complaints from those assigned elsewhere.[51] The situation was so bad that some statesmen were in favor of abolishing the office landholdings altogether. But Fan opposed their abolition because he sympathized with the underpaid local officials, who would "lose their integrity and succumb to corruption" in a period of inflation.[52] The fifth point in his memorial gave a vivid description:[53]

> In recent times, increased population has caused prices to rise. At the same time, the number of eligible candidates exceeds that of vacant positions. The waiting period for an office usually lasts more than one year or even two. With the high prices and the interruption of income while waiting, few families of officials with modest means are free from poverty. Often for that reason, their sons and daughters cannot get married and funeral services for deceased family members cannot be held. In waiting for an appointment, they have to borrow money to pay for food and clothing. As soon as they are assigned to a position, the creditors begin to exert relentless pressure. This drives many officials to violate the law, to receive bribes, to contract new loans or to engage in trade themselves. Being themselves guilty and with little integrity left, the officials dare not expose the corrupt clerks under them or punish the influential law violators under their jurisdiction. All these persons exploit the common people, who can neither expect justice nor seek to redress injustice.

This explained in part why many scholar-officials betrayed their Confucian training and became self-seeking, especially when the inflationary economy made them the victims of moneylenders. Fan was able to put into effect an equitable scale which assigned a definite acreage of office landholdings according to the rank of local government officials.[54]

The main curse of local government was not the low salary but the low quality of officials. This was a notorious feature which the Sung empire had inherited from the previous Five Dynasties period. It was described by Fan earlier in his memorandum of 1027:[55]

The prefects in recent times receive their appointment by routine promotion. Many of them lack both integrity and learning. The aged and incompetent ones concern themselves chiefly with security for their sons and grandsons. Gifts and bribes are shamelessly accepted. The young and ambitious prefects, who do not consider their present positions worthwhile, neglect their duties, except for those matters which may enhance their personal prestige. Looking into the administration of most subprefectures, one will find the files lying loosely about, the clerks and constables undisciplined, the labor service imposing much inequity, and justice miscarried. What is good for the people's livelihood is not done; what is hurting the people is left untouched. The poor and the widows receive no help while the loafers and the unproductive ones go free. Agricultural production is never increased and morality hardly encouraged. This is by no means an isolated case but probably true in seven or eight out of ten subprefectures.

The same memorandum advocated promotion strictly by merit and additional supervisory measures. The government should not be kind toward incompetent officials, because they were hard on the people. The offices of administrators and prefects must be filled only by those with proved ability. If the government wished to remain considerate toward those incumbents who were below standard, it should at least demote them to the office of inspector, which had less contact with the people and would not do much harm. On the other hand, so long as the incumbents were kept in officialdom, there would be little cause for them to complain.

Fan also noted the laxity of supervision. "Since the supervisory intendants hold about the same rank, they fear that strictness on their part will bring upon themselves the retaliation of those with equal political influence." This was why the officials tended to protect each other. In comparison with the beginning of the Sung empire, corruption was now punished less frequently and less severely.[56] Fan suggested that the emperor should send special envoys to investigate the prefects. "The censors should warn the local officials às well as the envoys to exchange neither greetings nor gifts. The envoys must take to the road as soon as the investigation is over. Favors must be strictly forbidden."

The memorandum of 1027 showed more youthful idealism than mature practicality. When Fan assumed power at court, he was ready with a more detailed scheme of sweeping reform. The fourth item in his ten-point memorial proposed: (1) The Secretariat-Chancellery and the Bureau of Military Affairs should each nominate a number of fiscal intendants, judicial intendants, and administrators of large prefectures. According to a separate memorial which followed, the Secretariat-Chancellery and the Bureau of Military Affairs should be allowed further to nominate three sponsors among the court officials who would assume the special responsibility of sponsoring a definite number of local government personnel at various ranks. The sponsors themselves would be rewarded or penalized depending on the performance of those whom they sponsored. (2) The Bureau of Academicians, the Special Drafting Office, the Finance Commission, the Censorate, the Metropolitan Prefect of K'ai-feng, and the circuit intendants should each recommend a certain number of administrators and vice-administrators. (3) Each of the latter should in turn recommend two prefects. In all these arrangements the candidates who received the largest number of recommendations from various offices and officials should be given priority in appointment.[57]

Attention was focused principally on the level of intendants who formed the crucial link between the imperial government and the local government. Fan lost little time in replacing many incompetent ones. When Fu Pi thought this might be too harsh on those dismissed, Fan retorted that to keep them would be too harsh on the people.[58] Fan further requested in another memorial that fiscal and judicial intendants should be given the power to recommend their subordinates as provisional administrators. If these provisional administrators were able to improve local conditions, they would be promoted to administrators.[59]

Fan's proposals had many significant points. First, the sponsorship system would institute collective responsibility. Second, the power to select local government personnel, though concentrated at the top, was at that level diffused enough to prevent any possible manipulation by a single group of high-ranking officials. Third, priority of appointment according to the number of recommendations was similar to a voting procedure. Thus a general or "public" opinion among the court officials would carry much weight. Finally, the principle of collective responsibility would apply in the local government hierarchy. Political responsibility would be matched by the necessary power to select one's own subordinates.

Fan's reform measures did bring good results to local government.[60] But it aroused fierce opposition at court. The entrenched bureaucrats, alarmed by the reform and numerous dismissals, resorted to the tactics of denouncing Fan's active leadership as personal ambition and of confusing the issue of collective responsibility with factional favoritism. The dispute was not confined to the matter of local government personnel alone. Part of the basic issue was whether the bureaucracy should be thoroughly reorganized.

5. Routine Promotion versus Responsible Sponsorship

A career bureaucrat looked mainly for promotion, but a true Confucian idealist hoped to discharge his political responsibility by rendering good service to the empire and its people. Fan was much dissatisfied with the prevailing system, which in effect encouraged officials to mind their own careers and discouraged political initiative. His memorandum of 1029 asserted that

in the morning the bureaucrats receive their new appointments; the same evening, they begin to maneuver for their next promotions. Offices are frankly regarded as career stepping stones. Officials, in their mutual self-interest, conceal each other's faults. No wonder the common people suffer so much from maladministration.[61]

The minimum period of office tenure was usually three years, at the end of which incumbents would be considered for promotion through a review of their personnel records (*mo-k'an*).[62] This routine procedure made promotion almost automatic. Fan attached great importance to this question and attacked it in the first point of his reform memorial:

An official of superior quality while in charge of a prefecture, subprefecture, or bureau may endeavor to initiate good measures and remove bad features. Others will accuse him of stirring up trouble, become jealous of him, obstruct him, criticize him and even make fun of him. If he should make a slight slip, the other officials will immediately jump at his throat. On the other hand, many mediocre officials, who do nothing besides draw their comfortable salaries and whose ignorance and cheap character no one respects, will be up for promotion at the end of every three years. In time they will reach high rank with ease. Such cases are far too numerous.[63]

Family influence was another cause of abuse. One vacancy at the capital might be coveted by several influential competitors, who would use every devious means in the hope of getting it. Should they fail, they would be satisfied for the time being with an appointment of administrative rank in local government. But they would delay their departure from the capital sometimes for over a year and soon after their actual arrival at the post ask for another promotion. With their family influence they usually got ahead without rendering real service, let alone the proof of merit.

Fan offered four proposals to reform the system of promotion.[64] First, the government should punish those who evaded actual performance and reward by promotion those who rendered worthy service. This would encourage more officials to take up their responsibility in local government instead of idling and competing with others in the capital. Second, in preferring sponsorship to routine promotion, Fan proposed that the bureau assistants, the division chiefs in the ministries, and the local officials of administrative rank should be promoted at the end of three years, as usual, only if they could find five sponsors among the military intendants, the fiscal intendants, the judicial intendants, and the academicians. Otherwise, they would have to wait five years instead of three for routine consideration of their promotion. Third, promotion by merit should be strictly on the basis of specific criteria such as lack of corruption, constructive policy proposals, promotion of education, no miscarriage of justice, increase in agricultural production, economy in fiscal matters, and the like. These should be carefully evaluated by the Ministry of Personnel. When opinions differed at the Ministry, the entire record should be reported to the emperor for his final decision. Each year the Bureau of Administrative Personnel should submit annual rating reports on a standard form listing merits and demerits under specific columns. Finally, for the purpose of drawing more learned scholars and people of exemplary conduct into government service, the Directorate of Education and the circuits throughout the empire should recommend such persons every year.

Some of these proposals were rather commonplace. The one especially worth noting was the proposed sponsorship, the key to Fan's whole program of reforming the bureaucracy and not a mere administrative measure. Fan wanted sponsorship to be a recognized, legitimate bond between the court officials and their sponsored subordinates. The former would exercise leadership in making policies, and the latter would respond by implementing them. With a common political outlook, mutual trust, and legal relationship, a political cohesion would emerge to revitalize the entire bureaucracy. The principle of collective or collegiate responsibility would hold the superiors responsible, as sponsors, for those whom they sponsored. They would rise and fall together on the basis of actual merit, which would be discussed openly at the Ministry of Personnel and be reviewed when necessary at the court before the emperor.

By some stretch of imagination, one may find in Fan's proposal of sponsorship a spirit akin to that in parliamentary democracy. A party in a democratic system is a formal organization which assumes the power and collective responsibility of government when it receives the approval of a majority in the electorate or parliament, or of the sovereign in the case of a limited democracy. According to Fan's proposal, the sponsors and those sponsored would form a legal bond and assume the power and collective responsibility of government whenever they received the esteem and approval, according to accepted standards, of their equals in the bureaucracy, as well as the

confidence of the emperor. It is not contended here that Fan's proposal was a step toward democracy. Bureaucracy by its very nature
leaves out the common people, the basis of democracy. Rather, there
is a resemblance in spirit.

The main significance of Fan's reform attempt lay in his effort to
turn into a dynamic political body the administrative mechanism
which had no political homogeneity. Only then would a responsible
administration emerge, with definite programs and effective action,
and be answerable to a consensus of opinion in the bureaucracy.
These were the ideals of Confucianism which unfortunately encountered determined opposition. The careerists, mindful of their own
promotions, discredited the reform measures as the cloak of a factionalism under which Fan's friends got rapid promotion. They criticized the sponsorship system as conducive to favoritism, since officials would try to seek favor from influential ministers.[65] They chose
to ignore completely the issue or the merit of the principle of collegiate responsibility.

Opposition to the reform became so strong that Fan chose to resign the next year and went once more to Shensi on a military assignment. He hoped that his departure would quiet the political storm.
Meanwhile, Han Ch'i and Fu Pi, who remained in power, might
manage to save some of his reform measures already in effect.[66] But
Fan's enemies gave no quarter. Since their charge of factionalism did
not dislodge all the reformers, another attempt was made to frighten
the emperor himself into taking a decisive step to end the reform.

6. *The Ultimate Power of the Emperor*

The power structure of the bureaucratic empire required delicate
handling to keep a proper balance. The derivative power exercised
by the officials might be so extended as to interfere with the ultimate
power of the emperor. This was true in the case of Fan Chung-yen.
Long before he became privy councilor, he had earned the penalty
of demotion by offending the sovereign no less than three times. He
protested in 1029 against the kneeling of the emperor in court before
the empress dowager on her birthday.[67] He objected in 1033 to the
dismissal of the empress.[68] And he was demoted in 1035 not only for
his attack on the prime minister's favoritism but also because of his
confidential suggestion that the younger brother of the emperor
should be designated as the heir apparent.[69] These setbacks in no
way discouraged Fan. He believed firmly that a good official should
commit no fault in private life but should never be afraid of being
blamed in his official career.[70]

The taming of the ultimate power is a permanent problem in history. Confucian idealism always sought to place it within the confines of proper institutional procedures under the sanction of ideological authority.[71] In practice, this meant that the emperor should follow the guidance of idealistic scholar-officials. Fan submitted, also in 1035, four famous essays on the proper exercise of the emperor's power.[72] The first essay held that the success of monarchs depended upon their inclination toward morality and upon virtuous ministers; the second essay called upon the emperor to seek the advice of the true Confucian scholars; and the third essay asserted the scholar's moral right to pronounce judgment. In short, the emperor had the ultimate power but the Confucian scholars had their independent ideological authority. In the final analysis, the Confucian scholars were more important than the emperor, for they did not necessarily depend upon the government for a living, whereas a dynasty in order to last must depend on their service. Incidentally, the generation of scholar-officials which came after Fan pressed the issue even further. Wang-An-shih and Lü Kung-chu, for example, requested the restoration of an old privilege—that the lecturers before the emperor should be seated.[73]

The last of the four essays, entitled "On the Delegation of Power," was the most important. Fan was not in favor of a concentration of power either in the emperor himself or in the prime ministers by delegation. Compared with previous dynasties, the power and prestige of the Sung prime ministers were already reduced. The control over military affairs and fiscal matters was given to separate offices. Fan felt, however, that the prime ministers still had too much power in personnel selection:[74]

Suppose the emperor should agree to nine out of ten promotion recommendations made by the prime minister; this would mean that the prime minister would control ninety per cent of the court positions. In a few years the emperor would be completely surrounded by the friends of the prime minister. If, on demotions, the emperor should agree nine out of ten times with the prime minister, it would mean that the latter would control ninety per cent of the power to punish. In a few years no one in the country would dare to offend him.

The emperor must maintain a balance between himself and his prime minister by retaining the essential function of his ultimate power, namely, "to distinguish the good officials from the bad ones, to select himself those who serve around him, to reward and to reprimand all officials and thus to control the destiny of all talents."[75] In addition, the emperor should redress the balance further by relying upon the censors and those officials in the Document Reviewing

Office who had the power of remonstrance and upon the academicians who in expressing their own views and that of many other officials had the power of opinion. Thus the selection of these officials must be made with utmost care. The emperor should ascertain their scholarship, and their standing by a consensus of opinion among numerous officials, and should verify both by imperial audience or special examination.[76]

In Fan's thinking, the power of remonstrance and the power of opinion were essential if the emperor was to maintain a proper balance against the executive power of his ministers. On the other hand, the ultimate power of the emperor according to Fan's scheme would also be restrained by its very reliance upon the power of remonstrance and the power of opinion.[77] Fan realized that the power of remonstrance had to be limited to the gentle art of persuasion. For example, he would not recommend his friend Shih Chieh to be a censor because Shih would make excessive demands on the emperor.[78] However, if the power of remonstrance should be supported by the power of opinion held by numerous bureaucrats, the pressure might be such that the emperor could ill afford to ignore it. When Fan was dismissed in 1035, many officials protested. Though the emperor ignored their remonstrances, he was uneasy enough to admit, "Now, Fan's friends keep on recommending him, what shall we do?"[79] The point is that, when an emperor ignored both the power of remonstrance and the power of opinion, he would be stripped of ideological authority and might actually find his ultimate power left naked and much weakened politically.[80]

Fan's extreme stress upon the power of opinion among the bureaucrats deserves attention. Confucian political idealism, in order to succeed, must permeate the bureaucracy in the form of opinion. This was precisely why Fan wanted more public schools to produce idealistically minded scholars, why he advocated an emphasis upon political opinions at the state examinations, and why he proposed the rule of priority according to the number of recommendations in the sponsorship system. If put into effect, the logical outcome of all these proposals combined would be a political cohesion based upon a sort of public opinion among a working majority of the officials. They would organize the derivative power of the bureaucracy and keep it in proper balance to tame the emperor's ultimate power. In essence, the entire power structure of the bureaucratic empire would be changed in the direction of realizing the Confucian ideals.

But Fan faced a dilemma: the changes toward a new power structure had to be worked out through the existing one. There his reform movement broke down. All his three proposals—on public schools, the examination system, and the sponsorship system—failed to go through. Fan realized his difficulties when he confided to Fu Pi, "We are here in the court. But how many others agree with us? Nor can we be sure in which direction His Majesty might turn."[81]

The emperor did eventually turn against the reform, when the career-minded bureaucrats frightened him into action by a dishonest and malicious maneuver. Hsia Sung, a veteran minister seeking political revenge, produced a forged letter. He claimed that Shih Chieh had feigned death and gone north to the Liao empire secretly. This letter was allegedly sent by Shih to Fu Pi, urging Fu to get an army ready for rebellion when Shih should bring in another army from Liao.[82] Normally, such fabricated allegation of high treason would hardly stand without corroborative evidence. Yet the burning zeal of Fan and his friends, especially the outspoken Shih, must have left Emperor Jen-tsung with some suspicion. When this allegation was brought forth, Fan's other political enemies, led by Wang Kung-ch'en, cast further doubts on and made other charges against the reformers.[83] Jen-tsung, though not convinced, was sufficiently aroused to take the precautionary step of dismissing Fu from the court, Fan from his military post in Shensi, and demoting other members of their faction in key offices to minor positions. The reformers were like fish "all caught in one net," and their opponents "enjoyed a hearty private celebration." The reform movement was at an end.[84]

The power struggle followed a clear pattern. The career-minded bureaucrats dealt their most devastating blow against the reform at the most sensitive spot in the power structure. The emperor, who feared a possible threat to himself, chose to believe at least partially in the fabricated allegation. He felt safer with those who advocated no reform, no extension of their derivative power, and no infringement upon his ultimate power.

7. An Analysis of the Reform Faction and Its Opponents

One important question remains: Were the two sides to the factional controversy both guilty of factionalism, favoritism, and the quest of power only for themselves? Are there some truly objective criteria by which to distinguish the reform faction from its adversaries other than what the traditional historiography offers? The word "faction," or *tang*, suffers from a bad connotation in both Chinese and English. Faction in English usage implies the subordinating of public good to private gain. However, its proper meaning is a group which rallies to the principles and policies of a leader and is without continuous organization.[85] This definition fits in this case, as well as in a rather similar case in British history, i.e., the two factions formed over the issue of imposing upon Queen Elizabeth some obligation to consult the Privy Council.[86]

Tang, in Chinese, was a term usually frowned upon. Confucius said that the superior man, "while sociable, does not identify himself with a faction."[87] Fan at times resented this obnoxious label. He complained bitterly that "recommending virtuous and capable officials was unjustly attacked as forming a faction."[88] On other occasions, Fan accepted the term "faction" as a political reality. In a funeral ode, Fan quoted Wang Chih as having said, "I am willing to be a member of the faction and suffer demotion with pride."[89] When the emperor questioned Fan on factional controversy, Fan replied, "The factions of the crooked and the straight . . . have always differed. If through friendship men should work together for the good of the state, what is the harm?" And "factions should not be banned, but it is up to Your Majesty to tell the difference."[90] Actually, this dichotomy of good versus bad, a characteristic of Chinese philosophy from ancient times, can be traced as far back as the *Book of Changes*, in which Fan and his many friends faithfully believed, with the notable exception of Li Kou. They unconsciously assumed themselves to be the "superior men" (*chün-tzu*) and their enemies to be the "mean men" (*hsiao-jen*).[91]

Objectively considered, the faction built around the leadership of Fan rested on several factors. As in any other political grouping, personal relations constituted an important one. The master-student relationship, though officially discouraged in early Sung as being conducive to nepotism,[92] was the tie between Fan and Yen Shu as well as between Sun Fu and Shih Chieh. The relationship between fellow students was the tie among the numerous disciples of Hu Yuan; at one time, 50 per cent of the candidates recommended by the Ministry of Rites had studied under Hu.[93] Another link was the marriage relationship between families. Fan arranged the marriage of Fu Pi, his protégé, to a daughter of Yen Shu, his patron. Wang Chih, who had joined Fan in demotion, later married his daughter to Fan's son.[94]

Sectionalism was another factor worth noting. The southeastern area, increasingly well developed during the Sung, produced more degree-holders than elsewhere. And it was mostly those who came from this area that initiated the factional controversy.[95]

Of much greater significance was the social factor of nonbureaucratic family background. Fan himself was raised in such a family, named Chu, because of the second marriage of his mother. While studying at a Buddhist temple in Shantung, he lived on a daily subsistence diet of two small rice cakes with a few slices of salted vegetables.[96] Later, Fan went away to a school at Suiyang originally founded by Ch'i T'ung-wen. Ch'i, who had never been an official, taught the Confucian classics in the spirit of their concern for the common people and also illustrated their teaching by his own exemplary conduct in his family, clan, and community. Though Fan arrived there shortly after the death of Ch'i,[97] the same school spirit much inspired Fan throughout his life. He would not permit his family the usual luxuries enjoyed by average bureaucratic families.[98] Yen Shu, the patron of Fan who recommended him on several crucial occasions in his career, also came up from a nonbureaucratic background. The same was true of many of Fan's friends, such as the scholars Hu, Sun, and Li or the statesmen Ou-yang Hsiu and Fu Pi. One notable exception was Han Ch'i. But it was well known that Han relied upon his own merit and served patiently in minor offices without using the influence of his large gentry family.[99]

None of these factors—personal, sectional, or social—played a role in the formation of Fan's faction as decisive as the factor of Confucian idealism. In fact, the ideals which Fan and his friends espoused kept the other factors at a minimum. Fan laid down the rule for himself that he would recommend only those who had enough scholarship to teach him and not someone who happened to be his friend.[100] When Fan recommended Ou-yang Hsiu, who had been demoted because of Fan, Fan specifically explained that his action was based on the consensus of public opinion and not his personal inclination. Even so, Ou-yang declined it as embarrassing. He believed that for two men to suffer demotion together on a matter of principle need not lead later on to their recommending promotions for each other.[101] When Fan, Han, and Fu were the ranking ministers together, they often differed and debated publicly in court. Public affairs and private friendship were not allowed to interfere in either direction.[102]

Confucian idealism definitely helped to maintain such high standards of conduct, though this does not mean that one who partook of the idealism was necessarily above criticism. According to the contemporary political literature, Fan was by no means faultless.[103] Among his political associates were undoubtedly persons of far less integrity and some opportunists who supported the reform not out of conviction but for their own advantage. Nevertheless, the chief characteristic of this faction was its leadership, whose idealism found much expression both in the reform proposals and in personal good conduct.

Such a faction was not self-seeking and cannot be equated with its opponents just because it was as vigorous on one side of a factional controversy as the opposing factions were on the other side. The opponents of the reform were not drawn together by a common political ideal but joined hands only temporarily for a common political objective. Much enmity existed among themselves. Lü I-chien and Hsia Sung accused each other. Wang Kung-ch'en attacked Hsia Sung as vigorously as he attacked Fan's friends.[104] These facts well substantiated the thesis of Ou-yang Hsiu, whose famous essay on faction, *P'eng-tang lun*, holds that only "superior men" form a real faction through a true association based on principles, whereas the "mean persons" either go together or go after each other as may be dictated by temporary expediency and selfish interest.[105]

Not all opponents of the reform were alike. The differences among them are clearly distinguishable from their biographies, which contain concrete information on their careers and political behavior. Chang Te-hsiang, for instance, a veteran minister well known for his quietness, opposed the reform in the firm belief that it would result in more controversies and little improvement. His prediction was not too mistaken. Other enemies of the reform, however, were more open to criticism.[106]

Lü I-chien was not a scholar. The examination which he took consisted of a number of simple questions much like the "objective type" questions in modern schools. And Lü got his degree even though he failed to answer a number of these questions.[107] Nor was Lü a "straight man" (*cheng-jen*), for he kept in close touch with eunuchs and flattered the empress dowager during her reign. As soon as she died, Lü tried to please the emperor by accusing the other ministers of having sided with the empress dowager.[108] For personal revenge, Lü encouraged the emperor to dismiss the empress without legitimate ground and arbitrarily demoted those officials who dared to oppose this. Lü was a most alert and circumspect politician. When he saw Fan's political star rising in spite of repeated demotions, he finally turned around to disarm Fan's antagonism by adding his own recommendation of Fan to those already made by others. This seeming generosity impressed not only the emperor, Fan himself, Ou-yang

Hsiu, and others, but also many scholars of later generations, including Chu Hsi.[109]

Lü represented the typical career-minded bureaucrat. He took tremendous pride in setting up regulations in such great detail that "from now on any mediocre person can take over the function of prime minister."[110] On the other hand, he relied on favoritism and opportunism to keep himself in power. His general rule was to initiate no innovation, so as not to be blamed for anything.[111] That was how he held the longest record of service, twenty years, in the Secretariat and became three times prime minister.[112] Many of his followers who were ministers at one time or another were much like him in this respect. Han Chen "had no merit to his credit."[113] Both Wang Sui and Chang Shih-hsun "suggested nothing significant to the emperor."[114] Wang Chü-cheng "was timid and evaded responsibilities."[115] Chang Kuan "did not distinguish himself in discharging administrative duties."[116] Sung Hsiang, who replaced Fan after the end of the reform, fell into the same category.[117] None of them showed traces of an idealistic outlook.

Hsia Sung was quite another type—learned but malicious. A scholar well versed in literature and history, he was once highly recommended even by Fan.[118] But his knowledge had nothing to do with his conduct. His corruption during official career made it possible for him to indulge in extreme luxuries.[119] Moreover, it was he who resorted to forgery in order to defeat the reformers. Typical careerists like Lü and his followers, who were gentlemen enough compared to Hsia, would hardly think of using such dishonorable means.

Wang Kung-ch'en was yet another type. A scholar-official without much personal fault, he was hardly distinguishable from the many followers of Fan. In fact, he was a relative of Ou-yang Hsiu. The only factor which prevented him from joining Fan's faction or being considered as a worthy equal on the other side of the political fence was his opportunism and lack of idealistic outlook.[120]

In summarizing the four different types among the opponents of reform, as represented by Chang, Lü, Hsia, and Wang, one may note some common characteristics. Whether they were themselves learned or not, they did not promote scholars and education. While their personal integrity and political conduct varied a great deal, from the quite honorable to the least honorable, they failed equally to make noteworthy contributions by improving either the administrative aspects of the government or the quality of the bureaucracy. Above all, they considered the bureaucracy to be nothing more than an administrative machine. All these characteristics must be traced to their lack of genuine Confucian idealism, which the reform leaders alone possessed. The traditional historiography which upholds this meaningful distinction is essentially correct.

This does not mean that the idealists and scholar-officials who worked for reform were saintly men free from certain biases due to factors such as personal, sectional, and social ties. Nor does this mean that the idealists were always in accord among themselves without personal friction and conflicts of opinion.[121] It may be added that Confucian idealism, like many other orthodox schools of thought, betrayed considerable shortcomings according to its own standard. For example, its idealistic fervor became a serious fault during the Sung period and more so during the Ming period because of the scholars' overworked habit of pronouncing judgment and criticism on the basis of small mistakes, with neither a careful verification of the facts nor any constructive purpose in mind, except to assert the personal superiority of the critics.[122]

8. Conclusions

The focal point of this short essay is the Confucian idealism which developed during the early Sung period. It should be pointed out, however, that the rise of the Confucian scholar-officials at this time had many aspects, among which their idealism was only one.

The revival of Confucianism was obviously motivated in part by a professional pride in the knowledge of the classics. This professional pride, from the broad cultural viewpoint, seems to have been rather narrow. Among educated people it caused some decline of interest in religion and art.

The scholar-officials during the Sung period favored a strong centralized government. While this was due partly to the state policy and the exigencies of the time, another reason was their own vested interest as members of the bureaucratic class. Consciously or unconsciously, they wanted more power for the government. In expressing their idealism, they made no criticism of the centralized form of empire.

The idealism which developed as a part of the revival of Confucianism was, however, basically incompatible with the power structure of the bureaucratic empire. The bureaucracy could not be transformed into an effective and cohesive political body, largely because it was not in the interest of either the career officials or the emperor's personal power. Between these two, there existed a close functional affinity such that they sought to keep the bureaucracy within the limits of an administrative mechanism. Nonetheless, Confucian idealism did inject its spirit into the system. While it definitely helped to raise the standard of government activity, it also paradoxically caused a constant tension between idealistic aspirations and the realities of power.

What the idealistic scholar-officials wished to realize may be described conceptually as a type of "ethocracy," a rule in which the elite in control is "characterized by a particular status and function with regard to moral values,"[123] just as a theocracy functions with regard to religious values. The reform movement which Fan Chung-yen led in the early Sung period was motivated basically by moral principles. It might be of interest to compare this reform movement with another one in the Christian church in eleventh-century Europe. The latter, according to some authorities, was also generated by a pious enthusiasm, against the influence of the Teutonic aristocracy.[124] It is interesting, though a mere coincidence, that both occurred in the same century.

The concept of the power structure seems worthy of further exploration. It should be pointed out, however, that it gives only a partial explanation of the question of why Confucian idealism failed to attain its major objectives. A more complete answer has to await the study of the socioeconomic structure of China. For example, the vocational limitations of the scholar-officials seem to have confined their activities to the bureaucracy and the schools. They failed to find a larger and more substantial socioeconomic base. One student whom Hu Yuan taught was the son of a millionaire merchant.[125] Why was it not possible for the scholars to find financial support for their schools from the merchant class? Fan Chung-yen introduced two new institutions into the clan organization. Other early Sung scholar-officials strengthened familism. How did the principles of familism fail to extend to the entire community and build up some degree of local autonomy against the political centralization imposed by the empire? Numerous questions which lie beyond the scope of this paper must be examined before the rich content of Confucian idealism can be fully understood.

THE TUNG-LIN MOVEMENT OF THE
LATE MING PERIOD

CHARLES O. HUCKER

1. Introduction

IN THE governmental system of imperial China there was no place for political parties as we know them today. Indeed, the system was such that partisanship inevitably suggested sedition. It is only occasionally, therefore, that so-called "partisan disasters" (tang-huo) enliven the annals of Chinese political history. But they have peculiar relevance to the study of relationships between thought and institutions in traditional Chinese life, because they represent deviations from the accepted patterns of political behavior and, also, because they tend to represent links between philosophical attitudes and political behavior. One of the most dramatic of these episodes, the subject of this paper, occurred toward the end of the Ming dynasty (1368–1644). It involved the so-called Tung-lin movement, which culminated during the 1620's in disastrous opposition among scholar-bureaucrats to a notorious eunuch dictator, Wei Chung-hsien.[1]

The Tung-lin movement might be of little interest, to Western students at least, if it could be considered merely an anti-eunuch struggle on the part of scholar-bureaucrats. But it was more than that. Opposition to Wei Chung-hsien was only the final stage of its history, and at no time was it dominated by anti-eunuch sentiment as such. The movement began some forty years before the era of Wei Chung-hsien in institutional friction that grew out of peculiarities in the Ming governmental structure. Then it quickly matured as a moral crusade on two planes, philosophical as well as political. It was represented on one plane by a group of men who gathered together at the Tung-lin Academy (Shu-yuan) in modern Kiangsu Province. These men, most of whom had been ousted from government during the period of institutional friction, devoted themselves to reaffirming the philosophical bases of public morality, which they thought to be tottering. On the political plane, the movement was represented by a group of men involved in continuing partisan controversies at court who sought to restore integrity to the government service. Because of their ties with the academic group, they were labeled by their enemies as the Tung-lin party (*tang*). The historical role of Wei Chung-hsien was to destroy the Tung-lin movement as a whole just when political success seemed within its grasp.

The present paper is an attempt to give a summary but coherent account of this Tung-lin movement in the context of the historical, institutional, and intellectual conditions out of which it arose.

2. China during the Late Ming Period

The period with which this study is concerned covers the reigns of the last four Ming emperors: Shen-tsung, who reigned from 1572 to 1620 under the era-name Wan-li; his son Kuang-tsung, who occupied the throne for only one month in 1620 under the era-name T'ai-ch'ang; Shen-tsung's grandson Hsi-tsung, who reigned from 1620 to 1627 under the era-name T'ien-ch'i; and Hsi-tsung's brother Ssu-tsung, who reigned from 1627 until the fall of the dynasty in 1644 under the era-name Ch'ung-chen. This period, from 1572 to 1644, witnessed a great cultural flowering. The era-name Wan-li, in particular, has become almost a synonym for elegance and prosperity. Nevertheless, the period was one of rapid deterioration in the stability of the Chinese state.[2]

During the first ten years of the Wan-li reign, while the emperor was in his adolescence, the central government was dominated by a civil minister named Chang Chü-cheng, one of the great men of Ming history.[3] The era is renowned as a time of exemplary government. The empire's enemies were subdued; its frontiers were well guarded and at peace. Its domestic administration was orderly, its economic affairs sound, and its treasuries overflowing. But the period following Chang's death in 1582, during which the Tung-lin movement rose and flourished, was one of deterioration.

Deterioration in one aspect was apparent in the character of Shen-tsung himself after he reached maturity. Released from the stern guidance and sometimes harsh tutorship of Chang Chü-cheng, who had overawed him, Shen-tsung rapidly became a self-willed, self-indulgent, extravagant, and irresponsible despot. He refused to have the traditional daily audiences with officials. For years at a time he even refused to see his highest-ranking ministers. He gradually developed a technique of simply ignoring the government; he refused to reply to requests for decisions and pigeonholed within the palace memorials of all sorts. Vacancies in the bureaucratic offices often went unfilled.[4] When Shen-tsung's fondness for an ambitious concubine involved him in a controversy over the establishment of his heir apparent, he childishly threatened new postponements at every request for action. When objections were made to his decisions to punish overly critical officials, he not only punished those who objected but increased the punishments of the original critics, hoping in this way to silence all opposition.

Funds that had been collected in the national treasuries during the regime of Chang Chü-cheng now dwindled steadily away. This was due in part to the extravagance of the imperial household[5] and in part to military campaigns that Shen-tsung ordered in the 1590's against Mongol rebels in the northwest, against aboriginal tribesmen in the southwest, and in support of China's vassal Korea, struggling with Japanese invaders under Toyotomi Hideyoshi.[6]

The campaigns of the 1590's, though costly, did not seriously endanger the security of the Ming empire. But there also began during the Wan-li period a long military contest that was in the end to destroy the Ming and place a new foreign dynasty on the Chinese throne. This was China's struggle with the Manchus,[7] who for two hundred years, as tributaries, had occupied the far northeastern frontier of the empire, north of Korea. The leading figure of the struggle was the great Manchu chieftain and organizer Nurhaci, who first disturbed the peace in 1583. After many campaigns and intrigues, Nurhaci succeeded in consolidating the Manchu tribes and subduing their immediate neighbors; and in 1616 he designated himself khan of a new dynasty. Two years later he published seven grievances against the Ming dynasty and set out in earnest to destroy it.

Hsi-tsung, who unexpectedly came to the Ming throne in 1620 at the age of fifteen, was an even less admirable emperor than his grandfather, Shen-tsung, had been.[8] Caring for nothing so much as puttering at carpentry, he permitted the ruthless eunuch Wei Chung-hsien, the favorite of the imperial governess, first to terrorize the imperial household and then to extend his authority into the central administration, the provinces, and the frontier marches. A eunuch army was organized and trained within the palace, and eunuchs were sent out to command frontier defenses. Government morale plunged to one of the lowest levels of the entire Confucian tradition. Officials who displeased the powerful eunuch or his friends were expelled from office by the hundreds, stripped of their status and traditional privileges, arrested, imprisoned, and in not a few instances tortured to death. Honors were heaped upon Wei Chung-hsien by sycophantic officials and the emperor alike, until men wondered who was emperor.

Meanwhile, China continued to be ravaged by scattered domestic revolts,[9] and the Manchus relentlessly advanced. At the death of Hsi-tsung in 1627 Ming authority had been effectively superseded in the northeast. When Ssu-tsung,[10] himself a youth of seventeen, took the throne, he got rid of Wei Chung-hsien and strove to quell the partisan squabbling that paralyzed the bureaucracy; but he was nevertheless unable to pull the government together sufficiently to enable it to overcome the challenges that it now faced.

It is difficult at present to calculate the extent to which basic social and economic conditions in China had deteriorated during these years. Literature, art, scholarship, and culture generally continued to flourish undiminished. The Chinese mind was being opened to new horizons through the activities of Jesuit missionaries, who first gained entry to the mainland in the time of Chang Chü-cheng. But social and economic dislocations, already evident long before, had concurrently become more severe.[11] Retired officials and the relatives and hangers-on of high-placed ministers increasingly took advantage of their prestige and of the special privileges and exemptions that were the traditional prerogatives of the literati. They found it easy in times of lax government to oppress the common people by extortion, by violence, and by the disruption of judicial processes; and conscientious local officials often found efforts to restrain them useless or dangerous because of the indolence or the susceptibility to bribery of their own superiors.

Tax inequities resulting from the privileged exemptions of the literati, and from the brazen evasions of great landlords generally, must have caused the common people to suffer under an all but intolerable burden at a time when tax levies were steadily increased. Expenditures on wars and palace construction work during the 1590's caused Shen-tsung to send out eunuch collectors to supervise tax matters and to levy a variety of special, new taxes—on mines, on shops, on boats, etc. Because of the requirements for defense against the Manchus, the basic land-tax rate was increased in 1618. Both salt taxes and domestic-customs taxes were increased during the reign of Hsi-tsung, and thereafter a series of special levies to meet defense costs was heaped upon the taxpayers. The concentration of land in fewer and fewer hands had been a tendency throughout the Ming period, and long-recognized problems of tenantry and bonded servitude seem to have intensified as the economic plight of the independent small farmer worsened.

Deterioration in all these aspects of national life culminated in the collapse of the Ming government in 1644, the suicide of Ssu-tsung, and the subjection of China to Manchu rule.

3. *Institutional Frictions of the Late Sixteenth Century*

Modern students tend to be distressed on finding that Chinese records of the late Ming period do not reveal a predominating concern about the military and socioeconomic problems that are clearly recognizable, in retrospect, as the crucial problems of the period. Contemporary records reveal a primary concern, rather, with the bureaucratic controversies that are dealt with in this paper,[12] which to the uninitiated seem to be characterized by little significance and less clarity. As was noted above, the controversies began in the form of institutional friction that grew out of peculiarities in the Ming governmental structure.[13] Most significantly, the troubles had to do with an institution known as the Grand Secretariat (*Nei-ko*).

A. THE MING GOVERNMENTAL STRUCTURE

The poles of power in the Ming governmental structure were what the Chinese informally call the "inner court" (*nei-t'ing*) and the "outer court" (*wai-t'ing*). "Inner court" was a general term used informally with reference to persons whose functions were intimately related to the imperial family, including palace ladies, eunuch attendants, and a group of civil service officials who served as readers-in-waiting, lecturers-in-waiting, proclamation drafters, and tutors of the imperial offspring, associated for the most part with a governmental organ known as the Hanlin Yuan. "Outer court" was a general term designating the functioning administrative agencies of the capital, the peak of the bureaucratic pyramid that directed the empire-wide activities of the government. Membership in the civil service bureaucracy was attained primarily through passing competitive examinations based on the Confucian classical literature, first at the provincial level (to attain the status of *chü-jen*) and then at the capital (to attain the status of *chin-shih*).

The founder of the Ming dynasty, T'ai-tsu (reigned 1368–98), erected an outer court largely after the pattern of preceding dynasties. It included at the top level an executive organ known as the Secretariat (*Chung-shu sheng*), whose head, the prime minister, was the first-ranking civil service official of the realm and the acknowledged spokesman of the bureaucracy. The Secretariat supervised the routine administrative work of six directly subordinate agencies called "ministries"—of civil service, of revenue, of rites, of war, of punishments, of works. Flanking this administrative hierarchy was a hierarchy of military service personnel and a separate hierarchy of civil service personnel constituting a special censorial branch of the government, represented by a Censorate proper and a group of six offices of scrutiny paralleling the six ministries.

The prime minister in this system had strong executive powers, sanctioned by regulations and by tradition; he could be in practice a substantial check on the absolutism of the emperor. Midway in his reign T'ai-tsu decided that the prime ministership was in fact a threat to his own position. He charged his prime minister with treason, put him to death, abolished the Secretariat, and gathered unto himself all executive authority. Moreover, he decreed that his successors must never permit re-establishment of the Secretariat and prescribed the death penalty for anyone who advocated doing so.

Chinese critics of the institutional tradition, from Huang Tsunghsi of the seventeenth century[14] to the present century's Ch'ien Mu,[15] have concluded that the subsequent lack of a prime ministership was a source of political weakness and, possibly, a cause of the eventual collapse of the Ming dynasty. T'ai-tsu's abolition of the Secretariat was based on the assumption that all Ming emperors would be as diligent and conscientious as he was himself. When, as a matter of fact, later emperors such as Shen-tsung and Hsi-tsung failed to fulfil this expectation, chaos resulted because the system did not permit any other hand constitutionally to take the helm.

One historical consequence of this beheading of the outer court was a great expansion of eunuch influence. T'ai-tsu had felt just as strongly about the dangers of eunuch influence as he had about the danger of competition from the prime ministership. He maintained only a small force of eunuchs, believed in keeping them illiterate, and forbade on pain of death their interference in governmental affairs.[16] Whereas his ban on the Secretariat was strictly heeded to the very end of the dynasty, however, later emperors paid little attention to his decrees concerning eunuchs. Perhaps they felt that eunuchs, being by their very nature unlikely to attract popular support in the event of a struggle for the throne, were singularly trustworthy. At all events, eunuchs came to be employed on a variety of special government commissions.

Since eunuchs did not have to answer to public opinion and had little reason to be concerned about anything other than pleasing the emperor, they found it relatively easy to win and hold imperial favor. And, since the emperor relied on them for the satisfaction of his personal, everyday wants, they were never troubled by failure to gain access to him. A strong eunuch consequently had every opportunity to dominate a weak emperor. Moreover, in the case of an emperor who, like Shen-tsung, declined to have audience with his ministers, eunuchs became go-betweens essential to the maintenance of even remote contact between the emperor and the bureaucracy.

B. THE GRAND SECRETARIAT AS A SOURCE OF FRICTION

Another historical consequence of the abolition of the Secretariat was the rise of the informal institution called "Grand Secretariat." Once the old-style Secretariat had disappeared, the six formerly subordinate ministries were left as the top-level organs of the administrative hierarchy. Although it was always understood that the minister of civil service took precedence over his counterparts in the other ministries, the ministries were in general of equal status, and no one but the emperor was in a position to co-ordinate their activities. And the ministries remained essentially administrative, not executive, organs; for decisions on almost all questions had to be obtained specifically from the emperor. The burden that such a system imposed on the emperor is indicated by a report that during one eight-day period late in T'ai-tsu's reign 1,160 documents dealing with 3,291 separate matters were presented for imperial action.[17] It need hardly be said that none but the strongest and most dedicated of emperors could bear such a burden of paper-work by himself.

Among the personnel of the inner court in T'ai-tsu's system was a group of grand secretaries (*ta hsueh-shih*), officially members of the Hanlin Yuan, who served within the palace grounds as consultants and editors. It was obviously T'ai-tsu's intention that these learned gentlemen should be no more than private secretaries. But later emperors, after the fashion of overburdened executives, found it convenient to delegate more and more work to their secretaries, with the result that this group came to serve as a buffer between the emperor and the outer court, with the unofficial designation of Grand Secretariat. Long before the time of Shen-tsung it had come about that all incoming documents were scrutinized first by the grand secretaries, who proposed decisions by drafting rescripts and attaching them to the original documents. When the documents were at last seen by the emperor, he was thus called upon for serious thought only in those cases where the decisions proposed by the grand secretaries did not appeal to him. The way was open, consequently, for a senior grand secretary to attain to almost the same level of authority as that enjoyed formerly by a prime minister. The Grand Secretariat even came to be referred to commonly as "the administration" (*cheng-fu*).

The Grand Secretariat, however, developed, as we would say, entirely outside the constitution. It was never regularized, never officially institutionalized, never recognized openly as an executive organ ranking above the six ministries. "On paper," as it were, there was no such thing as a Grand Secretariat; there were only individual grand secretaries, officially members of the Hanlin Yuan, ranking far down the civil service scale well below the senior officials of all the administrative organs of the central government. This obvious disadvantage was overcome by a practice of giving grand secretaries concurrent nominal ranks as vice-ministers or ministers in the various ministries, and their double ranks enabled them to take precedence at court assemblies over the functioning heads of the ministries.

But the manager's assistants, so to speak, never became assistant managers. The grand secretaries had no formal executive powers, and they were constantly subject to the whims of the emperor. Moreover, despite their nominal concurrent appointments in the ministries, they remained essentially members of the inner court and could not expect united support and co-operation from the outer court. Some grand secretaries nevertheless became strong and influential, usually in alliance with imperially favored eunuchs. But it would seem almost inevitable that they should have been frustrated and undone by resentment among officials of the outer court. The problem was how to become a prime minister under a system that did not permit a prime ministership.

One of the most successful grand secretaries was Chang Chü-cheng, who managed to dominate the government during the first ten years of Shen-tsung's reign. He accomplished many worthwhile things, but in the end he was corrupted—not so much by his power as by the constitutional illegitimacy of his power. Bureaucratic antagonism toward him became widespread.

C. THE RISE OF ANTIADMINISTRATION SENTIMENT

The occasion for open cleavage between Chang Chü-cheng and his supporters, on one side, and what might be called antiadministration (i.e., anti–Grand Secretariat) elements, on the other, was the death of Chang's father in 1577. The Confucian tradition required that on the death of a parent an official must leave office and observe mourning in retirement for twenty-seven months, and such was the general practice. Chang accordingly requested permission to depart. But the emperor Shen-tsung, who was fourteen years old at the time, ordered that the regular mourning procedure be waived and that Chang remain on duty. Many contemporaries and subsequent historians believed that Chang himself was responsible for this order. However that may be, Chang did not protest as dramatically as might have been expected but agreed to a compromise that permitted him to observe mourning and perform his Grand Secretariat duties simultaneously, merely being excused from personal participation in court audiences.

Four officials of the outer court immediately protested this "violation of human feelings," accusing Chang of being so jealous of his powerful position as to forget his parents. All were beaten in court, imprisoned, and in the end banished into frontier military service. A new *chin-shih* serving his apprenticeship in the Ministry of Punishments, Tsou Yuan-piao (eventually a leader of the Tung-lin party), was similarly beaten and banished when he memorialized in their defense.[18] In the remaining years of Chang's regime his supporters dominated the outer court, and his influence was so great that opposition was not shown openly. But anti-Chang feeling was strong and manifested itself in small ways, as when Ku Hsien-ch'eng (later a founder of the Tung-lin Academy) openly erased his own name from a list of sponsors appended to a prayer for the dying Chang's health after associates had written it there.[19] As soon as Chang had died in 1582, long-bridled censors began to attack his closest adherents. Shen-tsung, who, while maturing, had grown weary of Chang's unrelenting insistence upon his being conscientious and diligent, now listened to the critics with sympathy. Before a year had passed, Chang himself was posthumously disgraced and his household was confiscated. Officials who had been banished during the mourning controversy were recalled.

During the next twenty years Chang Chü-cheng's successors as senior grand secretary—notably Shen Shih-hsing,[20] Wang Hsi-chüeh,[21] and Shen I-kuan[22]—were constantly embroiled in court agitation. There occurred a series of frenzied controversies[23] over merit evaluations for civil service personnel, over the activities of eunuch tax commissioners, and over a host of seemingly trivial incidents related to what the antagonists called "the root of the state." This term referred to the status of the eldest imperial son, whose investiture as heir apparent was peevishly and repeatedly delayed by Shen-tsung, though increasingly insisted upon by the outer court. In general, Shen-tsung became steadily more inattentive, more irritable, and less manageable. Dozens of outer court spokesmen were degraded or banished, year after year; and the grand secretaries found themselves hopelessly caught in the cross-fire between the palace and the outer court.

By 1606, when Shen I-kuan left office under heavy attack, the controversies at the Ming court had gradually changed in character. No longer were they primarily expressions of friction between the Grand Secretariat and officials of the outer court intent on preventing the grand secretaries from attaining the predominance that Chang Chü-cheng had enjoyed. Moral issues had colored the controversies from the start, and now the institutional alignments tended to be submerged in a newly focused struggle, essentially within the outer court itself, that had a distinctly moral tone. What brought this moral tone into prominence was the development of the Tung-lin Academy.

4. The Tung-lin Academy and the Tung-lin Party

The flourishing of privately operated academies had been one of the notable phenomena of Chinese intellectual life since the Sung dynasty (960–1279).[24] Their function was to supplement the efforts of government schools in preparing young men for the civil service examinations and, in addition, to serve scholars of whatever status as gathering places for philosophical conferences. The establishment of such academies had been greatly stimulated by the evangelical work of the mid-Ming philosopher Wang Yang-ming (1472–1529). Now, despite an ineffective attempt at repression by Chang Chü-cheng, what can only be called an academy craze was sweeping the intellectual world in late Ming times.

A. THE FOUNDING OF THE ACADEMY

The Tung-lin Academy,[25] founded in Sung times but long since fallen into ruins, was re-established in 1604. It was located in the heart of one of traditional China's richest areas, economically and culturally, in the district of Wusih (Wu-hsi), of Ch'ang-chou Prefecture, in that part of modern Kiangsu Province that lies south of the Yangtze River inland from Shanghai. Wusih, in recent times a thriving commercial city, is some twenty-five miles northwest of Soochow, which was the greatest city of the area in Ming times. The academy consisted of an enclosed group of buildings beside Bow Creek in the eastern part of Wusih City, where there was a small grove of willow trees from which the name Tung-lin, meaning "Eastern Grove," was derived.[26]

Reconstruction of the academy at this time was brought about by a group of scholar-officials living in the area, almost all of whom had been ousted from the government during the controversies just described: Ku Hsien-ch'eng of Wusih, dismissed in 1594; his younger brother Yun-ch'eng,[27] degraded in 1593; Kao P'an-lung[28] of Wusih, degraded in 1594; Shih Meng-lin[29] of I-hsing District, on leave since 1593; Yü K'ung-chien[30] of Chin-t'an District, degraded in 1593; An Hsi-fan[31] of Wusih, dismissed in 1593; Hsueh Fu-chiao[32] of Wu-chin District, degraded in 1593; Ch'ien I-pen[33] of Wu-chin, degraded in 1592; and Liu Yuan-chen[34] of Wusih, who joined the group in 1605 after being dismissed for opposing Shen I-kuan. The only prominent members of the founding group who had no personal contact with the court controversies of the period were Yeh Mou-ts'ai[35] of Wusih, currently on leave from a Nanking post, and Hsü Shih-ch'ing[36] of Ch'ang-chou Prefecture, who, though a *chü-jen*, had never taken office.

Several members of this group, and other men who subsequently became associated with them, were significant thinkers,[37] but Ku Hsien-ch'eng was the dominant spirit. On completion of the construction work at the academy in 1604, Ku notified scholars throughout the area that on the ninth, tenth, and eleventh days of the tenth lunar month of that year a great assembly would be held. He also prepared and distributed a "meeting agreement" (*hui-yueh*)[38] establishing the fundamental philosophical aims of the group and rules of procedure for the assembly. He proposed that large-scale assemblies or philosophical conferences be held for three days annually, either in spring or autumn, and that lesser assemblies, primarily for the benefit of nearby residents, be held monthly except during the two coldest and the two warmest months of each year. Meetings of the sort prescribed were in fact held, though perhaps not with complete regularity, at least until 1621.[39]

Reports of the early conferences were printed,[40] and the group quickly won empire-wide renown. Ku Hsien-ch'eng, who remained the acknowledged master of the academy until his death in 1612, soon dominated a group of nearby satellite academies, at Wu-chin to the north, at I-hsing to the west, at Ch'ang-shu to the east, and at Chin-t'an to the northwest.[41] He made the rounds among them, lecturing, and in 1608 also lectured farther to the south in Chekiang Province.[42] Ku's death did not alter this relationship, for the philosophical ascendancy of the academy was maintained thereafter by his senior disciple and academy-founding colleague, Kao P'an-lung, who continued to visit the affiliated academies at I-hsing, Ch'ang-shu, and Chin-t'an, at least, on tour.[43]

It is not surprising that the ousted officials who dominated the Tung-lin Academy were concerned about politics. Ku Yün-ch'eng once complained that too many contemporary scholars who were devoted to philosophical disputation "would permit heaven to fall and earth to collapse and still would not care."[44] And Ku Hsien-ch'eng demanded that scholars must constantly keep their attention on worldly problems, even while discoursing on philosophy and cultivating themselves in retirement.[45] We find, consequently, that the Tung-lin academicians, besides talking about philosophical concepts, regularly discussed the personalities of the day and current governmental issues.[46] They did not have escapist inclinations. As the Chinese say, they were intent on "rescuing the world" (*chiu-shih*).

Ku Hsien-ch'eng recognized the institutional character of the political struggles of his time,[47] but he regarded these struggles primarily in the light of moral problems. Basically, he and his associates considered, there was developing a political cleavage, not between "ins" and "outs" or between different governmental organs, but between "good elements" (*shan-lei*) or "upright men" (*cheng-jen*) or "honest advocates" (*ch'ing-i*), on the one hand, and, on the other, men characterized by opportunism, sycophancy, and petty, vindictive partisanship based on selfish interest rather than on principles. The Tung-lin academicians correlated this political development with philosophical developments that, in their view, were undermining the whole structure of traditional morality. They hoped to rectify current philosophical errors and thus lay a foundation for a moral revival in politics.[48]

B. THE PHILOSOPHICAL CREDO OF THE ACADEMY

From the very beginning of the Ming dynasty, Neo-Confucianism, as systematized by Chu Hsi (1130–1200) in the twelfth century, had been the orthodox Chinese philosophy. This might be described as, in essence, a metaphysical rationalization of ancient Confucian morality, and it offered men as a goal the attainment in one's person of the *Tao* that is the controlling agent of the universe. The method it prescribed was cultivation (*hsiu*): literally, the extension of knowledge through the investigation of things. It was rather authoritarian, and it called for extensive study of the doctrines imbedded in the ancient Confucian texts.

The popular, early sixteenth-century philosopher-official Wang Yang-ming had given a new direction to Neo-Confucian thinking.[49] In opposition to the earlier emphasis on cultivation, Wang emphasized perception (*wu*); he advocated reliance on the innate knowledge of the individual mind, which he considered to be microcosmically identical with the universal principle (*li*), in which is manifested the *Tao*. Wang himself had studied Buddhism as well as Confucianism, and his doctrine of perception inevitably suggests the principle of attaining to Buddhahood through sudden enlightenment that had long been espoused by the Buddhist sect called Ch'an (Zen). Following Wang's death in 1529, Ch'an Buddhism had a significant revival in China,[50] and some of his disciples wedded Wang's brand of Neo-Confucianism to it. By the time of the Wan-li period, philosophical eclecticism was prevalent, and Wang's emphasis on the innate knowledge of the individual mind had been developed into an iconoclastic individualism that has a peculiarly "modern" flavor.

The most famous, if not the most representative, of these post-Wang iconoclasts was a Confucian official turned Ch'an Buddhist, Li Chih.[51] Li was a freethinker who completely renounced Confucius and the classics as standards of right and wrong, believed in the ready-made perfection of the individual's "child-mind," considered selfishness and profit to be worthwhile motivations, and advocated "naturalism" and "spontaneity." He denounced traditional Confucians as slavish job-seekers, was an ardent champion and student of the popular literature that orthodox Confucians publicly disdained, preached equality of the sexes, advocated marriage by free choice of the individuals concerned, and said that Confucianism, Buddhism, and Taoism were of equal truth and value. While holding public office, he sometimes conducted official business in Buddhist temples. His publications were popular, and the attitudes that he championed seem to have obtained widespread currency in his time. It is even reported that Shen-tsung himself, when urged to appoint tutors for his princes, said that innate, natural knowledge was after all the important thing, not instruction—an attitude that Li undoubtedly would have approved heartily.[52] Since anyone who preached such doctrines as these must have been anathema to all who believed in the traditional system of Confucian morality, which was the basis of the state, Li Chih was eventually denounced as a heretic and arrested; and in 1602 he committed suicide in prison. It is not surprising that the man who denounced him, Chang Wen-ta of Shensi province,[53] subsequently found himself aligned with the Tung-lin partisans at court.

Ku Hsien-ch'eng of the Tung-lin Academy repeatedly complained about Li Chih's attitudes and influence.[54] He was a fervent opponent of Confucian-Buddhist-Taoist eclecticism[55] and mourned that most of his contemporaries were Buddhists at heart and only superficially Confucians.[56] Ku felt that the current heterodoxy derived from mistakes made by Wang Yang-ming. Nevertheless, he was by no means solidly anti-Wang; he was himself a third-generation disciple of Wang. He took up a position as mediator between Chu Hsi and Wang, criticizing both but inclining toward Chu as the less objectionable. He said:

As for following the doctrines of K'ao-t'ing [i.e., Chu Hsi], the bad point is conservatism [*pao*]. As for following the doctrines of Yao-chiang [i.e., Wang Yang-ming], the bad point is recklessness [*tang*]. One who is conservative will not do some things; but there is nothing that one who is reckless will not do. For one who is conservative it is easy, obeying (his conservative inclination), to break off what is repugnant to the human emotions; but for one who is reckless it is difficult, going against (his reckless inclination), to turn from what is congenial to the human emotions. Of old, Confucius in discussing the bad points of ritual said that frugality is better than prodigality. Thus in discussing the bad points of scholarship one should say that conservatism is better than recklessness, and that is why I follow Chu-tzu.[57]

Ku Hsien-ch'eng defined the divergence of views about cultivation and perception as a difference of emphasis on the two corollary aspects of the mind, original substance (*pen-t'i*) and application (*kung-fu*).[58] Ku apparently believed that Wang Yang-ming, relying upon perception through the original substance of the mind as the means to attain the *Tao*, failed to appreciate the necessity of making up for the dissimilarity of human minds by assiduous cultivation in accordance with external standards; whereas Chu Hsi, relying upon assiduous cultivation through application of the mind, overestimated the value of external, objective investigation of things and perhaps failed to appreciate the efficacy of the original substance of the mind and thus of the innate knowledge that Wang emphasized.

In short, while recognizing the importance of both cultivation and perception, Ku insisted that cultivation must precede perception (in seeming contradiction to Wang) and yet insisted that external investigation of things is not the proper medium of cultivation (in seeming contradiction to Chu). "Things" (*wu*) did not interest him; "affairs" (*shih*) did. Therefore, he insisted that the *Tao* is to be attained by perception based on prior cultivation, that the proper medium of cultivation is investigation of "affairs" rather than "things," and that the investigation of affairs requires thorough study of the counsels of former sages and worthies to be found in the classics and, especially, courageous practice of their principles in the medium of practical human relationships. Believing the potential for evil of Wang's thought to be far more alarming than that of Chu's, he most vigorously rejected Wang's conception of the individual mind as the basis for moral judgment.

For almost all the Tung-lin philosophers, the heart of the philosophical problem was the conception of man's nature, and the Tung-lin spirit manifested itself in vigorous reaffirmation of the Mencian doctrine that man's nature is essentially good. The crucial section of Ku Hsien-ch'eng's "meeting agreement" of 1604, the manifesto and credo of the Tung-lin academicians, deals with this point. The argument has to do with a statement by Wang Yang-ming that "the absence of good and the absence of evil is the original substance of the mind; the presence of good and the presence of evil is the exercise of thought; the knowledge of good and the knowledge of evil is intuitive knowledge; the doing of good and the removing of evil is the investigation of things."[59] Ku considered this view to be self-contradictory and dangerous. His reasoning might be paraphrased as follows:

The original substance of the mind is bound up inseparably with the application of the mind. If the original substance of the mind (i.e., man's nature) is characterized by absence of good and evil, then how can one apply it so as to do good and remove evil? If the doctrine that the human nature is neither good nor evil prevails, then inevitably the necessity of doing good and removing evil must give way, and if this gives way, then inevitably contempt of proper human relationships and of proper procedures of study and practice must increase. How can it be otherwise? The doctrine that man's nature is good is the great wellspring of Confucianism, whereas the doctrine that man's nature is neither good nor evil is the source of Buddhism and Taoism. When these doctrines are blended together in an unnatural compromise into the concept that the absence of both good and evil is the supreme good, though it may be argued that this new "supreme good" is merely an extension and clarification of Mencius' "good," the fact remains that the similar-seeming nomenclature conceals a vastly altered reality, and what Mencius called "good" has been lost. Specious sycophancy and heterodox hermitry both result.[60]

This philosophical platform called, in effect, for a strengthening of the traditional virtue of moral integrity (*ch'i-chieh*); it called for a moral crusade. Its influence was felt in politics, in large part perhaps because of the extensive correspondence that Ku Hsien-ch'eng maintained with functioning officials. Injection of this philosophical note into the political situation makes political history from 1605 to 1615 confusing indeed to the modern reader, for clear-cut political or institutional issues tended to be submerged completely by questions of personal character and morality.

C. THE IMPACT OF THE ACADEMY ON POLITICS

Ku Hsien-ch'eng did not hesitate to call upon sympathetic officials to exert themselves in a common political cause, and all who associated themselves with the political causes he championed—whether or not in direct response to his urgings—came ultimately to be known as members of a Tung-lin party. Even during a controversy of 1603–4, Ku had tried to marshal support at court for an endangered friend, gravely annoying the senior grand secretary, Shen I-kuan;[61] and in 1607 Ku again took up a political cause.

After the controversies of the early 1600's, the prevailing mood at court was a hotly partisan one, but Shen I-kuan's attitude was considered by many to be inexcusably flagrant and vicious. In 1606, after being openly accused of treachery and avarice, he was permitted to retire. Chu Keng[62] was left as the sole incumbent in the Grand Secretariat. Chu is generally credited with preventing controversies of 1603–4 from developing into a widespread partisan disaster; but, being a cautious mediator by nature, he was not wholly trusted by either the Tung-lin partisans or their enemies.

In 1607 the emperor decided to appoint additional grand secretaries, and the Tung-lin partisans suffered a severe shock. New appointees were Li T'ing-chi[63] and Yeh Hsiang-kao;[64] in addition, Wang Hsi-chueh, senior grand secretary of 1593–94, was summoned out of retirement. Yeh Hsiang-kao had long been an outspoken critic of eunuch influence and had remonstrated with Shen I-kuan. Though Yeh was thus expected to be friendly, Li T'ing-chi was considered a protégé of Shen I-kuan; and the recall of the long-time antagonist Wang Hsi-chueh was anything but cheering to the Tung-lin followers, who could not restrain their irritation.

Ku Hsien-ch'eng, at home in Wusih, at this time wrote and widely distributed two small tracts that pointedly mourned the decay of court morality and that called upon Wang Hsi-chueh not to aggravate the situation by returning to the Grand Secretariat.[65] In the end Wang declined the emperor's summons and submitted a private statement urging the emperor to pay more attention to the personnel problems of the government. Ku Hsien-ch'eng's long-time friend Li San-ts'ai,[66] governor of the Huai River area, somehow learned the contents of Wang's statement and, apparently distorting its sense, spread word in the capital that Wang had slandered the censorial services by saying that censorial memorials lately had been no better than the squawking and growling of birds and beasts. Immediately an almost-universal furor against Wang arose, and his recall to service was not insisted upon.

Simultaneously, the Tung-lin group insistently memorialized against Li T'ing-chi. In 1608, after repeated attempts to retire, Li in despair shut himself up in his capital residence and refused to take any part in government. Denunciations never ceased, and at last in 1612 the emperor accepted his resignation after it had been submitted a hundred and twenty times. Though nominally a member of the Grand Secretariat for five years, he had actually taken part in its work for less than nine months.

Since Chu Keng died shortly before Li T'ing-chi went into seclusion, Yeh Hsiang-kao alone remained on duty in the Grand Secretariat. As expected, he was in general sympathetic with the Tung-lin, but he was not a very vigorous advocate and was unable to induce the emperor to act upon his proposals. Requests for the recall to service of Ku Hsien-ch'eng, Kao P'an-lung, and various early outer court heroes all went unheeded. Opposition factions warred against the Tung-lin partisans openly and incessantly. Since the emperor never took notice of their memorials and ignored Yeh's pleas for disciplinary action, there was nothing to restrain them. Denied the imperial vindication that their concept of ministerial honor seemed to demand, Tung-lin partisans began to follow Li T'ing-chi's precedent and abandon their posts; some submitted resignations and went home without waiting for imperial consent, which could not be expected.

There seem to have been three identifiable factions that harassed the Tung-lin group at this time. Predominant was a so-called Chekiang (*Che*) party, comprising the former outer court adherents of Shen I-kuan, a Chekiang man. The others were smaller groups known as the Hsuan party, supporters of the chancellor of the Nanking National Academy, T'ang Pin-yin of Hsuan-ch'eng District of modern Anhwei Province; and the K'un party, supporters of a Hanlin official, Ku T'ien-chün of K'un-shan District in Soochow Prefecture—thus a near neighbor of the Tung-lin Academy. A realignment soon submerged the latter two factions and brought about an alliance of the Chekiang party, a Shantung (*Ch'i*) party, and a Hukuang (*Ch'u*) party, all reportedly under the unifying guidance of T'ang Pin-yin.[67]

The Tung-lin party did not have clear-cut geographical associations. Among its most prominent men at this time were Yeh Hsiang-kao of Fukien, Wang T'u of Shensi,[68] Wang Yuan-han of Yunnan,[69] Ts'ao Yü-pien of Shansi,[70] Ting Yuan-chien of Chekiang,[71] Shih Chi-shih of Shensi,[72] and Sun Chü-hsiang of Shansi.[73] There is evidence to suggest that men from the northwestern province of Shensi allied themselves in these years with the Tung-lin partisans primarily because of provincial feeling, appearing as gratitude toward the southeasterner Yü Yü-li for his support of a Shensi man in an earlier controversy.[74] Yü Yü-li,[75] whom history has given the reputation of a cunning political strategist, was a resident of Chin-t'an District and thus a fellow-townsman and probably a clansman of Yü K'ung-chien, one of the founders of the Tung-lin Academy. His association with the Tung-lin group is clearly revealed by his attendance in 1612 at a Tung-lin Academy memorial service for Ku Hsien-ch'eng.[76] He had early been an outspoken critic of the grand secretary Shen Shih-hsing, and during a controversy of 1603–4 he had been first imprisoned and then dismissed.

The Tung-lin followers, not satisfied with Yeh Hsiang-kao's attempts to protect them during these years, apparently hoped that Li San-ts'ai, a powerful, popular, and politically minded governor who was their constant champion and had been a personal friend of Ku Hsien-ch'eng since the 1580's, might also be brought into the Grand Secretariat. This again reflects the institutional aspect of the partisan struggles; for grand secretaries were traditionally chosen from among men who had spent their careers in the Hanlin Yuan, within the inner court, whereas Li's career had been spent in the outer court and in the provinces. To forestall Li's nomination, opposition factions in 1610 launched a great attack on him, accusing him of corruption and insisting that he be tried. The Tung-lin partisans rallied immediately to his defense. Ku Hsien-ch'eng sent a letter to Yeh Hsiang-kao praising Li and demanding a full investigation of the charges, in the confidence that the governor would be exonerated. A well-meaning friend arranged for the publication of the letter in the *Peking Gazette*. Instead of helping Li's cause, however, this letter helped to ruin him; for the opposition factions promptly seized upon it as clear evidence of a great partisan conspiracy stemming from the Tung-lin Academy. This was apparently the first time that the academy and the name Tung-lin became publicly involved in the factional strife at court.

More than Li San-ts'ai's future was at stake in the controversy of 1610–11, for the time had come for a great merit evaluation of the capital officials. In preparation for this event, the emperor had recalled from retirement Sun P'ei-yang,[77] another Shensi man who had formerly been an anti-administration stalwart, to be minister of civil service. With Yeh Hsiang-kao alone in the Grand Secretariat and Sun in charge of the Ministry of Civil Service, the prospect of evaluations was an ominous one as far as T'ang Pin-yin and his partisans were concerned. On the assumption that offense is the best defense, they therefore supplemented their denunciations of Li San-ts'ai with attacks on several other key men of the Tung-lin party. They were, in turn, accused of trying to confuse the emperor concerning the forthcoming evaluations.

It was in the midst of this many-faceted struggle that the opposition began to draw the Tung-lin Academy into open politics and to speak publicly of a Tung-lin party. In 1611 a censor memorialized at length about the academy and its role in politics. He said that the perverted philosophers who attended conferences there devoted themselves to intimidating the local authorities and humiliating the local citizens; that Ku Hsien-ch'eng had spread his influence throughout the southeast by extensive correspondence and extensive travel; that Ku had corrupted scholarship by utilizing philosophical conferences to further political schemes and by allying himself with the allegedly corrupt Li San-ts'ai; and that his agents in the capital were now using the merit evaluations to serve their partisan aims with the co-operation of Sun P'ei-yang.[78]

D. TRIUMPH OF THE OPPOSITION

The evaluations were highly unfavorable to the three opposition factions. Both T'ang Pin-yin and Ku T'ien-chün, the opposition leaders, were marked for degradation, and a dozen or more of the men who for a decade had most openly harassed the Tung-lin partisans were similarly denounced. Yeh Hsiang-kao urged imperial approval of the ministry's evaluation recommendations, and the emperor after some hesitation did approve them. But what seemed at first to be a great victory for the Tung-lin party soon turned to disaster. So savage were the attacks on Li San-ts'ai that he withdrew into voluntary retirement without imperial consent. Sun P'ei-yang, old and tired, similarly retired on his own authority to escape the ceaseless accusations of the remaining opposition officials. And many other Tung-lin members rapidly followed suit. When Yeh Hsiang-kao was permitted to retire in 1614, the partisans were in almost total eclipse. Thereafter the only grand secretary on duty was Fang

Ts'ung-che,[79] and both he and the minister of civil service under him seem to have been little more than servile tools of the supervising secretary Chi Shih-chiao, a Shantung man who had become the acknowledged leader of the Shantung, Hukuang, and Chekiang factions. Meantime, the Tung-lin group had lost its vigorous intellectual leadership with the death of Ku Hsien-ch'eng. Kao P'an-lung, who succeeded as master of the academy, did not have Ku's intense interest in current politics.

5. The Tung-lin Party and Wei Chung-hsien

A. RE-EMERGENCE OF THE TUNG-LIN PARTISANS

The last years of Shen-tsung were marked by the almost unchallenged supremacy of the three opposition factions, but they could not entirely prevent the slow infiltration into the court of a new generation of "good elements" with Tung-lin sympathies. New "minority leaders," so to speak, appeared as Tung-lin spokesmen: Wang Wen-yen, a protégé of Yü Yü-li and a similarly skilled political tactician;[80] Yang Lien, a disciple of Ku Hsien-ch'eng and Kao P'an-lung;[81] and Tso Kuang-tou.[82] In 1615 and 1620 three great court controversies arose[83] that intensified partisan antagonisms. And in 1620, when Shen-tsung died, Kuang-tsung died after a reign of only one month, and Hsi-tsung came to the throne at the age of fifteen, the political tide turned. Kao P'an-lung, Yeh Hsiang-kao, and old Tung-lin friends and heroes such as Tsou Yuan-piao (critic of Chang Chü-cheng) and Chao Nan-hsing (an anti-administration martyr of 1593)[84] were recalled to service.

From 1620 into 1623 the Tung-lin party was predominant in the government. It owed much to the influence of a friendly eunuch, Wang An,[85] over Kuang-tsung and, temporarily, over Hsi-tsung. (Wang An's friendship had been carefully cultivated previously by Wang Wen-yen, who is said to have coached him on the intricacies of partisan politics.) In merit evaluations of 1623, under the leadership of Chao Nan-hsing, the Tung-lin men succeeded in removing from the capital many of their remaining enemies of former days, beginning with the Shantung faction leader, Chi Shih-chiao. By early 1624 the key posts at court were all held by Tung-lin partisans. The senior grand secretary was Yeh Hsiang-kao. Chao Nan-hsing was minister of civil service, and Kao P'an-lung was censor-in-chief.

The partisans, however, did not at any time have complete control of the government, and they had already suffered several setbacks. One setback was the result of a controversy over the establishment in

Peking of an academy in which philosophical conferences might be held. This was a project initiated by two of the most venerable "good element" heroes, Tsou Yuan-piao and Feng Ts'ung-wu of Shensi, a one-time disciple of Ku Hsien-ch'eng, who, like Tsou, had lived in retirement for more than twenty years after offending Shen-tsung by forthright remonstrance.[86] In 1622 these two men, then censor-in-chief and vice-censor-in-chief, respectively, opened a Shou-shan Academy in the capital and summoned their friends to meetings there. Kao P'an-lung and many other Tung-lin men participated. But enemies soon denounced even the idea of having philosophical conferences in Peking and accused Tsou and Feng of aggravating partisan antagonisms, and both were permitted to retire.

B. THE RISE OF WEI CHUNG-HSIEN

Much more ominous, however, was the rise to power within the palace of the eunuch Wei Chung-hsien. Wei was a man of Chihli who, in middle life during the Wan-li era, castrated himself and was accepted into palace service. He became an intimate friend of Madame K'o, nursemaid of the child who eventually became Hsi-tsung. When Hsi-tsung took the throne in 1620, Madame K'o and Wei Chung-hsien were both granted various honors and proceeded to make themselves masters of the imperial household. They plotted against Wang An, Wei's one-time patron, and in 1621 succeeded in having him first degraded and then murdered. Thereafter Wei's influence predominated. The young emperor, who had an absorbing interest only in carpentry, gradually tired of the demands that government made on him and let Wei be his go-between with the Grand Secretariat, with less and less supervision. Not all these developments were immediately appreciated by the outer court, for at all times outsiders had difficulty in knowing exactly what was happening in the palace. But the Tung-lin partisans did not like what little they learned about palace goings-on.

Dealing with eunuchs had long been a recognized practice, and often an inescapable one, of officials during the Ming dynasty, as a means to save emperors from their irresponsible inclinations or, at very least, to maintain contact with emperors. The Tung-lin partisans had no misgivings about co-operating with Wang An. It has been suggested that efforts were later made to cultivate another eunuch as a rival to Wei Chung-hsien.[87] But dealing with Wei Chung-hsien himself was another matter. As later events proved beyond dispute, Wei represented evil. Confucian ideology could permit no other judgment. Wei's purpose was not to grease the wheels of government by encouraging an unstable emperor to do his duty but to isolate the emperor from his ministers and pursue Wei's own aggrandizement. The Tung-lin men would not compromise with him. As early as 1621 objections were made to the favor that Madame K'o enjoyed, with the result that at least three men were sent away from the capital in disgrace and many others were rebuked. As Wei's influence grew, objections became sharper, and Wei then sought to find allies in the outer court who might join him in silencing his critics. Since the Tung-lin group at this time was busily rooting out "rascals," willing helpers were not difficult for Wei to find among the opposition officials, and unwitting tools were also at hand in the persons of officials who found partisanship distasteful and sought neutrality.

The years 1622 and 1623 were uneasy years. Despite their grasp on key positions, the Tung-lin partisans were steadily being undermined by a multitude of complicated intrigues that linked Wei Chung-hsien to dissatisfied elements in the outer court. The crisis came in 1624, when Yang Lien submitted a long denunciation of Wei in which he itemized twenty-four great crimes. These crimes included usurping imperial authority, intriguing against upright ministers, manipulating civil service appointment procedures, murdering opponents within the palace, and, by forced abortion, preventing the empress from giving Hsi-tsung an heir.[88] When subsequently Yang was severely rebuked, some seventy-five supporting memorials were submitted. One memorialist, Wan Ching,[89] was beaten in court and died a few days afterward.

C. THE TUNG-LIN PARTY COMES TO DISASTER

At about the same time, one of Yeh Hsiang-kao's protégés, a censor, flogged a eunuch and then went into hiding to escape the punishment that he knew would inevitably result. Wei Chung-hsien sent a small army of eunuchs to surround Yeh's residence, where he suspected the protégé was concealed. In humiliation, Yeh submitted his resignation and went home. This was followed almost immediately by a great purge of Tung-lin men. Chao Nan-hsing, Kao P'an-lung, Yang Lien, and Tso Kuang-tou all departed in disgrace. Those whom they had suppressed and removed were promoted or recalled. Long lists of Tung-lin members were drawn up, beginning with Ku Hsien-ch'eng and Li San-ts'ai and including men who had been on the side of the Tung-lin group in any of the controversies that had started with that over "the root of the state." The lists were presented to Wei Chung-hsien to guide him in the purge. In all, more than seven hundred names were listed.[90]

One of the men responsible for the compilation of these lists was a Shensi man and an old Tung-lin enemy, Wang Shao-hui.[91] A supervising secretary during the first decade of the century, Wang had become one of the strongest supporters of T'ang Pin-yin and had attacked Li San-ts'ai and Wang T'u during the controversies of 1610–11. Transferred to a provincial post by Sun P'ei-yang, Wang retired on sick leave and did not return to the service until 1620. Then he was vigorously denounced, notably by Wei Ta-chung, a one-time disciple of Kao P'an-lung and a friend of Wang Wen-yen.[92] Wang Shao-hui was forced to go home on sick leave. After the purge of the Tung-lin men in 1624, he was recalled to replace Tso Kuang-tou as assistant censor-in-chief and compiled the most significant Tung-lin blacklist.

Not all the men who now became active partisans of Wei Chung-hsien, however, were long-standing enemies of the Tung-lin group. Wei Kuang-wei,[93] for example, was the son of an old-time anti-administration champion—Wei Yun-chen, who had been disgraced in the 1580's because of offending Shen Shih-hsing, had again been disgraced in 1593 for defending Chao Nan-hsing, subsequently as governor of Shansi had been an outstanding opponent of eunuch tax commissioners, and was a friend of Li San-ts'ai. Wei Kuang-wei was nevertheless one of the earliest civil service officials to seek Wei Chung-hsien's favor and in 1623 entered the Grand Secretariat as Wei's spokesman. Chao Nan-hsing despised and repeatedly snubbed him; and, when he supported Wei Chung-hsien's determination to punish Yang Lien in 1624, he was impeached by Wei Ta-chung and also by Li Ying-sheng, a second-generation disciple of Ku Hsien-ch'eng.[94] Wei Kuang-wei thereupon, like Wang Shao-hui, devoted himself to the preparation of Tung-lin blacklists.

Another leading antagonist of this period was Ts'ui Ch'eng-hsiu,[95] a Chihli fellow-provincial of Wei Kuang-wei. At the very beginning of Hsi-tsung's reign, apparently sensing that the Tung-lin group was coming to power and wishing to get in its good graces, Ts'ui recommended the recall to service of Li San-ts'ai. Ignored, he was sent out by the Censorate to be a provincial inspector on a one-year tour. On his return to the capital, Wei Ta-chung and Kao P'an-lung enumerated cases in which Ts'ui had engaged in blackmail while on censorial duty, and Chao Nan-hsing joined them in recommending that he be disgraced by being put into the frontier military service. Ts'ui was suspended pending thorough investigation. He begged mercy and aid from Li Ying-sheng but was rejected. Then he went to Wei Chung-hsien, pleaded for rescue, and pledged himself to be Wei's adopted son. Wei had him restored to duty, and Ts'ui also prepared a Tung-lin blacklist for Wei's guidance in personnel matters.

As the purge went on, Wei Chung-hsien and his adherents ceased to be satisfied with mere dismissals. Their victims were pursued with more and more accusations. Honors were posthumously stripped from those who had died. Those who had been dismissed were now erased from the rolls. Chao Nan-hsing and some others were sent to serve as common foot soldiers at the frontier. But even this was not enough. Wang Wen-yen was arrested, imprisoned, beaten in court, and dismissed; then he was again imprisoned, tortured in an attempt to extort evidence of corruption on the part of Yang Lien and Tso Kuang-tou, and finally put to death in prison.

Though Wang Wen-yen had not given the desired evidence, early in 1625 Wei Chung-hsien ordered the arrests of Yang Lien, Tso Kuang-tou, Wei Ta-chung, and three other Tung-lin men.[96] All were brought to Peking, thrown into prison, and tortured. One committed suicide. The others did not survive their tortures. In the following year more arrests were ordered. Kao P'an-lung, learning that his time had come, drowned himself in a pond at his home to avoid the disgrace of arrest. Seven other men, including Li Ying-sheng, died of torture in prison that year.[97]

Simultaneously Wei Chung-hsien ordered compilation of a great "white book," the *San-ch'ao Yao-tien*, which is an anti–Tung-lin report on the "three great cases" of 1615 and 1620; and the empire's private academies were ordered demolished.[98] For a time Kao P'an-lung's influence with local authorities saved some of the Tung-lin Academy buildings, but after his suicide all were torn down.[99]

By such ruthlessness and terrorism Wei Chung-hsien reduced the entire civil service to acquiescent submission. Some of the earlier neutrals, disturbed by the brutalities of 1625 and 1626, dropped out of the government after helping to deliver control to Wei. Even such leaders as Wei Kuang-wei and Wang Shao-hui had misgivings; Wei Kuang-wei retired under suspicion late in 1626. But less scrupulous associates were found. Henceforth all memorials offered to the palace necessarily included specious praise of the powerful eunuch, and provincial authorities competed with one another in erecting temples to his honor and offering sacrificial prayers for his long life. Titles and honors were heaped upon him and his forebears; his relatives were granted official posts, then honorific titles, then higher and higher grades of noble rank. It was even proposed that Wei Chung-hsien be ranked on a par with Confucius in ritual observances, and a unicorn (*ch'i-lin*), an omen always associated with the emergence of a great sage, was speciously reported to have appeared in Shantung. Imperial edicts drafted by the Grand Secretariat for the emperor's approval usually began: "I and the palace minister. . . ." Finally one of Wei's nephews even substituted for the emperor in performing sacrifices in the imperial temple. It would appear probable that at no time in Chinese imperial history were court politics and ethics more debased.

D. THE AFTERMATH OF THE PARTISAN DEBACLE

The all but eclipsed emperor suddenly died in the autumn of 1627. What saved China from the humiliation that would have resulted from seizure of the throne by a eunuch is not known. One of Hsi-tsung's brothers, subsequently known as Ssu-tsung, was enthroned; and gradually conditions became somewhat better. Ssu-tsung, himself only seventeen years old, apparently did not feel secure enough or bitter enough to order an immediate and wholesale purge. Only after several months of tense waiting, during which time former supporters warily submitted criticisms of Wei to test the new emperor's attitude, did Ssu-tsung at last banish the eunuch to live in exile outside the capital. There were no protests. Rather, those who had previously glorified him now rushed to join in denunciations of him in the obvious hope of exonerating themselves. Soon Wei's arrest was ordered, and he committed suicide. Madame K'o was beaten to death. Their most notorious henchmen were punished, and their victims, if still alive, were recommended and recalled.

Thereafter the court was disrupted by continuous bickering over the guilt or innocence of individuals who held office during Wei Chung-hsien's regime, and in 1629 a "Roster of Traitors" (*Ni-an*) was prepared and promulgated throughout the empire, fixing guilt upon some two hundred and fifty persons.[100] Twenty-five men, in addition to Wei and Madame K'o, were sentenced to death.

Ssu-tsung, however, had no intention of turning the government over to the remnants of the old-line Tung-lin group. He hoped that partisanship could be done away with entirely, and the name Tung-lin seems to have been almost as distasteful to him as was that of Wei Chung-hsien. Throughout his reign the court was kept in a constant turmoil by pretty animosities between groups that sought to pin partisan labels on one another—Tung-lin or otherwise, no matter—in efforts to arouse the emperor's indignation. Partisan bickering had become a habit.

Although men who could rightfully claim to be heirs of the old Tung-lin party were active in these years, the party as a definable group nevertheless seems clearly to have passed out of existence during its suppression by Wei Chung-hsien. In this paper, therefore, no attempt will be made to trace the infinitely complex political history of Ssu-tsung's reign.

6. Conclusion

In presenting the Tung-lin movement as essentially a moral crusade, I have concurred in the traditional judgment of Chinese historians, but I have not done so uncritically. As I shall attempt to demonstrate, the judgment is an inescapable one. And there is perhaps no better justification for study of the Tung-lin movement than the fact that it serves as a concrete illustration of the inseparable link between ethics and politics in the traditional Confucian system.

An understanding of what the Tung-lin movement was can be facilitated by a clarification of what it was not. One of the most striking aspects of the movement, to a modern analyst, is that it completely lacked a specific and coherent political program. There is no question here of controversies such as those in the Sung dynasty over the administrative reforms of Fan Chung-yen (989–1052), discussed elsewhere in this volume by James T. Liu, or over the "new laws" of Wang An-shih (1021–86). Although the late Ming controversies began as manifestations of institutional frictions, the Tung-lin group was not consistently anti-administration and cannot be characterized by advocacy of any institutional reforms. The partisans accepted the institutional status quo so unquestioningly that they cannot be meaningfully characterized even as an anti-eunuch party. And the great socioeconomic dislocations and military challenges of the time were involved in the court controversies only in a most peripheral manner. The only clear-cut issue of the whole series of controversies in which the "good elements" engaged was that concerning Wei Chung-hsien, and it was clearly a moral issue, not a political one.

Provincialism has been so influential in traditional Chinese relationships that one is inclined to suppose that regional alignments might explain the partisan cleavage dealt with here. It has already been noted that geographic considerations were of some significance in the heyday of the Shantung, Hukuang, and Chekiang parties. But that the whole Tung-lin movement was essentially one of regional alignments is clearly disproved. The two best-known Tung-lin black-lists[101] yield the names of 317 men who are identifiable by native places; and 213 names on the "Roster of Traitors" (i.e., Wei Chung-hsien and his associates, in large part the consistent opponents of the Tung-lin group) are similarly identifiable by native places. Table 1 shows the geographical distribution of these men, in comparison with the geographical distribution of late Ming registered population in general.[102] These figures reveal a substantial representation among

TABLE 1

GEOGRAPHICAL DISTRIBUTION OF MING POPULATION AND OF
CONTENDING PARTISANS

(Figures in Parentheses Indicate Percentages of the Respective Totals)

Area	Population (In Millions)	Tung-lin	Opposition
Southern Metropolitan Area (Kiangsu and Anhwei)	10.5 (17.4)	89 (28.0)	29 (13.6)
Kiangsi	5.8 (9.6)	37 (11.7)	8 (3.8)
Shantung	5.6 (9.4)	19 (6.0)	25 (11.7)
Shansi	5.3 (8.7)	29 (9.1)	8 (3.8)
Honan	5.2 (8.6)	15 (4.7)	17 (8.0)
Chekiang	5.1 (8.4)	25 (8.0)	30 (14.1)
Shensi	4.5 (7.4)	33 (10.4)	4 (1.9)
Hukuang	4.4 (7.3)	26 (8.2)	9 (4.2)
Chihli	4.2 (6.9)	11 (3.5)	50 (23.5)
Szechwan	3.1 (5.1)	4 (1.3)	9 (4.2)
Kwangtung	2.0 (3.3)	11 (3.5)	5 (2.3)
Fukien	1.7 (2.9)	16 (5.0)	16 (7.5)
Yunnan	1.5 (2.5)	2 (0.6)	2 (0.9)
Kwangsi	1.2 (2.0)	. . . .	. . . .
Kweichow	0.3 (0.5)	. . . .	1 (0.5)
Total	60.4	317	213

Tung-lin men for the Southern Metropolitan Area and Shensi and low representation for Chihli. Conversely, there is a substantial representation among opposition partisans for Chihli and Chekiang, whereas their representation in the Southern Metropolitan Area and in Shensi does not come up to the norm suggested by over-all population distribution. The figures support the expectation that the influence of the Tung-lin Academy was strongest in its own area and that the influence of Wei Chung-hsien was strongest in his native area; but they fail to suggest a dominant regional distribution pattern among the contending partisans.

Analysis of the partisans in terms of their governmental status is even less fruitful; there is no evidence that the controversies represented any kind of class struggle. The early anti-administration and pro-administration partisans were equally members of the civil service bureaucracy, and the leading antagonists on both sides were men who had entered the service through the highest-level civil service examinations, with status as *chin-shih*. During the struggles concerning Wei Chung-hsien, eunuchs naturally became more prominent. So did members of the military service, who could have been expected to resist Wei's domination less vigorously than their civil service counterparts because of their lack of Confucian training. But, even so, substantial samplings from the Tung-lin blacklists and the "Roster of Traitors" reveal no significant differentiation based on governmental status (Table 2).

TABLE 2

GOVERNMENTAL STATUS OF CONTENDING PARTISANS

Status	Tung-lin	Opposition
Civil service, entry via—		
Chin-shih.	140	167
Chü-jen.	8	13
National Academy matriculation...		5
Purchase.	2	
Heredity.		6
Hereditary nobility.	1	1
Military service.	1	31
Eunuchs.	1	8
Women.		1
Total samples.	153	232

Similarly frustrating is any attempt to base partisan alignments on rivalries between "old families" and "new families" in the government service. One source, the *Tung-lin T'ung-nan Lu*,[103] includes data about direct paternal ancestry through the great-grandfather for seventeen men who lost their lives in the anti–Wei Chung-hsien struggle. Four of the seventeen men were the sons of functioning officials. In two of these four cases, the fathers, grandfathers, and great-grandfathers were all officials. Among the ancestors of all seventeen men, however, there were only three *chin-shih*, and only two other men got as far as *chü-jen* status. Four of the seventeen men had no ancestors with official status of any kind, even as students in government schools (*chu-sheng*, roughly equivalent to the status of *hsiu-ts'ai* in other periods). Ku Hsien-ch'eng's family had lived in Wusih since Sung times, but it was not an "old family" in terms of government service. Among Ku's direct paternal ancestors for three generations, no member of the family had been in government service, and only the great-grandfather had earned official status as a student in the local government school.[104] Kao P'an-lung's background was different. Kao's grandfather had been a *chü-jen* and a district magistrate, and Kao's father had been a student in the National Academy.[105] Thus there is no consistent pattern in the data available: the Tung-lin party cannot be considered either an "old family" group or a "new family" group.

It must be admitted that a wholly satisfactory interpretation of the Tung-lin movement is impossible without extensive study of the anti–Tung-lin groups at court. But it is difficult to escape the bias that permeates Chinese writings about the controversies, which categorize the opposition officials as immoral rascals and give little meaningful information about them. Even local gazetteers as often as not display a contemptuous silence toward anti–Tung-lin men, however exalted may have been their official positions. It would be a mistake, of course, to assume that everyone who at any time antagonized the Tung-lin group was necessarily an immoral rascal. Yet Shen Shih-hsing, Wang Hsi-chueh, and Shen I-kuan were compromisers. Shen I-kuan, moreover, is generally believed to have accepted bribes. T'ang Yin-pin is said to have stolen wives from young scholars in his native district, and both T'ang and Wang Hsi-chueh apparently corrupted the civil service examination procedures. Fang Ts'ung-che was irresolute. And men who eagerly served Wei Chung-hsien would seem, of course, to have deprived themselves of all honor, at least in any Confucian sense. Thus in many cases the attitude of the Tung-lin men, and of Chinese historians generally, can be appreciated.

As regards the Tung-lin men, even to speak of them as a party at all, though convenient for narrative purposes, is to perpetuate a slander originated by their enemies. The activities of men such as Ku Hsien-ch'eng, Yü Yü-li, and Wang Wen-yen suggest a rudimentary kind of party work and a distinct group consciousness; Ku himself repeatedly spoke of "our party" (*wu tang*).[106] Yet the Tung-lin leaders vehemently denied partisan motives, and among the men who suffered at the hands of Wei Chung-hsien there had certainly been no unanimity regarding specific problems. Tso Kuang-tou and Yang Lien disagreed so violently during a controversy in 1620 that Tso cursed Yang and spat in his face.[107] Tsou Yuan-piao disapproved of Chao Nan-hsing's determinedly partisan attitude in the early 1620's, feeling that old grudges should best be forgotten.[108] Yeh Hsiang-kao even objected to attacks on Fang Ts'ung-che[109] and shared with Huang Tsun-su[110] (who was eventually put to death by the eunuch partisans) the view that Yang Lien's denunciation of Wei Chung-hsien was untimely and tactically unwise.[111] Huang himself was constantly at odds with those whose fate he came to share. He disapproved heartily of philosophical conferences and never attended one,[112] and he feuded with Wei Ta-chung.[113] Feng Ts'ung-wu, though a disciple of Ku Hsien-ch'eng, insisted that academies were no place for political discussions.[114] It is probable that many men whose names appear on Tung-lin blacklists had no group consciousness whatever, no sense of belonging to any political entity.

Despite this lack of party coherence, especially apparent among the large group of men who ultimately offended Wei Chung-hsien, the name Tung-lin seems to have stood for something. Thus in the early 1620's Chou Shun-ch'ang,[115] who later was put to death by Wei Chung-hsien, was chided by a friend: "You are a latecomer; why do you hasten to align yourself with the Tung-lin?" And what the name stood for is clearly implied in the response that Chou made on this occasion—that it was a matter of spontaneous congeniality, not calculated partisanship.[116] The final struggle, against Wei Chung-hsien, clearly manifested what was only dimly seen in the earlier controversies, though always implied by the participants: that the men known as Tung-lin partisans had a fundamental uniformity of moral views. Whether conscious partisans or not, they must have recognized one another as men of good will, men of honor, and gentlemen.

In sum, presently available information suggests that (1) from the time of Chang Chü-cheng to that of Wei Chung-hsien, political morality at the Ming court deteriorated almost steadily to a very low level; (2) religious-philosophical eclecticism and iconoclastic individualism, having developed out of the teachings of Wang Yang-ming, were popular during the same period; (3) leaders of the Tung-lin Academy, believing that the decay of morality at court resulted directly from these philosophical trends, championed more orthodox philosophical attitudes partly in an effort to restore traditional morality in politics; (4) men active in politics whom their enemies called the Tung-lin party were generally characterized by common respect for the old moral standards; and (5) in many individual cases the resulting sense of common purpose among these men was reinforced by geographical relationships, friendships, or master-disciple bonds, all tending to associate the political partisans, directly or indirectly, with the philosophical conferences at the Tung-lin Academy.

The Tung-lin men engaged in a struggle for power with no program other than to "throw the rascals out." What they wanted—and what they could not willingly stop short of attaining—was merely a way of government that would permit men of integrity to serve uprightly in the company of like-minded gentlemen. They assumed that all national problems could then be solved without difficulty. They seemed to feel that failure in the partisan struggle, or death, or even destruction of the state, would be preferable to the compromise of personal ethics which would have been involved in yielding to an irresponsible emperor or a vicious and immoral eunuch.

Their political movement was in fact a glorious failure. It failed at least in part because of a fundamental incompatibility between traditional Confucian morality, which demanded resoluteness and integrity, and the Ming power structure, which did not permit success, under such emperors as Shen-tsung and Hsi-tsung, to any but the unprincipled.

The Tung-lin men were perhaps quixotic, but they were true Confucians.

CHINESE DESPOTISM AND THE CONFUCIAN IDEAL
A SEVENTEENTH-CENTURY VIEW

W. T. DE BARY

1. Introduction

NOT TOO long ago despotism in China was apt to be viewed by Chinese and Westerners alike as a decrepit institution with a long and wearisome past but certainly no future. The old order was crumbling fast, and whatever arose from the ruins of China in the twentieth century could not help being radically new and different. Communism, especially, promised to make a clean break with China's discredited past, vociferously proclaiming its determination to rebuild on the most modern foundations. Yet those who have observed the raising-up of this structure in the first five years of Communist rule are more and more impressed by its similarity to the centralized bureaucratic structures and almost unlimited despotisms of the past. The questions have had to be reopened, therefore, as to how far China has surmounted certain deep-seated historical tendencies and how far past experience may bear upon the future of the dynasty which Mao Tse-tung has founded. In this light, not only does the new party dictatorship take on unexpected proportions, but the traditional institutions of China emerge from temporary obscurity with a renewed significance for world history, which calls for a re-examination of their most characteristic features.

It would be unfortunate, however, if, in focusing attention upon the persistent features of Chinese despotism, the impression were to be created that all of Chinese history and civilization bears the mark of unrelieved oppression and totalitarian control. This danger besets, especially, our attempts to characterize Chinese society in general terms, which may highlight only those segments of the traditional order that lie close to the center, contributing to our sense of its massive unity. An example of this is the expression "Confucian state," which brings out the close historical association between the leading intellectual tradition and the dominant bureaucracy but may also have the effect of identifying Confucianism with autocratic institutions it had little part in creating and, thus, of emphasizing its susceptibility to despotic control. Confucianism was indeed wholly committed to the responsibilities of political leadership, even in the most unpromising circumstances, and cannot hope to escape entirely the judgment of history upon the imperial institutions its adherents held so long in custody. But before we hasten to render such a judgment, it would be well to consider what Confucianism may have contributed to the softening and humanizing of Chinese despotism, through its continuing efforts to restrain the exercise of absolute power by moral suasion and to reform the governmental structure itself. Cynics may deprecate the effectiveness of moral suasion in politics and grant to Confucianism, which placed such reliance upon it, less credit than it probably deserves. Now that we find China stripped of any such moderating influence and see despotic power in all its naked savagery, we may be better able to appreciate by comparison how much this humane teaching and its more courageous spokesmen tempered the absolutism of traditional China.

This paper presents an outstanding example of Confucian political thought in later times, which sought not only to analyze existing evils but to set forth in bold terms a new order inspired by traditional ideals. It is based upon a study the author has made of the life and thought of Huang Tsung-hsi (1610–95) and upon an annotated translation of his *Ming-i Tai-fang Lu* (freely rendered by me as *A Plan for the Prince*). Here Huang's ideas are discussed only in general terms and with a minimum of documentation. Those interested in a fuller treatment of these ideas in the original, as well as in the sources for the accompanying commentary, are referred to the translation itself.[1]

Huang Tsung-hsi needs no introduction to sinologists, who know him already as an outstanding figure in the history of Chinese thought and scholarship. Nevertheless, for the nonsinologist a few remarks about Huang's life and work are called for here. He was the son of a high official of the Ming dynasty who died in prison, some eighteen years before the fall of the dynasty, because of his opposition to the powerful eunuch Wei Chung-hsien. Huang himself spent many years in study, mostly under an outstanding philosopher of the Wang Yang-ming school, before he became involved in politics at the close of the dynasty. As a staunch supporter of the Ming refugee regime active along the southeast coast of China, he participated in guerrilla resistance to the Manchus for many years and did not settle down to serious intellectual production until comparatively late in life. The *Ming-i Tai-fang Lu* was his first important work, written in 1662 at the age of fifty-two. Thereafter Huang turned from politics and political writing to history, literature, and philosophy, leaving many works of lasting importance, among which his surveys of Confucian philosophy in the Sung, Yuan, and Ming dynasties (the *Ming-ju Hsueh-an* and *Sung-yuan Hsueh-an*) are the most highly regarded. His reputation as a scholar was well established years before his death, and the Manchu regime attempted to enhance its own prestige by patronizing him, though he declined the honors thus conferred upon him. In the history of Chinese philosophy Huang is important not as an original thinker or as the founder of a new school but as one who combined the broad scholarship characteristic of the Chu Hsi school with the active interest in contemporary affairs shown by the best of the Wang Yang-ming school. Accordingly, though a competent classical scholar, he gave more attention to the study of the recent past than did most scholars of his time, whose interests were increasingly antiquarian. In this sense, *A Plan for the Prince* may be considered truly representative of his best work.

A. AIM OF HUANG TSUNG-HSI'S WORK

A literal translation of the Chinese title *Ming-i Tai-fang Lu* does not convey its real significance. *Ming-i* has multiple meanings. Ordinarily *i* signifies "peace and order," and therefore *ming-i*, literally, suggests that the theme of this book is "an exposition of [the principles of] good government." But *ming-i* also means "brightness obscured" or "intelligence repressed," and is the title of the thirty-sixth hexagram in the Confucian classic, *Book of Changes* (*I Ching*), originally a divination text which later attracted much metaphysical and cosmological speculation. The *Ming-i* hexagram was considered to represent a phase in the cosmic cycle, during which the forces of darkness prevailed but the virtuous preserved their integrity, hopefully waiting for the power of evil to wane. Traditionally this was thought to symbolize a wise and virtuous minister of state, forced by a weak and unsympathizing ruler to hide his own brilliance and remain upright in obscurity. Chi-tzu, a legendary figure of classical times, exemplified this during the last reign of the Shang dynasty. Imprisoned for protesting against the decadent ways of his king, Chi-tzu was freed after the conquest of the Shang by King Wu. He refused to serve under the latter, considering him a usurper, but, when King Wu visited him to ask his advice in ruling the country, the veteran statesman communicated the political principles contained in the "Great Plan," a section of the *Book of History*. Thus Chi-tzu's knowledge of the ancient ideal of government did not die with him but was preserved and put into practice during the glorious reign of King Wu.[2]

In his preface to this work, Huang describes himself as living in a period of darkness such as that represented by the *Ming-i* hexagram, and says that he has written down a "Great Plan" (*ta-fan*) of ideal government for the benefit of posterity. He refers to an earlier writer, Wang Mien, who had written such a work in the hope that, if he lived a while longer and by some good fortune met an enlightened prince, he could accomplish great things with this plan as a guide. Huang was a veteran of the Ming, living under its conquerors, just as Chi-tzu had been of the Shang, so he says, "Though I am old, it may be that I, like Chi-tzu, will be visited by a prince in search of counsel!" The *tai-fang* in the Chinese title, which means "to await a visit," thus refers again to the Chi-tzu parallel.

Huang's likening of himself to Chi-tzu in this way has given rise to some controversy over the author's real intentions. A friend of Ch'üan Tsu-wang, his biographer, once pointed out, after reading the *Ming-i Tai-fang Lu* with Ch'üan, that Huang had put himself in an ambiguous position by this comparison to Chi-tzu. The latter had had no choice but to respond to the request of King Wu for advice, but how could Huang, who remained loyal to the Ming after the Manchu conquest, actually cherish the hope that his counsel might be sought out by some—presumably Manchu—ruler? Much later the scholar Chang Ping-lin, who took issue with Huang on many points, seized upon this reference to Chi-tzu as evidence of Huang's questionable loyalty to the Ming, alleging that he secretly hoped for a "visit" from a Manchu ruler.[3]

Nevertheless there is good reason to doubt that *A Plan for the Prince* was written for the Manchus. When Ch'üan's friend first raised this question, he did so not in such a way as to cast doubt on Huang's loyalty but as an example of the kind of careless slip, or lack of precision in expressing himself, of which even a great scholar might occasionally be found guilty.[4] Ch'üan Tsu-wang acknowledged this at the time, yet plainly regarded it as casting no reflection on Huang's integrity, which he reaffirmed on the basis of Huang's subsequent admonition to Wan Ssu-t'ung against offering any advice of a political nature to the Manchu court[5] and which is again upheld in Ch'üan's postface to *A Plan for the Prince*. Moreover, the testimony of Ku Yen-wu, who had read Huang's work shortly after it was written and, though himself a staunch Ming loyalist, betrayed no doubts on this score in his letter to Huang concerning it, would seem to be adequate evidence that Huang's contemporaries did not interpret the reference to Chi-tzu as a collaborationist gesture.

Of less significance, perhaps, are certain internal evidences of the work. It is not to be expected that *A Plan for the Prince* would contain any outright declaration of hostility to the Manchus, which would have provoked immediate suppression of both the work and the author. There may indeed have been such passages in Huang's original manuscript, but, as Ch'üan Tsu-wang indicates in his colophon, portions of the work which might give offense never appeared in the published version and were eventually lost. Still, in the book as we have it, there are hints that the new order he envisioned would not come about under Manchu auspices. In discussing the best location for the imperial capital, for example, Huang argues in favor of Nanking rather than Peking, and in the light of the Chinese dynastic traditions a change in the site of the capital was of so momentous and radical a nature as to imply a change of dynasties.[6] Another hint of Huang's attitude is his failure to observe the taboo on use of the characters in the personal name of the reigning emperor, Hsuan-yeh,[7] when referring to the Han commentator Cheng Hsuan.[8]

In any case, it seems most likely that *A Plan for the Prince* was meant to preserve the political wisdom of the past, as Huang Tsung-hsi conceived it, for the benefit of some resurgent Chinese power in the future, and, as we shall see, this new order was to have little in common with dynastic rule of any sort, past or present.[9]

B. A CYCLE OF CATHAY

A Plan for the Prince was Huang's first important literary effort after he had abandoned active opposition to the Manchus. Considering his past involvement in this struggle and his father's prominence as a Ming official, there was one immediate problem which must have been very much in his mind when he wrote this book, as it was in the minds of other dejected Ming loyalists: What were the real reasons for the Ming defeat by the Manchus? Why did this native Chinese dynasty, which had overthrown the Mongol conquerors of China, succumb to another invasion by foreigners who were inferior numerically and—so they were regarded—culturally to the Chinese? Though Huang never specifies this as one of the central problems of his work, in discussing other matters he constantly reverts to it. One common explanation for the downfall of the Ming—that it was due to factionalism among the officials and meddling of the schools in politics—particularly exercises him, as is shown by his defense of the Tung-lin in the *Survey of Ming Confucian Philosophers* (*Ming-ju Hsueh-an*). But it is clear that, for a writer with as broad a historical perspective as Huang's, the search for an answer to this question would carry him beyond consideration of any single factor in the Ming decline and, indeed, beyond the historical limits of the Ming dynasty itself. Huang's era was not unique in history; such disasters had befallen the Chinese people before.

In the opening lines of his preface Huang muses upon a statement in the book of Mencius: "Periods of order alternate with periods of disorder." How is it, he asks, that since the time of the ancient sage-kings China has never known a period of peace and order but only an unending series of disorders? Following Mencius and prompted by early speculation on the meaning of the *Book of Changes*, Confucian philosophers had tended toward a cyclical interpretation of human history, which was seen as governed by the alternating phases of the cosmic forces Yin and Yang. Among the many earlier attempts to work out mathematically the significance of the *Book of Changes* for the future, Huang cites the theory of the fourteenth-century writer Hu Han, who at least took into account what seemed to Huang an obvious fact of Chinese history: so far the phase of decline had not yet given way to a more auspicious one. "Since the death of Confucius and throughout the dynasties succeeding the Chou—the Ch'in, Han, Chin, Sui, T'ang, Sung, and so on down for two thousand years —the time has not come for a change."[10] It was on the basis of Hu's prediction of a change at the end of this two-thousand-year period that Huang hoped for a Chinese resurgence in the near future. He hoped in vain, but his reasoning at least demonstrates how he approached an explanation of the Ming failure. It was just one in a long series of dynastic failures, all of which, he went on to show, could be explained in much the same terms.

"Whether there is peace or disorder in the word does not depend on the rise and fall of dynasties but upon the happiness or distress of the people."[11] Contrary to the accepted view of history, which identifies the interests of the people with those of the dynasty and regards dynastic disorders as a calamity for the people, Huang maintains that the rise and fall of ruling houses ever since the end of the Chou (third century B.C.) has brought no fundamental change in the condition of the Chinese people. Again and again he reiterates this view; Chinese civilization underwent its great crisis with the rise of the Ch'in Empire and has never recovered. At one point he indicates that there were two such catastrophes, the first having come with the Ch'in and the second with the Mongol conquest, but he does not elaborate on this point, and nothing he says elsewhere suggests that Mongol rule effected a radical or decisive change in Chinese society.

What Huang probably meant was only that the Mongol conquest gave impetus to a process of degeneration set in motion long before. In the course of history less and less had survived of traditions deriving from the ideal society of the distant past, and this steady deterioration, accelerated by the Mongol conquest, probably accounted for the fact that the Ming dynasty suffered from certain evils even more acutely than preceding dynasties. But so far as the basic character of dynastic institutions is concerned, Huang in each case traces their evil origins back to the Ch'in. The weaknesses of the Ming are common to all preceding dynasties, though in differing degree, and it is in this light that he analyzes them. "Unless we take a long range view and look deep into the heart of the matter, changing everything completely until the ancient order is restored with its land system, feudal system, educational and military systems, then, even though minor changes are made, there will never be an end to the misery of the common man."[12]

At this point Huang places himself in the long line of Neo-Confucianists, and particularly those of the early Sung, who saw a re-establishment of the institutions of the early sage-kings as the only solution for the problems of their time. Like them, he takes as his model the feudal order outlined by Mencius and presented in a neat, symmetrical fashion by the classical books of rites, especially the *Rites of Chou*. But, like his predecessors, he must reckon with the vast and profound changes which China has undergone in the intervening centuries and with conditions which seem to render any such wholesale reform impracticable. And he must reckon too with the failure of these earlier advocates to accomplish their purpose. It is no longer alone the failure of the Han and T'ang to attain the ancient ideal but that of the Sung itself, and later dynasties, which hangs oppressively over the landscape of history. Against the long line of Neo-Confucian idealists in the past are probably arrayed by now at least an equal number of skeptics, who declare that return to the classical order is out of the question.

It cannot be said that Huang squarely faces all the obstacles between him and his objective; like many idealists he is more convinced that all other measures have failed than he is prepared to demonstrate that the same difficulties will not stand in the way of his own program. Nevertheless, he is forced to answer the question which had confronted the Sung reformers: Should the ancient feudal order be re-established in every aspect and every detail, or should we merely adapt certain fundamental principles or values embodied in that order, so that the same ends are achieved through different means? Huang's answers are not always consistent, but for the most part he accepts the latter view. When dealing with the problem in its most general terms, he is apt to be carried away by the sweep of his own fervent and oracular rhetoric and to insist, as in the passage just quoted, upon a complete restoration of the early system of government. But when he takes up one by one the specific institutions involved, Huang recognizes immediately that many of the classical prescriptions are inapplicable to his own time. The result is that his "Great Plan" as a whole represents, not a duplication of the book of Mencius or the *Rites of Chou*, but a new system of government based on classical principles.

What, then, are the classical principles which Huang seeks to uphold? For him, as for any true Confucianist, the most fundamental principles are involved in the conception of rulership, since Confucianism asserts that the key to any and all forms of social improvement, as well as to all social evils, is the personal example and influence of the king.

2. The Classical Principles of Confucian Rule

A. PRINCE AND DESPOT[13]

In man's original state, Huang says, there were no rulers. Each man took care of himself and left others alone. It was essentially the kind of life early Taoists had imagined it to be but not, as they thought, an idyllic existence, since no one promoted the good of all.[14] The first rulers to appear were men who attempted to remedy this defect, seeking not their own good but the benefit of others. These sage-kings taught men the arts of civilization, saw to it that their people had sufficient land from which to gain sustenance and clothing, established customs and ceremonies which would regulate their social intercourse, maintained schools for their education and moral training, and instituted military service for the common defense. But this was a burdensome task, and few men could be expected to undertake it. Some indeed—the heroes of the Taoists—refused to undertake it only because it was too great a responsibility and not, as the Taoists would have it, because government meant needless interference in the lives of others. This being the case, even those who accepted the office of ruler, like the emperors Yao and Shun, were eager to relinquish it to some worthy successor and had no desire to impose such a burden on their own sons.

Such, in essence, was the concept of rulership in ancient times. In later times, however, and especially with the rise of the Ch'in and Han dynasties, rulership was regarded as a great prize, not as a heavy responsibility. The emperor had no desire to serve others or to share with them, and therefore he abolished the feudal system, which to Huang had represented the natural means of sharing political leadership and property with others, as well as the most effective means of providing for the needs of others through the personal attention of the individual lord to the welfare of his people. With the abolition of feudalism all land was brought under the direct tax control of the emperor, so that he could exploit it for his own ends, through a new system of centrally administered provinces and prefectures. Thenceforth the ruler's only concern was to keep this vast personal estate intact and prevent it from falling into the hands of others than his own heirs.

The new relationship between ruler and ruled Huang likened to that between host and guest. In ancient times the people had been the hosts, the proprietors of the land, while the ruler was merely a guest on good behavior. Since the rise of the great empires, however, the ruler had become the host and the people the guests, possessing nothing in their own right. From what Huang tells us of this relationship, the analogy of master and servant or lord and tenant would seem to convey his meaning better than host and guest. In China as elsewhere the host is thought of as under an obligation to entertain and provide for his guests, in which sense it would apply exactly in reverse to the conditions Huang describes. In spite of this, his characterization of ruler and ruled as host and guest is what Huang has become most famous for, and later writers often cite it as the epitome of his political thought.

As a concept it is not at all new to the Confucian tradition. Mencius had said: "The people are the most important element in the nation; the spirits of the land and grain are next; the Prince is the last."[15] Hsün-tzu, the other great exponent of Confucius' teaching in classical times, had used an equally vivid and far more apt analogy than Huang Tsung-hsi: "When the people are satisfied with his government, then only is a prince secure in his position. It is said: 'The Prince is the boat, the common people are the water. The water can support the boat or the water can capsize the boat'—this expresses my meaning."[16] Therefore, if Huang had done no more than reiterate the primacy of the people and the consent of the governed as essential to successful rule, there would be little to recommend his work to the reader. His real contribution to Confucian thought lies in the application of this basic principle to political institutions which had undergone substantial changes since the time of Mencius and Hsün-tzu.

B. LAW

The rise of despotism in the Ch'in and Han dynasties represented the triumph of Legalism, a political philosophy abhorrent to Confucianists. This school of thought, whose exponents engineered the conquest and unification of China by the Ch'in, stressed the need for uniform law and its strict enforcement through heavy penalties. Law in this form expressed the will of an emperor ruling with absolute powers. Its purpose was to standardize the administration of the country, integrate the activities of the people, and organize all resources under the state. Whereas the Confucian ideal had been a decentralized feudal society, in which the unifying and regulating principle was the personal, moral influence of its rulers, the essence of this new order was its impersonality and its frank reliance on coercion. For this reason Confucianists traditionally held a strong antipathy for law, holding it responsible for all the excesses of the Ch'in regime and therefore merely an instrument of tyrannical rule. From their point of view, the fewer the laws, the better, since ultimately the successful execution of laws and policies depended on the moral authority of the ruler and his officials.

Huang Tsung-hsi joins earlier Confucianists in condemning the aims and methods of Ch'in rule, which he sees as perpetuated in substance by all subsequent dynasties. But he refuses to accept the traditional view that there is a basic antithesis between rule by law and rule by man. The law of the imperial dynasties is not true law but simply a mass of laws enacted for the benefit of the ruling house. True law was enacted for the benefit of the people by the sage-kings and is embodied in the system of government laid down in the classics. It consists not in multitudinous statutes, prescribing in detail what men should do and attaching a severe penalty to each infraction, but rather in a very simple and general set of institutions which are basic to proper functioning of government and to promotion of the general welfare.

Huang's recognition of the fundamental importance of law differentiates him from most Confucianists and is of far-reaching consequence to his political philosophy as a whole. Men of his school, whether in recent times they had followed Chu Hsi or Wang Yang-ming, had usually treated politics as if it involved no more than adherence to certain moral principles and cultivation of the Confucian virtues by the ruler and his officials. The laws and institutions of a dynasty were largely determined by its founder and regarded as unchangeable. All that remained was to insure proper administration of the established law through sound education of the emperor and selection of upright officials.[17] Huang, however, insists that dynastic law is not inviolate. Spreading further and further as morbid fears for its own security drive a dynasty to tie tighter the hands of its people and circumscribe further the powers of its officials, the complex net of laws serves only as a refuge for incompetents and clever scoundrels, while able men are deprived by it of any freedom of action. " 'Unlawful' laws fetter men hand and foot, and even a man capable of governing well cannot overcome the handicaps of senseless restraint and suspicion." Before men can govern well, Huang says, there must be laws which govern well.

Thus he resolves the false dilemma with which Confucianists had confronted themselves for centuries. The choice is not between men and laws but between true law and the unlawful restrictions of the ruler. In place of the existing mass of regulations and punishments a few basic laws must be established. These he conceives as more in the nature of a constitution or system of government than a legal code; they are laws which, serving the interests of the people and conforming to the moral law, can be maintained without resort to force, supplementary legislation, or endless litigation. To define the nature of these institutions is the purpose of *A Plan for the Prince.*

C. MINISTERSHIP

One Legalist concept which took hold and persisted at the imperial court long after Legalism itself died out was its view of ministership. Since this philosophy stressed the absolute supremacy of the ruler, it sought to deprive his ministers of any real authority which might limit the power of the throne. Officials were mere servants, to be rewarded or punished according to their usefulness to the emperor. One of the early Legalist philosophers, Han Fei-tzu, had put it: "If the ruler does not share the supreme authority with his ministers, the people will regard this as a great blessing." And, again, he advises the ruler, "Search the bosoms of ministers and take away their powers. The sovereign should exercise such powers himself with the speed of lightning and the majesty of thunder."[18]

What disturbs Huang is that in later times, not only does the ruler adopt this view, but his officials acquiesce in it. Instead of recognizing that they are colleagues of the emperor, sharing power with him in order that they may together with him serve the interests of the people, their only thought is to please him and, like courtesans, attempt to anticipate his every desire. They accept the fact that they, like all else in the land, are the Prince's property, to be disposed of as he pleases. And they take the lead in deifying the emperor, calling him their "Heavenly Father" and showing him the same filial devotion owed to one's own father. Thus they have been unable to provide the Prince with what he needs most: companionship and counsel. "The terms 'Prince' and 'Minister' derive their significance from service to all men. If I have no sense of duty to all men, I am an alien to the Prince. . . . If I do have the interests of all men at heart, then I am the Prince's mentor and colleague."[19]

Huang Tsung-hsi does not envision any general return to the feudal order, which would break up the empire into individual domains and distribute power among numerous autonomous rulers. But in the centralized state he does wish to maintain the same balance or distribution of power characteristic of feudal society. In this his aims are similar to those of Mencius, who regarded the minister or official as having status in his own right and entitled to a measure of respect from the emperor. He cites Mencius' account of the gradations of power in the Chou kingdom: there was an ordered hierarchy of rank descending from the Prince down through his officials at court and from the Prince down through the feudal nobility in outlying domains. In Huang's time no one had rank or dignity but the emperor, and, unless some attempt were made to approximate the feudal ideal of graduated authority, there would never be any curb on the Prince's abuse of his powers.

There can be no doubt that this question had become an especially serious one for the Ming dynasty. Not only had it inherited court traditions of long standing which compelled the minister utterly to abase himself before the throne, but it had developed more and more vicious practices for the degradation and intimidation of officials with any independence of mind. One practice which illustrates this trend is the chastising of ministers at court. In earlier years the flogging of officials was more a formality, intended only to humiliate the offender publicly, than a real corporal punishment. Before the dynasty was a century old, however, flogging had increased so in severity that on one occasion when thirty-five ministers were beaten en masse, though they wore heavy padding under their clothes for protection, many spent months in bed before they recovered. In the period styled, ironically enough, "True Virtue" (*Cheng-te*, 1506–22), for the first time officials were flogged naked. In the last year of that reign those who admonished the emperor against continuing his pleasure-seeking excursions to the south were beaten so unmercifully that many died.[20] Under such circumstances even the ablest of ministers could not be expected to act effectively in the people's interest.

D. THE OFFICE OF PRIME MINISTER

The attitude of Ming rulers toward their ministers was demonstrated very early in the dynasty, when its founder abolished the office of prime minister. At that time the official holding this position was found guilty of plotting against the throne and executed. To prevent anyone in the future from gaining such dominance in the government that he could seize the throne, Emperor Hung-wu decided to exercise the functions of the prime minister himself and deal directly with the various ministers in charge of the chief agencies of administration. In this decision Huang Tsung-hsi saw the origin of misgovernment in the Ming.

The office of prime minister was essential for three reasons. First, it gave recognition to the principle that ruling power was not to be held by the emperor alone but was to be shared with others, who themselves enjoyed a status of no mean degree. Second, with the adoption of hereditary succession to the throne by the imperial dynasties, the principle of succession according to personal merit, which had been observed by the sage-kings, was abandoned. Thereafter, the only check on an incompetent heir to the throne was the prime minister, whose selection was still based on merit. Third, ruling the empire and directing the government was such a burdensome job that the emperor could not possibly discharge this function alone. Failure to appoint a prime minister did not mean that his duties could be dispensed with but only that they fell to others by default, who discharged them in an irregular manner.

In the Ming the functions of the prime minister gradually came to be performed by an inner cabinet of close advisers to the emperor, a development rendered inevitable by the ruler's inability to cope with the burden of executive responsibilities. But from Huang Tsung-hsi's point of view the cabinet was no substitute for a prime minister. Since no single official had the authority to take positive leadership, power quickly fell into the hands of others close to the emperor with no official qualifications whatever—the eunuchs. To remedy this, Huang would have the office of prime minister restored, so that authority and responsibility would be fixed in a single executive. He should take a leading role in the discussion of state business with the emperor and, if necessary, should formulate policy decisions in writing for the emperor. To assist him in these duties he should set up his own administrative offices, which would facilitate a co-ordination of the regular Six Boards or Ministries and insure that all memorials submitted by the people received consideration, so that free discussion of political questions would be encouraged.

This recommendation is in sharp contrast to the general tendency of *A Plan for the Prince*. On the whole, Huang favors decentralized government and drastic limitations of the powers of the state bureaucracy. But he admits the need for positive leadership, which the emperor alone cannot give, and within the bureaucracy itself he advocates a stronger, more definite concentration of authority in the prime minister than had ever been granted in Chinese history.

E. EUNUCHS

Though Huang Tsung-hsi leaves until last his discussion of eunuchs in the imperial court, as if to indicate what their relative importance should be in the ideal order, again and again in his book eunuchs are singled out as responsible for many of the worst evils in the Ming dynasty, as well as in previous dynasties. "Throughout the Han, T'ang and Sung dynasties there was an endless series of disasters brought on by eunuchs, but none so frightful as those of the Ming. During the Han, T'ang and Sung there were eunuchs who interfered with the government, but no government which did whatever the eunuchs ordered [as in the Ming]."[21]

Among the several reasons given by Huang for the extraordinary power of eunuchs at court, the most basic is the emperor's inordinate lust for women. If the imperial harem were not so large, obviously there would be less need for eunuchs to attend them and therefore eunuchs would not be numerous enough to constitute a problem. But akin to the lust for women is the ruler's lust for personal power. This had led him to separate the management of his household from the regular civil administration, so that he need not be embarrassed by the intervention of state ministers desirous of curbing wastefulness and debauchery. Left to their own devices, however, eunuchs in the Ming had proceeded to encroach on the powers of the state administration. Behind the scenes they exerted a dominant influence on the emperor, now overburdened with the duties once performed by the prime minister, and because of the complex procedures involved in the drafting of state papers, they were able to intrude their own demands at crucial stages in the process. From this point of vantage they set up organs of administration paralleling those of the civil bureaucracy, gaining control over a large portion of the imperial revenues, over mining and a host of monopolies which nominally provisioned the palace but actually operated on a much wider scale, over the administration of justice through their own secret service and prison system, and finally over the army itself. Their most potent weapon in accomplishing all this, Huang says, was the argument that the wealth of the empire is the Prince's private possession and should be under direct control of the imperial palace. Convincing the emperor that they, rather than the state officials, had his personal interests at heart, and encouraged by the timid servility of civil officials themselves, the eunuchs gained for themselves the powers which should have been exercised by ministers of state, while the latter became virtual palace menials.

One proposal which had been advanced for the curbing of eunuchs was that they should be returned to the control of the state administration by placing them under the prime minister.[22] But Huang considers this inadequate and perhaps dangerous. Palace eunuchs were drawn, he says, from among criminals punished by castration, and they were too vicious and unscrupulous a lot to be restrained by this means. Indeed, because of their numbers and intimacy with members of the imperial family, they would soon dominate the prime minister himself. The only solution, therefore, was drastically to reduce the number of eunuchs, and this could not be done unless the emperor reduced the number of his wives. For those who object that this would limit the number of imperial offspring as well, and seriously endanger the dynastic succession, Huang points to the fate of the last emperor of the Northern Sung, whose many sons "served only as so much mincemeat" for their conquerors.

F. SCHOOL AND STATE

In China traditionally the state had put a high value on scholarship, and paradoxically the schools had suffered for it. Since scholarship was the primary qualification for office, schools were highly important in the training of a select number of students from among whom public servants were recruited, but they rarely served any other function. In spite of the fact that state-supported schools were maintained in the capital and the principal seats of provincial administration, their sole object was to prepare those who passed the district examinations for higher degrees leading to eventual employment in the bureaucracy, while an overwhelming majority of the people went uneducated. Except for the select number who gained admission to official schools and the Imperial Academy, instruction could be obtained only from private tutors whom few could afford. Thus the state's interest in scholarship did not have the effect of developing any general system of education.

But even without such universal education or a public school system, the state in China achieved a degree of control over education and thought comparable to that achieved by modern states through their centralized public schools. This was because virtually all education in China, whether public or private, was oriented toward the civil service examinations. These were the gateway to success in government and, in a society so dominated by state power, the main road to wealth and influence. The government did not need to maintain schools with a curriculum and texts of its own choosing. Simply by prescribing what was to be called for in the examinations, it could determine what most aspiring students would find it in their own interest to learn.

Against this background we can appreciate why Huang attached such great importance to educational reform. He wishes to remedy both these defects in traditional education by creating a universal public school system with functions much broader than the mere training of officials. In classical times, he attempts to show, schools were centers of all important community and state activities; they had a major role, too, in debating public questions and advising the Prince. Ideally, then, schools should serve the people in two ways: providing an education for all and acting as organs for the expression of public opinion. Likewise the Prince had two corresponding obligations: to maintain schools for the benefit of all and to give the people a voice in government through the schools. In ancient times "the emperor did not dare to determine right and wrong for himself, so he left to the schools the determination of right and wrong." But since the rise of the Ch'in, "right and wrong have been determined entirely by the court. If the emperor favored such and such, everyone hastened to think it right; if he frowned upon such and such, everyone condemned it as wrong."[23]

This argument is suggestive again of Confucian antipathy for Legalist doctrines which had been absorbed into the absolutist dogma of subsequent dynasties. Han Fei-tzu had said: "Whatever he [the ruler] considers good is regarded as good by the officials and people. Whatever he never considers good is not regarded as good by the officials and the people."[24] The Legalist statesman, Li Ssu, who was chiefly responsible for organizing the Ch'in empire, asserted the same principle in suppressing free speech:

> At present your Majesty possesses a unified empire and has laid down distinctions of right and wrong, consolidating for himself a single position of eminence. Yet there are those who . . . teach what is not according to the laws. When they hear orders promulgated, they criticize them in the light of their own teachings. . . . To cast disrepute on their ruler they regard as a thing worthy of fame; to hold different views they regard as high conduct. . . . If such conditions are not prohibited, the imperial power will decline. . . .[25]

According to Huang, the prevalence of this view, that the Prince determines what is right and wrong, deprived the schools of their most important function and created an unnatural separation between school and state. Thereafter the schools could not even fulfil the functions remaining to them of training scholars for office, because the true aims of education were lost sight of in the mad scramble for advancement and the desperate endeavor to conform. Thinking men, in their search for true education, turned more and more to the private academies which had become centers of Neo-Confucian thought in the Sung and Ming dynasties. But the independence and heterodox views of these academies brought repeated attempts at suppression by the state. Thus the arbitrary separation of school and state ended in open conflict between them, detrimental to the true interests of both.

Though Huang defends the private academies, which had been so much blamed for the political failure of the Ming, his real purpose is not to assert the need for independent private schools. These are of value only in the absence of true public education, which, according to the Confucian ideal, it is the duty of a ruler to provide. Instead he advocates a system of universal public education, maintained by the state but free of all centralized control. There are to be schools from the capital down through every city and town to even the smallest hamlets, but on each level supervision is to be independent of control from above. The principal units of administration, the prefectures and districts, will be presided over by superintendents of education chosen locally, not appointed by the court. These men need never have served as officials before or qualified for civil service. Not only should they have complete freedom in ordinary educational matters, including the right to override the provincial commissioner of education in the appointment of licentiates (those who have achieved the first degree in the prefectural examinations), but their pronouncements on any matter affecting the community should be listened to respectfully by the local magistrates. Similarly, at the capital the libationer (or chancellor) of the Imperial Academy should lecture each month on important questions, with the emperor and his ministers attending in the role of students. In addition, the local superintendent is to have wide authority over other aspects of community life—public ceremonies, family ritual observances, censorship over publications, and public entertainment. "If in any locality there are unorthodox sacrifices, or if unauthorized clothing is being worn, or if useless things are sold in the market place, or if the dead lie unburied on the ground, or if the actors' songs fill men's ears and the streets are full of vile talk, then the superintendent of education is not performing his job properly."[26]

These last stipulations are a reminder that the system Huang proposes, though it stresses decentralization and a kind of academic freedom, is nonetheless essentially authoritarian. The problem for Huang, as it must be for any true Confucian, is to place authority in the hands of those best qualified to exercise it, not to encourage unlimited freedom of expression or to make diversity of opinion an end in itself. In the final analysis, he is convinced that the interests and wishes of the people coincide with certain basic values that must be upheld. It is therefore quite possible for him to deny to nonpublic institutions he considers inimical to society the same freedom allowed public schools. Monks and nuns are to be secularized, and church lands expropriated so that the income from them may be used for the support of poor students.[27]

G. THE CIVIL SERVICE SYSTEM

Huang's views on the nature of education are more fully brought out in his essays on the selection of officials through the civil service examinations. It would be difficult to exaggerate the importance of this system, which had been the chief means of recruiting China's ruling class for centuries, and Huang, though he deplores the effect on education of too exclusive a concern with the preparing of candidates for the civil service, nevertheless recognizes what a vital role these examinations play in determining the make-up and outlook of those entrusted with the administration of the empire. The political failure of the Ming dynasty, he feels, is attributable in no small measure to the weaknesses of its civil service system. Indeed, this is one respect in which he finds Ming institutions subject to abuses even more extreme than in previous dynasties.

Huang's criticisms of the Ming system may be summarized under three main points. First, he believes that entrance to the civil service was restricted to only a few, whose qualifications were determined on too narrow a basis. On the other hand, once they had gained admittance, these officials were advanced far too rapidly and placed in posts of great responsibility before they had proved their ability or acquired sufficient experience as administrators. This procedure contrasted with the ancient method outlined in the *Book of Rites* (*Li-chi*), which was very liberal in admitting young men of talent to government service but strictly regulated their promotion by testing their capabilities while in office. Even in the Han, T'ang, and Sung dynasties, the ancient ideal was more closely approximated than in the Ming, and advancement was much slower. Therefore, in the system he proposed, Huang would have junior officials serve a sort of internship and be required to pass three successive fitness tests before being assigned to posts as local magistrates.[28]

Huang's second point concerns the content of the examinations and is related to the first. One of the principal limitations on the selection of candidates was the fact that civil service examinations in the Ming were devoted exclusively to the classics, particularly the *Four Books*. This meant that men who knew nothing else of value might gain admission to the official class through their knowledge of the classics, while men who had great talents in other fields would have no way to demonstrate them. Huang's remedy for this situation is twofold. He would greatly enlarge the scope of the regular examinations (i.e., the provincial examinations for the *chü-jen* degree and the metropolitan examinations held at the capital for the *chin-shih* degree) by adding three other subjects to the classics. These subjects were to embrace the more important philosophic writings, including the works of Hsün-tzu, which had not been dignified, like the book of Mencius, by inclusion in the *Four Books;* the more prominent Han, T'ang, and Sung philosophers; and even the heretical Taoist works, *Lao-tzu* and *Chuang-tzu.* Another subject would cover the classical historical writings, the voluminous dynastic histories up to the Sung, and the detailed court records of the Ming—truly a formidable array of literature! The last subject in the examinations was to be concerned with contemporary problems, which, like some of the above topics, had been a part of earlier examinations in the T'ang and Sung dynasties. Ironically enough, these recommendations, which are so much in contrast to the narrow range of the Ming examinations, follow in the main those proposed by the great Chu Hsi, whose commentaries on the classics were adopted as definitive by the Ming while his views on the content of the examinations were totally ignored.

Another method proposed by Huang for de-emphasizing knowledge of the classics as a qualification for office is to provide alternatives to the regular examination system, based on other criteria of selection. Among these, he suggests a system of special recommendations, whereby each prefecture would select a man to be examined personally by the prime minister to determine his fitness for office. A second method is for the provincial and district schools to send their best students to the Imperial Academy, where they would be examined and, upon graduation, be given posts on the same basis as graduates of the metropolitan examinations. Special consideration should also be shown to the sons of high officials in gaining entrance to official schools and the Imperial Academy, but they should be subject to the same examinations and advancement procedures as other students, so that incompetent ones would not be placed in positions of power through favoritism. Furthermore, promising young men are to be given minor posts in the prefectures and districts, and, after successive examinations, those qualified should be sent to the Imperial Academy or assigned to posts at the capital. A similar system is to be set up for interns serving by temporary appointment under the prime minister, the Six Boards, the military commanderies, and the provincial governors. If their performance in different posts shows them to be of high caliber, their temporary appointments are to be confirmed and made official. In addition to these types of selection based on administrative ability, men with special knowledge of certain branches of learning are to be sent to court for examination and appointment to the Imperial (Hanlin) Academy. Those who present memorials or books of special value to the throne also should be rewarded with official posts. Through all these different means Huang hopes to secure civil servants of varied talents or proved competence in office, and in most cases he specifies that they be further tested after taking office. From his insistence that the prime minister and others charged with actual administrative responsibility should be free to select, appoint, and promote their own subordinates, it is also apparent that he wants these officials to obtain assistants who they know are qualified for a particular assignment rather than be at the mercy of a Civil Service Board so impersonal in its operations that it cannot give adequate consideration to special needs. This is one more evidence of his concern to avoid bureaucratic centralization and to strengthen the hands of responsible officials.

Huang's third major criticism of the Ming civil service system has to do with the form in which the examinations were given, as represented by the famous "eight-legged" essays. That this aspect of the selection system was perhaps the most important to him is indicated by his treating it first and by his lengthy discussion of its historical origins in pre-Ming times. This is one case in which Huang makes us well aware that he is dealing with a question which has been the center of political and intellectual controversy for centuries. It has already been shown that reform of the examination system, in order to place greater emphasis on an understanding of the classics, was one of the chief aims of the early Neo-Confucian leaders in the Sung dynasty.[29] Huang's discussion of the problem focuses on the most ambitious attempt in the Sung to make this ideal a reality: the examinations instituted by Wang An-shih on the "general sense" of the classics.

Before Wang's time the examinations for the prized *chin-shih* degree had placed the greatest stress on skill in the composition of prose and poetry, while the examinations dealing with the classics were in disrepute. The reason for this was that in the T'ang dynasty, which instituted the types of examinations inherited by the Sung, the tests for the classics degree (*ming-ching*) had degenerated into a mere exercise in memorization of the classics and their commentaries and, therefore, were not considered as much of a demonstration of the candidate's intellectual attainments as the *chin-shih* examination. Wang An-shih (and others before him in the late T'ang and Sung, as Huang is careful to point out) wished to restore the classics to their rightful importance, and also to dispense with memorization of these texts and the commentaries, by requiring instead that the candidates show an understanding of the general purport of the classics. Wang therefore revised the *chin-shih* examination along these lines, but in doing so he found it necessary for the efficient and impartial administration of this vast examination system to introduce a large measure of standardization. His problem, which was a perennial one in the history of the Chinese examinations, is similar to the problem of American college instructors today in using objective-type and essay-type questions on examinations. The old classics examination was of the objective type, consisting mainly of completion-questions which required the candidate to finish a quotation or fill in specific details from the texts cited. Here only a precise answer would suffice, not an interpretive one, and consequently the student was forced to memorize texts. But if this approach were abandoned and interpretive essay questions adopted, the problem immediately arose in judging the answers of such a large number of candidates: "What form of essay and what interpretation of the classics is to be considered acceptable?" It was easy enough to dispense with the standard commentaries, but only if some other authoritative interpretation of the classics were set up as a criterion for judgment. Wang An-shih settled this by prescribing both the form of the essay and his own interpretation of the classics, which were disseminated for the guidance of all candidates.

In the Ming dynasty essentially the same procedure was followed. The commentaries of Chu Hsi were established as the authoritative interpretation, and the "eight-legged" essay was prescribed as the form to be followed. The result of this was that candidates did not bother to study any of the other commentators on the classics, and, since the essay form was so stereotyped, they took to memorizing the essays of previous successful candidates or of acknowledged experts in the "eight-legged" essay form. According to Huang's analysis, the effect of the existing type of examination was thus to exacerbate the evils it had originally been intended to reform.

Huang's solution for this dilemma reflects his basic philosophical position and his lifelong approach to classical scholarship. Just as in other works he advocates broad learning and exhaustive study of all sources, seeking to correct the widespread anti-intellectualism of the Ming, so in the examinations he considers it essential for the candidate to show a familiarity with all the important commentaries on the classics. It is better to memorize these, if need be, than stereotyped "eight-legged" essays. And just as he stresses in general the need for integrating one's knowledge and experience to make it truly one's own, so he specifies in this case that the candidate should offer his own interpretation of a question after he has noted the views of other authorities. By employing this method, Huang would have candidates master both the letter and the spirit of the classics, and, by extending the examination system to include other subjects of practical value to an administrator, he would secure officials who are men of ability as well as men of character.

H. PETTY BUREAUCRACY

Men of character and ability—this was the ideal of the Confucian scholar-official, who alone could be entrusted with political power.

Yet in the Ming dynasty, Huang tells us, the functions which should have been reserved to men of this class were increasingly usurped by a new type of petty bureaucrat. For this development Wang An-shih was again largely responsible. During his regime in the Sung dynasty, Wang had abolished the system by which many minor governmental functions, particularly on the local level, had been performed by drafting the services of persons in the locality, supposedly on a rotating basis to distribute the burden. These functions include such duties as those of tax collectors, custodians of official property, policemen, messengers, porters, and the like. For various reasons the most burdensome duties, or those involving the greatest financial liability, came to be borne by those who could least afford to meet the expense or labor involved. To remedy this, Wang put these services on a paid basis, the expense of which was met by a money-tax graduated to put the greatest burden on rich landlords and merchants. Though abandoned by Ssu-ma Kuang, this system was later restored and kept in modified form by the Ming dynasty.

According to Huang, once these minor functionaries obtained permanent, paid positions, they tended to become a class by themselves with vested interests and considerable power over the ordinary business of government. Those most successful even obtained positions on higher levels of administration which should have been reserved for regular civil officials. Many succeeded in making their jobs a family possession, turning them over to their sons when they retired. On the local level they were able, through their identification with the state bureaucracy, to oppress the people with impunity. In the agencies of provincial and central administration they became masters of bureaucratic red-tape and legalistic procedure, though actually they had little or no education to qualify them for the exercise of such power.

Huang would eliminate this class entirely by restoring the system of draft services at the local level and by placing true civil officials in the more important posts these subofficials had usurped. In effect, he would incorporate the miscellaneous draft services into the regular *li-chia* (or *pao-chia*) system, whereby they would be rotated regularly among the households of a locality. He believes that the local citizenry, particularly the responsible leaders of each 100-family unit, will refrain from oppressing their neighbors, as the petty bureaucrats do, because they themselves may suffer in turn when their neighbors take over the same posts. The people of a locality trust one of their own number as they never could an outsider who is a hireling of the state. The higher positions of fixed responsibility, whether at court or in the provinces, he would assign to graduates of the regular civil service system or men obtained through the other methods of selection he proposes. This fits in with his plan to make officials serve internships in subordinate positions before being placed in more important posts. It would also strip the Civil Service Board, which had been the bulwark of the petty bureaucracy, of its appointive powers over these numerous minor offices and thus serve his over-all aim of strengthening the position of responsible officials by allowing them to select and control their own assistants.

I. LAND REFORM

1. *Relation of land tenure to taxation.*—Perhaps nothing was of such vital concern to both the government and the people of China as the land tax, which for centuries had provided the state bureaucracy with its life's blood in revenue and, in doing so, had often deprived the peasantry of the life-sustaining fruits of their own labor. For this very reason it was also a matter of concern to Huang's Neo-Confucian predecessors, who generally regarded oppressive land taxes as just one more manifestation of the failure of later dynasties to rule according to the precepts of the sage-kings. But one such predecessor in the Sung, Su Hsün, upon examining this question concluded that tax rates in later times actually compared favorably with those of the classical age, and that the real difficulty of the peasants arose from their having to pay high rents along with land taxes, which had not been the case before the abolition of feudalism by the Ch'in. Huang's conclusion is substantially the same, but he takes issue with Su at many points along the line of his argument and is especially at pains to show why the tax rates of later times were not really as low as they might appear to be.[30]

During the Han dynasty (202 B.C.–A.D. 220) the land tax in grain had been based for the most part on a rate of one part in fifteen, or one-in-thirty, of the estimated yield. This was regarded by some persons as extremely low in comparison with the rate of one-in-ten which had prevailed in ancient times under ideal rule, and, therefore, if the tax were subsequently raised to one-in-ten, it was no more than could be expected in view of the ancient practice. Huang insists, however, that the Han tax rates are actually not comparable to those of ancient times, since they are based on a different system of land tenure. Under the sage-kings there was no private ownership of land; all land belonged to the king, who distributed it through the well-field system, so that everyone had enough to meet his needs. The tribute which they rendered to the king in return for the land he gave them was therefore not equivalent to taxes paid on private holdings in later times. After feudalism was abolished, the people no longer were granted land by the emperor but had to obtain it for themselves through purchase or the payment of rent. It was unreasonable, under this private property system which no longer assured the cultivator of a fair share of land, to expect him to pay as much to the ruler when he had received nothing in return. Moreover, under the ancient system, tribute was determined in accordance with the quality of the land held by the grantee, and, instead of a general tax rate for all, it was graduated so that those on poorer land paid less in tribute. The rate of one-in-ten, then, was actually what those holding the best land paid, while others paid much less.[31]

After the abolition of the well-field system, the Han adopted a general tax rate on all land. In this situation a rate of one part in thirty was fair enough—what even those holding the poorest land could afford. But a rate of one-in-ten was oppressive for two reasons: it could no longer be justified as a return on land granted the cultivator but was in addition to what he had to pay to purchase or rent his land, and it represented a tax on all holdings which only those best off could afford. Since those on poorer land lived close to the subsistence level, the same amount of tax would work a much greater hardship on them.

In this way Huang asserts that there is a fundamental relationship between the system of land tenure and what constitutes a fair tax. Under a system of private landownership, he regards a rate of one part in thirty or one-in-twenty as reasonable. If, however, the well-field system is restored, as he recommends, a rate of one-in-ten is allowable. But Huang is not at all so optimistic as are some advocates of the well-field system that its restoration alone will solve the tax problem. Throughout Chinese history he sees a tendency for taxes to proliferate and increase, often in hidden forms, as each dynasty conceives an urgent need for additional revenue. Special taxes imposed in times of crisis are rarely abolished when the crisis has passed. Tax reforms designed to consolidate existing taxes do not, in effect, reduce the burden on the people but merely clear the way for imposing still further levies. So downtrodden have the people become, generation after generation, that they themselves no longer have any conception of what a just tax is; in Huang's day, he says, they consider a three-tenths tax light and only a rate of five- or six-tenths is thought of as heavy.[32]

Thus it is essential, in Huang's view, to attack the problem from two sides: to redistribute the land so that all have a means of livelihood and to reform the administration of taxes so that those who obtain their own land will not lose it by falling heavily into debt.

2. *Land redistribution and the well-field system.*—Ever since the establishment of private landholding in the Ch'in and Han, the concentration of landownership in the hands of a few had been a recurrent problem, to which two main solutions were proposed by scholars and officials attempting to deal with it. The first was to restore the well-field system which supposedly had prevailed in earlier times. This would have involved the abolition of private property, the conscription of all land, its redistribution by the state in accordance with the "nine-squares" formula, and a permanent prohibition on the purchase or sale of land. Some who accepted this as the ideal, like the leading Han Confucianist, Tung Chung-shu, nevertheless conceded that conditions had so changed as to render a full return to the well-field system impracticable. As the next best solution, they proposed a simple limitation on the amount of land an individual could hold, the excess being distributed among those in need and with private ownership retained. As early as 7 B.C. a decree was promulgated embodying this latter proposal, but owing to powerful opposition at court it was never carried into effect.

Huang Tsung-hsi believes that this type of simple limitation on landownership is inadequate and, under the circumstances, unjust. For him it is essential that private ownership be abolished and that the people be "granted" land through the well-field system. Any attempt to retain private landholding, which means that men must buy their own land, and yet confiscate some of it for distribution to others, is certain to provoke opposition and could only be effected by the use of force. This is what Mencius called "doing an injustice," and, in keeping with the Confucian doctrine that coercion cannot be employed even for a good end, Huang rules it out. For essentially the same reason, he rejects the notion of others who had urged that restoration of the well-field system be held up until just after a period of chaos and bloodshed, when the population would be sufficiently reduced so that there would be enough land to go around. If restoration of the well-fields is truly desirable and practicable, Huang maintains, it need not wait until some dire calamity produces such a "favorable situation."

The question then becomes: "Is the well-field system truly practicable?" Su Hsün had said that it was not. The advocates of this system in his time had put much emphasis on the *Rites of Chou* (*Chou-li*) as a guide to re-establishment of the ancient order, and this text gave detailed specifications for the types of rivers and highways, canals and roads, ditches and lanes, and trenches and pathways which were to be maintained in connection with the division of land into well-fields. Su thought this beyond all hope of accomplishing. Only by "driving all men under Heaven, exhausting all revenues, and spending all efforts in this direction alone for several hundred years, without doing anything else, could one hope to see the empire converted into well-fields."[33] Therefore, like Tung Chung-shu, he reconciled himself to the method of limiting private landownership.

Huang is glad enough to credit Su Hsün with having presented "most fully the reasons why well-fields could not be restored," but he insists that the difficulties Su regards as so formidable are only minor details which in no way vitally affect the system and would take care of themselves once the well-fields were restored. On the other hand, he credits two later writers in the Ming, among them Hu Han,[34] with having most cogently argued in favor of the system, but declares that they failed to present a practical method for achieving this aim. His own contribution, Huang believes, is precisely in offering such a method. Hu Han had recommended that well-fields be adopted in one district, after which they might be extended to the whole empire. But Huang finds that all the essential principles of the well-field system have already been embodied and tested in the military farm system instituted at the inception of the Ming dynasty. Each soldier-cultivator received fifty *mou* of land, which was to provide for his needs and make it unnecessary for the government to pay or supply him from its own revenues. Huang is convinced that the same system could be extended to the empire as a whole. Basing his calculations on statistics for the late sixteenth century, which were available to him in an official compilation, the *Ming Hui-tien*, he first shows that military farmland already constitutes one-tenth of the total cultivated land of the empire, and concludes that what has already proved successful on such a large scale could easily be extended to the other nine-tenths. Then he shows that the total land under cultivation, when divided among the total number of households in the empire, would provide fifty *mou* for each with enough left over so that the rich could have a little extra. Such being the case, he is confident that the rich will raise no violent objections.

But one obvious objection still remained. The military farm system was not actually a proved success, since great numbers of the soldier-cultivators had abandoned their land and deserted from the army. This Huang explains as due not to any inherent defect in the system but rather to maladministration and simple homesickness among the deserters. The able-bodied soldiers were not allowed sufficient time to cultivate their farms, which consequently did not produce enough. On top of this, they were taxed at an excessive rate and were subject to the "squeezing" of rapacious military overlords. Such factors would not operate, however, on civilian farms.

3. *Tax reform.*—There are three chief tax evils which Huang would correct: the constant accumulation of taxes through the centuries, the payment of taxes in money rather than in kind, and the imposition of a uniform tax rate on all land regardless of the quality of the soil. In discussing the first two evils, he provides a review of the major tax developments in Chinese history, which demonstrates that he has studied carefully such sources as the economic treatises of the dynastic histories and such encyclopedic works on the history of Chinese social institutions as the *T'ung Tien* of Tu Yu, the *Wen-hsien T'ung-k'ao* of Ma Tuan-lin, its continuation by the Ming scholar, Wang Ch'i, the *Ming Hui-tien*, the *T'u-shu Pien* of Chang Huang, etc. To these he adds firsthand observations on contemporary developments.[35] Here only the high points of his analysis can be touched upon.

In ancient times the only tax was on land, payable in kind. By the early T'ang dynasty (A.D. 624), the land tax in grain had been supplemented by a tax on households, payable in cloth and a labor tax on adult males. By the middle of the T'ang, however, the collection of these separate taxes had become a complicated and inefficient procedure, so they were combined into one, the twice-a-year tax, payable in cash and grain. Thus the household and labor taxes were incorporated into the land tax. But by the Sung dynasty (960–1279) new taxes were imposed on adult males and households, without the people realizing that in effect they were being charged twice for the same items. During the Ming dynasty another great tax reform, which came to be known as the "single-whip" tax, again consolidated all existing taxes into the land tax, payable in silver so as to simplify collections. Subsequently the process of adding new forms of taxation to this basic one began again. A separate charge was made for miscellaneous labor services, and then, toward the end of the dynasty, special taxes were imposed in order to supply new troops raised to fight the Japanese in Korea and the Manchus in the north. A year before the fall of the Ming dynasty, these new pay-and-rations taxes for the army were combined into the single-whip collection. Thus, according to Huang's analysis, the effect of these reforms to simplify tax collections has only been constantly to increase the amount of the basic tax without putting a stop to the further proliferation of taxes. To correct this, he would repeal all such increases since ancient times and return to a basic land tax calculated at a rate of 5 per cent for private landholding and one-tenth for a well-field system.[36] The only other tax he would permit is one on households for the maintenance of a militia system he later proposes.

The crucial question then arises: Would such a low tax rate meet the needs of government? Huang's answer is revealing. Without attempting to estimate the legitimate expenses of government, even under his own plan, to see whether or not they would be provided for, he is content merely to show that the benevolent governments of ancient times got along with much less. Under feudalism, according to the Confucian texts, a much greater share of the tax proceeds was applied to the expenses of local government than to those of the court. Now, he implies, even though the central government has taken over many of the functions of the former feudal lords and is entitled to a larger proportionate share, still the over-all cost of government should not have increased. China has changed, he seems to admit, but China has not grown. The increasing cost of government is due not to expanded functions of state but to political degeneration, manifesting itself in waste and inefficiency.

Throughout Chinese history taxes had been paid for the most part in grain or cloth. Only with the adoption of the twice-a-year tax in the T'ang dynasty did payment in copper cash become a common practice in commutation of taxes in kind. And only with the single-whip tax did payment in silver become mandatory. A famous essayist of the T'ang dynasty, Lu Chih, had complained that people lost heavily in converting their produce into copper cash for the payment of taxes. "He thought that was bad!" exclaims Huang. "How much worse it is that all taxes should have to be paid in silver!" In earlier times money payment had in certain instances been authorized where it was a convenience to the people and where the rate of exchange for goods was favorable to the producer. But in the Ming dynasty the people often lost heavily when forced to convert their grain or cloth into silver at disadvantageous rates, and often a bountiful harvest would be of no benefit to the peasantry, since the value of their goods would drop sharply in relation to the silver they were forced to pay in taxes. Therefore it is essential to return to the an-

cient system of accepting in taxes whatever the land itself produced
rather than of asking the people to pay what they could obtain only
with difficulty.

Finally, Huang attacks the practice of fixing a uniform tax rate for
all land regardless of quality. Land values actually vary as much as
twenty to one, and a tax that is equitable when applied to productive
land may be ruinous when exacted from poor land. If an adjustment
were made for unproductive soil, it might be allowed to lie fallow for
a year or two and thus be gradually restored in fertility, but under
existing conditions the peasant is forced to work it continually in order
to meet his taxes. Consequently, Huang recommends the restoration
of a practice once tried by Wang An-shih, whereby the size of a Chinese acre (*mou*) varied for tax purposes according to the productivity
of the soil. This was called the system of "square fields" and provided
for five different land classifications. In this way a uniform rate
might be retained, but the taxable acreage would vary so that the
burden would be equally borne. Ultimately this should result in an
increase of tax revenue as the poorer land, allowed to lie fallow, gradually improved in quality and produced more.

J. OTHER REFORMS

The full scope of Huang's reform program cannot be adequately
presented here, but it is worth indicating at least that he had a wide
awareness of the other economic and social factors directly affecting
the exercise of political power. The maintenance of a sound monetary
system is one such problem which he analyzes in detail, showing that
the state had in the past failed to appreciate the importance of a
stable and convenient medium of exchange to the economy as a
whole and instead had rather shortsightedly manipulated or controlled the currency to its own immediate advantage. He therefore
urges the adoption of a sound system of paper money and copper
cash (which we recognize as essentially modern) and the abolition of
gold and silver as circulating media.

A considerable part of *A Plan for the Prince* is devoted to questions
of military organization, for Huang realizes that some of the basic
weaknesses of the Ming dynasty are attributable to an unsound defense system, which had disastrous repercussions on the political and
economic life of the nation. His fundamental thesis is that military
power should not be left to a separate class of professional soldiers
but that army organization and service should be integrated into the
regular pattern of civilian life and administration. At the same time,

Huang recommends the creation of autonomous commanderies—virtual feudal states—on the borders of China, which would serve as buffers against China's traditional enemies on her northern and western frontiers and thus eliminate the need for sending the home militia on campaigns in remote regions. The commanderies would also serve as counterweights to the court itself, constituting centers of power beyond the reach of those at court who might seek to monopolize such power for themselves.

3. Conclusion

In Huang's discussion of political principles and Chinese institutions, certain underlying themes appear. Certainly one of the most evident is his emphasis on government being conducted in the interests of the people, not of their rulers. And if having the people's interests at heart sufficed to make a thinker "democratic," then Huang would doubtless be among the first to qualify, for his analysis and condemnation of Chinese despotism, which had reached its peak in the Ming dynasty, are probably a more thoroughgoing and outspoken defense of the people's interests than any which has come down to us in Chinese literature. Nevertheless, we have reason to be dissatisfied with one recent appraisal of Huang Tsung-hsi which links him to John Locke and John Stuart Mill and concludes: "All three are democrats, believing as they do that the state is created for man, not man for the state."[37] There is indeed this much of a resemblance between the three, and yet democracy as we know it involves much more than simply "government for the people." Certainly Huang cannot be regarded as a proponent of political democracy as it is found in the West, with institutions designed to provide people with the means of freely expressing their will and in some way controlling the conduct of government. He advocates government "by the people" only in the sense that he asserts, with Mencius, the people's right to overthrow a tyrannical ruler and in the sense that, ideally, those he would entrust with political power will be sensitive to the desires of the people. But for representative government, in the form of legislative bodies, elections, referendums, political parties, and the like, he makes no provision.

It is true, however, that the institutions he does recommend would fulfil some of the same functions as do the organs of representative government in Western democracies. His emphasis upon law, for example, implies a sort of constitutional order, setting over-all limits to the powers of both the ruler and his officials. Especially as embodied in his proposal for a strong prime minister and for ministers who are servants of the people and cannot be arbitrarily overruled by the Prince, this constitutional order would have certain resemblances to the present English system of government. Moreover, in the great importance which he attaches to schools, going far beyond their immediate educative functions and setting them up as centers for the expression of public opinion, Huang intends that they should perform much the same purpose as political parties or parliaments. Indeed, considering the whole trend of Chinese political history, it is quite natural that he should think of them in this light. What were called "factions" at the Chinese court represented the nearest thing to the political parties of the West, and, in so far as these factions were alignments based on political principles rather than mere cliques held together by personal loyalties, they tended to become identified with certain schools, as in the late Ming dynasty. Unquestionably, Huang's conception of the high place of schools in the political sphere is inspired by the attacks which had been made in his time on precisely this role of the schools as organs of political expression.

A more fundamental reason, perhaps, why schools should seem to Huang the most suitable representatives of public opinion may be found in the traditional structure of Chinese society itself. In the absence of a strong middle class, which in the West has usually provided the basis for an effective party system, it was more natural to turn for this purpose to some institution indispensably bound up with the ruling class of literocrats. Statism had already gone so far in China that there was no real ground for political parties to stand on, no organized class or group for them to represent. Nor were there, beneath the ruling bureaucracy and its territorial agents, any corporate institutions or voluntary associations with sufficient economic power, social position, and established political rights to make themselves a force to be reckoned with. There was only the mass of common people, for the most part peasants, inarticulate and unaccustomed to political action except in the form of violent revolt. In such a situation the schools alone provided some mechanism for the expression of—not public, perhaps, but private—opinion, since schools were indispensable to the ruling class itself. Though attempts had often been made to make them, too, subservient to the ruling power, this very suppression testified to the fact that schools were potentially dangerous centers of opposition in a state which placed such a premium on learning. Even in modern times this has continued to be so, for, with all the apparent efforts to build up democratic institutions outside the schools in Republican China, the schools still remained the most articulate centers of political opposition.

If, therefore, we appreciate the forces with which Huang had to contend, it is not surprising that he should have proposed different means of achieving the same ends as Western democratic institutions. But having made allowances for the historical situation, there are still some deep-seated differences between Huang Tsung-hsi and Western proponents of "government by the people." In spite of his emphasis upon law and a quasi-constitutional order, the prime minister to whom he grants great powers and the ministers whom he calls servants of the people are still to be appointed by the Prince, not elected. Similarly, although he denies that "the principle of monarchy is inescapable," his denial implies only that a tyrant may be overthrown, not that monarchy should be abandoned and rulers elected. Of course, this might also be explained as an accident of history: he did not think of elections or responsible government in the Western sense only because history did not present this possibility to him. Yet we have good reasons for thinking that electoral processes, if not incompatible with Huang's fundamental Confucian beliefs, were at least unlikely vehicles for them. To him the Prince, and ideally the sage-king, remained a key figure. This is plain if only from the title of his work, which suggests that the hope of achieving his plan rests with some sympathetic ruler—traditionally the great hope of the Confucian writer or official. It is to the Prince and the scholar-official that Huang addresses this book, not to multitudes of common people among whom he would sow the seeds of a grass-roots democracy. Reform must come from above, because for any true follower of Confucius good government works from the top downward. The sage-king is the sun of virtue, from whom all goodness radiates down among the people. It is the moral authority and example of the Prince which rectifies all evils and maintains order in society.[38]

Huang Tsung-hsi would not have it any other way. Such limitations as he would place on the Prince's sovereignty are truly in the nature of moral restraints. They are intended not to make him less of a king but to help him to be a king. This is also why his ministers and officials are of such great importance. They are not simply co-administrators of the realm but colleagues and moral preceptors who will help the Prince be a real king. True, Huang has learned a lesson from Chinese dynastic history: he knows how rarely men of great virtue inherit the throne. Instead, however, of circumscribing the Prince's powers, instead of reserving certain rights to the people and their representatives, he offers a typically Confucian solution. Put others close to the throne who will make up for the Prince's deficiencies in virtue and ability. Thus, in contrast to the despot whose power is absolute and before whom all men, even the highest ministers, are no more than slaves, the Prince would be surrounded and supported by a hierarchy of merit and learning. It is for this reason that Huang would require the emperor and his ministers to sit as students at the lectures on politics of the chancellor of the Imperial Academy, in recognition of the latter's great moral and intellectual authority. The same thing would be true all down the line, with the lesser officials of the provinces paying the same homage to learning and virtue before the local superintendent of education, while also honoring mature wisdom and seniority at annual convocations for the elders of the region. There is no place here for mass meetings, monster rallies, or clambakes. Not through talking with the people and soliciting their support, but through consultation with the wise and virtuous in an aristocracy of merit, is the government to achieve its objective of ruling in the interests of all.

So long as we keep this basic principle in mind, we shall not make the mistake of interpreting Huang's reliance upon law and a well-defined system of government as placing him in a class with the advocates of constitutional government in the West. We have already seen that in calling for a restoration of the feudal order Huang did not intend so much the resurrection of specific feudal institutions or relationships as he did a decentralization or distribution of power which has often been the aim of constitutional movements in recent times. Yet here, too, a fundamental distinction should be made. Huang has in mind a sharing of power, so that its exercise would be left to competent individuals with sufficient freedom of action to meet their responsibilities. Sometimes this has the effect of concentrating great power in the hands of such individuals, as in the case of the prime minister, the ministers of the Six Boards, the local magistrates, the superintendents of education, the generals of the border commanderies, and so on. Thus what he retains of feudalism is what might be called "personalized" government. Its object is to put men of character and ability in positions of power and free them from any arbitrary restraints upon the discharge of their functions. In this way they can give full consideration to the needs of a situation and, if necessary, disregard prescribed procedures in order to solve particular human problems. Here, again, the inspiration and the aim are essentially Confucian.

This is all the more apparent if we consider how little this decentralization or diffusion of power is directed at maintaining a balance of power or a system of checks and balances. It is true that the ministers would serve as a check on the Prince, the superintendent of education as a check on the local magistrate, and the border commanders as a check on the court. But except in the case of the border commanderies the ideal is not a balance of interests or an equilibrium of countervailing powers. Power rests squarely with the ruler, yet in so far as he is an understanding person he will voluntarily heed the counsel of his ministers. The same is true for the magistrate, and, if he chooses to ignore wise counsel, the only recourse Huang offers is for the local inhabitants to rise up and drive him out. In some cases the effect of Huang's proposals is actually to do away with checks and balances incorporated into the Ming system of administration. For instance, he would strip the Civil Service Board of its power to direct a supposedly impartial and uniform civil service system, and grant appointive powers directly to administrators themselves. Huang likewise opposes the system of divided authority over the Ming armies, preferring to concentrate both administrative and operational control in the civilian Board of War. He has no confidence in a system of divided authority. The only secure system is one which places its reliance on men of character and ability.

Thus Huang does not look forward to a healthy give-and-take in politics and government. His ideal is the traditional Confucian one: harmony. Sound government is the product of a co-operative effort which strives for the good of all. Since this should be the only aim of men in government, he does not seek a balance of contending or competing interests or a reconciliation of opposing political forces. He defends freedom of expression for the schools but obviously does not consider diversity of opinion a good thing in itself. Different views may be held on questions of importance, and yet conflict itself is not productive. The thing to do when controversies arise is not to take a vote or arrive at a settlement in court (and this is probably the reason why supreme courts, like legislatures, have no place in his system). Ultimately, right and wrong are to be determined by scholar-philosophers in the schools, for they are custodians of the Truth, one and indivisible, handed down through generations of wise men from those who first revealed it, the sage-kings and Confucius.

Pursuing this ideal of social harmony, Huang seeks to solve many problems of Chinese society in ways which resemble more closely the approach of modern democracies. He advocates a universal school system, so that all may enjoy the benefits of education. Along the same line, his militia system would provide for universal military service, with a civilian army in which the people share equally the burdens of national defense and stand guard against the recurrent evils of warlordism. In the field of economic democracy, his recommendations in some respects go far beyond the demands of its noisiest champions in modern China. He sees the necessity of basic land reform, and, while the scheme he proposes leaves many practical difficulties unresolved, he is at least acute enough to realize that the equalization of landholdings alone would not lift the peasantry out of their misery. As long as the government which effected land reform did not reduce its demands for tax revenues, the peasant would find himself paying more in taxes to the state than he had paid in rents to the landlord. Huang had no desire to substitute an impersonal, all-powerful, tax-gathering machine for the local proprietor of tenant holdings.

RECENT APPRAISALS

Though Huang Tsung-hsi thus anticipated some of the most important economic and social reforms undertaken in modern China, it was for other reasons that Huang became an important figure in the reform and revolutionary movements of the last century. Liang Ch'i-ch'ao, probably the most influential writer of this period, acknowledges the relevance to his own time of proposals by Huang such as land equalization, currency and military reform, and the transfer of the capital to Nanking. But it is not to these ideas that Liang refers when he relates that Huang's writings proved "a powerful tonic for students in the 1890's" or when he says, "My own political activities can be said to have been influenced very early and very deeply by this book."[39] Rather it is the political principles asserted in *A Plan for the Prince* which make him appear to Liang as an early champion of democracy, a native authority from whom reformers could obtain sanction for the democratic ideas and institutions they wished to import from the West. For this reason, Liang tells us, he and his colleagues exhumed Huang's book, which had been suppressed during the literary inquisition of the Ch'ien-lung period (1736–96), and used it as a vehicle for spreading "democratic ideas" during the Kuang-hsü period (1875–1908).[40] When Liang and T'an Ssu-t'ung were "advocating popular sovereignty and republicanism, they printed several tens of thousands of copies of *A Plan for the Prince* and circulated it secretly, so that it had a most powerful effect on thought in the late Ch'ing dynasty."[41] Another contemporary source, setting forth the intellectual origins of the Chinese revolution, pictures Huang as the direct progenitor of the democratic and nationalist movement in modern times. "Viewed in proper historical perspective, the Chinese National Revolution was but the logical continuation of the struggle started by adherents of the late Ming Dynasty against the Manchu conquerors." Not only was Huang Tsung-hsi the most important philosopher of this "anti-imperialist" group, but, realizing that armed opposition to the Manchus was doomed to failure, he "conceived the plan of reorganizing the secret societies in China on a revolutionary nationalistic basis."[42]

From this idolization of Huang as the Chinese patriarch of the revolutionary movement, at least one leading thinker of the time, Chang Ping-lin, sharply dissented. In a long essay, "Against Huang," he analyzes the political aspects of *A Plan for the Prince* and opposes, in particular, his ideas concerning the importance of law, the prime ministership, and the schools. Though much of his criticism is abusive and unjust, inspired by what seems a deep-seated personal animosity, at times it serves as an illuminating commentary on the uses to which Huang's ideas were put by modern apostles of democracy and nationalism. In opposition, for instance, to the extremely active student movement of his time, some of whose champions found in Huang a justification for the intervention of students in politics,[43] Chang excoriates the notion that the opinions of immature and meddlesome students can be taken as representing the will of the people as a whole.[44] He also deplores the way in which Huang is acclaimed as an exemplar of the doctrine of constitutional government. "Today people who talk about making the government over anew, all base their ideas on Huang Tsung-hsi."[45] Huang he regards as an insincere and inept proponent of government based on law. The excessive power granted the prime minister by Huang and his undermining of the civil service system demonstrate that his form of government would be dominated by individual political leaders, not governed by law. In this respect he finds that Huang's proposals would indeed open the door to some of the worst features of the so-called constitutional democracies of the West, where the English cabinet is a rubber stamp for the prime minister, and the American president is a powerful demagogue whose followers will stop at nothing to get themselves and their party leaders elected.[46] "Today everyone talks about government according to law, but . . . among the Western powers today there is none which truly governs according to law. What Tsung-hsi advocates is what the Western world practices; they praise government according to law but stumble around because they overrate human intelligence."[47]

In spite of the absurd lengths to which he carries his argument, identifying Huang with all that is worst in the Western democracies where others had identified him with all that is best, Chang nevertheless inadvertently exposes the fundamental discrepancy between Huang's view of government by law and this doctrine as professed by modern proponents of political democracy. Subsequent criticism of Huang's work has not failed to observe this. One contemporary authority on Chinese political thought, Hsiao Kung-ch'uan, reveals his doubts over the enthusiasm which had been expressed for Huang as a champion of democracy and nationalism just a few decades earlier. Huang, he readily admits, was a stout foe of absolutism and would most likely have stood in the democratic camp had he been born in the nineteenth century. But, as it was, Huang failed to transcend the traditional limits of monarchism and was therefore simply "following in the ruts which Mencius had already worn in the road." Moreover, like Chang Ping-lin, Hsiao believes that in his attitude toward the Manchus and earlier foreign conquerors of China Huang failed to set an example of unqualified and unswerving loyalty to Chinese national and racial interests.[48]

To recent Marxist critics, however, this absence of an all-pervading racial loyalty has been less of a defect in Huang, and to one at least it has been a virtue.[49] Yet in spite of the fact that their evaluation of him is based on the same arbitrary view of seventeenth-century China as a "feudal" society, they have had as much difficulty as other writers in coming to agreement on his political significance. One such critic, for instance, classes Huang with Ku Yen-wu and Wang Fu-chih as a last-ditch defender of the crumbling feudal aristocracy, which sought to recoup something from its defeat by the Manchus and maintain the power of the landlord class through a "self-salvation" movement. This necessitated analyzing the causes of their previous failure and initiating reform measures which would stave off peasant revolt and complete collapse. Thus Huang's emphasis upon the "people" is no more than an attempt to placate the peasants and keep them from throwing off the domination of "feudal" landlords. All of Huang's proposed reforms partake of this character: land reform is merely an enticement to keep peasants on the land; tax reform is intended to head off the revolt of the peasants against high taxes; the abolition of gold and silver as money is designed to restore a natural, barter economy which will likewise keep the people on the land. And of course the schools, as much as the border commandery system, are to serve as instruments of class domination by the feudal aristocracy.[50]

On the other hand, a well-known writer[51] who accepts this same pseudo-Marxist view of Chinese society in Huang's time as essentially feudalistic[52] comes to precisely the opposite opinion concerning him. Centuries ahead of his time in his thinking, Huang had liberated himself from the shackles of "medieval dogma" and anticipated most of the important developments in modern thought and social reform. His revolutionary doctrines are expressed, it is true, in traditional terms, but this was characteristic also of the heralds of the modern age in the West. In fact, Huang is more truly an apostle of democracy than its Western advocates, because he sees the necessity for economic equality as well as government in the interests of the people.[53] His modern outlook is therefore most clearly apparent in the economic reforms he calls for: land reform, to give the peasants the means of production as is being done in the countries of Eastern Europe today (1946–47);[54] currency reform, to abolish the "feudalistic" money system and provide a circulating medium that will stimulate economic activity and development; and tax reforms to eliminate gross inequalities in the distribution of the tax burden.[55] Politically, Huang stands out for his attack on the "feudalistic" nature of the court bureaucracy, for his advocacy of a modern cabinet system giving extensive power to a prime minister chosen on a merit basis, and for his championing of free speech in the schools.[56] In short, Huang is "antifeudal," "enlightened," and, above all, "scientific" in his approach to the intellectual and social problems of his day.[57]

It is not surprising that Huang should mean different things to men of the same school of thought or that men of different schools should claim him as their own. The principles which he asserts in *A Plan for the Prince*—that government should be conducted in the interests of the people, that to this end restraints should be imposed on the exercise of power, that the state cannot be allowed to control men's minds, that political leadership should be entrusted to men who qualify on the basis of personal ability, and that ultimately the government must assume responsibility for the proper functioning of those economic and social institutions which vitally affect the people's welfare—are principles so general in application and appeal as to be accepted in some way by schools of thought which differ widely among themselves in other respects. On the other hand, since Huang did not confine himself to theory but tried to show how these principles applied to the problems of his own time, there are many points at which his work will be evaluated differently by those whose views vary on the historical questions involved. In this respect it seems safe to say that Huang's general analysis of Chinese institutions will be most compatible with interpretations of Chinese history and society which emphasize the dominant role of the state and bureaucracy from early times, only slightly less so with those who see absolutism as having fully matured at least by the Ming dynasty, and hardly compatible at all with characterizations of Chinese society in these times as essentially feudalistic.

But however Huang's own interpretations may stand up in the light of subsequent historical research, his attempt to make such an analysis will remain the principal contribution of *A Plan for the Prince*. Certainly no great claims can be made for it as a new departure in Chinese political theory, since so much that is basic to Huang's thought derives from the original deposit of Confucian doctrine, especially from Mencius. It is also true, however, that Confucius and Mencius did not have to cope with the problems of imperial China. Few, if any, of their later followers attempted to examine them in so comprehensive a manner as did Huang, or drew upon Confucian ideals more effectively in their critique of traditional institutions.

Others before him had certainly made the attempt, and no one is more conscious than Huang of his indebtedness to earlier writers, some famous and some comparatively obscure, who had wrestled with the same problems. In certain cases, indeed, it is quite apparent that his solution for a given problem was anticipated by others. It is also true that other men of his own time shared Huang's views. They were by no means generally accepted, and yet, among men with an intellectual inheritance similar to his, the same Confucian ideals inspired identical sentiments in regard to the critical questions of the day. Among them Ku Wen-wu is an outstanding example. He says, in his letter to Huang after reading *A Plan for the Prince*, that his own views are in agreement with "six- or seven-tenths" of what is set forth therein. A reading of Ku's essays on "Commanderies and Prefectures" (*Chün-hsien Lun*) and "Taxes in Money" (*Ch'ien-liang Lun*), as well as relevant passages in his great work *Jih-chih lu*, confirms that his views were extremely close to Huang's on most major issues.[58] Other contemporaries, such as Lü Liu-liang[59] and T'ang Chen,[60] are likewise outstanding exponents of the people's welfare against despotic rulers and oppressive institutions.

Nevertheless, it is still true that Huang's work is the most eloquent and comprehensive statement of this point of view. It draws together the ideas which others, in the past or present, had expressed in scattered or unsystematic form, and, while his discussion of certain problems is sometimes less exhaustive than the treatment of them by others (here the comparison to Ku Yen-wu is particularly apt), the balance which he achieves between general principles and their historical application adds considerably to the force of his presentation. It is for this reason, perhaps more than any other, that *A Plan for the Prince* has proved the most enduring and influential Confucian critique of Chinese despotism through the ages.

SYNARCHY UNDER THE TREATIES

JOHN K. FAIRBANK

1. Foreign Participation in the Government of China

ALIEN RULE is one of the commonplaces of the Chinese political tradition, but its implications for modern times have been generally disregarded. During the last seven centuries China has been ruled more than half the time by non-Chinese emperors—the Yuan dynasty of the Mongols (1279–1368) and the Ch'ing dynasty of the Manchus (1644–1912). Yet this alien rule was not an utterly new experience in Chinese history (witness the dynasties of the Northern Wei, Liao, and Chin in North China in earlier centuries), and China's socio-cultural entity was not basically transformed by it. These "dynasties of conquest" were somehow fitted into the Chinese scheme of things, their emperors ruled, on the whole, in the ancient Confucian tradition, and Chinese life went on with the "barbarian" conquerors playing a specialized military-political role as power-holders within the Chinese state. Indeed, since a million or so alien invaders were outnumbered a hundred or more to one by the Chinese populace, they could rule only with Chinese help. We may say that, in effect, the Mongols and Manchus *participated* in the government of China, albeit at the top level.

Inner Asian barbarians had in fact always participated in one way or another in the government of the Chinese empire, because the empire had normally embraced both China and the peripheral areas. In institutional terms we must think of agrarian China and nomadic Inner Asia as a single Sino-barbarian political universe, which in its periods of greatest integration and order could be ruled either by Chinese dynasties (like the Han, T'ang, and Ming) or by non-Chinese dynasties (like the Yuan and Ch'ing) but in either case had to be treated as a single interconnected imperial area.

Throughout East Asian history runs this motif of the marriage of the steppe and the sown, the indissoluble connections—military, political, economic—between China's densely populated farmlands and the sparsely populated grasslands of the peripheral regions. The complex reasons for this long historical relationship are grand subjects for speculation and difficult ones for research. The military superiority of mounted archers over peasant conscripts, the economic dependence of nomads on trade with settled areas, the greater political opportunity afforded to rebels on the periphery of empire (where they could develop effective administrations in comparative peace while rebels within China, obliged to keep fighting, had less chance to learn how to govern), all these are facets of this large problem of Sino-barbarian relations, which form the historical background of modern China's foreign relations.

As a result of this long tradition, the Chinese state came onto the international scene a century ago with a well-developed institution of *foreign participation* in its government. Under strong, expansive Chinese dynasties this had taken the form of vassalage on the part of the Inner Asian tribal chieftains, who maintained a tributary relationship to the Chinese emperor. Under non-Chinese dynasties ruling in China, this participation had taken the form of *joint administration* by a mixed Chinese and non-Chinese bureaucracy.

This phenomenon of joint administration, needless to say, had been extremely variegated. It had covered a wide spectrum, running from tyrannical forms of barbarian domination under the early Mongols to egalitarian forms of Sino-barbarian co-operation under the late Manchus. Many subtle factors had entered into it—cultural elements of language, dress, and custom; social considerations and economic interests; military strategy; political theory. I propose to call this intricate institution of "joint Sino-foreign administration of the government of China under a foreign dynasty" by the special name *synarchy*, not because it is a clearly known quantity but precisely because it is so largely unknown. (Later sections of this paper will attempt to define synarchy more fully; I prefer it to "dyarchy," because the latter term implies that only two parties are involved and already has a special meaning with reference to British India.)

Foreign rule in China under dynasties of conquest has thus far been studied almost entirely within the framework of the Chinese imperial tradition before modern times. Yet reflection suggests that the role played by non-Chinese in the Chinese state during the Northern Wei, Liao, Chin, Yuan, and Ch'ing periods, between the fourth and nineteenth centuries, has had some sort of historical relationship to the roles played in the nineteenth and twentieth centuries by the British and other Western powers under the unequal treaty system, by the Japanese invaders in their "co-prosperity sphere" subsequently, and perhaps by the Russians under communism most recently.

Just as synarchy became a recognizable political institution under the barbarian dynasties of conquest, so, I suggest, the treaty system after 1842 became for a time a major political institution of the Chinese state with certain "synarchic" features.

However, as we shall see, this tendency toward a brief *continuity of institutional practices*, before and after 1842, was not accompanied by a similar continuity of political theory concerning Sino-foreign relations. On the contrary, the *ideological discontinuity* created by Western contact eventually undermined and destroyed China's traditional political order, in its foreign as well as its domestic aspects.

In order to test out this analytic scheme, we will look first at certain traditional features of synarchy as an institution, both in theory and in practice; then note certain evidences of their persistence in the early years of the treaty system after 1842; and finally touch upon the decline of both the theory and the practice as a result of Western contact. In these speculations it will avail little either to assert the uniqueness of Chinese institutions (as sinologists sometimes do out of ignorance of other regions) or to stress their universal aspects and comparability with institutions elsewhere (which does not necessarily advance our knowledge of China). The problem is rather to formulate hypotheses that will more clearly illuminate the boundary of our ignorance and stimulate concrete research.

2. Synarchy as a Traditional Institution

A survey of the dynasties of conquest was attempted by a group of Japanese scholars a decade ago.[1] While their study by its nature was superficial and subject to wartime pressure for haste, it nevertheless brings out a consistent pattern in some detail. In the history of the Northern Wei (A.D. 386–556), Liao (907–1125), and Chin (1115–1234) there had already appeared certain features which recurred in the history of the Mongols and Manchus:

1. The barbarian invaders were able to seize power in North China usually after a period of disorder, at a time when a previous dynasty was collapsing and the need for unity and order was widely felt.

2. In organizing their effort at conquest, the barbarians inevitably enlisted Chinese advice and guidance, which they got most easily from Chinese of the border region.

3. Chinese army forces were similarly absorbed into the invading horde, even though the superior military striking power of the barbarians continued to be concentrated in their cavalry, which was supplied with more and better horses from the grazing land of the

steppe than could be maintained in the cultivated region of China.

4. As they acquired control over Chinese territory, the invaders pursued a policy both of terror and of appeasement of the Chinese local leadership. The alien regime had first to be built on the support of the Chinese upper class, principally the gentry-landlords. Frequently these latter groups had organized local self-defense corps by which to maintain local order and the old structure of social relationships in the village. The first aim of the alien conqueror was to appease these interests and secure their support. Chinese leaders must be used in order to enlist a larger corps of Chinese administrators.

5. Again in general terms, it seems characteristic of all these invaders from the north that they recognized the impossibility of imposing their own culture upon the settled masses of China, which of course was made the more difficult by the invaders' great inferiority in numbers. In varying degree, but to some extent in each case, the dynasties of conquest therefore conducted their administration of Chinese territory in the Chinese tradition of the day: they preserved the traditional forms of administration and of social and cultural life in China, even when, as under the Liao, they divided the region under their rule into two areas—one within North China and one outside the Wall, where the Liao culture and way of life could be preserved.

6. Thus, as a corollary to the principle of ruling China in a Chinese way, the invaders found it most essential to maintain a homeland of their own beyond the Wall whence they had come. In this way they attempted to preserve their own conscious existence as a people and avoid or postpone that "absorption" which a popular but superficial Western tradition used to assign as the ineluctable fate of foreigners who conquer China.

7. The preservation of Chinese ways in the government of China meant, in effect, that the administration should be conducted, at least on the local level, largely by Chinese under the supervision of the alien conquerors. The use of both types of personnel was an inevitable feature of every alien dynasty.

8. In addition, the invaders found it useful to employ other foreigners. Thus the Liao made use of the Hsi people of Mongolian stock from Jehol. The Chin used the Ch'itan Mongols widely in administration.

9. Once the conquest had been achieved, the barbarians' next task was to insure control through military force held in reserve. A territorial army had to be built up, into which Chinese could be recruited

and which would be completely loyal to the new dynasty. Units of this army could then be garrisoned to protect the capital and to hold key spots such as the Yangtze delta.

10. Toward the border peoples who remained behind them on the frontier of Inner Asia, meanwhile, the dynasties of conquest typically developed a divide-and-rule policy, setting tribe off against tribe, so as to insure their rear and prevent the rise of competitors in that quarter.

In addition to these various practices, and underlying them, was another factor which facilitated alien rule, namely, the political theory of the Chinese state—a similarly large and unstudied subject concerning which generalization must also be attempted.

In general, I suggest that the Chinese emperor as a political institution can be discussed most conveniently under the heading of the "Confucian monarchy." (While the monarchy owed much to the ancient, Legalist enemies of Confucius, its use of the ideology enshrined in the Confucian classics would seem to legitimize the adjective "Confucian." Similarly, the Roman Catholic Church may appear to be institutionally far advanced beyond the explicit teachings of Christ, yet it seems not inappropriate to call it "Christian.") The Confucian monarchy exercised the universal rule of the Son of Heaven, who in theory represented all mankind, and set no territorial limits to his sway. The Chinese emperor's role may be better described by calling him simply the Son of Heaven, rather than an emperor of any kind. His influence according to the Confucian-Mencian theory of government was held to emanate from the fact of his virtuous conduct. While his semireligious functions, signalized in the state cult of Confucius of which the emperor was the head, were centered in China, they were held to be valid also for the surrounding peoples. Whenever occasion offered, it was therefore appropriate in theory that the moral supremacy and as far as possible the actual rule of the Son of Heaven should be spread over the barbarians of Inner Asia. This extension of the rule of the Chinese Son of Heaven was often thwarted in practice by the Huns and their non-Chinese successors outside the Wall; yet the example of the universal and inclusive Confucian monarchy seems to have set the political style for barbarian rulers, from the Shan-yü of the Huns down to the unlimited sway of Chinghis Khan himself. At all events, as barbarian conquest became more frequent and thorough, the imperial institutions of China and of Inner Asia tended to coalesce—despite the continuing differences in social base, economy, and culture, barbarian

Sons of Heaven came to look very much like Chinese Sons of Heaven both in their administrative functions and in their theoretical position in the political order of East Asia. Thus by early modern times the Manchu rulers of Mongolia and China were able to use, over Mongolia, devices of divide-and-rule administration which they had inherited from the Ming and, over China, devices of centralized control which the Ming had originally inherited from the Mongols.

The result of all this was that the Confucian monarchy became a Sino-barbarian institution. The Mandate of Heaven (manifested in the tacit acquiescence of the Chinese populace) might be held by either a Chinese or a non-Chinese. Also, contenders for it might come either from within China or from outside.

The practice of joint administration or synarchy under a dynasty of conquest reached its most developed form under the Manchus. While it would be tedious to describe at length the dual system of administration which continued at Peking for well-nigh three centuries, certain bases of power which underlay it may be distinguished briefly in sequence.

A. THE EXTERNAL BASE

The barbarian power in China was most visibly represented by the military forces which were kept in readiness and in reserve with a demonstrable capacity to overcome any attempt at Chinese armed rebellion. Back of this, however, lay the fact of social and racial cohesion on the part of the barbarian minority group in China. Led by the reigning dynasty, the conquerors took great pains to maintain their identity and the special status and prestige which went with it. For this purpose it was important that they maintain a territorial base external to China proper. As successful rebels from the Manchurian pale, who had got ahead of competing Chinese rebels from within North China, the Manchus owed much to their territorial base outside the Wall. There they had imitated and taken over many features of Chinese economic life and government while retaining certain barbarian features of strength such as their military power. The secret of their success was that their external base gave them an opportunity for institutional development, especially the acquiring of the administrative skills necessary for the civil government of China. This was an opportunity often denied to Chinese domestic rebels—*vide* their competitor Li Tzu-ch'eng, who was strong enough to destroy the Ming in 1644 but not capable of recruiting upper-class scholar-gentry to help him govern in their place.[2]

B. THE USE OF THE GENTRY CLASS

Once in power, the conquerors' first needs were to revive civil administration by Chinese local magistrates and, for this purpose, to secure the co-operation of the local gentry both as a necessary adjunct of government and as a reservoir of potential officials. Whether one regards the key position of the scholar-gentry class as based primarily on landowning or, more broadly speaking, on its performance of local economic, social, cultural, and administrative functions, it is generally accepted that it was the central element in an elitist government conducted by the special class of literati-bureaucrats, over the politically inert mass of the peasantry. The ruling class of officials interpenetrated the scholar-gentry or literati, and the whole stratum of scholars and bureaucrats had special privileges and prerogatives which set them apart from the peasant mass (their personal connections, their competence in the written language, and their capacity to act in terms of Confucian ideology; also, their exemption from *corvée* labor and corporal punishment). The first task of every ruler was to act as the patron of the literati, maintain the examination system by which they qualified themselves, and choose his officials from among the successful candidates. The Manchu emperors proved extremely competent at this universalistic procedure.[3]

C. THE CIVIL CONTROL SYSTEM

To keep the civil government in working order, the barbarian dynasties used a "control system," as we may call it, of administrative practices which had been developed and used also by Chinese rulers and which went with the Confucian monarchy in the Chinese empire regardless of whether the monarch was Chinese or barbarian. In other words, the Manchu conquest consisted of their capture of the Chinese monarchy, leadership of the gentry class, and application of the control system.

To a considerable degree the control system of the Manchus was merely a continuation of that of the Ming. (What features the Ming had inherited from the Mongols is a question which needs further research.) Under it, the populace was held in check not only by military garrisons but mainly by the *pao-chia* system of mutual guaranty and responsibility among the village households. The literati were caught up in the examination system, which served both to recruit and to indoctrinate human talent that might otherwise become organized against the regime. To this the Manchus added a control of thought and literature. The institution of the censorate gave opportunity for the official schooled in orthodoxy to invoke the Confucian ideology against deviant conduct. Meanwhile the inveterate use of one man in several functions or part-functions, and the performance of every function by several men part-time, produced a situation of collegial or collective responsibility among officials such that one was obliged to check upon another. The administrative procedure by which provincial officials transacted their business through memorials directly to the emperor, rather than through the ministries at the capital, prevented the diffusion of central power. The "law of avoidance," by which a man could not serve in his native locality, checked family influence. At the top the emperor not only dispensed with a prime minister (as the Ming had also done) and retained the decisive position in the administrative procedure but also by custom was able to act as a despot without check or hindrance—promoting and discarding his officials arbitrarily as though his absolutism needed constantly to be demonstrated.[4]

D. CULTURALISM AS THE FOCUS OF LOYALTY

Without attempting to describe further this enormously complex and variegated governmental system, we may conclude, I think, that it exalted the exercise of central power by the Son of Heaven on a universal and nonnational plane. The Manchu rulers' patronage of the Chinese scholar-gentry exemplified traditional cultural values which also sanctioned their overlordship of the Mongol tribes, Turkestan, and Tibet. Just as the Mongols had used Arabs and other West Asians, Russians and other Europeans, so the Ch'ing had employed the Jesuits and would later hire Western advisers and civil servants. The touchstone of loyalty to the regime was a matter separate from one's origin or race. It was this emphasis upon the personal relationship between the Confucian ruler and his Chinese or foreign vassal which facilitated the use by the monarch of one barbarian against another, corresponding to his playing-off of one clique of Chinese officials against another. All of them were within the embrace of the universal empire.

As a consequence, the Confucian monarchy had a basis more cultural than national. Under it might function all those who had assumed a proper place with reference to the Confucian polity. Since Eastern Asia is the Chinese cultural area, where the Chinese type of writing system, bureaucracy, and intensive agriculture provide a common bond in the settled communities from Korea to Annam, this culturalistic basis of political order was no doubt to be expected. The greatest achievement of the Confucian monarchy, however, lay in its capacity to embrace the fighting nomads of Inner Asia within the same polity, no matter whether they were dominant or dominated. This capacity to bring the nomad into the Confucian state was undoubtedly a great accomplishment. Historically the nomad conquerors had made their contribution to it: for it had been forced upon the sedentary Chinese state through the instances of barbarian conquest.

The foregoing sketch will perhaps make it apparent that synarchy, as the "joint Sino-foreign administration of the government of China under a foreign dynasty," was no fly-by-night phenomenon but an old-established institution which stemmed from the very center of the Sino-barbarian political experience in East Asia, an integral aspect of the imperial Confucian order.

3. The Genesis of the Treaty System

The eventual upshot of British military superiority, as demonstrated in the Opium War of 1840–42, was a nexus of mutually supporting naval, legal, administrative, and commercial arrangements which for brevity we call the "treaty system." Its most conspicuous manifestations, the treaty ports, were produced by the confluence of two traditions—on the foreign side, that of European maritime expansion and, on the Chinese side, that of tribute relations. These two traditions had of course been in contact on the coast of China for several centuries, and their miscegenation had been no sudden act. Let us first note certain features of the Western maritime expansion and then see how it had been fitted into the tradition of tribute relations.

A. THE EARLY EUROPEAN FACTORY NETWORK IN ASIA

European adventuring overseas at first combined piratical seizure of goods and people with bartering for them as a less preferred alternative. Portuguese expansion paid its way around Africa largely by the traffic in slaves, and across the Indian Ocean by seizing the entrepôts of the Arab spice trade.[5] Early Portuguese freebooters on the China coast were quite comparable to their more formidable contemporaries, the pirates of Japan. In time, as trade became more profitable than buccaneering, the various joint-stock East India companies of the seventeenth century built up their trading posts (factories) at the focal points of Asian trade. Each Dutch, British, or French factory carried within it the seeds of colonial empire— namely, the company's wide prerogatives to monopolize the home country's trade in Asia, to exercise legal jurisdiction over its citizens there, to protect its goods and persons by naval and military forces, and, in short, to act as a government overseas by fiat of the national sovereign in Europe. These assorted prerogatives of government combined with the acquisitive motives of trade to make the European factories into dangerous nodes of expansion amid the political disunity of South and Southeast Asia. The same explosive danger remained locked within the factories at Canton, ready to burst forth whenever the government of China should lose its local military superiority vis-à-vis the Europeans there.[6]

B. THE FACTORIES IN CHINA UNDER THE TRIBUTE SYSTEM

From the Chinese point of view, barbarian ships arriving by sea seemed just as much inclined to raid the Middle Kingdom, when they were strong enough, as were nomad horsemen coming from Inner Asia. The early European sea-raiders were even more mobile and their home bases comparatively invulnerable through distance across the ocean. But a greater difference became apparent when they were eventually supplanted by regular traders whose sea-borne goods far exceeded the volume which came overland by Inner Asian caravans. Maritime trade soon became a form of Sino-barbarian contact entirely different from land trade—economically larger and more valuable, strategically less easy to control by the twin tools of military force and Confucian personal relationships (even though the big Ming naval expeditions of the early fifteenth century had made efforts in that direction).

The Chinese solution to this problem of sea trade was to quarantine the European merchants in their factories, restrict their factories to Canton, and control them through the prime motive which had brought them to China, their lust for commercial profit. This solution remained effective until the nineteenth century, because the Ch'ing power remained too formidable on its home soil and too remote from Europe to invite military attack.

The Western network of trading posts and naval bases, flung asross the Indian Ocean by Portugal and woven tighter by Holland, France, and Britain, thus frayed out when it came to China. The little outposts like that of the Dutch in seventeenth-century Formosa, which elsewhere in Asia expanded into colonial empires, could not pursue their inveterate tendencies on the mainland of China any more than in Japan. By the late eighteenth century the British East India Company, already restricted to Canton, found that the appearance of His Majesty's naval vessels hurt the trade more than helped it: the dominant incentive of Sino-British relations was mutual profit within the established Ch'ing political order, and the E.I.C. Select Committee could protect itself better by stoppages of trade within this framework than by bringing in British warships to try to change it. As it turned out, this situation was exceptional and temporary, in the history of Europe's world-wide colonial expansion, but it permitted China to assimilate the Western factories for the time being into the institutional framework of the tribute system, or at least to give the appearance of doing so.

For this purpose the precedents went far back, to the treatment accorded Arab merchants in ports like Canton and Ch'uan-chou (Zayton) as early as the Sung period. Arab traders in these ports had had their own quarter, within which they were expected to reside, and their own headmen, who acted responsibly for their community in its relations with Chinese officials. They also applied their own legal institutions among themselves and had their own mosque and religious practices. As the imperial tribute system developed in succeeding centuries under the Yuan, Ming, and early Ch'ing, it took account in practice of this type of foreign merchant community on the Chinese frontier. While merchants of Inner Asia, including eventually those from Russia, were expected to bring their caravans to certain centers of trade on the land frontier such as Yü-men-kuan or Mai-mai-chen, the maritime traders from Liu-ch'iu came regularly to Foochow, those of Siam to Canton, and so on for each of the overseas countries which sent tribute as the necessary concomitant of its trade.

When the tribute system was applied to Europeans, the foreign merchants in the Thirteen Factories at Canton, under their own recognized headmen, were left to practice their own legal arrangements and religious observances among themselves. Similarly the early Jesuits had been able to function within the Macao community long before they succeeded in breaking away from this commercial connection and getting Chinese consent for mission posts in the interior. The aim of the Manchu dynasty was to prevent Chinese contact with the European foreigner except as he entered into the Confucian scheme of things and played a proper tributary role. The early tribute missions from the Portuguese and Dutch served to confirm this principle. Care was taken to make the factories a point of economic contact only and to limit intellectual interchange. Thus there was a ban on teaching the Chinese language to foreigners or letting them secure gazetteers or other writings of strategic importance. By the early nineteenth century the custom was well established for the Ch'ing dynasty to cast the Western barbarians in a traditional role as tributaries of the Confucian monarchy. The chief element of discord which had emerged at Canton was that the Western barbarians, unlike their predecessors of Inner Asia, were not ready to accept the theoretical premises and political practices of this relationship. From this eventually flowed the conflict at Canton over practical matters of diplomacy, law, and trade.[7]

C. THE TREATY PORTS' CONTINUITY WITH TRADITION

The British after 1834 finally used gunfire to knock down the structure of the tribute system, including the Cohong trade monopoly and other restrictions at the Thirteen Factories of Canton, but, when the smoke of battle and the talk of the treaty negotiations had both subsided, they and their foreign colleagues of other treaty powers were left with the five treaty ports: foreign merchants and missionaries were still restricted to certain areas on the Chinese coast, which were measured by the distance which one might go inland and still return by evening to the treaty ports. These foreign communities were still under their own recognized headmen, who were now called "consuls." Among themselves they observed their own legal procedures, under the terms of what was now called extraterritoriality, as well as their own religious practices. They were in a more aggressive position with power to make further demands. But for the time being, in the 1840's and 1850's, they sought only treaty rights, the fulfilment of which in time would allow them to profit from the Chinese scene without being responsible for it.

On the political level, the institutional continuity of these early treaty ports with the preceding centuries of Sino-foreign relations is certainly very plain—plainer than the Westerners in nineteenth-century China ever realized. The most-favored-nation clause, for example, was not the sole invention of Western diplomats, as some of them believed, but embodied the Son of Heaven's traditional treatment of all barbarians with equal condescension, the better to manipulate them against one another.

If we now try to look at the early treaty system through traditional Confucian eyes (no easy feat), we may glimpse the persistent outlines of certain time-tested Sino-barbarian relationships, certain institutional tendencies which remained half-latent, half-emergent during the two decades after the Opium War of 1840. The essence of these postwar tendencies, I suggest, was for the Western participation in Chinese affairs to shift from the rejected forms of tribute relations toward those of synarchy—toward forms of "joint Sino-foreign administration." This tendency was manifested especially in the treaty ports, where the Western powers participated increasingly in the government of these small but strategic parts of China.

4. Synarchic Tendencies under the Early Treaties

My suggestion in what follows is that inveterate synarchic habits had some influence on Sino-foreign relations under the early treaties on the level of institutional practice. In this period the Ch'ing officialdom was still largely unaffected by the ideas of Western nationalism and clung to the Confucian view of foreign relations which had been coexistent with synarchy. While the Westerners in these two decades remained impervious to Confucian ideas, they found some practical usefulness in the synarchic tendencies in question.

For purposes of this analysis, we must deny any hard-and-fast causal relationship between thought and institutions. They are actually intermixed and interdependent, neither one existing in fact without the other, and the distinction between them is an analytic step taken by the observer on a high level of abstraction. Similarly the customary distinction between economics and politics, while implicit in most modern thinking, has limited usefulness and seems indeed to be breaking down. In the case of nineteenth-century China, economic determinists, by asserting the primary causal importance of economic factors like foreign trade, have persuaded a whole generation to look at the treaty system in mainly economic terms, thereby neglecting the important cognate approach to it in political terms. In what follows we need not deny the corrosive effect of Western trade on China, nor the contrast between the all-transforming industrial power of Britain and the comparatively innocuous influence of traditional invaders like the Manchus—all of which became more evident after the period here discussed.

The British were able after the Opium War to set forth a new structure of ideas including such elements as free trade and the equality of states, which were all expressed in the words of the treaties. However, the British and other Westerners in the treaty ports were not the only actors in the drama of Sino-foreign relations. Even after they had obtained the treaties on paper and were able to threaten the renewed use of superior force, they were far from dominant in the day-to-day situation and could not dictate Chinese action. In fact, the path of progress for the British often lay in a judicious accommodation of Western ways to those of the Middle Kingdom. As practical men representing their merchant compatriots, the British consuls not infrequently had to compromise with the institutional situation which confronted them.[8] This left the way open, during the interval from 1842 until the early 1860's, for a body of treaty-port practices and institutions to grow up which exhibited certain synarchic features reminiscent of Sino-barbarian relations in the past.

As an intellectual device for looking at these tendencies, let us compare aspects of the British opening of China in the 1840's with the Manchu conquest of the 1640's. If we acknowledge from the start that these invasions represent two very different traditions and social forces, far apart in time and cultural background, the similarities between them may take on added interest. The comparison will at least show more in common on the level of action and practice than on the level of theory and ideology.

THE MANCHU CONQUEST AND THE BRITISH OPENING OF CHINA

1. *Territorial bases on the Chinese frontier.*—Unlike domestic rebels, both the Manchus and the British before attacking China had built up their military striking power in territorial bases outside the area controlled by the dynasty then ruling at Peking. In what is now called Manchuria the nascent Ch'ing regime by 1644 had already developed its banner forces (totaling some 169,000 warriors), more than half of whom were Chinese and Mongols.[9]

The British territorial base in 1840 began with India, whence the China expedition was outfitted with a considerable proportion of Indian troops among its landing forces (Bengal and Madras infantry, artillery, sappers, and miners).[10] This base then extended through Singapore, where British administrators were already accustomed to dealing with a growing Chinese population, and Malacca, where British missionaries had first established the Anglo-Chinese College to train Chinese youths in Christianity and, incidentally, in the English language and customs.[11] This British external base was nonetheless territorial for being largely maritime—in it British war vessels dominated an area where the big Chinese junk fleets of Canton and Amoy[12] provided much of the economic activity and Chinese pirates much of the disorder. Operating from this sanctuary inaccessible to the dynasty in China, and with the unusual mobility of their fleet, the British, like the Manchus, were able to appear suddenly upon the Chinese frontier and demonstrate their military superiority, which became most evident when they captured walled cities and defeated imperial garrisons. Where the Manchus had established their border base by expelling the Ming power from Manchuria, the British established their advanced bases on islands like Hong Kong, Kulangsu at Amoy, and Chusan (south of Shanghai near Ningpo on the outer edge of the Hangchow estuary).

2. *Force in reserve: the maintenance of order.*—Once they had achieved their immediate ends (which in the case of the Manchu conquest of course went much further than the British), the invaders in each case distributed their military power at strategic spots where it was held ready to defend their position. The garrisons of Manchu bannermen at major cities like Chengtu and Foochow had their later counterparts in the British gunboats stationed at the treaty ports or patrolling the Yangtze. In both cases the military force held in reserve could be dispatched to suppress armed opposition in the areas of interest to the invaders. Where, for the Manchus, this included the entire country, for the British it included the treaty-port centers of residence and the coastal and later riverine routes of water-borne commerce. The British Navy's systematic suppression of Chinese piracy on the South China coast in the late 1840's and 1850's, by convoy and punitive expeditions, was a local police action. It was smaller in scope and aim than the Manchus' extirpation of the rebel Li Tzu-ch'eng after 1644 but similar in requiring the co-operation of the local Chinese populace and officials. During the two decades 1848–69 the British Navy paid 149,000 pounds sterling in bounties while carrying on this policing of the China coast. Usually, "the Viceroys of the maritime provinces . . . sent mandarins with the Queen's ships, who . . . sealed these undertakings with Imperial approval."[13]

3. *Enlistment of Chinese assistance.*—Neither invasion in practice was a purely military matter. In each case the invader sought to conciliate local Chinese sentiment and secure the aid of the local people as well as the expert help of a body of Chinese collaborators. The British felt little need for domestic military allies like General Wu San-kuei, who let the Manchus enter Shanhaikuan and assisted their subsequent conquest of the provinces. But the preliminary British commercial invasion of Central China, particularly the opium traffic, was carried on for them by their allies in trade, the Cantonese.

As the Manchu forces finally came within the Wall, according to their account, the local officials tendered their submission, which the invaders graciously accepted. On May 30, 1644, for example, when the Manchu invading force was at Fu-ning-hsien on the route to Peking, "the District Magistrate Hou I-kuang and his colleagues at the head of the local populace came out to welcome it. Robes (of office) were bestowed upon them and they were ordered to continue in the discharge of their official duties and to distribute grain from the storehouses for the relief of the populace."[14] The Manchus laid claim to the Mandate of Heaven by announcing that their mission was to save the Chinese people from disorder and bring them peace. Once installed in Peking, they used many of the Chinese members of the existing bureaucracy. As immediate acts indicating legitimate succession, the Manchu regent at Peking kotowed to Heaven and decreed mourning for the recently deceased Ming emperor. Toward the populace he showed the Son of Heaven's compassion by the remission of taxes.

In the case of the Opium War, even without the ceremonial vestments and the guidance supplied by the theory of the Mandate of Heaven and the record of previous dynasties, the British found it expedient to concentrate their attack on the ruling dynasty and announce that they had no quarrel with the common people. Even before the outbreak of hostilities, the British representative of the crown in China, Lord Napier, at Canton in 1834 had issued proclamations, addressed to the Chinese populace, which cast the blame for current difficulties upon "the perversity of their government" and by implication made it plain that Britain was no enemy of the people.[15] In 1841 British naval officers tried "to confine hostilities as much as possible to the servants and property of the Chinese government, leaving the people uninjured." The interpreters, J. R. Morrison and R. Thom, "frequently enlisted in our favour the people of the country, who might have offered great annoyance." They "knew well how to allay their fears, and conciliate even their good offices."

As a result the Canton delta populace even at close quarters seemed often "more moved by curiosity and astonishment" than by fear of the British steamers; they crowded the river banks, housetops, and surrounding hills and even helped clear the river passage, "the Chinese peasantry . . . coming forward to assist and even venturing . . . on board the steamer itself . . . undoubtedly, one of the good results of not having inflicted any injury upon the country people." Learning by experience, the British at Ningpo in October, 1841, after "the Chinese themselves voluntarily assisted to remove the obstructions . . . behind the city gates," called "some of the principal inhabitants" together and assured them that British hostility was directed "against the government, and not against the people." The Chinese of Ningpo thereupon welcomed British "protection," until they found themselves taxed to ransom the city.[16] The British invaders' success in securing co-operation from the local population was evident in their use of a Chinese coolie corps.

A type of Chinese leadership had already been recruited in the form of the "Chinese traitors" who assisted the early British interpreters in their correspondence and acted as go-betweens with local officials. The British merchants already had their compradors,[17] who assisted them in every form of commercial operation, and the opium trade had provided an incentive for both merchants and officials of the Middle Kingdom to collaborate with the foreign commercial invasion. Throughout the first two decades of the treaty system, the foreign establishments on the Chinese coast attracted a mixed body of Chinese collaborators, which ran the gamut from the early Christian converts (or would-be converts like the founder of the Taiping regime, Hung Hsiu-ch'uan) and translators like Dr. James Legge's assistant, Wang T'ao, to the many unknown and less savory characters who handled opium, scouted for coolies, or represented secret societies like the offshoots of the Triad.

Naturally, these points of comparison between the Manchu and British invasions are outnumbered by points of difference which in retrospect now seem to us far more significant. Yet such points of comparison should not for that reason be entirely overlooked, as has been the custom.

4. *The invaders' privileged and exploitative position.*—Extraterritoriality and the special status and immunities enjoyed by Westerners in modern China (which have helped to make the Western experience of life there often very pleasant) were new versions of the conquerors' traditional prerogatives. The Mongols had lived like overlords in the Middle Kingdom. The Manchus required all Chinese to shave their heads and wear the queue, bend the knee and render tribute. Manchu bannermen living on grain stipends in their special quarters of the big cities had become effete and impecunious by 1842, but institutionally they formed a precedent for the inviolable treaty-port communities which grew up after that date. For two centuries before the modern commercial exploitation by the imperialist powers, moreover, China had paid yearly tribute to alien rulers whose entire tribe and race lived off the Chinese surplus. The annual grain shipments from the Yangtze to Peking may well have been a greater

economic burden than the opium trade ever became (a detailed comparison would be of interest).[18]

Western privileges under the treaties have been too well advertised as part of Western imperialism to need recounting in detail. Yet it seems valid to note that many, if not most, of these privileges can also be viewed as traditional concomitants of barbarian conquest and synarchy, in modern dress. Thus China's eventual payment of most of her customs revenue to foreign bond-holders, while not termed "tribute" or paid in rice, was nothing new in principle. The exploitative financial power of the treaty-port banks might well be compared with that of the Moslem guilds during the century of Mongol synarchy, when China was drawn involuntarily into the international trade of the Mongol empire.

The modern tendency to stress the economic aspects of the imperialist situation has led us to ignore in retrospect the social and political aspects. Treaty-power nationals in recent decades (even though they have enjoyed the subtle satisfaction of extraterritorial status) have not really experienced the baronial life of the sometimes very ordinary Westerner who became a taipan, or at least managed to live like one, in a nineteenth-century treaty port. The Western superiority suggested by the (apocryphal) notice "Chinese and dogs not allowed" was effective not only in social life but also in politics, where the acceptability of late Ch'ing officials to the foreigners sometimes became a prime factor in their careers.

5. *Economic development.*—After the setting-up of their respective dispensations, both the Manchus and the British sought to make their new order work and fostered its economic prosperity. Where the Manchu emperors became the patrons of agricultural development, especially the reclamation or breaking-in of new land, and gave edifying advice to farmers, the British administrators in the treaty ports, on the contrary, sought to foster international and local free trade. The first consul at Shanghai lent assistance to the Canton broker, Alum, who energetically tried to bring the silk and tea exports of the interior to the new emporium on the Whangpu.[19] Chinese merchants were soon investing capital in foreign firms, just as the Canton hong merchant, Howqua, had put his money to work through Russell and Company of Boston. The British suppression of the piracy which formerly had handicapped coastal trade was only part of a general extension of orderly commerce, ships, telegraphs, and postal communications to China. In a port like Shanghai the consul soon secured the appointment of a harbor master and the establishment of

aids to navigation such as channel markings, and eventually helped dredge the Woosung bar. Meanwhile Shanghai's new international settlement, together with the adjoining French concession, entered on that phenomenal period of growth which has made it in a century one of the world's greatest cities. Where Manchu peace and order had been accompanied by the unfortunate doubling, if not the tripling, of China's population, Western trade and enterprise helped produce the giant, if not overgrown, city of Shanghai.[20]

6. *Joint administration.*—The development of administrative institutions involving a joint exercise of power by the invaders and the local regime is more fundamental for our purposes than the sometimes superficial similarities noted above. It seems unnecessary to describe the system of Manchu-Chinese rule which had been worked out with such care and balance at Peking, where each of the Six Boards had a Manchu and a Chinese president, two Manchu and two Chinese vice-presidents, and so on. Here it is of interest to notice comparable institutions built up under the treaty system. Since the British never had the slightest intention of themselves becoming the rulers of China, this development is all the more striking. It grew out of the local situation in the treaty ports, and the impetus arose in the field of practice from day to day rather than in the field of theory and policy aims.

First of all, let us note that in both the first and second China wars, whenever the British forces occupied a city, they were obliged to maintain Chinese local officials in office for purposes of local administration. The last occupation of Canton was followed by almost four years (January, 1858—October, 1861) of a so-called allied government over that metropolis, in which British and French officers, under the leadership of the energetic Harry Parkes, established the first puppet regime of modern times. Their chief puppet was the unfortunate governor of Kwangtung, Po-kuei, and the result was a thoroughly synarchic Sino-barbarian administration of the Canton area, using traditional Chinese forms.

The most striking form of joint administration became the Imperial Maritime Customs Service, in which the foreign commissioners of customs were employed by the emperor of China under the administrative supervision of the British Inspector-General, Robert Hart. The commissioners maintained a careful parallel relationship to the Chinese superintendents of customs, who continued during the nineteenth century to administer the "native customs" establishment and to receive the maritime customs duties at each port. In most cases this Chinese superintendent was concurrently a territorial official of considerable rank, like the taotai (intendant) in charge of the Shanghai area.[21] The foreign commissioners were early instructed by Hart to regard themselves as the "brother officers" of the native officials and, "in a sense, the countrymen" of the Chinese people. "The foreign staff," said Hart, "aids the Chinese Superintendent in the collection of the Revenue." The commissioner was "necessarily subordinate" to the latter official; he should act as the "head of the Superintendent's executive . . . be the Superintendent's adviser." A commissioner whose action or advice placed his "Superintendent in a false or untenable position" would lose his post. He should not "arrogate to himself the tone of the Superintendent" nor prejudice the latter's final decisions.[22]

Throughout its career until the end of the dynasty the foreign inspectorate of customs thus functioned in a partnership. The foreign employees of the emperor saw to it that the customs revenue was properly calculated and collected, but before 1911 they did not themselves receive or handle the funds. Their service was paid for by a fixed monthly allowance from the local superintendent of customs, who retained control over the essential operation of receiving the revenue at the customs bank and disposing of it at the order of Peking. This dual arrangement proved to be a great solution for the British problem of establishing optimum and reliable conditions for commercial expansion.

It is significant that the foreign inspectorate was invented at Shanghai and not in London and that the Foreign Office within two years after 1854 decreed the abolition of the system, on account of the fact that it had not yet been extended to the other ports.[23] H. N. Lay and Robert Hart, who created the inspectorate, both began their careers as British vice-consuls and interpreters, but they ceased to represent the British government directly. Both saw themselves as intermediaries between East and West, as indeed they were.

Joint administration also developed at Shanghai, which remained Chinese territory and was not made a "free city," as had been suggested in 1862. Quite aside from the extraterritoriality applied to foreigners, the Chinese authorities' powers over *Chinese* residents became "subject to certain definite restrictions" regarding law courts, police, taxation, and legislation.[24] While not seeking to remove luster from the Anglo-Saxon capacity for pragmatic governmental arrangements, we may well search for the roots of the Shanghai anomaly in Chinese as well as in Western tradition. Even allowing for the well-known historical fact that evidences properly selected will "prove" almost any point, our perspective on the treaty system may be usefully deepened by this exercise of viewing it against its synarchic background.

5. The Eclipse of Synarchy by Nationalism

While the British were drawn part way into the traditional Confucian orbit on the level of practice, they failed to accept Chinese political ideas. Viewed against the age-old synarchic tradition of China's foreign relations, the British invaders of 1840, once their superiority in warfare was evident, might well have been expected to seek imperial power and to try to supplant the Manchu dynasty. This had been the prize available in time past to tributaries who "rebelled" successfully (Ch'ing documents regularly referred to the British in wartime as *ni*, "rebels"). British conquest in India was no secret to Peking; even some Americans, like the anglophobic and overquoted Commissioner Humphrey Marshall,[25] foresaw a British attempt to take over China. But the British did not picture themselves as contenders for the Mandate of Heaven. Where the Manchus had made themselves the new managers of the old system, the British invaders tried to get a new system set up, but without becoming managers of it. They therefore worked with and through the Ch'ing regime, participated in its synarchic administration of China, but did not try to take its place.

The essence of the Western view was to approach China as an incipient nation. This was implicit in the treaties themselves, for they were each drawn up explicitly as between two equal states, one of which agreed to give unilateral privileges to the other. The treaties posited the equality of all nation-states even while creating a situation of inequality. But these unequal provisions came to be regarded by the West as temporary and transitional, imperfect arrangements along the road to China's eventual emergence as a modern sovereign nation. To the Western mind it was "normal" when Japan, saddled with a similar treaty system in the 1850's, succeeded in throwing it off by the end of the century.[26]

As a prime example of nation-state thinking in the Western approach to China, we may take the American development and expansion of the idea of the "Open Door for trade" into the idea of China's national independence. The conception of the Open Door which eventually caught on with the American public was not the demand for equal opportunity among the capitalist competitors in the commercial exploitation of China (embodied in John Hay's first notes of 1899) but rather the concept of Chinese "territorial and administrative entity" or "integrity" expressed more vaguely in the second set of notes in 1900.[27] We need not deny that the Open Door for equality of trading conditions as espoused by Hart and his deputy, Hippisley, who helped Rockhill draft the first notes, had an appeal for American business interests. The fact remains that the "integrity" of China, her national independence of the imperialist powers, her development as a nation-state, became the actual shibboleth of American policy.

Given these Western expectations, which go far back in Western thinking, it was inevitable that Western contact should bring nationalism to China just as disruptively as it brought industrialism. Sides of the same entering wedge, these cognate developments of nationalism and industrialism not only remade Chinese life but also remade the Western and modern Chinese evaluations of Chinese political institutions, including synarchy. This process may be seen at work if we look briefly at (a) the increasing foreign participation in the Ch'ing administration and economy under the policy of intra-Western and Sino-foreign "co-operation" after 1860, and (b) the Chinese intellectual response to this foreign influx.

A. SYNARCHIC ASPECTS OF THE CO-OPERATIVE POLICY

The tendency toward synarchic practices under the early treaties reached its last significant phase in the period of the "co-operative policy" of the 1860's at Peking, after the treaty system had finally been accepted by the dynasty. Here the British ministers Bruce and Alcock participated in measures which would strengthen the Ch'ing regime in a gradual progress toward stability and the meeting of its problems.[28] With the help of Bruce and Hart, the interpreter's college, or T'ung-wen Kuan, was staffed with foreign professors to train a Chinese body of Western specialists. With the blessing of Bruce and the American minister, Burlingame, the adventurous F. T. Ward of Salem and the British officer of engineers, C. G. Gordon, successively organized and led the "Ever-Victorious Army" which defended Shanghai against the Taipings in the early 1860's. In the same period H. N. Lay and Captain Sherard Osborn, with the support of the Foreign Office and the British Navy, were securing the building and manning of a fleet of powerful modern warships, which actually came to China before the project collapsed over the question of control and jurisdiction.[29] Already the imperial forces in the Yangtze Valley, under Tseng Kuo-fan, had procured Western steamers and the assistance of Western personnel to outmaneuver the rebels. Tseng and Li Hung-chang fostered the Kiangnan Arsenal at Shanghai to make foreign arms and gunboats, and at it John Fryer translated Western technical works into Chinese. As the climax of this period, Anson Burlingame toured the Western capitals as an envoy of the Ch'ing regime. All these activities, which were more various than is yet realized,[30] involved Sino-foreign co-operation and, specifically, the formal and informal acceptance by the Manchu-Chinese officialdom of Western officials' and private individuals' services and policy proposals.

One result, especially after the opening of the Yangtze to steamer traffic, was to place the major centers of Chinese economic development and so of political control—namely, the treaty ports both on the coast and on the inland waterways—under a mixed foreign and Chinese jurisdiction. The prototype of this development was under the Shanghai Municipal Council, which administered a Chinese city with the help of Chinese employees and eventually had a mixed Chinese and foreign membership. Amoy also developed an International Settlement on the island of Kulangsu.

As time went on, the participation of the foreigner in the Ch'ing administration was extended from the maritime customs to the new post office and salt gabelle. Meanwhile the modern economy was dominated by the foreign treaty-port banks and, after 1896, by foreign industrial establishments. Foreign domination of the carrying trade in Chinese waters was challenged only after the China Merchants Steam Navigation Company, founded in 1872, had purchased the steamship fleet of Russell and Company, which had been built up by Edward Cunningham of Boston with the help of Chinese merchant capital.[31] Education under government auspices was inaugurated with the aid of foreigners like W. A. P. Martin; eventually, the pace was set by Christian missionary colleges, which began as foreign-managed institutions and gradually "devolved" into the hands of Chinese staffs and trustees.

This Western participation in China's institutional development was so multifarious and varied as to give one the impression of a general influx of Western individuals and influences without, however, any center of political direction and control—much Western "participation" but little "joint rule." This view may be oversimplistic. The institutions of Western Europe and the United States in the latter part of the nineteenth century were highly pluralistic; the governments of the respective Western nations did not play as dominant a role in their foreign activities as did the Ch'ing officialdom in the corresponding lines of Chinese activity. The private enterprises of the mission boards, the trading companies, the treaty-port entrepreneurs, and sundry adventurers far outweighed the official acts and programs of the Western governments. Western participation in the conduct of affairs in late-nineteenth-century China must be seen in this larger context and not merely on the Western official plane. Timothy Richard was a private individual but influenced Ch'ing mandarins. W. A. P. Martin, another private citizen, headed a central government college, although he came from the American educational tradition of private colleges. F. T. Ward was a mere Yankee adventurer but received Ch'ing official rank. Chinese officialdom was corrupted by an opium trade founded by free-enterprise Scotsmen and never controlled by the Foreign Office. It is hard to find in this varied private activity of Westerners in China a tangible entity called "foreign rule" beyond the limits of the ports and foreign concessions, yet from the Chinese side it is plain that Ch'ing rule was greatly affected, circumscribed, and sometimes guided by foreign influences of various kinds. The possibility of "Sino-foreign rule" was thus left standing on one leg—the Manchu-Chinese side often felt forced into it and sometimes was willing, but the Western side never got it formally organized. Synarchy never became full-fledged.

B. THE INCREASING NATIONALISM OF CHINA'S INTELLECTUAL RESPONSE

Meanwhile, on the side of ideology and political ideals the potentialities of synarchy were gradually snuffed out by the growth of modern Chinese nationalism. This little-known process was first evidenced among the Canton populace and on a different level may also be traced in the writings of scholar-officials. In the 1840's the inauguration of the treaty system had been seen as an application, *faute de mieux*, of the traditional practice of "getting the barbarians under control through concessions" (*chi-mi*).[32] The Chinese reaction had been to attribute this disaster to the ineffectiveness of the Ch'ing regime rather than to emphasize the factor of foreign aggression. This attitude applied the traditional Confucian doctrine that barbarian invasion is inspired by domestic disorder and that domestic disorder results from the regime's lack of sufficient "men of ability" or "human talent" (*jen-ts'ai*). Tseng Kuo-fan's diary in 1862 notes, "If we wish to find a method of self-strengthening, we should begin by considering the reform of government service and the securing of men of ability." As he wrote to Li Hung-chang in the same year, "Confucius says, 'If you can rule your own country, who dares to insult you?' "[33]

In this period Tseng and his scholar-gentry colleagues were supporting the foreign (Manchu) dynasty and accepting foreign (Western) military aid to suppress the Chinese (Taiping) rebels, all in defense of the Confucian tradition and polity. Stigmatized today as unpatriotic "collaborators," these suppressors of native rebellion were merely demonstrating that Confucian "culturalism" was the focus of their loyalty: while imbued with a strong love of country and identification with "our mountains and rivers," they were yet premodern in their concept of the Chinese state. Indeed, its loose, decentralized social structure, the exclusion of the peasant masses from political life, the lack of modern communications and unifying symbols, kept China still below the level of nineteenth-century Western nationalism. Most of all, nationalism in the most developed form of *mass participation* in political life was antithetic to the tradition of the upper-class monopoly of government by emperor, bureaucracy, and gentry. Under the co-operative policy of the 1860's Confucian administrators like Tseng moved briefly in the direction of that community of interest between the Chinese gentry and the foreign invader which we have noted above as a hallmark of synarchy.

To Manchu leadership at Peking, meanwhile, the Taiping rebels were a disease within the Confucian body politic, while the Russians ("aiming to nibble away our territory like silkworms") and the British (seeking trade but "not covetting our territory and people") were lesser external dangers. In 1861 the policy was to "suppress the Taipings . . . first, get the Russians under control next, and attend to the British last."[34]

From this traditional point of view, the British invaders and their Western allies and hangers-on after 1860, having established themselves in a position of strategic, but not ubiquitous, military superiority, could be accorded a status analogous to that of border "allies." Like the Liao and Chin regimes in North China (eleventh and twelfth centuries), they ruled one part of a now divided empire. In the trading centers and on the waterways, their power made them potentially dominant, but they had made their peace with the Son of Heaven at Peking. In traditional terms the co-operative policy of the 1860's meant that the British and their foreign colleagues of other nations had been admitted into the power structure of the universal

Confucian state on a basis which, though uncertain for the future, was at least temporarily limited and stabilized. Thus it made sense for the British to co-operate, to the extent that they were permitted, in the suppression of the Taiping Rebellion. As barbarian allies on the maritime frontier who had been "pacified" by concessions, the British could be allowed to participate part way in the affairs of the dynasty without posing an immediate threat to it. This could be tolerated under the assumptions and attitudes connected with synarchy when it would not have been tolerable under the modern theory of nationalism, as indeed proved to be the case in the next century.

The theoretical rationale which was constructed to clothe the fact of British and other Western participation in a diluted form of synarchy was an application of the classical concept of *t'i* and *yung*. First applied to Sino-Western relations by Feng Kuei-fen about 1860, this formula became widely current through Chang Chih-tung's writings in the late 1890's. Stated by Chang as *Chung-hsueh wei t'i, Hsi-hsueh wei yung*, it may be translated, "Chinese studies for the essential principles and Western studies for the practical application."[35] Under this dichotomy, the continuation of the Confucian rule of the Manchu Son of Heaven, along with the Manchu-Chinese bureaucracy and the Chinese scholar-gentry, represented a basic principle, or *t'i*, while the whole process of modernization in which the Westerner participated, including the treaty-port system of trade regulations through the Maritime Customs and city administration in the foreign concessions, served as a mere "practical application," or *yung*.

The *t'i-yung* bifurcation was an unrealistic one from the beginning. The Western *yung* could not be imported without a considerable bit of Western *t'i* coming with it, and the Chinese *t'i* could not survive once the Chinese *yung* had been abandoned. It would be a mistake, however, to regard this famous dichotomy as a *source* of official action or even of policies; on the contrary, it was a formula which became widespread rather late, after modern contact had begun its inexorable course. The situation which it attempted to rationalize had come into being with the very advent of the treaty system. As described above, this situation was basically the early treaty-period adaptation of synarchy, which let the Westerner participate in the Confucian order. Unfortunately, the acceptance of anything Western proved to be a one-way ratchet which could serve only to draw the Confucian state further off its traditional base. When the British at Canton demanded the abolition of the Cohong monopoly and the inauguration of "free trade," they may have seemed to be introducing into the Chinese scene a mere Western practice (or *yung*), but the implication of the treaty clause which finally abolished the Cohong was that the Son of Heaven should turn his back upon the traditional hierarchy of classes which placed the merchant far below the official and should thus alter the ideological structure (or *t'i*) of the Confucian state. Similarly, when Commissioner Lin Tse-hsü and his literary colleague, Wei Yuan, advocated the use of foreign arms, which were the most obvious form of *yung*, they were in fact suggesting that China must develop an armament industry and embark on that process of industrialization which would inevitably destroy the traditional Confucian state and its agrarian economy administered by tax-gatherers. Once the treaty system and foreign contact had become established, it was already too late to save the old order by a distinction between *t'i* and *yung*. The theory was merely an insecure adjustment to a collapsing situation, a halfway house on the road to modernization.

Continued contact with the Western nation-states enforced the conclusion that nationalism was the only possible form of state organization for meeting the problems of the modern world. Learning by imitation, farsighted Chinese officials as early as 1861 were already holding up the examples of Peter the Great and other nation-builders and the object lesson of Turkey—a theme continued down to 1898 and after. The Western assumption about China's inevitable metamorphosis into a nation-state was thus taken over by modern Chinese themselves. The central theme of China's political history in the first half of the twentieth century, under Sun Yat-sen, Chiang Kai-shek, and even Mao Tse-tung, has been the struggle to create a nation-state which could take its place in the international order.

In retrospect we can see that the sentiments of nationalism were attached to almost every aspect of Westernization or modernization. Early Ch'ing efforts at armament against the West had to become nationalistic, at the very beginning of the modernization process, as soon as it proved impossible either to find Western allies who would fight against the British or to rely on Western mercenaries. Lin Tse-hsü and Wei Yuan in 1840–42, in the use-barbarians-against-barbarians tradition, had hopefully opined that "there is no better method of attacking England than to use France or America." But their successor as a "barbarian specialist," Feng Kuei-fen, was soon declaring, "It is utterly impossible for us outsiders to sow dissension among the closely related barbarians." Similarly his superiors, Tseng

Kuo-fan and Li Hung-chang, saw the need of becoming independent of foreign officers to lead modernized Chinese troops.[36] There was no way, in short, for contact to grow between China and the West except on the nation-state assumptions of sovereign independence or else colonialism. China's "semicolonial" echo of synarchy appeared increasingly anomalous.

In this way the treaty system, which began in the 1840's partly as a modified form of the traditional institution of synarchy, steadily, increasingly, and inexorably became a source of "disintegration and demoralization," as Generalissimo Chiang later so aptly phrased it,[37] which in the course of time undermined and destroyed the old Confucian order, including any possibility of permanent Sino-foreign administration of the Chinese state. Where the treaty system had begun by affecting mainly the Chinese economy, it ended by remaking Chinese political thought.

This reinterpretation leads to the final conclusion that synarchy proved to be the Achilles' heel of the universal Confucian empire. Once again, as so often before, the powerful barbarian invader had to be taken into the Chinese scheme of things. The tradition of synarchy made it at first relatively painless to do this. But while the Westerners in the treaty ports were inclined to welcome synarchic practices, which often seemed quaintly convenient, they denied the Confucian ideology which should have accompanied them. The eventual rise of modern Chinese nationalism led to the elimination, first, of the "unequal treaties" as documents, by Chiang Kai-shek in 1943, and, second, of the postwar American participation in the government of mainland China, by Mao Tse-tung in 1949. How far the ideology and institutions of Communist China may still show traces of the ancient synarchic tradition remains a question.

PART II

Thought and Officialdom in the Social Order

CHINESE CLASS STRUCTURE AND ITS IDEOLOGY

T'UNG-TSU CH'Ü

THIS PAPER uses Chou dynasty sources, together with a few Han works, to analyze certain theories of social stratification which had an enduring influence on Chinese political life. After the collapse of Chou feudalism, China's class structure was modified by historical changes in the degree and the channels of social mobility and in the factors which formed classes and determined the individual's status. Yet certain general patterns of social stratification persisted, together with traditional tenets of ideology.

1. Division of Labor and Social Stratification

The Confucian school denied that there could be a society of uniformity and equality. Instead it believed that human beings were different in intelligence, ability, and morality. Some were wise and some simple; some were virtuous and some vicious. There was a natural hierarchy. Consequently, people in a society could not all be given the same roles and treated as equals.

"Work is what people dislike; gain and profit are what they like," says Hsün-tzu. "If there is no distinction of occupation, then people will have difficulty in getting work done."[1] Social organization therefore required a division of labor and the assignment of different kinds of work to people, in a rational way.

Basically there were two types of work, the mental and the physical. Farmers, artisans, merchants, and others pursued the second type. It was their function to produce goods or render services. On the other hand, there was a group which was not expected to engage in production. This group included scholars and officials, whose function it was to study and to acquire virtue. Obviously the physical labor, which needed little training, could be performed by average men, whereas only the more talented were qualified to perform mental work. This kind of labor was considered to contribute the most to society and was therefore highly respected. The role of this class was characterized as that of the "great man," "the superior," or *chün-tzu*, in contrast to the role of the "small man," or *hsiao-jen*. The former group not only was superior but was also expected to be served and supported by the latter. This led to a relationship of subordination

235

and superordination. Statements such as the following were common in Chou times:

Superior men diligently attend to the rules of propriety [*li*], and men in an inferior position do their best.[2]

It is a rule of the former kings that superior men should labor with their minds and smaller men labor with their strength.[3]

The great men devote themselves to governing, and the small men devote themselves to labor.[4]

In an age of good government, men in high stations give preference to men of ability and give opportunity to those who are below them, and lesser people labor vigorously at their husbandry to serve their superiors.[5]

The commoners, the artisans, and merchants, each attend to their profession to support their superiors.[6]

Furthermore, the division of labor was politically oriented. Mental labor was linked with governing. This was clearly pointed out by Mencius in the following statement, which has been frequently quoted:

Great men have their proper business, and little men have their proper business. . . . Some labor with their minds, and some labor with their strength. Those who labor with their minds govern others; those who labor with their strength are governed by others. Those who are governed by others support them; those who govern others are supported by them. This is a principle universally recognized.[7]

Thus, to him, "if there were not men of a superior grade, there would be none to rule the countrymen. If there were not countrymen, there would be none to support the men of superior grade."[8]

Since the role of *chün-tzu* was more important to society, and since the *chün-tzu* assumed more responsibility than a member of the other group, naturally more rewards were distributed to him. He enjoyed more prestige. He was also given more and better material comforts.

Most ancient Chinese philosophers and statesmen merely argued that the labor of the two groups deserved different rewards. Probably Hsün-tzu was the only one who attempted to give a systematic explanation as to why consumption should be differentiated in society —an explanation which went beyond the usual argument that one's reward should correspond to one's contribution. He related it to the scarcity of things and the impossibility of satisfying all human beings without discrimination. "People desire and hate the same things. Their desires are many but things are few. Since they are few, there will inevitably be strife."[9] He also says:

Man by birth has desire. When desire is not satisfied, then he cannot be without a seeking for satisfaction. When this seeking for satisfaction is without measure or limits, then there cannot but be contention. When there is contention, there will be disorder; when there is disorder, then there will be poverty.[10]

Therefore the problem was how to meet human wants and keep society in order. Hsün-tzu thought that the problem could not be solved by treating all human beings alike and distributing things equally among them. In the circumstances, things would not be sufficient to satisfy all.

When social statuses are equal, there will not be enough for everybody. When men's power is equal, there will be no [way to achieve] unification. When people are equal, no one will be able to command the services of others. . . . Two nobles cannot serve each other, and two humble persons cannot command each other. This is a law of nature. When people's power and position are equal and their likes and dislikes are the same, things will not be sufficient to satisfy everyone, and hence there cannot but be strife. Strife will lead to disorder and disorder will lead to poverty.[11]

Thus the only way to solve the problem and to maintain the social order was to make social positions distinct and definite and to distribute things according to status. Hsün-tzu emphasized over and over the importance of "making social distinctions plain and keeping the people together."[12] The essential thing, then, was to have some way to insure that each one in the society would find his correct position, assume his duty, and satisfy his wants.[13] This was the function of *li*, the purpose of which was to make social distinctions clear and to regulate men's desires according to their statuses.[14] Only by establishing such a social system, Hsün-tzu observed, would it be possible to "nourish men's desires, to give opportunity for this seeking for satisfaction, in order that desire should never be extinguished by things, nor should things be used up by desire."[15] An ideal society in which a division of labor was well organized was described by the philosopher as follows:

To be honored as the Son of Heaven and to be so rich as to possess the empire, these are desired by all human beings alike. If these human desires are followed, it will be impossible for more than one authority to exist, and things will not be sufficient to supply them. Therefore the ancient kings formulated *li* and righteousness and made distinctions in order to have the grades of the noble and humble, the difference between the elders and the young, and discrimination between the intelligent and the stupid, the able and the incapable, thus making everyone assume his function and get into his proper position. Then the amount of one's salary will be in accordance [with his ability]. This is the way to have people live together in harmony and unity. Thereupon when the benevolent man is on his throne, the farmers will engage in cultivation with their strength; the merchants will engage in [using] wealth with their keenness; the various artisans will engage in [making] tools with their skill; from the *shih ta-fu* up to the dukes and marquises, all will fulfil their official duties with benevolence, generosity, intelligence, and ability. This may be called the utmost equality. Therefore the ruler whose reward is the whole empire will not think it too much for himself; any one who is a gatekeeper, an innkeeper, a guard at a pass, or a nightwatchman will not think his task too humble.[16]

2. Achievement as the Criterion

According to the above theories advocated by Confucianists, the criterion for social status should be achievement, not ascription. This has been described by Parsons as the "particularistic-achievement pattern."[17] Theoretically speaking, only the wise and virtuous were qualified for mental work and entitled to the task of governing. Virtue was the fundamental basis for appointing officials. Mencius thought that a ruler should "esteem virtue and honor virtuous scholars, giving the worthiest among them places of dignity, and the able, offices of trust."[18] To Hsün-tzu, "one's rank must correspond to his virtue, and his salary must correspond to his rank."[19] And the greater one's wisdom and virtue, the higher his rank and salary. It was remarked by Mencius that "when the state is in good order, men of little virtue are submissive to those of great, and those of little worth to those of great."[20] And Hsün-tzu put it this way:

One's grade should be determined by his virtue and his appointment to office should be according to his ability, making everyone assume his function and get into his proper position. The men of greater wisdom should be made feudal lords, and the men of lesser wisdom should be made ministers.[21]

It was said that in a kingly state "a man without virtue would never be honored; a man without ability would never be made an official; and a man without merit would never be rewarded."[22] On the other hand, "if a man's virtue does not correspond to his rank, or if his ability does not correspond to his office, or if his reward does not correspond to his merit," Hsün-tzu observes, "there is no misfortune greater than this."[23] A fair social order and good government could be attained only when it was certain that the virtuous were wealthy and honored and that the unworthy were poor and humble. In such an orderly society, poverty and humbleness would be indexes of unworthiness and inability, and things of which to be ashamed. That is why Confucius said, "When a country is well governed, poverty and a mean condition are things to be ashamed of."[24] A person would then be ashamed of his wealth and nobility only when the state was ill governed and corrupt.[25]

However, there is always a discrepancy between this ideal pattern advocated by the Confucianists and the actual system of stratification. Shun, who is frequently referred to by the Confucianists as an example of perfect co-ordination between virtue and reward, was a man of such great virtue that "it could not but be that he should obtain the throne, that he should obtain those riches, that he should obtain his fame, that he should attain to his long life."[26] However, a man of great virtue did not always enjoy such rewards. Confucius, whose virtue was that of a sage, did not hold a post corresponding to his virtue and ability. Thus there was no mechanism to guarantee that a man of great virtue would occupy a high post, no matter how orderly the society might be. This certainly puzzled the ancients, and reasons were sought to explain the discrepancy. Wang Fu, a Han scholar, says:

> It is not necessary that the so-called virtuous men or *chün-tzu* must always enjoy high position and high salary, must be wealthy, noble, and glorious. These are [attributes] which a *chün-tzu* should have, nevertheless they are not what a *chün-tzu* must have. It is not necessary that the small man always be poor, humble, and exposed to cold, hunger, humiliation, and distress. These are what a small man should be, nevertheless they are not what a small man must be.[27]

A similar attitude was held by another Han scholar, Wang Ch'ung, who attributed the unexpected discrepancy to opportunity.

> Integrity is always found among the virtuous; opportunity is not always there when one seeks to enter upon an official career. To be virtuous or not virtuous is a matter of ability; to meet or not meet [an opportunity] is a matter of chance. There is no guarantee that a person of great talent and pure behavior will be honored; there is no guarantee that a person of slight ability and impure behavior will be humbled; the talented and pure may not meet [with opportunity] and may be down in low positions; the incompetent and the impure may meet [with opportunity] and be up above others. . . . Entrance to official career depends upon meeting opportunity, and nonentrance depends upon not meeting it. One who is in an honorable post is not necessarily virtuous; it is because he has met [with opportunity]. One who is in an inferior post is not necessarily unintelligent; it is because he had not met [with opportunity].[28]

3. The Structural Background

The above are theories arguing that stratification is a requirement for the existence of society. Now let us discuss the structural background of this ideology.

First of all, it should be pointed out that the above-mentioned theories were formulated in the feudal period, in which the ranks and manors of the feudal lords and other nobles were hereditary. A commoner was born to be a commoner and never could become a nobleman. Thus it was remarked in the *Kuan-tzu* that the son of a *shih* was always a *shih*, that of a farmer always a farmer, that of an artisan always an artisan, and that of a merchant always a merchant.[29] These theories which emphasized the different roles of *chün-tzu* and small men and the importance of maintaining such differences obviously reflected the class structure of the society. They might be either an explanation of the situation expressed in the social structure or a rationalization of the privileges of the ruling class.

Here we are confronted with the most difficult problem involved in ideological analysis, for we have no way of identifying a rationalization. How can we prove one to be such unless an explicit confession is made by the person who advances the theory? However, any thought has an existential basis.[30] If we can locate the social bases of ideas and relate them to the ideas, we may be led to focus our attention on certain problems which would otherwise have been entirely overlooked. We may locate a man's social position and see whether he identifies himself with the characteristic thinking of the social group of which he is a member, i.e., whether he identifies himself with the interest of his own group. We may also explore the various social factors such as occupational role, style of life, relations of production, power structure, etc., to determine whether they are related to a man's verbal expression.

Now, we know that all statements found in the *Tso-chuan, Kuo-yü*, and other classics like those quoted above were voiced by members of the ruling class (e.g., Liu-tzu, Chih Wu-tzu, Yen-kung, and Kuo) or else by persons closely associated with that group (e.g., Mencius and Hsün-tzu). Their social position can be easily located. Our problems are: Do their statements represent the interest of a privileged group? Do they aim to justify its privileges, to consolidate its status and power, or to rationalize its control over and exploitation of the ruled class?

Creel has argued that Confucius was not an advocate of feudalism. However, he points out that "Confucius never directly denounced feudalism."[31] On the other hand, Confucius clearly stated, "I follow Chou."[32] His emphasis on the primacy of "ratifying names"[33] certainly was based on the concept that "there is government, when the prince is prince, and the minister is minister."[34] His statement which complained about the transfer of power from the Son of Heaven to the feudal lords, from the latter to the ministers, and from them to the subsidiary ministers, clearly indicates that he was not in favor of the disorder of his time and that he advocated the restoration of the traditional feudal order.[35] Mencius' advocacy of the "well-field" system[36] and of hereditary salaries for the descendants of officials[37] was also an indication of his attitude toward feudalism.

All of us are familiar with the principles of benevolent government and of governing by virtue advocated by the Confucian school. Confucius said that the people should be enriched and educated.[38] Mencius considered that "the people are the most important element in a nation, the spirits of the land and grain are the next, the sovereign is the lightest."[39] He emphasized over and over that a ruler should regard himself as the parent of his people, should always consider their welfare and livelihood, and should see that they were neither heavily taxed nor overworked, so that "all the people of the empire will be pleased and wish to come and be his people."[40] He severely attacked "tyrannizing over the people."[41] However, it does not follow that the ruling class should give up its privileges over the people. What the Confucian school emphasized was that the people should not be "exploited" to such an extent that they could not support their parents, wives, and children.[42] In other words, the "exploitation" must be mild and rational. Thus the view held by Confucius was one of "employing them only at the proper time and making the imposts light."[43] In a similar way, Mencius emphasized "taking from the people only in accordance with regulated limits."[44]

It should be pointed out that any theory which encourages the ruling class to give up its privileges is incompatible with feudalism. The productive system in a feudal society, by definition, calls for the exploitation of serfdom. Otherwise, it would be impossible for the feudal lords to be supported, and it would be impossible for the scholars of the lowest class (*hsia-shih*) to have "an emolument equal to what they would have made by tilling the field."[45] In short, the style of life which characterized the ruling class could not be maintained without feudalism. This point can best be illustrated in Mencius' own case; he was once a minister in the state of Ch'i and, while not holding an office, as pointed out above, was closely associated with the ruling class. This kind of association made it possible for Mencius "to go from one prince to another and live upon them, followed by several tens of carriages and attended by several hundred men."[46] Without some explanation or rationalization, this style of life, which was clearly marked off from that of the masses, certainly could not be justified. Questions might even be raised among those who were closely associated with the privileged class, not to mention the unprivileged and the exploited groups. Thus one of Mencius' disciples was puzzled by his extravagant way of life and questioned whether it was proper for a scholar performing no service to accept such support. To this Mencius replied:

"If there be not a proper ground for taking it, a single bamboo-cup of rice may not be received from a man. If there be such proper ground, then Shun's receiving the kingdom from Yao is not to be considered excessive. Do you think it was excessive?"

[P'eng] Keng said, "No. But for a scholar performing no service to receive his support notwithstanding is improper." Mencius answered, "If you do not have an intercommunication of the productions of labor, and an interchange of men's services, so that one from his over-plus may supply the deficiency of another, then husbandmen will have a superfluity of cloth. If you have such an interchange, carpenters and carriage-wrights may all get their food from you. Here now is a man, who at home is filial and abroad respectful to his elders; who watches over the principles of the ancient kings, awaiting the rise of future learners—and yet you will refuse to support him. How is it that you give honor to the carpenter and carriage-wright, and slight him who practices benevolence and righteousness?" P'eng Keng said, "The aim of the carpenter and carriage-wright is by their trades to seek for a living. Is it also the aim of the superior man in his practice of principles thereby to seek for a living?" "What have you to do," returned Mencius, "with his purpose? He is of service to you. He deserves to be supported and should be supported."[47]

In another case, Mencius was asked by another disciple why it was that the superior man ate without laboring in the fields. Mencius answered:

When a superior man resides in a country, if its sovereign employs his counsel, he comes to tranquility, wealth, honor, and glory. If the young in it follow his instructions, they become filial, obedient to their elders, true-hearted and faithful—vhat greater example can there be than this of not eating the bread of idleness?[48]

The above two quotations may be examined as expressing theories formulated by Mencius to explain the important role performed by the *chün-tzu* in his society. The situation in which these statements were made may give us some hints as to their motivation, although these may be far from conclusive. We may assume that, when one's privilege is questioned and challenged, it is necessary to find reasons with which to defend it or justify it. The element of rationalization seems more explicit in this case than in other cases where the situation in which statements were made remains obscure to us. Mencius may or may not have been conscious of his rationalization, but his statements, whether we call them rationalizations or theories, apparently were put forward by him to defend and to justify the privileges of the upper class. They represented the class interest of the privileged group.

Our discussion shows that the theories expressed in connection with the division of labor and social stratification corresponded to the structure of the feudal society; they fit each other harmoniously. However, there was one point of discrepancy between the social structure and one aspect of these theories, namely, that the achievement pattern advocated by the Confucianists, which emphasized the importance of virtue and merit, was in conflict with the ascription pattern, which was characteristic of feudalism. If one's status and reward were determined at birth, then they had nothing to do with personal qualification and achievement. These theories could not be justified unless all nobles were men of virtue and intelligence. This could not always be the case. Confucius' and Mencius' remarks on the government conducted by the ruling class implied that it fell far short of the ideal pattern. Confucius and his followers emphasized that the government should be in the hands of the most virtuous, such as Yao and Shun. This was their Utopia; yet they could do little about it.

On the other hand, Confucius was successful in causing some changes in class structure and social mobility by extending to commoners the kind of education which hitherto had been accessible only to nobles. He educated a group of commoners and made them members of the *shih* group, qualified to enter on official careers.[49] Most of his disciples were men of humble origin.[50] When knowledge was no longer monopolized by the nobles, then the commoners were given a new opportunity for social mobility. As a matter of fact, a number of his disciples, such as Jan Ch'iu, Tzu-lu, Tzu-yu, Tzu-hsia, Yuan-Ssu, Tzu-chien, Tzu-kao, Tsai Wo, and Tzu-kung, either became stewards (*chia-ch'en* or *tsai*) of the nobles or occupied official posts of higher rank.[51] Under the principle that, when one has "completed his learning [he] should apply himself to be an officer,"[52] the cultivation of virtue and the special training for the *chün-tzu* had a practical value in promoting one's status and changing one's role. However, one could enter only the lower stratum of the political hierarchy. Power was still in the possession of the big families.

A more radical change took place in the late Chou period of the Warring States. The feudal order was greatly weakened, if not completely destroyed, through the violent process of political struggle. As the legitimate order of the feudal system was no longer respected by the powerful feudal lords and their ministers, the top stratum of the political hierarchy was upset. At the same time, there was also a change at the bottom of the stratified order. A number of commoners with extraordinary talent and unusual ability were able to impress the rulers of the various states and push their way into the upper stratum. Many prominent intellectuals, including Tzu-hsia, Shun-yü K'un, P'eng Meng, Hsün-tzu, Tsou Yen, and other scholars, who were honored as guests or teachers of the rulers, enjoyed superior prestige as well as material comfort, although they were not appointed officials.[53] Some others were able to become high officials. Fan Sui, Ts'ai Tse, Su Ch'in, Chang I, Lü Pu-wei, Sun Pin, Po Ch'i, Wang Chien, and others whose background was that of commoners became chancellors and generals of the state. As pointed out by Chao

I, this was the first time in Chinese history that men of humble origin could ever occupy such top posts.[54]

This unprecedented change certainly gave a new basis for the justification of the theories of achievement and social mobility. It was for this reason that the situation was somewhat redefined by Hsün-tzu. In the earliest days, as seen in the usage of Confucius and others, the meaning of *chün-tzu* referred to either virtue or status or both.[55] The new definition given by Hsün-tzu, however, almost completely disregarded status; his emphasis was on the side of virtue, that is, personal qualification. Thus we read in his works:

> Although a man is the descendant of a king, duke, or *shih ta-fu*, if he does not observe the *li* and righteousness, he must be classified as a commoner; although he is a descendant of a commoner, if he accumulates learning, rectifies himself and his conduct, and is able to observe the *li* and righteousness, then he must be classified as a minister, chancellor, or *shih ta-fu*.[56]

Another change occurred in Han times. First of all, with the exception of a limited number of kings and marquises, official posts were not hereditary. Thus they were no longer monopolized by the big families. Although there was no regular system of civil service examination, the offices were bestowed, in principle, according to merit. Men of special qualifications could be either recommended as students in the Imperial Academy or directly recommended as candidates for official appointment. In the first case, those students of the Erudits who had excellent academic records were qualified for official appointment.[57] In the second case, people could be recommended by the local governments and the offices of the central government under various categories such as "virtuous, wise, square, and upright," "filial and pure," or "extraordinary fine talent."[58] Besides, scholars of extraordinary reputation were sometimes summoned to court by special decree.[59] By these means a formal channel for social mobility was set up. These opportunities had been unknown in the past.

A mechanism to facilitate and regulate "free competition" by means of a regular examination system was not set up until the Sui and T'ang periods. Theoretically, this opportunity was, with a few exceptions, open to all. This system was considered the most rational measure ever worked out to select men of ability. It was assumed that the talented and the learned would be able to pass the examinations; on the other hand, if one failed, it meant that he was not qualified. This popular belief at least served one purpose. It minimized the discrepancy between the actual degree of social mobility and the ideal pattern.

4. Class Structure: Officials and Commoners

Now let us examine the class structure after Chou times. Did the theories discussed above continue to play an important role in the actual stratification of Chinese society after the collapse of feudalism? To what extent was the social order conditioned by these social theories? Did the class structure correspond closely to the ideal pattern? Can the theory of two classes, i.e., the ruling class and the ruled, serve to describe the class structure? Were there only two classes in the society, or were there more?

The doctrine which distinguished between mental and physical labor was widely accepted and played a dominant part in China's social stratification for many centuries as a criterion in determining the prestige of one's occupation. Mental labor was highly respected, whereas physical labor was looked down upon. Physical labor was, so to speak, a status disqualification.

At the same time, the sharp demarcation between the ruling class and the ruled continued to operate. The officials, the backbone of the ruling class, were the superiors; commoners were inferiors. Officials themselves were conscious of their superior status, which was also admitted by the commoners. There was little social communication between the two groups, and intermarriage was rare.

The difference between the two groups can also be observed by objective criteria. The officials, together with their family members, had a style of life quite different from that of commoners, so that they could be clearly marked off from the latter. The style of life was not conditioned economically, as is the situation in modern capitalist society. Instead, it was regulated legally under sumptuary laws.[60] Thus a monopoly over the superior way of life by a privileged group was legitimized. The official class was guaranteed the exclusive enjoyment of it, unthreatened by any propertied class. The sumptuary laws served to minimize or limit the exercise of economic power to such an extent that wealth alone did not guarantee the right to consume. For example, it was emphasized in the *Kuan-tzu* that "one may have a virtuous and honorable body, but he dare not use [a nobleman's] garment if he does not possess a noble rank; one's family may be wealthy, but he dare not use his money if he does not receive an official salary."[61] It was also mentioned in an edict of Emperor Ch'eng of Han that "the sage kings distinguish the *li* so as to put the superior and the inferior in order, and they differentiate the carriages and horses so as to mark out the virtuous. Though one has wealth, if he has not a superior [status], his use of it is not allowed to go beyond the regulations."[62]

Officials were also given other legal privileges. They were exempted from *corvée* service. They could not be arrested and investigated without the approval of the emperor.[63] Neither were they subject to corporal punishment. The punishment could be canceled by giving up official rank or by paying a fine. These procedures were given in detail in the codes of various dynasties.[64] The inequality between the officials and the commoners was most striking in the fact that the punishment of a commoner who injured an official was heavier than in ordinary cases in which both parties were commoners.[65]

From the above discussion we may conclude that the officials and the commoners were two different status groups, whether in terms of prestige, or style of life, or legal privileges.

However, it would be a mistake to think that China was a two-class society. Were there only two classes? The answer must be in the negative. All the theories seeking to justify the privileges of the ruling class were focused on the respective statuses and roles of the rulers and the ruled. They were not concerned with the different statuses within the ruled class. From the standpoint of the power structure, all the "four people" (*ssu min*) might be considered as one homogeneous group—all of them were the ruled. However, sociologically speaking, in terms of social stratification they could not be considered one class. First, not all persons in the same occupational group enjoyed the same status. Witness the difference between wealthy merchants and small shopowners or peddlers. Similar variations also characterized the farmers: to include landowners, owner-cultivators, tenants, and hired laborers in a single class would certainly be misleading. Furthermore, numerous occupational groups were all classified as commoners. Obviously, neither their roles in the society nor their statuses were the same. Different occupations were accorded different degrees of prestige. The traditional order of scholars, farmers, artisans, and merchants itself already suggested that there was a stratified difference in prestige. The status of the non-official scholars was the highest among the commoners, because they were the only group engaged in mental labor. They were considered the best elements among the commoners—the elite. The occupation of farmer, artisan, merchant, butcher, and the like was considered physical work, and their statuses were therefore inferior. This kind of classification, in which the officials were distinguished from the commoners and, among the latter group, the scholars were again marked off from the others, is quite similar to Pareto's classification of governing and nongoverning elites, on the one hand, and the nonelite, on the other.[66]

Among those who performed physical labor, farmers were held to be the most productive, and therefore their status came next to that of the scholars. Artisans and merchants, whose efforts were considered less productive, had an unfavorable position and were looked down upon by the society, especially by the intellectuals. An example may be cited from the *Family Instructions* of Lu Yu, in which he advised his descendants that they should devote themselves to study and make a living by teaching, that it was all right for them to become farmers, but that they should never be engaged in the "small men's business of the marketplace," which he considered would be a great disgrace to his family. He also expressed concern about the fate of his descendants who might be "degraded to the marketplace or reduced to government runners."[67] During certain periods, merchants were particularly discriminated against. They were allowed neither to wear silk nor to use horses in Han times.[68] Similar restrictions against horseback-riding were also invoked against merchants and artisans in the T'ang dynasty.[69] And at times, these two occupational groups, as well as butchers and sorcerers, were forbidden to take the civil service examinations or enter upon an official career.[70] However, the stratified order described above was an ideal pattern. The actual situation was much more complicated. The inferior status of merchants in Chinese history has usually been exaggerated. In spite of the fact that their class position did not correspond to their status,[71] the influence of their wealth cannot be overlooked. It must have had some effect on their status and style of life.

Statesmen frequently complained that the merchants, by the possession of great wealth, had violated the sumptuary laws and enjoyed what they were not entitled to. Merchants in Han times were accused of wearing embroideries and silks.[72] It was also mentioned in a T'ang edict that many merchants and artisans rode on horses which bore rich decorations.[73] With these deviations in mind, it is not difficult for us to imagine what status a wealthy merchant actually had in the society. For, if the style of life peculiar to the privileged class was no longer monopolized by it, then the status order was already threatened. Their trespass against the regulations meant that the merchants were successful in sharing the honor of the superior status group, to which they were not entitled legally. The fact of close communication between merchants and officials can also be documented.[74] Association with the most honored group must have greatly enhanced the prestige of merchants in society. In these circumstances we can hardly imagine that merchants had an inferior status among the commoners. That a wealthy merchant usually had a status superior to that of a farmer, who was supposed to be in a higher position but was actually exploited by him, was well illustrated in a Han memorial of Ch'ao Ts'o.[75]

All these facts lead us to think that probably the merchants were discriminated against not simply because they were despised by the ruling class but because their economic power constituted a constant threat to those whose privileges were legally protected. All the efforts at discriminations and the repeated warnings may be looked upon as a reaction on the part of the elite to the danger of the merchants' intrusion into the status group. The latter made jealous and vigorous efforts to guard their status and privileges.[76]

It may also be pointed out that the status of merchants did not remain the same all the time. They must have enjoyed a higher status in periods such as the Ming and Ch'ing, when there was no unfavorable sumptuary law against them, when they were not excluded from the privilege of taking the civil service examinations, and when there was a growth of industry and commerce which greatly strengthened their financial power. All these factors must have contributed to the improvement of their status and the enhancement of their social mobility.

Thus it is obvious that the commoners, though as a group they had a social and legal status inferior to that of the officials, may be subdivided. There were differences in occupational prestige. Moreover, wealth, though not a determining criterion of Chinese stratification, nevertheless influenced in some degree the status of different occupational groups as well as that of persons in the same occupational group. Unfortunately, we have only fragmentary knowledge about the prestige of various occupations. There are evidences that certain occupations were superior in prestige, whereas certain other occupations were inferior.[77] But we are unable to compare the prestige of the various occupations and thus to reconstruct a scale of occupational prestige in stratified order. Such a study would require the subjective judgment and evaluation of the various occupations in the society, either in terms of accorded status or in terms of subjective self-ranking, and these are impossible to obtain in a historical study.

5. Class Structure: "Mean" People

Finally, there was the lowest stratum in the social pyramid. This group was comprised of slaves, prostitutes, entertainers, government runners, and such regionally defined groups as the *yueh-hu*, or singers and music players, in Shensi and Shansi, the "beggars" in Kiangsu and Anhwei, the "lazy people"[78] in Chekiang, the boatmen[79] in Kwangtung, the "permanent servants"[80] in Hui-chou, Ning-kuo, and Ch'ih-chou of Anhwei Province, and others. Their occupations, which were merely to serve or entertain others, were considered non-productive and as making the least contribution to society. They were therefore placed lowest on the prestige scale and labeled "mean" people. Certain families ruled that any one of their members who chose to become an actor, prostitute, or government runner was to be expelled from the clan, since engaging in any of these mean occupations was considered a serious disgrace to the whole group.[81] The social distance between the "mean" people and the common people was great. Intermarriage between the two strata was socially and legally forbidden. Social mobility was very slight. In fact, the "mean" people formed a caste more than a class.

Moreover, the "mean" people were the negatively privileged class. They were excluded from taking the civil service examinations,[82] a prohibition which made it impossible for them to enter upon an official career. Their children were similarly deprived.[83] Thus the best avenue for social mobility was closed to them. Under sumptuary law they were allowed to have only the most humble style of life. If the style of life peculiar to the officials gave them special social honor, then we may say that the style of life peculiar to the "mean" group, such as a certain specified color or decoration, was designed particularly to give the bearers social dishonor, so that they would not be mixed up with the "good" people. For instance, a black gown[84] or green scarf[85] was a symbol of humiliation and an indication of inferior status. Nor were the "mean" people given the same treatment as commoners before the law. Every dynastic code held that a slave who had injured or killed a commoner was to be punished more severely than in ordinary cases between equals, whereas a commoner who had injured or killed a slave was to be punished less severely.[86] The same principle also operated in cases of illicit intercourse.[87]

6. The Bureaucratic Power Basis

From the above discussion it is obvious that the superior-inferior relationship in traditional Chinese society was based on occupational categories. The officials had the highest status. The scholars, farmers, artisans, merchants, and other occupational groups, known as the common people or "good" people, came next. They may be divided into substrata. Then, in the lowest stratum, there were the "mean" people.

There was a close correlation between the distribution of power and the distribution of statuses.[88] In other words, bureaucracy was the source of prestige and privilege. Those persons permitted to enter the bureaucracy had the highest social status and enjoyed the most privileges. The scholars had the highest status among the commoners because their training constituted the basic qualification for civil administration. Thus they were the potential candidates for membership in the bureaucracy. That was why the possessor of a degree under the examination system had a status superior to that of a scholar without a degree; he was a step closer to the power structure than the ordinary scholar. It has been keenly observed by Max Weber that "social rank in China has been determined more by qualification for office than by wealth."[89] Unlike the commoners who, with a few exceptions, at least in theory could take the examination and enter officialdom, the "mean" people were excluded from such privileges. In terms of political power they were permanently barred from entering the power structure. Thus they had the most inferior status in society. It is not exaggerating to say that the hierarchy of prestige corresponded closely with the hierarchy of power. We cannot understand and interpret social stratification in traditional China if the stratification system is not considered in terms of power. In this sense, then, the "ruling class and the ruled class" dichotomy is a key concept in Chinese social and political thought, and its sociological significance should not be overlooked.

REGION, FAMILY, AND INDIVIDUAL IN THE CHINESE EXAMINATION SYSTEM

E. A. KRACKE, JR.

THE TRADITIONAL Chinese examination system occupies a central place in Chinese political theory and in the practical structure of Chinese society and was one of the earliest of Chinese institutions to attract the attention and inspire the imagination of Western political thinkers. It has symbolized dramatically the ideal of a public career open to all in the measure of their worth and ability. Yet the relation between the ideal and the reality of the examinations remains in some ways elusive. As with the broad pattern of Chinese social relationships, discussed by Dr. T. T. Ch'ü elsewhere in this volume, the continued appeal to early statements and precedents has somewhat deceptively cloaked changes in function, and the resulting shifts in relation between ideal and reality have inevitably modified the real meaning of the ideals within Chinese thought.[1] To understand the real meaning of the examinations in Chinese political thought, therefore, it is necessary to trace the change in their actual practice over the centuries. The present study is concerned with a single aspect of this change—the variation in interpreting the concept of free opportunity and the differing results of this for the several regions of the empire.

1. The Ideal of Free Opportunity and Its Realization

Behind the concept of competitive examinations for office lies the ideal of Confucius that only ability and virtue qualify a man for service in government—an ideal inherited by such divergent Confucian schools as that of Hsün-tzu, authoritarian in its trend, and that of Mencius, whose more liberal principles predominated in Chinese thought from the T'ang dynasty onward. Since the more favored Confucian doctrine held that human nature (including the mind) was inherently capable of perfection, it followed that ability and virtue were independent of the status into which one might be born. Therefore the means should be provided, and the way left open, for any man to rise from low birth-status to the highest rank.[2]

We must not read into this concept certain connotations apt to accompany it in the Occident. In Confucian theory, once men's charac-

251

ter and status were established, their differing needs and moral attainments made it natural that they should receive differing material advantages, prerogatives, responsibilities, and liberties. Certain occupations—including in earlier periods commerce and handicrafts—brought ethical disqualification for an official career. Freedom of opportunity to develop one's abilities, in short, was quite compatible with strong class distinction. To the Chinese thinker this was not inconsistent. To him the need of society took priority over the will of the individual. It was a man's duty, rather than his right, to place his services at the ruler's disposal; he should accept office but not seek it.[3]

Practical conditions at all times modified the operation of the theory, however. On one hand, although universal education would seem to follow logically from Confucian political doctrines, the creation of schools and the support of students on such a scale were scarcely conceivable with the material resources available to traditional Chinese society in the best of times. Diversity in economic development, increasing the disparity of educational resources among groups and places, necessarily made opportunity more unequal. Differences in examination methods and requirements also favored some groups and places over others. On the other hand, the educated Chinese in normal times sought office, whether as his right or as his duty, almost as eagerly as his occidental counterpart. Since in most periods no other career could rival the prestige offered by the civil service, the examinations, which gradually became the pre-eminently honored gateway to the service, assumed a unique importance. Above all other ways of entrance, they represented the principle of recruitment through merit. But they never quite won either an exclusive control of the recruitment process or unchallenged approval as an ideal. Testing ability rather than character, they failed to satisfy some of the more zealous Confucians, and they were always obliged to compete with other recruitment methods such as recommendation, protection (*yin-pu*), promotion from the clerical service, or sale of official rank. The changing balance among methods was of course intimately involved with the political movements of different periods. The honor accorded to the examination system, its practical importance, and the zeal and honesty of its administration saw successive periods of rise and decline. While the story of the examinations reflected in some degree the history of social mobility in the bureaucracy as a whole, the reflection was never complete.[4]

The length of the present study permits only brief and inadequate reference to most of the factors mentioned above. Primary emphasis will be placed on discernible relationships between available data of three kinds: population concentrations and changes, regional representation among examination graduates, and regional patterns of vertical social mobility among the graduates. The focus in time will be on the period from the mid-seventh century A.D. to the end of the nineteenth, with somewhat greater attention to the earlier periods when competition in the examinations was free from regional limitations. It is scarcely necessary to emphasize that explanations of the examination system based on investigations thus limited in scale and scope can arrive only at partial and tentative conclusions. These are presented in the hope of contributing toward the fuller study that is needed.

2. Regional Representation under Free Interregional Competition, 655–1279

The examinations were at first, in the Han dynasty, primarily a method of classifying candidates who had been recommended for governmental service. They were slow to assume the role of a major recruitment method, and during earlier centuries the numbers who passed annually were rather few. Even during the earlier reigns of the T'ang dynasty, before 655, there seem never to have been more than twenty-five men so selected in any single year; the annual average during this time was less than nine men. (Because of irregularities in the spacing of examinations, both before and after the triennial rule was adopted in 1067, the annual *average* of graduates during a period of years, including the years between examinations, is the only practical unit for comparison.) The first significant increase came abruptly with the rise to power of the ambitious empress Wu Tse-t'ien. Her sharp eye discerned in the technique of examination, it seems, a tool for her projected usurpation of power. It might serve to tap the heretofore neglected source of trained men in the Southeast and help to dislodge from power the tightly knit clique from the capital region, which was devoted to the interests of the reigning dynasty. In 655 she caused forty-four doctoral examination degrees to be conferred, and, in a seven-year period before the proclamation of her new dynasty, the annual average exceeded fifty-eight men. She thus, perhaps unintentionally, established the quantitative importance of examinations for recruitment. At the same time, by the favored treatment of the graduates, she enhanced the prestige of the new method as the accepted channel to power. The process of opening opportunities to wider groups had begun.[5]

After the fall of Empress Wu, the restored T'ang rulers employed the same tool and, for a brief time, raised still higher the annual average of degrees conferred. The disorders of the later T'ang and of the succeeding Five Dynasties period (907–60) brought a hiatus in the growth of the system, and practices that facilitated favoritism in examination-grading restricted the opportunity of men who were without influential connections. At the end of the tenth century, however, the Sung rulers, who had now reconstituted the empire, took new steps to develop the system. They instituted a series of measures to insure the greatest possible objectivity in grading the examination papers. Simultaneously, they expanded the number of degrees annually awarded until these more than doubled the highest T'ang averages. The numbers of degrees remained high during most of the remaining years of the dynasty for which we have statistics. Usually around two hundred or more per annum, at times they averaged nearly two hundred and forty.[6]

In using the examination technique to further her plans for usurpation, Empress Wu had not only opened a governmental career to wider groups. By bringing in new men from the Southeast to compete with those of the capital region, she had also consciously or unconsciously created a situation that would continue to strengthen the imperial position through the balancing of potentially rival regional groups within the bureaucracy. Equitable recruitment of officials from all areas also offered advantages beyond this: it might strengthen the allegiance of well-represented regions and avoid the antagonism of frustrated literati; it might insure that interests of all regions would find a voice in government councils; it might encourage the development of an educated local leadership to assist the centrally appointed regional officials. It is hard to say how far rulers or officials were aware of these advantages. There is ample evidence that regional feeling was strong in the civil service, and any inequities in recruitment were fully noticed. We see this in the discussion of the subject between Ssu-ma Kuang and Ou-yang Hsiu in the eleventh century. Regional inequality still existed, but its patterns were now quite different from those of five centuries before, as we may see from figures preserved in a memorial of Ssu-ma Kuang. These figures concern the distribution of both the competing and the successful candidates for the degree of doctor of letters (*chin-shih*) in the years 1036, 1038, and 1040. They represent scattered illustrative examples, from varying circuits for different years, but their trend is surprisingly clear. The area of the capital produced, in all the years named, between 170 and 270 doctors of letters for each million house-holds of its population. But the areas along the North border, those in the Southwest (excepting the vicinity of Chengtu in modern Szechwan), and the South Central area produced, in the examples given, roughly one to four such graduates per million households. No figures are given for the remaining seven circuits in the flourishing East Central and Southeast areas, but at a conservative estimate these must have supplied close to twelve per million households, sev-

TABLE 1

NUMBERS QUALIFYING AS CANDIDATES FOR DOCTORATE OF LETTERS ("CHIN-SHIH") IN 1036, 1038, AND 1040, AND NUMBERS WINNING THE DEGREE

CIRCUIT OR ADMINISTRATIVE UNIT	POPULATION *ca.* 1100 (MILLION HOUSEHOLDS)	NUMBER OF CANDIDATES			NUMBER OF GRADUATES		
		1036	1038	1040	1036	1038	1040
South Central:							
Kuang-nan Tung	.57	97	84	77	3	2	0
Ching-hu Nan	.95	69	69	68	2	2	2
Chin-hu Pei	.58	.....	24	23	.....	0	1
Southwest:							
Kuang-nan Hsi	.24	38	63	63	1	0	0
K'uei-chou	.25	28	32	.....	1	0	.....
Tzu-chou (T'ung-ch'uan)	.56	63	.....	.....	2	.....	.....
North and West border:							
Ching-tung	1.34	157	150	.....	5	5	.....
Ho-pei	1.17	152	.....	154	5	.....	1
Ho-tung	.61	44	41	45	0	1	1
Shensi	.56	.....	123	124	.....	1	2
Li-chou	.30	26	.....	28	1	.....	0
Capital area:							
K'ai-feng Fu	.26	278	266	307	44	69	66
Directorate of Education (Kuo-tzu Chien)	.....	118	108	111	22	28	30
Remaining seven circuits	8.98	.....	.....	.....	.....	.....	.....
Total	16.37	.....	.....	.....	.....	.....	.....

eral times the ratio of the rest of the empire, excluding the capital. While these seven circuits held somewhat over half the empire's population, they included a much smaller proportion of its territory; among them were the densely populated areas of the Szechwan Basin, on the west, and the fertile Yangtze delta. It may be particularly significant that they held many of the empire's greatest cities, including the trade emporia of the southeastern coast. Ou-yang Hsiu's discussion of the subject makes clear that the Southeast already rivaled the capital as a cultural center and dominated the examinations to a degree that incurred the envy of other parts of China.[7]

The significance of these facts becomes clearer in the light of fuller statistics derived from lists of graduates for two later Sung examinations. Two examinations, out of more than a hundred held during the Sung period, afford a slender basis for generalization, but the particular selection (made by chance preservation) is a rather fortunate one. The two examinations—one of 1148 and one of 1256—came near the beginning and near the end, respectively, of the era during which the Sung rulers reigned at Hangchow, after most of North China had fallen to the Jurchen invaders in 1127. During the years immediately following the northern debacle, much of South China was also ravaged by Jurchen raids, but with the return of peace after 1141 the administrative system was largely restored to order. The following century was relatively undisturbed, and Sung culture flourished despite the persistence of serious economic problems until after 1233, when a new threat appeared in the North. The Mongols raided Szechwan in 1253 and invaded it more seriously in 1258. Fifteen years later the main Sung defenses were breached and the remaining Chinese resisters driven to the mountains and seas. The examination of 1148 thus fell in a time of peace following disorder, and that of 1256 at the threshold of disorder after long peace. Where the graduate lists of the two examinations agree in their testimony concerning Chinese society, it is not improbable that they typify the intervening century as well; and, since they are relatively complete, they supply an invaluable cross-section of the successful candidates in their respective years.[8]

Among the most striking parallels between the two lists is their indication of the dominant place held by the regions with denser population, larger numbers of great cities, and more advanced commercial development. Among the sixteen circuits of the empire at that time, the two southeastern coastal circuits, Fu-chien and Che-tung, containing the outstanding commercial cities of the age, stand out above all others, supplying together more than 40 per cent of the empire's total in both years. The share of the empire's graduates that came from these circuits was even greater than their share of the empire's population; in both years they were far ahead of all other circuits in numbers of graduates per million households.[9]

In other circuits the correlation between a dense population and a high ratio of graduates to population is less consistent, perhaps because the smaller numbers of graduates permitted greater accidental fluctuations, or because of factors outside of our present consideration. But such a correlation is still strongly suggested. And when we

TABLE 2

POPULATION AND REGIONAL REPRESENTATION AMONG
DOCTORAL GRADUATES, 1148 AND 1256

REGION AND CIRCUIT	POPULATION (THOUSAND HOUSEHOLDS)*		NUMBER OF GRADUATES		GRADUATES PER 1,000,000 HOUSEHOLDS		PREFECTURES OF OVER 100,000 HOUSEHOLDS
	1162	1223	1148	1256	1148	1256	ca. 1100
Southeast China:							
Fu-chien	1,391	1,599	66	114	48	71	5
Che-tung	ca. 1,090	ca. 1,080	52	82	45	72	7
Che-hsi	ca. 1,150	ca. 1,140	38	26	35	24	5
Chiang-nan Tung	966	1,046	30	30	31	29	6
Chiang-nan Hsi	1,891	2,268	23	53	12	23	7
Regional total	6,492	7,134	209	305	32	43	30
South Central China:							
Kuang-nan Tung	514	446	5	17	10	38	1
Ching-hu Nan	969	1,251	1	9	1	7	2
Ching-hu Pei	254	370	1	15	4	41	0
Regional total	1,737	2,067	7	41	4	20	3
Southwest China:							
Kuang-nan Hsi	489	528	0	19	0	36	0
K'uei-chou	387	208	4	4	10	19	0
T'ung-ch'uan Fu	805	841	28	48	35	57	1
Ch'eng-tu Fu	1,098	1,140	35	34	32	30	3
Regional total	2,779	2,717	67	105	24	39	4
Free North China:							
Li-chou	371	401	2	16	5	40	0
Ching-hsi	43	6	0	3	0	480	0
Huai-hsi	52	218	0	7	0	32	3
Huai-tung	111	127	3	7	27	55	1
Regional total	577	753	5	33	9	44	4
Total with relevant information	11,584	12,671	288	484	25	38	41
Occupied North China	....	....	26	1	......	......	....
Imperial clan	....	....	16	76	......	......	....
Relevant data lacking	....	....	......	40	......	......	....
Total for year	....	....	330	601	......	......	....

* Since all census figures have been reduced to the nearest thousand households, the regional and national totals do not in all cases equal the exact sum of the circuit figures given.

compare evidence on the relative urban development of the several circuits, we find again that a greater number of large prefectures tends to be associated with more degrees per capita.[10]

Clearly the disparity in representation between the border regions and the central, noted by Ssu-ma Kuang in the eleventh century, still existed in the twelfth and thirteenth. The large proportion of unsuccessful candidates from the border areas, seen in the eleventh century, was surely not accidental. As Ou-yang Hsiu had then pointed out, the greater chance for success enjoyed by each candidate from the more populated regions reflected the more rigorous selective process through which he had qualified in the preliminary local tests. But the situation was now modified in two respects. The region of the new Southern Sung capital (at Hangchow in Che-hsi) was extremely modest in its share of the degrees as compared with the old Northern Sung capital at K'ai-feng. And the men of four southwestern circuits appear to have progressed very significantly in their ability to compete with candidates from the more developed areas. There is evidence that a natural process of regional equalization was under way, apparently without resort to any formal action toward this end.

3. Social Group Representation under Free Interregional Competition

Beyond indicating the local distribution of the successful candidates, the Sung examination lists give us in most cases little specific indication of their social background. Only one group is clearly singled out—that of the graduates who traced their descent to the founder of the Sung dynasty or his house. In the centuries since the dynasty was founded the imperial descendants had of course multiplied rapidly. Direct descendants of recent emperors, with titles of prince or duke, constituted the only true nobility of the age. Later generations of the imperial family, normally untitled, also enjoyed a special social status and were subject to imperial clan administration rather than to the ordinary units of local government. To insure that imperial descendants should not monopolize an undue share of the examination degrees, they were examined separately; very possibly they also escaped in this way some of the intensity of the regular competition. They provided 16 of the 288 successful candidates on whom we have relevant information in 1148, and 76 of the 484 in 1256. All of those in the earlier year, and 51 of those in the latter, had fathers, paternal grandfathers, or great-grandfathers (in many cases all three forebears) who had held official rank or office.[11]

For the candidates other than the imperial descendants, the two lists are less specific. But they do supply important clues to the relative numbers of candidates descended from officials and of those without such ancestry. They state regularly the offices held in the candidates' direct paternal line for the three previous generations,

TABLE 3

POPULATION CHANGE AND SOCIAL MOBILITY AMONG
DOCTORAL GRADUATES, 1148 AND 1256

REGION AND CIRCUIT	PER CENT OF POPULATION GROWTH OR DECLINE		PER CENT OF NEW MEN*	
	ca. 1100–1162†	1162–1223	1148	1256
Southeast China:				
Fu-chien.............	31	15	70	52
Che-tung⎱	14	− 1	⎰74	⎰62
Che-hsi ⎰			⎱30	⎱62
Chiang-nan Tung.....	− 5	8	71	67
Chiang-nan Hsi.......	14	15	68	70
South Central China:				
Kuang-nan Tung......	− 11	− 13	....	59
Ching-hu Nan........	2	29	....	78
Ching-hu Pei.........	− 56	45	....	53
Southwest China:				
Kuang-nan Hsi.......	107	8	....	84
K'uei-chou..........	57	− 46	....	....
T'ung-ch'uan Fu......	43	4	56	67
Ch'eng-tu Fu.........	24	4	54	50
Free North China:				
Li-chou..............	− 17	8	....	75
Ching-hsi............	− 81	− 86	....	....
Huai-hsi.............	− 93	320	....	71
Huai-tung............	− 80	15	....	57
Occupied North China...	....	....	30	....
Imperial clan........	....	....	....	33
Total with relevant information......	− 8	9	56	58

* Percentage of new men not given when a circuit total of six or less graduates is involved.

† Because of certain circuit boundary changes after 1127, in order to make a valid comparison, the circuit population figures for 1100 are based not on the circuit boundaries as they existed at that time but on the boundaries of 1162.

and in 1148 also specify the absence of such offices. Data on collateral relatives are unfortunately lacking or too sporadic for comparative purposes, but the completeness of the data on the direct paternal line makes it possible to use them as a yardstick for comparing the degree of official-family influence in different periods and areas. The variations of such influence that appear in this limited category of information may reflect with reasonable accuracy the variations of official-family background in a more general sense. For the sake of convenience, we may refer to the graduates who had officials in the three direct generations of their paternal ancestry as "officially-connected men," and those with no such indications as "new men," remembering that these terms are used in this restricted sense only.[12]

Having in common only the negative quality of nonofficial paternal ancestry, the "new men" with whom we have to do were certainly not a homogeneous group. Apart from the fact, already noted, that some of our "new men" had or may have had officials among their relatives in collateral lines, other incomplete data indicate, as we might expect, that a number of them came from families with a past tradition of education. Some had forebears who had passed examinations, although they do not seem to have held office. Some had brothers, or in one case a nephew, who had passed examinations or held office—suggesting, though not conclusively, a family background of education. Recorded instances of relatives with degrees are, however, few and scattered and serve only to suggest that the line separating the officially-connected from the outsiders may have been a rather shadowy one at this period.[13]

The regional variations in the proportion of new men are much more instructive.[14] As we might expect, the twenty-three traceable cases whose legal residence in 1148 was given as the occupied area of North China—largely, no doubt, refugees or sons of refugees from the Jurchen invasion—were nearly 70 per cent officially-connected. In 1256 there was only one such case, a new man from a place near the Sung border. For the territories under Sung control, the regions having high proportions of new men seem to share certain characteristics which are rather different from the unifying characteristics we saw in regions with many degrees per capita. The several regions vary greatly in the backgrounds of their graduates, but on the whole a high proportion of new men seems as likely to appear in a thinly populated region as in one more densely populated and economically developed. There does, however, seem to be a correlation between population *change* and the proportion of new men. In general, a long-range population rise tends to accompany a higher proportion of new men, while a long period of population stability or fall seems often to accompany a larger proportion of officially-connected graduates. There were nine circuits whose population rose between 1162 and 1223 by more than 5 per cent. If we discard as unreliable the percentages based on fewer than six graduates per circuit, and if we count the 1148 and the 1256 cases separately, we have twelve examples there: seven show 70 per cent or more new men, three show proportions of new men close to the national average or somewhat above (57–69 per cent), and two examples are below average. Among the circuits of stable or declining population, on the other hand, we find eight examples: one with 70 per cent or more new men, three near or above the national average, and four below the average (including both years for Ch'eng-tu circuit).[15]

To oversimplify the picture somewhat, under the circumstances of free interregional competition a given circuit tended to fall into one or another of the following patterns of associated characteristics:

Population	Dense, Rising	Sparse, Rising	Dense, Not Rising	Sparse, Not Rising
Graduates per capita	Many	Few	Many	Few
Ratio of new men....	High	High	Low	Low
Number of new men..	Many	Rather few	Rather many	Few

The coincidence of rising populations and high proportions of new men may be explainable as the result of greater social mobility among new settlers, who were able in their new homes to raise both their economic and their social status. In this connection it is interesting to note that three southeastern circuits with many new men in one year or both—Che-tung, Fu-chien, and Chiang-nan Tung—show in 1256 an unusually high number of graduates whose actual homes are elsewhere than their official residences. (Data on this are not available for 1148.) These may well be either immigrants or descendants of immigrants. This possibility in itself would have interesting implications for Sung society; it is linked with another factor that gives it still greater interest. For we find that in the Sung dynasty there were important areas that fell into the pattern of dense and rising population and higher proportions of new men. These areas included two of the most populous and urbanized circuits—Che-tung and Fu-chien. These two together furnished over a third of the new men from all of China in both 1148 and 1256. Even in the eleventh century we saw that they contributed a high proportion of the doctors of letters.

Do we have here, in the fact that southeastern urbanization was in its *active* phase, the controlling factor in the social mobility of the Sung civil service? Before a final answer can be given, it will be necessary to look into additional factors not here considered which may also have influenced the accessibility of the examinations to different social groups. The relative availability of educational facilities, the subject matter prescribed, and the examiners' methods all contributed to the result. The currents of economic development were themselves complex. But we can scarcely doubt that the degree of free opportunity present in the Sung examinations owed much to a combination of circumstances peculiar to the period—the continued growth of population in the urbanized and commercial southeastern coastal regions and a freedom of competition that allowed this region to dominate the examinations as a whole.

From what social groups did these new men come? If commercial development and city growth were related to the influx of new blood into the bureaucracy through the examinations, to what extent were the merchants or their families represented? Evidence on this point is not yet sufficient for a satisfactory answer; it seems at least quite possible that the share of the merchants among the new men was considerable. Social bars against them were weakening, and we know that a number held government positions. Yet, if they contributed any significant number to the civil service, there is as yet little evidence that they retained their group identity or exercised any strong influence on government policies. In many ways the sources of the new men among Sung graduates, and their political role, remain an enigma.

4. The Era of Regional Quotas

The extinction of the Sung dynasty in 1279 marked, in one sense, the end of an era in the Chinese examination system. The regime of relatively unrestricted competition among candidates, with the empire as a single arena, gave way to systems of regional quotas. Apart from the rivalry for high placement, the individual candidate was now really pitted only against others of his region. The distribution of opportunity among regions was now subject to political decision. The southeastern coast lost its preferential position, and new factors came to affect the rise of new men.

As we have already seen, the idea of imposing regional quotas was not new. When Ssu-ma Kuang complained of the disproportionate share of graduates enjoyed by the capital and the Southeast, he proposed to equalize the regional distribution by instituting a system of circuit quotas. An important feature of this plan was its linking of a circuit's quota not to population but to number of qualified candidates. One degree should be conferred for every ten qualified candidates from each circuit, and one degree when candidates were fewer than ten but more than five. This proposal would have gained a better representation for the circuits whose men were weaker competitors, without discriminating too severely against those with more numerous candidates.[16]

While this scheme failed to win acceptance in the Sung, the idea of regional quotas was not forgotten. When the Mongol rulers decided in 1315 to revive the examinations, then long suspended, they adapted the quota principle to purposes of their own. Obliged to use Chinese administrative skills in running their new empire, yet distrusting Chinese loyalty, they balanced carefully the several racial elements that comprised their bureaucracy. They curtailed the number of examination degrees to a yearly average of a little over twenty-one, which contrasted sharply with the Sung yearly average of around two hundred. The examinations now clearly played a more limited role in the recruitment of the bureaucracy. The degrees were divided equally among the four recognized racial groups: Mongols, foreign collaborators of the Mongols (*Se-mu jen*), North Chinese (*Han-jen*), and South Chinese (*Nan-jen*). In terms of population, and no doubt of potential candidates, this division greatly favored the Mongols and their foreign collaborators, the most trusted groups, and, among the Chinese, it favored those of the North over those of the South. While the empire now included Mongolia, Manchuria, and Korea as well as China, the population of Mongols and foreign collaborators was certainly far smaller than that of the Chinese; and census figures of 1290 give less than two million households for North China as against nearly twelve million for the South.

The 300 candidates permitted to take the triennial doctoral examination similarly included 75 of each racial group, whose numbers were further allocated by provinces. Here the discrimination against the men of the southeastern coast becomes still clearer. That area— the old circuits of Fu-chien, Che-tung, Che-hsi, and Chiang-nan Tung—was then credited with some 48 per cent of China's population. But its native residents (the technically South Chinese) were allowed only 28 candidates, in addition to 15 allowed to Mongols and foreign collaborators living there. The rest of China furnished 225 candidates.[17]

The Ming house, which expelled the Mongols and restored China's independence in 1368, tended to pursue a policy of modifying Mongol practices without reverting entirely to previous Chinese traditions. The examination system, which gradually regained its importance, illustrates this trend. The number of doctoral degrees rose gradually until, during the last century of the dynasty, the yearly average reached nearly 110. (Under the Manchu dynasty it rose further to an average a little under 120.) The Ming at first discarded the Mongol system of regional quotas, but the men of the Southeast soon began once more to win the lion's share of the degrees, and in 1425 fixed proportions were allocated to the North and to the South. The division was later made threefold, allowing for a Middle Quota Region in addition to the Northern and Southern. The new Middle Region included a small but populous area in the East, roughly equivalent to the part of modern Anhwei north of the Yangtze, and a large area in the Southwest, where Szechwan and Yunnan had become under the Mongols more closely identified with the North than with the South. The *chü-jen*, or "master's," degrees, qualifying a candidate to compete in the doctoral examinations, increased in importance. Under the Ming, as under the Mongols, each province was allowed a fixed number of these.

TABLE 4

REGIONAL QUOTAS OF CANDIDATES FOR ADMISSION TO
DOCTORAL EXAMINATIONS IN THE MONGOL PERIOD

	South-east China	South Central China	South-west China	North China	Non-Chinese Areas	Total
Mongols..................	8	3	2	47	15	75
Foreign collaborators.......	16	7	5	38	9	75
North Chinese.............	0	0	7	60	8	75
South Chinese.............	50	18	0	7	0	75
Total..............	74	28	14	152	32	300

The threefold division of doctoral quotas remained, with temporary interruptions, for the rest of the dynasty. Under the Ch'ing dynasty of the Manchus, the division was further elaborated by the assignment of numerical doctoral quotas for each province, in lieu of the regional percentages, and by the addition of quotas for Chinese, Mongol, and Manchu bannermen who chose the examinations as a path of advancement.[18] It is not altogether clear how far the Ming and Ch'ing quotas reflected the local distribution of potential candidates. In terms of the total regional populations, the quotas assigned seem for the most part rather fair. The 55 per cent assigned to the Southern Quota Region and the 10 per cent assigned to the Middle in 1426 may well have been close to their respective shares of the population at that time, although the northward migration perceptible in the Mongol and Ming periods may have left the South with a more favorable ratio of quota to population during the later Ming. The provincial quotas for master's degrees in the Ming and for doctor's in the Ch'ing period (varying slightly from year to year) in general appear to recognize the changed population pattern; the numbers assigned to the individual provinces during the nineteenth century, however, tend to favor the more thinly settled at the expense of the more populous.[19]

But representation in terms of population was only one aspect of regional representation. We must remember that the distribution of potential candidates might be quite unequal in different regions; in terms of the quality of their preparation, it might be still more unequal. Where opportunities for education varied locally, regional

TABLE 5

PERCENTAGE REGIONAL QUOTAS OF DOCTORAL DE-
GREES AND RELATIVE POPULATIONS IN THE
MING AND CH'ING DYNASTIES

	Southern Region	Middle Region	Northern Region
1426 quota.............	55	10	35
1393 population.......	64	8	28
1578 population.......	41	15	44
1889 quota.............	49	16	35
1885 population.......	49	25	25

quotas that ignored this variation necessarily created differences in the intensity of competition. These differences would favor the man in the region which had fewer and inferior candidates (in terms of the standards then accepted). As we have seen, the evidence of the Sung examination lists tends to confirm the supposition that the more numerous and better qualified candidates came from regions of denser population. In these regions, if quotas were equalized on a per capita basis, the competition would be keenest. Which candidates would win out? Very possibly those with official connections and the associated advantages of education, family tradition, and experience. In the twelfth and thirteenth centuries, at least, the men without official connections tended to appear more frequently among the lower grade-brackets of the examination lists, and this situation may well have persisted.[20] Thus in more densely populated regions the quota restriction, other things being equal, would tend to eliminate larger numbers of new men. Other regional conditions affecting social mobility might modify this effect or exaggerate it.

For the Mongol and Ming periods there seems to be as yet no

quantitative evidence to test the outcome. For the Ch'ing period, however, we are more fortunate. For some years scholars at the University of Washington have gathered from many sources an impressive body of evidence on nineteenth-century Chinese institutions. (Highly significant results of this work will soon appear in a volume of studies on the social background of the bureaucracy, by Dr. C. L. Chang.[21]) This evidence throws interesting light on certain aspects of the problem of social mobility in the later Ch'ing period. In the nineteenth century, as in the twelfth and thirteenth, the proportions of new men in the several areas show much evidence of constancy within limited periods, but there are noticeable contrasts between the prequota periods (before 1279) and the nineteenth century. In the latter, there is a rather constant tendency toward higher ratios of new men among the doctoral graduates in the provinces of lesser population density, notably Kweichow, Shensi, and Kansu. There is also, it is true, some tendency toward a similar higher ratio of new men in provinces that show more rapid population growth during the century. But while such growing and relatively urbanized provinces as Kwangtung and Hupeh show such a combination of social mobility and growth, they are also among those with more limited per capita representation among the graduates, so that they do not affect the national averages as much as they otherwise might. It is tempting to find here an example in which the quota system worked to reduce social mobility in the examinations as a whole. But since the doctoral figures are based on a study still in progress, such inferences must be tempered with caution.

The holders of lower degrees and equivalent ranks in the Ch'ing offer in some ways a better comparison with the Sung doctoral degrees, although factors other than the regular examinations affect the picture. The proportion of new men as a whole is significantly greater among lower-degree holders than among the doctoral-degree holders of the same period; there are also other differences. Dr. Chang notes several factors that throw light on the regional pattern.[22] The relative administrative importance of an area plays a large role. It would appear that the generous quotas accorded the border provinces were meant to encourage the supply of trained men to help in the informal chores of local administration in those underpopulated areas. Some of the highest proportions of new men are found in Ch'ing provinces whose people had received expanded graduate quotas after 1850, either because they had played a more active part in fighting the Taiping and other rebels or because they had contributed generously to the depleted state treasury. In this category may fall the province of Hunan, with its population of medium density, as well as the border provinces of Yunnan and Kweichow. Commercial wealth also may have accounted for the high proportions of new men from such populous provinces as Anhwei and Kwangtung. Increasingly generous examination quotas were now specially reserved for the merchants as a group. In addition, degrees and ranks were now opened to purchase on a far greater scale than before, and provinces such as Anhwei and Kwangtung were high among the beneficiaries of this practice. Merchants may well have been among the leading purchasers.

Through one channel or another, it appears from this evidence that the emergency caused by the rebellions opened an opportunity to previously untapped sources of new men and, in doing so, underlined the fact that these men might otherwise have had no opportunity for entrance into the civil service. While the examinations clearly remained a vital tool of state policy, the emphasis and purposes of the system had changed since the thirteenth century in significant respects. Perhaps the expansion of the educated group over the intervening centuries made it less vital to seek out qualified men, regardless of their region, solely on the basis of their qualifications. The merit principle could now be tempered by political considerations. At the same time, as we have seen, other ways of advancement assumed greater importance for the new men as alternative entrances into the bureaucracy.[23]

The shifting balance of regional importance may also have contributed to the changing examination policies. It would seem that in a sense the pendulum had returned, in the course of twelve centuries, to its original position. The movement away from regional discrimination had begun in the T'ang, when the growing importance of the South enabled it to serve as a useful political counterweight to the hitherto dominant northern groups. The examinations served the southerners well, and seemingly furthered the growth of their own political and intellectual leadership even before the North was lost by conquest.[24] After the fall of the Sung, however, the North reasserted its political role, and at the same time the southward flow of population was reversed. A century and a half of separation and divergent experience no doubt strengthened regional differences and sharpened regional rivalries, present even in earlier times. But since the men of the South were not easily surpassed in the literary skills, the quota was a convenient weapon for a Northern reassertion of political influence.

Thus, in the single narrow aspect of the examination system that has been the focus of this paper, we find that in the course of centuries the dominant trend of Chinese opinion has continued for the most part to recognize the need for equal opportunity in the examinations. In defining the desirable form of "equal opportunity," however, political conditions of different periods have led to shifting formulations, which have stressed variously equality for the individual, the racial group, or the region. Regional equality has in turn assumed the various forms of equality among administrative areas, among populations of similar size, or among similar numbers of potential candidates. Continuing to invoke the same classical authority and the same tradition, the Chinese political theorist has been able in fact to modify the tradition and construe the authority with the freedom demanded by changing circumstances. If the Confucian tradition has acted as a limiting force on political experimentation, the limits imposed have proved, in this case, flexible.

THE FUNCTIONAL RELATIONSHIP BETWEEN CONFUCIAN THOUGHT AND CHINESE RELIGION

C. K. YANG

THIS PAPER deals with the nature of the functional relationship between Confucian thought and religion in traditional Chinese society and with the leading factors which made this relationship possible. This issue is a part of the broader problem of the functional role of religion in Chinese social life and social organization.

In this discussion the term "Confucian thought" refers not only to the views of Confucius and Mencius but also to those of the Confucian school as it has developed down to modern times. "Religion" here is taken to mean simply man's interrelations with the superhuman and supernatural powers.[1] Much broader definitions can of course be found, such as Thomas Carlyle's conception of religion as man's relation with the greater world, hence man's relation with his duty and his destiny.[2] Carlyle and other like-minded thinkers put forward this and similar definitions of religion during the period of rising rationalism, as an antidote to the earlier dominance of religion in Europe. But to evaluate the role of religion in a traditional social order like that of China, the supernatural powers must be the principal consideration because of their dominance in the religious life of the people.

1. Religious Elements in Confucianism

A. "RATIONALISTIC" CONFUCIANISM VERSUS THE FACTS OF RELIGIOUS LIFE

The relationship between Confucianism and religion, and the broader problem of the place of religion in Chinese society, have long claimed the attention of scholars of Chinese culture. In the spectrum of opinions already expressed on the matter, one may discern one leading view, which dwells upon the rationalistic and agnostic nature of Confucianism. This has been maintained by a long line of Western scholars from Voltaire to James Legge, as well as by modern oriental scholars such as Suzuki in Japan and Liang Ch'i-ch'ao and Hu Shih in China.[3] Some modern Chinese have even considered that, because of the dominance of Confucianism over the Chinese social and political order, the rationalism of Confucianism has logically given rise to a rationalistic Chinese society in which religion plays only an unimportant part, if it is admitted to exist at all. Liang Ch'i-ch'ao was one of the first to advance this view:

> Whether China has any religion at all is a question that merits serious study. . . . Confucius confined his attention to reality, and his views are incompatible with religious matters. . . . Since China's indigenous culture contains no religion, the history of Chinese religion is made up mainly of foreign religions introduced into China. . . . The Ch'an [Zen] school of Buddhism is a Chinese product, but it belongs more properly to the realm of philosophy than of religion. . . . Taoism is the only religion indigenous to China . . . but to include it in a history of Chinese religion is indeed a great humiliation . . . for it has repeatedly misled the people by its pagan magic and disturbed the peace and security.[4]

This statement is significant, for it lays bare an attitude common among modern Chinese intellectuals, who seem overeager to justify Chinese civilization in the face of the stronger and rationalistically oriented Western world, where magic and mysticism are contemptuously held to be the very symbols of backwardness and inferiority.

Though supported by an impressive array of scholarly names, this view cannot easily be reconciled with the social facts. It is generally recognized that, even in the modern period, the highly religious *Almanac* (*Li-shu*) enjoys a much wider sale in China than the "rationalistic" Confucian classics. Religion penetrates the concepts and structure of every social institution. Astrology, chronomancy, and numerous other forms of magic and animism profoundly influence the average man's outlook on life and his workaday routine activities. As late as 1953, the Chinese Communist government still had to launch a propaganda campaign to forestall the politically disturbing influence of an eclipse of the sun on New Year's Day of the old lunar calendar, a phenomenon traditionally considered to be an omen portending the anger of Heaven at the governing power for its misrule.[5]

The strong influence of religion is manifest in the numerous temples and shrines which dot the entire landscape of China. Tinghsien of Hopei Province may serve as an example. There was an average of 7 temples per village in 1882, and 1.7 temples per village in 1928, with about 600 persons per village at the latter date.[6] In terms of families, there was an average of 24 families per temple in 1882, and 50 families in 1928.[7] In spite of the secularization trend of recent decades, the ratio of temples to population is still high. Furthermore, a functional classification of these temples and their gods shows their influence on all phases of life, from the struggle with nature, and questions of peace or war, health or sickness, wealth or poverty, to every crisis in public as well as private life.[8]

As the official orthodoxy of the traditional social order, Confucianism could not avoid forming some sort of working relationship with such pervasive religious phenomena; yet, if Confucianism is considered to have been a body of purely rationalistic principles, we may well ask how it was fitted into the facts of Chinese religious life. In what follows, the compatibility and working relationship between Confucianism and the rest of traditional social life will be examined under the following heads: (1) the question of Confucius' agnosticism; (2) Confucianism's relation to the concepts of Heaven, predetermination, divination, the theory of Yin-Yang and the Five Elements; (3) Confucianist sponsorship of sacrifices and ancestor worship. In the following, many classical quotations are used because of the influence they have exercised, throughout most of the historical period, in conditioning the Confucian mind. For the present discussion, the question of what Confucius and Mencius actually said or meant is not as important as what subsequent Confucianists have reported them to have said as the most eminent authority on all questions.

B. THE QUESTION OF CONFUCIUS' AGNOSTICISM

Many seemingly agnostic statements by Confucius have been repeatedly employed by Western as well as Chinese scholars to establish the agnostic nature of Confucianism and to divest it of any supernatural concepts. Such familiar statements include:

The Master did not talk about extraordinary forces and disturbing spirits.[9]

While you are not able to serve men, how can you serve their spirits? . . . . While you do not know life, how can you know about death?[10]

To give one's self earnestly to the duties due to men, and, while respecting spiritual beings, to keep aloof [at a distance] from them, may be called wisdom.[11]

A quarter of a century ago, Creel made a revealing study of this subject by pointing out that none of the pre-Sung Chinese commentaries on these and similar passages of the *Lun-yü* considered Confucius to be agnostic and that, among the Sung and later Chinese commentaries, only four passages even suggested it. The agnostic impression of Confucius, according to Creel, is mainly the result of a trend toward rationalism within the Confucian school which reinterpreted Confucius' personal Heaven as "an immanent . . . impersonal directive principle of the universe."[12] This "rationalization" of Confucius is particularly apparent in the case of modern Chinese scholars who have been heavily influenced by Western rationalism and the general social trend toward secularization in a period of revolution.

Whatever the interpretation of these statements by Confucius, it should be noted that, while they grant priority to knowledge about man in this world, they do not attempt to disprove the existence of supernatural forces. Instead, Confucius carefully kept the supernatural alive in the background in his admonition to "respect the spiritual beings," in his emphasis on sacrificial ceremonies, in his attitude toward Heaven and fate. Supernatural conceptions loomed large in people's minds during Confucius' time, in spite of certain tendencies toward secularization.[13] Confucius himself can hardly have escaped entirely this concern for the supernatural, nor can he have ignored its contemporary importance in human affairs. Thus Confucianism leaves ample room for the development of a working relationship with supernatural conceptions.

In spite of its preoccupation with this-worldly matters, Confucianism cannot be considered a completely rationalistic system of thought. It does not make a thorough attempt to transform the world into a disenchanted, causal mechanism, to the complete exclusion of supernatural elements.[14] A working relationship can be developed between "rationalistic" Confucianism and religion without logical contradiction.

C. CONFUCIANISM IN RELATION TO CERTAIN MAJOR CONCEPTS

A concrete bond between Confucianism and religion lies in the former's acceptance of the supernatural concepts of Heaven, predetermination, divination, and the theory of Yin-Yang and the Five Elements. In recent decades a whole polemical literature has grown up on the relationship between these concepts and Confucianism.[15] The following somewhat oversimplified argument is arranged to throw light upon the working relationship between Confucianism and the religious institution of Chinese traditional society.

1. *Heaven and predetermination.*—It should first be recognized that the concepts of Heaven, predetermination, divination, and the theory of Yin-Yang and the Five Elements form a logical system of thought by themselves. The system begins with Heaven as the personified supreme governing force of the universe—hence the belief in Heaven as the predeterminer of human fate and the conception of predetermination or fatalism. Divination and the theory of Yin-Yang and the Five Elements are both devices for peeping into the secret course predestined for the human world, so as to help man attain well-being and avoid calamity. Closely bound up with this effort to glean information from the secrets of Heaven and fate are

the interpretation of portents from extraordinary phenomena of nature,[16] the concept of *feng-shui* ("wind and water," or geomancy), and the degeneration of these efforts into other forms of magic and animism.

Amid a profusion of opinion, there is a general agreement that, in the pre-Confucian period, Heaven was taken as a personified supreme force, dictating the events of nature and man, wielding the power of reward and punishment.[17] In the general intellectual trend toward secularization during the Ch'un-ch'iu and Warring States periods, there was an increasing tendency to identify Heaven as an impersonal, natural, and self-operating force. This is reflected in statements by Confucius, Mencius, Hsün-tzu, and their contemporaries.[18] But such a naturalistic notion of Heaven was limited to small groups of the advanced thinkers of the time and was adopted in a sporadic fashion. It did not become the central theme of a system of empirical knowledge, worked through to the "disenchantment of the world" and transforming it into a causal mechanism.[19] Both Confucius and Mencius repeatedly attributed to Heaven the misfortunes of their age and the disappointments of their personal careers. Above all, the inclusion of the Five Classics as a fundamental part of the Confucian doctrine is tantamount to Confucian endorsement of the many supernatural notions of Heaven contained in them.

It is, therefore, no logical contradiction to find that Tung Chung-shu of the Han dynasty, who was so instrumental in establishing Confucianism as the state orthodoxy, wrote a large number of essays on Heaven as a personified supreme being, such as "The Conduct of Heaven and Earth."[20] It is similarly logical to find full Confucianist support for the state cult of Heaven worship, which, down to this day, has carried with it a highly supernatural connotation.

A sequel to the supernatural conception of Heaven is the belief in predetermination or fate (*ming*), which has occupied a prominent place in Confucianism. This concept was a vital part of early Chinese culture, and, by Confucius' time, a variety of theories of predetermination had emerged.[21] Confucian acceptance of this cultural legacy is reflected in statements about fate made by Confucius, Mencius, and subsequent Confucianists. One of the most frequently quoted sayings, "Death and life have their determined appointment; riches and honor depend upon Heaven," comes from the text of the Confucian *Analects*.[22] And Confucius asserted, "If my principles are to advance, it is so ordered. If they are to fall to the ground, it is so ordered."[23] The phrases "determined appointment" and "so ordered" are Legge's translations of the same Chinese character *ming* ("fate" or "predetermination"). Mencius was even more frequent and explicit in taking Heaven as a personified predeterminer. For example, "To advance a man or to stop his advance is really beyond the power of other men. My not finding in the prince of Loo a ruler who would confide in me, and put my counsels into practice, is from Heaven."[24] Again from Mencius, "But Heaven does not yet wish that the empire should enjoy tranquillity and good order. If it wished this, who is there besides me to bring it about? How should I be otherwise than dissatisfied?"[25]

These and other similar statements from the two Masters indicate that they retained the supernatural, personified notion of a Heaven that governed the fate of man. The above statements share a common ground. Both men started with tremendous confidence in the superiority of their own abilities. Why, then, should they still fail, when they, as the best of men, had done their utmost? Their this-worldly doctrine could produce no answer. It must be that beyond man there was a supreme determinant: fate, as ordained by Heaven. It is perhaps no accident that Confucius, after a long disappointing career, turned to that mystic book, the *I-ching*, in his old age.

In recent times predetermination has underlain the stereotyped stories about who would and who would not pass the imperial examinations.[26] Even the modern K'ang Yu-wei was deeply imbued with a belief in predetermination. There is a story that he once walked under a scaffold where a falling brick missed his head by a few inches, but he came through the incident with perfect serenity, saying that his safety had been predetermined.

2. *"Knowing fate."*—Following upon the assumption of fate is the logical attempt to learn the predetermined course of events in advance so as to enable man to gain success and avoid failure. This matter of "knowing fate" obviously engaged the attention of Confucius, for he considered the ability to recognize fate as a necessary quality of a superior man.[27] Again he said, "The mean man does not know the ordinances of Heaven, and consequently does not stand in awe of them."[28] And he claimed he knew the decrees of Heaven at the age of fifty.[29] But how can one know fate? If there were such secrets, Confucius divulged none, and it is an unsettled problem whether Mencius founded the school of Yin-Yang and the Five Elements as such a means.[30]

Here comes the puzzle of the *I-ching*. What did Confucius try to learn from the obscure lines of this mystic volume when, if we trust the traditional account, he thumbed it so persistently that the binding broke three times? The answer depends on one's view of the nature of the book, and there is a variety of interpretations on this point. There is the naturalist interpretation of it as protoscientific. But there is also the traditional use of the book for divination, and there is the interpretation that the book represents a simplified, standardized method to decipher the meaning of configurations of heat cracks on oracle bones.[31]

Aside from the *I-ching*, which occupies an important place in the Confucian mind, divination is a frequent subject in the other four of the Five Classics. Divination was an important trait of early Chinese culture, and, as a part of the Five Classics, it was inherited to some degree by Confucianism. This may explain the widespread belief in divination among Confucianists, as attested by many biographical accounts and traditional stories.

3. *The theory of Yin-Yang and the Five Elements.*—As a means of "knowing fate," divination is not always dependable, and the *I-ching* is too obscure to understand; even Confucius wished to have more years to his life to study and understand it.[32] By the third and second centuries B.C., the theory of Yin (negative), Yang (positive), and the Five Elements (metal, wood, water, fire, and earth) rose rapidly to prominence as a means of deciphering the secrets of Heaven. By the Han period, books devoted wholly or partly to the discussion of this theory account for one-fourth to one-third of all books listed in the "Bibliography" section (*I-wen chih*) of the *History of the Former Han Dynasty*.[33] And there are twenty-three essays on the same subject, accounting for one-half of all the essays, in the volume *Ch'un-ch'iu Fan Lu*, written by Tung Chung-shu, the arch-Confucianist whose success in helping to instal Confucianism as the state orthodoxy is clearly inseparable from his effective use of this theory in his argument.

Following this came the widespread application of the theory to the study and interpretation of the Five Classics by Confucianists from the Han period on down.[34] Since then, few Confucianists have escaped coloring of their thought by this theory. An expression of this influence is visible in the Confucian historiographical tradition of the Five Emperors[35] and in numerous Confucian terms, like the "Five Cardinal Relations," the "Five Rituals," "Five Punishments," all bearing the semisacred number five from the original Five Elements.[36]

While there were early naturalistic notions of the Yin-Yang and the Five Elements,[37] the effective theory developed after the Han period centered on the supernatural theme of "interaction between Heaven and man" (*t'ien jen hsiang ying*).[38] Man's deeds may anger or please Heaven, and Heaven metes out punishment or reward accordingly. By assigning moral significance to each of the factors of Yin and Yang and the Five Elements, it was possible to work up a frame of reference by which to interpret the intentions behind the phenomena of the supernatural forces in the sky, the earth, the seasons, the crops, the governing of the state, the rise and fall of a dynasty, life and death, health and sickness, poverty and prosperity, divination, palm reading and physiognomy, astrology, chronomancy, and geomancy. From the activities of the sun and the moon to the intimate deeds of the individual's private life, all may be interpreted by this theory of Yin-Yang and the Five Elements; it deeply penetrated the minds of the common men as well as those of most Confucianists.

Here, one has to recognize the relatively independent status of Yin-Yang and the Five Elements as a separate school of thought, which was blended also into magical Taoism and, to a lesser extent, into Buddhism. To Confucianism, nevertheless, the theory is an important sequel to the supernatural conceptions of Heaven and fate, hence the intimate alliance between Confucianism and the theory.

D. THE CONFUCIAN EMPHASIS ON SACRIFICE AND ANCESTOR WORSHIP

If the theory of Yin-Yang and the Five Elements may be considered a development outside the main context of Confucianism, the matter of sacrifice is an integral part of Confucianism. Sacrifice is a most stable complex in the Chinese culture which was endorsed and elaborated by Confucius, Mencius, and subsequent Confucianists.

Basically, sacrifice is a form of man's ritualistic behavior toward the gods and spirits for the purpose of inducing their protection and blessing. Such is plainly the meaning of sacrifice in early pre-Confucius sources like the *Shu-ching* and the *Shih-ching*. With the trend toward secularization during the Ch'un-ch'iu and Warring States periods, the moral and social significance of sacrifice received growing emphasis. It is as part of this trend that Confucius made sacrifice a vital part of the *li* ("ritualism") for the control and regulation of social conduct. Early books, like the *Li-chi* and *Kuo-yü*, contain many passages discussing the secular functions of sacrifice, such as the cultivation of filial piety, the encouragement of honesty and loyalty, and the idea of *ch'ung te pao kung* ("to honor the virtuous and to repay the service [of outstanding men]").[39] Recently, the secular function of sacrifice in fostering desirable social values has also been emphasized by modern Confucianists like Liang Sou-ming.[40]

There is no dispute here on the secular function of sacrifice. But why is the religious rite of sacrifice used, instead of other secular means, to inculcate social values? On this point, even early classics contain fairly explicit explanations. Thus the *Li-chi* said, "When the scholars show respect [in sacrifice], the people will believe." Believe in what? Very likely, in spirits and gods, the objects of sacrifice. Widely quoted in the religion sections of local histories (*hsien-chih*) is a statement from the commentary to the *I-ching* attributed to Confucius: "The sages devised guidance in the name of the gods, and [the people of] the land became obedient." But Hsün-tzu put it most plainly:

> The Sage plainly understands it [sacrificial rites]; the scholar and Superior Man accordingly perform it; the official observes it; and among the people it becomes an established custom. Among Superior Men it is considered to be a human practice; among the common people it is considered to be a serving of the spirits. . . .[41]

And so, for two millenniums since Hsün-tzu gave this explanation, sacrifice has all along been a serving of the spirits, in the view of common men, while rationalistically inclined Confucian scholars have probably regarded it as merely a practice among men. The dual principles underlying sacrifice, one for the superior men and the other for the common men, make it clear that the supernatural element in sacrifice is a valuable tool in enforcing social values and in taming the masses. Awe of the supernatural is inescapable for the untutored mind when it participates in the religious activities of sacrifice, the burning of candles and papers, the offering of food and drink, the kotow, the taboos, the prayers and other acts, all carefully prescribed to please the spirits.

One who faithfully observes the prescribed procedure of sacrifice cannot escape from mystic influence even if he be a Superior Man. The *Li-chi* has this passage on the procedure for sacrifice:

> The severest vigil and purification is maintained and practised in the inner self, while a looser vigil is maintained externally. During the days of such vigil, the mourner thinks of the departed, how and where he sat, how he smiled and spoke, and what were his aims and views, what he delighted in, and what he desired and enjoyed. By the third day he will perceive the meaning of such exercise.
>
> On the day of sacrifice, when he enters the apartment (of the temple), he will seem to see (the deceased) in the place (where his spirit-tablet is). After he has moved about (to perform his operations), and is leaving by the door, he will be

arrested by seeming to hear the sound of his movements, and will sigh as he seems to hear the sound of his sighing. . . .

. . . Still and grave, absorbed in what he is doing, he will seem to be unable to sustain the burden, and in danger of letting it fall. . . . Thus he manifests his mind and thought, and in his dreamy state of mind seeks to commune with the dead in their spiritual state. . . .[42]

The "dreamy state of mind," acquired by three days of vigil and concentrated meditation with the dead person's image in mind, is typical of the procedure used in many cultures to induce mystic experience, to obtain spiritual communion with the spirits and gods.[43] It is an interesting question whether the ritualistic use of liquor in Chinese sacrifice was not originally designed to induce the above "dreamy state of mind."[44]

Sacrifice is a central element in ancestor worship. The latter is used by Confucianism as one of the means to integrate the kinship group, which is a strategic point for carrying out the Confucian scheme of social organization. The dual nature of sacrifice holds true also for ancestor worship. The secular function of ancestor worship is to cultivate kinship values like filial piety, family loyalty, and continuity of the family lineage, aims which some Confucianists may be well satisfied to achieve. But, for the common men, the welfare of the soul of the departed kinsman is a large factor compelling him to undertake sacrifice even when poverty-stricken and unable to afford the expense. In a harsh and niggardly world, the hope for supernatural help and the fear of supernatural punishment have been powerful influences stabilizing the kinship system within the operation of the Confucian scheme of social organization.

The above discussion should suffice to show how the largely rationalistic Confucian doctrine contains elements that enable it to work with the religious elements in traditional Chinese society. Certain supernatural notions in the doctrine that keep the spirits and gods alive in the background, the theory of Yin-Yang and the Five Elements that penetrated into the vitals of Confucian thought, and the prominence of sacrificial rites and ancestor worship in the Confucian system of social control—all predispose the Confucian mind favorably toward religious matters. In fact, they may be considered the religious aspects of Confucianism which made possible the coexistence of Confucianism, Taoism, and Buddhism, as in the period of the Six Dynasties.[45] They helped make it possible for Confucianism to function as the official orthodoxy of the social and political order. For these religious conceptions not only served as tools for the carrying-out of Confucian principles and values; they also helped justify many discrepancies between the real world and the ideal Confucian values, such as the occasional moral failure of even the best and most conscientious of men.

2. The Separation between Ethics and Religion

The dominant influence of religion in many cultures stems from religious dominance over ethical values. In Chinese culture a striking difference lies in the dominance of Confucianism over the ethical values, while religion tends to lend supernatural sanction to the Confucian values. This gives Confucianism and religion a mutually supporting function.

To facilitate discussion, it is suitable here to distinguish between diffused and specialized religions. A diffused religion is organizationally diffused in secular institutions, such as ancestor worship in the family, worship of Heaven in the state, and the worship of patron gods in guilds. A specialized religion, on the other hand, has an independent status and organization to serve specifically religious functions, though it may perform many derivative functions also. Buddhism, Taoism, *feng-shui*, and other forms of professionalized magic and animism, like sorcery and divination, belong to this type.

The separation between ethics and religion, and the mutual support between the two, are apparent in the case of diffused religions. The theology of ancestor worship, for example, does not evolve a system of kinship ethics from its supernatural premises but, rather, lends support to the Confucian values designed for the kinship group. Again, in the state cult of Heaven worship, the moral and social connotations of political power are defined by Confucian values which Heaven and the associated deities are believed to approve and support. The Mandate of Heaven is a piece of blank paper on which the Confucianists write an ethical content. Just as they have no independent organizational existence, diffused religions possess no independent system of ethical values.

With specialized religions, the case is somewhat more complicated, but the above assumption on the separation between ethics and religion still generally holds true. The leading specialized religions in China, like Buddhism and Taoism, have their own systems of ethical values, which at times tend to contradict Confucian values. But their ethical values as a system are generally put into practice only by priests and devotees, and are not systematically observed by common men, who may come under the influence of one or more religions. For the common men, the main influence of these religions is much more magical than ethical. Thus, an average Chinese observes Confucian ethics, but simultaneously he may pray to Buddha or hire a Taoist priest to perform magic for the benefit of his body or soul.

Even more important is the fact that Confucianism possessed a far more comprehensive, consistent, and practical system of ethical values for secular life than any traditional religion in China. The Taoist Five Commandments and Ten Virtues,[46] for example, represent only a rather chaotic mixture of Confucian and Buddhist values. The Buddhist ethical system is much more elaborate and consistent than the Taoist, but, when applied to the kinship-oriented Chinese social structure, it is still inferior to the Confucian system in consistency and practicability. It is no accident that the Confucian ethical system came to dominate Chinese social institutions.

One may also note that the tacit or explicit acceptance of many Confucian values by Buddhism and Taoism makes these religions sources of support for Confucianism. Thus, Kuang Hsiao Ssu ("Monastery for the Glorification of Filial Piety") is a common name for Buddhist monasteries, in spite of the kinship-renouncing doctrine of Buddhism. Filial piety heads the Taoist Ten Virtues, and it is a frequent point for approbation in the official biographies of Taoist popes.[47]

Magical and animistic cults contribute even less to the development of comprehensive ethical systems, because they are basically not dogmatic religions and do not impose broad social doctrines or rules of conduct that possess general validity in social life.[48] Rather, they represent procedures for the utilitarian control of natural or human forces.

The cult of Wind and Water, for instance, possesses no ethical system of its own other than that taken mainly from Confucianism. And the majority of the functional deities in China, such as Kuan Ti (the god of justice and bravery) or Niang Niang (the goddess of fertility), are the product rather than the cause of established values and ideals. Because of this, there is a general tendency for magical and animistic religiousness to support rather than challenge the established values, thus reinforcing the interdependence between the two separate systems of religion and ethics.

3. Structural Features of Chinese Religions

It is an observable fact that, while the largely rationalistic Confucianism occupied a dominant organizational position in the Chinese social and political order, religious influence permeated every aspect of Chinese social life. The coexistence of these two situations was due, among other factors, to the organizational weakness of Chinese religions, which facilitated the establishment of a dominant-subordinate relationship between Confucianism and religion in most periods of Chinese history. It is therefore necessary to examine the organizational features of both specialized and diffused religions in China.

A. SPECIALIZED RELIGIONS

With the exception of the numerically small Christian and Islamic religions, the leading specialized religions in China have developed no centrally organized priesthood and no organized congregation or parish among laymen. The basic independent unit of organization among Buddhist and Taoist priests is the temple, the monastery, or the nunnery. There may be occasional associations of a local nature among the temples, but they have no hierarchical authority outside and do not alter the essentially independent status of the individual temples. The so-called Taoist pope, Chang T'ien-shih, may have high religious or magical prestige, derived from the assumed ability, for example, to make rain or to harness evil spirits, but he commands no organizational subordination from Taoists or Taoist temples in different parts of the country.[49] The same holds true for Buddhist 'high monks.''

Until recent decades, there was no central system of schooling for the priesthood in either Buddhism or Taoism. Instead, the system of acolytes or apprenticeship was followed, a system that restricts the expansion of the priesthood. In fact, under the Ch'ing dynasty the law permitted each qualified priest to train and ordain only one pupil.[50] This teacher-pupil relationship was a central factor in the local organization of priests and was limited in scale. When the chief priest died, he was succeeded by the pupil whom he had previously chosen, or by someone elected by members of the temple, or by other methods of succession based on age and rank. At times, neighboring temples might participate in selecting a successor. But, in any case, the successor was not appointed by a higher authority in a hierarchy, since such did not exist.

Another important feature is the economic independence of the individual temples. They are built with the help of one of the four major types of financial benefactors: single private donors, a group of private donors, the government, or collective organizations, like the clans. There is no central religious authority controlling financial resources. Once built, a temple sustains itself by the income from the temple property, contributions of "incense and oil money," special donations by worshipers, or remuneration for religious services rendered.

Reflecting this decentralization is the lack of clear religious affiliation for many, perhaps most, of the small temples in the countryside. When one asks the priest in a small temple to what religion his temple belongs, such as Taoist or Buddhist, the answer is often that he does not know.[51] This indicates that such temples exist as independent units, not as parts of a religious system. In a way, when gods of many faiths are present in the same temple, as is frequently the case, it would be difficult to identify the temple with any one faith.

If the organization of the priesthood is weak, the religious organization of the laymen is weaker. The general absence of an organized congregation or parish among laymen has long been noted.[52] Aside from a small number of devotees, there is no organizational affiliation between the lay worshipers and the temples. A worshiper may worship in many temples of different faiths without having an organizational affiliation with any one of them. A person may pray in a Buddhist temple of the Goddess of Mercy for fertility and in a Taoist temple of the God of Medicine (Hua T'o) for health, depending on the magical power desired for the occasion. He goes to a temple, lights candles and incense, mumbles a prayer for the benefit or benediction desired, burns papers, pays the priest (if there is one) for the incense and for oil for the "everburning lamp," and leaves the temple without further obligation. When one hires Buddhist or Taoist priests or professional magicians to pray and to perform magic at home or elsewhere, the obligation also ends at the conclusion of the service. Such a relationship between the worshiper, on the one hand, and the temple or the priest, on the other, is an "over-the-counter" deal, and the worshiper is free to shop in the religious market according to his taste and convictions.

In fact, in the broad countryside there are numerous temples without priests in attendance. The temple is an empty establishment with only idols in it, and the village people give it the necessary physical maintenance. Only on special occasions, such as the birthday of the temple's main god, does a priest come to attend service.[53] In such cases, there is no nucleus about which to integrate the individual worshipers into any form of organization.

B. DIFFUSED RELIGION

In a metaphorical sense, diffused religions may be considered as having an organized following as well as an organized priesthood. Thus, ancestor worship has both an organized priesthood, in the hierarchy of ceremonial elders who officiate in sacrificial rites, and an organized congregation, in the membership of the family or clan. But the major function of ancestor worship is to integrate and strengthen the essentially secular kinship group, and the control of worship is in the hands of secular members within the family whose vocation is not religious. Hence, competition from a religious group for control of the kinship system does not arise. Furthermore, the kinship body is inherently a localistic organization. It is incapable of developing into an effective large-scale centralized system and so offering any threat to the Confucianist domination of the social and political order. Hence, however pervasive its influence, ancestor worship as a religion diffused in the kinship structure cannot become anything but a tool of Confucianism, which dominates the kinship structure.

A similar analysis applies to other diffused religions in China. As a general category, diffused religions have no priesthood or following independent of the structure and membership of the secular institution into which they are diffused. Diffused religions as such do not possess independent structural importance in social organization.

The lack of an independent, centrally organized priesthood and an organized laity deprives Chinese religions of any important structural position in the general framework of social organization. This leaves Confucianism to play the central role in the traditional Chinese social and political order. Similarly, organizational weakness tends to limit religion to a supporting role for Confucian thought in the operation of Chinese social institutions. Confucianism has had much less to fear from religious competition than would have been the case if Chinese religions had developed strong organizational features. This is a feature of the long co-operation between Confucianism and religion in China.

4. Some Factors in the Organizational Weakness of Chinese Religion

The working relationship between religion and Confucianism has not been always smooth or harmonious, and struggles between them have broken out time and again in Chinese history right down to the modern period. But the result of these contests has been the continued dominance of Confucianism. One apparent cause is, again, the organizational weakness of religions in China, without which their historical subordination would have been unstable—hence the relevance of a brief consideration of some of the factors underlying this organizational weakness. Two sets of factors may be mentioned here. One concerns the political suppression and control of religious organizations, and the other relates to the characteristics of major Chinese religions that may affect their organizational strength.

A. POLITICAL SUPPRESSION AND CONTROL OF RELIGIOUS ORGANIZATIONS

Among social groups, organized religion has been one of the most persistent contestants for political dominance, and its competition and conflict with secular power groups have marked the course of development of every major civilization. In China the relative lack of open, protracted struggle between religion and the state has been partly the result of the ceaseless suppression and control of religious organizations by secular power groups. Consequently, Chinese religion has lacked the opportunity to organize and seek to develop a more important structural position in society. There have been periods, such as those of the Six Dynasties, Sui, and the early part of T'ang, when religious organizations played a more important structural role in society than in most eras of Chinese history.[54] But such historical situations developed when the secular political power had undisputed supremacy over religion, and religious organizations were permitted to exist because they served the political ends of the ruling groups or at least did not threaten the latter's security. In no major period did a specialized religion develop a strong structural position on its own, without dependence on the patronage and favor of a secular political power.

Political suppression of religious organizations has taken place in every major period of Chinese history, from the suppression of the Taoist Yellow Turbans in the Han, the leveling of Buddhist temples in the T'ang, the suppression of the many religious-political movements in the nineteenth century, including the Taiping Rebellion, down to the current liquidation of many religious societies by the Chinese Communist government. The endless struggle for political power by religious groups in the past led to a situation where any unlicensed religious organization was regarded with suspicion and antagonism by the government.[55] Since it was extremely difficult to obtain official approval for new religious movements, the suppression policy produced secret or semisecret practices in almost all religious organizations outside the officially recognized temples and monasteries. In spite of the change in the legal regulation of religion during the Republican period, the traditional social situation has continued to a considerable extent down to the present day. In Ting-hsien in North China, for instance, secrecy still shrouds most religious organizations outside the temples and the churches of the Christian and Moslem religions. Membership in many religious societies is not to be disclosed even to one's own parents, wife, and children.[56] Religious organizations were driven underground in traditional China.

The motivation for such suppression has been practical instead of theoretical or theological. It is to remove any possible threat against the established political power and the sociopolitical order. Religious suppression because of open rebellion by religious organizations is a phenomenon too obvious to need explanation. The T'ang persecution of Buddhist organizations was caused partly by the growing strength of such groups and partly by the large proportion of the people who had joined the Buddhist religion mainly to enjoy exemption from taxation and the *corvée*, thus endangering the state's revenue and the supply of free labor. From the times of Han Yü in the T'ang, Chu Hsi in the Sung, and the commentators on the *Ta-Ch'ing Lü-li* ("The Laws and Regulations of the Ch'ing Dynasty"), the theoretical ground against Buddhism has consistently been the Buddhist renunciation of kinship relations and avoidance of productive labor. This endangers the Confucianist foundation of social organization, the kinship system, and the economic order. Aside from such practical grounds, Confucianists have had little quarrel with religion, especially when religion has served as a support for Confucian values. In most historical situations Confucianism has not been against religion or magic on purely theoretical grounds.

To be tolerated, religion had to be a willing tool of the secular political power and its Confucian orthodoxy. This was clearly expressed in Emperor Ch'ien-lung's many edicts to the Taoist pope, commanding the latter to help control dissident religious heresies.[57] Aside from issuing edicts and outright suppression, there was an extensive list of means of control to ensure the subordination of religion to the secular political power. To mention a few, emperors in the Ch'ing and earlier periods bestowed honorific titles on prominent religious figures and on efficacious gods,[58] in order to demonstrate the superiority of the secular over the spiritual power. The old system of government licensing of every ordained priest was devised to keep a vigilant watch over the size and activities of the religious population,[59] though the system was discontinued in the Republican period. In the pre-Republican period, official approval was necessary for the construction of a temple even with private funds, so as to weed out any heretical religious elements subversive of the official orthodoxy.[60] A certain degree of social and political discrimination against priests, magicians, sorcerers, and seers, except those of high prestige, was obviously Confucian-inspired.

But suppression and control somehow never succeeded in eliminating officially unrecognized religious organizations or preventing new ones from arising. Secret and semisecret religious groups have come into widespread existence even down to the present period. There can be many factors in such situations, including man's persistent quest for spiritual salvation, which earthly Confucianism or even existing religions fail to satisfy. But, organizationally, Confucian orthodoxy has failed to provide an intimate brotherhood for man's social needs beyond the kinship system; for, beyond the kinship system, the only other organization that received elaborate development at the hands of Confucianism was the state, and the state was not an intimate group that could meet the individual's many immediate needs. What would happen to the individual should the kinship system fail in its brotherly function was a question that the Confucian scheme of social organization never adequately dealt with.

It is significant to note that the membership of the religious societies in Ting-hsien is found to be composed mainly of lonely men and women without a normal family, such as widows, widowers and single persons, and married persons without children.[61] In times of extensive misery or calamity, when the family cannot provide help for the individual, secret religious organizations flourish for the same reason, and rebellions and uprisings have stemmed from them. The religious associations provide individuals with intimate brotherly assistance in material and spiritual ways; they are extrafamilial brotherhoods. Socially and economically helpless persons join monasteries or nunneries for substantially the same reasons.[62] But this often requires those individuals to sever relations with the secular world, as in the case of Buddhist monasteries, and this is difficult even for desperately needy individuals. Besides, membership in monasteries is usually too limited to accommodate a misery-stricken world. Against this, secret religious societies, in spite of a certain amount of political and social risk, allow the individual to keep his secular life and are much less restricted in membership.

B. INTERFAITH POLYTHEISM AS A WEAKENING FACTOR

It is a familiar fact that Chinese religions are generally polytheistic and eclectic in nature and that the exclusiveness of worshiping only one god is foreign to the Chinese tradition. What needs to be stressed here is the interfaith character of polytheism in China, which tends to obfuscate the boundary of each religion. The average Chinese layman believes in the friendly and ordered coexistence of all gods, regardless of their religious identification. The layman's spiritual world comprises gods and spirits from Taoism, Buddhism, the worship of Heaven and its associated cult of Yin-Yang and the Five Elements, ancestor worship, and numerous local cults of magic and animism. In this grand pantheon, the boundary between religions hardly exists, and the gods and spirits are arranged in a hierarchy according to their magical powers.

Motivated by this magical notion, the Chinese layman worships a Taoist god today, a Buddhist god tomorrow, and the gods and spirits of different religions on other occasions, all to suit his practical purpose and convenience. Consequently, it is difficult for any one religion to develop a loyal and well-organized following among laymen, for many religions would simultaneously claim loyalty and affiliation from the same individual. The inability of even many temple priests to identify the religion of their own temple or gods, as noted above, is an indication of the independent status of each temple and its lack of organizational affiliation with any broad religious body. If this is the case with some trained priests, the layman's ability to recognize the distinction between religions is much weaker, and the lack of affiliation with religious organizations among the laity appears to be a logical consequence.

The organizational strength of many monotheistic religions lies partly in the undivided loyalty paid to one god as a single object of spiritual devotion without rival claims. It perhaps can be argued that, if a group can be persuaded to be loyal to one god, it can also become loyal to a group of gods, as is attested by many strong polytheistic organizations, such as Tibetan Lamaism. This seems to be true only on condition that the gods are organized into a well-defined independent system. But if the gods from different systems are all mixed together, to the obfuscation of the independent character of each system, the bond of loyalty between each system and its followers cannot escape weakening.

Another aspect of this interfaith polytheism is the mutual theological contamination among major Chinese religions. There has been extensive adoption of Buddhist theology, liturgy, and organization by Taoism. Buddhism, in turn, has adopted many Taoist magical concepts and practices. Both, but especially Taoism, have been influenced by the theory of Yin-Yang and the Five Elements. And, judging from the phraseology and concepts, the Taoist *T'ai-p'ing Ching* ("Scripture of the Great Peace"), expounding the Yin-Yang theory, could well have been penned by a Confucianist like Tung Chung-shu. The broad tolerance in Mahāyāna Buddhism is in harmony with what Confucius said in the *Doctrine of the Mean:* "All things are nourished together without their injuring one another. The courses of the seasons, and of the sun and moon, are pursued without any collision among them."[63] While Confucianism is not considered a religion, in this paper, its eclectic tendencies have influenced all traditional Chinese thinkers, religious or secular, and this may have some bearing on the eclectic character of Chinese religious life and thought.

C. MAGIC AND RELIGIOUS ORGANIZATION

The widespread existence of generally unorganized magical cults in China raises the question whether magic has been a factor in the unorganized state of such cults, for some qualities of magic seem to be unfavorable to the development of extensive systems of religious organization.

For example, magic tends to have an impersonal quality. Its success depends upon the correct performance of magical procedures which are used to manipulate and to induce action from the supernatural forces, and it does not depend so much on personal loyalty and devotion to a superhuman being. Magical practices lack the strong bond generally found between a religion of the personal, salvational type and its followers, where there is a direct and exclusive tie between the worshiper and his god. In an interfaith polytheistic setting, this impersonal character of magic tends to further the development of the "market situation" in Chinese religious life as noted above.

In addition, the incredible nature of Chinese magical superstitions is a well-known fact. This feature of Chinese magical religion at times attracted mass followings from the untutored among the masses, particularly among those caught in the tight grip of misery and eager for relief from otherwise hopeless circumstances; this is attested by the rise of religious movements based on incredible miracles in troubled times when there was extensive misery. But, in the long run, this alienates intelligent minds, thus depriving magical religion of an educated leadership for the development of permanent, routinized organizations.

Magic constantly has to prove its efficacy in order to maintain confidence among its followers. The undependable efficacy of magic accounts partly for the rise and fall of the influence of cults based mainly on magic, and this quality appears to be unfavorable for the development of stable and strong organizations.

The above hypothetical points are based on the assumption that magic is the central factor of a cult, unsupported by a higher theology or doctrine. Magic is but a means to an end. When the end sought by the believers is to relieve personal or local suffering, magical activities proceed in unorganized, or temporarily organized, form, such as the "rain processions" praying for precipitation during a drought.[64] But, when the end sought is a universal one or concerns society in general, such as ends advocated by dogmatic theologies or salvation religions, magic then may become an asset for organizational purpose by providing a focus of interest and by generating confidence among the followers. Impersonalized magic can be made to serve a personalized god, and the failings in its immediate efficacy can be mitigated by the promise of an unverifiable other-world. Hence, many great organized religions have their magical aspects, and many magical cults in Chinese history developed into widespread organized religious movements through the acquisition of a universal purpose, as exemplified by the White Lotus sect. However, in such organized movements, magic no longer remains the central factor but becomes the means to a higher end. Magic itself, unsupported by a dogmatic theology or a higher purpose, and set in an interfaith polytheistic background, does not appear to be a factor that would inspire organizational strength.

5. Conclusion

Confucianism, with its largely rationalistic structural principles and ethical value system, holds a dominant position in Chinese social institutions. Meanwhile, religious influence, in the supernatural sense, permeates every aspect of Chinese social life, but without developing a position of general structural importance in social organization. This religious influence gives a supernatural sanction to, and hence becomes an operational tool of, Confucian structural principles and ethical values.

Such a dominant-subordinate working relationship between religion and a largely rationalistic system of thought is made possible by: (1) the presence of certain religious elements in Confucian thought; (2) the separation between ethics and religion that calls for co-operation between Confucianism and religion; and (3) the organizational weakness of Chinese religions that helps to keep religion in a subordinate structural position among social institutions, thus preventing any successful attainment by religion of structural dominance. This weakness is rooted partly in the constant political suppression and control of religious organizations, and also possibly in some of the characteristics of Chinese religions, such as interfaith polytheism and magic. But perhaps the most important factor lies in the dominance of diffused religions in Chinese social life, since diffused religions possess no independent personnel and organization of their own and are under the constant control of the secular leadership of social institutions into which they are diffused.

It should be recognized that the dominance of a largely rationalistic thought such as Confucianism, and the organizational weaknesses of religions, have not made the traditional Chinese social order a "rational" one. Religious influence remains pervasive and strong, and powerful religious movements have risen from time to time in Chinese history to challenge the supremacy of Confucianism. Such religious movements did not arise suddenly from a "rationalistic" social foundation but, rather, stemmed from religious roots already deep in Chinese society.

THE CONCEPT OF *PAO* AS A BASIS FOR
SOCIAL RELATIONS IN CHINA

LIEN-SHENG YANG

THE CHINESE word *pao* as a verb has a wide range of meanings including "to report," "to respond," "to repay," "to retaliate," and "to retribute." The center of this area of meanings is "response" or "return," which has served as one basis for social relations in China. The Chinese believe that reciprocity of actions (favor and hatred, reward and punishment) between man and man, and indeed between men and supernatural beings, should be as certain as a cause-and-effect relationship, and, therefore, when a Chinese acts, he normally anticipates a response or return. Favors done for others are often considered what may be termed "social investments," for which handsome returns are expected. Of course, acceptance of the principle of reciprocity is required in practically every society.[1] Nevertheless, in China the principle is marked by its long history, the high degree of consciousness of its existence, and its wide application and tremendous influence in social institutions.

The Confucian classic, the *Book of Rites*,[2] contains the famous passage:

In the highest antiquity they prized (simply conferring) good; in the time next to this, giving and repaying was the thing attended to. And what the rules of propriety value is that reciprocity. If I give a gift and nothing comes in return, that is contrary to propriety; if the thing comes to me, and I give nothing in return, that also is contrary to propriety.

This passage has been quoted so many times that it has become a proverb. In Smith's *Proverbs and Common Sayings from the Chinese*,[3] he quotes the *Book of Rites* and adds, among others, the following common sayings:

Reciprocity, in theory, signifies that one person honors some other person a linear (or other) foot, and the other person should in return honor him ten feet 你敬我一尺，我敬你一丈. Reciprocity means giving a horse in return for an ox, and that a case of presents received is to be acknowledged by a case of presents in return, 得人一牛，還人一馬，一盒子來，必須一盒子去.

In the same work by Smith (p. 73), the following four lines are cited and labeled

Poem. Showing the necessity of Reciprocity, elucidating the true functions of Friendship, explaining one of the fundamental principles of the Chinese Empire:

天上下雨地上滑　　　When heaven sends rain earth turns to mire, each mortal slips and falls:

各人栽倒各人爬　　　In struggling to regain his feet, each mortal creeps and crawls;

親戚朋友拉一把　　　Dost thou expect thy friends and kin to lend a hand to thee,

酒換酒來茶換茶　　　Repay each sip of wine with wine, and each cup of tea with tea.

The response or return in social relations need not always be immediate. For instance, the exchange of gifts during the New Year and other annual festivals is almost immediate. Presents given on other occasions such as birthdays, weddings, and funerals, however, can be returned only when similar occasions are available. Of course, the food and drink provided for the guests on such an occasion may be considered a partial return for the gift already received, and, in cases where the gift is trivial and the entertainment lavish, the response would already be excessive. Ordinary entertainment, not on a particular occasion, is counted the same way, by quality and by quantity.

Response may be postponed, because social relations in China are normally on a family basis, and a family, like a legal person, is expected to last a long time. Between two families which have established friendly relations, social transactions need not be settled every time, because both parties can afford to be liberal in the short run. The Chinese phrase for such a liberal friendship is *kuo-te-chao*, which means that "there is enough reciprocity passing between us to allow some liberty." In the long run, however, the social balance sheet should be kept in balance. It is extremely important not to owe others what may be called "human feelings," termed in Chinese *jen-ch'ing*, which covers not only sentiment but also its social expressions such as the offering of congratulations or condolences or the making of gifts on appropriate occasions. Lest he fail to fulfil his social obligations and thus bring shame upon his family, a thoughtful head of a household may prepare a special social calendar,[4] which may be placed on the wall by the side of his washbowl as a daily reminder. In extreme cases, a poor scholar may decline all invitations to dinner simply because it is beyond his means to make the appropriate responses.[5]

The question of what is an appropriate response or return is considered differently in Confucianism and in Taoist philosophy. In the Confucian *Analects*[6] we read: "Some one said, 'What do you say concerning the principle that injury should be recompensed with kindness?' The Master said, 'With what then will you recompense kindness? Recompense injury with justice, and recompense kindness with kindness.' " The phrase "to recompense injury with kindness," or *i-te pao-yuan*, is found in the *Tao-te Ching*, attributed to Lao-tzu. This has been pointed out by James Legge, the famous translator of the Chinese classics, who adds: "But it is possible that Confucius' questioner simply consulted him about a saying which he had himself heard and was inclined to approve. . . . How far the ethics of Confucius fall below our Christian standard is evident from this chapter, and even below Lao-tzu."

Legge's criticism is not necessarily justifiable, because forgiveness, or *shu* (sometimes referred to as *k'uan*, "spacious," or as having *liang*, "capacity"), certainly has an important position in the Confucian system. Chinese ethics advise the gentleman to overlook minor wrongs or injuries. The highest ideal, of extending one's help without seeking reward, is honored in Confucianism, but it is also considered somewhat impractical. Here the point stressed is that justice should not be infringed upon by mercy.

According to the *Book of Rites*,[7] Confucius also permitted *i-yuan pao-yuan*, "to recompense injury with injury." It is not clear whether this principle appeared to Confucius to be the same as that of *i-chih pao-yuan*, "to recompense injury with justice." If Confucius actually recommended both principles, his position has been modified by later Confucianists, who consider it repulsive for a gentleman to talk about recompensing injury with injury. It is possible that the change was brought about under the influence of Taoism. But, if that was the case, it should not be understood as Taoist idealism winning over Confucian realism, because both Confucianism and Taoism have their idealistic and realistic aspects and because the arguments advanced against "injury for injury" can be realistic as well as idealistic. The realistic argument is *yuan-yuan hsiang-pao ho-shih te-liao*, "If injury is recompensed with injury, when will mutual retaliation come to an end?" This fear of endless retaliation is often expressed in government orders prohibiting revenge or blood feuds.[8] It supplements the legal argument that injustice should be corrected only through the state authority.

Anyhow, the statement "to recompense injury with injury" was

very rarely quoted by later Confucianists, who must have wished
that there had been a misprint in that part of the text of the *Book of
Rites*. In a famous Sung work, *Yuan-shih Shih-fan*, or the *Social Code
for the Yuan Family*,[9] we find the following passage entitled "Pao-
yuan i-chih nai kung-hsin" ("It is public spirited to recompense injury with justice"):

> The Sage (i.e., Confucius) said, "Recompense injury with justice." This is the
> middle way which is most practical. Generally speaking, to recompense injury with
> injury is of course not worth recommending. Yet there are literati-officials (*shih ta-
> fu*) who, wishing to win fame for being gentlemanly and generous, sometimes leave
> the wicked unpunished because they happen to have been their own personal ene-
> mies. This is entirely artificial and does not conform to human feelings. What the
> Sage calls justice is that if a man is good, he is not to be rejected because he is an
> enemy, and if the man is bad, he is not to be protected because he is a friend. Judg-
> ments and decisions should in every case correspond to the facts. To recompense
> injury in this manner certainly will not lead to an endless process of mutual retalia-
> tion.

The author of this passage ably defends the orthodox Confucian
tradition. However, when he denounces the principle of recompensing injury with injury, he obviously forgets that the saying is also
labeled as by Confucius in the *Book of Rites*. Incidentally, the fact
that the *Book of Rites* contains this statement supports the point
made by modern scholars like Fung Yu-lan[10] that the *Book of Rites*
agrees more with the Realistic Wing of Confucianism, represented by
Hsün-tzu, than with the Idealistic Wing, represented by Mencius.

Another tradition which has influenced the concept of *pao* is that
of the *hsia* or *yu-hsia*, a term translated as "knights-errant." These
people were first recognized as a group during the period of the Warring States. At that time, the old feudal order had disintegrated, and
many hereditary warriors had lost their positions and titles. As brave
and upright individuals, and joined by strong sons of lower origin,
they scattered throughout the country and made a living by offering
their services (and even their lives) to anyone who could afford to
employ them. The knights-errant were distinguished by their absolute reliability, which was their professional virtue. As described by
Ssu-ma Ch'ien in his *Historical Memoirs:* "Their words were always
sincere and trustworthy, and their actions always quick and decisive.
They were always true to what they promised, and without regard to
their own persons, they would rush into dangers threatening
others."[11] This is the way they responded to friends who really appreciated their worth. Always seeking to right wrongs, the knights-
errant proved most helpful to people who desired to secure revenge.

After China became a unified empire under Ch'in and Han, the government made attempts to check the activities of the knights-errant. This policy was chiefly based on the principle that justice should be administered only by legal authorities responsible to the emperor. Similar attempts were made by later dynasties, and on the whole they were quite successful. People who avenged themselves were brought to court, and, as offenders of the law, they would be punished accordingly (except for cases in which a filial son took vengeance upon the murderer of his parent, whereupon, as the avenger, he might be sentenced to exile rather than death).

The chivalrous spirit of the ancient knights-errant, however, did not die. The celebrated models recorded in the *Historical Memoirs* never failed to inspire later generations, which have produced from time to time both genuine and fake examples of the knight-errant tradition. The following story[12] illustrates the emphasis placed on the concept of *pao* by the knight-errant.

In the middle of the T'ang dynasty, Ts'ui Yai and Chang Hu, two candidates for the *chin-shih* degree, having failed in their examinations, wandered in the region of the Yangtze and the Huai Valley. They both loved wine and boastfully recognized each other as knights-errant. Ts'ui Yai once, when intoxicated, wrote a poem which reads:

太行嶺上三尺雪

崔涯袖中三尺鐵

一朝若遇有心人

出門便與妻兒別

Over the T'ai-hang range lie three feet of snow;
In the sleeve of Ts'ui Yai lies a three-foot sword.
One day when he meets a warm-hearted and warm-blooded man,
He will rush away with him, leaving at home his wife and children.

This poem and other big talk made both men quite famous. Chang Hu, who was rather wealthy, one night received a distinguished-looking warrior who had a sword at his waist and a bag in his hand containing something quite bloody. Entering the house, the warrior asked whether this was the residence of Knight Chang. Chang said, "Yes," and treated the visitor with great respect. When seated, the visitor said, "I had an enemy on whom I tried to get revenge without success for ten years. I just got him tonight, and here is his head." Then he asked, "Have you got wine?" Chang served him wine. Drinking it, the visitor said, "About a mile from here lives a right-eous person whose kindness I have always wanted to return. If I can do it, then the injuries received and kindnesses paid during my whole life will be recompensed. I have heard of your generosity. Can you lend me 100,000 strings of cash so that I can repay him right away? That will fulfil my last wish. From then on, I shall have no hesitation to rush into boiling water or burning fire for you or to serve you like a dog or a rooster." Chang was completely charmed by these remarks, and, under the candlelight, he searched his valuables and gave the visitor silks and other things which approximated the sum. The visitor said, "Excellent! This is most satisfactory!" Then he went away without the bloody bag, saying that he would come back for it before dawn. Chang waited and waited until daybreak, but the warrior never returned. Fearing to keep a human head in a bag, Chang ordered a servant to bury it. Only then was it discovered that what was in the bag was only the head of a pig.

According to the ethical code of genuine knights-errant, although they themselves were entirely dependable in returning the kindness of others, they would not expect any reward when they did favors to others. Many of them would even reject such a reward. This virtue is called *i*, which is normally rendered "righteousness," but here it is used in a special sense referring to any virtue that is above the normal requirement. Following is an analysis of this meaning of *i* by Fung Yu-lan:[13]

People who are said to practice *hsia*, or *i*, adopt a standard of conduct which is sometimes higher than what is prescribed by morality in the society. For example, in the novel *Erh-nü Ying-hsiung Chuan*, or *Heroic Lovers*, the heroine of the novel, Shih-san Mei, bestowed kindness and rejected any reward. She was lectured at length by the old gentleman Mr. An (who later became her father-in-law) on the middle way of the sages and the wise. That is a good example. Mr. An said, "All those who distinguish themselves as *hsia* and *i* are extraordinarily gifted in personality and talent and want to behave on a level even higher than that of the sages and the wise." The sages and the wise "take pleasure in treading comfortably the middle way," in following what is prescribed by the morality of the society. But to behave on a level even higher than that of the sages and the wise is to be supermoral. To bestow kindness and not to expect a reward is moral. To bestow kindness and to reject any reward is supermoral.

The principle of reciprocal response, or *pao*, has been applied to social relations of all kinds, beginning with that between the ruler and his subjects, the first of the *Wu-lun*, or Five Relationships. Even in ancient times, *pao-en*, or the return of grace, was already recognized as a basis for good government. Particularly explicit are the following remarks by the Han scholar Liu Hsiang in his *Shuo-yuan*, or *Garden of Sayings*:[14]

Confucius said, "Virtue is not left to stand alone. (He who practices it) will have neighbors."[15] Worthy bestowers of kindness will not expect gratitude, while grateful receivers of grace will certainly make a return. Thus ministers toil to serve there ruler but do not seek rewards. The ruler uses the power to bestow grace as a means of government but does not consider it particularly virtuous (to do so). Therefore, says the *Book of Changes*,[16] "To toil without complaint and to be meritorious without boasting of one's virtue constitute the height of generous goodness." When the ruler and his ministers treat each other in the manner of the marketplace 以人市道接 (i.e., on a strict business basis), the ruler uses salary as an inducement and the ministers exert themselves in return. If a minister achieves unusual merit, the ruler will bestow upon him handsome rewards. If the ruler bestows extraordinary grace, the minister (who receives it) will repay it even by death. . . . Now even birds, beasts, and insects understand the principles of co-operation and reciprocity, how much the more so in the case of educated gentlemen whose aim it was to bring fame and welfare to the empire! When ministers no longer return the grace of the ruler but merely line their own pockets, that is the source of disaster. When the ruler fails to repay the ministers' merits and hesitates in his use of rewards and punishments, that is also the root of disorder. All sources and roots of disaster and disorder come from failure in returning grace.

The first part of the passage describes the ideal situation, "the height of generous goodness." But "the manner of the marketplace" that comes next appears more practical. The comparison to birds, beasts, and insects makes return or response a universal law of nature. A similar observation was made by Tung Chung-shu. This famous theorizer of the Han empire developed a remarkable theory of the unity of the cosmic and the human order. In his comprehensive system the fabric of the state and society is considered analogous to the structure of the universe. Explaining the responses of nature and man, he writes:

If now water be poured on level ground, it will avoid the parts that are dry and move toward those that are wet. Whereas if (two) identical pieces of firewood are exposed to fire, the latter will avoid the one that is wet and catch to that which is dry. All things avoid that from which they differ and cleave to that to which they are similar. Thus forces that are similar meet each other. . . . (Likewise) a thing that is beautiful will call to itself another beautiful thing the same in kind, whereas an ugly thing will call to itself another ugly thing of the same kind. For example, when a horse neighs, another horse will respond; when an ox lows, another ox will respond. In the same way, when an emperor or king is about to arise, auspicious omens first appear. Thus it is that things of the same kind call to one another.[17]

According to Tung Chung-shu, governmental institutions are justifiable when they are modeled after the way of Heaven. What he calls "four ways of government" correspond to the four seasons:

In Heaven's course, spring with its warmth germinates, summer with its heat nourishes, autumn with its coolness destroys, and winter with its cold stores up. Warmth, heat, coolness and coldness are different forces but their work is identical, all being instruments whereby Heaven brings the year to completion. The sage, in his conduct of government, duplicates the movements of Heaven. Thus with his beneficence he duplicates warmth and accords with spring, with his conferring of rewards he duplicates heat and accords with summer, with his punishments he duplicates coolness and accords with autumn, and with his executions he duplicates coldness and accords with winter. . . . Therefore I say that the king is co-equal with Heaven, meaning that Heaven in its course has its four seasons, while the king in his, has his four ways of government. Such are what Heaven and man share in common.[18]

The term "Heaven," or T'ien, for Tung Chung-shu and for the majority of Chinese thinkers as well, refers to both nature and the divinity which presides over nature, with emphasis sometimes on the one and sometimes on the other.[19] We may say that, whether personal or impersonal, Heaven has been believed to be bound by the rule of response.

This leads us to the belief in natural or divine retribution, a deep-rooted tradition in Chinese religion. In the *Book of Documents*[20] we read, "The way of Heaven is to bless the good and to punish the bad," and "On the doer of good, he sends down all blessings, and on the doer of evil, he sends all calamities." Retribution is believed to operate on a family basis. As is said in the *Book of Changes*,[21] "The family which stores up virtue will have an exuberance of happiness: the family which stores up vice will have an exuberance of calamity." A proverb in ancient China says, "A family that has produced generals for three (i.e., several) generations will bring disaster to its descendants." Ch'en P'ing, a brilliant strategist and politician of the Former Han dynasty, once remarked, "I have done too much secret plotting. My sons and grandsons will not flourish."[22]

Experience, however, does not always confirm this belief in the certainty of retribution. Consequently, doubts of the principle have been raised from time to time. For instance, Wang Ch'ung, the famous naturalistic thinker of Later Han times, once observed:

In conducting affairs men may be either talented or stupid, but when it comes to calamity or good fortune, there are some who are lucky and some unlucky. The things they do may be right or wrong, but whether they meet with reward or punishment depends on chance. . . . There are many persons who wish to display their loyalty (to a ruler), yet he rewards some and punishes others; there are many who wish to do him benefit, yet he trusts some and distrusts others. Those whom he rewards and trusts are not necessarily the true ones, nor are those whom he punishes and distrusts necessarily the false. It is simply that the rewarded and trusted ones are lucky, while those who are punished and distrusted are unlucky.[23]

To this theory of fatalistic uncertainty, early religious thinkers had no adequate answer until Buddhism converted China with its concepts of karma and transmigration of souls, which explain retribution not only in one life but through a chain of lives. Before this ingenious interpretation became available, native thinkers had relied largely on the explanation that fate was shared by members of the same family or clan or by people who lived in the same area. The principle of joint responsibility of family or neighborhood has been applied in Chinese government and law since ancient times. It is only natural to assume that the principle is approved by Heaven as well as by man.

This sharing of fate is called *ch'eng-fu*, "transmission of burdens," in the *T'ai-p'ing Ching,* or *Classic of the Great Peace,*[24] which contains ideas dating back to Later Han times and hence may be considered the first book on the Taoist religion. According to this work, Heaven often sends down calamities because it has been angered by wicked deeds of man. One example is the drilling of wells, which, according to a common belief, involves penetrating into the blood vessels of Mother Earth. Another example given in this book is the killing of baby girls, which is said to have reduced the female population to such a point that it became impossible for a man to have two wives and so realize the principle of one Yang matching two Yin. Such crimes may have been committed by only a few persons of earlier times, but the consequences involved later generations of the offenders' families and their neighborhoods. (This term *ch'eng-fu* is not found in other books. The context of the passages which include this term suggests that it was most likely of Han origin.)

In the first part of the period of the Six Dynasties (220–589) there was a considerable revival of naturalism, and doubt about the validity of divine retribution became strong among certain intellectuals. This led to several lively debates concerning karma. The Buddhist karma originally was supposed to work on an individual rather than on a family basis. The theory of transmigration of souls covers not only mankind but all living beings. The elevation of animals to the level of human beings was against the Confucianist tradition, which placed man in the center of the world. The Buddhist law against taking life made it difficult to justify sacrificial offerings as a means of worship. It was by a gradual process of give-and-take that the newly introduced concepts of retribution became reconciled with the native tradition.[25] Since about the T'ang and certainly from the Sung period, it has been generally accepted that divine retribution works on a family basis and through a chain of lives. Compared with the rather primitive idea of *ch'eng-fu* in the *T'ai-p'ing Ching,* this enriched concept of response marks an increase in sophistication.

Another early Taoist work, the *Pao-p'u-tzu*[26] of the fourth century, stresses the mechanical, quantitative aspect of retribution. Basing itself on still earlier Taoist texts which are no longer extant, the *Pao-p'u-tzu* says:

It is said that heaven and earth are possessed of crime-recording spirits. According to the lightness or gravity of his transgressions, the sinner's term of life is reduced. . . . The great offenses cause a loss of a *chi*, i.e., three hundred days; small ones of a *suan*, i.e., three days [one tradition says one day].[27] . . . If one dies before the total deductions are made, the evil luck will be transferred to children and grandchildren.

The book also contains an optimistic note which makes fate seem improvable:

For those who have committed various crimes and later repented, if one has wrongly killed another person, he should try to save a person who is about to die in order to redeem himself. If one has stolen valuables from another, he should try to recommend and promote a virtuous person to redeem himself. In every case, the merit should double the amount of demerit which has been committed. Then one will be able to receive good fortune. This is the way of transforming curses into blessings.[28]

Most of the above ideas have been incorporated, practically word for word, into the popular Sung work *T'ai-shang Kan-ying P'ien*, or *Treatise of the Exalted One on Response and Retribution*. For centuries it was the most highly esteemed of all *shan-shu*, i.e., books devoted to moral teachings, and its distribution was considered a religious duty. According to an estimate made in the early years of the present century,[29] the editions of the *Treatise on Response and Retribution* possibly were even more numerous than those of the Bible or the works of Shakespeare have been.

Another popular Sung work is the *Kung-kuo Ko*, or *Table of Merits and Demerits*, which was often appended to the *Treatise on Response and Retribution* but also circulated independently. It contains a list of standard good and evil deeds and marks their value in positive and negative figures. At the end of the book there are provided for the reader blanks for lists of demeritorious and meritorious deeds, for the sum total on both sides, and for a statement of the balance. A study of the standard list has been found illuminating for the understanding of Chinese moral values.[30]

Social relations purely worldly in nature are also subject to a quantitative analysis and in most cases can be translated into terms of money. This may be illustrated by the following joke taken from a book called *Hsiao-te-hao*, or *Good Laughs*, in a series of moralistic compilations called *Ch'uan-chia Pao*, or *Family Treasures*, by the early Ch'ing author Shih T'ien-chi of Yang-chou (pp. 3a–4a):

There was an old man who was generous and philanthropic. One day, during a snowstorm, he saw a young man taking shelter at his gate. He pitied the young fellow and invited him in. Having given him some wine to ward off the cold, he put him up for the night. The next day found the snowfall still heavy; he kept the young man again. This was repeated until the fourth day, when the weather became clear. While taking his leave, the young man asked the old man to lend him a sword. With it in hand, the young man said to his host, "I have never known you before, but you have treated me so kindly. I am so overwhelmed that I can repay you only by killing myself." The old man was shocked and tried to stop him, saying, "Then you will bring me trouble." The young man asked why. The old man said, "If a man is found dead in my house, the officials may decide that I am innocent, but even then I shall have to pay at least twelve taels of silver as *shao-mai ch'ien* ['burn-and-bury money'], not to speak about the other miscellaneous fees." The young man said, "Since you have been so kind to me, I shall omit the miscellaneous fees. You can give me the twelve taels of 'burn-and-bury money' and I will leave you." The old man was greatly angered and shouted loudly to argue his case. When the neighbors heard him, they came and offered to arbitrate, and finally it was settled that the young man should receive six taels, i.e., half what he demanded. When he was about to leave, the old man sighed, "I never guessed that I should meet such a mean person." The young man said, "You yourself are mean." The old man asked why. The young man said, "If you are not mean—you kept me for only three nights—you should not have taken from me a charge of two taels per night."

Shih T'ien-chi used this joke to introduce his moral instruction that we should not merely laugh at this young man but should also think of the numerous ungrateful sons and officials who have turned their backs on their parents or ruler. Perhaps one can also use the joke to illustrate the Chinese saying *Shan-men nan-k'ai*, "It is difficult to keep open the door of philanthropy." In America, people may recall cases in which a hitchhiker murdered the driver who was kind enough to give him a lift. In the above story, the point which throws light on our discussion is the application of a kind of hotel rate to friendly shelter for the night.

The influences of the concept of *pao* over Chinese institutions are many and various. Trying to classify such influences by categories, one finds it profitable to use some of the generalizations made by modern scholars about Chinese society. Especially noticeable are the following three: (1) familism, (2) worldly rationalism, and (3) ethical particularism. The first two are generally accepted as characteristic of Chinese society. Since they have already been illustrated above, only a few supplementary remarks are necessary. The contrast between particularism and universalism was first pointed out by Max Weber in his famous *Religionssoziologie*. In the United States his theory has been ably expounded by Talcott Parsons. The relationship between the concept of *pao* and the principles of universalism and particularism, however, remains to be made explicit.

1. For familism, it should be clear from the above that the principle of response or return works on the basis of the family system. Rewards and punishments, curses and blessings, are all transferable within a family. Among political and legal institutions, we find such examples as *yin* or *yin-hsü* favors extended to lower generations in the family of an official; *feng-tseng i-erh-san tai*, honors extended to one, two, or three upper generations; *i-tseng*, honors transferred from himself to his ancestors by an official's request (instead of having the honor bestowed upon himself); and *tsu-hsing*, punishments involving a whole family or even a clan.[31]

The principle of reciprocity in turn strengthens the family system. For instance, the basic virtue of filial piety has a ready justification in the concept of response. A son should be filial even on a strict business basis because he has received so much from his parents, especially during childhood. The Chinese proverb says, "Men rear sons to provide for old age; they plant trees because they want shade."[32] Another version says, "Men rear sons to provide for old age: they store up grain to provide for years of famine."[33] Bringing up children may be considered the commonest form of social investment. An unfilial son is also a bad businessman who fails to pay his parents' old age insurance.[34] In matters of ritual, according to Confucius, the explanation for the mourning period of three years for each parent is because "a son, three years after his birth, ceases to be carried in the arms of his parents."[35]

2. Worldly rationalism ascribes the same reasoning to Heaven and to man and, in doing so, brings Heaven down to earth rather than lifts man up to the heights above. Divine retribution and worldly retribution are believed to work hand in hand, the former supplementary to the latter. The word *pao*, in the sense of thanksgiving, is used many times in the *Book of Rites* to explain the religious institution of sacrificial offering. The following observation by the modern scholar Liang Ch'i-ch'ao[36] is well supported in the Chinese classics:

The Confucian *Analects* say, "For a man to sacrifice to a spirit which does not belong to him is flattery."[37] The conceptions of "a spirit which belongs to one" and "a spirit which does not" create a point of view different from the Westerners'. It means simply that spirits and deities cannot influence our fortune, and that our offering sacrifices to them is to revere virtue and recompense merit. Sacrifices are offered to parents because they give birth to us and bring us up; to heaven and earth because they give us numerous facilities. Parents should be sacrificed to; so are heaven and earth, mountains and rivers, the sun and the moon. Extending this principle to persons, we want to offer sacrifices to all those who have warded off disasters or promoted the welfare of the state or the locality.[38] Extending this principle to things, even the deities [i.e., spiritual representatives] of cats, dogs, cattle, and horses should be sacrificed to. This single conception of *pao* penetrates the whole [institution] of sacrificial offerings.

In one place, however, Liang has overrationalized the institution when he says spirits and deities cannot influence our fortune. Here he is reading the ethics of the educated gentlemen into the mind of the masses, of whom the majority certainly would expect blessings from worship. This point is rather important, and its significance will become clear when we are through with our discussion of universalism and particularism.

3. According to Weber and Parsons, one of the fundamentals of the modern Western social order is its ethical universalism:

To a very high degree both in theory and in practice our highest ethical duties apply "impersonally" to all men, or to large categories of them irrespective of any specific personal relation involved. . . . In this respect the Puritan ethic represents an intensification of the general Christian tendency. It has an extremely powerful animus against nepotism and favoritism. To this the Confucian ethic stands in sharp contrast. Its ethical sanction was given to an individual's *personal* relations to particular persons—and with any strong emphasis *only* to these. The whole Chinese social structure accepted and sanctioned by the Confucian ethic was a predominantly "particularistic" structure of relationships.[39]

The Chinese principle of response prescribes reciprocity for all social relations and in this sense may be considered universalistic in nature. The working of the principle, however, has tended to be particularistic, because a social response in China is rarely an independent single transaction but rather an additional entry in a long balance sheet which registers the personal relations between two individuals or two families. Conditioned by already established personal relations, a given response can easily have an effect, or at least an appearance, of nepotism or favoritism.

Generally speaking, personalized relations have a tendency to particularize even institutions which were intended to apply in a universalistic manner. Thus in traditional China, even in a case of fulfilment of an official duty, if it happened to be beneficial to a particular person, he would be expected to cherish a sense of indebtedness to the person who was instrumental in the outcome. For instance, when the civil service examinations were the chief channels to officialdom, the relationship between successful candidates and the examiner who passed them was extremely close. It was compared to the relation between disciples or apprentices and their beloved master. In the Chinese ethical code, a master is one of the five most respectable persons, the other four being Heaven, Earth, one's lord, and one's parents. To the five, one is obliged to be respectful and grateful, because one owes them so much that it is beyond one's power to return it.

The following story[40] illustrates how an examiner in traditional China could make social investments out of his duties. In the first years of the ninth century, Ts'ui Ch'ün was prime minister and very famous for his incorruptibility. Once he served as commissioner of examinations. Sometime afterward, when his wife advised him to buy some real estate to be left to children and grandchildren, he replied smiling, "I have thirty excellent manor houses with rich fields spreading all over the empire. Why should you worry about real estate?" His wife was puzzled and said she had not heard anything like that. The minister said, "You remember the year before last I served as examiner and passed thirty candidates. Are they not excellent estates?" His wife said, "If that is the case, you yourself passed examinations under Minister Lu Chih, and yet, when you served as commissioner of examinations, you especially sent a messenger to ask Lu's son not to take them. If candidates are fertile fields, one of the estates of the Lu family has been laid waste." Upon these remarks, Ts'ui felt greatly ashamed of himself and even lost his appetite for several days.

It must be explained that the reason Ts'ui asked Lu's son not to take the examinations was to avoid the suspicion of favoritism. The uncorrupted minister was following the rule of the Chinese gentleman to keep one's self out of every situation that might lead to doubt. On the other hand, as suggested by his wife, in doing so, he could be criticized as being selfish and ungrateful because he had failed to return the kindness of his examiner and master. The important point here is that the minister's comparison of candidates to real estate was not exactly a joke. It pointed to the common practice during the era of imperial China for examiners to expect considerable returns from fulfilling their own duties.

This kind of relationship between an examiner and candidates was accepted as normal in traditional China. But in the modern West it probably would be considered to approach favoritism because of its failure to distinguish public duties from private personal relations. Whether certain conduct constitutes favoritism, bribery, or any other form of corruption is of course a matter of degree. In addition, judgment also depends upon whether the moral standard is high or low, single or multiple.

This leads us to the interesting problem of the dual standards of Confucianist ethics, one for the "gentlemen," or *chün-tzu*, and the other for the "small men," or *hsiao-jen*. Confucian idealism advocates the way of the gentleman as praiseworthy, whereas Confucian realism defends, or at least tolerates, the way of the small man as normal. Since Confucianism in imperial China was a combination of its idealistic and realistic elements, it naturally permitted the co-existence of two different ethical standards. A discussion of these dual standards and their significance in the history of Chinese thought will conclude this paper.

According to Confucius, "The mind of the gentlemen is conversant with righteousness; the mind of the small men is conversant with gain."[41] Consequently, the gentlemen and the small men would respond differently to the same challenge or stimulus. The gentleman "requires much from himself and little from others,"[42] said Confucius. Obviously that is because the others may or may not be gentlemen like himself. Following this old tradition, the *Treatise on Response and Retribution* also prescribes, "Extend your help without seeking reward. Give to others and do not regret or begrudge your liability."[43] The normal small man extends his help and seeks reward. He who receives help but offers no reward falls even below the standard of the normal man. Such a person is a *hsiao-jen* in the sense of a wicked rather than merely a small man. The normal small man would regret his liability if he had benefited an ungrateful or wicked man.

As for a gentleman, in the words of Mencius, "If he treats others politely and they do not return his politeness, let him turn inward to examine his own (feeling of) respect,"[44] in other words, to make sure whether his own outward politeness came from true respect. For this inward examination, Mencius gives a lengthy illustration which may be summarized as follows: If a gentleman who is benevolent and observant of propriety is treated by a man in a perverse and unreasonable manner, the gentleman will first reflect upon himself, asking whether he himself has been wanting in benevolence or propriety, and also whether he has been failing to do his utmost. After he is satisfied with himself, if the man still repeats his perversity and unreasonableness, the gentleman will say, "This is a man utterly lost indeed! Since he conducts himself so, what is there to choose between him and a brute? Why should I go to contend with a brute?"[45]

In the case of a small man, his ethical code permits him to retaliate against unreasonableness with unreasonableness. In the first part of this paper where the virtue of the knight-errant is described, we have quoted Ssu-ma Ch'ien: "Their words were always sincere and trustworthy, and their actions always quick and decisive." The same description appears also in the works of Mo-tzu, whose teachings, according to Fung Yu-lan, were closely connected with the tradition of the knight-errant.[46] Interestingly enough, the same words *yen pi hsin, hsing pi kuo* 言必信, 行必果 are also found in the *Analects*, where such people are labeled "small men" by Confucius, although he did give them a grade of "fair" following what may be called the "excellent" and the "good."[47] Here we note a significant difference between the ethical code of the knight-errant and that of Confucius.

The difference comes from the objection raised by Confucianists to the word "always" in the description. Mencius makes this clear when he says, "The great man does not insist that his words should always be sincere and trustworthy, or that his action always be quick and decisive. He only speaks and acts according to what is right."[48] The word for "what is right" is *i*, i.e., righteousness or the right decision after deliberation. Compare the character *i*, "to discuss, to deliberate," in which *i*, "righteousness," is a phonetic but probably also a signific component.

Commenting on the Mencius passage, the Han Confucianist Chao Ch'i says: "The great man sticks to what is right, which may not always require sincere words or decisive action. An example for the former is that a son may lie to conceal his father's stealing.[49] One for the latter is that one should not promise his own life to a friend while his own parents are alive."[50] These examples are excellent illustrations of filial piety put above sincerity, and universalism modified by particularism.

In the ethical code of the knight-errant, the principle of response is universalistic. He is determined to repay every meal served with kindness and to return every angry glance from the eyes of another person, irrespective of whether the latter is a gentleman or a small man, a relative or a stranger. The Confucian gentleman, however, refuses to fight against an unreasonable person, whom he compares with a mere brute. That is why Confucianists in ancient China were known as "weaklings," which was the original meaning of the word *ju*.[51]

Among leading Confucianists in ancient China, Mencius is especially famous for his advocacy of the principle of *i*, the desirability of doing what is exactly right. He applied the principle in a very deliberate and delicate manner, as is illustrated in the following example: A prince who was serving as the guardian of a neighboring state, and a minister of another state, independently sent presents to Mencius, who accepted both but in neither case returned the courtesy. Later, when Mencius went to the respective neighboring states, he paid a visit to the prince but not to the minister. This difference in response puzzled a disciple, who asked Mencius whether it was because the minister was merely a minister. Mencius said, "No," and hinted that the minister's presents had not been accompanied with sufficient respect. The disciple then realized that, as the guardian of a state, the prince could not leave it to pay a visit in another. There was no reason, however, why the minister should not have paid his respects to Mencius in person.[52]

This kind of deliberate and delicate response was obviously intended to provoke the thought not only of the disciples but also of the person involved. Because no response is also a kind of response, one who expected a response from a gentleman but received none should begin to reflect upon himself. In this light we may interpret the remark of Mencius that his refusal to teach somebody was also a way of teaching him.[53]

Such a deliberate and delicate way of response is not characteristic of the realist Hsün-tzu. On the other hand, Hsün-tzu's teaching was rather close to universalism in his emphasis on the institutional aspects of life, such as the observation of mourning periods and the making of sacrificial offerings. It was not accidental that among his pupils we find the Legalist Han Fei-tzu, who advocated a uniform law for the whole empire. There is a sharp contrast between this universalistic concept of *fa*, or law, and the Confucianist concept of *li*, propriety or the way of life of the gentleman (for the gentlemen only),[54] or the concept of *i*, i.e., what is right after deliberation, or as one might say, particularistic righteousness.

This difference in ethical codes of course had its social background. If we remember that in Chou times the term *chün-tzu* referred to nobles as well as to gentlemen, and *hsiao-jen* to commoners as well as to small people, we can easily reach the conclusion that the dual standard of ethics arose from a two-class society. In early Chou times, the person who had a noble status and the person who had gentlemanly virtue were believed to be normally if not invariably identical. The same identification was applied to the commoner and the small man. The gentleman and the small man each had his own moral standard. With the decline of the Chou feudal order, the social classes and their respective ways of life, including their moral standards, ceased to correspond. This became noticeable by the time of

Confucius, when the words *chün-tzu* and *hsiao-jen* were used each in two distinct connotations. The knights-errant may have been nobles themselves. But, since they had lost their old status, they tended to identify themselves with the commoners, and their ethical code also blended with that of the commoners.[55] Another possible interpretation is that there may have been a difference between the ethical code of the knightly nobles and that of the gentlemanly nobles, which led subsequently to the different principles held by the knights-errant and by the Confucianists. But this could not have been much earlier than the time of Confucius, because this process of social differentiation or specialization among the nobles had just begun in his time. In the early Chou period, the terms "knight" and "gentleman" pointed to one and the same noble.

In the twenty-one centuries after the fall of Chou and the unification of China under the Ch'in dynasty in 221 B.C., the imperial system provided the superstructure of Chinese society, while the family system served as its basic unit. Duties to the emperor and to one's parents therefore tended to receive increasing attention. Particularism along these two lines became still more predominant, and the principle of reciprocity was further modified. Confucianism in this era was inclined to place one's nominal status and role, *ming-fen*, above reality. The mere position of a ruler or a parent guaranteed his privilege to receive respect and service from his subject or son. In extreme cases, when a loyal official was punished for no reason, he might still say to his emperor, "Your minister deserves his punishment. Your majesty is sagacious and just."[56] To justify the absolute piety required from a son, Confucianists invented the sweeping generalization, "There are no wrongdoing parents in the world."[57] The son or the subject was always the one to blame, no matter whether there was kindness from the parent or the ruler.

The attitudes of early Confucianism toward the ruler and the parent were different. For ill treatment from a ruler, Mencius approved retaliation with dissertion, disloyalty, or even rebellion.[58] Tyrannicide was justified on the ground that in being tyrannical the ruler had reduced his own status to that of an isolated single individual.[59] Mencius also permitted a filial son to murmur against his parent when the latter's fault was great, the reason being that if the son responded to his father's cruelty with indifference that would increase the distance and alienation between them.[60] Confucius also allowed a son to remonstrate with his parents, though he should do so only gently.[61] The attitude of Confucius toward the ruler-subject relationship could not have differed widely from that of Mencius.[62] To Confucius and Mencius the modifications made by later Confucianists would have seemed very strange.

The imperial China which developed particularism and continued the dual standard of ethics was not a two-class society in any strict sense. Nevertheless, the term "two-class society" may be applied to it in a loose sense, because the contrast between the literati-officials and the common people (or gentry and peasantry, as some writers would prefer) was quite striking. Still, we must remember, in any period of traditional China there were more small men than gentlemen, because only a limited portion of the population could afford an education. For the not-so-well-educated small men, whose ethical code is preserved in proverbs and other forms of folklore, reciprocity was always the normal standard. Since it also served as a low but tolerable standard for the Confucianists, the principle provided a common ground for both gentlemen and small men—in other words, for the whole society. Here rests its real significance.

In the last few decades, Chinese society has been undergoing a process of tremendous transformation or revolution, which has had far-reaching influence in many aspects of life. As yet, it is difficult to ascertain whether people will limit the wide application of the principle of reciprocity or whether they will lose their high degree of consciousness of the existence of the principle and, if so, to what extent. Under the influence of the ethical standards of the modern West, it is unlikely that the principle will continue to function in the same manner, although it is also unlikely that the Chinese will wish entirely to abandon the principle as a basis for social relations.

THE SCHOLAR'S FRUSTRATION: NOTES
ON A TYPE OF *FU*

HELLMUT WILHELM

EVERY STUDENT of Chinese literature has been struck by the sudden emergence of the *fu* as a literary genre in early Han times. It seems to have arisen almost out of a vacuum to become the dominant form of literary expression within less than a generation. From the very beginning it was endowed with certain features which have remained characteristic of this genre down to the present. Among them are its rather strict prosodic pattern, in rhythm as well as rhyme, its tendency to quote abundantly from earlier literature, especially the classics, its often highly sophisticated language, its general inclination to display the author's learning, and its wide use of metaphor and symbolism.[1] This sudden emergence is all the more astonishing when one notes that there is only one *fu* in existence that undisputedly goes back to late Chou times.[2] With the rise of Han, however, the art of *fu* writing was immediately practiced so widely that it overshadowed all other literary genres.[3] In later periods the *fu* remained one of the accepted types of literary expression. It underwent, however, specific changes, prosodically as well as in content and purpose. And never again did it dominate the literary scene as it had done in the Han period.

It is not the purpose of this paper to analyze the prosodic features of the Han *fu*. It is a very highly stylized composition with rhythmic and rhyme patterns that make it come close to poetry. Actually, it is classed together with poetry in the earlier bibliographies, and only later was it put at the head of prose genres. The term *fu* has been quite aptly translated as "prose-poetry" or "rhyme-prose."

Nor does the present paper undertake to evaluate the literary merits of the *fu*, even though some examples are hauntingly beautiful. It is restricted, rather, to a line of argument which may throw light on the reason for the sudden emergence of the *fu* in the Han period.

Actually, only a small percentage of the Han *fu* have come down to our times. Of these, again, the majority survive only in short fragments. An analysis of the content and the purpose of the Han *fu* is thus restricted to a very limited amount of evidence, and there is no way of knowing whether the lost *fu* would corroborate or qualify the suggestions presented here.[4]

A perusal of the surviving *fu* of Han times reveals that the topics discussed and their main purport are rather limited. Identical topics are taken up over and over again by writers of the same or succeeding generations. Quite frequently the titles used by different authors are identical or almost identical, but, even when this is not the case, the Han *fu* can easily be classified into a limited number of types. All these types have one feature in common: almost without exception they can be and have been interpreted as voicing criticism—either of the ruler, the ruler's behavior, or certain political acts or plans of the ruler; or of the court officials or the ruler's favorites; or, generally, of the lack of discrimination in the employment of officials. The few examples that are positive in tone recommend the authors or their peers for employment, or even contain specific political suggestions. In short, almost all *fu* have a political purport, and, in addition, almost all of them deal with the relationship between the ruler and his officials.

It hardly needs stressing that "political" topics in China have provided content for pure literature not only in Han times and that other literary genres also have been used for this purpose. Already the *Odes* of the Chou era complain frequently about political oppression and social injustice; many T'ang writers give vent in their poems to emotions engendered by bad government; and in later periods the novel has repeatedly been used as a vehicle for extreme political criticism. However, it appears to this writer that in no other period has the predominant literary type been so exclusively used for political purposes as was the *fu* in Han times. Furthermore, in no other period were the topics thus discussed so limited and, throughout, so specific. It is not political oppression or social injustice that is treated —these *fu* revolve around one central problem: the position of the scholar in government and his relations to the ruler, on whom, in turn, his position depends. This seems to have been the problem that monopolized the literary mind in that period to the exclusion of almost everything else, to the exclusion even of many of the topics traditionally treated in pure literature. Even if we knew nothing about the stage of historical development of the Chinese society in which these writers wrote, we would be forced to assume that this exclusive preoccupation of the literary mind reflected a historical situation in which important decisions were at stake concerning the structure of

Chinese society and, more particularly, concerning the position within that society of the group which these writers represented.

Another even more specific inference that could be drawn from the available facts is that the *fu* was a literary form particularly suited to the writer's purpose. An investigation of the antecedents of the *fu* may throw light on the question why it was a particularly suitable literary vehicle for the types of political criticism mentioned. It is now and has been for some time a rather widely adopted custom to link the *fu* to the Ch'u school of literature, symbolized by the name Ch'ü Yuan.[5] This custom is so firmly established that, retroactively, the compositions of the Ch'u school have been called *fu*.[6] There is no doubt that the influence of this school on the *fu* was very strong. The two types of composition have many stylistic features in common; many Han *fu* are written on patterns established by the Ch'u school; Ch'ü Yuan was the hero—or villain, depending on one's political inclinations—of many *fu* writers; and the Ch'ü Yuan legend became part and parcel of the political ideology of most of them. One source of inspiration of the Ch'u school, however, and possibly the most important source, was the religious usage and popular tradition of its region of South China. Frequently reinterpreted, these figure large in the content of almost the entire production of the Ch'u school.

This last point, among others, makes one wonder whether the influence of the Ch'u school on the Han *fu* was really as exclusive as we are asked to believe. The assumption of this exclusive influence is in fact contradicted by the earliest discussions of the prehistory of the *fu*.

Pan Ku's postscript to his section on *shih* and *fu* in the *History of the Former Han* reads:[7]

The commentary[8] says: "To recite without singing is called *fu*. Climbing high,[9] if one is able to write *fu*, he can become a great official." This means that if one brings into proper arrangement the emotion called forth by reality, and if one [garbs] in profound beauty one's talent and knowledge, with such a man it is possible to plan affairs and therefore he can be introduced [to the rank of] a great official.

The ministers and great officials of the feudal lords in ancient times tried to exert influence with subtle words when they dealt with a neighboring country. When it came to bowing complacently, they would recite a poem in order to express their intentions, as in this way the wise and the stupid could be distinguished, and rise and decay could be foreseen. This is why Confucius said: "If you do not learn the *Odes*, you will not be fit to converse with."[10]

After the Spring and Autumn period, the way of Chou gradually decayed; to recite poetry when on a mission went out of fashion in the states, and scholars who had learned the *Odes* were idle amongst the commoners. This was the time when *fu* [expressing] the disappointment of the sages came into being. The great Confucianist Hsün Ch'ing, and the Ch'u official Ch'ü Yüan, when they encountered slander, and mourned about their country, both made *fu* in order to criticize by indirection; all of them had the meaning of commiseration of the old poems.

After them came Sung Yü and T'ang Lo; but when Han arose, Mei Sheng, Ssu-ma Hsiang-ju, and others, down to Yang Hsiung, all competed with each other in composing texts of luxurious beauty and vast length, thereby drowning out the purpose of criticizing by indirection. That is why Yang Hsiung remorsefully said: "The *fu* of the poets (*shih-jen*) are beautiful on account of their holding on to standards, the *fu* of the rhapsodists (*tz'u-jen*) are beautiful on account of their licentiousness.[11] If the Confucianists had employed the *fu*, then Chia I would have ascended to the hall and Ssu-ma Hsiang-ju would have passed into the inner apartments;[12] but they did not employ them, so what of it?"[13]

After Emperor Wu of Han instituted the Yüeh-fu office to collect folk songs, the ballads (*ou*) of Tai and Chao and the odes (*feng*) of Ch'in and Ch'u became known, all of which were composed to express sorrow or joy over matters of fate, but in them also folk customs can be observed, and meanness and generosity can be recognized.

[The preface] says that there are five kinds of poems and *fu*.

Pan Ku's postscript to his section on the School of Politicians reads:[14]

The tradition of the School of Politicians developed out of the office of the ambassadors (*hsing-jen*). Confucius said: "Though a man be able to recite the 300 *Odes*, and yet, when sent to any quarter on a mission, he cannot give his replies unassisted, notwithstanding the extent of his learning, of what practical use is it?"[15] And again he said: "An envoy! An envoy!"[16] [The meaning of] these words is that when [the politicians] attend to political affairs, they should receive an order [to carry out] but should not receive the [precise] terms [in which to put their message]. This is their strong point. If, however, unprincipled people attend to this profession, they will first of all practice deceit and relinquish their sincerity.

These statements by Pan Ku do not, of course, all have to be taken at their face value. When he claims that the great purposeful tradition of the *fu* had been adulterated at the hands of the *fu* writers of Western Han, it is probably due to the fact that he, as one of the Old Text school, did not want to give credit to these authors who mostly stood in the other camp. But some of the points he makes are worthy of attention. He stresses first of all the political purpose of the *fu*. To make or recite *fu* is an ability that goes with high position. He links it further to the custom in polite conversation of reciting poetry in order to make a point by indirection;[17] this custom was specifically current among envoys,[18] who, in turn, traditionally belonged to, or at least closely followed the discipline of, the School of Politicians. Of particular interest, he says that to criticize by indirection is the main purpose of the *fu* and that, to achieve this, the display of learning is necessary.

Other indications reinforce the impression that Pan Ku's points are well taken. The biography of Tsou Yang, traditionally considered to be one of the molders of the Han *fu*, is combined by Ssu-ma Ch'ien with that of Lu Chung-lien, a protagonist among the traveling salesmen of political ideology;[19] and Pan Ku, in his bibliography, lists him under the School of Politicians.[20]

Ssu-ma Ch'ien's postscript to the biography of Ssu-ma Hsiang-ju, perhaps the foremost *fu* author of early Han, reads:

> The *Ch'un-ch'iu* traces appearances back to what is hidden; the *Book of Changes* is based on the hidden, and goes from there to the apparent. The *Ta-ya* odes speak about kings, dukes, and great officials, [showing how] their power [of example] filters down to the lowly people; the *Hsiao-ya* odes ridicule the strong and weak points of the small individual, [showing how] this influences those above. Although the reasons for the statements [of these different books] are seemingly different, they all coincide in their accumulative aim. Even though Ssu-ma Hsiang-ju frequently used fantastic descriptions and an overflowing rhetoric, his main purpose can be reduced to the [conception of] restraint. In what way does that differ from the indirect criticism of the *Book of Poetry?*
>
> (Yang Hsiung was of the opinion that a *fu* of extravagant beauty would praise a hundred times and criticize by indirection only once.[21] It is as if one galloped around among the [licentious] tunes of Cheng and Wei and at a final turn played the *Ya* odes; is that not also amiss?[22] I therefore collected here in this chapter those of his words worthy of discussion.)[23]

In his justification for writing a biography of Ssu-ma Hsiang-ju, Ssu-ma Ch'ien states:

> The affairs dealt with in the *Tzu-hsü-fu* and the rhetoric in the *Ta-jen-fu* are of extravagant beauty [overly elegant] and frequently overstated; [Ssu-ma Hsiang-ju's] aim, however, was criticism by indirection, and he reduced [everything] to the doctrine of non-action.[24] Therefore I wrote the biography of Ssu-ma Hsiang-ju as number 57 [among the biographies].[25]

The evidence presented above suggests that the Han *fu* was a legacy of the School of Politicians and of their art of conveying things by indirection. Actually, the School of Politicians was far from extinct in the first two or three generations of Han, even though they no longer practiced their craft at the courts of sovereign lords but merely at those of rather independent imperial princes.[26]

Unfortunately, the literary remains of this important school are, with one possible exception, practically nonexistent. There is, of course, the *Chan-kuo-ts'e*, in which persuasion by indirection is presented in many superb examples. But it appears rather definite that the accounts of the *Chan-kuo-ts'e* are highly fictionalized, and, in any case, they show only the practice of the politicians' art and not their theory. There is one book, however, which, if we follow Theunissen's argument,[27] is a product of one of the great old masters of the School of Politicians, Su Ch'in himself—the book known by the name *Kuei-ku-tzu*.[28] But even regardless of the authorship of this work and its specific school relationship, it has a strong bearing on our problem because it contains many detailed instructions on the art of persuasion, derived from conceptions that come close to those of the *Book of Changes* and of Taoism.[29] Other theoretical recipes for the technique of the political orator are found in the writings of those schools that are closely related to the School of Politicians. I refer particularly to the chapter "Chuan-tz'u" in the book *Teng-hsi-tzu*,[30] and to the chapter "Shui-nan" in the book *Han-fei-tzu*.[31] The chapter "Shun-shui" in the *Lü-shih Ch'un-ch'iu*[32] could also be referred to in this context. From all these writings it becomes evident that there existed a discipline of political rhetoric[33] with a technique for conveying things by indirection. And it is in this tradition that the Han *fu* matured from a technique into an art.

The close connection between the Han *fu* and the School of Politicians seems to have been lost sight of rather soon. Later literary criticism was more interested in the style and the literary value of the *fu* than in its main purpose. It was only in comparatively recent times that this connection was stressed again rather vigorously.[34] Some modern authors have taken up the point or developed a similar idea independently.[35]

As indicated above, the main problem that preoccupied the literary mind of Han times was the position of the scholar in society and particularly his relationship to the ruler. It is by now a truism that Han was the period in which the scholar's position began to be institutionalized.[36] Actually, it was not only during the Han that the problem of the scholar's position was in debate. Already in the Ch'un-ch'iu period a certain degree of at least ideological protection of this position had been agreed upon. If we can believe Mencius, one of the injunctions of the Convention of K'uei-ch'iu in 650 B.C. was: "Honor the worthy and maintain the talented, to give distinction to the virtuous."[37] Already at that time it was recognized that status alone did not determine a man's position and that ability and talent, based on learning, were one of the ways to distinction. Ever afterward *all* schools vied with one another to produce ability and talent for just that purpose. The *chün-tzu* type, produced by the Confucian school, is a well-known example and does not have to be elaborated here. No state could dispense with the advice and service of scholars, and even the nihilistic authoritarianism of Ch'in had to make use of them.

The second injunction of the Convention of K'uei-ch'iu was, however, too weak a sanction to confirm the scholar's position in society or government. It expressed a growing realization of the importance of scholars but did not guarantee their security as a group. To strengthen their standing, the Confucian school tried, with success, to produce a spirit of solidarity among them.[38] But even so, their situation depended on their personal performance as individuals, and on the personal, frequently momentary, inclination of the ruler; and, although traveling scholars could as a rule count on some sustenance from princely courts, no amount of political philosophy produced by different schools to stabilize the status and influence of the scholars could do away with the fact that they stood unprotected against the ruler's whim.

By Han times, the great and exciting task of the scholars was to attempt this stabilization of their status and influence by securing institutional recognition. In other words, they wanted to establish themselves as a new class which would be the ruling class in Chinese society. They were successful to a considerable degree. But it must be said at once that their much-heralded victory was double-edged.[39] Their position, beginning in the Han and elaborated and refined in later times, was based upon the premise of their dependence upon government and their becoming a bureaucracy. Thus, even in their new garb, they found their old problem never solved.

To explain the attitude of the scholars during this development, very little use has thus far been made of purely literary materials, yet from them, if properly interpreted, the scholars' personal reactions can be deduced with much more insight than from their expository writings. As an example, I want to discuss here one type of *fu* that could be styled the *fu* of the "Scholar's Frustration." Later pieces of this type are entitled "Shih pu yü fu," a title taken from a passage in the oldest *fu* in existence, that of Hsün Ch'ing, which is in itself one of frustration.[40] Here Hsün says about Confucius, "How completely was the time he met impropitious."[41] And the term, "Not meeting [the proper time]" has thence become the title of these *fu*.

Hsün Ch'ing, in the first five sections of his *fu*, displays in a veiled form his personal qualifications for holding office: knowledge of social principles, wisdom, agility, assiduity, and critical faculty, the particular properties of these qualifications being very skillfully expounded. Then, in the coda, he bemoans the times which are not

propitious for a man of his qualifications, bringing in historical references to similar situations, and finishing with the sigh:

> I think of that distant region,[42]
> How arrogant it is![43]
> Humane people are impeded and restrained,
> And the violent are abundant.
> Loyal officials are in danger,
> And slanderers roam around at pleasure.[44]
> Precious jades and pearls,
> People do not know how to wear them.
> Simple cloth and brocade,
> People do not know how to distinguish them.
> Lü-ch'ü and Tzu-she,[45]
> There is nobody to make the match for them;
> Mo-mu and Li-fu,[46]
> By these the marriage is consummated.
> The blind are called sharp of hearing.
> Danger is called security,
> And luck is called disaster.
> Alas, Great Heaven
> How can I consort with them?

The *"Fu* on Dry Clouds," "Han-yun-fu," the earliest "frustration
fu" of Han times, is by Chia I.[47] It makes abundant use of the symbolism from the *Book of Changes* and bemoans the fact that celestial
grace is not forthcoming. It closes with the following lines:

> Considering in my mind the white clouds:
> It rends my bowels!
> They persist in their resentment and do not rain,
> This is utterly inhumane!
> They are spread [all over the sky] and do not come forth,
> This is utterly unreliable!
> White clouds, what do you resent?
> And what shall we people do?

The two most important Han pieces of this type, however, are
those by Tung Chung-shu and Ssu-ma Ch'ien.[48] (Since both have
recently been superbly translated by J. R. Hightower, they need not
be quoted here.)

Tung Chung-shu's *fu* sheds clear light on the dilemma which the
scholars had to face in that period. Furthermore, it demonstrates
definite progress in the development of this type of *fu*, consistent
with the development of the scholars' problem. Hsün Ch'ing had felt
frustrated on account of one event in his personal career, and, even
though he delights in putting himself alongside some of the great
heroes of the past, it is in the last analysis his personal misfortune

that he bemoans. Chia I, in his "Han-yun-fu" above quoted, has already enlarged the problem and does not speak about his personal experience only, but about the general relationship between ruler and official. In his mind, however, it is clearly the ruler who is to blame. Tung Chung-shu puts the problem into a still broader context. The ruler is no longer attacked personally, but the idea of timeliness, already touched upon by Hsün, is taken up and emphasized. This puts the problem beyond the volition of any of the interested parties. The two rationally possible solutions are then discussed, and both are shown to be dead-end roads, thus pointing to the insolubility of the problem.[49] There is one more point in Tung's *fu* that deserves attention. (I do not want to overinterpret this work of Tung; it is possible that, with the idea of the solidarity of scholars which he brings in, and with his ultimate cry for friendship, he perhaps did not want to indicate a possible solution, but only a personal escape. Still, it is interesting that this note is touched upon.)

The appeal of Tung Chung-shu's *fu* lies not only in the intimacy with which his personal position is expressed. It lies more particularly in the fact that such an outburst came from just that man, who was, after all, the foremost political thinker and philosopher of his age.[50] More than any other person, he was responsible for bringing about the incipient institutionalization of scholardom, referred to above.[51] He was the founder and head of that school of Confucianism that later became known as the New Text school.[52] Grossly simplified, it may be stated that this school always fought for a greater degree of independence on the part of the scholars—personally, regionally, and socially—whereas the Old Texters threw in their lot with the central government without reserve. One weapon in this fight of the New Texters was their embracing of the mantic arts and the tradition of the *Book of Changes*.[53] Their preoccupation with the *Book of Changes* reinforced their belief in the concept of change in society and in social institutions, which they had drawn from the *Spring and Autumn Annals* and the *Kung-yang* commentary.

Against this background, the treatment of the problem in Tung's *fu* appears consistent and profound. Although basically a lament, his *fu* uses the idea of timeliness[54] to give the problem an aspect that makes it, though personally insoluble, less formidable for scholardom as a whole. Time, after all, changes, and, if one man is hit by its impropitiousness, others may find the door open.

Ssu-ma Ch'ien's personal experience was more bitter than that of any of the other writers mentioned. His philosophy of life also differs to a certain extent from that of Tung. Rather than fight for any particular philosophical or political attitude, he fought for the purity of what appeared to him as "the Chinese tradition," which included so many non-Confucianist elements that he can almost be called a Taoist. In his temperament, however, he was even more Confucianist than Tung. His great pride pushed him further along the path of ambition and made him look upon himself as a link in the chain of the chosen few whose vocation it was to maintain the Chinese tradition.[55]

In his *fu*, therefore, Ssu-ma Ch'ien, even more than Tung, lays the insolubility of the problem to fate. Time, change in time, and timeliness are to him things with which the individual can have no personal relationship; they are expressions of blind destiny. Thus to him the problem seems still more desperate of solution than it seemed to Tung. The divergence between his temperament and his attitude makes him at one point even blame his own ambitions, which he immediately turns around to defend again, thus showing the complete hopelessness of any attempt to co-ordinate scholarly ambition and performance.

That Ssu-ma Ch'ien was aware of the fact that the *fu* indicated that suicide would be the only logical solution is directly mentioned in his postscript to the biographies of Ch'ü Yuan and Chia I[56] and is discussed at length in his famous letter to Jen An.[57] That he did not choose this way out is explained in that letter with two reasons. The first is that the sheer terror of the procedure which he has had to go through has crippled him also psychologically, so much so that he has lost any consciousness of his dignity; the second is that he wants to remain true to his vocation. In view of the stark realism of the first argument and the supreme rationalization of the second, the Taoist wisdom at the end of his *fu* seems almost artificial. However, it too expresses the determination to go ahead in spite of the hopelessness of the situation. This was an attitude for which Confucius was famous, of whom it was said: "There's a man who is undertaking something even though he knows it can't be done."[58] It was this attitude that made officialdom in China possible.

THE AMATEUR IDEAL IN MING AND EARLY CH'ING SOCIETY: EVIDENCE FROM PAINTING

JOSEPH R. LEVENSON

The master said, "The accomplished scholar is not a utensil."
—*Lun-yü*, II, 12.

Another common and important feature of these functions is their *political* character; they do not demand particular, special knowledge, but a *savoir-vivre* and a *savoir-faire*. . . .—ÉTIENNE BALÁZS, "Les aspects significatifs de la société chinoise," *Asiatische Studien*, VI (1952), 83.

1. Introduction

WHILE THE alien Mongols ruled in China (Yuan dynasty, 1279–1368), Confucian literati were at one of their relatively low points of social importance. The Ming dynasty raised them high again, and as a ruling intelligentsia they naturally cherished an ideal of social stability.[1] As a corollary, in matters of taste they deprecated the idea of change and the quest for originality.[2] By and large, the literati were classicists, like Jonathan Swift in England, and in Swift's defense of the ancients against the moderns, in his vast preference for the humanities over the natural sciences, and in his patrician uneasiness with material utility as the touchstone of value, we see the pattern of literati culture with significant clarity.[3]

Swift died in savage indignation and derangement. The moderns were taking his world, and he knew it. Science, progress, business, and utility, the combination he deplored, would soon be ruling concepts in modern Western culture. But in Ming and early Ch'ing China, the China of the four or five centuries before Westerners came in force, science was slighted, progress denied, business disparaged and (with possibly increasing difficulty) confined; and with these three went the fourth of Swift's desiderata, an antivocational, retrospective humanism in learning. Artistic style and a cultivated knowledge of the approved canon of ancient works, the "sweetness and light" of a classical love of letters—these, not specialized, "useful" technical training, were the tools of intellectual expression and the keys to social power. These were mainly the qualities tested in the state examinations, which qualified the winners for prestige and opportunities.[4]

The elite, in short, were not permitted (as Balázs puts it) to "impoverish their personalities in specialization."[5] The Ming style was the amateur style; Ming culture was the apotheosis of the amateur.

2. The Ming Style in Society and Art

A. IN SOCIETY

Probably more in the Ming period than ever before, as the extreme aestheticism of the Ming "eight-legged" essay suggests, Chinese officials were amateurs in office. They were trained academically, but not directly for specific tasks to be undertaken; whatever the case among aides in official yamens, mere hirelings without the proper Confucianist's claim to leadership, the higher degree-holding members of the bureaucracy—the ruling class par excellence—were not identified with expertise. The prestige of office depended on that fact. A scholar's belle-lettristic cultivation, a type of learning divorced from the specialized, technical programs which it qualified him to direct, was essential, not to performance of official functions with technical efficiency (there it was rather inhibiting), but to the cultural celebration of those functions.

If the knowledge characteristic of officials had been a vocational, technical, "useful" knowledge, then it would have been only a professional means, with no intrinsic quality to dignify the bureaucratic end. But when office could be taken to symbolize high culture, knowledge for its own sake, the terminal values of civilization, then officeholding was clearly superior to any other social role. No other sort of success (commercial, military, technological, or the like), which might be assumed to depend on a body of professional knowledge devised as a logical means to produce it, could compete in prestige with success in winning office; for the peculiar preparation for the latter success, by its independent aestheticism, its very irrelevance, logically, to the bureaucratic end—at least in a specialized, technical sense, if not in a broadly moral one—made of that end the end of life.[6]

In China, of course, because of the nature of its institutions, this aesthetic brand of knowledge really was for the sake of something: office. But it was a symbolic, not a logical, qualification. To see the significance of this distinction, let us compare the Ming situation with the modern English one, for in England, too, classical training has frequently given entree to civil office. A recent tribute to a British civil servant, after praising his classical scholarship, attempted, rather defensively, it seems, to make an ordinary logical reference of his classical training to his official role:

He read classics at Malvern and became a humanist. . . . Then in 1932, like many a classical scholar before him, he entered the Home Civil Service. . . . He is certainly a great civil servant, and I have no doubt whatever that he owes his quality to his humanism. It is that which gentles his will and disciplines his mind to the delicacies of human relationships.[7]

Living, as he does, in a highly specialized society, in which the amateur yields to the expert almost all along the line, a society in which "amateur" as a term, in fact, has developed rather its connotation of imperfect skill than of disinterested love, the writer here must strike us as quasi-apologetic (which no Ming classicist, in a similar case, would ever have been) in making such a "professional" plea for the classical curriculum: he writes as though he feels that his public— a practical, vocationally minded public with a common-sense indifference to educational frills—must be doubting the genuine relevance of antique studies to modern professional tasks. He cannot simply assume a general public acceptance of an obvious affinity between classical education and a managerial office. The prestige of letters, it is true, has lent a greater prestige to the higher bureaucracy of England than it has to its Western counterparts. But in England—and here it has differed from China—the bureaucracy, though thus enhanced, has not been able to reflect its glory back to the source. For, while the social facts of Chinese history made bureaucracy the central point of power, the social facts of English history have relegated bureaucracy to a role of service to other powers in the English state. Socially, the rise of "business" (which Swift had seen with such distress), with its antitraditional, antihumanist bias, put bureaucracy in the shade, while intellectually it forced the classics from their solitary eminence. In England, instead of the splendid, symbolic Ming alignment of the highest cultural values with the highest social power, we find bureaucracy rather more just a useful employment, while the classics, in so far as they preserve vestigial links with power, tend to be justified as a professionally useful means to an end which is only a means itself.

"Culture," "the best that has been thought and known" (as Matthew Arnold paraphrased "sweetness and light"),[8] has a bad time in a world of utilitarians. When the "yahoos" and "philistines" of Swift and Arnold dominate society, the defense of culture may tend to lean on philistine criteria. An amateur's love of the liberal arts, his belief that they justify themselves, may be complicated by society's insistence that he find a professional point in their cultivation. But, in China, the men of social consequence in the Ming and early Ch'ing periods were hardly cultural philistines; the professional point in their humanistic studies was in their failing to have any specialized professional point. They were amateurs in the fullest sense of the word, genteel initiates in a humane culture, without interest in progress, leanings to science, sympathy for commerce, or prejudice in favor of utility. Amateurs in government because their training was in art, they had an amateur bias in art itself, for their profession was government.

Long before, in the Sung dynasty, Wang An-shih (1021–86) had tried, among other things, to make the civil service examinations more practical than aesthetic. Although Wang was unquestionably a dedicated Confucianist, trying to revive in Confucianism its primal concern with political science, his finest official and scholarly contemporaries, who began by largely sharing his convictions, finally turned away, and ordinary Confucianists never forgave him. Was it only impracticability they saw in his sweeping program, or disputable points in his classical exegesis, or an immediate material challenge to their perquisites; or did they also sense that a Confucian landed bureaucracy would rule as intellectual amateurs, or not at all?

Su Tung-p'o (1036–1101), one of the foremost serious opponents of Wang An-shih, seems to have been the first painter to speak of *shih-ta-fu hua*, the "officials' style" in painting, a term which became in the Ming era one of the several interchangeable terms for the "amateur style."[9]

B. IN PAINTING

By the end of the Ming dynasty, one rule had been firmly established in the world of painting: officials themselves were painters, and they liked their painting best. Painters *by profession* were disparaged. The Ming emperors had revived the court academy of painting (*Hua-yüan*), associated mainly with the names of Hui-tsung (regn. 1101–26, the last real emperor of the Northern Sung) and his Southern Sung successors.[10] But the Ming academy differed from the Sung in that the latter had merely honored painters with official titles, while their Ming counterparts were genuinely court painters, working to specifications.[11] Accordingly, the Ming academy, unlike Hui-tsung's, was never put on an equal footing with the Hanlin Yuan, the highest circle of literary scholars, and Ming *Hua-yuan* painters by no means had the rank or prestige of Hanlin literati.[12]

Wen Cheng-ming (1470–1567), a scholar who had the *Han-lin* rank, and a famous painter as well, clearly expressed the amateur's creed. "The cultivated man," he said, "in retirement from office, frequently takes pleasure in playing with the brush and producing landscapes for his own gratification."[13] Mo Shih-lung, a very important late Ming critic, highly approved of some earlier artists for looking at painting as a joy in itself, not as their profession.[14] His friend Tung Ch'i-ch'ang (1555–1636) echoed Mo in praising one of the fourteenth-century Yuan masters as the first to make the painter's pleasure as well as expression the end of his art.[15] Tung himself, painter and calligrapher as well as the foremost critic of his time, was perfectly careless about what became of his own productions. It was said of him that if a person of station asked directly for some of his work, the petitioner might be fobbed off with anything—Tung's signature, perhaps, or a poem from his brush, on a painting by somebody else. If people wanted a Tung original, they learned to seek it from the women of his household, for whom he would frequently, idly, paint or write.[16]

Tung had, quite simply, a contempt for professionalism. One of its connotations, he felt, was narrowness of culture. The true *wen-jen*, the "literary man," the amateur, had a feeling for nature and a flair for both painting and poetry.[17] It was a familiar thing for painters to deprecate their special talents by offering themselves as rounded personalities; the sixteenth-century painter Hsü Wei, for example, said of himself (though critics disagreed) that his poetry came first, other literature second, and painting last.[18] The Ch'ing scholar Shen Tsung-Ch'ien (fl. *ca.* 1780?) summed up the persisting amateur's bias against narrow specialization: "Painting and poetry are both things with which scholars divert their minds. Generally, therefore, those who can participate in the writing of poetry can all take part in painting."[19]

The amateur's scorn of professionals had an aspect, too, of patrician contempt for the grasping climbers who were not the gentry's sort. There were overtones of anticommercial feeling in the scholar's insistence that the proper artist is financially disinterested. Mi Fu (1051–1107), the famous intuitive Sung artist who was a classical hero to the Ming amateur school, had written, "In matters of calligraphy and painting, one is not to discuss price. The gentleman is hard to capture by money."[20] Much later, the "Mustard-Seed Garden" manual (*Chieh-tzu Yuan Hua Chuan*), an encyclopedic instruction book for painters, appearing in several parts between 1679 and

1818 (though its earliest stratum was late Ming), made the same equation between professionalism and a nonliterati culture. "When one has the venal manner," it loftily proclaimed, "one's painting is very vulgar."[21] And the Ch'ing painter Tsou I-kuei (1686–1772) laid down the rule that the *shih-ta-fu* painter, the amateur painter-official, "is not acquisitive in the world, nor does he distract his heart with considerations of admiration or detraction."[22]

In short, in the amateur's culture of the Ming and early Ch'ing, officials as critics commended officials as painters to officials as connoisseurs. "Wang Yü, *tzu* Jih-ch'u, *hao* Tung-chuang Lao-jen, painted landscapes and grasped in them the very marrow of the vice president of the Board of Revenue's art."[23] A remark like this, ordinary enough in its own day, will joyously strike the modern reader as comically incongruous; he could hardly sense more vividly the individual quality of the culture which knew it as commonplace.

3. The paradox of an academic antiacademicism

A. THE "NORTHERN" AND THE "SOUTHERN" SCHOOLS OF PAINTING

Since they were intellectual leaders and social leaders at the same time, the painting elite formed a school of thought as well as a league of amateurs. By the end of the Ming dynasty an aesthetically expressive term, *nan hua*, "southern painting," had become assimilated to *wen-jen hua* and *shih-ta-fu hua*, sociologically expressive, equivalent terms for the painting of the "gentleman." Not its inventor, but the scholar who made the distinction between northern and southern styles a canon of connoisseurship, was the antiprofessional Tung Ch'i-ch'ang, the acknowledged doyen of calligraphers, painters, and critics in late Ming times, "master of a hundred generations in the forest of art," whose reputation as the arbiter of elegance had spread as far as Liu-ch'iu and Korea.[24]

He traced the northern and southern schools through various masters, from the T'ang dynasty's Li Ssu-hsün (651–716 or 720) and Wang Wei (698–759), respectively, down to his own day. The names "northern" and "southern" referred, not to a geographical distribution of painters, but to two T'ang dynasty schools of Ch'an (or Zen) Buddhism, whose philosophical principles were said to color the two aesthetics.[25] However, the term *Ch'an-hua*, Ch'an painting, came to be reserved for the southern style, as a term contrasting with *yuan-hua*, academic painting of the northern school.[26] The idealist landscape of the southern school was inspired by the artist's "sudden awakening" (a concept usually called in the West *satori*, from the Japanese Buddhist terminology), the shock of intuition of the nature of reality; and Tung considered that paintings in this style were superior to those of the northern school, which was intellectual rather than intuitive, more meticulous in detail, and interested rather in the formal relations of objects than in their spirit. "True classic elegance," he said, "does not lie in exact and punctilious execution."[27]

This sort of caveat against painstaking, conscious workmanship was the first commandment in the southern aesthetic. According to theory, the literati-painter, without design, hurled his inner conception of landscape on the silk.[28] Spontaneity was all, and the elliptical phrase *ch'i-yun*, "spirit-consonance," from the first of the famous "six laws" of painting of Hsieh Ho (fl. *ca.* 500), was taken over as the southern concept of intuitive communion of the painter with his subject; intellectual apprehension was "academic" and despised. "*Ch'i-yun* is the result of something which is inborn; the more the skill that is applied, the further *ch'i-yun* recedes," said Tung Ch'i-ch'ang,[29] and, while Mo Shih-lung would allow that the academic style was *ching-miao*, refined and subtle, he found it correspondingly deficient in *tzu-jan*, the priceless spontaneity.[30] "There are painters," he said, "who take the old masters as teachers. But whoever wants to make forward strides himself must choose Heaven and Earth as teachers."[31] *Hsiung-chung i-ch'i*, "spirit flashing into the mind," was the motto professed in the *wen-jen hua*[32]—not cool knowledge, but searing insight.

B. THE CONFUCIANIST CHOICE OF A BUDDHIST AESTHETIC

A question now arises of true importance for the understanding of Ming culture: how could Ming Confucian intellectuals, the most academic of men in their literary practice, committed to the preservation of recorded wisdom—and a wisdom, at that, which referred in the main to human relations in civilization—how could such a group reject the theory of painting which they associated with learning, and prize instead an anti-intellectual theory of mystical abstraction from civilized concerns? One might expect that Confucian traditionalists, who looked for the gradual education of man in society, would feel an affinity with the academic northern aesthetic and oppose the southern Ch'an; for the latter, after all, in its original emphasis on the sudden enlightenment of man in nature, challenged the whole Confucian view of life and culture.

Yet, what is logically curious is sociologically comprehensible. An idea's meaning depends not only on what a thinker affirms but on what he denies, and for Ming Confucianists, with their amateur leanings, the intuitive Ch'an need not mean—as it could not mean to such bookish custodians of an intellectual tradition—anti-intellectualism;[33] *antiprofessionalism* would fill the bill. A flash of intuitive insight is nothing if not "natural," and how could a professional painter, who worked to order, be natural? How could the academic be natural, planning his strokes and carefully painting them in? The very idea of a special vocation of "fine arts" was equally distasteful to Ch'an mystics and Confucian literati: "natural" is opposed to "artistic," and the latter word has a queasy, professional sound.[34]

The southern aesthetic, then, took hold in literati circles not because they were *philosophically* committed, committed to inspiration over tradition, but because they were *socially* committed, committed to genteel amateurism over professionalism. At least one writer has suggested that it was practical compulsion, especially in early Ch'ing times, which made the officials such southern enthusiasts; deep literary culture was obligatory, painting could only come second, as an amateur's pastime, and the scholars made a virtue of necessity, opting for intuition since a really rigorous painter's training was impossible.[35] Such a view is doubtless inadequate—many literati-painters, after all, were exquisitely accomplished virtuosi—but nevertheless, though for reasons less practical than symbolic (and not philosophical at all), an antiacademic aesthetic was the popular choice of the amateur. The Ch'an of the Ming Confucianists was not serious.

Buddhism in general had ceased to be serious for Confucian literati as long ago as the Sung period. The intellectual synthesis of Chu Hsi (1130–1200) was a Confucian raid on Buddhism and a blunting of its point as an intellectual rival; and organized Buddhism—ecclesiastical, iconological, and always repellent socially to the gentry-official class—was relegated to the peasant masses and finally lost its one-time intellectual lure. Ch'an ideas, which were antiecclesiastical, anti-iconological, and thereby divorced from an anti-Confucian social organization, remained in the gentry's world and animated its landscape painting (Buddhist figure painting, once an important branch of Chinese art, languished almost completely in the Ming phase of the church's decline and the amateur painter's rise).[36] But this last shred of Buddhism was not a foreign body in the gentry's Confucian environment. The Ch'an intuitive nature-cult of the Ming painters was not an antithesis to Confucian humanism, but a tame, learned element in the Confucian humane culture—not a bold challenge to didacticism, but a cultural possession of didactically educated men.

C. THE ROUTINIZATION OF INTUITION

An ostensibly Buddhist doctrine, once embraced in that Confucian spirit, must be changed in itself. The real paradox of the Ming aesthetic was not in the harmonizing of two warring creeds but in the self-contradiction of one of them. Peace was easy to arrange when one of the pair of rivals denied itself. In the last analysis, the conventionally learned *shih-ta-fu* painter felt quite at ease in the southern school of individual inspiration—because the southern school had conventional rules for manufacturing inspiration. An antiacademicism which was socially vital to the amateur gentry-officials, but intellectually alien, was safely academicized.

Ambivalence was built into the Ming intuitive southern theory, for it was a theory not intuited but learned. Sung literati, predecessors of the Ming in the Confucian taming of Buddhism, had already made the basic statements of the credo which the Ming called southern. The academic uselessness of the imitation of outward form, the indispensable oneness of immediate perception and immediate execution, the impossibility of learning *ch'i-yun*, that "spirit-consonance" which man derives solely from innate knowledge—all these were Sung lessons to Tung Ch'i-ch'ang and his fellow-critics of the Ming and Ch'ing.[37]

And behind the Sung was Hsieh Ho, whose six principles were handed down (especially the first: "spirit-consonance, life-movement") as prescriptions for the unprescribable, binding rules for untrammeled intuitive genius. "In painting there are six canons . . . ," a Ming southern treatise flatly began.[38] That was the law—all the rest was commentary. Wang Yü (fl. *ca.* 1680–1724), whose painting was said to betray him as "a parasite on others," solemnly preached about quite unconscious creative activity.[39] His aesthetic, opposed to stereotype, was a stereotype as an aesthetic; his painting, failing to follow it, was consistent with it.

There was no getting around it. The free, natural, southern souls of literati-amateurs were pervaded with traditionalism. It was said of Tung Ch'i-ch'ang that he copied the works of the old masters (especially those of his Sung namesake, the Ch'an artist, Tung Yuan) with such a zeal that he forgot to eat and sleep.[40] A late Ming source reported that a wonderful scroll by Shen Shih-t'ien (1427–1509), an

eminent scholar-painter, had been executed, in the true amateur
spirit, as a gift for a friend on his travels; that the scroll was modeled
completely after Tung Yuan; and that it later became the outstanding treasure of a famous connoisseur.[41] Obviously, with the antiacademic Ming and Ch'ing critics, no painting failed of an accolade
just for its being patently derivative. It was right and proper to imi-
tate the ancients—because the ancients were spontaneous.

This is why, in the Ming and early Ch'ing China of the gentry-
scholar-official, who was antiprofessional in his outlook but never
antitraditional, the implications of antiacademicism were so far from
what they were in the West. By definition, antiacademicism any-
where depends on a common conception of genius: that genius, a
general quality, is shared only by artists who spontaneously choose
their individual ways to express it.

> A good work of art must be *mehr gefüllt als gemessen.* . . .[42]
> . . . He that imitates the divine *Iliad*, does not imitate Homer. . . .[43]
> . . . The men who have reduced locomotion to its simplest elements, the trotting
> wagon and the yacht *America*, are nearer to Athens at this moment than they who
> would bend the Greek temple to every use. . . .[44]

Pronouncements on genius like these seemed to be made in China
as in the West. The warning against missing Homer by hitting the
Iliad was paraphrased, in effect, by Wang K'en-t'ang, a *chin-shih* of
1589: "If one paints water, mountains, trees, and stones and roams
'only thus' with the brush, such is not the old method."[45] Yun Shou-
p'ing wrote in the seventeenth century about the intuitive southern
technique of *hsieh-i*, the representation of the idea, the immanent
form, of visible objects: "It was said in the Sung period: 'If one can
reach the point where he creates unconsciously, like the ancients,
this is called *hsieh-i*. . . . If the artist creates unintentionally, then he
attains the unconscious creativity of the ancients.' "[46] And Ou-yang
Hsiu (1007–72), perhaps the very Sung spokesman to whom Yun
referred, had begun a poem in the following way: "In ancient painting, they painted *i*, the idea, not *hsing*, the (mere) outer appearance."[47] Presumably then, by this token, only a spark of intuitive
insight, not a copyist's talent, could bring an artist close to the works
of ancient genius.

But in the West these reflections were arguments of an *avant-garde;*
in China they were arguments of traditionalists. Given the social
context in China of antiacademicism, its intellectual sequence was
twisted around. Spontaneous creativity was as much the prize in one

society as in the other. Yet it became in China, not the means of reaching the ancient end of genius, but the end reached through the ancient means of genius. The very words which acclaimed the Chinese ancients for their spontaneity were really acclaiming spontaneity for its ancient embodiment. In the poem of Ou-yang Hsiu, the "mere-ness" of *hsing*, or outer appearance, in comparison with *i*, the idea, was conveyed by the linking of *ku-hua*, ancient painting, with *i*.

In Western antiacademicism, then, fidelity to the inner voice of genius justified abandonment of ancient outer appearances. In Chinese antiacademicism, it was fidelity to the outer voice, the voice of antiquity, speaking through outer appearances, which justified fidelity to the inner voice. Small wonder that southern theory seemed to chase itself in circles, and that Tung Ch'i-ch'ang appealed to master-models, while he solemnly intoned that genius could not be taught.

How could antiacademicism in Ming China take the form it did in the West, where an *avant-garde* in the arts, straining against the conventional taste of an outside public, was part of a general vaguely displaced intelligentsia, iconoclastically restless in a world it could not dominate? In China, where the intelligentsia (artists among them) did dominate, as gentry-officials, disdain of elders and contempt for the public were unlikely, to say the least. The easy Western association of antiacademicism with youthful individualism was impossible there. No higher praise could be meted out, by Tung Ch'i-ch'ang or any other southern critic, than to say of a painter that he entered completely into the spirit of some old master.[48]

It was not that he should copy his master directly; that would be pedantic, academic, entirely unsuitable. Nevertheless, as a Ch'ing literati-painter significantly put it, he had to copy old examples in a certain fashion, as a student of literature must thoroughly examine the productions handed down from the past.[49] He was supposed to copy in a manner called *lin-mo*, which would divine the spirit of the master-work, not repeat the letter. One Ming critic mentioned four great painters who had studied a painting of Tung Yuan, copied it in the *lin-mo* way, and produced works quite dissimilar among themselves. If "vulgar men" (i.e., academics, professionals, not literati) had been set this task, the critic said, their works would all have been quite the same as the original model.[50]

What has happened here? Unmistakably, the field for Buddhist artistic intuition has been subtly transferred by Confucian literati from nature to art itself. The academic is still condemned. Careful surface copying of visible phenomena is properly anathematized, in accordance with southern principles. But communion with masters in a great tradition (a congenial Confucian idea) has superseded the Buddhist communion with nature. It was not the persistence of the old landscape themes which compromised the amateurs' creed of antiacademicism. Chinese painters, from Wang Wei on (at least those whom the *wen-jen* mainly honored), had forsworn individualism in subject-matter in order to ignite and reveal their individuality of soul, their personal intuition of an already existing beauty.[51] But to the traditional subjects, Ming literati-painters come to adapt traditional insights. A painter's "spirit-consonance" need not be with mountains but with a classic painter of mountains. The southern artist's immersion in nature through landscape painting is not a Ch'an rejection of cultural sophistication but a Confucian extension of it.

Once art had been thrust between the artist and nature, he was diverted in his quest for intuitive knowledge. Unless an act of cognition is a directly experienced *knowledge of* . . . , it is not intuitive; the only alternative form of cognition, relational *knowledge about* . . . , is intellectual, and it disrupts the single whole of experience which, theoretically, the southern aesthetic envisaged.[52] In the true artist of "sudden enlightenment," art and contemplation are indistinguishable; what he sees is not external; he becomes what he represents.[53] The object of such enlightenment is a "thing-in-itself," a supersensible reality, beyond sensation; for thing-in-itself, the nonephemeral ideal, is implied in intuitive understanding with absolute necessity, and can only be grasped, as Kant put it, by "art's free conformity to rule." The "imposition of rules on art" is not intuitive, and Cézanne, who affirmed this completely, proclaimed a significant corollary: "Les causeries sur l'art sont presques inutiles."[54]

But the Ming and early Ch'ing period was the great age of *causeries*, treatises which precisely did impose rules on art.[55] In the foreword to the last section (1818) of the *Mustard-Seed Garden*, the painter's manual which epitomized the movement, the author made the fatal promise that genius could be taught, "spirit-consonance" and "life-movement" distilled in explanation. "Thus can he [the reader] enter the 'divine class' and the 'skilled class,' and follow in the steps of painters like Ku K'ai-chih and Wu Tao-tzu."[56]

It was another passage in the same foreword, but from a different hand, which plainly exposed the intellectual corruption of the intuitive process. In a dialogue, a question was raised about portraiture. Why was there no manual for this most difficult form of art, when there seemed to be a manual for everything else? The answerer stated that everything else—mountains, rivers, grasses, trees, birds, beasts, fish, insects—had fixed forms. If one studied them assiduously, one could reach the point of reproducing them by rules. But the human face had most varied forms, not lending themselves to stereotyping, and it was hard to convey these forms in words.[57]

Fixed forms, then, were presumably easy to convey in verbal formulas. But fixed forms are the Kantian things-in-themselves, ideals beneath the sensible surface of phenomenal life. The very concept of the type-form is correlated essentially with the concept of intuitive apprehension. And the latter is the antithesis of intellectual apprehension, the fruit of didactic exposition, which were just what artists were invited to find in the *Mustard-Seed Garden*.

In itself, of course, the mere will to deal with technical problems of execution, and to study their resolutions, need not bar intuitive penetration. Every art has a technical language, upon which even the most personal of artists depends for communication, and even, perhaps, for seeing. Freed from concern with the hand when technique is automatic, the mind may be free for vision, and a codification of technical knowledge can assist in this liberation.

Accordingly, the role of technique in Chinese painting, intellectually formulated and transmitted, has occasionally been compared with the creative musician's standard equipment in harmony or fugue.[58] For the most part, however, Ming-Ch'ing painters' technical mastery tends to seem a larger part of their art than that, as another analogy drawn from music illustrates: "When a Chinese artist reproduces a composition of an old master or paints in his style, it is no more plagiarism than when Horowitz plays a composition by Brahms."[59] Such a statement quite properly reduces any "moral" question about *lin-mo* representation to absurdity. But in the aesthetic realm of questions, if Ming is to Sung as pianist to composer, then Ming knowledge of technical rules, vocabulary of type-forms, and the like is not a simple precondition of creativity but an interpreter's key to what was once created. The later landscapist's technical lore opened the way, not directly from mind to nature, but to records of earlier sudden meetings of nature and mind. Insight into silence, for music which must be there, is not the same as insight into music.

The sum of the matter is this: Ming and early Ch'ing aesthetic antiacademicism was academically perpetuated. While thus inconsistent internally, it was appropriate to its exponents in their character as part of a dominant social class, traditionalistic, humanistic, and fundamentally opposed to specialization. No other society had an aesthetic ostensibly more favorable to genius, the foe of the academy; and no other society was less likely to practice what it preached—or even to preach what it said it did. This society, which had come to its antiacademicism naturally, not philosophically logically but socio-logically, was the home of authority, prescription, and routine, restraints on genius but spurs to conventional learning. Matthew Arnold, who took from Swift, the Ming scholar-gentleman *manqué*, his definition of culture as "sweetness and light," said what the Ming scholar-gentleman-painters could never say, though in practice they proved it—that cultural continuity depends on intelligence, which is more transferable than genius, and which academies cause to thrive.[60]

D. BUREAUCRACY AND THE STEREOTYPED AESTHETIC: A NEGATIVE CONFIRMATION OF THE LINK

In the seventeenth century, three eccentric painters flourished whose devotion to Ch'an was much more freely given than that of the ordinary southern painter, and whose work was far less stereotyped than their contemporaries'. They were the Buddhist priests Shih-t'ao (Tao-chi), Shih-ch'i, and Pa-ta-shan-jen.

It was said of the two Shih, in awe, that they were *san-seng ju-sheng che*, beings for whom no space of time existed between their leaving priesthood and entering sagehood.[61] They were painters, that is, who had reached the heights, not step by step, with progressive learning, but in a leap of sudden enlightenment. "Only so might I paint landscapes," Shih-ch'i wrote on a painting, "so, as if I conversed with mountains."[62] He was said to have been "naturally intelligent" (*su-hui*, a Buddhist phrase) from early youth and to have read no Confucian books.[63]

"Knowledge is secondary, natural gifts are primary, and acquired gifts are not gifts,"[64] Shih-t'ao wrote, and, "I am I, and in me there is only I!"[65] Schools and models were death to art. What he longed to establish was a method of painting so natural that it would prove to be no method.[66]

He felt a real affinity with Pa-ta-shan-jen, and unconventionally praised him as unprecedented: "In his manner of calligraphy and painting, he stands ahead of earlier men; and his eye has none to compare with it in antiquity, to a height of more than a hundred generations."[67] Pa-ta-shan-jen was of Ming royal lineage and became a priest after 1644. One day he wrote "Dumb" on his door and never spoke a word again to anyone. "His brush was very free and did not adhere to rules."[68]

It is surely no accident that these free spirits, whose southern aesthetic was straight and undistorted, should have led peculiar civil existences. They were not of the normal intelligentsia, conventional Confucian officials (like Tung Ch'i-ch'ang) or retired gentlemen (like Shen Shih-t'ien) who owed their cultured ease to their official affiliations, and whose Apollonian temperaments were hardly attuned to frenzy. If their theory and practice of painting had an uncommon logical consistency, they themselves had an uncommon sociological status. As deviants in society and deviants in art, they confirm the correlation between the gentry-scholar's domination and an amateur, unadmitted academicism.

These early Ch'ing eccentrics, then, had no unsettling influence in the world of painting, for the Manchu conquest left the *shih-ta-fu*, *wen-jen* position socially unimpaired. Many scholars, in the first generation of Manchu rule, were disturbed and disaffected. A few partisans of the Ming, disillusioned, like Pa-ta-shan-jen, might leave the great world, and reflect their resignation in their painting. But the main body of the literati accepted the Ch'ing as the conventional type of dynasty it was, kept their careers with their sense of proportion, and maintained, with all its implications for their southern style of painting, their antiprofessional, traditionalistic cultural continuity.

Indeed, the independence of even these painting rebels may be overestimated. Shih-t'ao, for one, quite like a literatus, frequently used phrases of Li Po, Tu Fu, and other early writers in his own poetic inscriptions on his paintings.[69] And in any case, if he really did revive the pure southern spirit, subsequent generations of undisturbed traditionalists failed to understand. "How could he [Shih-t'ao] have attained such deep merit and strength," asked an early nineteenth-century scholar, "if he had not absorbed all the masters of T'ang and Sung in his heart and spirit?"[70]

4. Eclecticism and Connoisseurship

A. THE SOFTENING OF PARTISAN LINES

Tung Ch'i-ch'ang's aesthetic distinction between south and north implied tension between intuition and intellect, nature and books. But since southern intuitive theory was compromised by the social commitments of its highly intellectual adherents, north-south tension was inevitably relaxed. For all his southern sympathies, Tung believed that a fusion of northern and southern procedures was possible; that reality, to some extent, could be not merely seized upon but learned about. "If one has studied ten thousand volumes, walked ten thousand li, and freed one's mind from all dust and dirt, beautiful landscapes will rise quite naturally in the mind."[71]

Even Shih-ch'i, one of the intensely southern Buddhist painters of the seventeenth century, injected a northern note in an inscription on a painting: "In peace we discussed the ideas of the Buddhists and the fine points of the six laws [of Hsieh Ho]. Whoever wishes to say anything about them must have absorbed a great deal from books and history, and must climb mountains, to push on to the essence of the sources."[72] And Yun Shou-p'ing, his contemporary, also reflected on the need to harmonize intuition and intellect. He repeated a saying of Ni Tsan (1301–74), one of the four Yuan masters who were heroes of the southern school. Ni had said, "Making a picture is nothing other than drawing one's inner spontaneity." Yun went on, "This remark is most subtle"—and, after this genuflection to the approved concept of intuition—"and yet, one must speak with cognoscenti."[73]

This flexibility in theory was matched by a certain catholicity in taste. Tung Ch'i-ch'ang found himself admiring a scroll by the emperor Hui-tsung, the arch-northern founder of the Sung academy. Somewhat embarrassed at seeing his preferences outrun his principles, he questioned the attribution.[74] But Mo Shih-lung, professedly just as sternly discriminating as Tung—and equally the architect of the system of discrimination—sometimes frankly owned to his basically eclectic taste. Theoretically, he rejected the northern school; in practice, when he was faced with actual productions of great painters whom he called northern, like Li T'ang of the Sung and Tai Chin of the Ming, he simply commended them.[75]

But the low temperature of aesthetic controversy in the Ming and early Ch'ing periods was indicated not only by relaxed discrimination but by confused discrimination. For example, Lan Ying (fl. *ca.* 1660), always classified as a painter of the Che (Chekiang) school, a perpetuator of the northern traditions of the Sung academy, was said to resemble Shen Shih-t'ien, one of the great literati-painters of the Wu (Wu-hsien, modern Soochow—by extension, southern Kiangsu) school, which was considered safely southern. The fact of the matter was that Lan Ying, like hosts of others, eluded rigid classification. The north-south dichotomy, a formal abstraction imposed on the history of Chinese painting for extra-aesthetic reasons, could prove suggestive for identification of differing elements of style, but it could not be fitted to the body of work of individual artists. Lan Ying did, in fact, range in his painting all the way from Che to Wu. He and so many others, by abstract southern standards, were eclectics.[76]

More famous than Lan Ying were his predecessors, Ch'iu Ying (fl. 1522–60) and T'ang Yin (1470–1524). They, too, were usually numbered among the academics, but were sometimes among the angels of the southern school.[77] For they could be labeled northern, southern, and syncretic, in turns. Ch'iu Ying, in particular, was felt to have magnificent talents in *lin-mo* copying, which he exercised especially in reinterpreting the masterpieces of the renowned Yen collection. It was said that of the famous brushes of T'ang, Sung, and Yuan, there were none, whatever their tendencies, whose essence he could not grasp.[78] Essentially uncommitted stylistically, he produced, for example, a picture book of sixteen paintings, illustrations of T'ang poems, in which he exhibited various methods. Both northern style and southern style, according to the canons of the later critics, were represented, and types of line both "thick and turbid," as the experts called it, and "pure and elegant."[79] T'ang Yin, too, changed methods and models according to impulse.[80] And Wen Cheng-ming, universally considered a pillar of the Wu school, the southern stronghold, roamed like the others through a wide variety of Sung and Yuan styles, and was said to have mastered them all.[81]

Eclecticism, however, meant more than divided loyalties between the northern and southern styles; it meant the fusion of them in individual works. For instance, one of the Ch'iu Ying paintings in his album of T'ang illustrations shows an emperor's visit to a newly built mansion. This is executed in the right foreground in a meticulous academic style, while in the background, and on the left, suggestively misty pale-wash mountains taper off toward southern infinity.[82] Such stylistic complexities were common. The late Ming painter Sheng Mao-yeh (fl. *ca.* 1635) was described by connoisseurs as painting northern pines, detailed and stylized, among southern rocks and mountains.[83]

The movement toward the joining of the two styles culminated in Wang Hui (1632–1717), celebrated during his lifetime as the *hua-sheng*, the painter-sage, and later on as the greatest genius among the "six great masters" of the early Ch'ing. All question of trends or schools aside, Wang Hui beyond a doubt was a superb painter, one of the most compelling figures in art history, but the grounds on which he was early appreciated were more truly expressive of his age than was his own individual mastery. An accepted proof of his merits, his claim to special appreciation, was this: "In painting there were northern and southern schools: Wang Hui brought them together."[84] He was avowedly an eclectic, drawing on legions of the old masters, and his favorite model, significantly enough, was the earlier many-sided eclectic, T'ang Yin.[85]

The eclecticism of T'ang Yin has been described as that of a transitional figure, standing midway in time between the domination of the Che school (which, led by Tai Chin [fl. *ca.* 1446], the "modern Ma Yuan," had early Ming imperial favor, for its revival of the style of the Southern Sung imperial academy) and the Wu school, citadel of the amateurs.[86] If this was so of T'ang Yin, Wang Hui's eclecticism was of a different order, with special implications. Whether or not T'ang Yin should really be seen as an unconscious figure, adrift in a process of qualitative change between one vogue and another, Wang Hui can only be seen as a deliberate, syncretic figure, reintegrating the first vogue into the second, consciously striving for harmony and an end to conflict (however unspirited) which might have led to renewal of process, and change.

B. VIRTUOSI AND CONNOISSEURS

Syncretism is not by definition (and unquestionably not in Wang Hui) a source of artistic sterility. It is certainly possible to express a genuine aesthetic insight by combining techniques which were once exploited to different ends. But the late Ming—early Ch'ing syncretism came in general, not from an arrival at a new insight to which earlier techniques were adapted, but from a virtuoso's fascination by techniques.

The techniques of painting which the syncretists pieced together had each existed, in the first instance, because the painter had seen his subject in a certain way and had used the brush in a manner contrived to convey it. In the eclectic spirit which had come by the seventeenth century to dominate Chinese painting, however, interest in the brushwork itself transcended interest in the subject, the aesthetic vision which brushwork might presumably have been intended to realize. To the connoisseur, variety of brush strokes became an important criterion of value, and critics were as ready to analyze single strokes as to contemplate a composition as a whole. They expressed their refined discriminations in vague and elusive language ("his brushwork manner was exceedingly elegant and smooth, fine and close, but it was slightly weak"), as if to imply the exquisite subtlety of their aesthetic appreciations.[87]

The spirit which invested this eclectic connoisseurship—whether one's principles were supposed to be southern, northern, or in between—was the traditional Chinese inclination to follow early models. We have observed how Ch'iu Ying had diverted the painter's efforts from divining the spirit of nature to divining the spirit of previous paintings. It became a virtue, really, to have no stylistic commitment; all styles were simply like natural features, whose essence the genius captures. Tung Ch'i-ch'ang, with his practically canonical pronouncements, made this vogue of *ni-ku*, imitation of the ancients, all-prevailing, and he approved the methods of eclectics who sought to make masterpieces by synthesizing details from the works of different masters.[88] It was a virtuoso's task, and a connoisseur's delight.

When the painter's emphasis was on fidelity to models instead of on fidelity to vision—which is what moved the men who created the models—there was no stylistic, aesthetic reason why various techniques developed in the past could not be mixed. And so the modern painter could throw everything into the pot, all the technical elements devised by men who had been aesthetically serious, committed to some end behind their technical means. By late Ming times, the end of the approved painter was the demonstration of his mastery of means. Style became a counter in an artist's game of self-display, while gentry-literati-officials and their set were the self-appreciative happy few who recognized the rules and knew the esoterica.[89]

5. Conclusion: Modernization as the Corrosion of the Amateur Ideal

A. THE RELATIVITY OF JUDGMENTS OF "DECADENCE"

Historians of the arts have sometimes led their subjects out of the world of men into a world of their own, where the principles of change seem interior to the art rather than governed by decisions of the artist. Thus, we have been assured that seventeenth-century Dutch landscape bears no resemblance to Breughel because by the seventeenth century Breughel's tradition of mannerist landscape had been exhausted.[90] Or we are treated to tautologies, according to which an art is "doomed to become moribund" when it "reaches the limit of its idiom," and in "yielding its final flowers" shows that "nothing more can be done with it"—hence, the passing of the grand manner of the eighteenth century in Europe and the romantic movement of the nineteenth.[91]

How do aesthetic values really come to be superseded? This sort of thing, purporting to be a revelation of cause, an answer to the question, leaves the question still to be asked. For Chinese painting, well before the middle of the Ch'ing period, with its enshrinement of eclectic virtuosi and connoisseurs, had, by any "internal" criteria, reached the limit of its idiom and yielded its final flowers. And yet the values of the past persisted for generations, and the fear of imitation, the feeling that creativity demanded freshness in the artist's purposes, remained unfamiliar to Chinese minds. Wang Hui was happy to write on a landscape he painted in 1692 that it was a copy of a copy of a Sung original;[92] while his colleague, Yun Shou-p'ing (1633–90), the flower-painter, was described approvingly by a Ch'ing compiler as having gone back to the "boneless" painting of Hsü Ch'ung-ssu, of the eleventh century, and made his work one with it[93] (Yun had often, in fact, inscribed "Hsü Ch'ung-ssu boneless flower picture" on his own productions).[94] And Tsou I-kuei, another flower-painter, committed to finding a traditional sanction for his art, began a treatise with the following apologia:

When the ancients discussed painting, they treated landscape in detail but slighted flowering plants. This does not imply a comparison of their relative merits. Flower painting flourished in the northern Sung, but Hsü (Hsi) and Huang (Ch'üan) could not express themselves theoretically, and therefore their methods were not transmitted.[95]

The lesson taught by this Chinese experience is that an art form is "exhausted" when its practitioners think it is. And a circular explanation will not hold—they think so, not when some hypothetically objective exhaustion occurs in the art itself, but when outer circumstance, beyond the realm of purely aesthetic content, has changed their subjective criteria; otherwise, how account for the varying lengths of time it takes for different publics to leave behind their worked-out forms? Suspicion of sterility in modern Chinese painting, embarrassment about the extent of traditional discipleship (instead of a happy acceptance of it) began in China only late in the nineteenth century, when Chinese society began to change under Western pressure and along Western lines, and when modern Western value-judgments, accordingly—like praise of "originality"—were bound to intrude their influence. We have seen how the amateur commitments of the literati-official class in early-modern China brought Chinese painting to its late Ming—early Ch'ing condition. A reassessment of that condition never came until a change of role was thrust on the official class, and a change in its education, and a change in the general currency of its amateur ideal.

B. NATIONALISM: CULTURE CHANGE AND THE
PROFESSIONALIZATION OF BUREAUCRACY

The world of painting in early-modern, pre-Western China issued from and reflected a broader world of social institutions. Behind the amateur painter and the southern critic was the antiprofessional official, whose socially high estate was the mark of his deeply respected humanistic culture, not a technically specialized one. It was felt, of course, that Confucian moral learning was especially appropriate to government service, since administration was supposed to be less by law than by example. Still, the official's education failed to make him professional, it was not vocational, for this important reason: his learning was not just valuable for office but happened to be *the* body of learning, artistic as well as moral, which was valuable in itself, and which lent itself more easily, for examination purposes, to aesthetic exposition than to practical implementation. It was this intimate association of bureaucracy with the mastery of nonvocational high culture which was cracked by modern Western pressure and its concomitant, Chinese nationalism.

As the Chinese nation began to supersede Chinese culture as the focal point of loyalty,[96] sentiment grew for changing, and finally for abandoning, the examination system. An education sacrosanct in the old heyday of the amateurs, when "the accomplished scholar was not a utensil," came to be criticized more and more, toward the end of the nineteenth century, as being far too predominantly literary—as failing, that is, to equip officials with specialized, useful knowledge for the national defense.[97] The Chinese state was changing its identity, from that of a world, an environment in which the officials' culture flourished, to that of a nation, whose needs should color its bureaucracy's educational purposes. It meant the end of the "aesthetic value" and self-sufficiency of the bureaucratic Confucian "princely man," which had been at opposite poles (as Weber saw it) from the Puritan—and capitalist—"vocation."[98]

With the pressure, then, of modern Western industrialism (and those attendant concepts—science, progress, business, and utility—unhonored, we have noticed, in the Ming literati culture) on Chinese society and Chinese consciousness, the charge of formalism came to be leveled at the official examinations and at the intellectual ideals which the latter sustained. But objectively, at the time such censure began to be effective, the examinations were no more formalistic than in Ming and early Ch'ing times, when the "eight-legged" essay, such a scandal to the moderns, was perfected and prescribed. Minds had changed, more than the institutions minds dwelt upon; the spirit of the amateur was fleeting.

Only then (almost, only now) was the scholar-official's emphasis on form, on the subtleties of style, in the literati-painting as in the literary essay, felt to be the symptom of a weak concern with content. Only when the modern West impinged on China and undermined the position of the gentry-literati-officials, who had set the styles in art and expression as they set the rates in taxes and rents— only then did the concept of "amateur" slide into its modern sense of something less than "specialist," and what had once been precious to traditionalists and classicists seem mainly preciosity to a new youth in a new world of science and revolution.

NOTES

NOTES

NOTES TO THE INTELLECTUAL HISTORY OF CHINA

1. *K'o-hsueh yü jen-sheng-kuan* (Shanghai, 1923), Preface by Ch'en Tu-hsiu and Hu Shih.

2. Karl Mannheim, *Man and Society* (London, 1940), Parts IV and V ("Thought at the Level of Planning" and "Planning for Freedom"), pp. 147–381.

3. *Reconstruction in Philosophy* (New York: Mentor Books, 1950), p. 44.

4. See Herbert A. Hodges, *The Philosophy of Wilhelm Dilthey* (London, 1952).

5. The reference is to the central thesis of C. P. Fitzgerald's book, *Revolution in China* (New York: Praeger, 1952).

NOTES TO THE POLITICAL FUNCTION OF ASTRONOMY AND ASTRONOMERS IN HAN CHINA

1. Th. W. Danzel, *Magie und Geheimwissenschaft* (Stuttgart, 1924) and *Der magische Mench* (Potsdam, 1928).

2. K. A. Wittfogel, "Die Theorie der orientalischen Gesellschaft," *Zeitschrift für Sozialforschung*, VII (1938), 90–122. See also E. Erkes, *China und Europa* (Leipzig, 1947), pp. 11 ff., and J. Prušek, in *Archiv Orientalni*, XXII (1954), 1–2 ("Ce sont surtout des bésoins spéciaux de la société chinoise, comme la lutte contre les inondations et la sécheresse, la construction de digues de canaux, de voies de communication et de greniers publics ... qui ont provoqué la création d'un état centralisé puissant, administré par des fonctionnaires lettrés ...").

3. See H. Franke, "Das Begriffsfeld des Staatlichen im chinesischen Kulturbereich," *Saeculum*, IV, No. 2 (Munich, 1953), 231–39, and H. H. Dubs, "Chinese Imperial Designations," *Journal of the American Oriental Society*, LXV, No. 1 (1945), 26–33.

4. The definition of "despotism" used here and in earlier publications is not "one-man rule" (É. Balázs, in *Pacific Affairs*, XXVII, No. 1 [1954], 75) but "unlimited rule of an autocrat who does not feel himself bound by laws nor the consent of the ruled. Typical for the despot is that he rules by personal decrees, that he exercises the administration not by offices with responsibility of their own, but by persons (often favorites) who depend upon him, and that he relies less upon forces of tradition and upon the native elite than upon military power, often foreign mercenaries. By these points despotism differs from monarchy" (*Der Grosse Brockhaus* [16th ed.; Wiesbaden, 1953], III, 121). (My translation.)

5. K. A. Wittfogel, "Oriental Despotism," *Sociologus*, III, No. 2 (1953), 96–108, especially p. 97 ("A hydraulic economy was probably a prerequisite for the origin of Oriental despotism"). É. Balázs, too, seems to regard the Chinese emperors of the Ch'in and Han periods as despots (cf. *Études asiatiques*, Nos. 3/4 [1953], p. 163).

6. As Wittfogel ("Oriental Despotism," *op. cit.*, pp. 104–5), Balázs (*loc. cit.*, p. 163), and J. Prušek (*loc. cit.*) seem to assume. A clearly different position is taken by D. Bodde ("Authority and Law in Ancient China" in *Authority and Law in the*

Ancient Orient [Suppl. No. 17 to the *Journal of the American Oriental Society* (1954)], p. 54), who speaks of "benevolent paternalism" and of "government as the particular preserve of a small ruling elite"

7. Cf. B. Sinogowitz, "Die Begriffe Reich, Macht und Herrschaft im byzantinischen Kulturbereich," *Saeculum*, IV, No. 4 (1953), 451 ff., and M. Hellman, "Staat und Recht in Altrussland," *Saeculum*, V, No. 1 (1954), 61 ff.

8. G. E. von Grunebaum, "Islamic Studies and Cultural Research" in G. E. von Grunebaum (ed.), *Studies in Islamic Cultural History* (American Anthropological Association Memoir No. 76 [Menasha, Wis., 1954]), pp. 5–6.

9. The following societies are selected, because they are sometimes grouped together as "Oriental societies."

10. A. Coomaraswami, *Spiritual Authority and Temporal Power in the Indian Theory of Government* (New Haven, Conn., 1942), pp. 12, 16, 69.

11. See *Bulletin of the Ramakrishna Mission Institute of Culture*, Vol. IV, No. 5 (1953), and H. Hoffmann, "Die Begriffe 'König' und 'Herrschaft' im indischen Kulturkreis," *Saeculum*, IV, No. 3 (1953), 334–39.

12. H. Frankfort, *Kingship and the Gods* (Chicago, 1948), p. 36, and J. A. Wilson, "Authority and Law in Ancient Egypt" in *Authority and Law in the Ancient Orient* (Suppl. No. 17 to the *Journal of the American Oriental Society* [1954]), p. 1.

13. Frankfort, *op. cit.*, p. 39.

14. *Ibid.*, p. 51

15. *Ibid.*, pp. 51–52. See also E. Lüddeckens in *Jahrbuch 1953, Akademie der Wissenschaften und der Literatur* (Wiesbaden, 1945), p. 182.

16. Frankfort, *op. cit.*, pp. 58–59.

17. *Ibid.*, p. 245.

18. *Ibid.*, p. 277.

19. *Ibid.*, pp. 252–54.

20. E. A. Speiser, "Authority and Law in Mesopotamia" in *Authority and Law in the Ancient Orient* (Suppl. No. 17 to the *Journal of the American Oriental Society* [1954]), p. 13.

21. *Ibid.*, p. 12.

22. We do not include a discussion of the Shang period here.

23. Wittfogel, "Oriental Despotism," *op. cit.*, p. 98.

24. K. Bünger, "Die Rechtsidee in der chinesischen Geschichte," *Saeculum*, III, No. 2 (1952), 198.

25. *Ibid.*, p. 203.

26. *Ibid.*, p. 199, n.

27. *Ibid.*, p. 209. Bünger points out that the legitimacy of succession of a new ruler or a new dynasty to the throne was regarded as extremely important by the Chinese from the Han period on. This is another sign of the importance which the law had in ancient China (*ibid.*, p. 214); it also indicates that a ruler felt bound by the law and could not arbitrarily create law.

28. This term seems to have been in use during the Han period (cf. *Hou-Han-shu*, chap. 112a, p. 3a; *Shui-ching-chu*, Vol. V, chap. 30, p. 67, quoting an event of the first century B.C.; *Shui-ching-chu*, Vol. VI, chap. 34, p. 18, referring to Sung Yü), while the term *t'ien-shen* seems to refer to uncanonic deities or non-Chinese deities (*Hou-Han-shu*, chap. 80, p. 1b, and chap. 119, p. 3a; commentary to *Hou-Han-shu*, chap. 117, p. 1b).

29. This term is, according to Karlgren, never used in Shang documents (B. Karlgren, *Yin and Chou in Chinese Bronzes* [Stockholm, 1936], p. 32). It was never an official term.

30. Such stories and legends were probably little believed by the scholars of the time; they served in the main to legitimize claims of clans and families to the accession to the throne (W. Eberhard, "Geschichte Chinas bis zum Ende der Han-Zeit," *Historia mundi*, II [Bern, 1954], 557–68). An interesting parallel is the stories of the deceased in the "Book of the Dead," *Odyssey* ii.

31. A number of examples, but by no means all, are enumerated and discussed by E. Erkes in "Der Chinese und das Tier," *Sinologica*, I (1948), 278–83. Professor Erkes' explanation differs from mine.

32. The tradition of the second century B.C. at least attributed similar ideas to K'ung-tzu, who was credited with the development of a theory of dynastic change. In general, cf. Ku Chieh-kang in Lo Ken-tse (ed.), *Ku-shih-pien* (Shanghai, 1938), II, 137.

33. See Tjan Tjoe Som, *Po Hu T'ung*, I (Leiden, 1949), 218. The *Shuo-wen* (chap. 12b, p. 1a), on the other hand, still expresses the older view that the holy mothers of antiquity "sensed" Heaven and got children by this; it is for this reason, the *Shuo-wen* says, the term "Son of Heaven" is used.

34. This may have already taken place in the fourth to third centuries B.C. In general, cf. Bodde, *op. cit.*, pp. 47–49.

35. References in W. Eberhard, *Beiträge zur kosmologischen Spekulation der Chinesen der Han-Zeit* (Berlin, 1933), p. 72.

36. *Han-shu*, chap. 99b, p. 3a.

37. Mentioned, e.g., in *Chuang-tzu*, chap. 10, p. 3 (R. Wilhelm trans., p. 70), and in *Lü Pu-wei*, chap. 19, p. 5 (R. Wilhelm trans., p. 333).

38. Found in Korea; see *Museum Exhibits Illustrated*, Vol. VIII (1936). In Tun-huang documents, however, other forms, such as finger marks, were preferred.

39. Parallels to this concept are still alive among China's neighbors (cf. L. Schram, "The Mongours of the Kansu-Tibetan Frontier," *Transactions of the American Philosophical Society*, N.S., XLIV, No. 1 [1954], 48, and Rintchen in *Acta orientalia*, III, No. 1 [Budapest, 1953], 25). It is of great importance for our problem that during the T'ang period imperial princes, empresses, and imperial concubines, as well as high officials, used seals of offices, not personal seals (Noboru Niida, *The Critical Study on Legal Documents of the T'ang and Sung Eras* [Tokyo, 1937], pp. 79–80). Seals were also used against evil spirits and prevented them from doing harm to men. For the *Hou-Han* period, see J. J. M. de Groot, *The Religious System of China* (Leiden, 1892–1921), VI, 1048.

40. Described in *Han-shu*, chap. 98, p. 7a–b.

41. A general history of the imperial seal is given in *Yü-chih-t'ang T'an-wei* (*Pi-chi hsiao-shuo ta-kuan* ed.) (Shanghai, n.d.), compiled by Hsü Ying-ch'iu in the sixteenth century, chap. 27, p. 16b. See also *T'ien-hsia Monthly*, X (1940), 9–22. On Han seals see also *Nen-chen-tzu*, chap. 3, p. 3a–b. A case of forgery, the earliest known to me, is reported in *Hou-Han-shu*, chap. 78, p. 7a. This report is similar to the report in the *Neng kai-chai man-lu*, chap. 3, p. 5b, a Sung text, which clearly describes the seal as the symbol of the legitimacy of the dynasty because it is used in sacrifices which the emperor has to perform. It is significant that the first seal was made by the "First Emperor" (Shih-huang-ti). This seal was lost in the early fourth century A.D.; the Sui made a new one which was lost by the Hou-T'ang

rulers of the tenth century; the Sung seal was made by the Hou-Chou ruler. In al cases a dynasty with clear imperial aspirations created the new seal.

42. The last act before this ceremony is often the investment with the "nine bestowals" (*chiu-hsi*). It is interesting that these bestowals have great similarity to the privileges of the Tarkhan among Turkish and other Central Asian nations (enumerated in Han Ju-lin, "Le Titre official darhan de l'époque mongole," *Studia Serica*, I [1940], 171). The Title Tarkhan occurs for the first time among the Juan-juan (*Yü-kung*, VII, No. 8 [1937], 86–88, but it is possible that earlier references, from A.D. 300 on, are hidden behind names of non-Chinese from Central Asia. The nine bestowals seem to be mentioned from the Han period on. They played an important role for the first time in connection with Wang Mang (*Han-shu*, chap. 99a [H. O. H. Stange trans., pp. 71–73]).

43. We consciously ignore here some passages in Mo Ti and other early writers, in which a kind of "selection" of the worthiest is mentioned for the beginning of an organized state and society. These passages would seem to belong to "sociological theory" only.

44. Speiser, *op. cit.*, p. 8.

45. On the role of astronomy see H. Bielenstein, *The Restoration of the Han Dynasty* (Stockholm, 1953), pp. 150, 156.

46. Cf. H. Reichenbach, *The Rise of Scientific Philosophy* (Berkeley, 1951), pp. 32 ff.

47. A general discussion of this problem and its history in the West is given by B. Sticker, "Weltzeitalter und astronomische Perioden," *Saeculum*, IV (1953), 241–49.

48. Modern scientific philosophy has begun to pay more attention to this phenomenon on the basis of new discoveries (see Reichenbach, *op. cit.*, chap. 16).

49. Eberhard, *Beiträge zur kosmologischen Spekulation*.

50. In "An Interpretation of the Portents in the Ts'ien Han Shu," *Bulletin of the Museum of Far Eastern Antiquities*, XXII (1950), 133.

51. This analysis was done for me by Professor Duncan McRae, to whom I want to express my gratitude.

52. Lo Chen-ying, *Une famille d'historiens* (Paris, 1931), p. 43 ff., and H. H. Dubs in *Isis*, No. 111/112 (1947), p. 63.

53. O. Franke, *Geschichte des chinesischen Reiches* (Berlin, 1930), I, 308–9.

54. For detailed analysis see Eberhard, *Beiträge zur kosmologischen Spekulation*.

55. Cf. W. Eberhard, "Beiträge zur Astronomie der Han-Zeit," *Sitzungsberichte der Preussischen Akademie der Wissenschaften, phil.-hist. Kl.*, 1933, Part II, pp. 22–45; and "Neuere Chinesische und Japanische Arbeiten zur altchinesischen Astronomie," *Asia Major*, IX (1933), 601 ff.

56. See further Ku Chieh-kang, "Wu-tê chung-shih-shuo-hsia-ti chêng-chih ho li-shih," *Tsing Hua Journal*, VI, No. 1 (1930), 191–208. Already *Hou-Han-shu* (chap. 66, pp. 4a–7a) remarks that the *Tso-chuan* is in agreement with the apocryphal texts. These texts are typical for the first century B.C. and the early first century A.D. See also Bielenstein, *Restoration*, p. 156.

57. E.g., the first phenomenon recorded under Emperor Chao in *Han-shu*, chap. 26.

58. E.g., Sui Meng in 78 B.C.; see *Han-shu*, chap. 75, p. 546c–b, and many other cases.

59. "Historians" means not the chairman of the final editing committee or the

final editors but all their predecessors, beginning with the man who made the first rearrangement of the data recorded by the archivist.

60. See Eberhard, "Astronomie," *op. cit.*, Part II, pp. 36 and 39. It might be remarked here that a correct understanding of the *Shih-chi* and the *Han-shu* can be reached only when the connections of both books with the *Ch'un-ch'iu* are recognized. In Han times the *Ch'un-ch'iu* was (*a*) a book which contained a collection of precedents of political behavior (*Han-shu*, chap. 78, p. 4*a*, and chap. 76, p. 6*b*), and (*b*) a collection of abnormal phenomena and their relations to human political action (*Han-shu*, chap. 75, p. 7*a;* chap. 62, pp. 3*b* and 4*a;* chap. 81, p. 7*a;* chap. 97*b*, p. 2*b;* chap. 21*a*, p. 8*b*). In Han times it was generally known (see *Han-shu*, chap. 62, p. 5*a*) that the *Shih-chi* came to an end with the capture of a *ch'i-lin*, exactly as the *Ch'un-ch'iu* had come to an end centuries earlier. Behind both appearances of the *ch'i-lin* lie astronomical speculations (see W. Eberhard, "Contributions to the Astronomy of the Han Period III. Astronomy of the Later Han Period," *Harvard Journal of Asiatic Studies*, I [1936], 229–30). The structure and diction of the *Shih-chi* and *Han-shu* were deeply influenced by the *Ch'un-ch'iu;* this influence was strongest in the annalistic parts of both books.

61. On the office which discussed the advisability of political action see Yen Keng-wang in *Ta-lu Tsa-chih*, IV, No. 8 (1952), 1*b*.

62. The office proposing political action (*ibid.*). We do not discuss here *when* the Han system was changed.

63. These parts have been translated and analyzed in my "Astronomie," *op. cit.* Please refer to this publication for all details, including details of individual phenomena.

64. Although it might seem logical to bring together a sufficient number of such casually linked portent-events and develop standards by which safe inferences might be made when the link is not explicit, the great imprecision of the "explanations" does not warrant such a procedure. If the link is not explicit, we can only "guess."

65. In some of the official histories, such as the *Chiu Wu-tai Shih*, the annals (*pen-chi*) are indeed not much more than lists of promotions or demotions of officials and lists of other court activities. The *pen-chi* of Han times could perhaps be regarded as collections about important activities of the ruler, to be used as guides for political behavior based on ethical principles. The posthumous name of each ruler, such as "the warlike Emperor" or "the peace-loving Emperor," given to him after his death and upon evaluation of all his actions, would then serve as a "caption" to help those who might want guides for behavior in special situations. Here we see another system of checks upon the ruler: How will posterity paint his picture? How will he stand in history? We do not discuss this system of checks here but want to point out that this same consideration still motivates many contemporary rulers.

66. The fact that the "biography" of Emperor Wu was compiled from data to be found in other parts of the *Shi-chi*, mainly the chapter on the *Feng* and *Shan* sacrifices, does not alter this. Other rulers of the Earlier Han dynasty, for whom we have *pen-chi* in the *Shih-chi* and *Han-shu*, show similarly different character traits, although less explicitly. A comparison, from this point of view, of those annals for which we have an older and a later official history (*T'ang-shu*, etc.) might prove interesting.

67. O. Franke, *Studien zur Geschichte des konfuzianischen Dogmas* (Hamburg, 1920).

68. Cf. Eberhard, "Astronomie," *op. cit.*, Part II, p. 39, where one such case is discussed. Bielenstein (*Restoration*, p. 159 ff.) has not taken into account that the increase in portents under Emperor Ch'eng and his successors was regarded by the historians as a bad sign for the Han, but actually most of the portents were at the same time lucky omens for Wang Mang. It is only logical that the omens should decrease when Wang actually came into power (from A.D. 6). Like Emperor Kao of the Han, Wang Mang had omens before his accession, but after the accession both rulers were given a "chance." The omens against Wang Mang, i.e., the omens in favor of the coming dynasty of the Later Han, begin only toward the end of his government. The relatively low number of portents in the early part of Wang Mang's regime compared to the high number before his accession, therefore, does not mean that the last Han rulers were extremely bad and the beginning of Wang Mang's rule was very beneficial.

69. They are connected with periods of discussion about a change of basic dynastic symbols and can be regarded as signs initiating a "new beginning."

70. A list of recorded and calculated eclipses is published in Eberhard, "Astronomie," *op. cit.*, pp. 88–89; a similar list was later prepared by H. H. Dubs, *History of the Former Han Dynasty*, Vols. I, II (Baltimore, 1933–44), appendixes. Bielenstein has used Dubs's list.

71. This invalidates argument 3 of Bielenstein in "An Interpretation of the Portents in the Ts'ien Han Shu," *op. cit.*, p. 143. If it were possible to use modern science to check upon the other reported portents, the number of "falsifications" would certainly be much higher.

72. *Han-shu*, chap. 9, p. 312a, as one example out of many.

73. Ching Fang was already dead at this time and is quoted from his writings.

74. And in such cases it becomes questionable to assume that the phenomenon itself was reported to the emperor; he certainly would have asked the reporter for an explanation.

75. *Han-shu*, chap. 27a, p. 405d.

76. *Ibid.*, chap. 36, p. 451.

77. *Ibid.*, chap. 9, p. 312c.

78. *Ibid.*, chap. 4, p. 301a.

79. *Ibid.*, chap. 36, p. 450c–d.

80. Even if, in cases like the one discussed above, the different explanations offered for the same event may have been dictated by political considerations only, it is often clear that different schools had different techniques of explanation—but these schools at the same time also represented different political constellations. In this field, further work can be done.

81. In the Sumerian world-view, too, a clear cause-effect relationship seems not to have existed; Speiser (*op. cit.*, p. 10) therefore states that "divine and human societies interfused," asserting that cause and effect could work both ways.

82. *Han-shu*, chap. 4, p. 301a–b.

83. The assumption of Bielenstein (*Restoration*, pp. 150 ff.) that a very large flood had occurred as a result of a change in the course of the Yellow River between A.D. 2 and 6 but was not recorded because at that time no one wanted to criticize the emperor, young Emperor P'ing, seems, therefore, to be very bold. There are a number of portents reported in these years, all of them of little real importance if compared with a catastrophe which, if it occurred, would have killed and dislocated millions of persons. On the other hand, we know of examples from later

periods that certain events on which the court historians had data were omitted in the later compilations of the history because the chancellor objected to reporting "a national shame" (*Chiang-lin chi tsa-chih*, chap. 1, p. 6a, for the Sung period).

84. Wang Mou, who in his *Yeh-k'o ts'ung-shu*, chap. 4, p. 1a discusses this, disagrees with Chang Fu.

85. Analyzed in Eberhard, "Astronomie," *op. cit.*

86. Some materials on popular calendars are collected in W. Eberhard, *Lokalkulturen im alten China* (2 vols.; Leiden and Peking, 1943).

87. Fragments of Han calendars have been published in Lao Kan, *Chü-yen Hanchien k'ao-shih* (4 vols.; Nanking: Academia Sinica, 1948), and in Bruno Schindler "Preliminary Account of the Work of Henri Maspero concerning the Chinese Documents on Wood and Paper Discovered by Sir Aurel Stein on His Third Expedition in Central Asia," *Asia Major*, N.S., I (1950), 222. We have fragments of popular calendar books from 760 (Lionel Giles, "Dated Chinese Manuscripts in the Stein Collection," *Bulletin of the School of Oriental and African Studies*, IX [1937], 15; text S. 3824), 877 (*ibid.*, p. 1033; text p. 6), 882 (*ibid.*, pp. 1036–37; text p. 10), 926 (Liu Fu, *Tun-huang To-so* [3 vols.; Nanking, 1931–34], 88/3247), 945 (Giles, *op. cit.*, X, 343; text S. 560), 956 (*ibid.*, XI, 154; text S. 95), 978 (*ibid.*, p. 162; text S. 612), 982 (*ibid.*, p. 166; text S. 1473), and 986 (Liu Fu, *op. cit.*, 89/3403).

88. Similar to our "nautical almanacs," the Chinese in later periods had a book containing the basic tables from which to calculate the details for the popular calendars without the necessity for taking actual observations. The name of this book was *Po-chung-ching* (*Cho-keng-lu*, chap. 29, pp. 13b–15b). In the late T'ang period an "Indian" calendar, the "Calendar of the Seven Luminous Stars" ("Ch'i-yao Li"), was introduced and used unofficially among the people until the middle of the tenth century (*K'un-hsüeh Chi-wen*, chap. 9, p. 10a). The name indicates without doubt that this calendar was influenced by Mazdaist speculations. It may, therefore, have been a solar calendar, practical for farmers.

89. Ku Chieh-kang, "Wu-tê chung-shih-shuo-hsia-ti chêng-chih ho li-shih," *op. cit.*, pp. 104–5.

90. *Ibid.*

91. All details have been discussed in my *Beiträge zur kosmologischen Spekulation*.

92. See W. Eberhard and R. Müller, "Contributions to the Astronomy of the San Kuo Period," *Monumenta Serica*, II (1936), 156.

93. We agree here fully with J. Needham, *Science and Civilization in China* (Cambridge, 1954), I, 9.

94. These books are mentioned in *Hou-Han-shu*, chap. 45, p. 1a; chap. 45, p. 4a; chap. 53, p. 2a; chap. 58, pp. 1a–3a; chap. 59, p. 5b; chap. 60a, pp. 1a–2a; chap. 78, p. 3a; chap. 84, p. 7b; chap 87, p. 6b; chap. 87, p. 7b; chap. 60b, pp. 4b and 10b; chap. 66, p. 2b; chap. 65, pp. 2a and 4ab; chap. 83, p. 4b; chap. 84, p. 9b; chap. 87, p. 6a; chap. 89, pp. 5b–6a; chap. 109a, p. 3a; chap. 109b, p. 2b.

95. Details on this school are in my article in *Harvard Journal of Asiatic Studies*, I (1936), 227 ff.; in Eberhard and Müller, "Contributions to the Astronomy of the San Kuo Period," *op. cit.*, pp. 149–64; and especially in my "Sinologische Bemerkungen zu den Türkischen Kalenderfragmenten," in G. R. Rachmati (ed.), *Türkische Turfan-Texte* (Berlin, 1936), VII, 83–99; and *Lokalkulturen im alten China* (Peking, 1943), II, 438–39.

96. The books were officially prohibited in A.D. 267 (*Chin-shu*, chap. 3, p. 1084a). This, of course, refers only to that sector of this "science" which publicly was known in the Later Han times.

97. Cf. E. Rousselle, "Konfuzius und das archaische Weltbild der chinesischen Fruhzeit," *Saeculum*, V (1954), 5.

98. Eberhard, *Beiträge zur kosmologischen Spekulation*.

NOTES TO THE FORMATION OF SUI IDEOLOGY, 581–604

ABBREVIATIONS.—References to the "Dynastic Histories" are to the photo-lithographic edition of the T'ung-wen Shu-chü, 1884.

HKSC   The *Hsü Kao-seng Chuan*, by Tao-hsüan, completed shortly after 645. *Taisho*, Vol. 50, pp. 425–707.

KHMC   *Kuang Hung-ming Chi*, also by Tao-hsüan. *Taisho*, Vol. 52.

LTSPC   *Li-tai San-pao Chi*, by Fei Ch'ang-fang, who was an ex-monk, returned to lay life by the Northern Chou persecution of Buddhism. Completed 597. *Taisho*, Vol. 49, pp. 22–127.

PCL   *Pien-cheng Lun*, by Fa-lin (572–640). *Taisho*, Vol. 52.

SS   *Sui-shu*, compiled between 629 and 644 by an imperial commission headed by Wei Cheng.

T   *Taisho Shinshū Daizōkyō* (55 vols.; Tokyo, 1924–29).

TC   *Tzu-chih t'ung-chien*, with Hu San-hsing's commentary, punctuation by Yamana Zenjō (Tokyo, 1882).

I am grateful to the Guggenheim Foundation, which made possible the year of research during which the draft of this paper was written. I am deeply indebted to the hospitality and learned assistance of Professors Miyakawa Hisayuki, Tsukamoto Zenryū, and Yamazaki Hiroshi. I have profited, in my revision, by the criticism of my conference colleagues and by the comments of Professor Étienne Balázs.

1. Cf. Étienne Balázs, "Le Traité économique du 'Souei-chou,'" *T'oung Pao*, XLII (1953), 2–4 (hereinafter cited as "Balázs"). This brilliant study of the institutional and social background of the Sui unification is the most important Western language work on the period.

2. The testimony of the Japanese monk-pilgrim Ennin significantly alters the picture of the great Buddhist persecution of 845 as given by the dynastic histories (cf. Arthur Waley, *The Real Tripitaka* [New York, 1952], pp. 154–59). Yet for a full understanding of the impact of this measure on communities all over China, one should take account of local histories, inscriptions, and Buddhist chronicles.

3. Ideology, in the sense in which I shall use it, means the sum of assertions, in words or in ritual-symbolic acts, of ideas and principles intended to sanction and justify power and elicit the consent or support of various social groups. An ideological measure means a single assertion with such an intent.

4. My friend, Shunsuke Tsurumi, observes that the working principles of American advertising resemble the Chinese view of symbols. The belief in the potency of certain compact reiterated symbols to produce—directly and immediately—certain desired behavior is shared by both. There is surely a similarity between the point of view of one who fills an office with signs reading "Think," in the expectation of

inducing this process, and the Chinese householder who has the character *hsiao* displayed in every room, in the hope that it will produce filial behavior.

5. Cf. Étienne Balázs, "Entre révolte nihiliste et évasion mystique," *Études asiatiques*, Nos. 1/2 (1948), pp. 39 and *passim*.

6. In current academic usage the words "Confucian" and "Confucianism" are employed with so many different meanings that a major effort to specify and clarify the variant meanings is now urgently necessary.

7. See Arthur Waley's essay on the fall of North China to the Huns in *History Today* (London, 1952). This is particularly valuable because it makes use of the third-party, privately directed observations of the Sogdian merchants whose letters have been reconstructed.

8. For simplicity I shall use the word "South" for the area south of the Yangtze; this was the term which northerners and southerners at the time used to refer to the regimes centered at Nanking. Of course, in terms of China's present geography, the area referred to is Central China.

9. Cf. *Chin-shu Chiao-chu* (Peiping, 1928), chap. 105, pp. 8*b*–9, text and commentary.

10. SS, chap. 24, p. 2; Balázs, p. 131 and n. 21.

11. Cf. W. Eberhard, *Das Toba-Reich Nordchinas* (Leiden, 1949), p. 73. The ethnic origins of the Yang family are not established beyond doubt.

12. SS, chap. 1, p. 1; TC, chap. 117, p. 1; P. Boodberg, "Marginalia to the Histories of the Northern Dynasties," *Harvard Journal of Asiatic Studies*, IV (1939), 253–70 (hereinafter cited as "Boodberg").

13. SS, chap. 1, p. 1*b*. The temple, in 584, became one of the officially supported *Ta-Hsing-kuo Ssu*. Cf. HKSC, chap. p. 26, 667*c;* PCL, chap. 3, p. 508*c*.

14. HKSC, chap. 26, p. 667*c*. This account adds certain further facts as well as considerable pious embroidery. It states that Chih-hsien was born in the Liu family of P'u-fan (southern Shensi) and that she became a specialist in meditation. Instances of her wonderful clairvoyance are not greatly different from those of people of other persuasions who claimed to have predicted a man's rise to the imperial position. But the fact that Yang Chien was brought up under Buddhist influence is not disputed. That the nun's supervision continued until he was 13 *sui* is also attested by the *Sui K'ai-huang Ch'i-chü Chu*—an official compilation which the court chronicler Wang Shao wrote under imperial orders. The relevant passage is quoted in Tao-hsuan's (596–667) *Chi Ku-chin Fo-tao Lun-heng,* chap. 2; T, chap. 52, p. 379*a*. The *Ch'i-chü Chu*, originally in 60 *chüan*, had disappeared by the time of the writing of the *Hsin-T'ang-shu*, save for 6 *chüan* covering the first year of K'ai-huang. Cf. *Sui-shu ching-chi-chih k'ao-cheng* (hereinafter cited as "SCKC"), chap. 15, p. 264*b*. I am inclined to rule out the possibility that the eminent Buddhist cleric Tao-hsuan doctored or fabricated this quotation from a work which was probably known to many of his contemporaries.

15. *Ch'i-chü Chu, loc. cit.*, and HKSC, chap. 26, p. 667*c*.

16. *Ibid.* This incident is to be viewed with skepticism but is perhaps not to be altogether ruled out.

17. SS, chap. 1, p. 1*b*.

18. *Ibid.*

19. Cf. the references to his governorship (*tz'u-shih*) in northwestern Anhwei (*ibid.*, chap. 69, p. 4*b*).

20. *Ibid.*, chap. 36, pp. 4–6; PS, chap. 61, p. 8. The empress' mother was Chinese, née Ts'ui (*Pei-shih*, chap. 61, p. 9). On the important Tu-ku clan of the Toba cf.

Eberhard, *op. cit.*, pp. 323–24. Eberhard suggests (p. 324) that this family was descended from the ruling house of the Hsiung-nu. On the powerful Chinese gentry family of Ts'ui cf. *ibid.*, pp. 66–68.

21. On the contrast between northern and southern women cf. *Yen-shih Chiahsün*, chap. 1, p. 18, and Moriya Mitsuo, "Nanjin to Hokujin" ("Northerners and Southerners"), *Tōa Ronsō*, VI (1948), 54 and *passim*.

22. SS, chap. 36, p. 5b.

23. *Ibid.*, p. 5.

24. *Ibid.*, p. 4b.

25. *Ibid.*, p. 5.

26. *Ibid.*, chap. 41, p. 4b.

27. She received the vows from Fa-shen, one of the monks favored by the imperial house (cf. HKSC, chap. 18, p. 575b–c). Her participation in the munificent imperial donations to Buddhism is recorded in the edict of January 5, 594 (eighth day, twelfth moon, K'ai-huang 13) (cf. LTSPC, chap. 12, p. 108b).

28. SS, chap. 69, p. 5; Boodberg, p. 268, n. 179.

29. *Pien-cheng Lun*, by Fa-lin (572–640), *Taisho* 52, chap. 3, p. 509a (hereinafter cited as "PCL"); HKSC, chap. 30, p. 701b–c; the life of Fa-ch'eng recounts his participation in the daily sutra readings at the palace; it also remarks that the auditors took advantage of breaks in the readings to ask questions on the meaning of the sutra. For another monk's participation cf. HKSC, chap. 18, p. 572c. Cf. also *Ta T'ang Nei-tien Lu*, chap. 5; T, chap. 55, p. 279c. These texts are discussed in Yamazaki Hiroshi, *Shina Chūsei Bakkyō no tenkai* ("The Development of Medieval Chinese Buddhism") (hereinafter cited as "Yamazaki, *Chūsei*") (Tokyo, 1942), pp. 283–96. They are all written by Buddhist authors, and there is no doubt that they invariably make the most of manifestations of imperial piety. But the variety of references to these palace observances and the wealth of circumstantial detail argue for the credibility of these accounts. Further the Confucian historians do *not* record—as they do for other successful rulers—that he enjoyed reading or discussing the Chinese classics and histories; rather they repeatedly mention his lack of taste and learning in the Confucian tradition.

30. Yamazaki, *Chūsei*, pp. 291–94, discusses the Buddhist affiliations of the imperial princes. All five of the sons had such affiliations, but this does not mean that they were devout believers. Their heavy-handed parents demanded such observances. However, Chün, prince of Ch'in (571–600) asked his father for permission to become a monk and was (as he had expected?) refused (SS, chap. 45, p. 11b). According to TC, chap. 178, this occurred in 597.

31. The most concise statement of Wen-ti's attitude is found in SS, chap. 36, p. 30: "Kao-tsu was a steadfast believer in Buddhism and was contemptuous of the Taoist adepts." J. Ware, "The Wei-shu and the Sui-shu on Taoism," *Journal of the America Oriental Society*, LIII (1933), 249, misses the meaning of this passage.

32. Boodberg, pp. 255–56. Boodberg's account of the fast-moving complex events and the crises of Yang Chien's route to supreme power make Chao I's observation that Yang Chien's rise was of unprecedented ease seem fatuous. Cf. also Yamazaki's discussion of this (*Chūsei*, p. 274).

33. Boodberg, p. 255.

34. *Ibid.*, pp. 258–59. The sequence of these two events follows TC, chap. 174, pp. 2b–3.

35. Cf. Boodberg, p. 260 and n. 133. TC (chap. 174, p. 5) and SS (chap. 36, p. 4)

(different wording) both attribute this to his wife. SS (chap. 78, p. 4) has him using the saying in a consultation with the diviner Yü Chi-ts'ai. It would hardly be surprising, from what we know of their relationship, if Yang Chien was, in the second instance, quoting his wife.

36. Boodberg, p. 262. On Kao Chiung's role see below.

37. *Ibid.*, p. 264. The child ex-emperor of Chou died, presumably murdered, on July 10, 581.

38. *Ibid.*, pp. 264–65.

39. For a good statement of his views cf. TC, chap. 175, p. 5–5b. The empress also favored such a policy (cf. SS, chap. 36, p. 5).

40. Balázs (p. 222, n. 159) takes the view that Su Wei was the third most important counselor of Wen-ti, after Kao Chiung and Yang Su. My present impression is that Yang Su is more important as an executor of policy than as a formulator, but this view may well be modified through further research. Professor Yamazaki, in a conversation of May 6, 1954, expressed the view that Su Wei was the dominant figure of Sui officialdom. Yet about 592 Yang Su regarded him as *mieh-ju*, a nonentity (cf. TC, chap. 178, p. 2).

41. Eberhard (*op. cit.*, pp. 45–46) gives the history of two branches of the powerful Kao family which had become rich as colonists in Korea and served as high court officials in the Northern Wei.

42. Kao Chiung's biography (SS, chap. 41, pp. 1–6b). It was probably at the time of the order for Chinese to take Hsien-pi surnames, in 549, that Tu-ku Hsin allowed the Kaos to take his name. Wen-ti called Kao Chiung "Tu-ku." Was this to suggest their kinship by marriage and adoption through the empress? After her father's death in 557, the future empress was in the care of Kao Chiung's father (cf. *ibid.*, p. 1).

43. *Ibid.*, p. 6b.

44. Balázs, p. 155.

45. Cf. *T'ung-tien*, chap. 7, p. 42, and Kanai Yukitada, *Zui no Kōkei no saijutsu to Tsūden no shokkaten* ("Kao Chiung's Statecraft and the Section on Economics of the *T'ung-tien*"), *Bunka*, Vol. III (1937).

46. On Su Ch'o, cf. Balázs, pp. 281–302, and Chauncey Goodrich, *Biography of Su-ch'o* (Berkeley, 1953).

47. The Six Articles are translated by Balázs, pp. 284–302, and by Goodrich, *op. cit.*, pp. 16–36.

48. On Kao Chiung's relation to Su Ch'o cf. Kanai, *op. cit.*, p. 424. Kanai's argument, especially on the influence of Su Ch'o on Kao's economic policies, is persuasive, but further study of the sources is necessary. Kanai maintains that Kao Chiung's repeated efforts to resign his posts in favor of Su Wei reflected Kao's reverence for Su Wei's father.

49. Cf. Balázs, *Le Traité juridique du "Souei-chou"* (Paris, 1954), *passim*.

50. SS, chap. 75, p. 2b.

51. *Ibid.*, chap. 41, p. 4b.

52. Cf. HKSC, chap. 16, pp. 559c–560b: chap. 10, p. 505b–c: chap. 18, p. 573a. Wei Shu's (d. 757) *Liang-ching Hsin-chi* (p. 15) records Kao Chiung's donation of a residence which became the *Hua-tu ssu* (and p. 16) his wife's building of a nunnery on the site of her family's mansions. Collected fragments of this work are found in *Yüeh-ya-t'ang Ts'ung-shu*, Part II, Sec. 12. Yamazaki (*Chūsei*, pp. 295–96) discusses the Buddhist activities of leading Sui statesmen.

53. SS, chap. 41, pp. 7–13.

54. *Ibid.*, p. 7*b;* TC, chap. 175, p. 4.

55. TC, chap. 175, p. 4*b*.

56. *Ibid.*, p. 6*b*. Cf. also Balázs, *Traité juridique*, pp. 160–61.

57. Cf. *Pei-shih*, chap. 63, p. 18*b*. This is the only source that mentions the offensive phrasing. The text and the precise content of the "five teachings" are unknown. I am inclined to believe that they were some form of restatement of the five traditional Confucian norms of behavior and that it was the insulting phrasing and the forced memorization which enraged the southerners. It is interesting to note that Su Ch'o had forced all Northern Chou officials to memorize his Six Articles on pain of dismissal (cf. Balázs, p. 283). When the southerners disemboweled Sui officials, they said to their victims, "The better to memorize the five teachings" (*Pei-shih*, chap. 63, p. 18*b*, and TC, chap. 177, p. 15–15*b*).

58. He enjoyed retiring to a mountain temple to read (SS, chap. 41, p. 7). He is said to have received religious instruction in his leisure hours (cf. HKSC, chap. 18, p. 573*a*). Su Wei's *tzu* was Wu-wei (Sanskrit "abhaya"), a Buddhist epithet meaning "dauntless." Su Ch'o had written a *Fo-hsing Lun* in collaboration with the monk Ming-tsang. For a guess as to its contents, cf. *Sui-shu Ching-chi-chih Pu* (*Erh-shih-wu Shih Pu-pien* ["Supplements to the Twenty-five Histories"], Vol. 4), chap. 2, p. 9b.

59. The data on Wen-ti's behavior are sufficient for systematic psychological analysis, but the situation at present is that the historian lacks the skill and the psychologist lacks the interest to attempt such a study.

60. Boodberg's suggestion (p. 266) that the Turco-Mongol custom of gerontoctony influenced Wen'ti's relations with his sons has still to be followed up.

61. Cf. the memorial relating dynastic and social decay to literary refinement (SS, chap. 63, pp. 2–3). Wen-ti had this promulgated throughout the empire (TC, chap. 176, p. 2). Note the similar views held by Su Ch'o and his royal master (Balázs, p. 284; Goodrich, *op. cit.*, pp. 7, 36, 44). When the educated Confucian official Li Te-lin protested Wen-ti's plan to liquidate the Northern Chou princes, the emperor, enraged, called him a "bookworm" (*Shu-sheng*), and thereafter Li was not promoted (TC, chap. 175, p. 3).

62. Wen-ti was morbidly fearful of the withdrawal of Heaven's favor, but he was also sensitive about his public reputation. When, after their estrangement, he was advised to execute Kao Chiung, he recalled his recent executions of other high officials and said, "If, on the top of these, I execute Chiung, what will the empire say of me?" (SS, chap. 41, p. 5*b*).

63. Boodberg, p. 266.

64. SS, chap. 69, p. 8*b*. TC (chap. 178, pp. 6*b*–7*a*) adds that it included a fortunate interpretation of the names of the Yang family. The SS describes Wang Shao's interpretation of these symbols but does not say that this went into the book. I am not certain what the "texts" of the *Lo-shu* and *Ho-t'u* may have been at this time.

65. SS, chap. 69, p. 8*b*.

66. Cf. *Han-shu*, chaps. 99*B* and 100*A*. Pan Piao, the great historian, was ordered to compile the work justifying Wang Mang's usurpation. The *Han-shu* accounts of this "classic" usurpation have been translated by Burton Watson and will appear in Columbia University's volume of readings in Chinese thought. Wen-ti was hyper-

sensitive to criticism that hinted at any resemblance between himself and Wang Mang (cf. TC, chap. 177, p. 14).

67. *Chou-shu*, chap. 5, p. 19b; J. J. M. De Groot, *Sectarianism and Religious Persecution in China* (Amsterdam, 1903), p. 35. Cf. also Tsukamoto Zenryū, "Hokushū no Haibutsu ni tsuite" ("On the Northern Chou Suppression of Buddhism"), Part I in *Tōhō Gaku-hō*, XVI (1948), 29–101. Part II appeared in *Tōhō Gaku-hō*, XVIII (1950), 78–111. "Hokushū no Shūkyō Haiki Seisaku no Hōkai" ("The Failure of the Northern Chou Policy for the Suppression of Religion") appeared in *Bukkyō Shigaku*, I (1949), 3–31. These important articles will be referred to by sequence as "Tsukamoto, *Pers*" I, II, or III.

68. Cf. *Li-tai Ch'ung-tao Chi; Tao-tsang, T'ung-hsüan Pu.*

69. Cf. *Liang-ching Hsin-chi.*

70. Described in Sung Min-ch'iu, *Ch'ang-an Chih*. Cf. Adachi Kiroku, *Chōan Shiseki no Kenkyū* (Tokyo, 1933), pp. 200–201. See also Yamazaki Hiroshi, "Tsūdō-kan to Daikeizenji oyobi ni Gentokan" ("The T'ung-tao-kuan, the Ta-hsing-shan ssu and the Hsuan-tu kuan"), *Shigaku Zasshi*, Vol. LVII (1948).

71. Yamazaki, "Tsūdōkan . . . ," *op. cit.*

72. The branches of T'ung-tao kuan learning are not directly known. The inferences on which this is based are given in A. F. Wright, "Fu I and the Rejection of Buddhism," *Journal of the History of Ideas*, XII [1951], p. 38. Tsukamoto (*Pers* II, p. 103) sees it as a device to pacify Taoist and Buddhist believers by the token preservation, under official auspices, of some of the traditions of the two faiths.

73. Cf. TC, chap. 176, p. 1–1b (year 581), and Yabuuchi Kiyoshi, *Zuitō Rekihō no Kenkyū* ("A Study of the Sui-T'ang Calendar") (Tokyo, 1944), p. 8. The Taoists' virtual monopoly of calendar-making in the period of disunion is well known. Cf. Yü Hsun, "Tsao-ch'i Tao-chiao Cheng-chih Hsin-nien" ("Political Beliefs of Early Taoism"), *Fu-jen Hsueh-chih*, X (1942), 133–36.

74. Cf. Tokiwa Daijo, *Bukkyō to Jūkyō Dōkyō* ("Buddhism, Confucianism, and Taoism") (Tokyo, 1930), p. 617.

75. TC, chap. 175, pp. 4b–5.

76. SS, chap. 69, p. 7. Wang Shao maintains in one of his memorials presenting the prognostic rationalization of Sui power that the era-name coincides with that in the sacred Taoist work *Ling-pao Ching* (on which cf. Ware, *op. cit.*, p. 222). The Buddhists made a distinctly forced effort to show that the era-name symbolized the revival of Buddhism (cf. LTSPC, chap. 12, p. 102a).

77. This is the edict establishing Buddhist monasteries at the sacred mountains (see below). Text in LTSPC, chap. 12, p. 107b; PCL, chap. 3, p. 509a–c.

78. Cf. Ware, *op. cit.*, pp. 218–19. A thorough study of Taoist inscriptions from the period of disunion would be rewarding. Two inscriptions, of 587 and 592, reproduced in Omura Seigai, *Shina Bijutsushi Chōsōhen* ("History of Chinese Art: Sculpture") (Tokyo, 1915), pp. 419–20, are from votive images erected to Lao-tzu. They show a fusion of Lao-tzu devotion and the family cult which parallels the fusion found in so many Buddhist images.

79. Cf. Hsueh Tao-heng, "Lao-shih pei," and Introduction, *Ch'uan Sui-wen*, chap. 19, pp. 6–8b. Wang Shao made much of the fact that Yang Chien had once been governor of Hao-chou and reported a large number of miraculous occurrences at the Lao-tzu shrine which signified that Wen-ti's rise was a fulfilment of one of Lao-tzu's prophecies (cf. SS, chap. 69, p. 4–4b). This is paralleled on the Buddhist

side by solemn arguments that Wen-ti's rise is a fulfilment of one of Buddha's prophecies.

80. Cf. Tokiwa, *op. cit.*, pp. 511–15; Ware, *op. cit.*, p. 221.

81. SS, chap. 40, p. 8–8*b*; TC, chap. 176, p. 5*b* (583). In 598 Taoist adepts in Szechwan encouraged the subversive designs of Wen-ti's fourth son, Prince Hsiu, and this must have strengthened the emperor's antipathy toward the adepts (cf. SS, chap. 45, p. 16–16*b*, and *Fa-lin Pieh-chuan*, chap. 3; T, Vol. 50, p. 208*b*). This man's biography is rich in materials on Sui Taoism.

82. TC, chap. 178, p. 3 (593). I suspect that Fu I, serving a Sui prince as official diviner, had the use of such texts (cf. *Hsin T'ang-shu*, chap. 107, p. 1). It may have been to control the distribution of these texts as well as the activities of their interpreters that Taoist adepts had to receive official permission to practice their profession (cf. Wright, "Fu I . . . ," *op. cit.*, 39).

83. In 583 he made a progress to a Taoist temple, where he saw a painting on that popular theme of Taoist polemics, "Lao-tzu Converting the Barbarians"—a graphic representation of the argument that Buddha had been Lao-tzu's disciple. The emperor, it is said, was greatly astonished, ordered a discussion between Buddhist monks and Taoist adepts, and appointed a committee of officials to investigate. From his general outlook and from his other actions, we may infer that he found for the Buddhist side of the argument. The influential cleric Yen-tsung presented the Buddhist case, "exposing the arrant heterodoxy of the Taoists" (cf. HKSC, chap. 2, pp. 436*c*–437*a*).

84. It is usually said that his official nomenclature marked a return to Han and San-kuo Wei precedents, but as in all other aspects of Sui institutions the real—as distinct from the avowed—derivations are far more complex.

85. SS, chap. 75, p. 2*b*.

86. TC, chap. 174, p. 14; Boodberg, p. 264.

87. TC, chap. 175, p. 1–1*b*; Boodberg, p. 264.

88. TC, chap. 175, p. 2–2*b*; SS, chap. 7, pp. 12*b*–13.

89. TC, chap. 176, p. 10*b*, and Hu San-hsing's commentary.

90. Cf. TC, chap. 177, p. 15; chap. 178, p. 3. See also SS, chap. 69, p. 7, for Wang Shao's rationalization of the Five Virtues of the Sui. On the Five Elements and the five emperor-virtues cf. Kano Naoki, *Dokushō Senyo* (Tokyo, 1947), pp. 63–132. Liu Hsiang and Liu Hsin are usually credited with the dynasty-element succession theory, and it was their view that the Han ruled by the virtue of fire. The Later Chao and the Liang had both ruled by the virtue of fire, but in both cases the "virtue" had not been long sustained.

91. SS, chap. 8, p. 6. The Northern Ch'i tradition was in fact authoritative in the decisions of the commission.

92. TC, chap. 178, p. 3; SS, chap. 6, p. 18*b*.

93. SS, chap. 6, p. 19. Cf. also SS, chap. 68, pp. 2 ff. Yü-wen K'ai, the leading engineer of the Sui, was the principal designer (cf. Balázs, p. 221, n. 155). Despite his copious references to the prescriptions of canonical texts, Yü-wen K'ai's design called for a twelve-storied *ming-t'ang*—one story for each month—and this was a daring innovation. W. E. Soothill's *The Hall of Light* (London, 1951) is an unsatisfactory history of the *ming-t'ang*. The sections in Marcel Granet, *La Pensée chinoise* (Paris, 1934), which deal with the *ming t'ang* are a brilliant statement of its symbolic ramifications.

94. Cf. Édouard Chavannes, *Le Tai Chan* (Paris, 1910), pp. 158–69.

95. *Ibid.*

96. SS, chap. 2, p. 5*b;* TC, chap. 177, p. 11*b.*

97. SS, chap. 7, p. 17; TC, chap. 178, p. 6*b.* Chavannes (*op. cit.*, p. 169) translates the passage from *Chiu T'ang-shu,* chap. 23, on these observances.

98. SS, chap. 2, p. 10*b;* TC, chap. 178, p. 7.

99. SS, chap. 7, p. 17; Chavannes, *op. cit.*, pp. 120, 169. A further deterrent may have been another kind of superstitious dread. In popular Buddhism the mountain T'ai-shan had been fused with the Buddhist hell called T'ai-shan, where evildoers suffered the most violent torments. Cf. Tsukamoto, *Shina Bukkyōshi no Kenkyū* ("Studies in the History of Chinese Buddhism") (Kyoto, 1942), pp. 307–8.

100. SS, chap. 24, p. 11*a–b;* Balázs, p. 152. I take the latter two categories of virtuous people in a somewhat narrower sense than does Balázs, who translates "les époux équitables et les épouses chastes."

101. SS, chap. 2, p. 16. This information is from the emperor's disillusioned review of his efforts at Confucian education (see below).

102. See text above and Robert des Rotours, *Le Traité des examens* (Paris, 1932), p. 37. In the T'ang, the provincial scholars were escorted and presented, along with "tribute," by the provincial representatives on their annual trip to the capital.

103. As late as 603 Wen-ti was still ordering special measures to get qualified people from the provinces, suggesting, as does his own review in the edict of 601, that the regular arrangements had not been effective: "Select the worthy and the wise, choose all those who have a clear knowledge of the ancient and the modern and a comprehensive grasp of the basis of government and of chaos, those who have comprehended the fundamentals of political doctrine, who have a full understanding of Rites and of Music" (SS, chap. 2, p. 20*b*).

104. TC, chap. 175, p. 8–8*b.* Although this account is placed under the year 581, it is included by Ssu-ma Kuang to illustrate the working of government in the K'ai-huang period, 581–600. There is interesting evidence of improvement in the condition of the Yeh area in SS, chap. 30, and in Balázs, p. 315.

105. TC, chap. 175, pp. 8*b*–9.

106. *Ibid.*, chap. 176, pp. 11*b*–12.

107. *Ibid.*, p. 11*b;* SS, chap. 2, pp. 1–2*b.*

108. SS, chap. 41, p. 3.

109. Tsukamoto (*Pers* II, p. 102) analyzes the groups disaffected by the persecution: (1) secularized clergy whose way of life had been abruptly changed and who were at a disadvantage in lay society; (2) lay adherents of all classes who had supported clergy, temples, the copying of scriptures, etc., in the hope of salvation; (3) military and civil officials whose loyalty to the throne was shaken by oppressive measures against their personal religion; (4) the vast numbers of artists, artisans, copyists, provisioners, and others, who depended for their livelihood on serving Buddhist establishments. I would add those who profited, directly or indirectly, from the tax-free, corvée-free status of Buddhist lands. Summarized from Wright, "Fu I . . . ," *op. cit.*, p. 37, n. 7.

110. PCL (chap. 3, p. 509*b*) says that 230,000 monks were ordained in Wen-ti's reign. This would hardly create a clergy-ridden society in an empire that a few years after his death had a population of at least 46,000,000 (cf. Balázs, pp. 308–10).

111. Tsukamoto, *Pers* III, pp. 10–12. The Ting-hsien inscription of 585 reprinted

in the *Ting-hsien Chih* of 1934 is discussed by Tsukamoto Zenryū in his *Nisshi Bukkyō Kōshōshi* ("Studies in Buddhist Intercourse between China and Japan") (Tokyo, 1945), p. 43; it piously states that Chou Wu-ti died of jaundice (*Chia-mo-lo;* Sanskrit *kāmalā*) as retribution for his suppression of Buddhism and that the era-name Ta-hsiang, chosen in 579, symbolized his son's remorse for his father's acts and the new emperor's vow to build a "great [Buddha] image." There is naturally also a Taoist interpretation of this era-name based on the *I-ching* (cf. SS, chap. 69, pp. 2*b*–3). On Cheng I cf. SS, chap. 38, pp. 5–8*b*.

112. HKSC, chap. 8, p. 491*a*. Tsukamoto (*Pers* III) gives good reasons why the date in this passage should be emended to Ta-hsiang 1. See also KHMC, chap. 10.

113. Tsukamoto, *Pers* III, pp. 9–10.

114. *Ibid.*, pp. 15–18.

115. HKSC, chap. 19, p. 581*b;* Tsukamoto, *Pers* III, p. 18; Yamazaki, *Chūsei*, p. 285.

116. *Chou-shu*, chap. 8; TC, chap. 174, p. 5*b*.

117. E.g., Yen-tsung and T'an-yen. Cf. HKSC, chap. 2, pp. 436*b*–439*c;* chap. 8, pp. 488*a*–489*c*. See also Tsukamoto, *Pers* III, pp. 20–22.

118. The elaborate Sui system of state controls of Buddhism has been studied in Yamazaki Hiroshi, "Zuidai Sōkan Kō" ("Study of the Sangha-Officials of the Sui"), *Shina Bukkyō Shigaku*, VI (1942), 1–15, and in "Zui no Daikeizenji ni Tsuite" ("Concerning the *Ta-hsing-shan ssu* of the Sui"), *Shichō*, Vol. XLII (1949). The administrative machinery of control was centered in the Chao-hsüan ssu in the capital, which was staffed by a bureaucratic hierarchy of monks headed by the Ta-t'ung. There were branch bureaus of Buddhist affairs in the provinces and districts (*chou* and *hsien*), known as the Sha-men tsao (cf. SS, chap. 27, p. 8). These institutions were adopted, with minor changes, from those that had developed under the northern dynasties.

119. *Liang-ching Hsin-chi*, p. 2*a*.

120. Based on the descriptions in the *Liang-ching Hsin-chi*. Cf. Tsukamoto, *Pers* III, p. 30. The social status of donors of Buddhist establishments of Sui date compiled from data in the *Liang-ching Hsin-chi* shows this distribution: high officials (including in one instance a wife)—11; members of the imperial family—7; palace ladies of Northern Chou and Sui—4; merchants—2; eunuchs—1; emperor's physician—1; commoner—1; T'u-ch'ueh dignitary—1.

121. Cf. HKSC, chap. 16, pp. 559*c*–560*b*. On this movement cf. Yabuki Keiki, *Sankaikyō no Kenkyū* ("Study of the San-chieh Chiao") (Tokyo, 1927), pp. 68, 90, and *passim*, and Tokiwa Daijo, in *Shina Bukkyō no Kenkyū*, I (1938), 179–98. For a critical estimate of sources cf. Tsukamoto Zenryū, in *Shina Bukkyō Shigaku*, I (1937), 57–74, 96–110.

122. LTSPC, chap. 12, p. 107*b;* PCL, chap. 3, p. 509*a*–*b*.

123. Cf. Chavannes, *op. cit.*, pp. 3–9. For many instances of Taoist sacred writings received on mountaintops cf. Ware, *op. cit.*, *passim*.

124. Buddhist monks had from very early times been the rivals of Taoist adepts in dealing with the unseen forces of nature (cf. Wright, "Fo-t'u-teng, a Biography," *Harvard Journal of Asiatic Studies*, XI [1948], 324–27). I have found one case of Wen-ti's use of monks for rain-making and expect to find more (cf. HKSC, chap. 21, p. 660*b*–*c*). Provisions of 594 and later, for the cults of the mountains and the seas, involve the use of Taoist nuns and shamans. In addition to Buddhist monks? Cf. SS, chap. 7, p. 17*a*–*b*.

125. Evidence on the date, which is conflicting, is reviewed in Yamazaki, *Chūsei*, pp. 287–89. According to PCL (chap. 3, p. 509a), Wen-ti built an official temple in each of the *chou* through which he had passed in the years before his accession.

126. LTSPC, chap. 12, p. 108a. In 603, on his own birthday, Wen-ti ordered that on this day throughout the empire there should be a suspension of all killing, this on behalf of his father and mother (SS, chap. 2, p. 18)—an interesting fusion of the cult of imperial ancestors and Buddhism.

127. LTSPC, chap. 12, p. 107c. For the edict of the eighth moon cf. LTSPC, chap. 12, pp. 107c–108a.

128. Such claims had earlier been made by Liang Wu-ti. For canonical statements on the role and destiny of a Čakravartin cf. *A-yu-wang Chuan* ("Aśoka Avadana"), translated *ca.* 300 (T, chap. 50, p. 100b and *passim;* also Jean Przyluski, *La Légende de l'EmpereurAçoka* [Paris, 1923], p. 233 and *passim*).

129. The author of LTSPC, chap. 12, p. 108, regards this action of Wen-ti as unprecedented. In China? Cf. Jules Bloch, *Les Inscriptions d'Açoka* (Paris, 1950), p. 30, and Rock Edict XIII, pp. 125–32. Bloch (p. 30, n. 1) points out that T'ang T'ai-tsung in 630 set up seven temples on battlefields, and he cites another instance in Northwest China about the year 800, recorded in a Tun-huang document. Wen-ti's son, after the disasters of the second expedition against Korea, in 614 ordered decent burial, a Buddhist temple, and services on behalf of the war dead (SS, chap. 4, p. 8). Cf. also Yamazaki Hiroshi, "Zui no Koguryō Ensei to Bukkyō" ("The Sui Expedition against Kao-chü-li and Buddhism"), *Shichō*, LIX (1953), 1–10. I have not yet found the precise textual link between Aśokan precedent and Wen-ti's act. Neither Chinese version of the *Aśoka Avadana*, despite their apparent relation to Wen-ti's other acts, specifically mentions battlefield monuments. This is part of a larger problem I hope to investigate: the parallels between the problems facing the two monarchs, their respective policies and achievements. As the historic Aśoka emerges from the work of many scholars, these parallels become ever more arresting. *But* Wen-ti, as far as we know, knew only the Aśoka of the pious Buddhist legendary accounts and apparently could have known little of the historic Aśoka, whose temporal problems and achievements so closely paralleled his own.

130. Order of 585 providing for regular Buddhist services at the palace (PCL, chap. 3, p. 509a).

131. Edict of 583 (*ibid.*, p. 508c).

132. Edict of 584 (LTSPC, chap. 12, p. 108a).

133. Edict of 585 (PCL, chap. 3, p. 509a). This was accompanied by an order for the large-scale amnesty of prisoners.

134. Cf. the letter of transmittal of the *Chung-ching Mu-lu* dated 594 (T, chap. 54, p. 149a).

135. LTSPC, chap. 12, p. 107b, quoting the *Te-hu Chang-che Ching*. Other canonical texts are quoted by the author of LTSPC to support the idea of Wen-ti as the Buddha-ordained monarch. The author gives a special interpretation of the "extinction of the dharma" referred to in Buddha's prophecy. According to him, this referred to the Northern Chou persecution.

136. Cf. *A-yu-wang Chuan* (T, chap. 50, p. 99c; Przyluski, *op. cit.*, p. 228). The long and widespread persistence of Aśoka legends in China—centered in the so-called Aśoka pagodas—would indicate a popular basis of belief on which such an appeal might be posited. On the Aśoka stupas in China cf. Alexander Soper in *Monumenta Serica*, IV (1939), 638–79.

137. This contrast, which dates back to the early fifth century, is admirably reviewed in Takao Giken, *Chūgoku Bukkyōshiron* ("Essays in the History of Chinese Buddhism") (Kyoto, 1952), pp. 37–53.

138. Tsukamoto Zenryū, "Zui no Kōnan Seifuku to Bukkyō ("The Sui Conquest of the South and Buddhism"), *Bukkyō Bunka Kenkyū*, III (1953), 2–3.

139. HKSC, chap. 10, p. 501*c*. According to this passage, "fifty-odd tens of thousands" were ordained, and Tsukamoto ("Zui no Kōnan . . . ," *op. cit.*, p. 3) makes the reasonable inference that this order at this time, plus the resulting sudden enlargement of the clergy, is to be explained only as a measure directed at the south.

140. Wen-ti told the greatest of southern Buddhist clerics, Chih-i, at the beginning of 590, that he, Wen-ti, had vowed to revive Buddhism after the Chou persecution and that the conquest of the south had been accomplished out of reverence for the true law and the desire to bring peace to all creatures (*Kuo-ch'ing Pai-lu*, chap. 2, par. 22, quoted in Tsukamoto, "Zui no Kōnan . . . ," *op. cit.*, pp. 7–8).

141. LTSPC, chap. 12, p. 108*a*. The concentration of "unity" terms in the Chinese text creates a still stronger effect.

142. *Ibid.*, p. 108*b*. It is this edict that contains the passage which, misconstrued, led to the belief that printing existed in the Sui (cf. Paul Pelliot, *Les Débuts de l'imprimerie en Chine* [Paris, 1953], pp. 9–10).

143. Boodberg, p. 267. As Boodberg points out (n. 175), Buddhist seers predicted he would not live beyond 599 (SS, chap. 41).

144. SS, chap. 2, p. 16. The Kuo-tzu hsueh in the capital, with a quota of seventy students, was retained. SS, chap 75, p. 2*b*, says seventy-two students.

145. KHMC, chap. 17, p. 213*b*.

146. *Ibid.*

147. The tireless collector and interpreter of portents, Wang Shao, compiled a *She-li Kan-ying Chi*. This is quoted from the more circumstantial section (KHMC, chap. 17, p. 214*b*).

148. *Ibid.*

149. *Ibid.*, p. 217*a–b*. Some sources say fifty-three localities.

150. HKSC, chap. 21, p. 611*c*.

151. Sasaki Kosei, "Jinshu Sharitō Kō" ("A Study of the Reliquary Pagodas of the Jen-shou Era"), *Ryūkoku Daigaku Ronsō*, CCLXXXIII (1928), 62–71; Yamazaki, *Chūsei*, pp. 333–36.

152. Sasaki (*op. cit.*, p. 71), having surveyed the geographical distribution, points out (*a*) that the effort was empire-wide; (*b*) that the missions were more numerous in the north than south of the Yangtze (in my view reflecting differences in population density); (*c*) that there was, notably in the third distribution of 604, a strong emphasis on the old capitals of the Northern dynasties—centers of vigorous Buddhist communities; and (*d*) that there was a strong concentration of enshrinements at places which already had centers of religious interest. Yamazaki (*Chūsei*, pp. 333–36) has identified 101 out of the 111 sites at which imperial reliquaries were built; the map (Fig. 1) showing their distribution is reproduced, with his kind permission, from the one which appeared in *Chūsei*, opposite p. 444.

153. Sasaki, *op. cit.*, pp. 73–75. Yamazaki (*Chūsei*, pp. 333–36) has identified a total of 95 participants, but has not traced the connection of all of these with the Northern Chou persecution.

154. Prince Hsiung's compilation is found in KHMC, chap. 17, pp. 216*a*–221*a*,

where the accounts of wonders by the historian and omen specialist, Wang Shao, also appear (*ibid.*, pp. 213*b*–215*c*).

155. *Ibid.*, p. 217*c*.

156. Cf. *A-yu-wang chuan*, p. 102*b*, and Przyluski, *op. cit.*, p. 244.

157. Cf. *A-yu-wang chuan*, p. 102*a*, and Przyluski, *op. cit.*, pp. 242–43.

158. HKSC, chap. 18, p. 573*c*.

159. This relationship is thoroughly analyzed in Tsukamoto, *Nisshi Bukkyō Kōshōshi*, pp. 1–47.

160. Wang Shao, *She-li Kan-ying Chi*, KHMC, chap. 17.

161. Cf. Bloch, *op. cit.*, p. 31. Toynbee, reflecting on the period of disunion says: "The contrast between this political failure of the Mahāyāna in Northern China in a post-Sinic Age and the success with which the Christian Church seized and harvested its corresponding opportunities in Western Europe in a post-Hellenic Age brings out the fact that—at any rate by comparison with Christianity—the Mahāyāna was a politically incompetent religion. The patronage of the parochial princes in Northern China during the best part of three centuries . . . was of no more avail than the more potent patronage of the Kushan Emperor Kanishka had been" (*A Study of History* [London, 1954], IX, 40–41). I hope to show in a later paper that one of the principal reasons for the political incompetence of Buddhism was that it was not a "church"—a fact which Toynbee implicitly recognizes by his choice of words in this quotation.

NOTES TO AN EARLY SUNG REFORMER: FAN CHUNG-YEN

1. The composition and the operation of the Sung bureaucracy are well discussed in a definitive work: E. A. Kracke, Jr., *Civil Service in Early Sung China, 960–1067* (Cambridge, Mass., 1953). The basic source materials are found mainly in *Sung Hui-yao Chi-kao* (Shanghai, 1936), especially the sections under the headings *Hsuan-chü* ("Recruitment and appointment") and *Chih-kuan* ("Organization and operation of the Government Offices"). One may consult for convenient reference the *T"ung-k'ao* and *Hsü T'ung-chih* (*Wan-yu wen-k'u* ed.; Shanghai, 1937), under the same headings as above.

On the social background of the bureaucrats see E. A. Kracke, Jr., "Family vs. Merit in the Chinese Civil Service Examination," *Harvard Journal of Asiatic Studies*, X (1947), 118–24; also his essay in the present volume.

2. Hsiao-t'ung Fei, *China's Gentry* (Chicago, 1953), p. 58; see also a review by Arthur W. Hummel in *Far Eastern Quarterly*, XIII (1954), 333–34.

3. Several theoretical works are helpful to the study of the power structure. They begin with Max Weber, *The Theory of Social and Economic Organization*, trans. A. R. Henderson (London, 1947), and *The Religion of China*, trans. Hans H. Gerth (Glencoe, Ill., 1951). Talcott Parsons has gone further than Weber in theoretical analysis (see his *The Social System* [Glencoe, Ill., 1951]). Harold D. Lasswell and Abraham Kaplan, *Power and Society* (New Haven, Conn., 1950), is a systematic study of power by different theoretical approaches. Numerous new theoretical aspects are raised by more recent researches, which are conveniently found in a collective work: Robert K. Merton (ed.), *Reader in Bureaucracy* (Glencoe, Ill., 1952). For the clarification of basic concepts, one may consult Robert M. MacIver,

The Web of Government (New York, 1947). Bertrand Russell's *Power* (New York, 1938) is rather superficial but makes certain penetrating points.

4. The power structure approach has been applied to a limited extent by Wang Yü-ch'üan, "Central Government of the Former Han Dynasty," *Harvard Journal of Asiatic Studies*, XII (1949), 180–85.

5. Cf. Weber, *Religion of China*, p. 68, and Kracke, *Civil Service*, pp. 190–98. However, both neglect to discuss the political significance inherent in administrative reforms.

6. This classification of bureaucrats has been suggested by Ch'ü T'ung-tsu.

7. The importance of Confucian idealism has been ably pointed out by W. Theodore de Bary, "A Reappraisal of Neo-Confucianism," in Arthur F. Wright (ed.), *Studies in Chinese Thought* (Chicago, 1953). The practical utilitarian spirit and active political interest of the revived Confucianism during the Sung period are emphasized in Hsiao Kung-ch'üan, *Chung-kuo Cheng-chih Ssu-hsiang Shih* (Shanghai, 1946), II, 143–45.

8. See article by Charles O. Hucker in this volume.

9. See article by W. Theodore de Bary in this volume.

10. Fan Chung-yen, *Fan Wen-cheng-kung Chi* (1910 ed.), NP, p. 18*b*. For the sake of brevity, the contents of this primary source are indicated by the following abbreviations: CFTI (*Cheng-fu Tsou-i*), CT (*Ch'ih-tu*), H (*Hsü*), ICKC (*I-chuang Kuei-chü*), NP (*Nien-p'u*), PC (*Pieh Chi*), PHC (*Pao-hsien Chi*), PP (*Pu-pien*), WC (*Wen-chi*), YHL (*Yen-hsing Lu*).

The present essay has been completed for some time. For factual information on Fan Chung-yen, a lengthy historical study is now available: J. Fischer, "Fan Chung-yen (989–1052), das Lebensbild eines chinesischen Staatsmannes," *Oriens Extremus*, 1955, pp. 39–85 and 142–56.

11. Fan, H, p. 1*a;* Huang Tsung-hsi and Ch'üan Tsu-wang, *Sung Yuan Hsueh-an* (*Wan-yu Wen-k'u* ed. [hereinafter cited as "SYHA"]), chap. 1, pp. 96–97.

12. Fan, CFTI, chap. 1, pp. 1*a*–15*a;* cf. a short summary in De Bary, "Reappraisal," *op. cit.*, p. 93.

13. Ch'en Yin-ch'üeh, *T'ang-tai Cheng-chih Shih Shu Lun-kao* (Chungking, 1943), pp. 59–62.

14. Fan, H, p. 1*a*.

15. Yeh Meng-te, *Pi Shu Lu Hua* (*Ts'ung-shu Chi-ch'eng* ed. [hereinafter cited as "TSCC ed."]), chap. 1, p. 41; Fan, PHC, chap. 1, pp. 18*b*–19*b*.

16. Fan, PHC, chap. 5, p. 14*a*.

17. SYHA, chap. 1, pp. 25 and 31; Hu Ming-sheng, "*An-ting Hsien-sheng Nien-p'u*," *Wen-shih Ts'ung-k'an*, I (1932), 19–35; De Bary, "Reappraisal," *op. cit.*, pp. 88–91 and 94.

18. SYHA, chap. 1, p. 66; De Bary, "Reappraisal," *op. cit.*, pp. 91–93; Fan, WC, chap. 18, p. 6*a*–*b*, and CT, chap. 3, pp. 4*b*–5*a*.

19. SYHA, chap. 1, p. 96; De Bary, "Reappraisal," *op. cit.*, p. 92.

20. Fan, PHC, chap. 5, p. 19*b*; CFTI, chap. 2, pp. 22*b*–23*a*; YHL, chap. 1, p. 4*b*; SYHA, chap. 2, p. 24; Hsiao, *Ssu-hsiang Shih*, pp. 145–49.

21. Fan, WC, chap. 19, pp. 4*a*–5*a;* Feng Ch'i, *Sung-shih Chi-shih Pen-mo* (1874 ed. [hereinafter cited as "*Pen-mo*"]), chap. 18, pp. 8*b*–11*b*.

22. Fan, PHC, chap. 5, pp. 15 ff.

23. Chao I, *Nien-erh Shih Cha-chi* (1934 ed.), pp. 274–75; Ssu-ma Kuang, *Su-shui Chi-wen* (TSCC ed.), chap. 15, p. 163, records how courteous Fu Pi was toward scholars.

24. Fan, PHC, chap. 5, 18*b*.

25. *Ibid.*, chap. 2, pp. 11*a*–14*a*.

26. This quotation is found in "Yueh-yang-lou Chi" (Fan, WC, chap. 7, p. 4*a*), which Fan composed for his friend T'eng Tsung-liang in 1046, after both had fallen from power. Cf. Ssu-ma Kuang, *Su-shui Chi-wen*, chap. 9, p. 101; Fan Kung-ch'eng, *Kuo T'ing Lu* (TSCC ed.), p. 5. The popular impression that Fan uttered this quotation during his youth is due to an erroneous assertion by Chu Hsi (see Fan, PHC, chap. 5, pp. 17*b*–18*a*).

27. Fan, WC, chap. 7, p. 4*b;* SYHA, chap. 1, p. 2 and chap. 2, p. 5; *Hsü T'ung-tien (Wan-yu Wen-k'u* ed.; Shanghai, 1937), p. 1453.

28. Ch'ien Mu, *Kuo-shih Ta-kang* (Shanghai, 1947), chap. 2, pp. 573–79.

29. Fan, NP, pp. 37*a*–38*a;* CT, chap. 1, p. 2*a;* ICKC, pp. 1*a*–3*a;* PP, chap. 1, 17*a*–*b;* PHC, chap. 4, pp. 7*a*–9*b;* Hui-chen Wang Liu, "An Analysis of the Chinese Clan Rules" (Ph.D. thesis, University of Pittsburgh, 1956).

30. Fan, PHC, chap. 3, p. 2*b*.

31. Ch'ien, *Kuo-shih*, chap. 2, pp. 569–70.

32. Wang Ming-ch'ing, *Hui-chu Ch'ien Lu* (TSCC ed.), chap. 2, p. 82.

33. Fan, CT, chap. 1, p. 7*a*.

34. Ch'ien, *Kuo-shih*, chap. 2, p. 611.

35. Chao, *Nien-erh Shih*, pp. 329–30 and 332–33; Fan, WC, chap. 7, pp. 9*b*–10*a;* chap. 8, p. 16*a;* and chap. 13, p. 4*a*.

36. Fan, CFTI, chap. 1, pp. 4*a*–5*b*, 37*b*–40*a;* cf. Kracke, *Civil Service*, p. 74; *Hsü T'ung-tien*, p. 1452; *Hsü T'ung-chih*, p. 4117.

37. Ch'ien, *Kuo-shih*, chap. 1, p. 354.

38. Fan, WC, chap. 9, pp. 1*b*–2*b*.

39. Ting Ch'uan-ching, *Sung-jen I-shih Hui-pien* (Shanghai, 1930), chap. 9, p. 379.

40. Fan, CFTI, chap. 1, pp. 6*a*–7*a;* CT, chap. 1, p. 7*a*.

41. Feng, *Pen-mo*, chap. 38, p. 3*a;* Fan Chen, *Tung-chai Chi-shih* (TSCC ed.), chap. 1, p. 6.

42. *T'ung-k'ao*, pp. 289–90; *Hsü T'ung-tien*, p. 1214.

43. Fan, PP, chap. 1, p. 16*a;* WC, chap. 8, p. 5*a*.

44. Fan, WC, chap. 9, p. 22*a*, and chap. 11, p. 13*a;* Fan Chen, *Tung-chai*, chap, 3, p. 19.

45. Fan, WC, chap. 9, p. 17*b*.

46. *Ibid.*, chap. 8, p. 10*a;* chap. 9, p. 19*b;* chap. 12, p. 11*a;* YHL, chap. 1, p. 6*a;* CFTI, chap. 1, pp. 49*b*–50*a;* chap. 2, p. 11*b*.

47. Fan, WC, chap. 8, p. 21*a;* CT, chap. 1, pp. 1*b*–4*a;* PC, chap. 4, pp. 1*a*–2*a*.

48. Fan, WC, chap. 8, pp. 8*a*–9*a*.

49. Fan, NP, p. 38*a*–*b*.

50. Chao, *Nien-erh Shih*, pp. 330–31.

51. *Hsü T'ung-chih*, p. 4089.

52. Fan, NP, p. 10*a;* PP, chap. 1, p. 1*a*–*b*.

53. Fan, CFTI, chap. 1, p. 9*a*–*b*.

54. *T'ung-k'ao*, p. 592; Fan, CFTI, chap. 1, pp. 41*a*–42*a*.

55. Fan, WC, chap. 8, pp. 5*a*–8*b;* Wei T'ai, *Tung-hsuan Pi-lu* (TSCC ed.), chap. 3, p. 19.

56. Chao, *Nien-erh Shih*, p. 327.

57. Fan, CFTI, chap. 1, pp. 8*a*–*b* and 19*a;* YHL, chap. 3, p. 3*a*–*b*.

58. Fan, NP, pp. 31*b*–32*a*.

59. Fan, PP, chap. 1, pp. 15*b*–16*b*; *Pen-mo*, chap. 29, p. 16*a*.

60. Wei, *Tung-hsuan*, chap. 3, p. 19; Chang-Lui, *Ming-tao Tsa-chih* (TSCC ed.), pp. 21–22.

61. Fan, WC, chap. 8, p. 16*a*.

62. Kracke, *Civil Service*, pp. 86–88.

63. Fan, CFTI, chap. 1, pp. 1*b*–4*a*.

64. *Ibid.*, pp. 3*b*–4*b*, 21*a*–*b*, and 42*a*–44*b*; cf. Kracke, *Civil Service*, p. 114.

65. *Hsü T'ung-tien*, p. 1230.

66. Ch'en Shih-tao, *Hou-shan Lu* (TSCC ed.), chap. 18, pp. 5–6.

67. *Pen-mo*, chap. 24, pp. 2*b*–3*b*; Fan, NP, p. 9*a*–*b*.

68. *Pen-mo*, chap. 25, pp. 1*b*–3*b*.

69. *Ibid.*, chap. 29, p. 6*a*.

70. Ch'ao Shui-chih, *Ch'ao-shih K'o Yü* (TSCC, ed.), p. 14.

71. Weber, *Theory*, p. 301.

72. Fan, WC, chap. 5, pp. 10*a*–16*a*.

73. Yeh Meng-te, *Shih-lin Yen-yü* (TSCC ed.), chap. 1, p. 9.

74. Fan, YHL, chap. 3, p. 7*a*; WC, chap. 5, p. 4*a*.

75. Fan, WC, chap. 5, p. 13*a*.

76. Fan, CFTI, chap. 2, pp. 26*b*–27*b*; WC, chap. 5, pp. 14*a*–15*a*; K'ung P'ing-chung, *K'ung-shih T'an Yuan* (TSCC ed.), chap. 4, p. 94.

77. Fan, PC, chap. 2, pp. 5*b*–6*b*; WC, chap. 20, pp. 9*a*–10*a*.

78. Fan, YHL, chap. 1, p. 6*b*; Wei, *Tung-hsuan*, chap. 13, p. 98.

79. Fan, PP, chap. 2, p. 10*b*; *Hsü T'ung-chih*, p. 5231.

80. Russell, *Power*, p. 97.

81. Fan, NP, p. 31*a*.

82. *Pen-mo*, chap. 29, pp. 16*a*–19*b*; SYHA, chap. 1, pp. 96–97 and 103; Fan, NP, p. 33*a*.

83. Wei, *Tung-hsuan*, chap. 4, pp. 23–25.

84. Fan, NP, p. 35*a*; *Pen-mo*, chap. 29, pp. 20*a*–23*a*.

85. MacIver, *op. cit.*, p. 209.

86. Conyers Read, "Factors in the English Privy Council under Elizabeth," *Annual Report of the American Historical Association*, I (1911), 109–19.

87. Kracke, *Civil Service*, p. 130, n. 43.

88. Fan, WC, chap. 17, p. 7*a*.

89. *Ibid.*, chap. 13, p. 4*a*.

90. Fan, NP, p. 32*b*; compare with Kracke, *Civil Service*, p. 130, n. 43.

91. Derk Bodde, "Harmony and Conflict in Chinese Philosophy," in Arthur Wright (ed.), *Studies in Chinese Thought* (Chicago, 1953), pp. 41–43; T'ang Yung-t'ung, "Wang Pi's New Interpretation of the *I-ching* and *Lun-yü*," *Harvard Journal of Asiatic Studies*, X (1947), 124–61; Fan, WC, p. 5 and *passim*.

92. Chao, *Nien-erh Shih*, p. 310.

93. SYHA, chap. 1, pp. 26–29.

94. Fan, WC, chap. 10, pp. 4*b*–5*a*, and chap. 13, p. 5*a*. Wang (*Hui-chu Ch'ien Lu*, chap. 2, p. 77) mentions that the Sung high-ranking officials usually married their daughters to promising young officials.

95. *Pen-mo*, chap. 37, p. 16*a*; Ch'ien, *Kuo-shih*, chap. 2, pp. 415–17.

96. Fan, NP, p. 3*b*.

97. Ch'ien, *Kuo-shih*, chap. 2, p. 397, corrects the mistake in SYHA, chap. 2, p. 4, which alleges that Fan studied under Ch'i himself.

98. Fan, YHL, chap. 1, p. 2*a*.

99. Wang, *Hui-chu Ch'ien Lu*, chap. 2, p. 82.

100. Fan, YHL, chap. 1, p. 3*b*.

101. Fan, WC, chap. 18, p. 3*a–b;* YHL, chap. 3, p. 1*a*.

102. Fan, YHL, chap. 1, p. 3*b;* PHC, chap. 5, pp. 3*b–*4*a*.

103. Yeh, *Pi Shu Lu Hua*, chap. 1, p. 33.

104. *Sung-shih* (*Po-na-pen* ed.), chap. 318; K'o Wei-ch'i, *Sung-shih Hsin-pien* (1557 ed. [hereinafter cited as "*Hsin-pien*"]), chap. 86.

105. *Pen-mo*, chap. 29, pp. 7*b–*8*a*.

106. *Sung-shih*, chap. 311; Ting, *Sung-jen I-shih*, chap. 7, p. 260.

107. *T'ung-k'ao*, p. 283; Ch'ien, *Kuo-shih*, chap. 2, p. 416.

108. *Pen-mo*, chap. 24, pp. 6*a–*9*b;* Ssu-ma Kuang, *Su-shui Chi-wen*, chap. 5, p. 45.

109. Fan, PHC, *passim;* Ting, *Sung-jen I-shih*, chap. 8, p. 310.

110. Ssu-ma Kuang, *Su-shui Chi-wen*, chap. 3, p. 31.

111. *Pen-mo*, chap. 29, pp. 13*b–*14*a*.

112. *Sung-shih*, chap. 311; *Hsin-pien*, chap. 39.

113. *Hsin-pien*, chap. 100.

114. *Sung-shih*, chap. 311.

115. *Ibid.*, chap. 266.

116. *Hsin-pien*, chap. 90.

117. *Sung-shih*, chap. 284.

118. Fan, YHL, chap. 2, p. 9*b*.

119. *Sung-shih*, chap. 283; *Hsin-pien*, chap. 86.

120. *Sung-shih*, chap. 318.

121. Yuan Chiung, *Feng-ch'uang Hsiao Tu* (TSCC ed.), chap. 2, p. 28.

122. Ch'ien, *Kuo-shih*, chap. 2, p. 429.

123. Lasswell and Kaplan, *op. cit.*, p. 210.

124. Talcott Parsons has made some observations, though only in a general way from the viewpoint of structural conflict, on the Chinese bureaucratic empire and on the victory of the medieval church in the eleventh century (*op. cit.*, pp. 178–80).

125. SYHA, chap. 1, pp. 54–55.

NOTES TO THE TUNG-LIN MOVEMENT OF THE LATE MING PERIOD

No attempt has been made to burden this paper with the extensive bibliographical impedimenta that a full-scale study of the Tung-lin movement would require. Major sources for various parts of the paper are listed, but citations of sources for specific statements, and especially sources of biographical information about individuals, are reduced to a minimum.

In 1955, after the conference for which this paper was prepared, Father Heinrich Busch published a study of the Tung-lin Academy, its leading philosophers, and some of the political controversies with which it was associated, together with an extensive bibliography, under the title "The Tung-lin Academy and Its Political and Philosophical Significance," in *Monumenta Serica*, XIV (1949–55), 1–163. Working independently over substantially the same sources, Busch and I have arrived, perhaps not surprisingly, at similar conceptions of the Tung-lin movement, though we differ somewhat in approach and emphasis.

I have not undertaken in this paper to explore the problem of contacts between the Tung-lin movement and Jesuit missionaries. That there were significant contacts is suggested by Henri Bernard, "Whence the Philosophic Movement at the Close of the Ming?" *Bulletin of the Catholic University of Peking*, No. 8 (December, 1931), pp. 67–73. That contacts existed but that they were peripheral and of little significance for Tung-lin history has been shown in a still unpublished article entitled "Tung-lin Tang Yü T'ien-chu Chiao," written in 1937 by Fang Hao and kindly made available to me by the author, now on the faculty of National Taiwan University. Cf. Busch, *op. cit.*, pp. 156–63.

1. *Ming-shih* (*T'ung-wen* ed. [hereinafter cited as "MS"]), chap. 305, pp. 18a–28a; Ku Ying-t'ai, *Ming-shih Chi-shih Pen-mo* (*Wan-yu wen-k'u* ed.), chap. 71; T. K. Chuan, "Wei Chung-hsien," *T'ien Hsia Monthly*, III, No. 4 (November, 1936), 330–40; biographical notice in A. W. Hummel (ed.), *Eminent Chinese of the Ch'ing Period* (Washington, D.C.: Government Printing Office, 1943–44).

2. No over-all study of the decline and fall of the Ming dynasty has yet been published, but surveys can be found in most modern general histories of China, especially those in Chinese and Japanese. Standard references are Ku Ying-t'ai (*op. cit.*) and the annals and biographies in MS. An excellent modern bibliography of late Ming historical materials is Hsieh Kuo-chen, *Wan Ming Shih-chi K'ao* (Peking, 1933).

3. MS, chap. 213, pp. 14a–25a; Ku Ying-t'ai, *op. cit.*, chap. 61; Chu Tung-jun, *Chang Chü-cheng Ta-chuan* (Kaiming Book Store, 1945 [reprinted 1947]). A long review of the latter work by Shih-hsiang Chen, entitled "An Innovation in Chinese Biographical Writing," is to be found in *Far Eastern Quarterly*, XIII (November, 1953), 49–62.

4. MS, chap. 218, pp. 15a–16b; Li Wen-chih, *Wan Ming Min-pien* (Special Publication No. 23, Academia Sinica Institute of Social Sciences, 1948), p. 10, n. 1.

5. When Shen-tsung married, the ceremonies cost the state an estimated 90,000 taels. Celebration of the birth of a daughter in 1577 required 100,000 taels. The investiture of various princes involved the expenditure of more than 12,000,000 taels, and the marriages of imperial princesses required another 120,000 taels. When the reconstruction of burned-down palace buildings was undertaken, expenditures on wood alone are reported to have amounted to 9,300,000 taels; and similar construction work within the palace during the reign of Hsi-tsung required 5,950,000 more taels (Li Wen-chih, *op. cit.*, pp. 1–2).

6. Ku Ying-t'ai, *op. cit.*, chaps. 62–64. These "three great expeditions of the Wan-li era" required total expenditures by the central government of an estimated 10,000,000 taels (Li Wen-chih, *op. cit.*, pp. 1–2).

7. For general information about the Manchu conquest of China see Hsiao I-shan, *Ch'ing-tai T'ung-shih* (Shanghai, 1927), Vol. I; Franz Michael, *The Origin of Manchu Rule in China* (Baltimore: Johns Hopkins Press, 1942); and Hummel, *op. cit.*, especially under biographical notice of Nurhaci.

8. See Hummel, *op. cit.*, under Chu Yu-chiao.

9. Ku Ying-t'ai, *op. cit.*, chaps. 69 and 71.

10. Hummel, *op. cit.*, under Chu Yu-chien.

11. Li Wen-chih, *op. cit.*, pp. 1–14; Wang Te-chao, *Ming-chi Chih Cheng-chih Yü She-hui* (Chungking, 1942).

12. An abundance of literature concerning late Ming political struggles is available in Chinese. The narrative given in this paper is based on a variety of standard sources written soon after the events, which primarily include: Wen Ping (1609–69), *Hsien-po Chih-shih* (2 *chüan, Chieh-yueh Shan-fang Hui-ch'ao* ed.); Wu Ying-chi (1594–1645), *Tung-lin Pen-mo* (3 *chüan, Kuei-ch'ih Hsien-che I-shu* ed.); Liu Hsin-hsueh (1599–1674), *Ssu-ch'ao Ta-cheng Lu* (2 *chüan, Kuo-hsueh Wen-k'u* reprint, 1937); Ku Ling (fl. in the 1640's), *San-ch'ao Ta-i Lu* (*Kuo-hsueh Wen-k'u* reprint, 1937); Chiang P'ing-chieh, *Tung-lin Shih-mo* (*Hsueh-hai Lei-pien* ed., identical with Ku Ying-t'ai, *op. cit.*, chap. 66).

Events within the palace are described by a eunuch observer in Liu Jo-yü, *Cho-chung Chih* (24 *chüan, Ts'ung-shu Chi-ch'eng* ed.). Also see the *Ming Shih-lu* (1940 photolighographic reprint) for the reigns of Shen-tsung, Kuang-tsung, and Hsi-tsung; Ku Ying-t'ai, *op. cit.*, chaps. 61, 65, 66, 67, 68, and 71; and biographies of the individuals concerned in works such as MS; Ch'en Ting, *Tung-lin Lieh-chuan* (24 *chüan*, 1711 ed.); and Tsou I, *Ch'i-chen Yeh-ch'eng* (16 *chüan*, 1936 Peking reprint). The most comprehensive modern survey is Hsieh Kuo-chen, *Ming Ch'ing Chih Chi Tang-she Yun-tung K'ao* (Shanghai, 1934 [reprinted 1935]). Also see Wang T'ung-ling, *Chung-kuo Li-tai Tang-cheng Shih* (Peking, 1922 [reprinted 1931]), pp. 173–211.

Sketches of some of the partisan controversies are given in Lin Yutang, *A History of the Press and Public Opinion in China* (Chicago, 1936), pp. 65–73; and E. Backhouse and J. O. P. Bland, *Annals and Memoirs of the Court of Peking* (London: William Heinemann, 1914), pp. 46–78.

13. The following discussion of Ming governmental structure is based primarily on MS, chaps. 72–74; Ch'ien Mu, *Chung-kuo Li-tai Cheng-chih Te-shih* (Hongkong, 1952), pp. 76–101; and Chou Ku-ch'eng, *Chung-kuo Cheng-chih Shih* (Shanghai, 1940), pp. 183–91. Hsieh Kuo-chen has also discussed the relationship of governmental structure, and particularly of the censorial organs, to the partisanship of the late Ming period in his *Ming Ch'ing Chih Chi Tang-she Yun-tung K'ao*, pp. 1–7. Also see Tilemann Grimm, "Das Neiko der Ming-Zeit, von den Anfängen bis 1506," *Oriens Extremis*, I, No. 2 (1954), 139–77.

14. Huang Tsung-hsi, *Ming-i Tai-fang Lu* (*Wan-yu Wen-k'u* ed.), pp. 5–6. Cf. W. Theodore de Bary's study of this work in the present volume.

15. Ch'ien Mu, *op. cit.*, pp. 79–85.

16. MS, chap. 304, p. 1*a*.

17. Ch'ien Mu, *op. cit.*, p. 79.

18. MS, chap. 243, pp. 5*b*–11*a*. Tsou Yuan-piao (*chin-shih* 1577) was recalled to service after Chang Chü-cheng's death but was soon degraded by one of Chang's successors and went home on leave. He became a famous teacher at his own academy in Kiangsi Province. Recalled in 1620, he retired after being denounced by opposition partisans and died at home in 1624. In 1625 he was posthumously erased from the civil service rolls by order of Wei Chung-hsien.

19. *Ibid.*, chap. 231, pp. 1*a*–5*a*. Ku Hsien-ch'eng (*chin-shih* 1580) was degraded in 1587 and finally erased from the rolls in 1594 because of his anti-administration activities. He was the guiding spirit among the philosophers of the Tung-lin Academy, of which he was master until his death in 1612.

20. *Ibid.*, chap. 218, pp. 1*a*–4*b*.

21. *Ibid.*, pp. 4*a*–9*a*.

22. *Ibid.*, pp. 9*a*–14*a*.

23. For data on some of these controversies see Lin Yutang, *op. cit.*, pp. 64–68. I hope to publish separately a detailed analysis of the Wan-li court controversies, which space limitations prevent dealing with here.

24. A handy survey of the history of Chinese academies is Sheng Lang-hsi, *Chung-kuo Shu-yuan Chih-tu* (Shanghai, 1934).

25. The basic source of information on the academy is *Tung-lin Shu-yuan Chih* (22 *chüan*, 1881 rev. ed.). Also see Busch, *op. cit.*, pp. 27–42.

26. *Tung-lin Shu-yuan Chih*, chap. 1, p. 2*a*–*b*. The academy included a front hall, an assembly hall, and a temple, erected amid trees behind a large front gate. Books and sacrificial utensils were housed in rooms added as wings to the temple, and verandas extended from the temple wings at the rear to the front gate, enclosing the academy compound. Study rooms for individual scholars were eventually built along the verandas. Adjoining the academy compound was a temple dedicated to the Sung dynasty Neo-Confucian Yang Shih, who had taught at the site and remained the patron saint of local academicians.

27. MS, chap. 231, pp. 6*a*–8*a*. A *chin-shih* of 1583, Ku Yun-ch'eng had repeatedly denounced current abuses, had been erased from the rolls and then had been restored, and in 1593 had gone home on leave after being degraded. He died in 1607.

28. *Ibid.*, chap. 243, pp. 15*b*–19*b*. Kao P'an-lung (*chin-shih* 1589) had left office after being degraded in 1594 for denouncing the Grand Secretariat's evaluations abuses. His fame as a philosopher was second, in the Tung-lin group, only to that of Ku Hsien-ch'eng. He was recalled to court in 1621 and helped Chao Nan-hsing root out opposition partisans. He left office when denounced for partisanship, was erased from the rolls in 1625, and in 1626 committed suicide.

29. *Ibid.*, chap. 231, pp. 16*b*–18*a*. A *chin-shih* of 1583, Shih Meng-lin had almost immediately returned home on his own initiative after denouncing the administration. Recalled, he had denounced monopolization of power by the Grand Secretariat in 1592 and had been active in controversies in 1593. After living at home on leave for many years, he was subsequently recalled to service in time to participate in a controversy in 1615. He was promptly degraded. Under Hsi-tsung he was restored to office but soon died.

30. *Ibid.*, pp. 14*a*–16*a*. Yü K'ung-chien (*chin-shih* 1580) had been degraded in 1593 and never again took office.

31. *Ibid.*, pp. 19*b*–20*b*. An Hsi-fan (*chin-shih* 1586) in 1593 had protested against successive removal of honest officials by the partisans of Wang Hsi-chueh. He died when he was about to be recalled to service under Hsi-tsung.

32. *Ibid.*, pp. 18*a*–19*b*. A *chin-shih* of 1589, Hsueh Fu-chiao did not again take office after his degradation in 1593. He had been an intimate friend of Ku Hsien-ch'eng and Ku Yun-ch'eng since his boyhood, when his grandfather, Hsueh Ying-ch'i, tutored the Ku brothers.

33. *Ibid.*, pp. 8*b*–13*a*. A *chin-shih* of 1583, Ch'ien I-pen had bitterly criticized Shen Shih-hsing's monopolization of authority and had demanded prompt enfeoffment of the heir apparent. He never took office again after having been erased from the rolls in 1592.

34. *Ibid.*, pp. 21*b*–23*a*. A *chin-shih* of 1595, Liu Yuan-chen was degraded in 1605 after an evaluations controversy. In 1620 he was recalled to service but soon died.

35. *Ibid.*, pp. 23*b*–24*a*. A *chin-shih* of 1589, Yeh Mou-ts'ai did not again enter

service until the opposition factions were in power, and he promptly retired under attack. Under Hsi-tsung he was repeatedly summoned, but he did not respond until the Wei Chung-hsien partisans were about to take control, and he promptly took sick leave in disgust. He was overlooked in the partisan disaster of 1625–26 and died in retirement in 1631.

36. Huang Tsung-hsi, *Ming-ju Hsueh-an* (*Kuo-hsueh Chi-pen Ts'ung-shu* ed.), XII, 11–12 (chap. 60).

37. In his *Ming-ju Hsueh-an* (chaps. 58–61), Huang Tsung-hsi enumerated seventeen members of the Tung-lin school of philosophy. These were Ku Hsien-ch'eng, Kao P'an-lung, Ku Yun-ch'eng, Ch'ien I-pen, Shih Meng-lin, Hsueh Fu-chiao, Yeh Mou-ts'ai, Hsü Shih-ch'ing, Liu Yuan-chen, Wu Chung-luan (MS, chap. 276; p. 12a–b), Wu Kuei-shen (*Tung-lin Shu-yuan Chih*, chap. 9, pp. 1a–4b), Sun Shen-hsing (MS, chap. 243, pp. 11a–15a), Liu Yung-ch'eng, Keng Chü, Hua Yun-ch'eng (MS, chap. 258, pp. 4a–6a), Ch'en Lung-cheng (*ibid.*, pp. 37a–38b), and Huang Tsung-hsi's own father, Huang Tsun-su (MS, chap. 245, pp. 12a–15b).

In the 1620's Kao P'an-lung placed, in the temple of the academy, memorial tablets for Ku Hsien-ch'eng, Ku Yun-ch'eng, Ch'ien I-pen, Hsueh Fu-chiao, An Hsi-fan, and Liu Yuan-chen; and, subsequently, similar tablets were added for Kao himself, Yeh Mou-ts'ai, Hsü Shih-ch'ing, Wu Kuei-shen, and Hua Yun-ch'eng (see *Wu-hsi Chin-kuei Hsien Chih* [41 *chüan*, 1881 ed.], chap. 6, pp. 16b–17a). These men, consequently, should be considered the core of the philosophical movement associated with the academy.

38. Reproduced in *Tung-lin Shu-yuan Chih*, chap. 2, pp. 1a–14b. The document begins with prolegomena praising the ancient Confucians and Chu Hsi. Then it proposes four essentials or "musts" (*yao*) that the academicians should uphold; two "points of confusion" (*huo*) that they should remove from their minds; nine "advantages" (*i*) that might accrue to them through philosophical conferences; and nine "disadvantages" (*sun*), kinds of conduct that might detract from the optimum success of the conferences. Key philosophical points are made in the discussion of the four "musts": (1) "know the root" (*chih-pen*, an argument that human nature must be considered fundamentally good); (2) "establish the aim" (*li-chih*, emphasizing the efficacy of determination); (3) "venerate the classics" (*tsun-ching*); and (4) "investigate motivation" (*shen-chi*, a plea for sincerity). The meeting agreement closes with detailed rules of procedure for the conferences. Cf. Busch, *op. cit.*, pp. 34–40.

39. The academy assemblies were by no means casual gatherings. Ku's rules of procedure (*Tung-lin Shu-yuan Chih*, chap. 2, pp. 13a–14b) required that announcements of the annual meetings be distributed half a month in advance, that participants submit cards of acceptance to designated registrars, and that, as guests arrived at the academy, they be welcomed by the registrars and introduced to the group. Daily assemblies began at noon, with obeisances to a portrait of Confucius hung in the assembly hall and to the shrine of Yang Shih in the adjacent temple. The assemblies ended only in late afternoon. Participants were seated according to a fixed order, with precedence for those who had come from the greatest distance and for the aged. Regular participants served in rotation as hosts, and at each assembly the host was required to give an address on a theme chosen (by himself?) from the Four Books. The address was followed by questions, by discussion, and, in conclusion, by the singing of one or two songs "as an aid in purging stiffness and stagnation and giving outlet to the spirit." Eventually, and per-

haps from the beginning, the singers were assisted by a choir made up of young pupils being tutored at the academy. During the afternoon, tea and cakes were served, and lunch and dinner were provided for guests from afar—four dishes (two of meat) for lunch and six dishes for dinner, with soup, sweetmeats, and four varieties of fruits added at dinner on the final day. "Several servings" of wine were available at dinner; and, though the regulations were strict about such breaches of decorum as interrupting speakers or changing the subject during the afternoon discussions, it was permitted that in the evening guests drink wine according to their individual capacities. Cf. Busch, *op. cit.*, pp. 36–40.

40. The academy discourses of Ku Hsien-ch'eng and Kao P'an-lung are reproduced in *Tung-lin Shu-yuan Chih*, chaps. 3–6.

41. Huang Tsung-hsi, *Ming-ju Hsueh-an*, XI, 50 (chap. 58). At Wu-chin was a newly built Ching-cheng Academy (*t'ang*), sponsored by Ch'ien I-pen (see *ibid.*, p. 95 [chap. 59]; *Chiang-nan T'ung-chih* [204 *chüan*, 1736 ed.], chap. 163, p. 22*b*). Master of the Ming-tao Academy at I-hsing was another Tung-lin associate, Shih Meng-lin, who established it in 1608 on the Tung-lin pattern (see *Tung-lin Shu-yuan Chih*, chap. 22, p. 26*a*). At Ch'ang-shu a Yü-shan Academy was built, during the period when the Tung-lin group flourished, by the philosophically inclined local magistrate, Keng Chü (see n. 37 above), for the specific use of Ku Hsien-ch'eng; and, after Ku's death in 1612, sponsorship was continued by local personages (see Huang Tsung-hsi, *Ming-ju Hsueh-an*, XII, 12 [chap. 60]). At Chin-t'an was a Chih-chü Academy (*t'ang*), established by Yü K'ung-chien (see *Chin-t'an Hsien Chih* [17 *chüan*, 1885 movable-type ed.], chap. 9, pp. 4*b*–5*b;* and Ku Yü-mu *et al.*, *Ku Tuan-wen Nien-p'u* [4 *chüan*, appended to K'ang-hsi ed. of *Ku Tuan-wen Kung I-shu*], chap. 3, p. 36*b*). For reports of Ku's discourses in these satellite academies see *Ku Tuan-wen Kung I-shu*, Vols. IV, V; or *Ku Tuan-wen Kung Chi* (22 *chüan* plus supplementary 4th vol., Ch'ung-chen ed.), Vol. IV.

In 1609 it was apparently agreed that the grand annual assemblies should be held in rotation at Wusih, Wu-chin, I-hsing, and Chin-t'an (see Ku Yü-mu, *op. cit.*, chap. 3, p. 19*b*).

42. This was in the Jen-wen Academy at Chia-hsing, under the sponsorship of Ku's friend Yueh Yuan-sheng, a resident there (see *Ku Tuan-wen Kung Chi*, Vol. IV; or *Ku Tuan-wen Kung I-shu*, Vol. V; and Tsou I, *op. cit.*, chap. 6, pp. 17*a–b*).

43. Hua Yün-ch'eng, *Kao Chung-hsien Kung Nien-p'u* (appended in Vol. XII of 1690 ed. of *Kao-tzu I-shu*), *passim.*

44. Ku Yü-mu, *op. cit.*, chap. 3, p. 14*b*.

45. Jung Chao-tsu, *Ming-tai Ssu-hsiang Shih* (Shanghai, 1940), pp. 298–99.

46. Huang Tsung-hsi, *Ming-ju Hsueh-an*, XI, 50 (chap. 58).

47. See, e.g., Ku Yü-mu, *op. cit.*, chap. 2, p. 20*a–b*.

48. The following discussion of the Tung-lin philosophy is based primarily on Jung Chao-tsu, *op. cit.*, pp. 284–314; Huang Tsung-hsi, *Ming-ju Hsueh-an*, chaps. 58–61; Okada Takehiko, "Tōringaku no Seishin," *Tōhōgaku*, VI (June, 1953), 77–90; and, especially, Ku Hsien-ch'eng's "meeting agreement." Cf. Ch'ien Mu, *Sung Ming Li-hsueh Kai-shu* (Taipei, 1953), II, 272–301; Ch'ien Mu, *Chung-kuo Chin San-pai-nien Hsueh-shu Shih* (Shanghai, 1937 [reprinted 1948]), I, 7–21; and Busch, *op. cit.*, pp. 73–97.

49. For general information about Wang Yang-ming's thought see F. G. Henke, *The Philosophy of Wang Yang-ming* (Chicago, 1916).

50. See Huang Ch'an-hua, *Chung-kuo Fo-chiao Shih* (Shanghai, 1940), pp. 345–46; and Ch'en Yuan, *Ming-chi Tien Ch'ien Fo-chiao K'ao* (Peking, 1940).

51. The following discussion of Li Chih's thought is based on Jung Chao-tsu, *op. cit.*, pp. 231–56. Also see Jung Chao-tsu, *Li Cho-wu P'ing-chuan* (Shanghai, 1936); Shimada Kenji, *Chūgoku ni okeru Kindai Shii no Zasetsu* (Tokyo, 1949), pp. 178–251; and K. C. Hsiao, "Li Chih, an Iconoclast of the Sixteenth Century," *T'ien Hsia Monthly*, VI, No. 4 (April, 1938), 317–41.

52. Shen Shih-hsing, *Sheng-ch'u Hui-lu* (Wan-li ed.), chap. 1, p. 13*b*.

53. MS, chap. 241, pp. 3*b*–7*a*. A *chin-shih* of 1583, Chang Wen-ta was an early critic of Shen-tsung's laxity and extravagance and of the eunuch tax commissioners. He was involved in a court controversy in 1615, and in 1625 he was erased from the rolls. For Chang's denunciation of Li Chih see Jung Chao-tsu, *Li Cho-wu P'ing-chuan*, pp. 50–51.

54. Jung Chao-tsu, *Li Cho-wu P'ing-chuan*, pp. 58–59.

55. See, e.g., Ku Yü-mu, *op. cit.*, chap. 3, pp. 1*a*–2*a*.

56. *Ibid.*, p. 1*b*.

57. Ku Hsien-ch'eng, *Hsiao-hsin Chai Cha-chi* (6 vols., 1608 ed.), chap. 2, p. 7*b*. Cited in Jung Chao-tsu, *Ming-tai Ssu-hsiang Shih*, p. 287.

58. "Expression très employée par les philosophes moralistes des Song et des Ming, pour désigner d'une façon plus concrète l'*étude*, la poursuite de la perfection morale. Nous traduisons cette expression par le *travail (moral)*" (Wang Tch'ang-tche, *La Philosophie morale de Wang Yang-ming* ["Variétés sinologiques," No. 63 (1936)], p. 206).

59. Cf. Fung Yu-lan, *A History of Chinese Philosophy*, trans. Derk Bodde (Princeton, N.J., 1953), II, 624.

60. This is a condensation, in paraphrase, of Ku's long argument about "knowing the root" (*chih-pen*) in his "meeting agreement" (*Tung-lin Shu-yuan Chih*, chap. 2, pp. 4*a*–7*a*).

61. Ku Yü-mu, *op. cit.*, chap. 3, p. 9*b*.

62. MS, chap. 219, pp. 11*a*–13*b*.

63. *Ibid.*, chap. 217, pp. 13*b*–15*b*.

64. *Ibid.*, chap. 240, pp. 1*a*–9*a*. Yeh Hsiang-kao (Fukien, *chin-shih* 1583), as grand secretary, regularly supported the Tung-lin partisans. He retired in 1614, was recalled in 1621, and retired again in 1624. Some notes on Yeh's life are given in Gustav Ecke, "Two Ashlar Pagodas at Fu-ch'ing in Southern Fu-chien," *Bulletin of the Catholic University of Peking*, No. 8 (December, 1931), pp. 49–66.

65. See *Ku Tuan-wen Kung Chi*, III, 2*b*–9*b*, and Busch, *op. cit.*, pp. 52–53.

66. MS, chap. 232, pp. 7*b*–13*b*. Li San-ts'ai (Chihli, *Chin-shih* 1574) was a long-time personal friend of Ku Hsien-ch'eng and a controversial figure from 1608 on. He was considered by its enemies the political generalissimo of the Tung-lin party.

67. *Ibid.*, chap. 224, pp. 14*a*–19*b*; chap. 236, pp. 19*b*–20*a*.

68. *Ibid.*, chap. 216, pp. 13*a*–14*a*. A *chin-shih* of 1583, Wang T'u antagonized Shen I-kuan in 1603–4, supported Sun P'ei-yang in the evaluations of 1611, was denounced by opposition partisans, and went home on leave. He returned to service in 1623 but was impeached in 1624 by Wei Chung-hsien partisans and was erased from the rolls. His brother, Wang Kuo, was another prominent Tung-lin partisan. See MS, chap. 232, pp. 5*a*–6*a*.

69. *Ibid.*, chap. 236, pp. 10*a*–13*a*. A *chin-shih* of 1601, Wang Yuan-han was a notoriously forthright remonstrator. He repeatedly criticized Shen-tsung's laxity,

objected to the eunuch tax commissioners, denounced Li T'ing-chi, and recommended the recall of Tsou Yuan-piao, Ku Hsien-ch'eng, and others. Repeatedly attacked by opposition partisans, he finally left office on his own authority and subsequently was degraded. Under Wei Chung-hsien's regime, he was erased from the rolls.

70. *Ibid.*, chap. 254, pp. 3b–5b. A *chin-shih* of 1592, Ts'ao Yü-pien was a leading figure in the evaluations controversy of 1611, defended Li San-ts'ai, and went home on leave. Recalled in 1620, he supported Chao Nan-hsing in weeding out opposition partisans. While on leave at home in 1624, he was denounced as a Tung-lin ringleader and erased from the rolls.

71. *Ibid.*, chap. 236, pp. 16b–17b. A *chin-shih* of 1586, Ting Yuan-chien was an early disciple of Ku Hsien-ch'eng and subsequently a participant in conferences at the Tung-lin Academy (Ku Yü-mu, *op. cit.*, chap. 2, 11a; chap. 4, pp. 1b–2a). Dismissed from office in the 1590's after denouncing Wang Hsi-chueh, he was recalled and supported Sun P'ei-yang in the evaluations controversy of 1611. Denounced by a fellow-provincial as an ambition-goaded adherent of Ku Hsien-ch'eng and Li San-ts'ai, he was erased from the rolls in 1617. Recalled by Hsi-tsung, he was again erased from the rolls in 1625.

72. Chiang P'ing-chieh, *op. cit.*, *passim; Shan-hsi* [Shensi] *T'ung-chih* (100 *chüan*, 1735 ed.), chap. 60, p. 59a–b; *Shan-hsi* [Shansi] *T'ung-chih* (184 *chüan*, 1892 ed.), chap. 108, p. 24a; *Ch'ung-chi Wei-nan Hsien Chih* (18 *chüan*, 1829 ed.), chap. 13, pp. 25a–29b. Shih Chi-shih was a *chin-shih* of 1595.

73. MS, chap. 254, pp. 5b–7a. A *chin-shih* of 1592, Sun Chü-hsiang successively denounced Shen I-kuan, T'ang Pin-yin, and Fang Ts'ung-che. In 1617 he was transferred to a provincial post and retired. He was recalled in 1621. While on sick leave in 1624, he was denounced as a henchman of Li San-ts'ai, Shih Chi-shih, Chao Nan-hsing, and Yang Lien and was erased from the rolls.

74. See Wu Ying-chi, *op. cit.*, *passim*.

75. MS, chap. 236, pp. 17b–19a.

76. Ku Yü-mu, *op. cit.*, chap. 4, pp. 1b–2a.

77. MS, chap. 224, pp. 14a–19b.

78. *Shen-tsung Shih-lu*, chap. 483, pp. 4b–6b.

79. MS, chap. 218, pp. 14a–20b.

80. Chin Jih-sheng, *Sung-t'ien Lu-pi* (24 *chüan*, *Ch'ung-chen* ed.), chap. 22, pp. 24a–25b.

81. MS, chap. 244, pp. 1a–11a; biographical notice in Hummel, *op. cit.* A Hu-kuang man, Yang Lien was a *chin-shih* of 1607. Early in his official career, while magistrate of a district near Wusih, he had regularly attended conferences at the Tung-lin Academy.

82. MS, chap. 244, pp. 11a–15a. Tso Kuang-tou was an Anhwei man and a *chin-shih* of 1607.

83. See Wen Ping, *op. cit.*, chap. 1, pp. 25b–34a, 39a–41a; Ku Ying-t'ai, *op. cit.*, chap. 68; Tso Tsai, *Tso Chung-i Kung Nien-p'u* (2 *chüan;* appended to *Tso Chung-i Kung Wen-chi* [3 *chüan*, Ch'ing ed.]); Lin Yutang, *op. cit.*, pp. 69–70; and biographical notices of Wang Chih-ts'ai and Yang Lien in Hummel, *op. cit.*

84. MS, chap. 243, pp. 1a–5b. Chao Nan-hsing (Chihli, *chin-shih* 1574) had resolutely refused to flatter Chang Chü-cheng. Erased from the rolls in 1593, he became a symbol of the anti-administration cause. In 1620 he was recalled, and during the early 1620's he vigorously led the Tung-lin struggle to oust opposition partisans.

In 1624 he was dismissed by order of Wei Chung-hsien; then he was erased from the rolls and banished into frontier military service, which he did not survive.

85. *Ibid.*, chap. 305, pp. 17*a*–18*a*.

86. *Ibid.*, chap. 243, pp. 19*b*–21*a*.

87. This was Li Shih, who entered palace service in 1578 and eventually became companion-reader to Shen-tsung's heir apparent. Under Hsi-tsung he apparently lost favor, for he was not originally a partisan of Wei Chung-hsien, and in 1621 he was sent out to be supervisor of textile manufactures in Soochow and Hangchow. It has been suggested that the Tung-lin partisan Huang Tsun-su connived with Li Shih in the hope of using him as a lever to oust Wei Chung-hsien. Subsequently, however, Li was in part responsible for the arrests of many Tung-lin men in the Soochow area (see Wen Ping, *op. cit.*, chap. 2, p. 21*a;* Liu Jo-yü, *Cho-chung Chih*, chap. 15, pp. 19*a*–20*a;* Wu Ying-chi, *op. cit.*, chap. 3, pp. 5*b*–6*a;* MS, chap. 245, pp. 12*a*–15*b*). Cf. pp. 230 ff. in C. O. Hucker, "Su-chou and the Agents of Wei Chung-hsien," *Silver Jubilee Volume of the Zinbun-Kagaku-Kenkyusyo* (Kyoto, 1954), pp. 224–56.

88. This memorial is reproduced in Yang's collected works, *Yang Ta-hung Chi* (2 *chüan, Ts'ung-shu Chi-ch'eng* ed.). A condensed translation is given in Backhouse and Bland, *op. cit.*, pp. 68–72.

89. MS, chap. 245, pp. 18*b*–20*a*.

90. Versions of at least eight such lists are extant:

   a) Tung-lin Tang-jen Pang: 309 names, reproduced in Ch'en Ting, *op. cit.* Three other complete texts are known, not entirely identical (see Chu Tan, "Tung-lin Tang-jen Pang K'ao-cheng," *Yen-ching Hsueh-pao*, XIX [1936], 157–71).

   b) Tung-lin Tien-chiang Lu: 109 names, reproduced in Wen Ping, *op. cit.* Four other complete texts are known, also not identical (see Chu Tan, "Tung-lin Tien-chiang Lu K'ao-i," *Kuo-li Chung-shan Ta-hsueh Wen-shih-hsueh Yen-chiu So Yueh-k'an*, II, No. 1 [October, 1933], 33–65).

   c) Tung-lin P'eng-tang Lu: 94 names, reproduced in Liu Jo-yü, *Cho-chung Chih Yü* (2 *chüan, Cheng-chueh Lou Ts'ung-k'o* ed.), chap. 1, pp. 7–12.

   d) Tung-lin Hsieh-ts'ung: 53 names (*ibid.*, pp. 13–15).

   e) Tung-lin T'ung-chih Lu: 319 names (*ibid.*, pp. 24–29).

   f) Tung-lin Chi-kuan: 162 names (*ibid.*, pp. 30–33).

   g) Tao-ping Tung-lin Huo: 393 names (*ibid.*, pp. 34–57).

   h) Huo-huai Feng-ch'iang Lu: 35 names (*ibid.*, pp. 58–59).

Old manuscript versions of lists *c, d, e, f, g,* and *h,* almost identical in content with the *Cho-chung Chih Yü* texts, are owned by the Seikadō Library, Tokyo. Almost all the lists that are extant seem to have been altered in transmission.

Another Tung-lin party roster, this compiled by a friendly hand, is one entitled *Chung-cheng Piao-t'i.* I have seen only two versions:

   a) In Vol. IV of the old manuscript collection *Pi-ts'e Ts'ung-shuo,* now in the possession of the Academia Sinica Institute of History and Philology, Taiwan: 378 names, without attribution of authorship.

   b) In Vol I of the Naikaku Bunko (Tokyo) copy of Chin Jih-sheng, *Sung-t'ien Lu-pi:* 389 names, with preface and postface both by Chin Jih-sheng, dated 1633. This roster is not included in two other copies of *Sung-t'ien Lu-pi* that I have seen— in the Kyoto University Library and in the Sonkeikaku Bunko, Tokyo.

91. MS, chap. 306, pp. 28*a*–29*a*.

92. *Ibid.*, chap. 244, pp. 15*b*–19*a*. Wei Ta-chung, a Chekiang man, was a *chin-shih* of 1616.

93. *Ibid.*, chap. 306, pp. 11*b*–14*a*.

94. *Ibid.*, chap. 245, pp. 15*b*–18*b*. Li Ying-sheng was a native of Ch'ang-chou Prefecture and a *chin-shih* of 1616. He was a student of Wu Chung-luan (see n. 37 above).

95. MS, chap. 306, pp. 15*b*–18*a*.

96. Besides Yang, Tso, and Wei, the group included Chou Ch'ao-jui, Yuan Hua-chung, and Ku Ta-chang.

Chou Ch'ao-jui (Shantung, *chin-shih* 1607) had treated palace eunuchs with complete contempt, remonstrated forthrightly, and denounced Wei Chung-hsien and his adherents (MS, chap. 244, pp. 20*a*–21*b*).

Yuan Hua-chung (Shantung, *chin-shih* 1607) had impeached Fang Ts'ung-che in 1620, denounced growing eunuch influence in 1621, and had followed Yang Lien in attacking Wei Chung-hsien in 1624. He had thereupon been transferred to a provincial post (*ibid.*, pp. 21*b*–23*a*).

Ku Ta-chang (Soochow, *chin-shih* 1607) had been acquainted with the Tung-lin Academy group since 1607, if not before, though he perhaps did not participate in philosophical conferences there. In the early 1620's he repeatedly antagonized Wei Chung-hsien. He committed suicide in prison (*ibid.*, pp. 23*a*–24*b*; *Su-chou Fu Chih* [160 *chüan*, 1824 ed.], chap. 89, pp. 19*b*–21*a*; *Chiang-nan T'ung-chih*, chap. 153, pp. 11*b*–12*a*).

97. Besides Kao and Li, men imprisoned in 1625 included Chou Tsung-chien, Miao Ch'ang-ch'i, Chou Ch'i-yuan, Chou Shun-ch'ang, Wang Chih-ts'ai, and Huang Tsun-su (see n. 37 above).

Chou Tsung-chien (Soochow, *chin-shih* 1613) had remonstrated with Hsi-tsung about the influence of Madame K'o and had denounced Wei Chung-hsien. In 1625, while at home in mourning, he had been erased from the rolls (MS, chap. 245, pp. 7*b*–11*b*).

Miao Ch'ang-ch'i (Ch'ang-chou Prefecture, *chin-shih* 1613) was allegedly a protégé of Yü Yü-li. He was an active participant in the controversy of 1615. Subsequently he supported Yang Lien's denunciation of Wei Chung-hsien and was dismissed (*ibid.*, pp. 3*a*–5*a*).

Chou Ch'i-yuan (Fukien, *chin-shih* 1601) had been one of the most active Tung-lin partisans in the controversies of 1610–11 and had subsequently been transferred to a provincial post by Fang Ts'ung-che. He became governor of the Soochow area in 1623 and was erased from the rolls after controversies with a local eunuch dignitary, Li Shih, and a henchman of Wei Chung-hsien (*ibid.*, pp. 1*a*–3*a*).

Chou Shun-ch'ang (Soochow, *chin-shih* 1613) had helped restore Tung-lin partisans to power in the early 1620's. Subsequently, while living at home on leave, he had denounced Wei Chung-hsien in indignation at the treatment accorded his friends Chou Ch'i-yuan and Wei Ta-chung (*ibid.*, pp. 5*a*–6*b*). My article, "Su-chou and the Agents of Wei Chung-hsien" (see n. 87 above), is a study of a popular uprising that followed Chou Shun-ch'ang's arrest.

Wang Chih-ts'ai (Shensi, *chin-shih* 1601) was a central figure during the court controversies of 1615 and 1620 and one of the most vigorous Tung-lin partisans during the early 1620's. He had been removed from the rolls in opposition-controlled

merit evaluations in 1617 but restored to service by Hsi-tsung (MS, chap. 244, pp. 25a–30b; biographical notice in Hummel, *op. cit.*).

98. *Hsi-tsung Shih-lu*, chap. 57, pp. 7a–8a; Sheng Lang-hsi, *op. cit.*, pp. 87 ff.

99. In 1628, after the era of persecution had ended, Wu Kuei-shen, a disciple of Kao P'an-lung and a long-time participant in the Tung-lin conferences (see n. 37 above), rebuilt the academy's front hall, wrote a supplement to Ku Hsien-ch'eng's "meeting agreement," and revived the philosophical conferences. From Wu's death in 1632, until 1653, the academy seems to have been neglected, but then one of Kao's nephews, Kao Shih-t'ai, again revived the conferences, rebuilt the temple in the rear of the academy compound, and wrote yet another supplement to the old "meeting agreement." Finally, in 1693–94 the assembly hall was rebuilt. But the academy never again flourished as it had under Ku Hsien-ch'eng and Kao P'an-lung (*Tung-lin Shu-yuan Chih*, chap. 1, pp. 2b–3a).

100. Several variant versions of this roster are extant: (a) in Wen Ping, *op. cit.*, chap. 2; (b) in Liu Jo-yü, *Cho-chung Chih Yü*, chap. 2; (c) in *Pi-ts'e Ts'ung-shuo*, Vol. XIII; and (d) in an old manuscript owned by the Seikadō Library, Tokyo. It appears likely that these lists, like the Tung-lin rosters, have been altered in transmission.

Another list of anti–Tung-lin men is *T'ien-chien Lu*, compiled about 1625 to show Wei Chung-hsien who were his friends. Perhaps the only extant version of this roster is that included in Liu Jo-yü, *Cho-chung Chih Yü* (chap. 1, pp. 60–61), which lists 105 names. A not quite identical roster, without a title but with an identical introductory statement, is appended to the *Pi-ts'e Ts'ung-shuo* version of the *Tung-lin Tien-chiang Lu*.

In all, 377 different anti–Tung-lin men are identified in these various lists.

101. *Tung-lin Tang-jen Pang* and *Tung-lin Tien-chiang Lu* (see n. 90 above).

102. The general population figures are those for 1578, as modified by O. B. van der Sprenkel in his article, "Population Statistics of Ming China," *Bulletin of the School of Oriental and African Studies, University of London*, XIV, No. 2 (1953), 289–326.

103. By Miao Ching-ch'ih (*Yen-hua-tung T'ang Hsiao-p'in* ed.). The seventeen men dealt with are Yang Lien, Tso Kuang-tou, Wei Ta-chung, Chou Ch'ao-jui, Yuan Hua-chung, Ku Ta-chang, Wan Ching, Chao Nan-hsing, Miao Ch'ang-ch'i, Chou Tsung-chien, Chou Shun-ch'ang, Chou Ch'i-yuan, Kao P'an-lung, Huang Tsun-su, Li Ying-sheng, Hsia Chih-ling, and Wu Yü-chung.

Hsia Chih-ling, a Honan man, was a censor who repeatedly offended Wei Chung-hsien and Ts'ui Ch'eng-hsiu. He was impeached, erased from the rolls, impeached again, arrested, imprisoned, and tortured to death (MS, chap. 245, p. 20b).

Wu Yü-chung, a Hukuang man, was another censor who offended Wei. He died after being beaten in court (*ibid.*, pp. 20b–21a).

104. Ku Yü-mu, *op. cit.*, chap. 2, pp. 1a–2a.

105. Hua Yun-ch'eng, *op. cit.*, pp. 1a–1b; *Tung-lin T'ung-nan Lu*, chap. 1, pp. 29a–30b.

106. See, e.g., Ku Yü-mu, *op. cit.*, chap. 2, pp. 9b, 11b, 13a. Ku Hsien-ch'eng's use of this term generally appears to suggest the philosophical group rather than the political group.

107. MS, chap. 244, p. 3b.

108. *Ibid.*, chap. 243, pp. 5b–11a.

109. Hua Yun-ch'eng, *op. cit.*, p. 18*b*.

110. See n. 37 above.

111. MS, chap. 240, pp. 1*a*–9*a;* chap. 245, pp. 12*a*–15*b*.

112. Huang Tsung-hsi, *Ming-ju Hsueh-an*, XII, 18–19 (chap. 61).

113. MS, chap. 245, pp. 12*a*–15*b*.

114. Huang Tsung-hsi, *Ming-ju Hsueh-an*, VIII, 50–51 (chap. 41); Jung Chao-tsu, *Ming-tai Ssu-hsiang Shih*, p. 299.

115. See n. 97 above.

116. Yin Hsien-ch'en, *Chou Chung-chieh Kung Nien-p'u* (in *Ts'ung-shu Chi-ch'eng* ed. of *Chou Chung-chieh Kung Chin-yü Chi*), chap 4, p. 34.

NOTES TO CHINESE DESPOTISM AND THE CONFUCIAN IDEAL: A SEVENTEENTH-CENTURY VIEW

1. To be published in the "Records of Civilization, Oriental Series," by Columbia University Press, in Spring, 1957. The original text of the *Ming-i Tai-fang Lu* (abbreviated "MITFL") consulted for present purposes is the woodblock edition of the Erh-lao ko, edited by Cheng Hsing and published between 1737 and 1743.

2. Cf. James Legge, *The Chinese Classics* (Oxford, 1893–95), III, 269, 278, 320 ff.; *The Sacred Books* (Oxford, 1899), XVI, 269, 242, 311.

3. Chang Ping-lin, *T'ai-yen Wen-lu* (*Chang-shih Ts'ung-shu* ed.), chap. 1, p. 116*b*. Liang Ch'i-ch'ao attempted to defend Huang from this charge by claiming that the death of the first Manchu emperor and the immaturity of his heir had in 1662 encouraged Ming adherents to believe that the new dynasty would soon collapse (*Chin San-pai-nien Hsueh-shu Shih* in *Yin-ping Shih Chuan-chi* [*Chung-hua Shu-chü* ed.], XVII, 48). The reference in Huang's preface to Hu Han's prediction of a new cycle, which was about to usher in a Golden Age, lends some credence to this view. However, Ch'üan Tsu-wang, who had studied Huang's writings carefully and was acquainted with members of Huang's family, asserts that Huang wrote this book precisely because he had given up hope for the Ming cause and could do nothing else to perpetuate the best traditions of that dynasty.

4. Ch'üan Tsu-wang, *Chi-ch'i T'ing-chi* (Commercial Press, *Kuo-hsueh Chi-pen Ts'ung-shu* ed. [hereinafter cited as "KHCPTS"]), chap. 22, p. 267.

5. *Ibid.*, wai-pien, chap. 44, p. 1331.

6. It is true that the Ming capital had been changed from Nanking to Peking, but this was done by a virtual usurper of the throne, Yung-lo.

7. Reign title: K'ang-hsi (1662–1722).

8. During the Ch'ing dynasty the name of this famous scholar, Cheng Hsuan, was rendered Cheng Yuan because of the taboo in force during the long reign of K'ang-hsi and the great awe in which he was held thereafter. Cf. *Tz'u-hai*, tzu 284*c*, No. 7; [Sung-pen], *Shih-san-ching Chu-su Fu Chiao K'an Chi* (hereinafter cited as "SSCCS") (*Mai-wang Hsien Kuan* ed., 1887), *Chou Li*, p. ia.

9. On this point cf. Hou Wai-lu, *Chin-tai Chung-kuo Ssu-hsiang Hsueh-shuo Shih* (Shanghai, 1947), II, 116–77.

10. Hu Han, *Hu Chung-tzu Chi* (*Ts'ung-shu Chi-ch'eng* ed. [hereinafter cited as "TSCC"]), chap. 1, p. 2.

11. MITFL, p. 4*b*, ll. 9–10.

12. *Ibid.*, p. 7*b*, ll. 3–5.

13. Topics discussed generally follow Huang's order of presentation in the original. Exceptions to this are the inclusion of his ideas on eunuchs (found at the end of the work) with other topics on the central administration; of his view on petty bureaucracy (next to last in the original) with those on the civil service generally; and of his discussion of border commanderies and location of the capital (found in the middle of the work) at the end along with his observations on military affairs.

14. Lin Mou-sheng misses this fundamental distinction between Taoist romanticism and Confucian idealism when he states (*Men and Ideas* [New York, 1942], p. 196): "Rousseau, father of modern liberalism, Marx, father of modern communism, and Proudhon, father of modern anarchism—all great revolutionary philosophers—assume the primitive state to be the utopian existence. So does Huang."

15. Mencius, Book VII, Part 2, chap. 14.

16. H. H. Dubs, *Works of Hsüntze* (London, 1928), p. 125.

17. Not all Confucianists took this view, however. Fang Hsiao-ju (1357–1402) takes essentially the same position as Huang in his essay on government administration (*Kuan-cheng*). Cf. *Hsün-chih-chai Chi* (SPTK, 1st ser.), chap. 3, p. 9*b*.

18. W. K. Liao, *Complete Works of Han Fei Tzu* (London, 1931), I, pp. 57, 61.

19. MITFL, p. 5*b*, ll. 9–6*a*, l. 2.

20. *Ming Shih*, chap. 95, pp. 1*a* and 3*a*, in [*Ch'in Ting*] *Erh-shih-ssu Shih* (*Han Fen Lou* facsimile reprint of Palace ed. of 1739 [Shanghai, 1916] [all subsequent references to the dynastic histories are from this edition]). Cf. also Ch'en Teng-yuan, "Shu Ming-i Tai-Fang Lu Hou," *Nanking Journal*, IV, No. 2 (1934), 277.

21. MITFL, p. 47*b*, l. 7.

22. Ku Yen-wu was one who subscribed to this view. Cf. *Jih-chih Lu* (Commercial Press, *Kuo-hsueh Chi-pen Ts'ung-shu* ed.), chap. 5, p. 28; chap. 9, p. 33.

23. MITFL, p. 10*b*, l. 10, and p. 11*a*, l. 2.

24. Liao, *Han Fei Tzu*, p. 65. This is essentially a restatement of the view advanced earlier by Mo-tzu: "What the superior thinks to be right all shall think to be right; what the superior thinks to be wrong all shall think to be wrong" (Yi-pao Mei, *Works of Motse* [London, 1929], p. 56).

25. Derk Bodde, *China's First Unifier* (Leiden, 1938), p. 82.

26. MITFL, p. 15*a*, ll. 3–6.

27. If we are to judge from his prefaces to the *Ming-ju Hsueh-an*, Huang's conception of orthodoxy changed later in life, and he would presumably have allowed Buddhism and Taoism a greater measure of toleration.

28. In this essay on schools Huang reveals that he has a special grudge against conceited young magistrates who fail to show sufficient respect to local civilians older and wiser than they.

29. See W. T. de Bary, "A Reappraisal of Neo-Confucianism," in Arthur F. Wright (ed.), *Studies in Chinese Thought* (Chicago, 1953), pp. 88 ff.

30. In only one instance does he cite Su specifically, but the issues he raises had been discussed earlier in Su's essay on "The Land System" (*Chia-yu Chi* [SPTK, 1st ser.], chap. 5, pp. 7*a*–9*b*), and Huang undoubtedly had this in mind when he wrote.

31. In *A Plan for the Prince* this argument is presented in an extremely elliptical manner ("Land System," Books I, II). An essay on taxes in Huang's *P'o-hsieh Lun*

(chap. 1, p. 6b), written much later as a postscript to the present one, clarifies his position somewhat.

32. This assertion is made in the *P'o-hsieh Lun*, chap. 1, p. 6b.

33. *Chia-yu Chi*, chap. 5, p. 8b.

34. His essay on the well-field system, *ching-mou* (*Hu Chung-tzu Chi* [TSCC ed.], chap. 1, pp. 7–11), anticipates many of the points made here by Huang, who was obviously much indebted to his work, and suggests a solution similar to Huang's based on earlier statistics for the Sung dynasty.

35. Huang's work has been cited as an important source for the study of Chinese tax history by modern writers. Cf. Wu Chao-hsin, *Chung-kuo Shui-chih Shih* ("History of Chinese Tax Systems") (Shanghai: Commercial Press, 1937), II, 141; Takashima Katsumi (ed.), *Shina Zeisei no Enkaku* ("The Development of Chinese Tax Systems") (Dairen: South Manchuria Railway, 1933), p. 155.

36. In other words, on land granted the cultivator by the government an additional 5 per cent could be charged as rent.

37. Lin Mou-sheng, *op. cit.*, p. 199.

38. For Confucius the "grass-roots" unit is the family, and the *Great Learning* especially stresses that no state can be well ordered unless the families living in it are first put in order. But in the political sphere what this means is that the ruler must tend to this basic problem before he can achieve harmony on a higher level. It does not mean that the ruler takes his lead from the householders of the land. Rather "the ruler is like the wind, the people like grass; when the wind blows across it, the grass must bend" (*Analects*, XII, 19; Legge, *Chinese Classics*, I, 123).

39. Liang Ch'i-ch'ao, *Chin San-pai-nien Hsueh-shu Shih*, p. 47.

40. *Ibid.*, According to L. C. Goodrich, whose *Literary Inquisition of Ch'ien-lung* (Baltimore, 1935) is the most exhaustive study of the books banned in this period, Huang's *Ming-i Tai-fang Lu* does not appear on any of the extant lists of proscribed books.

41. Liang Ch'i-ch'ao, *Ch'ing-tai Hsueh-shu Kai-lun* (Tokyo, 1938), pp. 32, 141.

42. T'ang Leang-li, *Inner History of the Chinese Revolution* (London, 1930), p. 2. Needless to say, the role of Huang as the ideological and organizational genius of the anti-imperialist struggle is a mythical creation, by which T'ang, as a nationalist, attempts to naturalize and dignify the revolutionary movement. For a more sober statement of Huang's influence on the revolutionary movement see Naitō Torajirō, *Shina Ron* (Tokyo, 1914), pp. 271–73.

43. Hu Shih, *Hu Shih Wen-ts'un Erh-chi* (10th ed.; Shanghai, 1947 [1st ed., 1924]), chap. 3, pp. 11–14 (*Huang Li-chou Lun Hsueh-sheng Yun-tung* ["Huang Tsung-hsi on the Student Movement"]).

44. Chang Ping-lin, *T'ai-yen Wen-lu*, chap. 1, p. 125a.

45. *Ibid.*, chap. 1, p. 128b.

46. Including bribery, "squeeze," extortionate taxation, embezzlement of public funds, and prostitution of their wives (cf. *ibid.*, p. 129a).

47. *Ibid.*

48. Hsiao Kung-ch'üan, *Chung-kuo Cheng-chih Ssu-hsiang Shih* (Shanghai, 1947), p. 264.

49. Hou Wai-lu, *op. cit.*, II, 116.

50. T'an P'i-mo, *Ch'ing-tai Ssu-hsiang Shih-kang* (3d ed.; K'ai-ming, 1947), pp. 8–20.

51. Hou Wai-lu, *op. cit.*, II, 104–64.

52. Hou's application of this view to the interpretation of Ch'ing thought is far less rigid and doctrinaire than that of T'an P'i-mo and shows a much closer acquaintance with Huang's writings. Since in other respects Hou's work is done in a conscientious and thoroughgoing manner, with due regard for his source materials, it is unfortunate that he should be burdened with a theory that tends to obscure, instead of clarify, the real issues. If, for instance, to present Huang in a favorable light he must be characterized as "antifeudal," it becomes extremely difficult to appreciate what he found of value in the Confucian feudal ideal.

53. Hou Wai-lu, *op. cit.*, II, 119.

54. *Ibid.*, p. 113.

55. *Ibid.*, pp. 108–9, 112–13.

56. *Ibid.*, pp. 120, 122, 124.

57. *Ibid.*, p. 128.

58. For a convenient summary of Ku's political beliefs see Hsiao Kung-ch'üan, *op. cit.*, pp. 269–74; and Matsui Hitoshi, *Shina Kinsei Seiji Shichō* ("Sekai Kōbō Shiron," Vol. XV [Tokyo, 1931]), pp. 145–356, 376–94.

59. (1629–83.) Lü's political ideas are discussed in Ch'ien Mu, *Chin San-pai-nien Hsueh-shu Shih* (Shanghai, 1937), I, 69–87.

60. (1630–1704.) For T'ang's political views see his *Ch'ien Shu;* see also Hsiao Kung-ch'üan, *op. cit.*, II, 265–68; and Ch'en Teng-yuan, *op. cit.*, which also presents other parallels to Huang Tsung-hsi's thought on specific issues.

NOTES TO SYNARCHY UNDER THE TREATIES

1. This comprehensive, systematic effort to analyze the dynasties of conquest comparatively was made by a group of fourteen scholars at Kyoto and Tokyo in a wartime research project for the Tōa Kenkyūjo. Some nineteen papers were reduced and revised to form the volume *Iminzoku no Shina Tōchishi* ("History of the Rule of Alien Peoples over China") (Tokyo, 1944; 424 pp.). (The first edition, *Iminzoku no Shina Tōchi Gaisetsu* [1943; 312 pp.], is practically identical.) Contributors included Momose Hiromu, Miyazaki Ichisada, Abe Takeo, Tamura Jitsuzō, and Sudō Yoshiyuki. The chief monographic study in this field (with broad implications) is by Karl A. Wittfogel and Feng Chia-sheng, *History of Chinese Society: Liao (907–1125)* (Philadelphia: American Philosophical Society, 1949; 752 pp.). The important pioneer work is by Owen Lattimore, *Inner Asian Frontiers of China* (New York: American Geographical Society, 1940; 2d ed., 1951; 585 pp.). In revising this paper, I have been much indebted to comments, among others, of James T. C. Liu, Owen Lattimore, and Wolfram Eberhard; note the latter's chapter, "Patterns of Nomadic Rule," in his *Conquerors and Rulers* (Leiden: Brill, 1952).

2. The chief analytic study is by Franz Michael, *The Origin of Manchu Rule in China* (Baltimore: Johns Hopkins Press, 1942; 127 pp.). The chief source has been translated by Erich Hauer as *Huang-Ts'ing K'ai-kuo Fang-lüeh, Die Gründung des Mandschurischen Kaiserreiches* (Berlin and Leipzig, 1926; 710 pp.).

3. On the relation of gentry to dynasty, suggestive theories have been put for-

ward by Wolfram Eberhard, *A History of China* (Berkeley and Los Angeles: University of California Press, 1950; 374 pp.), *passim*.

4. It is a commentary on political science studies of China in the West that the most thorough work in English on the Ch'ing administration is now thirty years old, that of Pao-chao Hsieh, *The Government of China (1644–1911)* (Baltimore: Johns Hopkins Press, 1925; 414 pp., no index), while the chief Japanese work has remained unused, namely, the Taiwan Government-General's eight-volume *Shinkoku Gyōseihō* (Tokyo and Kobe, 1910–14; 3,046 pp.).

5. On the early Portuguese depredations see Richard Thurnwald, *Koloniale Gestaltung: Methoden und Probleme überseeischer Ausdehnung* (Hamburg: Hoffmann und Campe, 1939; 492 pp.), pp. 57–68 and *passim*.

6. On European sea expansion into Asia generally see G. B. Sansom, *The Western World and Japan* (New York: A. A. Knopf, 1950; 504 pp.), Part I, "Europe and Asia."

7. The above developments are dealt with at greater length in J. K. Fairbank, *Trade and Diplomacy on the China Coast* (2 vols.; Cambridge, Mass.: Harvard University Press, 1953; 577 pp.), Part I, "China's Unpreparedness for Western Contact."

8. See *ibid.*, Parts II and III, on the first treaty settlement and its application.

9. See tables in Chao-ying Fang, "A New Technique for Estimating the Numerical Strength of the Early Manchu Military Forces," *Harvard Journal of Asiatic Studies*, XIII (June, 1950), 192–215.

10. References to the sepoys are in, e.g., John Ouchterlony, *The Chinese War* (London, 1844), pp. 39, 92, 152–56 and *passim*.

11. The Anglo-Chinese College was founded in 1818 by the pioneer Protestant missionary Robert Morrison. It was continued under W. C. Milne and remained closely connected with missions in China.

12. The Chinese junk trade played an important economic role in Far Eastern economic history and could be (but has not been) studied in a variety of gazetteers and special sources. See bibliography in J. K. Fairbank and S. Y. Teng, "On the Ch'ing Tributary System," *Harvard Journal of Asiatic Studies*, VI (June, 1941), 135–246.

13. Grace Fox, *British Admirals and Chinese Pirates, 1832–1869* (London: Kegan Paul, 1940), p. 126 and *passim*.

14. See *Huang-Ch'ing K'ai-kuo Fang-lüeh* (*Kuang-pai-sung-chai* movable type ed.; Shanghai), chap. 32, p. 5b; cf. Hauer, *op. cit.*, p. 584.

15. See the British bluebook, *Correspondence and Papers Relating to China* (1840), p. 33, Napier's lithographed statement of August 26, 1834. For this example I am indebted to Mr. Hsin-pao Chang.

16. W. D. Bernard, *Narrative of the Voyages and Services of the Nemesis* . . . (1-vol. ed.; London, 1844), pp. 183, 180, 188, 185, and 331, successively. Cf. Alexander Murray, *Doings in China* (London, 1843), p. 219: "The people, in general, were civil and seemed well-disposed to us, when none of their authorities or soldiers were near . . . readily supplying our men with water or tea."

17. Japanese scholars have gone furthest in study of the comprador system (see Negishi Tadashi, *Baiben Seido no Kenkyū*, and other works described in J. K. Fairbank and Masataka Banno, *Japanese Studies of Modern China* [Tokyo: Tuttle & Co., for the Harvard-Yenching Institute, 1955]).

18. The grain shipments have recently been studied by Harold C. Hinton, "The Grain Tribute System of the Ch'ing Dynasty," *Far Eastern Quarterly*, XI (May, 1952), 339–54.

19. Fairbank, *op. cit.*, p. 220.

20. The latest study of this growth is Rhoads Murphey, *Shanghai, Key to Modern China* (Cambridge, Mass.: Harvard University Press, 1953; 232 pp.).

21. Cf. Stanley F. Wright, *Hart and the Chinese Customs* (Belfast, 1950), p. 220.

22. Inspector-General's circular No. 8 of June 21, 1864. Also in H. B. Morse, *International Relations of the Chinese Empire*, III, 453–60. These sanguine instructions breathed the spirit of the "co-operative policy" then being pursued at Peking (see below).

23. See J. K. Fairbank, "The Definition of the Foreign Inspectors' Status, 1854–55 . . . ," *Nankai Social and Economic Quarterly*, IX (April, 1936), 125–63.

24. See Justice Richard Feetham, *Report of . . . to the Shanghai Municipal Council* (2 vols.; Shanghai, 1931), I, 99–111.

25. Marshall's anglophobia has been widely disseminated through Tyler Dennett's influential volume, *Americans in Eastern Asia* (New York: Macmillan Co., 1922, 725 pp.).

26. On the British and American assistance to Japan in her abolition of extrality see F. C. Jones, *Extraterritoriality in Japan* (New Haven, Conn.: Yale University Press, 1931), p. 155, and Dennett, *op. cit.*, p. 530.

27. As George Kennan (*American Diplomacy, 1900–1950* [Chicago: University of Chicago Press, 1951]) points out, "None of these communications had any perceptible practical effect" at the time. See also Charles S. Campbell, Jr., *Special Business Interests and the Open Door Policy* (New Haven, Conn.: Yale University Press, 1951).

28. This period has been studied by Dr. Mary C. Wright in her manuscript, "The T'ung-chih Restoration," now in process of publication. See also S. Y. Teng and J. K. Fairbank, *China's Response to the West: A Documentary Survey, 1839–1923* (Cambridge, Mass.: Harvard University Press, 1954; 296 pp.).

29. The most recent study is by John L. Rawlinson, "The Lay-Osborn Flotilla," *Papers on China* (Harvard Committee on Regional Studies), IV (April, 1950), 58–93.

30. See the extensive sources described in S. Y. Teng and J. K. Fairbank, *Research Guide for "China's Response to the West"* (Cambridge, Mass.: Harvard University Press, 1954; 84 pp.).

31. Mr. Kwang-ching Liu is making an illuminating study of this Sino-foreign enterprise. See his article, "Financing a Steam-Navigation Company in China, 1861–62," *Business History Review*, XXVIII (June, 1954), 154–81.

32. On this concept (*chi-mi*) see Fairbank, *Trade and Diplomacy*, p. 94.

33. Teng and Fairbank, *China's Response to the West*, pp. 62–63.

34. *Ibid.*, p. 48.

35. *Ibid.*, chaps. vb and xvii.

36. *Ibid.*, p. 53 (quoting Feng's *Chiao-pin-lu K'ang-i*) and p. 68 (quoting *Ch'ing Shih-lu*, edict of November, 1862).

37. Chiang Kai-shek, *China's Destiny* (authorized Wang trans.; New York: Macmillan Co., 1947, p. 77.

NOTES TO CHINESE CLASS STRUCTURE AND ITS IDEOLOGY

1. *Hsün-tzu* (*Ssu-pu Ts'ung-k'an* ed. [hereinafter cited as "SPTK ed."]), chap. 6, p. 2b; H. H. Dubs, *The Works of Hsüntze* (hereinafter cited as "Dubs") (London: Arthur Probsthain, 1928), p. 152.

2. A statement of Liu-tzu. See *Ch'un-ch'iu Tso Chuan Chu-su* (*Ssu-pu pei-yao* ed. [hereinafter cited as "SPPY ed."]), chap. 27, p. 6a; James Legge, *The Chinese Classics* (hereinafter cited as "Legge") (5 vols.; London, 1861–72), V, Part I, 381–82.

3. A statement of Chih Wu-tzu. See *Tso Chuan Chu-su*, chap. 30, p. 16a; Legge, V, Part II, 440.

4. A statement of Yen-kung. See *Kuo-yü* (SPTK ed.), chap. 4, p. 1a.

5. *Tso Chuan Chu-su*, chap. 32, p. 2b; Legge, V, Part II, 458.

6. A statement of Kuo. See *Kuo-yü*, chap. 1, p. 16a.

7. *Meng-tzu Chu-su* (SPPY ed.), chap. 5B, pp. 1b–2a; Legge, II, 125–26.

8. *Meng-tzu Chu-su*, chap. 5A, p. 5a; Legge, II, 120.

9. *Hsün-tzu*, chap. 6, pp. 1b–2a; Dubs, p. 152.

10. *Hsün-tzu*, chap. 13, p. 1a; Dubs, p. 213.

11. *Hsün-tzu*, chap. 5, p. 3b. Cf. Dubs, pp. 123–24.

12. *Hsün-tzu*, chap. 6, p. 2a. Cf. Dubs, p. 152.

13. *Hsün-tzu*, chap. 2, p. 22a–b; Dubs, p. 65.

14. Thus *li* was defined by Hsün-tzu as follows: "*Li* is to nourish. A great man enjoys nourishment and also likes discrimination. And what is meant by discrimination? The answer is that a graded sequence be set up for the noble and the humble, that there is a difference between the elders and the young, and that whether the individuals are poor or rich, unimportant or important, all will be appropriate" (*Hsün-tzu*, chap. 13, pp. 1b–2a; cf. Dubs, p. 214). For a more detailed discussion on the meaning and function of *li* see Ch'ü T'ung-tsu, *Chung-kuo Fa-lü Yü Chung-kuo She-hui* (Shanghai: Commercial Press, 1947), pp. 217 ff.

15. *Hsün-tzu*, chap. 13, p. 1a; Dubs, p. 213.

16. *Hsün-tzu*, chap. 2, p. 22a–b. Cf. Dubs, pp. 65–66.

17. Talcott Parsons, *The Social System* (Glencoe, Ill.: Free Press, 1951), pp. 195–98.

18. *Meng-tzu Chu-su*, chap. 3B, p. 1b; Legge, II, 73.

19. *Hsün-tzu*, chap. 6, p. 4b. Cf. Dubs, p. 121.

20. *Meng-tzu Chu-su*, chap. 7A, p. 6a; Legge, II, 172.

21. *Hsün-tzu*, chap. 8, p. 7a–b.

22. *Hsün-tzu*, chap. 5, p. 9a–b. Cf. Dubs, p. 131.

23. *Hsün-tzu*, chap. 12, pp. 7b–8a. Cf. Dubs, p. 194.

24. *Lun-yü Chu-su* (SPPY ed.), chap. 8, p. 3a; Legge, I, 76.

25. *Lun-yü Chu-su*, chap. 8, p. 3a.

26. *Li-chi Chu-su* (SPPY ed.), chap. 52, p. 7b; Legge, I, 263.

27. Wang Fu, *Ch'ien-fu Lun* (SPTK ed.), chap. 1, p. 10a.

28. Wang Ch'ung, *Lun-heng* (SPTK ed.), chap. 1, p. 1a.

29. *Kuo-yü*, chap. 6, pp. 3b–5a.

30. For the significance of this concept in approaches to the sociology of knowledge see R. K. Merton, *Social Theory and Social Structure* (Glencoe, Ill.: Free Press, 1949), p. 223.

31. H. G. Creel, *Confucius, the Man and the Myth* (New York: John Day, 1949), p. 148.

32. *Lun-yü Chu-su,* chap. 3, p. 5a; Legge, I, 24.

33. *Lun-yü Chu-su,* chap. 13, p. 1a–b; Legge, I, 127–28.

34. *Lun-yü Chu-su,* chap. 12, p. 4a; Legge, I, 120.

35. *Lun-yü Chu-su,* chap. 16, pp. 2b–3b; Legge, I, 174–75. Cf. Hsiao Kung-ch'üan, *Chung-kuo Cheng-chih Ssu-hsiang Shih* (2 vols.; Shanghai: Commercial Press, 1945), I, 43–44.

36. *Meng-tzu Chu-su,* chap. 5A, p. 5a–b; Legge, II, 120–21.

37. *Meng-tzu Chu-su,* chap. 2A, p. 8a; 5A, p. 4b; Legge, II, 38, 118.

38. *Lun-yü Chu-su,* chap. 13, p. 3a; Legge, I, 130–31.

39. *Meng-tzu Chu-su,* chap. 14A, p. 4b; Legge, II, 359.

40. *Meng-tzu Chu-su,* chap. 3B, p. 3a; Legge, II, 76.

41. *Meng-tzu Chu-su,* chap. 1A, p. 6b; 2B, p. 5a; Legge, II, 9, 47.

42. *Meng-tzu Chu-su,* chap. 1A, p. 7a; IB, p. 4a; Legge, II, 11–12, 24.

43. *Li-chi Chu-su,* chap. 53, p. 12a; Legge, I, 274.

44. *Meng-tzu Chu-su,* chap. 5A, p. 4a; Legge, II, 116.

45. *Meng-tzu Chu-su,* chap. 10A, p. 3a; Legge, II, 250–52.

46. *Meng-tzu Chu-su,* chap. 6A, p. 4b; Legge, II, 145. In another instance, the king of Ch'i was willing "to give Mencius a house, somewhere in the middle of the kingdom and to support his disciples with an allowance of 10,000 *chung*" (*Meng-tzu Chu-su,* chap. 4B, p. 4a; Legge, II, 226).

47. *Meng-tzu Chu-su,* chap. 6A, pp. 4b–5a; Legge, II, 145–46.

48. *Meng-tzu Chu-su,* chap. 13B, p. 3a–b; Legge, II, 343–44.

49. Confucius himself made the remark that "in teaching there should be no distinction of classes" (*Lun-yü Chu-su,* chap. 15, p. 6a; Legge, I, 169). Cf. Feng Yu-lan, *A History of Chinese Philosophy,* trans. Derk Bodde (Peiping: Henri Vetch, 1937), pp. 47–52.

50. Ch'ien Mu, *Hsien-Ch'in Chu-tzu Hsi-nien K'ao-pien* (Shanghai: Commercial Press, 1935), p. 77.

51. *Lun-yü Chu-su,* chap. 6, pp. 2a, 3b; chap. 11, pp. 3b, 5b; chap. 13, p. 4a; Legge, I, 50, 53, 106–7, 110; *Shih-chi* (Po-na ed.), chap. 67; *Han-shu* (Po-na ed.), chap. 88, p. 2a.

52. *Lun-yü Chu-su,* chap. 19, p. 2b; Legge, I, 208.

53. Here we may cite the case of Marquis Wen of Wei, who honored Tzu-hsia as his teacher, and the case of the group of scholars who were received by the rulers of Ch'i at Chi-hsia. They were not officially appointed, but they received the salary of *shang ta-fu* and were treated nicely (see *Shih-chi,* chap. 46, pp. 13b–14a; chap. 74, p. 5a; Huan K'uan, *Yen-t'ieh Lun* [SPTK ed.], chap. 2, 13b; cf. Ch'ien Mu, *op. cit.,* pp. 215–21).

54. Chao I, *Nien-erh Shih Cha-chi* (SPPY ed.), chap. 2, p. 9a–b.

55. Cf. Hsiao Kung-ch'üan, *op. cit.,* I, 49–50.

56. *Hsün-tzu,* chap. 5, p. 1b.

57. *Han-shu,* chap. 88, pp. 4b–6a.

58. Hsü T'ien-lin, *Hsi-Han Hui-yao,* chaps. 44, 45; *idem, Tung-Han Hui-yao,* chap. 26.

59. *Hsi-Han Hui-yao,* chap. 44; *Tung-Han Hui-yao,* chap. 26.

60. For details see Ch'ü T'ung-tsu, *op. cit.,* chap. 3.

61. *Kuan-tzu* (SPTK ed.), chap. 1, p. 14a.

62. *Han-shu,* chap. 10, p. 13b.

63. *Ibid.*, chap. 1B, p. 10*b;* chap. 8, p. 24*a;* chap. 12, p. 3*a; Hou-Han-shu* (Po-na ed.), chap. 1A, p. 30*b; Hsü Han-chih* (Po-na ed.), chap. 26, p. 12; *Sung-shih* (Po-na ed.), chap. 199, p. 22*a; Ming-lü Chi-chieh Fu-li* (1908 ed.), chap. 1, pp. 6*a,* 11*a–b; Ta-Ch'ing Lü-li Hui-chi P'ien-lan* (1872 ed.), chap. 4, p. 25*a.*

64. *Wei-shu* (Po-na ed.), chap. 111, p. 12*b; Sui-shu* (Po-na ed.), chap. 25, pp. 9*a,* 18*a; T'ang-lü Su-i* (Lan-lin Sun-shih ed.), chap. 2, pp. 10*b–13a; Sung Hsing-t'ung* (Liu-shih Chia-yeh-t'ang ed.), chap. 2, p. 11*a; Ming-lü Chi-chieh,* chap. 1, pp. 19*a–* 23*a; Ta-Ch'ing Lü-li,* chap. 4, pp. 7*a–b,* 10*a,* 48*a–b,* 60*a.*

65. *T'ang-lü Su-i,* chap. 21, pp. 11*a,* 14*a–b; Sung Hsing-t'ung,* chap. 21, pp. 10*a,* 12*b; Ming-lü Chi-chieh,* chap. 20, p. 11*a–b; Ta-Ch'ing Lü-li,* chap. 27, pp. 31*a–* 32*a.*

66. Vilfredo Pareto, *The Mind and Society,* trans. Andrew Bongiorno and Arthur Livingston (4 vols.; New York: Harcourt, Brace & Co., 1935), III, 1419 ff.

67. Lu Yu, *Fang-weng Chia-hsün (Chi-pu-tsu-chai Ts'ung-shu* ed.), pp. 2*a,* 9*b.*

68. *Han-shu,* chap. 1B, p. 11*b;* 24B, p. 3*a.*

69. *Hsin T'ang-shu* (Po-na ed.), chap. 24, p. 12*b.*

70. Merchants were not permitted to enter on an official career, according to Han regulations (*Han-shu,* chap. 11, p. 3*b;* chap. 24B, p. 3*b;* chap. 72, p. 16*b; Hou-Han-shu,* chap. 81, p. 36*a);* neither were sorcerers (*Hou-Han-shu,* chap. 83, p. 15*a).* Artisans and merchants were not permitted to be officials in Sui and T'ang times (*Sui-shu,* chap. 2, p. 10*b; Chiu T'ang-shu* [Po-na ed.], chap. 43, pp. 3*b,* 7*a;* chap. 177, p. 18*b; Hsin T'ang-shu,* chap. 45, p. 1*a;* chap. 181, p. 5*a).* Under Sung, artisans and merchants were not qualified for the *chin-shih* examination (*Sung-shih,* chap. 155, p. 3*a).* In the Liao dynasty, physicians, diviners, butchers, and merchants were also excluded from the privilege of taking examinations (*Liao-shih* [Po-na ed.], chap. 20, p. 4*b;* chap. 27, p. 4*b).*

71. Here we adopt the terminology of Max Weber. "Class" refers to the possession of property, and "status" refers to prestige (see H. H. Gerth and C. W. Mills, *From Max Weber: Essays in Sociology* [New York: Oxford University Press, 1946], pp. 181 ff.; A. M. Henderson and Talcott Parsons, *Max Weber: The Theory of Social and Economic Organization* [New York: Oxford University Press, 1947], pp. 424–29).

72. *Han-shu,* chap. 48, p. 14*a.*

73. Wang P'u, *T'ang Hui-yao (Wu-ying-tien Chü-chen-pan* ed.), chap. 31, p. 15*a–b.*

74. *Han-shu,* chap. 24A, p. 11*b;* chap. 57A, p. 1*b;* chap. 59, p. 4*b;* chap. 91, p. 8*a–b.* It was remarked in an early Ch'ing source that two wealthy families of Wan-p'ing, Ch'a and Sheng, were fond of associating with the *shih ta-fu* and that they were accused by the censors for this reason (Chao-lien, *Hsiao-t'ing Hsü-lu* [1880 ed.], chap. 1, pp. 63*b–*64*a).*

75. Ch'ao Ts'o's memorial reads: "At the present time the laws and regulations (of the government) disesteem the merchant, but the merchant is already rich and honored. (Laws and regulations) dignify the farmer, but the farmer is already poor and disesteemed. Thus what usage honors is what rulers disesteem; what offices (*li*) debase is what law dignifies" (*Han-shu,* chap. 24A, pp. 11*b–*12*a;* N. L. Swann, *Food and Money in Ancient China* [Princeton, N.J.: Princeton University Press, 1950], p. 166).

76. Max Weber has noted the effect of economic power on status as follows: "Yet if such economic acquisition and power gave the agent any honor at all, his

wealth would result in his attaining more honor than those who successfully claim honor by virtue of style of life. Therefore all groups having interests in the status order react with special sharpness precisely against the pretensions of purely economic acquisition. In most cases they react the more vigorously the more they feel themselves threatened" (Gerth and Mills, *op. cit.*, p. 192).

77. Cf. nn. 67 and 78.

78. The "lazy people" (*to-min*) in Chekiang and the "beggars" (*kai-hu*) in Kiangsu and Anhwei were the same kind of people. Actually they were not beggars. Their main occupation was to render services to others at weddings or funerals. Most of the women supported themselves by dressing the hair of women of ordinary families or by being the *Pan-niang*, the maid who accompanied a bride (Shen Te-fu, *Yeh Hou Pien* [1827 ed.], chap. 24, pp. 29b–30a; idem, *Pi-chou-hsuan Sheng-yü* [*Hsueh-hai Lei-pien* ed.], chap. C, p. 10a.

79. The boatmen (*tan-hu*) are said to have been aborigines of the south, the *Nan-man*. Fishing, gathering of oysters, and collecting pearls were their major occupations. They were not treated as equals by the common people and were not allowed to live on the land by the native Chinese. The boats were their homes (T'ao Tsung-i, *Cho-keng Lu* [*Ching-ti Pi-shu* ed.], chap. 10, p. 5a; Ku Yen-wu, *T'ien-hsia Chün-kuo Li-ping Shu* [SPTK ed.], ts'e 29, pp. 107–8; Ch'ü Hsuan-ying, *Chung-kuo She-hui Shih-liao Ts'ung-ch'ao* [3 vols.; Shanghai: Commercial Press, 1937], II, 389–91).

80. Legally the "permanent servants," *shih-p'u* or *pan-tang*, were neither considered slaves nor classified as "mean" people. However, they were treated by the local populace as "mean" people and were compelled to render services to a family. When they enrolled for examination or purchased an official title, they were always accused by the commoners, who complained that they were "mean" people and not entitled to such privileges. An edict was issued in 1727 to assure their free status. Later, in 1810, however, a distinction was made in the law between two categories: those who were still kept by a master and rendered service in the latter's family were treated as slaves and were allowed to enter the examinations or to purchase an official title only three generations after manumission. On the other hand, those who were not kept by a master and did not render service at the time were treated as free people and were entitled to the above-mentioned privileges three generations later (for details see *Ch'ing Shih-lu* [1937 ed.], Shih-tsung, chap. 56, pp. 23b–28b; Jen-tsung, chap. 223, p. 25a–b; *Ta-Ch'ing Hui-tien Shih-li* [1886 ed.], chap. 158; *Hu-pu Tse-li* [1831 ed.], chap. 3, p. 27a–b; *Hsueh-cheng Ch'üan-shu* [1812 ed.], chap. 43, pp. 29a–30a; *Ta-Ch'ing Lü-li*, chap. 8, p. 18a–b; chap. 27, pp. 59a–62b).

81. E.g., see *Yun-yang Chang-shih Liu-hsiu Tsung-p'u* (1887), chap. 3, p. 2b.

82. *Liao-shih*, chap. 20, p. 3b; *Yuan-shih* (Po-na ed.), chap. 81, p. 9a; *Yuan Tien-chang* (*Ta-Yuan Sheng-cheng Kuo-ch'ao Tien-chang*, 1908), chap. 31, p. 15b; *Ming-shih* (Po-na ed.), chap. 3, p. 9a; *Hsueh-cheng Ch'üan-shu*, chap. 43, pp. 1a ff.

83. According to Ch'ing law, the children of prostitutes, entertainers, and government runners were not allowed to participate in the civil service examinations. Any member of such a family who entered for an examination or purchased an official title was dismissed and given one hundred strokes (*Ta-Ch'ing Lü-li*, chap. 8, p. 16b; *Hsueh-cheng Ch'üan-shu*, chap. 43, pp. 1a, 4a, 5a–b). Although the *yueh-hu* in Shensi and Shansi, the *kai-hu* in Kiangsu and Anhwei, the *to-min* in Chekiang, and the *tan-hu* in Kwangtung were removed from the category of "mean" people in 1723, 1729, and 1730, respectively, they were not allowed to participate in the examinations immediately. Their descendants could have this privilege only after a lapse of

four generations from the time of their change of occupation (*Ta-Ch'ing Hui-tien Shih-li*, chap. 158; *Hsueh-cheng Ch'üan-shu*, chap. 43, pp. 4a–5a).

84. In Ming and Ch'ing times black gowns were worn by the government runners, the so-called *tsao-li* (*Ming Hui-tien* [1587 ed.], chap. 61, p. 39b; *Ming-shih*, chap. 67, p. 23a).

85. It was required in the Yuan dynasty that a male member of the family of a prostitute wear a blue scarf (*Yuan Tien-chang*, chap. 29, p. 8b; *T'ung-chih T'iao-ko* [Peiping: National Peiping Library, 1930], chap. 9, pp. 4a–5a). In the Ming dynasty a green scarf was worn by the actors belonging to the *Chiao-fang-ssu* (*Ming Hui-tien*, chap. 61, 39b; *Ming-shih*, chap. 67, p. 23a).

86. *T'ang-lü Su-i*, chap. 17, p. 7a; chap. 22, pp. 2a–5b; *Sung Hsing-t'ung*, chap. 17, p. 6b; chap. 22, pp. 2b–5a; *Yuan-shih*, chap. 104, p. 7a; chap. 105, p. 13a–b; *Ming-lü Chi-chieh*, chap. 19, p. 5b; chap. 20, pp. 22a–b, 25a–26a; *Ta-Ch'ing Lü-li*, chap. 26, p. 17b; chap. 27, p. 58a–b; chap. 28, pp. 2a–4a.

87. *T'ang-lü Su-i*, chap. 26, pp. 11b–12a, 13b; *Sung Hsing-t'ung*, chap. 26, pp. 14b, 16a; *Yuan-shih*, chap. 104, p. 10a–b; *Ming-lü Chi-chieh*, chap. 25, pp. 8b, 11b; *Ta-Ch'ing Lü-li*, chap. 33, pp. 31a, 40a.

88. For a discussion of the correlation between power and status in a society, see Kingsley Davis, *Human Society* (New York: Macmillan Co., 1949), p. 95.

89. Gerth and Mills, *op. cit.*, p. 416.

NOTES TO REGION, FAMILY, AND INDIVIDUAL IN THE CHINESE EXAMINATION SYSTEM

1. See pp. 239 ff.

2. See p. 238 of this volume; H. G. Creel, *Confucius, the Man and the Myth* (New York, 1949), p. 159; Derk Bodde, "Harmony and Conflict in Chinese Philosophy," in A. F. Wright (ed.), *Studies in Chinese Thought* (Chicago, 1953), p. 51.

3. See, for instance, Chu Hsi in Dschu Hsi, *Djin-si lu, Die sungkonfuzianische Summa*, trans. Olaf Graf, O.S.B. (3 vols.; Tokyo, 1953), II, 461–62. This general Confucian tendency to stress duties rather than rights appears in the emphasis on the subject's duty to criticize an errant ruler rather than on his right of free speech. The duty-doer here merits protection, because he acts for duty's sake.

4. On Confucian objections to examinations see W. T. de Bary, "A Reappraisal of Neo-Confucianism," in A. F. Wright (ed.), *Studies in Chinese Thought* (Chicago, 1953), esp. 92–94. For the *yin-pu* system see K. A. Wittfogel, "Public Office in the Liao Dynasty," *Harvard Journal of Asiatic Studies*, X, No. 1 (June, 1947), 13–40; Ch'ien Mu stresses the merits of this system and the disadvantages of examination measures, to insure objectivity in his *Chung-kuo Li-tai Cheng-chih Te-shih* ("Pros and Cons of Chinese Political History") (2d ed.; Hong Kong, 1954), esp. pp. 64–66. On recommendation see E. A. Kracke, Jr., *Civil Service in Early Sung China* (Cambridge, Mass., 1953), esp. pp. 6–7. For recruitment methods in Sung, *ibid.*, pp. 57–76.

5. See Ch'en Yin-k'o, *T'ang-tai Cheng-chih Shih Shu-lun Kao* ("Notes on the Political History of the T'ang Period") (Chungking, 1943), pp. 10–15; Ma Tuan-lin, *Wen-hsien T'ung-k'ao* (*Chekiang Shu-chü* ed., 1882–96), chap. 29; these numbers do

not include degrees in the classics (*ming-ching*), as noted by Robert des Rotours, *Traité des examens* (Paris, 1932), p. 117.

6. The later T'ang system, under which candidates were known to the examiners, did not effectively prevent patronage of doctoral candidates by leading officials. Note that the loss of Sung population in 1127 meant that the number of graduates per capita actually increased during the Southern Sung. For the T'ang see Des Rotours, *op. cit., passim;* Arthur Waley, *The Life and Times of Po Chü-i* (London, 1949), pp. 18–19, 23. For the tenth century, after the fall of the T'ang, see Wolfram Eberhard, *Conquerors and Rulers* (Leiden, 1952). For the early Sung see Kracke, *op. cit.*, pp. 58–72. For later periods see nn. 18–22.

7. See Ssu-ma Kuang, *Wen-kuo Wen-cheng Ssu-ma Kung Wen-chi* (*Ssu-pu ts'ung-k'an* ed.), chap. 30, pp. 1*a*–5*b;* Ou-yang Hsiu, *Ou-yang Wen-chung Kung Wen-chi* (*Ssu-pu ts'ung-k'an* ed.), chap. 113, p. 10*a*. See also Table 1. The doctorate of letters was only one—but the most important—of several doctoral degrees given at this time. The numbers of doctoral degrees in letters at this time suggest an average of over 200 for a two-year period (cf. Ma Tuan-lin, *op. cit.*, chap. 32, pp. 31*b*–33*b*). For population see below, n. 9. The figures used are earlier than 1100 for some of the Southwest and South Central circuits, so that their ratio of graduates to population may be relatively still lower.

8. The lists of 1148 and 1256 appear in the *Sung-Yuan K'o-chü San Lu* ("Three Records of Sung and Yuan Examinations"), ed. Hsü Nai-ch'ang (1929). For a discussion of other aspects of the lists and their history see Kracke, "Family vs. Merit in Chinese Civil Service Examinations under the Empire," *Harvard Journal of Asiatic Studies*, X, No. 2 (September, 1947), 103–23. The 1148 list is complete for its year, although there are a few scattered items of information lacking. The 1256 list lacks entirely about 5 per cent of its entries, and a number of entries are incomplete, as noted below, but it supplies certain details lacking in the earlier list and supports many of its indications.

9. See Tables 2 and 3. Circuit populations for the period about 1100 follow Chao Hui-jen, "Sung Shih Ti-li-chih Hu-k'ou Piao" ("Table of Sung History Geographic Monograph Populations"), *Yü-kung*, II, No. 2 (September, 1934), 19–30; and *Sung-shih* (Po-na ed.), chap. 88, p. 1*a–b*. For 1162, *Sung Hui-yao Chi-kao*, "Shih-huo," chap. 69, p. 71*a*. For 1223, Ma Tuan-lin, *op. cit.*, chap. 11, pp. 18*b*–20*a*. For 1290, *Yuan-shih* (Po-na ed.), chap. 62, *passim*. Separate figures for Che-tung and Che-hsi are available only for about 1100 and for 1290; for 1162 and 1223, known combined increases are here conjecturally allocated. Data on population changes through the Sung are sufficiently full and consistent to give us some confidence in the general reliability of the figures in terms of households (making allowance for certain obvious errors and assuming some inaccuracy in census reports, especially in border regions). For further discussion of Sung population data see my article, "Sung Society," *FEQ*, XIV, No. 4 (August, 1955), 479–88. The residence data provided by the 1148 and 1256 lists probably indicate most often the actual homes of graduates. In 1256, in many cases both legal and temporary residence are given; in such cases the temporary residence is followed in these tabulations. The one man listed as from occupied North China, without residence in the South, is from a border region, suggesting that in other cases the legal residence is usually the actual. The 1148 list distinguishes between legal and temporary residence in only one case. In others it seems on the whole probable that the legal residence is commonly the actual

or recent residence of the candidate's family (as in the case of those listed from occupied North China). For example, Chu Hsi is known to have moved his actual residence several times, but the legal residence given is that where he probably lived at the time of the examination. Imperial descendants are tabulated separately and not counted under the circuit of their residence.

10. See Table 2. Eight of the sixteen circuits had markedly denser populations: Fu-chien, Che-tung, Che-hsi, Chiang-nan Tung, Chiang-nan Hsi, Ching-hu Nan, Ch'eng-tu, and T'ung-ch'uan. These eight contained all six circuits that in 1148 exceeded the average representation by five men or more per million households, and three of the five similarly above average in 1256 (all three were also among the six of 1148). In the absence of exact city population figures, their relative size can only be inferred approximately from the relative populations of the prefectures in which they are located. The eight circuits with higher ratio of graduates to population in one year or the other held 28 of the 41 prefectures with over 100,000 households as of *ca.* 1100 (the latest full prefectural population data available for the Sung). Among these eight circuits were four of the five with the largest numbers of prefectures of such size.

11. See Table 3. Civil servants also received noble titles as a reward for service, of course, but these did not constitute a separate class in the same way. All imperial clan candidates in 1148 had official forebears in all three generations; in 1256 there was much variation, explained perhaps by the growth of the clan in the interim. One graduate of 1148 was descended from the T'ang rulers, but showed no official forebears in the last three generations. All imperial clan graduates in 1148 received grades in the third and fourth examination groups (of five). In 1256 they were scattered in the first four, over 66 per cent being in the fourth.

12. In the 1256 list the absence of notation that a given forebear held office may indicate in some cases missing information rather than nonofficial status. The resemblance between the two lists in the distribution of official and nonofficial forebears suggests, however, that such cases were not numerous. In tabulating the 1148 data, all cases lacking a definite statement on any one forebear's official service or its absence are excluded. No data on maternal ascendants are available. Nine "new men" by our definition in 1148 and thirteen in 1256 showed officials among three generations of collateral male ascendants. These few cases do not affect the general group totals materially and, being fragmentary, would distort the data for statistical purposes if included. They are all heads of the candidates' households; this atypical relationship would also make them somewhat misleading examples of collateral ascendants in general. Tables of candidates by examination group and by exact degree of relationship in the paternal line for the empire as a whole will be found in Kracke, "Family vs. Merit," *op. cit.* An interesting case of maternal influence on scholarly success in the Ming appears in L. C. Goodrich, "Maternal Influence: A Note," *Harvard Journal of Asiatic Studies*, XII, Nos. 1–2 (June, 1949), 226–30.

13. Twenty new men in 1256 show forebears with examination degrees of some sort; no such data are available for 1148. Ten brothers of new men and one nephew had degrees or offices in 1148, and twenty-three brothers in 1256.

14. See Table 3. Excluding imperial descendants and men from occupied North China, combined residence and official connection data are available on 240 cases in 1148 and on 484 in 1256.

15. The changes in circuit populations between 1100 and 1162 must be strongly

influenced by the devastation of some areas (fighting extended even south of the Yangtze) and the movement of refugees to others. The changes from 1162 to 1223 should represent the long-term changes more faithfully. The population rises reported in 1290—of Chiang-nan Tung to 1,644,369 households and Che-hsi to 2,142,289—might help to explain the high proportion of new men there, while the decline of new men in Fu-chien may be compared with the fall in 1290 to 1,300,817 households. Excluding the imperial clan, graduates whose homes were elsewhere than their legal residences numbered 14 in Fu-chien, 16 in Che-tung, 7 in Chiang-nan Tung. All other circuits combined had 10.

16. See n. 7. The students of the Directorate of Education (Kuo-tzu Chien) were to receive a similar quota, and students related to examining officials would receive a test by another examiner without distinction of circuit.

17. See Table 4. There were also 47 racial South Chinese from other areas. Note that areas for the Mongol period show the following changes from those used for Sung: the old Kuang-nan Tung now moved from South Central to Southeast; the old Kuang-nan Hsi now moved from Southwest to South Central. Quotas in *Yuan-shih* (Po-na ed.), chap. 81, p. 5*b*. For population data see Herbert Franke, *Geld und Wirtschaft in China unter der Mongolen-Herrschaft* (Leipzig, 1949), p. 128. For Southeast see *Yuan-shih*, chap. 62, *passim. Se-mu jen.*

18. See Table 5. The Mongols were the first to incorporate Yunnan in the empire; they occupied Szechwan some time before the fall of the Southeast, and classified the Chinese of the two provinces as North Chinese. The Ming provincial *chü-jen* quotas, in contrast with the Mongol, followed fairly closely the relative provincial populations. There were some clear deviations. Proportionately higher quotas appeared in certain highly developed areas (especially the regions of the Northern and Southern capitals and Fukien) and also in the southwestern border areas (Kwangsi, Yunnan, Kweichow), probably reflecting, in the first case, a larger educated group and, in the second, the wish to insure at least a minimum representation for all areas (see also n. 22). For numbers of degrees see Huang Ch'ung-lan, *Ming Kung-chü K'ao-lueh* ("Outline Study of Ming Examinations") (Ching-ling, 1879), *passim;* P. C. Hsieh, *The Government of China, 1644–1911* (Baltimore, 1925), pp. 162–63. For Ming quotas, *Ming-shih* (Po-na ed.), chap. 70, pp. 5*b*–6*a*. The 1425 rule gave 60 per cent of its places to the South, 40 per cent to the North. The regions defined in 1454 were: *South:* Chekiang, Kiangsi, Fukien, Hu-kwang, Kwangtung, and the places of Ying-ti'ien, Su-chou, and Sung-chiang; *Middle:* Szechwan, Kwangsi, Yunnan, Kweichow, and the places of Feng-yang, Lu-chou, Ch'u-chou, Hsü-chou, and Ho-chou; *North:* Shun-t'ien, Shantung, Shansi, Honan, and Shensi. The quotas were applied at the *hui-shih* examinations. Later deviations from this rule were generally short-lived. Southerners swept the field in 1397; the emperor suspected favor and replaced them entirely with Northerners (*ibid.* and Ku Chieh-kang, "A Study of Literary Persecution in the Ming," trans. L. C. Goodrich, *Harvard Journal of Asiatic Studies*, III, Nos. 3–4 [December, 1938], 254–311, esp. 274–77). For suggestions concerning the Ming data I am indebted to Dr. C. O. Hucker; he is not, however, responsible for any interpretations offered here. For Ch'ing *hui-shih* quotas, Étienne Zi, *Pratique des examens littéraires en Chine* (Shanghai, 1894), pp. 178–79 and *passim*. Note that in Table 5, on nineteenth-century quotas and population, the populous northern Anhwei and northern Kiangsu areas are moved from the Middle Region to the Northern and Southern regions, respectively.

19. For Ming populations see O. B. van der Sprenkel, "Population Statistics of Ming China," *Bulletin of the School of Oriental and African Studies*, XV (1953), 289–326; and Wang Ch'ung-wu, *Yen-ching Hsueh-pao*, XX (1936), 331–73. The nineteenth-century population data are relatively unsatisfactory. See articles of W. F. Willcox in *Journal of the American Statistical Association*, March, 1928, pp. 18–30, and September, 1930, pp. 255–68; S. Couling, *Encyclopedia Sinica* (Shanghai, 1917), p. 488; and sources supplied in C. L. Chang (n. 21 below). The 1885 figures for Szechwan (in the Middle Region) appear improbably large.

20. See tables in Kracke, "Family vs. Merit," *op. cit.*

21. I am greatly indebted to Dr. Chang, Dr. Franz Michael, and Dr. Hellmut Wilhelm for their kindness in arranging for me to consult the manuscript of Dr. Chang's "Studies on the Gentry of Nineteenth-Century China" before its publication and in making available to me rough data from still incomplete studies of nineteenth-century examination lists made by Dr. C. K. Yang and Dr. Chang. Some aspects of the nineteenth-century analysis are suggestive for the interpretation of earlier periods as well. Data on doctoral (*chin-shih*) examinations are drawn from the lists of 1835, 1868, and 1894, and those on the master's (*chü-jen*) examinations from the lists of 1834 and 1851. In estimating the proportion of new men, not only the offices or ranks held by three generations of patrilineal forebears but also any degrees held by them have been used as criteria of official connection, so that the proportions of new men thus obtained (14 per cent for these three examinations, or 19 per cent if another of 1907 be also included) are not easily comparable with figures of the twelfth and thirteenth centuries. In any case, the latter figures would be more comparable to those of the nineteenth-century *chü-jen*, since the nineteenth-century doctoral numbers were more restricted than in the Sung, and lower offices in particular had come to be filled by *chü-jen* as well. Using the same criteria as for the doctors, the proportion of new men here comes to 32 per cent in the two nineteenth-century examinations, and 35 per cent for a similar group based on a biographic analysis (see below). We may note that an earlier study, based on a much smaller number of examination papers gathered at random in Peiping and applying similar criteria, reached a figure of 16.2 per cent for a mixed group, largely of the later nineteenth century, including holders of all kinds of degrees (P'an Kuang-tan and Fei Hsiao-t'ung in *She-hui K'o-hsueh* ["Social Science"], IV, No. 1 [October, 1947], 1–21). Generalizations and inferences concerning the regional distribution of new men among nineteenth-century doctoral graduates are my own, based on the rough notes of Drs. Chang and Yang.

22. The less rigorous competition for the lower degrees would naturally be another factor. Detailed data concerning holders of lower degrees (including those who also passed higher examinations) are to appear in Dr. Chang's forthcoming book, which deals with many aspects of the subject beyond the scope of the present study. Holders of title, grade, degree, or official rank are designated by the term "gentry"; in a strict sense that excludes persons of wealth or prominence not so qualified. Data here cited are based on Dr. Chang's analysis of over 5,000 biographies of the period from 1796 to 1908 (over 2,000 with relevant data).

23. The speculations in this paragraph and those following are my own.

24. The South already dominated Confucian scholarship by the end of the Northern Sung (see Yü Ying, "Sung-tai Ju-che Ti-li Fen-pu Ti T'ung-chi" ["Statistics on the Geographic Distribution of Sung Confucianists"], *Yü-kung*, I, No. 6, [May, 1934], 17–22). See also above, n. 7. The rise of the Southern political power

was slower, but also clear; among the councilors of state (*tsai-chih*) the North supplied about 90 per cent from 960 to 1022, 61 per cent from 1022 to 1085, and 48 per cent from 1085 to 1127. The proportion from the South (including Szechwan) was greatest under Shen-tsung (*ca.* 56 per cent) and Hui-tsung (*ca.* 62 per cent). See Sudō Yoshiyuki, *Sōdai Kanryōsei to Daitochi Shoyū* ("The Rules Governing Officials in the Sung Dynasty and Great Landholdings") (Tokyo, 1950). This book, which was called to my attention by Dr. L. S. Yang after the completion of the present paper, also includes an analysis of data on the regional distribution and social mobility of Sung examination graduates according to the 1148 and 1256 examination lists. Professor Sudō's findings coincide in part with those here presented, but he analyzes the data under somewhat different categories and from a different point of view.

NOTES TO THE FUNCTIONAL RELATIONSHIP BETWEEN CONFUCIAN THOUGHT AND CHINESE RELIGION

1. Alfred Bertholet, "Religion," *Encyclopaedia of the Social Sciences.*

2. Joachim Wach, *Sociology of Religion* (London, 1947), pp. 393 ff.; also William James, *The Varieties of Religious Experience* (London, 1902), pp. 26 ff.

3. Cf. James Legge, *Life and Teachings of Confucius* (London, 1867); D. S. Suzuki, *A Brief History of Early Chinese Philosophy* (New York, 1914); Hu Shih, "Shuo Ju" ("On Ju"), *Academica Sinica Bulletin*, IV, No. 3, 233–84; Liang Ch'ich'ao, *Yin-ping-shih Ch'üan-chi* ("Complete Works of the Ice-drinker's Studio"), XXIII, 138–41.

4. Liang, *op. cit.*; cf. also Chan Wing-tsit, *Religious Trends in Modern China* (New York, 1953), chaps. 1 and 6.

5. *Jen-min Jih-pao* ("People's Daily") (Peiping), January 28, 1953.

6. Sidney D. Gamble, *Ting Hsien, a North China Rural Community* (New York, 1954), pp. 406–7.

7. *Ibid.*

8. *Ibid.*, chap. 10.

9. *Lun-yü*, VII, 20. This interpretation and translation of the Chinese text *kuai li luan shen* is different from most commentaries and Legge's translation of it: "The subjects on which the Master did not talk were . . . extraordinary things, feats of strength, disorder, and spiritual beings." The latter version is contradictory to the fact that the Master did talk a great deal about disorder and refer frequently to spiritual beings. Hence the adoption of the version in the text above. In other places throughout this paper, translations from the *Lun-yü*, *Chung-yung*, and *Meng-tzu* are Legge's.

10. *Lun-yü*, XI, 11.

11. *Ibid.*, VI, 20.

12. H. G. Creel, "Was Confucius Agnostic?" *T'oung pao*, XXIX (1932), 55–99.

13. See the numerous miracles in *Tso-chuan.* Also Fung Yu-lan, *History of Chinese Philosophy*, trans. Derk Bodde (Princeton, N.J., 1952), Vol. I, chap. iii.

14. Max Weber, *Essays in Sociology*, trans. and ed. H. H. Gerth and C. Wright Mills (London, 1947), pp. 350 ff.

15. Leading opinions on this issue have been reprinted in Ku Chieh-kang (ed.),

Ku-shih Pien ("Critical Studies of Ancient History") (Peiping, 1935), V, 343–753.

16. Cf. paper by Wolfram Eberhard in the present volume.

17. Fung, *op. cit.*, chap. iii; H. G. Creel, "Shih T'ien" ("The Meaning of T'ien"), *Yenching Journal*, No. 18 (1935), pp. 59–71; Wen I-to, "T'ien-wen Shih T'ien" ("The Meaning of Heaven in T'ien-wen"), *Tsing Hua Journal*, IX, No. 4 (1934), 873–95.

18. Chan, *op. cit.*, chap. vi.

19. Weber, *op. cit.*, pp. 350 ff.

20. See the Table of Contents, Tung Chung-shu, *Ch'un-ch'iu Fan Lu.*

21. Ma Hsü-lun, "Shuo Ming" ("On Fate"), *Hsueh-lin*, No. 9 (July, 1941), pp. 15–34; also Fu Ssu-nien, *Hsing Ming Ku-hsun Pien-cheng* ("Critical Study of the Ancient Teachings on Human Nature and Fate"), a summary of which appears in Chan, *op. cit.*, pp. 27–29.

22. *Lun-yü*, XII, 5.

23. *Ibid.*, XIII, 38.

24. *Meng-tzu* ("Works of Mencius"), I, 16.

25. *Ibid.*, II, 13.

26. Cf. Lu Fu-ch'en, *K'o-ch'ang I-wen Lu* ("Strange Stories from the Imperial Examination Halls") (Shanghai, 1863).

27. *Lun-yü*, XX, 3.

28. *Ibid.*, XVI, 8.

29. *Ibid.*, II, 4.

30. Fan Wen-lan, "Yü Chieh-kang Lun Wu-hsing-shuo ti Ch'i-yuan" ("A Discussion with Chieh-kang on the Origin of the Theory of the Five Elements"), *Ku-shih Pien*, V, 642.

31. Fung, *op. cit.*, pp. 26–30, 380.

32. *Lun-yü*, VII, 16.

33. Liang Ch'i-ch'ao, "Yin-yang Wu-hsing Shuo Chih Lai-li" ("The Origin of the Theory of Yin-Yang and the Five Elements"), *Ku-shih Pien*, V, 353–59.

34. *Ibid.*

35. Ku Chieh-kang, "Wu-te Chung-shih Shuo Hsia Chih Cheng-chih Ho Li-shih" ("Politics and History under the Cyclical Theory of the Five Virtues"), *Ku-shih Pien*, V, 404–617, esp. tables on pp. 463 and 585.

36. Hsü Wen-shan, "Ju-chia Ho Wu-hsing ti Kuan-hsi" ("The Relation between Confucianism and the Five Elements"), *Ku-shih Pien*, V, 669–703.

37. *Ku-shih Pien*, V, 335–59.

38. Tung Chung-shu, *op. cit.*

39. *Li-chi*, XIV, 3–4; also see the paper by Yang Lien-sheng in the present volume.

40. Cf. Liang Sou-ming, *Chung-kuo Min-chu Tzu-chiu Yun-tung Tsui-hou Chih Chueh-wu* (1932).

41. *Hsün-tzu*, XIII, 24–26, as translated by D. Bodde in Fung, *op. cit.*, p. 351.

42. *Li-chi*, XIV, 5–7, as translated by D. Bodde in Fung, *op. cit.*, p. 352. The present writer has substituted, for the Chinese term *huang fu*, "dreamy state" of mind for Bodde's "lost abstraction" of mind. The term "dreamy state" has been used by William James to describe similar religious experience (see James, *op. cit.*, p. 382).

43. Compare with Robert H. Lowie, *Primitive Religion* (London, 1936), pp. 3–14; also James, *op. cit.*, pp. 6–10.

44. Compare with James, *op. cit.*, pp. 386–88.

45. Cf. the paper by Arthur F. Wright in the present volume.

46. Fu Ch'in-chia, *Chung-kuo Tao-chiao Shih* ("History of Chinese Taoist Religion") (Shanghai, 1946), pp. 145–48.

47. *Ibid.*, pp. 84–93.

48. Lowie, *op. cit.*, p. 30.

49. *Ch'ing-ch'ao Hsü Wen-hsien T'ung-k'ao*, CLIV, 9109.

50. *Ta-ch'ing Lü-li Tseng-hsiu T'ung-tsuan Chi-ch'eng* ("The Laws and Regulations of the Ch'ing Dynasty") (rev. ed.; Shanghai, 1905), Vol. VIII.

51. A similar observation is made by John Shryock in his *The Temples of Anking and Their Cults* (Paris, 1931), p. 35.

52. *Ibid.*

53. Gamble, *op. cit.*, chap. 10.

54. Wright, *op. cit.*

55. *Ta-ch'ing Lü-li*, chap. xvi.

56. Gamble, *op. cit.*

57. *Ch'ing-ch'ao Hsü Wen-hsien T'ung-k'ao*, Vol. CLXVI.

58. *Ibid.*

59. *Ta-ch'ing Lü-li*, Vol. VIII.

60. *Ibid.*, p. 61.

61. Gamble, *op. cit.*

62. Chan, *op. cit.*, p. 81.

63. *Chung-yung*, chap. xxx.

64. See also the example of magic used in an epidemic crisis in Yunnan Province in Francis L. K. Hsü, *Religion, Science and Human Crises* (London, 1952).

NOTES TO THE CONCEPT OF *PAO* AS A BASIS FOR SOCIAL RELATIONS IN CHINA

1. For a general discussion see Marcel Mauss, "Essai sur le don, forme archaïque de l'échange," *Année sociologique*, N.S., Vol. I (1923–24), or English translation by I. Cunnison, *The Gift: Forms and Functions of Exchange in Archaic Societies* (1954). I am indebted to Professor Wolfram Eberhard for this reference.

2. *Li-chi*, "Ch'ü Li," *A*, chap. 1, p. 6a; Legge, *Li Ki*, chap. 1, p. 65. The edition for the Chinese classics is that of the *Shih-san Ching Chu-su*.

3. Arthur H. Smith, *Proverbs and Common Sayings from the Chinese* (rev. ed.; 1902), pp. 289–90.

4. For instance, see Shih T'ien-chi, *Ch'uan-chia Pao, Chih Shih-shih*, p. 31a–b.

5. An early example was Fu Hsien of the Later Han dynasty. See *Hou-Han-shu* by Hsieh Ch'eng, quoted in *Pei-t'ang Shu-ch'ao*, chap. 53, p. 13a.

6. *Lun-yü*, "Hsien Wen," 14, 6a; Legge, *Confucian Analects*, p. 288.

7. *Li-chi*, "Piao Chi," chap. 54, p. 2a; Legge, *Li Ki*, chap. 2, p. 332.

8. On revenge and blood feuds see Ch'ü T'ung-tsu, *Chung-kuo Fa-lü Yü Chung-kuo She-hui* (1947), pp. 50–65. On pp. 50–51 is a list of important Western works on the subject.

9. *T'u-shu Chi-ch'eng* ed., p. 42.

10. Fung Yu-lan, *A Short History of Chinese Philosophy*, ed. Derk Bodde (1948), pp. 148–50.

11. *Ibid.*, p. 50.

12. *T'an-yen* (*Shuo Fu* ed.), pp. 3a–4a. A modified version of this story is in the novel *Ju-lin Wai-shih* (chaps. 12–13), where the warrior is described as jumping into the courtyard from a roof instead of entering by the gate.

13. Fung Yu-lan, *Hsin Shih-lun* (1940), p. 78.

14. *Shuo-yuan* (*Ssu-pu ts'ung-k'an* ed. [hereinafter cited as "SPTK ed."]), chap. 6, pp. 1a–2a.

15. *Lun-yü*, "Li Jen," 4, 10b; Legge, *Confucian Analects*, p. 172.

16. *I Ching*, "Hsi-tz'u," A, chap. 7, p. 8b.

17. *Ch'un-ch'iu Fan-lu* (SPTK ed.), chap. 13, pp. 3b–4a; translated by D. Bodde in Fung Yu-lan, *A History of Chinese Philosophy* (1953), II, 56.

18. *Ch'un-ch'iu Fan-lu*, chap. 13, p. 1a–b; translated by Bodde in Fung, *op. cit.*, p. 48.

19. This definition of *T'ien* has been proposed by Professor Chin Yueh-lin. See Fung, *A Short History of Chinese Philosophy*, p. 192.

20. *Shu-ching*, "T'ang Kao," chap. 8, p. 5a, quoted in Smith, *op. cit.*, p. 43.

21. *I Ching*, chap. 1, p. 11b, quoted in Smith, *op. cit.*, p. 46.

22. *Shih-chi* (*T'ung-wen Shu-chü* ed.), chap. 56, p. 10b; *Hung-ming Chi* (SPTK ed.), chap. 13, p. 5a–b.

23. *Lun-heng* (SPTK ed.), chap. 2, p. 1a–b; translated by Bodde in Fung, *A History of Chinese Philosophy*, II, 163–64.

24. *Tao-tsang* ed., esp. chaps. 35, 45, 92.

25. For a summary of the debates see Kenneth Ch'en, "Anti-Buddhist Propaganda during the Nan-ch'ao," *Harvard Journal of Asiatic Studies*, XV (1952), 166–92. I have touched upon the problem of interpretation of karma in my article, "Hostages in Chinese History," *Harvard Journal of Asiatic Studies*, XV (1952), 520.

26. *Pao-p'u Tzu* (SPTK ed.), *Nei-p'ien*, chap. 6, p. 5a–b.

27. According to commentaries to the *T'ai-shang Kan-ying P'ien*, a *chi* covers 12 years and a *suan* 100 days. See Paul Carus and Teitaro Suzuki, *Treatise of the Exalted One on Response and Retribution* (1906), p. 52.

28. *Pao-p'u Tzu*, *Nei-p'ien*, chap. 6, p. 7b.

29. Carus and Suzuki, *op. cit.*, p. 3.

30. *Ibid.*, pp. 132–34. Tachibana Shiraki, *Shina Shisō Kenkyū* (1936), pp. 39–92.

31. On *yin* see Karl A. Wittfogel, "Public Office in the Liao and the Chinese Examination System," *Harvard Journal of Asiatic Studies*, X (1947), 13–40; E. A. Kracke, Jr., "Family vs. Merit in Chinese Civil Service Examinations under the Empire," *Harvard Journal of Asiatic Studies*, X (1947), 103–23. On *yin-hsü* and *feng-tseng* in later periods see *Ming Hui-tien* (*Wan-li* ed.), chap. 6, and *Ta-Ch'ing Hui-tien Shih-li* (*Kuang-hsü* ed.), chaps. 127–28. On *tsu-hsing* see Niida Noboru, *Shina Mibunhō Shi* (1942), pp. 225–36.

32. Smith, *op. cit.*, p. 302.

33. *Ch'uan-chia Pao*, *Li Yen*, p. 3a.

34. On filial duties as old age insurance, a predominant attitude of village life, see D. H. Kulp II, *Country Life in South China: The Sociology of Familism* (1925), pp. 135–37.

35. *Li-chi,* "San-nien Wen," chap. 58, p. 22*a;* Legge, *Li Ki,* chap. 2, p. 294; *Lun-yü,* "Yang Huo," 17, 4*a–b;* Legge, *Confucian Analects,* p. 328.

36. *Chung-kuo Li-shih Yen-chiu-fa Pu-pien* (1933), p. 201.

37. *Lun-yü,* "Wei Cheng," 2, 4*b;* Legge, *Confucian Analects,* p. 154.

38. *Li-chi,* "Chi Fa," chap. 46, p. 17*a;* Legge, *Li Ki,* chap. 2, pp. 207–8.

39. Talcott Parsons, *The Structure of Social Action* (1949), pp. 550–51.

40. *Tu-i Chih (Pai hai* ed.), *C,* p. 2*a–b,* and *T'ang Yü-lin (Ts'ung-shu Chi-ch'eng* ed.), chap. 4, p. 120. This story has been discussed by Ch'en Yin-k'o, *T'ang-tai Cheng-chih-shih Shu-lun Kao* (1944), p. 61.

41. *Lun-yü,* "Li Jen," 4, 2*b;* Legge, *Confucian Analects,* p. 170.

42. *Lun-yü,* "Wei Ling-kung," 15, 3*a;* Legge, *Confucian Analects,* p. 299.

43. Carus and Suzuki, *op. cit.,* p. 53.

44. *Meng-tzu,* "Li Lou," A, 7A, 4*a; The Works of Mencius,* pp. 294–95.

45. *Meng-tzu,* "Li Lou," B, 8B, 2*b–3a; Mencius,* pp. 333–34.

46. Fung, *A Short History of Chinese Philosophy,* pp. 50–52.

47. *Lun-yü,* "Tzu-lu," 13, 3*b–4a;* Legge, *Confucian Analects,* pp. 271–72.

48. *Meng-tzu,* "Li Lou," B, 8A, 3*b; Mencius,* pp. 322–23.

49. *Lun-yü,* "Tzu-lu," 13, 3*b;* Legge, *Confucian Analects,* p. 271.

50. *Li-chi,* "Ch'u Li," A, chap. 1, p. 10*a; Li Ki,* chap. 1, p. 69.

51. In *The Doctrine of the Mean* (pp. 389–90), or *Chung Yung,* there is an interesting discussion between Confucius and his knightly disciple Tzu-lu on the various types of *ch'iang,* "energy, strength." Although interpretation of the passage is uncertain, it seems probable that the "energy of the South" and the "energy of the North" referred, respectively, to the tradition of the "weakling" gentlemen and that of the knights-errant. The third type of energy, preferred by Confucius, was between the two.

52. *Meng-tzu,* "Kao Tzu," B, 12A, 4*a–b; Mencius,* pp. 431–32.

53. *Meng-tzu,* "Kao Tzu," B, 12A, 6*a–b; Mencius,* p. 448.

54. On this point see the able discussion by Ch'ü T'ung-tsu, *op. cit.,* pp. 214–27.

55. Lao Kan, in his article on knights-errant of the Han dynasty (in *T'ai-ta Wen-shih-che Hsueh-pao,* chap. 1, pp. 1–16), makes the interesting suggestion that ideologically the ancient knights-errant may have been closely related to Taoist philosophy. Proofs for this point, however, are not conclusive.

56. *Han Ch'ang-li Chi (Kuo-hsueh Chi-pen Ts'ung-shu* ed.), chap. 6, p. 54; chap. 7, pp. 37–39.

57. *Hsiao-hsueh Chi-chu (Ssu-pu pei-yao* ed.), chap. 5, p. 8*a.*

58. *Meng-tzu,* "Li Lou," B, 8A, 2*a–b; Mencius,* p. 318.

59. *Meng-tzu,* "Liang Hui-wang," B, 2B, 12*a; Mencius,* p. 167.

60. *Meng-tzu,* "Kao Tzu," B, 12A, 2*b; Mencius,* p. 428.

61. *Lun-yü,* "Li Jen," 4, 2*b;* Legge, *Confucian Analects,* pp. 170–71.

62. In *Lun-yü,* "Yen Yuan," 12, 3*a,* the lines 君君臣臣父父子子 i.e., "(There is government) when the prince is prince, and the minister is minister; when the father is father, and the son is son" (Legge, *Confucian Analects,* p. 256), apparently refer to two pairs of reciprocal virtues rather than four independent, unilateral requirements. Also compare *Kuan-tzu* (SPTK ed.), chap. 2, p. 6*a,* and *Han-shu,* chap. 63, p. 3*a,* where we have 君不君則臣不臣, 父不父則子不子.

NOTES TO THE SCHOLAR'S FRUSTRATION: NOTES
ON A TYPE OF *FU*

1. General information on the *fu* may be found in the Introduction to Georges Margoulies, *Le Fou dans le Wen-siuan* (Paris, 1926); the Introduction to Arthur Waley, *The Temple and Other Poems* (New York, n.d.); the Introduction to Cyril Drummond le Gros Clark, *The Prose Poetry of Su Tung-po* (Shanghai, 1935); the Introduction to Lim Boon Keng, *The Li Sao* (Shanghai, 1935); and an unpublished paper by Ch'en Shih-hsiang, "The Meaning and Origin of the *Fu* as a Literary Genre," which the author was kind enough to put at my disposal. More extensive surveys are contained in the following monographs: Chin Chü-hsiang, *Han-tai Tz'u-fu Chih Fa-ta* (Shanghai, 1934); Suzuki Torao, *Fu-shi Daiyō* (Tokyo, 1936); and T'ao Ch'iu-ying, *Han-fu Chih Shih ti Yen-chiu* (Shanghai, 1939). The last three titles have been used extensively for the compilation of this paper. In addition, for corrections and valuable suggestions I am indebted to Ch'en Shih-hsiang, Hsiao Kung-ch'uan, Vincent Shih, and Yang Lien-sheng.

2. The one contained in chap. 28 of the *Hsün-tzu*. In the *I-wen-chih* of the *Han-shu* (Wang Hsien-ch'ien [ed.], p. 54*b*), Hsün Ch'ing is credited with ten *fu*, which is probably a copyist's error. It lists, in addition, the following *fu* authors of Chou times: Ch'ü Yuan, Sung Yü, T'ang Lo. The reliable pieces of Ch'ü and Sung are not considered *fu* by this writer. The pieces by Sung called *fu* are all doubtful. Of T'ang no piece remains. That he was a contemporary of Sung is attested several times in the old literature, for instance, in the Ch'ü Yuan biography in the *Shih-chi*. The *I-wen-chih* attributes four *fu* to him. The *Hsiao-yen-fu* (Waley, *op. cit.*, p. 27) contains a passage supposedly by T'ang Lo, which is of course just as doubtful as the whole piece. No doubt his writing was similar to the genuine pieces by Ch'ü and Sung. The Ch'ü Yuan biography in the *Shih-chi* mentions one Ching Ch'a as an author contemporary to Sung and T'ang. This name also crops up occasionally in other contexts, as that of a camp follower of King Hsiang of Ch'u. It is also mentioned that he competed with Sung and T'ang in the composition of a *Ta-yen-fu*. But this information is just as doubtful as the *Ta-yen-fu* itself. The *I-wen-chih* then mentions nine *fu* of Ch'in times without naming any authors. This information found its way into the *Wen-hsin Tiao-lung*, which contains a passage stating: "The Ch'in period was not literary minded, but they had some mixed *fu* (*tsa-fu*) (Wang Li-k'i [ed.], p. 23). Thus even if they were real *fu*, their literary value could not have been very high. We have no way of judging what they really were like.

3. The *Han-shu, I-wen-chih*, in its section on *shih* and *fu* lists for Chou and Western Han 106 authors, of whom 78 are authors of *fu*. This figure is not complete; for instance, Tsou Yang, one of the molders of the *fu* style of Han, is not included. This list includes altogether 1,318 pieces, of which 1,004 are *fu* and only 314 are poems. Pieces from both the Han periods that survived whole or in fragments include 230 *fu* as against slightly over sixty poets' poems (in this figure only *fu* in the strictest sense are included, and related genres such as the *ch'i* and the *chiu* have not been counted). These figures have to be evaluated in the light of the fact that the *fu* is usually a composition of considerable length, whereas the *shih* ("poems") are generally rather short.

4. In particular, the 233 titles listed in the section "Tsa-fu" in the *I-wen-chih* may have been of a type that would not lend itself so easily to the interpretation put forward in this paper. None of them survives, however.

5. The following statements are representative of many others: "Le ... Li-sao ... est à juste titre considéré comme l'origine du fou ..." (Margoulies, *op. cit.*, p. 8). On the following page Margoulies links the so-called descriptive *fu* to other pieces of the same body of literature. "They [the *fu* authors] all emulate Ch'ü Yuan and Sung Yü but do not grasp Ch'ü's and Sung's poetic ideas" (Cheng Chen-to, *Chung-kuo Wen-hsüeh Shih* [Peiping, 1932], I, 129). "The poetic genre known as *fu* may be regarded as a development from the *sao*" (J. R. Hightower, *Topics in Chinese Literature* [Cambridge, Mass., 1950], p. 26).

6. Already the *Han-shu, I-wen-chih*, does this.

7. *Han-shu, I-wen-chih*, pp. 58*b*–59*a*.

8. Mao's commentary to Ode 50, stanza 2. Actually the first sentence is Pan Ku's own, and the quotation starts only with the words "climbing high." Mao lists the ability to write *fu* as one of nine prerequisites to becoming a great official.

9. K'ung Yin-ta's subcommentary explains this as ascending a high place, such as a tower or a hill, from which to gain a wide view. The same explanation is given in the *Wen-hsin Tiao-lung*, p. 24. K'ung's explanation is probably due to the fact that, by this time, *fu* which dealt with ascending a high place and describing the view had become one of the most popular types. As far as I can ascertain, the earliest *fu* of this type is the *Teng-lou-fu* by Wang Ts'an, whose dates are 177–217. Thus Mao could not very well have had this kind of *fu* in mind. *Teng-kao* probably stands here for *Teng-t'ai*, i.e., ascending the platform where business of state was transacted.

10. *Lun-yü*, 16, 3; Legge, *Confucian Analects* (hereinafter cited as "Legge"), p. 315.

11. According to the preceding sentence: Ching Ch'a, T'ang Lo, Sung Yü, and Mei Sheng.

12. Obviously with reference to *Lun-yü*, 11, 15 (in Legge's count, 14 [Legge, p. 242]), even though the reading there is *Sheng-t'ang*, not *Teng-t'ang*. The meaning is that Ssu-ma Hsiang-ju would have to be considered superior to Chia I.

13. The quotation is from *Fa-yen*, p. 2; see E. von Zach, *Sinologische Beitrage IV* (Batavia, 1939), p. 7.

14. *Loc. cit.*, pp. 45*b*–46*a*.

15. *Lun-yü*, 13, 5; Legge, p. 265.

16. *Lun-yü*, 14, 25 (in Legge's count, 26 [Legge, p. 286]); this exclamation was meant to be a comment on the smoothness of the envoy Ch'ü Po-yü.

17. This custom is documented in the *Tso-chuan* by a great number of specific cases (see *Concordance to Ch'un-ch'iu*, *s.v.*). It is tempting to link this meaning of the word *fu*, "to recite," from which the name of our literary genre has been derived, to the original meaning of the word as "a military contribution," "a tribute in kind or in service." Reciting poetry may have been considered a tribute to the lord on the part of the learned who were able to do it. Compare the semantics of the English word "tribute." Cases where odes were recited as a genuine tribute, and not yet with a hidden barb, occur in the *Tso-chuan*, e.g., Wen, 3, 6; Legge, I, 237.

18. *Hsing-jen* (Confucius still calls them *Shih-che*). This position is again amply attested in the *Tso-chuan* and the *Shih-chi*: see *Concordance to Ch'un-ch'iu* and *Shih-chi Index*. A highly institutionalized picture of this office is given in *Chou-li*. chap. 38 (Biot, II, 395–417). Here, as in other cases, *Pan Ku* delights in linking a particular school of thought to particular offices in this bible of the Old Texters. It need not be stressed that this in itself is an anachronism. But the fact remains that he can point to a historically well-documented custom.

19. Chap. 83 (Lu Chung-lien's biography and the remnants of his writings have been translated by Frank Kierman in "The Historiographical Attitude of Ssu-ma Ch'ien," a thesis at the University of Washington, 1953). Derk Bodde (*China's First Unifier* [Leiden, 1938], p. 108) follows Ssu-ma Cheng's suggestion that this may not have been the original arrangement; but the rearrangement proposed is entirely historical and would tend to impede Ssu-ma Ch'ien's purpose of characterizing by affinity.

20. *Loc. cit.*, p. 45. I have purposely used the rather vague term "School of Politicians" as a translation of *Tsung-heng-chia*. The strict categorization of Chou thinkers into schools, represented in the *Han-shu, I-wen-chih*, is of late Western Han date. It is in itself inconsistent and does not tally with earlier classifications found, for instance, in the *Shih-chi*. I would include in this school not only those writers listed under the *Tsung-heng-chia* but also those of related schools whose main purpose was political thought and political rhetoric.

21. I have not located this quotation from Yang Hsiung. In the passage quoted above, however, a similar idea is expressed: "Someone asked: Have you not my master, in the days of your youth cherished the writing of *fu?* [Yang] answered: Yes, as a boy I indulged in such petty [pedantic] endeavors. And after a while he added: A grown-up man does not do such things. Someone asked: Can one not through a *fu* criticize by indirection? [Yang] answered: Criticize by indirection indeed! Criticism by indirection may make [the one who is criticized] desist [from the criticized behavior]. If it does not, I am afraid it may not avoid abetting [the criticized behavior]" (see Zach, *op. cit.*, p. 6). The commentator Li Kuei adduces here the story of how Emperor Wu of Han was impressed with the elegance of Ssu-ma Hsiang-ju's *Ta-jen-fu* rather than with its supposed political purport.

22. The *Han-shu* version reads *hsi*, "frivolous," instead of *k'uei*.

23. Chap. 117. The biography contains the texts of most of Ssu-ma Hsiang-ju's *fu*. The last paragraph, of course, is not Ssu-ma Ch'ien's but was added here from the Ssu-ma Hsiang-ju biography in *Han-shu*. The *Han-shu* biography, save for stylistic differences, is almost identical with the one in *Shih-chi*. Bodde (*op. cit.*, pp. 108–9) draws the inference that the *Shih-chi* biography was copied in its entirety from the *Han-shu*. A detailed stylistic analysis of the two biographies by Wong Kai-sau, in an unpublished manuscript, would not bear this out.

24. The reference seems to be to *Lun-yü*, 15, 4 (Legge, p. 296), where Shun is credited with having governed by nonaction.

25. *Shih-chi*, chap. 130.

26. For documentation see T'ao, *op. cit.*, pp. 102–4. T'ao shows that all those known for their political rhetoric are at the same time known as *fu* writers. The official toleration of this school was withdrawn in 140 B.C.; see O. Franke, *Geschichte des chinesischen Reiches* (Berlin, 1930), p. 1297.

27. Peter Theunissen, "Su Ts'in und die Politik der Läng- und Quer-Achse (Tsung-Heng-Schule)" (thesis, Breslau, 1938), pp. 14–16.

28. *Kuei-ku-tzu*. A German translation of this book, by Ch. S. Kim, is to be found in *Asia Major*, IV (1927), 108–46. The manuscript of an English translation by van Gulik was lost during the war.

29. This makes it unnecessary to count Taoism as an independent influence on the *fu*, as T'ao does (*op. cit.*, p. 21).

30. *Chuan-tz'u*, trans. H. Wilhelm in *Monumenta Serica*, XII (1947), 81–83.

31. *Shui-nan*, trans. Hsü Dauling in *Sinica* (1929), 116–20.

32. *Shun-shui*, trans. R. Wilhelm, *Frühling und Herbst des Lü Bu We*, pp. 220–23.

33. According to *Lun-yü*, 11, 2 (Legge, pp. 237–38), political rhetoric was regarded as a discipline even by the Confucianists.

34. By Chang Hsueh-ch'eng (1738–1801). Cf. A. Hummel (ed.), *Eminent Chinese of the Ch'ing Period* (Washington, D.C., 1943–44), 38–41; see especially the section *Shih-chiao* in his *Wen-shih T'ung-i*, in *Chang-shih I-shu* (Commercial Press ed.), I, 17–25. Chang Ping-lin (1868–1936), sections Wen-tzu Ts'ung-lun and Pien Shih of his *Kuo-ku Lun-heng* (Ku-shu Liu-t'ung-ch'u ed., Shanghai, 1924), XIII, 42, 67, 70–71.

35. See Chin, *op. cit.*, p. 409; T'ao, *op. cit.*, pp. 17–21; Liu Hou-tz'u, *Chung-kuo Wen-hsueh-shih Ch'ao* (Peking, n.d.), pp. 111–12. Waley (*op. cit.*, pp. 16–18) hints at the connection without making much of it. Suzuki (*op. cit.*, p. 5) tries to save both theories by making the Ch'u school of poetry dependent upon the School of Politicians. This is rather far-fetched. The origins of the Ch'u school are well known; they have to be looked for in very different quarters.

36. See W. Seufert, "Urkunden zur staatlichen Neuordnung unter der Han Dynastie," *MSOS*, Vols. XXIII–XXV; Hu Shih, "The Establishment of Confucianism as a State Religion during the Han Dynasty," *Journal of the North China Branch of the Royal Asiatic Society*, LX (1929), 20–41; Franke, *op. cit.*, pp. 1,295–320; John K. Shryock, *The Origin and Development of the State Cult of Confucius* (New York, 1932), chaps. 3 and 4; H. H. Dubs, "The Victory of Han Confucianism," *Journal of the American Oriental Society*, LVIII (1938), 435–39.

37. *Meng-tzu*, 6B, 7; Legge, p. 437. The last clause, *i-chang ch'i-te*, could be translated more succinctly as "in order to manifest their power." The *Tso-chuan* does not enumerate these injunctions.

38. See particularly the famous words of Tzu-hsia, *Ssu-hai chih nei chieh-hsiung-ti yeh*, commonly translated as, "Within the four seas, all men are brothers" (*Lun-yü*, 12, 5; Legge, pp. 252–53), which, as the context makes abundantly clear, refer to the brotherhood of *chün-tzu*, and not, as commonly assumed, to the brotherhood of men.

39. By the end of Wu-ti's reign, the scholar's position was still not far advanced. The Shih-ch'ü Discussions and the Discussions on Salt and Iron show that the scholars were a force to be dealt with, but they show also how little tainted with Confucianism government ideology was at that time.

40. In the recent literature I have not yet found a proper interpretation of Hsün-tzu's *fu*. Nobody, as far as I know, has taken up the remark in the *Han-shu* which labels it clearly as a *fu* of frustration. Of course, the *fu* should not be divided up (the parts then being called "riddles in rhyme" [cf. Hightower, *op. cit.*, p. 27]; Hu Shih has translated one of these "riddles" in *Harvard Journal of Asiatic Studies*, II [1937], 383). The *fu* pattern requires that one interpret the piece as a whole, including the "poems" at the end, which correspond to the "coda," *luan*, of many other *fu*.

41. *yü yü hu ch'i yü shih chih pu hsiang yeh*. The *yü-yü-hu* is taken from *Lun-yü*, 3, 14 (Legge, p. 160).

42. Apparently referring to Ch'u, where he was dispossessed after the death of the *Ch'un-shen-chün* in 238.

43. I accept Lu Wen-chao's emendation.

44. I again accept Lu Wen-chao's emendation.

45. Lü-ch'ü was a proverbial beauty.

46. Mo-mu was a proverbially ugly woman. According to the symbolism of the *Book of Changes*, the official stands to the ruler in the relationship of Yin to Yang.

Love affairs are therefore frequently used to symbolize a ruler-official relationship.

47. Chia I (*ca.* 200–168). Biography in *Shih-chi*, chap. 84, and *Han-shu*, chap. 48, translated by Bönner in his *Alte asiatische Gedankenkreise* (Berlin, 1912), pp. 175–94; see R. Wilhelm, *Literatur*, pp. 111–12; Georges Margoulies, *Prose artistique*, pp. 51–54; Alfred Forke, *Geschichte der mittelalterlichen chinesischen Philosophie* (Hamburg, 1934), pp. 11–24.

48. Tung Chung-shu's *fu* is recorded in the *I-wen Lei-chü* and the *Ku-wen-yuan*, and one of its passages is quoted in *Wen-hsuan* commentaries. This makes its position rather trustworthy. Ssu-ma Ch'ien is credited with eight *fu* in the bibliography of the *Han-shu*. This is the only one left. It is recorded in the *I-wen Lei-chü* with passages quoted in *Wen-hsuan* commentaries. Both are translated by Robert Hightower in *Harvard Journal of Asiatic Studies*, XVII, Nos. 1/2 (June, 1954), 200–203 and 197–200, respectively.

49. Chia I, in his *Fu-niao-fu* (translated by Bönner, *op. cit.*, pp. 186–92; by Giles in *Adversaria Sinica*, II, No. 1 [1915], 1–10; by R. Wilhelm, *Literatur*, pp. 111–12), took one way out which Tung Chung-shu rejects: acquiescence in a Taoist attitude. Ssu-ma Ch'ien had much sympathy for this attitude. The closing sentences of his biography of Ch'ü Yuan and Chia I read: "Having read the *Li-sao*, the *T'ien-wen*, the *Chao-hun*, and the *Ai-ying*, I was moved by the intention [expressed in these pieces]. Coming to Ch'ang-sha and seeing the place where Ch'ü Yuan drowned himself, I never can withhold my tears, realizing what a personality he was. Now I have seen Chia I's lamentation for him, and I have begun to wonder why Ch'ü Yuan, who, with all his talent, if he had traveled around to the courts of the sovereign lords, would not have been rejected by any of the states, acted toward himself as he did. After having read the *Fu-niao-fu*, in which life and death are considered equal, and going and leaving [position] are treated lightly, I realize clearly that I was mistaken." (The last clause is misinterpreted by Biallas, *Asia Major*, IV [1927], 66: "Dass er [Chia I] geirrt hat." Bönner, *op. cit.*, translates: "Dass mein Leben verfehlt war.") But Ssu-ma Ch'ien's attitude still differs from that of Chia.

50. Tung Chung-shu's political and historical philosophy has been dealt with in two monographs: O. Franke, *Studien zur Geschichte des konfuzianischen Dogmas und der chinesischen Staatsreligion, das Problem des Tsch'un-ts'iu und Tung Tschungschu's Tsch'un-ts'iu fan lu* (Hamburg, 1920), and Kang Woo, *Les trois théories politiques du Tch'ouen-ts'ieou interprétés par Tong Tchong-chou* (Paris, 1932). Two chapters from the *Ch'un-ch'iu Fan-lu* are translated in *Lectures chinoises*, I (1945), 1–17. Some remarks on his general philosophy may be found in Yao Shan-yu, "The Cosmological and Anthropological Philosophy of Tung Chung-shu," *Journal of the North China Branch of the Royal Asiatic Society*, LXXIII (1948), 40–68; and in Fung Yu-lan, *A History of Chinese Philosophy*, trans. Derk Bodde (Princeton, N.J., 1953), II, 7–87. Neither of the two monographs does justice to Tung as a philosopher.

51. I do not want to enter here into the problem of "the scholar at home." It might be pointed out, however, that the scholars were to be sent up from the provinces by a machinery which the central government at that time could not directly control. The regional point of view, that was expressed by this arrangement, was of course one of the levers with which to lift the position of the scholars— if not to a large degree of independence, at least to a level from which pressures could be applied.

52. Tung Chung-shu's stature was so towering that not even the Old Texters could refuse him his due. I cannot escape the impression, however, that Pan Ku's biography of Tung definitely colors some of Tung's ideas. It is significant that Fung

Yu-lan quotes so frequently from Pan Ku's biography in his interpretation of Tung. Ssu-ma Ch'ien's biography of Tung was translated by Franke (*Studien zur Geschichte des Konfuzianischen Dogmas* . . . , pp. 91–93) and by Woo (*op. cit.*, pp. 15–33); Pan Ku's biography, by Pfitzmaier (*loc. cit.*, 39, 345–84). On the whole question of the tradition of Old Text and New Text scholars see Tjan Tjoe Som's excellent monograph, *Po Hu T'ung: The Comprehensive Discussions in the White Tiger Hall* (2 vols.; Leiden, 1949–52). I differ from Tjan in my interpretation of the political stand of the two schools.

53. Compare the frequent references to the *Book of Changes* in Tung's *fu*. This particular aspect of the New Text school has earned the New Text scholars much ridicule; see, for instance, Bodde, in Fung Yu-lan, *op. cit.*, p. 7. These criticisms overlook the fact that by these means the New Text scholars were supposed to make themselves *masters of their fate*.

54. See H. Wilhelm, "Der Zeitbegriff im Buch der Wandlungen," in *Eranos Jahrbuch*, 1951, 321–48.

55. For an expert characterization of Ssu-ma Ch'ien's ambitions see Kierman, *op. cit.*

56. See above, n. 49.

57. Translated by Chavannes, *Mémoires historiques*, 1, CCXXVI–CCXXXVIII.

58. *Lun-yü*, 14, 38. The translation is from James R. Ware, *The Best of Confucius* (Garden City, N.Y., 1950), p. 143.

NOTES TO THE AMATEUR IDEAL IN MING AND EARLY CH'ING SOCIETY: EVIDENCE FROM PAINTING

1. Cf. Plato's *Republic*, a consistent model for a timeless, permanent social order. Plato held that philosophy, as soon as it turned from the study of nature to set up standards for human things, was at war with the state, potentially; and to banish the chance of conflict between the state, which has the authority, and philosophers out of office, he made the philosophers rulers of the Republic. See Werner Jaeger, *Paideia: The Ideals of Greek Culture* (New York, 1943), II, 71.

2. For the link between constancy of the social structure and constancy of taste see Levin L. Schücking, *The Sociology of Literary Taste* (New York, 1944), pp. 64 ff.

3. For Swift's humanistic attack on "originality" see the famous passage about the "modern" spider (bringing dirt and poison, spun and spat wholly from himself) and the "ancient" bee (pretending to nothing of his own, but ranging through nature to make honey and wax, or sweetness and light) in *An Account of a Battel between the Antient and Modern Books in St. James' Library* (first published in 1704). For his antipathy to science see *Gulliver's Travels*, Part III, chap. 5 ("The Grand Academy of Lagardo"), directed against the Royal Society, the citadel of science, which was challenging the humanities as an intellectual fashion. The conflict between science and letters was already established as a literary theme, e.g., in Shadwell's seventeenth-century play, *The Virtuoso* (i.e., scientist), in which the rhetorician Sir Samuel Formal remarks of Sir Nicholas Gimcrack: "He is an enemy to wit as all Virtuosos are." See C. S. Duncan, "The Scientist as a Comic Type," *Modern Philology*, XIV (September, 1916), 92; and, for the necessarily ephemeral quality of a combined literary and scientific amateurism in that century and the next, B. Ifor Evans, *Literature and Science* (London, 1954), pp. 22–25, 72. For Swift's distaste for utilitarian criteria, and the contrast on this issue between Swift and such

antitraditionalistic "moderns" and devotees of science as Bacon and Locke, see Miriam Kosh Starkman, *Swift's Satire on Learning in "A Tale of a Tub"* (Princeton, N.J., 1950), pp. 72, 9, and Walter E. Houghton, Jr., "The English Virtuoso in the Seventeenth Century" (Part 2), *Journal of the History of Ideas*, III (April, 1942), 215.

4. It should be noted that the formalistic "eight-legged" essay, with its strong emphasis on rhetorical skill and literary culture, became a prominent feature of the examination system in 1487.

5. Étienne Balázs, "Les aspects significatifs de la société chinoise," *Asiatische Studien*, VI (1952), 84.

6. On this suggestion that the cultural prestige of office in China (its economic value is another subject) depended on the external associations of bureaucracy cf. C. Wright Mills, *White Collar: The American Middle Classes* (New York, 1951), p. 247: "The rationalization of office and store undermines the special skills based on experience and education. It makes the employee easy to replace by shortening the training he needs: it weakens not only his bargaining power but his prestige. It opens white-collar positions to people with less education, thus destroying the educational prestige of white-collar work, for there is no inherent prestige attached to the nature of any work; it is, Hans Speier remarks, the esteem the people doing it enjoy that often lends prestige to the work itself."

7. Kenneth Bradley, "Personal Portrait: Sir Andrew Cohen," *London Calling*, No. 745 (February 11, 1954), p. 13.

8. Matthew Arnold, *Culture and Anarchy* (new ed.; London, 1920), p. 31.

9. Victoria Contag, "Tung Ch'i-ch'ang's *Hua Ch'an Shih Sui Pi* und das *Hua Shuo* des Mo Shih-lung," *Ostasiatische Zeitschrift* (hereinafter cited as "OZ"), IX (May–August, 1933), 86.

10. The *Han-lin T'u Hua Yuan*, to give it its full Sung title, was actually founded by the minor dynasty of the Southern T'ang (923–36). See Taki Seiichi, "Shina e no Ni Dai Chōryū ("The Two Main Currents of Chinese Painting"), *Kokka* (hereinafter cited as "KK"), No. 458 (January, 1929), p. 3. It should be noted, however, that A. G. Wenley has expressed doubts that a *hua yuan*, by that name or by variants of it, in fact existed in the Sung dynasty, although various contemporary and near-contemporary sources refer to it. Mr. Wenley infers from a study of the *Sung-shih* that not a *yuan*, or official academy, independent of other governmental departments, but *hsueh*, or schools, under various superior departments, existed then. See A. G. Wenley, "A Note on the So-called Sung Academy of Painting," *Harvard Journal of Asiatic Studies*, VI (June, 1941), 269–72.

11. Contag, *op. cit.*, p. 92.

12. Osvald Sirèn, *A History of Later Chinese Painting* (London, 1938), I, 24.

13. Hu Man, *Chung-kuo Mei-shu Shih* ("History of Chinese Art") (Shanghai, 1950), p. 151.

14. Contag, *op. cit.*, p. 88.

15. Sirèn, *op. cit.*, I, 7.

16. *Ku-kung Shu-hua Chi* (Peiping, 1930), ts'e 1, Pl. 15.

17. Contag, OZ, IX (October, 1933), 178.

18. Fang-chuen Wang, *Chinese Free-hand Flower Painting* (Peiping, 1936), p. 19.

19. Shen Tsung-ch'ien, "Chieh-chou Hsueh Hua Pien," in Yü Hai-yen (ed.), *Hua-lun Ts'ung-k'an* ("Collection of Treatises on Painting") (Peiping, 1937), ts'e 3, chap. 2, p. 1a.

20. Tanaka Toyozō, *Tōyō Bijutsu Dansō* ("Discussions of Far Eastern Art") (Tokyo, 1949), p. 69. For Tung Ch'i-ch'ang's admiration of Mi Fu see *Ku-kung Shu Hua Chi*, ts'e 1, Pl. 15, and Contag, "Schriftcharacteristeken in der Malerei, dargestellt an Bildern Wang Meng's und anderer Maler der Südschule," OZ, XVII (1941), 49.

21. Raphael Petrucci (trans.), *Encyclopédie de la peinture chinoise* (Paris, 1918), p. 48. See Introduction, pp. vi–viii, for dating of the work.

22. Tsou I-kuei, "Hsiao-shan Hua-p'u," in Chang Hsiang-ho (ed.), *Ssu T'ung Ku Chai Lun-hua Chi K'o* (Peking, 1909), ts'e 3, chap. 2, p. 4b.

23. Osvald Sirèn, "An Important Treatise on Painting from the Beginning of the Eighteenth Century," *T'oung pao* (hereinafter cited as "TP"), XXXIV (1938), 154. The reference is to Wang Yuan-ch'i (1642–1715).

24. For these references to the high standing of Tung Ch'i-ch'ang see Naitō Konan, "Tō Kishō Sai Bunki Ezō" ("Tung Ch'i-ch'ang's Portrait of Ts'ai Wen-chi"), *Tōyō Bijutsu* (hereinafter cited as "TB"), I (April, 1929), 64, and Tajima Shiichi (ed.), *Tōyō Bijutsu Taikan* ("General View of Far Eastern Art"), XI (Tokyo, 1912), Pl. 16.

25. The *locus classicus* for the origins of the north-south dichotomy in Chinese painting is Tung Ch'i-ch'ang, *Hua Ch'an Shih Sui-pi*, ed. Wang Ju-lu (Peking, 1840), chap. 2, pp. 14b–15a. This passage has been quoted or paraphrased in almost every serious modern history of Chinese art. One can see Tung's identification of the southern style with the amateur style in a slightly earlier passage in the same work, where he states that *wen-jen chih hua*, "literati-painting," began with Wang Wei (*ibid.*, p. 14a). The earliest extant appearance of the term *wen-jen hua*, as a synonym first for *shih-ta-fu* (or *shih-fu*) *hua* and later also for *nan-hua*, seems to be in the *Hua-p'u* ("Treatise on Painting") of T'ang Yin (1466–1524), where it is recorded as an expression of Wang Ssu-shan, of the Yuan period. See Ise Senichirō, *Ji Ko Baishi Shi Kei Kō Shina Sansuiga Shi* ("History of Chinese Landscape Painting from Ku K'ai-chih to Ching Hao") (Kyoto, 1933), p. 147.

For a discussion of the growing post-Sung correlation between painting style and personal status of the painter, and of Tung Ch'i-ch'ang's friend, Mo Shih-lung, as the original theorist about northern and southern schools and their beginnings, see Yoshizawa Tadashi, "Nanga to Bunjinga" ("Southern Painting and Literati Painting") (Part 1), KK, No. 622 (September, 1942), pp. 257–58.

The following are among the major pre-Ming painters who were later identified as representative figures in one or the other school: *Northern*—the colorist landscapists Chao Po-chü and his brother Chao Po-su and the academicians Liu Sung-nien, Li T'ang, Ma Yuan, and Hsia Kuei, all of the Sung dynasty; *Southern*—the Sung painters Li Ch'eng, Fan K'uan, Tung Yuan, and Chü-jan and the "four masters" of the Yuan dynasty, Huang Kung-wang, Wu Chen, Ni Tsan, and Wang Meng. See T'eng Ku, "Kuan-yü Yuan-t'i Hua Ho Wen-jen Hua Chih Shih ti K'ao-ch'a ("An Examination of the History of 'Academic' and 'Literati' Painting"), *Fu-jen Hsueh-chih*, II (September, 1930), 68.

26. Taki Seiichi, "Shin Keinan *Kudan kinga satsu* ni tsuite" ("On the Picture-Album *Chiu-tuan chin-hua-ts'e*, by Shen Shih-t'ien"), KK, No. 495 (February, 1932), p. 33.

27. Contag, "Schriftcharakteristeken . . . ," *op. cit.*, p. 49.

28. Contag, "Tung Ch'i-ch'ang's . . . ," *op. cit.*, p. 96.

29. Sirèn, *Later Chinese Painting*, I, 182.

30. Yoshizawa (Part 3), KK, No. 624 (November, 1942), p. 346.

31. Victoria Contag, *Die Beiden Steine* (Braunschweig, 1950), p. 37.

32. Ise Senichirō, "Bunjinga—Nanga yori Bunjinga e no Suii" ("Literati Painting—the Transition from Southern Painting to Literati Painting"), TB, III (September, 1929), 7.

33. This description holds true even for most of the scholars in the prominent *Lu* (Hsiang-shan)—*Wang* (Yang-ming) tradition, which was more introspective than the examination-sanctioned Chu Hsi tradition, but which was still in the world of conventional cultural standards, whatever the allegations made by orthodox critics of its antisocial implications. What happened to the relatively rare Ming literatus who embraced Ch'an as though he really meant it, with all its aura of apostasy from Confucian morality and rejection of its textual underpinnings, is suggested by Mr. Hucker's account, in this volume, of the persecution of Li Chih (see pp. 144–45). Obviously, the authoritative exponents of a southern aesthetic in painting met with no such strictures.

34. For the disparagement of the concept of fine arts because of its connotation of conscious planning cf. the late-sixteenth-century scholars Kao Lien and T'u Lung, quoted in Contag, "Tung Ch'i-ch'ang's . . . ," *op. cit.*, p. 95.

35. Ch'in Chung-wen, *Chung-kuo Hui-hua-hsueh Shih* ("History of Chinese Painting") (Peiping, 1934), p. 150.

36. P'an T'ien-shou, *Chung-kuo Hui-hua Shih* ("History of Chinese Painting") (Shanghai, 1935), pp. 161–62; Liu Ssu-Hsün, *Chung-kuo Mei-shu Fa-ta Shih* ("History of the Development of Chinese Art") (Chungking, 1946), p. 98. It is true that, especially in the early Ming period, some fine Buddhist figure-paintings were executed; but these seem to have derived rather from the early Ming passion for imitating T'ang works than from Buddhist religious commitment.

37. For these as Sung concepts of Su Tung-p'o *et al.* see, respectively, J. P. Dubosc, "A New Approach to Chinese Painting," *Oriental Art* (hereinafter cited as "OA"), III (1950), 53; Louise Wallace Hackney and Yau Chang-foo, *A Study of Chinese Paintings in the Collection of Ada Small Moore* (London, New York, and Toronto, 1940), p. 197; and Alexander Coburn Soper, *Kuo Jo-hsü's "Experiences in Painting"* (*T'u-Hua Chien-Wen-Chih*) (Washington, D.C., 1951), p. 15.

38. T'ang Chih-ch'i, *Hui Shih Cheng-yen* (Shanghai, 1935), chap. 1, p. 1a.

39. Sirèn, "An Important Treatise . . . ," *op. cit.*, pp. 155, 161.

40. Friedrich Hirth, *Native Sources for the History of Chinese Pictorial Art* (New York, 1917), p. 11; Florence Wheelock Ayscough, *Catalogue of Chinese Paintings Ancient and Modern by Famous Masters* (Shanghai, n.d.), p. 19.

41. "Shin Sekiden Hitsu *Zō Go Kan Gyō* Emaki Kai" ("Analysis of Shen Shih-t'ien's Scroll-Painting, 'A Gift to Wu K'uan upon His Making a Journey' "), KK, No. 545 (April, 1936, p. 113.

42. Goethe, quoted in Nikolaus Pevsner, *Academies of Art* (Cambridge, 1940), p. 191.

43. Edward Young, "Conjectures on Original Composition," in Mark Schorer, Josephine Miles, and Gordon McKenzie, *Criticism: The Foundations of Modern Literary Judgment* (New York, 1948), p. 15.

44. Harold A. Small (ed.), *Form and Function: Remarks on Art by Horatio Greenough* (Berkeley and Los Angeles, 1947), p. 22.

45. Contag, "Tung Ch'i-ch'ang's . . . ," *op. cit.*, p. 96.

46. Yun Shou-p'ing, "Ou Hsiang Kuan Hua Pa" (*chüan* 11–12 of *Ou Hsiang*

Kuan Chi), in Chiang Kuang-hsü (ed.), *Pieh Hsia Chai Ts'ung-shu* (Shanghai, 1923), ts'e 16, p. 4a.

47. T'eng, *op. cit.*, p. 80.

48. Yukio Yashiro, "Connoisseurship in Chinese Painting," *Journal of the Royal Society of Arts*, LXXXIV (January 17, 1936), 266.

49. Sheng, *op. cit.*, ts'e 3, chap. 2, p. 3b.

50. Tanaka, *op. cit.*, p. 81.

51. Serge Elisséev, "Sur le paysage à l'encre de Chine du Japon," *Revue des arts asiatiques*, II (June, 1925), 31–32.

52. For this distinction see Michael Oakeshott, *Experience and Its Modes* (Cambridge, 1933), pp. 21–23.

53. Ananda K. Coomeraswamy, "The Nature of Buddhist Art," in *Figures of Speech or Figures of Thought* (London, 1946), p. 177. Cf. Croce's distinction between intuitive and intellectual activity, as the distinction between apprehending the individuality of a thing by thinking one's self into it, making its life one's own, and analyzing or classifying it from an external point of view. See R. G. Collingwood, *The Idea of History* (Oxford, 1946), p. 199.

54. H. W. Cassirer, *A Commentary on Kant's "Critique of Judgment"* (London, 1938), p. 19; and Christopher Gray, *Cubist Aesthetic Theories* (Baltimore, 1953), pp. 47–49. For the iron law of correlation between ideal and intuition, note also the place of *Ion* (in which art is "the god speaking through one," hence art cannot be taught) among the dialogues of the greatest idealist, Plato.

55. The literature of art criticism ran riot in the Ming era, so that no attempt has since been made to collect it all (see Hirth, *op. cit.*, pp. 25–26).

56. Victoria Contag, "Das Mallehrbuch für Personen-Malerei des Chieh Tzu Yüan," TP, XXXIII (1937), p. 18. The critics' division of painters into three classes, according to talent, went back at least to the T'ang dynasty.

57. *Ibid.*, p. 20.

58. Elisséev, *op. cit.*, p. 32. For descriptions of Ming and Ch'ing recorded vocabularies of abstractions—epitomes of natural forms and rules for reproducing them—see Victor Rienaecker, "Chinese Art (Sixth Article) Painting—I," *Apollo*, XL (October, 1944), 81–84; Benjamin March, *Some Technical Terms of Chinese Painting* (Baltimore, 1935), pp. xii–xiii; Wang, *op. cit.*, pp. 98–99; William Cohn, *Chinese Painting* (London and New York, 1948), p. 18.

59. Laurence Sickman, in *Great Chinese Painters of the Ming and Ch'ing Dynasties* (catalogue of an exhibition, March 11–April 2, 1949, at Wildenstein Galleries, New York); concurred in by Benjamin Rowland, in *Masterpieces of Chinese Bird and Flower Painting* (catalogue of an exhibition, October 30–December 14, 1951, at the Fogg Art Museum, Cambridge), p. 4.

60. Matthew Arnold, "The Literary Influence of Academies," in his *Essays in Criticism* (Boston, 1865), pp. 47–51.

61. Naitō Torajirō, *Shinchō Shoga Fu* ("Treatise on Ch'ing Calligraphy and Painting") (Osaka, 1917), p. 3 (text in Chinese).

62. Contag, *Die Beiden Steine*, p. 10.

63. *Ming-jen Shu Hua Chi* (Shanghai, 1921), p. 4, Pl. 2.

64. Osvald Sirèn, *The Chinese on the Art of Painting* (Peiping, 1936), p. 188.

65. Werner Speiser, "Ba Da Schan Jen," *Sinica*, VIII (March 10, 1933), 49.

66. Sirèn, "Shih-t'ao, Painter, Poet, and Theoretician," *Bulletin of the Museum of Far Eastern Activities*, XXI (1949), 55.

67. Yawata Sekitarō, *Shina Gajin Kenkyū* ("Study of Chinese Painters") (Tokyo, 1942), p. 170.

68. *Chung-kuo Jen-ming Ta Tzu-tien*, quoted in Speiser, *op. cit.*, p. 46.

69. Bokuyūsō Shujin, *Sekitō to Hachidaisenjin* ("Shih-t'ao and Pa-ta-shan-jen") (Kanagawa ken, 1952), p. 3.

70. Sirèn, "Shih-t'ao . . . ," *op. cit.*, p. 41.

71. Sirèn, *The Chinese on the Art of Painting*, p. 164. As an example of the literati's disinterest in originality, the same reference to the "ten thousand volumes" and the "ten thousand *li*" may be found in a contemporary treatise by Mo Shih-lung and in the later work, the *Mustard-Seed Garden* (see Yoshizawa, *op. cit.*, [Part 1], p. 260, and Petrucci, *op. cit.*, pp. 4–5). The English critic Sir Herbert Read puts the emphasis just wrong, and misses the strain in Tung Ch'i-ch'ang which makes him such a revealing figure, when he writes: "But one of the great artists of the Ming epoch, Tung Ch'i-ch'ang, said with perhaps obvious truth that no one was likely to gain such a state of grace, even if he read ten thousand books and ranged over ten thousand leagues; the artist is born, not made" (*A Coat of Many Colours* [London, 1945], p. 266).

72. Contag, *Die Beiden Steine*, p. 10.

73. Yun, *op. cit.*, ts'e 16, p. 8a–b.

74. Hackney and Yau, *op. cit.*, p. 56.

75. Yoshizawa, *op. cit.* (Part 3), p. 346.

76. See "Ran Ei Hitsu: *Hisetsu senzen* Zu Kai" ("Analysis of 'Flying Snow and a Thousand Mountains,' by Lan Ying"), KK, No. 477 (August, 1930), p. 228. For the distinction among the Che school (in the Ma-Hsia tradition of monochrome landscape of the Southern Sung academy), the Yuan school (particularly figure-painting and decorative color landscape, "blue-green," etc., more meticulous than Che), and the Wu school (for whom both preceding schools were academic)— and for an account of their intermingling—see Hu, *op. cit.*, pp. 150–51, and P'an, *op. cit.*, pp. 167–70. For Shen Shih-t'ien as the very embodiment of the "Wu taste" in sixteenth-century and subsequent opinion see Tempō Imazeki, "Shin Sekiden Jiseki" ("Biographical Note on Shen Shih-t'ien") (Part 1), KK, No. 457 (December, 1928), pp. 349–50.

77. For varying Ming and Ch'ing assignments of these painters to schools see Tajima, *op. cit.*, Vol. X (1911), Pl. 16; Yawata, *op. cit.*, pp. 68–69; Ichiuji Giryō, *Tōyō Bijutsu Shi* ("History of Far Eastern Art") (Tokyo, 1936), p. 215; Huang Pin-hung, *Ku Hua Cheng* ("Evidence on Old Painting") (Shanghai, 1931), pp. 30–32; and Werner Speiser, "Tang Yin" (Part 2), OZ, XI (May–August, 1935), 109.

78. Yonezawa Yoshiho, "Kyū Ei Hitsu: Hakubyō *Tan ran tei* Zu" ("The *Chuan lan ting*, a Picture in the *Pai-miao* Method, by Ch'iu Ying"), KK, No. 708 (March, 1951), p. 122; Lin Feng-mien, *I-shu Ts'ung-lun* ("Essays on Art") (Shanghai, 1937), p. 121; Arthur Waley, "A Chinese Picture," *Burlington Magazine*, XXX (January, 1917), 10.

79. Unzansei, "Kyū Ei no Gasatsu ni Tsuite" ("On a Picture Book by Ch'iu Ying"), KK, No. 475 (June, 1930), pp. 159–60; "Kyū Ei Tōjin Shii e Kai" ("Explanation of Ch'iu Ying's Paintings on Themes from T'ang Poetry"), KK, No. 481 (December, 1930), pp. 344–45. There is a similar album by Shen Shih-t'ien, one of nine paintings, each after an individual early artist (see Taki, "Shin Keinan . . . ," *op. cit.*, p. 35).

80. Sirèn, *Later Chinese Painting*, I, 133–34; Werner Speiser, "T'ang Yin" (Part

1), OZ, XI (January–April, 1935), 21. Cf. the note on T'ang of the famous sixteenth-century collector, Wang Shih-chen, which mentions as a matter of course T'ang's derivations (all Wang's notes have an account of derivations at the beginning of his brief biographical sketches). Wang acknowledges a thoroughly eclectic background for T'ang, in which Sung academicians like Li T'ang, Ma Yuan, *et al.*, and Yuan intuitive masters like Huang Kung-wang all figure. See Wang Shih-chen, *I-yuan Chih Yen Fu-lu*, in Shih Ching T'ang (ed.), *Yen-chou Shan Jen Ssu Pu Kao*, chap. 155, pp. 16*b*–17*a*.

81. Tajima, *op. cit.*, XI (1912), Pl. 6.

82. See KK, No. 481 (December, 1930), No. 5 painting in the illustrated set. Cf. a late Ming account of a Ch'iu Ying painting, which identified the styles (and praised the combinations) of various masters in Ch'iu Ying's stones and mountains, trees, figures, and coloring (see Sirèn, *Later Chinese Painting*, I, 146).

83. "Sei Moyō Hitsu: *Sankyo Hōmon* Zu Kai" ("Analysis of 'A Visitor to a Mountain Abode,' by Sheng Mao-yeh"), KK, No. 543 (February, 1946), p. 53.

84. Wada Mikio (ed.), *Tōyō Bijutsu Taikan*, Vol. XII (1913), Pl. 6; Contag, "Tung Ch'i-ch'ang's . . . ," *op. cit.*, pp. 181–82. The quotation is from the *Kuo Ch'ao Hua Cheng Lu* (1739), by Chang Keng.

85. "Ōō Sekikoku Hitsu: Semmen Sansui Zu" ("Landscape Painted on a Fan, by Wang Hui"), KK, No. 614 (January, 1942), p. 24; Yonezawa Yoshiho, "Ōō Sekikoku Hitsu: Kambaku Zu" (" 'Looking at a Waterfall,' by Wang Hui"), KK, No. 702 (September, 1950), p. 306.

86. Aimi Shigeichi, *Gumpō Seigan* (Tokyo, 1914), Vol. II, Pl. 5; Nakamura Saku-tarō and Ojika Bukkai, *Shina Ega Shi* ("History of Chinese Painting") (Tokyo, 1923), p. 163; P'an, *op. cit.*, p. 167.

87. Wang Shih-chen on T'ang Yin (see Wang Shih-chen, *op. cit.*, chap. 155, p. 17). Generally, for the Ming-Ch'ing connoisseurs' cult of brushwork—its sensitivity to nuance, feeling for extra-aesthetic suggestiveness in the painter's strokes, elaborate systems of classification, tendency to proliferate detail (the subject of brushwork) in what might have been truly southern empty space, and gradual change of emphasis from typical motives in an intellectually regulated composition to more individualized motives in free arrangement, more suitable to the range of virtuosity—see, successively, A. Bolling and John Ayers, "Chinese Art of the Ming Period in the British Museum," OA, III (1950), 79; Victoria Contag, *Die Sechs Berühmten Maler der Ch'ing-Dynastie* (Leipzig, 1940), p. 17; Kojiro Tomita, "Brush-Strokes in Far Eastern Painting," *Eastern Art*, III (1931), 29–31; Arthur Waley, *An Introduction to the Study of Chinese Painting* (London, 1923), p. 247; Fang-chuen Wang, *op. cit.*, p. 102; Victor Rienaecker, "Chinese Art (Seventh Article) Painting—II," *Apollo*, XL (November, 1944), 109; Tsou, *op. cit.*, ts'e 3, chap. 2, p. 6*a;* Arthur von Rosthorn, "Malerei und Kunstkritik in China," *Wiener Beiträge zur Kunst- und Kultur-Geschichte*, IV (1930), 22; George Rowley, "A Chinese Scroll of the Ming Dynasty: Ming Huang and Yang Kuei-fei Listening to Music," *Worcester Art Museum Annual*, II (1936–37), 70–71; Cohn, *op. cit.*, p. 92; John C. Ferguson, *Chinese Painting* (Chicago, 1927), p. 62; Édouard Chavannes and Raphael Petrucci, *La Peinture chinoise au Musée Cernuschi, avril-juin 1912* (*Ars Asiatica I*) (Brussels and Paris, 1914), pp. 49–50; Edgar C. Schenck, "The Hundred Wild Geese," *Honolulu Academy of Arts Annual Bulletin*, I (1939), 6–10.

88. For details on this prescription of Tung *et al.* for the painting of synthetic pictures see Tung, *op. cit.*, chap. 2, pp. 5*a*–8*a;* Alan Houghton Broderick, *An Out-*

line of Chinese Painting (London, 1949), p. 32; Waley, *An Introduction* . . . , pp. 246–50; Contag, "Schriftcharakteristeken . . . ," *op. cit.*, p. 48, and *Die Sechs* . . . , p. 20; Sirèn, *The Chinese on the Art of Painting*, p. 143, and *Later Chinese Painting*, I, 187; John C. Ferguson, "Wang Ch'uan," OZ, III (April-June, 1914), 58–59.

89. As an example of the latter, Waley refers to the transfer of the ideals of literary study to art in this fashion: a certain river having been mentioned in the *Shih-ching* in connection with autumn, it must always be represented by the painter in an autumn scene (see Waley, *An Introduction* . . . , p. 246). Sirèn speaks of the Ming taste as demanding an inscription on a painting in a literary style appropriate to the motif and a calligraphic style corresponding to the manner in which the picture was painted, i.e., *k'ai-shu* (formal style) calligraphy for *kung-pi* (highly finished, meticulous) painting, and *ts'ao-shu* (cursive style) calligraphy for *hsieh-i* (intuitive) painting (see Sirèn, "Shih T'ao . . . ," *op. cit.*, pp. 35–36).

90. Kenneth Clark, *Landscape into Art* (London, 1949), p. 30.

91. C. M. Bowra, *The Creative Experiment* (London, 1949), p. 2.

92. Werner Speiser, "Eine Landschaft von Wang Hui in Köln," OZ, XVII (1941), 170.

93. "Abe Kojirō Zō: Un Nanden Hitsu Kaki Satsu" (" 'Flowers' by Yun Shou-p'ing in the Abe Kojirō Collection"), *Bijutsu Kenkyū*, XCII (August, 1939), 306.

94. "Hashimoto Shinjirō Zō: Un Nanden Hitsu Kahin Seikyō Zu" (" 'Fruits' by Yun Shou-p'ing in the Hashimoto Shinjirō Collection"), *Bijutsu Kenkyū*, VII (July, 1932), 237.

95. Tsou, *op. cit.*, ts'e 3, chap. 1, p. 1a.

96. For discussions of this process see Joseph R. Levenson, *Liang Ch'i-ch'ao and the Mind of Modern China* (Cambridge, Mass., 1953), *passim*, esp. pp. 109–28; and " 'History' and 'Value': Tensions of Intellectual Choice in Modern China," in Arthur F. Wright (ed.), *Studies in Chinese Thought* (Chicago, 1953), pp. 169–73.

97. For a discussion of nineteenth- and early twentieth-century utilitarian criticism, and proposals for modification, of what had come to appear the aestheticism of the examination system, see Ssu-yü Teng and John K. Fairbank, *China's Response to the West* (Cambridge, Mass., 1954), esp. pp. 139, 145, 178, and 205.

That specialization and practical purposes in education were essentially uncongenial to the traditional Confucian intellectual world, so that their late Ch'ing appearance in China must represent a significant change in that world, is corroborated by the fact that earlier Ch'ing thinkers like Yen Yuan (1635–1704) and Chang Hsueh-ch'eng (1738–1801), in advocating specialization, were consciously attacking their intellectual milieu and were considered eccentric within it. See David S. Nivison, "The Literary and Historical Thought of Chang Hsüeh-ch'eng (1731–1801): A Study of His Life and Writing, with Translations of Six Essays from the 'Wen-shih t'ung-i,' " (Ph.D. thesis in the Department of Far Eastern Languages and Literatures, Harvard University, Cambridge, Mass., May, 1953), p. 18; and " 'Knowledge' and 'Action' in Chinese Thought since Wang Yang-ming," in Arthur F. Wright (ed.), *Studies in Chinese Thought* (Chicago, 1953), pp. 128–29.

98. Max Weber, *The Religion of China* (Glencoe, Ill., 1951), p. 248.

INDEX

PHOENIX BOOKS
in History